Table of Contents

What do you think of this book? We want to hear from you!

Microsoft is interested in hearing your feedback so we can continually improve our
books and learning resources for you. To participate in a brief online survey, please visit:

microsoft.com/learning/booksurvey

Microsoft®

Programming Microsoft® LINQ in Microsoft .NET Framework 4

Paolo Pialorsi

Marco Russo

Published with the authorization of Microsoft Corporation by:
O'Reilly Media, Inc.
1005 Gravenstein Highway North
Sebastopol, California 95472

Printed and bound in the United States of America.

1 2 3 4 5 6 7 8 9 M 5 4 3 2 1 0

Microsoft Press titles may be purchased for educational, business or sales promotional use. Online editions are also available for most titles (*http://my.safaribooksonline.com*). For more information, contact our corporate/institutional sales department: (800) 998-9938 or *corporate@oreilly.com*. Visit our website at *microsoftpress.oreilly.com*. Send comments to *mspinput@microsoft.com*.

Acquisitions and Development Editor: Russell Jones
Production Editor: Adam Zaremba
Editorial Production: OTSI, Inc.
Technical Reviewer: Debbie Timmins
Indexing: Ron Strauss
Cover: Karen Montgomery
Compositor: Octal Publishing, Inc.
Illustrator: Robert Romano

978-0-735-64057-3

To Andrea and Paola: thanks for your everyday support!

—Paolo

Contents at a Glance

Part IV **Advanced LINQ**

What do you think of this book? We want to hear from you!

Microsoft is interested in hearing your feedback so we can continually improve our
books and learning resources for you. To participate in a brief online survey, please visit:

microsoft.com/learning/booksurvey

Preface

We saw Language Integrated Query (LINQ) for the first time in September 2005, when the LINQ Project was announced during the Professional Developers Conference (PDC 2005). We immediately realized the importance and the implications of LINQ for the long term. At the same time, we felt it would be a huge error to look to LINQ only for its capability to wrap access to relational data. This would be an error because the important concept introduced by LINQ is the growth in code abstraction that comes from using a consistent pattern that makes code more readable, without having to pay in terms of loss of control. We liked LINQ, we could foresee widespread use for it, but we were worried about the possible misperception of its key points. For these reasons, we started to think about writing a book about LINQ.

Our opportunity to write such a book began when our proposal was accepted by Microsoft Press. We wrote an initial short version of this book, *Introducing Microsoft LINQ* (Microsoft Press), which was based on beta 1 code. A second book, *Programming Microsoft LINQ* (Microsoft Press), comprehensively discussed LINQ in .NET 3.5. Readers provided a lot of feedback about both these books. We took both the positive and more importantly, the negative comments as opportunities to improve the book. Today, we are writing the preface to the third book about LINQ, *Programming Microsoft LINQ in Microsoft .NET Framework 4*, which we believe is a more mature book, full of useful content to help people develop real-world .NET solutions that leverage LINQ and new .NET 4.0 features!

After spending almost five years working with LINQ, this book represents a tremendous goal for us, but it is just the beginning for you. LINQ introduces a more declarative style of programming; it's not a temporary trend. Anders Hejlsberg, the chief designer of C#, said that LINQ tries to solve the impedance mismatch between code and data. We think that LINQ is probably already one step ahead of other methods of resolving that dilemma because it can also be used to write parallel algorithms, such as when using the Parallel LINQ (PLINQ) implementation.

LINQ can be pervasive in software architectures because you can use it in any tier of an application; however, just like any other tool, it can be used effectively or not. We tried to address the most beneficial ways to use LINQ throughout the book. We suspect that at the beginning, you—as we did five years ago—will find it natural to use LINQ in place of relational database queries, but you'll soon find that the ideas begin to pervade your approach to programming. This turning point happens when you begin writing algorithms that operate on in-memory data using LINQ to Objects queries. That should be easy. In fact, after only three chapters of this book, you will already have the knowledge required to do that. But in reality, that is the hardest part, because you need to change the way you think about your code. You need to start thinking in LINQ. We have not found a magic formula to teach this. Probably, like any big change, you will need time and practice to metabolize it.

Enjoy the reading!

Acknowledgments

A book is the result of the work of many people. Unfortunately, only the authors have their names on the cover. This section is only partial compensation for other individuals who helped out.

First, we want to thank Luca Bolognese for his efforts in giving us resources and contacts that helped us to write this book and the two previous editions.

We also want to thank all the people from Microsoft who answered our questions along the way—in particular, Mads Torgersen, Amanda Silver, Erick Thompson, Joe Duffy, Ed Essey, Yuan Yu, Dinesh Kulkarni, and Luke Hoban. Moreover, Charlie Calvert deserves special mention for his great and precious help.

We would like to thank Microsoft Press, O'Reilly, and all the publishing people who contributed to this book project: Ben Ryan, Russell Jones, Jaime Odell, Adam Witwer, and Debbie Timmins. Russell has followed this book from the beginning; he helped us to stay on track, answered all our questions, remained tolerant of our delays, and improved a lot of our drafts. Jaime and Adam have been so accurate and patient in their editing work that we really want to thank them for their great job. Debbie has been the main technical reviewer.

We also want to thank the many people who had the patience to read our drafts and suggest improvements and corrections. Big thanks to Guido Zambarda, Luca Regnicoli, and Roberto Brunetti for their reviews. Guido deserves special thanks for his great job in reviewing all the chapters and the code samples during the upgrade of this book from .NET 3.5 to .NET 4.0.

Finally, we would like to thank Giovanni Librando, who supported us—one more time in our life—when we were in doubt about starting this new adventure. Now the book is here, thanks Giovanni!

Introduction

This book covers Language Integrated Query (LINQ) both deeply and widely. The main goal is to give you a complete understanding of how LINQ works, as well as what to do—and what not to do—with LINQ.

To work with the examples in this book, you need to install both Microsoft .NET Framework 4.0 and Microsoft Visual Studio 2010 on your development machine.

This book has been written against the released-to-market (RTM) edition of LINQ and Microsoft .NET 4.0. The authors have created a website (*http://www.programminglinq.com/*) where they will maintain a change list, a revision history, corrections, and a blog about what is going on with the LINQ project and this book.

Who Is This Book For?

The target audience for this book is .NET developers with a good knowledge of Microsoft .NET 2.0 or 3.x who are wondering whether to upgrade their expertise to Microsoft .NET 4.0.

Organization of This Book

This book is divided into five parts that contain 19 chapters.

The authors use C# as the principal language in their examples, but almost all the LINQ features shown are available in Visual Basic as well. Where appropriate, the authors use Visual Basic because it has some features that are not available in C#.

The first part of this book, "LINQ Foundations," introduces LINQ, explains its syntax, and supplies all the information you need to start using LINQ with in-memory objects (LINQ to Objects). It is important to learn LINQ to Objects before any other LINQ implementation because many of its features are used in the other LINQ implementations described in this book. Therefore, the authors strongly suggest that you read the three chapters in Part I first.

The second part of this book, "LINQ to Relational," is dedicated to all the LINQ implementations that provide access to relational stores of data. In Chapter 4 "Choosing Between LINQ to SQL and LINQ to Entities," you will find some useful tips and suggestions that will help you choose between using LINQ to SQL and LINQ to Entities in your software solutions.

The LINQ to SQL implementation is divided into three chapters. In Chapter 5, "LINQ to SQL: Querying Data," you will learn the basics for mapping relational data to LINQ entities and how to build LINQ queries that will be transformed into SQL queries. In Chapter 6, "LINQ to SQL:

Managing Data," you will learn how to handle changes to data extracted from a database using LINQ to SQL entities. Chapter 7, "LINQ to SQL: Modeling Data and Tools," is a guide to the tools available for helping you define data models for LINQ to SQL. If you are interested in using LINQ to SQL in your applications, you should read all the LINQ to SQL chapters.

The LINQ to Entities implementation is also divided into three chapters. In Chapter 8, "LINQ to Entities: Modeling Data with Entity Framework," you will learn how to create an Entity Data Model and how to leverage the new modeling features of Entity Framework 4.0. Chapter 9, "LINQ to Entities: Querying Data," focuses on querying and retrieving entities using LINQ to Entities, while Chapter 10, "LINQ to Entities: Managing Data," shows how to handle changes to those entities using LINQ to Entities, how to manage data concurrency, and how to share entities across multiple software layers. If you are interested in leveraging LINQ to Entities in your software solutions, you should read all the LINQ to Entities chapters.

Chapter 11, "LINQ to DataSet," covers the implementation of LINQ that targets ADO.NET DataSets. If you have an application that makes use of DataSets, this chapter will teach you how to integrate LINQ, or at least how to progressively migrate from DataSets to the domain models handled with LINQ to SQL or LINQ to Entities.

The third part, "LINQ to XML," includes two chapters about LINQ to XML: Chapter 12, "LINQ to XML: Managing the XML Infoset," and Chapter 13, "LINQ to XML: Querying Nodes." The authors suggest that you read these chapters before you start any development that reads or manipulates data in XML.

The fourth part, "Advanced LINQ," includes the most complex topics of the book. In Chapter 14, "Inside Expression Trees," you will learn how to handle, produce, or simply read an expression tree. Chapter 15, "Extending LINQ," provides information about extending LINQ using custom data structures by wrapping an existing service, and finally by creating a custom LINQ provider. Chapter 16, "Parallelism and Asynchronous Processing," describes a LINQ interface to the Parallel Framework for .NET. Finally, Chapter 17, "Other LINQ Implementations," offers an overview of the most significant LINQ components available from Microsoft and third-party vendors. For the most part, the chapters in this part are independent, although Chapter 15 makes some references to Chapter 14.

The fifth part, "Applied LINQ," describes the use of LINQ in several different scenarios of a distributed application. Chapter 18, "LINQ in a Multitier Solution," is likely to be interesting for everyone because it is an architecturally focused chapter that can help you make the right design decisions for your applications. Chapter 19, "LINQ Data Binding," presents relevant information about the use of LINQ for binding data to user interface controls using existing libraries such as ASP.NET, Windows Presentation Foundation, Silverlight, and Windows Forms. The authors suggest that you read Chapter 18 before delving into the details of specific libraries.

Conventions and Features in This Book

This book presents information using conventions designed to make the information readable and easy to follow:

- Boxed elements with labels such as "Note" provide additional information or alternative methods for completing a step successfully.

- Text that you type (apart from code blocks) appears in bold.

- A plus sign (+) between two key names means that you must press those keys at the same time. For example, "Press Alt+Tab" means that you hold down the Alt key while you press the Tab key.

- A vertical bar between two or more menu items (e.g., File | Close), means that you should select the first menu or menu item, then the next, and so on.

System Requirements

Here are the system requirements you will need to work with LINQ and to work with and execute the sample code that accompanies this book:

- Supported operating systems: Microsoft Windows Server 2003, Windows Server 2008, Windows Server 2008 R2, Windows XP with Service Pack 2, Windows Vista, Windows 7

- Microsoft Visual Studio 2010

The Companion Website

This book features a companion website where you can download all the code used in the book. The code is organized by topic; you can download it from the companion site here: *http://examples.oreilly.com/9780735640573/*.

Find Additional Content Online

As new or updated material becomes available that complements this book, it will be posted online on the Microsoft Press Online Developer Tools website. The type of material you might find includes updates to book content, articles, links to companion content, errata, sample chapters, and more. This website will be available soon at *www.microsoft.com/learning/books /online/developer*, and will be updated periodically.

Errata & Book Support

We've made every effort to ensure the accuracy of this book and its companion content. If you do find an error, please report it on our Microsoft Press site at oreilly.com:

1. Go to *http://microsoftpress.oreilly.com*.

2. In the Search box, enter the book's ISBN or title.

3. Select your book from the search results.

4. On your book's catalog page, under the cover image, you'll see a list of links.

5. Click View/Submit Errata.

You'll find additional information and services for your book on its catalog page. If you need additional support, please e-mail Microsoft Press Book Support at *mspinput@microsoft.com*.

Please note that product support for Microsoft software is not offered through the addresses above.

We Want to Hear from You

At Microsoft Press, your satisfaction is our top priority, and your feedback our most valuable asset. Please tell us what you think of this book at:

http://www.microsoft.com/learning/booksurvey

The survey is short, and we read every one of your comments and ideas. Thanks in advance for your input!

Stay in Touch

Let's keep the conversation going! We're on Twitter: *http://twitter.com/MicrosoftPress*

Part I
LINQ Foundations

Chapter 1
LINQ Introduction

By surfing the web, you can find several descriptions of Microsoft Language Integrated Query (LINQ), including these:

- LINQ provides a uniform programming model for any kind of data. With it, you can query and manipulate data by using a consistent model that is independent of data sources.

- LINQ is another tool for embedding SQL queries into code.

- LINQ is another data abstraction layer.

All these descriptions are correct to a degree, but each focuses on only a single aspect of LINQ. LINQ is much easier to use than a "uniform programming mode"; it can do much more than embed SQL queries; and it is far from being just another data abstraction layer.

What Is LINQ?

LINQ is a programming model that introduces queries as a first-class concept into any Microsoft .NET Framework language. Complete support for LINQ, however, requires some extensions to whatever .NET Framework language you are using. These language extensions boost developer productivity, thereby providing a shorter, more meaningful, and expressive syntax with which to manipulate data.

 More Info Details about language extensions can be found on the Microsoft Developer Network (MSDN), located at *msdn.microsoft.com*.

LINQ provides a methodology that simplifies and unifies the implementation of any kind of data access. LINQ does not force you to use a specific architecture; it facilitates the implementation of several existing architectures for accessing data, such as:

- RAD/prototype
- Client/server
- N-tier
- Smart client

LINQ made its first appearance in September 2005 as a technical preview. Since then, it has evolved from an extension of Microsoft Visual Studio 2005 to an integrated part of .NET Framework 3.5 and Visual Studio 2008, both released in November 2007. The first released version of LINQ directly supported several data sources. Now with .NET Framework 4 and Visual Studio 2010, LINQ also includes LINQ to Entities, which is part of the Microsoft ADO.NET Entity Framework, and Parallel LINQ (PLINQ). This book describes current LINQ implementations from Microsoft for accessing several different data sources, such as the following:

- LINQ to Objects
- LINQ to ADO.NET
- LINQ to Entities
- LINQ to SQL
- LINQ to DataSet
- LINQ to XML

Extending LINQ

In addition to the built-in data source types, you can extend LINQ to support additional data sources. Possible extensions might be LINQ to Exchange or LINQ to LDAP, to name just a couple of examples. Some implementations are already available using LINQ to Objects. We describe a possible LINQ to Reflection query in the "LINQ to Objects" section of this chapter. Chapter 15, "Extending LINQ," discusses more advanced extensions of LINQ, and Chapter 17, "Other LINQ Implementations," covers some of the existing LINQ implementations.

LINQ is likely to have an impact on the way applications are coded, but it would be incorrect to think that LINQ will change application architectures; its goal is to provide a set of tools that improve code implementation by adapting to several *different* architectures. However, we expect that LINQ will affect some critical parts of the layers of an n-tier solution. For example, we envision the use of LINQ in a SQLCLR stored procedure, with a direct transfer of the query expression to the SQL engine instead of using a SQL statement.

Many possible evolutionary tracks could originate from LINQ, but we should not forget that SQL is a widely adopted standard that cannot be easily replaced by another, just for performance reasons. Nevertheless, LINQ is an interesting step in the evolution of current mainstream programming languages. The declarative nature of its syntax might be interesting for uses other than data access, such as the parallel programming that is offered by

PLINQ. Many other services can be offered by an execution framework to a program written using a higher level of abstraction, such as the one offered by LINQ. A good understanding of this technology is important because LINQ has become a "standard" way to describe data manipulation operations inside a program written in the .NET Framework.

> **More Info** PLINQ is covered in Chapter 16, "Parallelism and Asynchronous Processing."

Why Do We Need LINQ?

Today, data managed by a program can originate from various data sources: an array, an object graph, an XML document, a database, a text file, a registry key, an email message, Simple Object Access Protocol (SOAP) message content, a Microsoft Excel file.... The list is long.

Each data source has its own specific data access model. When you have to query a database, you typically use SQL. You navigate XML data by using the Document Object Model (DOM) or XPath/XQuery. You iterate an array and build algorithms to navigate an object graph. You use specific application programming interfaces (APIs) to access other data sources, such as an Excel file, an email message, or the Windows registry. In the end, you use different programming models to access different data sources.

The unification of data access techniques into a single comprehensive model has been attempted in many ways. For example, by using Open Database Connectivity (ODBC) providers, you can query an Excel file as you would a Windows Management Instrumentation (WMI) repository. With ODBC, you use a SQL-like language to access data represented through a relational model.

Sometimes, however, data is represented more effectively in a hierarchical or network model instead of a relational one. Moreover, if a data model is not tied to a specific language, you probably need to manage several type systems. All these differences create an "impedance mismatch" between data and code.

LINQ addresses these issues by offering a uniform way to access and manage data without forcing the adoption of a "one size fits all" model. LINQ makes use of common capabilities in the *operations* in different data models instead of flattening the different *structures* between them. In other words, by using LINQ, you keep existing heterogeneous data structures, such as classes or tables, but you get a uniform syntax to query all these data types—regardless of their physical representation. Think about the differences between a graph of in-memory objects and relational tables with proper relationships. With LINQ, you can use the same query syntax over both models.

Here is a simple LINQ query for a typical software solution that returns the names of customers in Italy:

```
var query =
    from   c in Customers
    where  c.Country == "Italy"
    select c.CompanyName;
```

The result of this query is a list of strings. You can enumerate these values with a *foreach* loop in Microsoft Visual C#:

```
foreach ( string name in query ) {
    Console.WriteLine( name );
}
```

Both the *query* definition and the *foreach* loop are regular C# 3.0 statements, but what is *Customers*? At this point, you might be wondering what it is we are querying. Is this query a new form of Embedded SQL? Not at all. You can apply the same query (and the *foreach* loop) to a SQL database, to a *DataSet* object, to an array of objects in memory, to a remote service, or to many other kinds of data.

For example, *Customers* could be a collection of objects:

```
Customer[] Customers;
```

Customer data could reside in a DataTable in a DataSet:

```
DataSet ds = GetDataSet();
DataTable Customers = ds.Tables["Customers"];
```

Customers could be an entity class that describes a physical table in a relational database:

```
DataContext db = new DataContext( ConnectionString );
Table<Customer> Customers = db.GetTable<Customer>();
```

Or *Customers* could be an entity class that describes a conceptual model and is mapped to a relational database:

```
NorthwindModel dataModel = new NorthwindModel();
ObjectSet<Customer> Customers = dataModel.Customers;
```

How LINQ Works

As you will learn in Chapter 2, "LINQ Syntax Fundamentals," the SQL-like syntax used in LINQ is called a *query expression*. A SQL-like query mixed with the syntax of a program written in a language that is not SQL is typically called *Embedded SQL*, but languages that implement it do so using a simplified syntax. In Embedded SQL, these statements are not integrated into the language's native syntax and type system because they have a different syntax and several restrictions related to their interaction. Moreover, Embedded SQL is limited to querying data-bases, whereas LINQ is not. LINQ provides much more than Embedded SQL does; it provides a query syntax that is integrated into a language. But how does LINQ work?

Let's say you write the following code using LINQ:

```
Customer[] Customers = GetCustomers();
var query =
    from   c in Customers
    where  c.Country == "Italy"
    select c;
```

The compiler generates this code:

```
Customer[] Customers = GetCustomers();
IEnumerable<Customer> query =
        Customers
        .Where( c => c.Country == "Italy" );
```

The following query is a more complex example (without the *Customers* declaration, for the sake of brevity):

```
var query =
    from   c in Customers
    where  c.Country == "Italy"
    orderby c.Name
    select  new { c.Name, c.City };
```

As you can see, the generated code is more complex too:

```
var query =
        Customers
        .Where( c => c.Country == "Italy" );
        .OrderBy( c => c.Name )
        .Select( c => new { c.Name, c.City } );
```

As you can see, the generated code apparently calls instance members on the object returned from the previous call: *Where* is called on *Customers*, *OrderBy* is called on the object returned by *Where*, and finally *Select* is called on the object returned by *OrderBy*. You will see that this behavior is regulated by what are known as *extension methods* in the host language (C# in this case). The implementation of the *Where*, *OrderBy*, and *Select* methods—called by the sample query—depends on the type of *Customers* and on namespaces specified in relevant *using* statements. Extension methods are a fundamental syntax feature that is used by LINQ to operate with different data sources by using the same syntax.

> **More Info** An extension method appears to extend a class (the *Customers* class in our examples), but in reality a method of an external type receives the instance of the class that seems to be extended as the first argument. The *var* keyword used to declare *query* infers the variable type declaration from the initial assignment, which in this case will return an *IEnumerable<T>* type.

Another important concept is the timing of operations over data. In general, a LINQ query is not executed until the result of the query is required. Each query describes a set of operations that will be performed only when the result is actually accessed by the program. In the following example, this access is performed only when the *foreach* loop executes:

```
var query = from c in Customers ...
foreach ( string name in query ) ...
```

There are also methods that iterate a LINQ query result, producing a persistent copy of data in memory. For example, the *ToList* method produces a typed *List<T>* collection:

```
var query = from c in Customers ...
List<Customer> customers = query.ToList();
```

When the LINQ query operates on data that is in a relational database (such as a Microsoft SQL Server database), it generates an equivalent SQL statement instead of operating with in-memory copies of data tables. The query's execution on the database is delayed until the query results are first accessed. Therefore, if in the last two examples *Customers* was a *Table<Customer>* type (a physical table in a relational database) or an *ObjectSet<Customer>* type (a conceptual entity mapped to a relational database), the equivalent SQL query would not be sent to the database until the *foreach* loop was executed or the *ToList* method was called. The LINQ query can be manipulated and composed in different ways until those events occur.

> **More Info** A LINQ query can be represented as an expression tree. Chapter 14, "Inside Expression Trees," describes how to visit and dynamically build an expression tree, and thereby build a LINQ query.

Relational Model vs. Hierarchical/Network Model

At first, LINQ might appear to be just another SQL dialect. This similarity has its roots in the way a LINQ query can describe a relationship between entities, as shown in the following code:

```
var query =
    from   c in Customers
    join   o in Orders
           on c.CustomerID equals o.CustomerID
    select new { c.CustomerID, c.CompanyName, o.OrderID };
```

This syntax is similar to the regular way of querying data in a relational model by using a SQL *join* clause. However, LINQ is not limited to a single data representation model such as the relational one, where relationships between entities are expressed inside a query but not in the data model. (Foreign keys keep referential integrity but do not participate in a query.) In a hierarchical or network model, parent/child relationships are part of the data structure. For example, suppose that each customer has its own set of orders, and each order has its own list of products. In LINQ, you can get the list of products ordered by each customer in this way:

```
var query =
    from   c in Customers
    from   o in c.Orders
    select new { c.Name, o.Quantity, o.Product.ProductName };
```

This query contains no joins. The relationship between *Customers* and *Orders* is expressed by the second *from* clause, which uses *c.Orders* to say "get all *Orders* for the *c Customer*." The relationship between *Orders* and *Products* is expressed by the *Product* member of the *Order* instance. The result projects the product name for each order row by using *o.Product.ProductName*.

Hierarchical and network relationships are expressed in type definitions through references to other objects. (Throughout, we will use the phrase "graph of objects" to generically refer to hierarchical or network models.) To support the previous query, we would have classes similar to those in Listing 1-1.

LISTING 1-1 Type declarations with simple relationships

```
public class Customer {
    public string Name;
    public string City;
    public Order[] Orders;
}
public struct Order {
    public int Quantity;
    public Product Product;
}
public class Product {
    public int IdProduct;
    public decimal Price;
    public string ProductName;
}
```

However, chances are that we want to use the same *Product* instance for many different *Orders* of the same product. We probably also want to filter *Orders* or *Products* without accessing them through *Customer*. A common scenario is the one shown in Listing 1-2.

LISTING 1-2 Type declarations with two-way relationships

```
public class Customer {
    public string Name;
    public string City;
    public Order[] Orders;
}
public struct Order {
    public int Quantity;
    public Product Product;
    public Customer Customer;
}
public class Product {
    public int IdProduct;
    public decimal Price;
    public string ProductName;
    public Order[] Orders;
}
```

Let's say we have an array of all products declared as follows:

```
Product[] products;
```

We can query the graph of objects, asking for the list of orders for the single product with an ID equal to 3:

```
var query =
    from    p in products
    where   p.IdProduct == 3
    from    o in p.Orders
    select o;
```

With the same query language, we are querying different data models. When you do not have a relationship defined between the entities used in a LINQ query, you can always rely on subqueries and joins that are available in LINQ syntax just as you can in a SQL language. However, when your data model already defines entity relationships, you can use them, avoiding replication of (and possible mistakes in) the same information.

If you have entity relationships in your data model, you can still use explicit relationships in a LINQ query—for example, when you want to force some condition, or when you simply want to relate entities that do not have native relationships. For example, imagine that you want to find customers and suppliers who live in the same city. Your data model might not provide an explicit relationship between these attributes, but with LINQ you can write the following:

```
var query =
    from    c in Customers
    join    s in Suppliers
            on c.City equals s.City
    select new { c.City, c.Name, SupplierName = s.Name };
```

Data like the following will be returned:

```
City=Torino      Name=Marco       SupplierName=Trucker
City=Dallas      Name=James       SupplierName=FastDelivery
City=Dallas      Name=James       SupplierName=Horizon
City=Seattle     Name=Frank       SupplierName=WayFaster
```

If you have experience using SQL queries, you probably assume that a query result is always a "rectangular" table, one that repeats the data of some columns many times in a join like the previous one. However, often a query contains several entities with one or more one-to-many relationships. With LINQ, you can write queries like the following one to return a graph of objects:

```
var query =
    from   c in Customers
    join   s in Suppliers
           on c.City equals s.City
           into customerSuppliers
    select new { c.City, c.Name, customerSuppliers };
```

This query returns a row for each customer, each containing a list of suppliers available in the same city as the customer. This result can be queried again, just as any other object graph with LINQ. Here is how the *hierarchized* results might appear:

```
City=Torino      Name=Marco        customerSuppliers=...
  customerSuppliers: Name=Trucker          City=Torino
City=Dallas      Name=James        customerSuppliers=...
  customerSuppliers: Name=FastDelivery    City=Dallas
  customerSuppliers: Name=Horizon         City=Dallas
City=Seattle     Name=Frank        customerSuppliers=...
  customerSuppliers: Name=WayFaster        City=Seattle
```

If you want to get a list of customers and provide each customer with the list of products he ordered at least one time and the list of suppliers in the same city, you can write a query like this:

```
var query =
    from   c in Customers
    select new {
        c.City,
        c.Name,
        Products = (from   o in c.Orders
                    select new { o.Product.IdProduct,
                                 o.Product.Price }).Distinct(),
        CustomerSuppliers = from   s in Suppliers
                            where  s.City == c.City
                            select s };
```

You can take a look at the results for a couple of customers to understand how data is returned from the previous single LINQ query:

```
City=Torino      Name=Marco        Products=...     CustomerSuppliers=...
   Products: IdProduct=1    Price=10
   Products: IdProduct=3    Price=30
   CustomerSuppliers: Name=Trucker           City=Torino
City=Dallas      Name=James        Products=...     CustomerSuppliers=...
   Products: IdProduct=3    Price=30
   CustomerSuppliers: Name=FastDelivery      City=Dallas
   CustomerSuppliers: Name=Horizon           City=Dallas
```

This type of result would be hard to obtain with one or more SQL queries because it would require an analysis of query results to build the desired graph of objects. LINQ offers an easy way to move data from one model to another and different ways to get the same results.

LINQ requires you to describe your data in terms of entities that are also types in the language. When you build a LINQ query, it is always a set of operations on instances of some classes. These objects might be the real containers of data, or they might be simple descriptions (in terms of metadata) of the external entity you are going to manipulate. A query can be sent to a database through a SQL command only if it is applied to a set of types that maps tables and relationships contained in the database. After you have defined entity classes, you can use *both* approaches we described (joins and entity relationships navigation). The conversion of all these operations into SQL commands is the responsibility of the LINQ engine.

> **Note** When using LINQ to SQL, you can create entity classes by using code-generation tools such as SQLMetal or the Object Relational Designer in Visual Studio. These tools are described in Chapter 7, "LINQ to SQL: Modeling Data and Tools."

Listing 1-3 shows an excerpt of a *Product* class that maps a relational table named *Products*, with five columns that correspond to public properties, using LINQ to SQL.

LISTING 1-3 Class declaration mapped on a database table with LINQ to SQL

```
[Table("Products")]
public class Product {
    [Column(IsPrimaryKey=true)] public int IdProduct;
    [Column(Name="UnitPrice")] public decimal Price;
    [Column()] public string ProductName;
    [Column()] public bool Taxable;
    [Column()] public decimal Tax;
}
```

When you work on entities that describe external data (such as database tables), you can create instances of these kinds of classes and manipulate in-memory objects just as if the data from all tables were loaded in memory. You submit these changes to the database through SQL commands when you call the *SubmitChanges* method, as shown in Listing 1-4.

LISTING 1-4 Database update calling the *SubmitChanges* method of LINQ to SQL

```
var taxableProducts =
    from   p in db.Products
    where  p.Taxable == true
    select p;
foreach( Product product in taxableProducts ) {
    RecalculateTaxes( product );
}
db.SubmitChanges();
```

The *Product* class in the preceding example represents a row in the Products table of an external database. When you call *SubmitChanges*, all changed objects generate a SQL command to synchronize the corresponding data tables in the database—in this case, updating the corresponding rows in the Products table.

> **More Info** You can find more detailed information about class entities that match tables and relationships in Chapter 5, "LINQ to SQL: Querying Data," in Chapter 6, "LINQ to SQL: Managing Data," and in Chapter 9, "LINQ to Entities: Querying Data."

Listing 1-5 shows the same *Product* entity, generated using LINQ to Entities and the Entity Framework that ships with .NET Framework 4 and Visual Studio 2010.

LISTING 1-5 The *Product* entity class declaration using the Entity Framework

```
[EdmEntityType(Name = "Product")]
public class Product {
    [EdmScalarProperty(EntityKeyProperty = true)] public int IdProduct { get; set; }
    [EdmScalarProperty()] public decimal Price { get; set; }
    [EdmScalarProperty()] public string ProductName { get; set; }
    [EdmScalarProperty()] public bool Taxable { get; set; }
    [EdmScalarProperty()] public decimal Tax { get; set; }
}
```

In Chapter 4, "Choosing Between LINQ to SQL and LINQ to Entities," we will compare the main features of LINQ to SQL and LINQ to Entities. However, you can already see that there are different attributes applied to the code, even if the basic idea is almost the same.

Listing 1-6 shows the same data manipulation you have already seen in LINQ to SQL, but this time applied to the *Product* entity generated using the Entity Framework.

LISTING 1-6 Database update calling the *SaveChanges* method of the Entity Framework

```
var taxableProducts =
    from p in db.Products
    where p.Taxable == true
    select p;

foreach (Product product in taxableProducts) {
    RecalculateTaxes(product);
}
db.SaveChanges();
```

Once again, the main concepts are the same, even though the method invoked (*SaveChanges*), which synchronizes the database tables with the in-memory data, is different.

XML Manipulation

LINQ has a different set of classes and extensions to support manipulating XML data. Imagine that your customers are able to send orders using XML files such as the ORDERS.XML file shown in Listing 1-7.

LISTING 1-7 A fragment of an XML file of orders

```
<?xml version="1.0" encoding="utf-8" ?>
<orders xmlns="http://schemas.devleap.com/Orders">
    <order idCustomer="ALFKI" idProduct="1" quantity="10" price="20.59"/>
    <order idCustomer="ANATR" idProduct="5" quantity="20" price="12.99"/>
    <order idCustomer="KOENE" idProduct="7" quantity="15" price="35.50"/>
</orders>
```

Using standard .NET Framework 2.0 *System.Xml* classes, you can load the file by using a DOM approach or you can parse its contents by using an implementation of *XmlReader*, as shown in Listing 1-8.

LISTING 1-8 Reading the XML file of orders by using an *XmlReader*

```
String nsUri = "http://schemas.devleap.com/Orders";
XmlReader xmlOrders = XmlReader.Create( "Orders.xml" );

List<Order> orders = new List<Order>();
Order order = null;
while (xmlOrders.Read()) {
    switch (xmlOrders.NodeType) {
        case XmlNodeType.Element:
            if ((xmlOrders.Name == "order") &&
            (xmlOrders.NamespaceURI == nsUri)) {
                order = new Order();
                order.CustomerID = xmlOrders.GetAttribute( "idCustomer" );
```

```
                  order.Product = new Product();
                  order.Product.IdProduct =
                      Int32.Parse( xmlOrders.GetAttribute( "idProduct" ) );
                  order.Product.Price =
                      Decimal.Parse( xmlOrders.GetAttribute( "price" ) );
                  order.Quantity =
                      Int32.Parse( xmlOrders.GetAttribute( "quantity" ) );
                  orders.Add( order );
              }
              break;
        }
    }
```

You can also use an XQuery to select nodes:

```
for $order in document("Orders.xml")/orders/order
return $order
```

However, using XQuery requires learning yet another language and syntax. Moreover, the result of the previous XQuery example would need to be converted into a set of *Order* instances to be used within the code.

Regardless of the solution you choose, you must always consider nodes, node types, XML namespaces, and whatever else is related to the XML world. Many developers do not like working with XML because it requires knowledge of another domain of data structures and uses its own syntax. For them, it is not very intuitive. As we have already said, LINQ provides a query engine suitable for any kind of source, even an XML document. By using LINQ queries, you can achieve the same result with less effort and with unified programming language syntax. Listing 1-9 shows a LINQ to XML query made over the orders file.

LISTING 1-9 Reading the XML file by using LINQ to XML

```
XDocument xmlOrders = XDocument.Load( "Orders.xml" );

XNamespace ns = "http://schemas.devleap.com/Orders";
var orders = from o in xmlOrders.Root.Elements( ns + "order" )
             select new Order {
                         CustomerID = (String)o.Attribute( "idCustomer" ),
                         Product = new Product {
                             IdProduct = (Int32)o.Attribute("idProduct"),
                             Price = (Decimal)o.Attribute("price") },
                         Quantity = (Int32)o.Attribute("quantity")
                     };
```

Using LINQ to XML in Microsoft Visual Basic syntax (available since Visual Basic 2008) is even easier; you can reference XML nodes in your code by using an XPath-like syntax, as shown in Listing 1-10.

LISTING 1-10 Reading the XML file by using LINQ to XML and Visual Basic syntax

```
Imports <xmlns:o="http://schemas.devleap.com/Orders">
' ...

Dim xmlOrders As XDocument = XDocument.Load("Orders.xml")
Dim orders =
    From o In xmlOrders.<o:orders>.<o:order>
    Select New Order With {
        .CustomerID = o.@idCustomer,
        .Product = New Product With {
            .IdProduct = o.@idProduct,
            .Price = o.@price},
        .Quantity = o.@quantity}
```

The result of these LINQ to XML queries could be used to transparently load a list of *Order* entities into a customer *Orders* property, using LINQ to SQL to submit the changes into the physical database layer:

```
customer.Orders.AddRange(
    From o In xmlOrders.<o:orders>.<o:order>
    Where o.@idCustomer = customer.CustomerID
    Select New Order With {
        .CustomerID = o.@idCustomer,
        .Product = New Product With {
            .IdProduct = o.@idProduct,
            .Price = o.@price},
        .Quantity = o.@quantity})
```

And if you need to generate an ORDERS.XML file starting from your customer's orders, you can at least use Visual Basic XML literals to define the output's XML structure. Listing 1-11 shows an example.

LISTING 1-11 Creating the XML for orders using Visual Basic XML literals

```
Dim xmlOrders = <o:orders>
    <%= From o In orders
        Select <o:order idCustomer=<%= o.CustomerID %>
                        idProduct=<%= o.Product.IdProduct %>
                        quantity=<%= o.Quantity %>
                        price=<%= o.Product.Price %>/> %>
    </o:orders>
```

Note This syntax is an exclusive feature of Visual Basic. There is no equivalent syntax in C#.

You can appreciate the power of this solution, which keeps the XML syntax without losing the stability of typed code and transforms a set of entities selected via LINQ to SQL into an XML *Infoset*.

> **More Info** You will find more information about LINQ to XML syntax and its potential in Chapter 12, "LINQ to XML: Managing the XML Infoset" and in Chapter 13, "LINQ to XML: Querying Nodes."

Language Integration

Language integration is a fundamental aspect of LINQ. The most visible part is the query expression feature, which has been present since C# 3.0 and Visual Basic 2008. With it, you can write code such as you've seen earlier. For example, you can write the following code:

```
var query =
    from    c in Customers
    where   c.Country == "Italy"
    orderby c.Name
    select  new { c.Name, c.City };
```

The previous example is a simplified version of this code:

```
var query =
        Customers
        .Where( c => c.Country == "Italy" );
        .OrderBy( c => c.Name )
        .Select( c => new { c.Name, c.City } );
```

Many people call this simplification *syntax sugaring* because it is just a simpler way to write code that defines a query over data. However, there is more to it than that. Many language constructs and syntaxes are necessary to support what seems to be just a few lines of code that query data. Under the cover of this simple query expression are local type inference, extension methods, lambda expressions, object initialization expressions, and anonymous types. All these features are useful by themselves, but if you look at the overall picture, you can see important steps in two directions: one moving to a more declarative style of coding, and one lowering the impedance mismatch between data and code.

Declarative Programming

What are the differences between a SQL query and an equivalent C# 2.0 or Visual Basic 2005 program that filters data contained in native storage (such as a table for SQL or an array for C# or Visual Basic)?

In SQL, you can write the following:

```
SELECT * FROM Customers WHERE Country = 'Italy'
```

In C#, you would probably write this:

```
public List<Customer> ItalianCustomers( Customer customers[] )
{
    List<Customer> result = new List<Customer>();
    foreach( Customer c in customers ) {
        if (c.Country == "Italy") result.Add( c );
    }
    return result;
}
```

> **Note** This specific example could have been written in C# 2.0 using a *Find* predicate, but we are using it just as an example of the different programming patterns.

The C# code takes longer to write and read. But the most important consideration is expressivity. In SQL, you describe *what* you want. In C#, you describe *how* to obtain the expected result. In SQL, selecting the best algorithm to implement to get the result (which is more explicitly dealt with in C#) is the responsibility of the query engine. The SQL query engine has more freedom to apply optimizations than a C# compiler, which has many more constraints on how operations are performed.

LINQ enables a more declarative style of coding for C# and Visual Basic. A LINQ query describes operations on data through a declarative construct instead of an iterative one. With LINQ, programmers' intentions can be made more explicit—and this knowledge of programmer intent is fundamental to obtaining a higher level of services from the underlying framework. For example, consider parallelization. A SQL query can be split into several concurrent operations simply because it does not place any constraint on the kind of table scan algorithm applied. A C# *foreach* loop is harder to split into several loops over different parts of an array that could be executed in parallel by different processors.

> **More Info** You will find more information about using LINQ to achieve parallelism in code execution in Chapter 16.

Declarative programming can take advantage of services offered by compilers and frameworks, and in general, it is easier to read and maintain. This single feature of LINQ might be the most important because it boosts programmers' productivity. For example, suppose that you want to get a list of all static methods available in the current application domain that return an *IEnumerable<T>* interface. You can use LINQ to write a query over Reflection:

```
var query =
    from     assembly in AppDomain.CurrentDomain.GetAssemblies()
    from     type in assembly.GetTypes()
    from     method in type.GetMethods()
    where    method.IsStatic
             && method.ReturnType.GetInterface( "IEnumerable'1" ) != null
    orderby method.DeclaringType.Name, method.Name
    group    method by new { Class = method.DeclaringType.Name,
                             Method = method.Name };
```

The equivalent C# code that handles data takes more time to write, is harder to read, and is probably more error prone. You can see a version that is not particularly optimized in Listing 1-12.

LISTING 1-12 C# code equivalent to a LINQ query over Reflection

```
List<String> results = new List<string>();
foreach( var assembly in AppDomain.CurrentDomain.GetAssemblies()) {
    foreach( var type in assembly.GetTypes() ) {
        foreach( var method in type.GetMethods()) {
            if (method.IsStatic &&
                method.ReturnType.GetInterface("IEnumerable'1") != null) {
                string fullName = String.Format( "{0}.{1}",
                                    method.DeclaringType.Name,
                                    method.Name );
                if (results.IndexOf( fullName ) < 0) {
                    results.Add( fullName );
                }
            }
        }
    }
}
results.Sort();
```

Type Checking

Another important aspect of language integration is type checking. Whenever data is manipulated by LINQ, no unsafe cast is necessary. The short syntax of a query expression makes no compromises with type checking: data is always strongly typed, including both the queried collections and the single entities that are read and returned.

The type checking of the languages that support LINQ (starting from C# 3.0 and Visual Basic 2008) is preserved even when LINQ-specific features are used. This enables the use of Visual Studio features such as IntelliSense and Refactoring, even with LINQ queries. These Visual Studio features are other important factors in programmers' productivity.

Transparency Across Different Type Systems

If you think about the type system of the .NET Framework and the type system of SQL Server, you will realize they are different. Using LINQ gives precedence to the .NET Framework type system, because it is the one supported by any language that hosts a LINQ query. However, most of your data will be saved in a relational database, so it is necessary to convert many types of data between these two worlds. LINQ handles this conversion for you automatically, making the differences in type systems almost completely transparent to the programmer.

> **More Info**   There are some limitations in the capability to perform conversions between different type systems and LINQ. You will find some information about this topic throughout the book, and you can find a more detailed type system compatibilities table in the product documentation.

LINQ Implementations

LINQ is a technology that covers many data sources. Some of these sources are included in LINQ implementations that Microsoft has provided—starting with .NET Framework 3.5—as shown in Figure 1-1, which also includes LINQ to Entities.

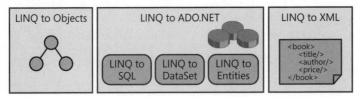

FIGURE 1-1 LINQ implementations provided by Microsoft starting with .NET Framework 3.5.

Each implementation is defined through a set of extension methods that implement the operators needed by LINQ to work with a particular data source. Access to these features is controlled by the imported namespaces.

LINQ to Objects

LINQ to Objects is designed to manipulate collections of objects, which can be related to each other to form a graph. From a certain point of view, LINQ to Objects is the default implementation used by a LINQ query. You enable LINQ to Objects by including the *System.Linq* namespace.

> **More Info**   The base concepts of LINQ are explained in Chapter 2, using LINQ to Objects as a reference implementation.

However, it would be a mistake to think that LINQ to Objects queries are limited to collections of user-generated data. You can see why this is not true by analyzing Listing 1-13, which shows a LINQ query that extracts information from the file system. The code reads the list of all files in a given directory into memory and then filters that list with the LINQ query.

LISTING 1-13 LINQ query that retrieves a list of temporary files larger than 10,000 bytes, ordered by size

```
string tempPath = Path.GetTempPath();
DirectoryInfo dirInfo = new DirectoryInfo( tempPath );
var query =
    from    f in dirInfo.GetFiles()
    where   f.Length > 10000
    orderby f.Length descending
    select  f;
```

LINQ to ADO.NET

LINQ to ADO.NET includes different LINQ implementations that share the need to manipulate relational data. It also includes other technologies that are specific to each particular persistence layer:

- **LINQ to SQL**   Handles the mapping between custom types in the .NET Framework and the physical table schema in SQL Server.

- **LINQ to Entities**   An Object Relational Mapping (ORM) that—instead of using the physical database as a persistence layer—uses a conceptual Entity Data Model (EDM). The result is an abstraction layer that is independent from the physical data layer.

- **LINQ to DataSet**   Enables querying a DataSet by using LINQ.

LINQ to SQL and LINQ to Entities have similarities because they both access information stored in a relational database and operate on object entities that represent external data in memory. The main difference is that they operate at a different level of abstraction. Whereas LINQ to SQL is tied to the physical database structure, LINQ to Entities operates over a conceptual model (business entities) that might be far from the physical structure (database tables).

The reason for these different options for accessing relational data through LINQ is that different models for database access are in use today. Some organizations implement all access through stored procedures, including any kind of database query, without using dynamic queries. Many others use stored procedures to insert, update, or delete data and dynamically build SELECT statements to query data. Some see the database as a simple object persistence layer, whereas others put some business logic into the database by using triggers, stored procedures, or both. LINQ tries to offer help and improvement in database access without forcing everyone to adopt a single comprehensive model.

More Info   The use of any LINQ to ADO.NET implementation depends on the inclusion of particular namespaces in the scope. Part II, "LINQ to Relational," investigates LINQ to ADO.NET implementations and similar details.

LINQ to XML

You've already seen that LINQ to XML offers a slightly different syntax that operates on XML data, allowing query and data manipulation. A particular type of support for LINQ to XML is offered by Visual Basic, which includes XML literals in the language. This enhanced support simplifies the code needed to manipulate XML data. In fact, you can write a query such as the following in Visual Basic:

```
Dim book =
    <Book Title="Programming  LINQ">
        <%= From person In team
            Where person.Role = "Author"
            Select <Author><%= person.Name %></Author> %>
    </Book>
```

This query corresponds to the following C# syntax:

```
dim book =
    new XElement( "Book",
        new XAttribute( "Title", "Programming LINQ" ),
        from   person in team
        where  person.Role == "Author"
        select new XElement( "Author", person.Name ) );
```

More Info   You can find more information about LINQ to XML in Chapters 12 and 13.

Summary

In this chapter, we introduced LINQ and discussed how it works. We also examined how different data sources can be queried and manipulated by using a uniform syntax that is integrated into current mainstream programming languages such as C# and Visual Basic. We took a look at the benefits offered by language integration, including declarative programming, type checking, and transparency across different type systems. We briefly presented the LINQ implementations available since .NET Framework 3.5—LINQ to Objects, LINQ to ADO.NET, and LINQ to XML—which we will cover in more detail in the remaining parts of the book.

Chapter 2
LINQ Syntax Fundamentals

With Microsoft Language Integrated Query (LINQ), you can query and manage sequences of items (objects, entities, database records, XML nodes, and so on) within your software solutions, using a common syntax and a unique programming language—regardless of the nature of the items handled. The key feature of LINQ is its integration with widely used programming languages, an integration made possible by the use of a syntax common to all kinds of content.

As described in Chapter 1, "LINQ Introduction," LINQ provides a basic infrastructure for many different implementations of querying engines, including LINQ to Objects, LINQ to SQL, LINQ to DataSet, LINQ to Entities, LINQ to XML, LINQ to SharePoint, and so on. All these query extensions are based on specialized extension methods and share a common set of keywords for query expression syntax that you will learn in this chapter.

Before looking at each keyword in detail, we will walk you through various aspects of a simple LINQ query and introduce you to fundamental elements of LINQ syntax.

LINQ Queries

LINQ is based on a set of query operators, defined as extension methods, that work with any object that implements the *IEnumerable<T>* or *IQueryable<T>* interface.

This approach makes LINQ a general-purpose querying framework, because many collections and types implement *IEnumerable<T>* or *IQueryable<T>*, and developers can define their own implementations. This query infrastructure is also highly extensible, as you will see in Chapter 15 "Extending LINQ." Given the architecture of extension methods, you can specialize a method's behavior based on the type of data you are querying. For instance, both LINQ to SQL and LINQ to XML have specialized LINQ operators to handle relational data and XML nodes, respectively.

Query Syntax

To introduce query syntax, let us start with a simple example. Imagine that you need to query an array of objects of a *Developer* type by using LINQ to Objects. You want to extract the names of the developers who use Microsoft Visual C# as their main programming language. The code you might use is shown in Listing 2-1.

LISTING 2-1 A simple query expression in C#

```csharp
using System;
using System.Linq;
using System.Collections.Generic;

public class Developer {
    public string Name;
    public string Language;
    public int Age;
}

class App {
    static void Main() {
        Developer[] developers = new Developer[] {
            new Developer {Name = "Paolo", Language = "C#"},
            new Developer {Name = "Marco", Language = "C#"},
            new Developer {Name = "Frank", Language = "VB.NET"}};

        var developersUsingCSharp =
            from    d in developers
            where   d.Language == "C#"
            select  d.Name;

        foreach (var item in developersUsingCSharp) {
            Console.WriteLine(item);
        }
    }
}
```

When you run this code, it writes the names Paolo and Marco.

In Microsoft Visual Basic, you can express the same query against the same *Developer* type with syntax such as that shown in Listing 2-2.

LISTING 2-2 A simple query expression in Visual Basic

```vbnet
Imports System
Imports System.Linq
Imports System.Collections.Generic

Public Class Developer
    Public Name As String
    Public Language As String
    Public Age As Integer
End Class
```

```
Module App
    Sub Main()

        Dim developers As Developer() = New Developer() {
            New Developer With {.Name = "Paolo", .Language = "C#"},
            New Developer With {.Name = "Marco", .Language = "C#"},
            New Developer With {.Name = "Frank", .Language = "VB.NET"}}

        Dim developersUsingCSharp =
            From    d In developers
            Where   d.Language = "C#"
            Select d.Name

        For Each item in developersUsingCSharp
            Console.WriteLine(item)
        Next
    End Sub
End Module
```

The syntax of the queries (shown in bold in Listings 2-1 and 2-2) is called a *query expression*. In some LINQ implementations, an in-memory representation of these queries is known as an *expression tree*. A query expression operates on one or more information sources by applying one or more query operators from either the group of standard query operators or domain-specific operators. In general, the evaluation of a query expression results in a sequence of values. A query expression is evaluated only when its contents are enumerated. For further details on query expressions and expression trees, refer to Chapter 14, "Inside Expression Trees."

> **Note** For the sake of simplicity, we will cover only the C# syntax in the following examples; however, you can see that the Visual Basic version of this sample is very similar to the C# one.

These queries look similar to a SQL statement, although their style is a bit different. The sample expression we have defined consists of a selection command:

```
select d.Name
```

That command is applied to a set of items:

```
from d in developers
```

The *from* clause targets any instance of a class that implements the *IEnumerable<T>* interface. The selection applies a specific filtering condition:

```
where d.Language == "C#"
```

The language compilers translate these clauses into invocations of extension methods that are sequentially applied to the target of the query. The core library of LINQ, defined in assembly System.Core.dll, defines a set of extension methods grouped by target and purpose. For example, the assembly includes a class named *Enumerable*, defined in the namespace *System.Linq*, which defines extension methods that can be applied to instances of types implementing the *IEnumerable<T>* interface.

The filtering condition (*where*) defined in the sample query translates into an invocation of the *Where* extension method of the *Enumerable* class. This method provides two overloads, both of which accept a delegate to a *predicate* function that describes the filtering condition to check while partitioning the resulting data. In this case, the filtering *predicate* is a generic delegate that accepts an element of type *T*, which is the same type as the instances stored in the enumeration we are filtering. The delegate returns a *Boolean* result stating the membership of the item in the filtered result set:

```
public static IEnumerable<T> Where<T>(
    this IEnumerable<T> source,
    Func<T, bool> predicate);
```

As you can see from the method signature, you can invoke this method against any type that implements *IEnumerable<T>*; therefore, you can call it on the *developers* array as follows:

```
var filteredDevelopers = developers.Where(delegate (Developer d) {
    return (d.Language == "C#");
});
```

Here, the *predicate* argument passed to the *Where* method represents an anonymous delegate to a function called for each item of type *Developer* taken from the source set of data (*developers*). The result of invoking the *Where* method will be a subset of items: all those that satisfy the *predicate* condition.

C# and Visual Basic can define an anonymous delegate in an easier way, using a *lambda expression*. Using a lambda expression, you can rewrite the sample filtering code more compactly:

```
var filteredDevelopers = developers.Where(d => d.Language == "C#");
```

The *select* statement is also an extension method (named *Select*) provided by the *Enumerable* class. Here is the signature of the *Select* method:

```
public static IEnumerable<TResult> Select<TSource, TResult>(
    this IEnumerable<TSource> source,
    Func<TSource, TResult> selector);
```

The *selector* argument is a projection that returns an enumeration of objects of type *TResult*, which is obtained from a set of source objects of type *TSource*. As described previously, you can apply this method to the whole collection of *developers* using a lambda expression, or invoke it on the collection that is filtered by the programming language (named *filteredDevelopers*)—because it is still a type implementing *IEnumerable<T>*:

```
var csharpDevelopersNames = filteredDevelopers.Select(d => d.Name);
```

Based on the sequence of statements we have just described, here is the sample query rewritten without using the query expression syntax:

```
IEnumerable<string> developersUsingCSharp =
    developers
    .Where(d => d.Language == "C#")
    .Select(d => d.Name);
```

The *Where* method and the *Select* method both receive lambda expressions as arguments. These lambda expressions translate to predicates and projections based on a set of generic delegate types defined within the *System* namespace, in the System.Core.dll assembly.

Here is the entire family of available generic delegate types. Many extension methods of the *Enumerable* class accept these delegates as arguments, and we will use them throughout the examples in this chapter:

```
public delegate TResult Func< TResult >();
public delegate TResult Func< T, TResult >( T arg );
public delegate TResult Func< T1, T2, TResult > (T1 arg1, T2 arg2 );
public delegate TResult Func< T1, T2, T3, TResult >
    ( T1 arg1, T2 arg2, T3 arg3 );
public delegate TResult Func< T1, T2, T3, T4, TResult >
    (T1 arg1, T2 arg2, T3 arg3, T4 arg4 );
...
public delegate TResult Func<T1, T2, T3, T4, T5, T6, T7, T8, T9, T10, T11, T12, T13, T14,
    T15, TResult>(T1 arg1, T2 arg2, T3 arg3, T4 arg4, T5 arg5, T6 arg6, T7 arg7, T8 arg8,
    T9 arg9, T10 arg10, T11 arg11, T12 arg12, T13 arg13, T14 arg14, T15 arg15);
public delegate TResult Func<T1, T2, T3, T4, T5, T6, T7, T8, T9, T10, T11, T12, T13, T14,
    T15, T16, TResult>(T1 arg1, T2 arg2, T3 arg3, T4 arg4, T5 arg5, T6 arg6, T7 arg7, T8
arg8,
    T9 arg9, T10 arg10, T11 arg11, T12 arg12, T13 arg13, T14 arg14, T15 arg15, T16 arg16);
```

A final version of the original query in this chapter might look something like Listing 2-3.

LISTING 2-3 The original query expression translated into basic elements

```
Func<Developer, bool> filteringPredicate = d => d.Language == "C#";
Func<Developer, string> selectionPredicate = d => d.Name;
IEnumerable<string> developersUsingCSharp =
    developers
    .Where(filteringPredicate)
    .Select(selectionPredicate);
```

The C# compiler, like the Visual Basic compiler, translates the LINQ query expressions (Listings 2-1 and 2-2) into something like the statement shown in Listing 2-3. After you become famil-iar with the query expression syntax (Listings 2-1 and 2-2), it is simpler and easier to write and manage this syntax, even if it is optional—and you can always use the equivalent, more verbose version (Listing 2-3). Nevertheless, sometimes it is necessary to use the direct call to an extension method because query expression syntax does not cover all possible extension methods.

> **Important** In Chapter 3, "LINQ to Objects," we will cover in more detail all the extension methods available in the *Enumerable* class defined in the *System.Linq* namespace.

Full Query Syntax

The previous section described a simple query over a list of objects. Query expression syntax, however, is more complete and articulate than shown in that example, providing many differ-ent language keywords that satisfy most common querying scenarios. Every query starts with a *from* clause and ends with either a *select* clause or a *group* clause. The reason to start with a *from* clause instead of a *select* statement, as in SQL syntax, is related (among other technical reasons) to the need to provide IntelliSense capabilities within the remaining part of the query, which makes writing conditions, selections, and any other query expression clauses easier. A *select* clause projects the result of an expression into an enumerable object. A *group* clause projects the result of an expression into a set of groups, based on a grouping condition, where each group is an enumerable object. The following code shows a prototype of the full syntax of a query expression:

```
query-expression ::= from-clause query-body

query-body ::=
join-clause*
(from-clause join-clause* | let-clause | where-clause)*
orderby-clause?
(select-clause | groupby-clause)
    query-continuation?

from-clause ::= from itemName in srcExpr

select-clause ::= select selExpr

groupby-clause ::= group selExpr by keyExpr
```

The first *from* clause can be followed by zero or more *from*, *let*, or *where* clauses. A *let* clause applies a name to the result of an expression; it is useful whenever you need to reference the same expression many times within a query:

```
let-clause ::= let itemName = selExpr
```

A *where* clause, as already discussed, defines a filter that is applied to include specific items in the results:

```
where-clause ::= where predExpr
```

Each *from* clause generates a local "range variable" that corresponds to each item in the source sequence on which query operators (such as the extension methods of *System.Linq.Enumerable*) are applied.

A *from* clause can be followed by any number of *join* clauses. The final *select* or *group* clause can be preceded by an *orderby* clause that applies an ordering to the results:

```
join-clause ::=
join itemName in srcExpr on keyExpr equals keyExpr
(into itemName)?

orderby-clause ::= orderby (keyExpr (ascending | descending)?)*

query-continuation ::= into itemName query-body
```

You will see examples of query expressions throughout this book. You can refer to this section when you want to check specific elements of their syntax.

Query Keywords

The following sections describe the various query keywords available in query expression syntax in more detail.

From Clause

The first keyword is the *from* clause. It defines the data source of a query or subquery and a range variable that defines each single element to query from the data source. The data source can be any instance of a type that implements the interfaces *IEnumerable*, *IEnumerable<T>*, or *IQueryable<T>* (which implements *IEnumerable<T>*). The following excerpt shows a sample C# statement that uses this clause:

```
from rangeVariable in dataSource
```

The language compiler infers the type of the range variable from the type of the data source. For example, if the data source is of type *IEnumerable<Developer>*, the range variable will be of type *Developer*. In cases that do not use a strongly typed data source—for example an *ArrayList* of objects of type *Developer* that implement *IEnumerable*—you should explicitly provide the type of the range variable. In Listing 2-4, you can see an example of a query that explicitly declares the *Developer* type for the range variable named *d*.

LISTING 2-4 A query expression against a nongeneric data source, with type declaration for the range variable

```
ArrayList developers = new ArrayList();
developers.Add(new Developer { Name = "Paolo", Language = "C#" });
developers.Add(new Developer { Name = "Marco", Language = "C#" });
developers.Add(new Developer { Name = "Frank", Language = "VB.NET" });

var developersUsingCSharp =
    from    Developer d in developers
    where   d.Language == "C#"
    select  d.Name;

foreach (string item in developersUsingCSharp) {
    Console.WriteLine(item);
}
```

In Listing 2-4, the casting is mandatory; otherwise, the query will not compile because the compiler cannot automatically infer the type of the range variable, thereby losing the ability to resolve the *Language* and *Name* member access in the same query.

Queries can have multiple *from* clauses that define joins between multiple data sources. In C#, each data source requires a *from* clause declaration, as you can see in Listing 2-5, which joins customers with their orders. Note that the relationship between *Customer* and *Order* is physically defined by the presence of an *Orders* array of type *Order* in each instance of *Customer*.

LISTING 2-5 A C# query expression with a join between two data sources

```
public class Customer {
    public String Name { get; set; }
    public String City { get; set; }
    public Order[] Orders { get; set; }
}

public class Order {
    public Int32 IdOrder { get; set; }
    public Decimal EuroAmount { get; set; }
    public String Description { get; set; }
}

// ... code omitted ...

static void queryWithJoin() {
    Customer[] customers = new Customer[] {
        new Customer { Name = "Paolo", City = "Brescia",
            Orders = new Order[] {
                new Order { IdOrder = 1, EuroAmount = 100, Description = "Order 1" },
                new Order { IdOrder = 2, EuroAmount = 150, Description = "Order 2" },
                new Order { IdOrder = 3, EuroAmount = 230, Description = "Order 3" },
            }},
```

```
        new Customer { Name = "Marco", City = "Torino",
            Orders = new Order[] {
                new Order { IdOrder = 4, EuroAmount = 320, Description = "Order 4" },
                new Order { IdOrder = 5, EuroAmount = 170, Description = "Order 5" },
            }}};

    var ordersQuery =
        from    c in customers
        from    o in c.Orders
        select new { c.Name, o.IdOrder, o.EuroAmount };

    foreach (var item in ordersQuery) {
        Console.WriteLine(item);
    }
}
```

In Visual Basic, a single *from* clause can define multiple data sources, separated by commas, as you can see in Listing 2-6.

LISTING 2-6 A Visual Basic query expression with a join between two data sources

```
Dim customers As Customer() = {
    New Customer With {.Name = "Paolo", .City = "Brescia",
        .Orders = New Order() {
            New Order With {.IdOrder = 1, .EuroAmount = 100, .Description = "Order 1"},
            New Order With {.IdOrder = 2, .EuroAmount = 150, .Description = "Order 2"},
            New Order With {.IdOrder = 3, .EuroAmount = 230, .Description = "Order 3"}
        }},
    New Customer With {.Name = "Marco", .City = "Torino",
        .Orders = New Order() {
            New Order With {.IdOrder = 4, .EuroAmount = 320, .Description = "Order 4"},
            New Order With {.IdOrder = 5, .EuroAmount = 170, .Description = "Order 5"}
        }}}

Dim ordersQuery =
    From    c In customers,
            o In c.Orders
    Select c.Name, o.IdOrder, o.EuroAmount

For Each item In ordersQuery
    Console.WriteLine(item)
Next
```

Important When you use multiple *from* clauses, the "join condition" is determined by the structure of the data and is different from the concept of a join in a relational database. (For this, you need to use the *join* clause in a query expression, which we will cover later in this chapter.)

Where Clause

As discussed earlier, the *where* clause specifies a filtering condition to apply to the data source. The predicate applies a *Boolean* condition to each item in the data source, extracting only those that evaluate to *true*. Within a single query, you can have multiple *where* clauses or a *where* clause with multiple predicates combined by using logical operators (*&&*, *||*, and *!* in C#; or *And, Or, AndAlso, OrElse, Is,* and *IsNot* in Visual Basic). In Visual Basic, the predicate can be any expression that evaluates to a *Boolean* value, so you can also use a numeric expression that will be considered *true* if it is not equal to zero.

Consider the query in Listing 2-7, which uses the *where* clause to extract all the orders with a *EuroAmount* greater than 200 Euros.

LISTING 2-7 A C# query expression with a *where* clause

```
var ordersQuery =
    from   c in customers
    from   o in c.Orders
    where  o.EuroAmount > 200
    select new { c.Name, o.IdOrder, o.EuroAmount };
```

In Listing 2-8, you can see the corresponding query syntax using Visual Basic.

LISTING 2-8 A Visual Basic query expression with a *where* clause

```
Dim ordersQuery =
    From   c In customers,
           o In c.Orders
    Where  o.EuroAmount > 200
    Select c.Name, o.IdOrder, o.EuroAmount
```

Select Clause

The *select* clause specifies the shape of the query output. It is based on a projection that determines what to select from the result of the evaluation of all the clauses and expressions that precede it. In Visual Basic, the *Select* clause is not mandatory. If it is not specified, the query returns a type that is based on the range variable identified for the current scope. Listings 2-7 and 2-8 used the *select* clause to project anonymous types made up of properties or members of the range variables in scope. As you can see by comparing the C# syntax (Listing 2-7) and the Visual Basic syntax (Listing 2-8), the Visual Basic version looks more like a SQL statement in its select pattern, whereas the C# version appears more like programming language syntax. In fact, in C# you must explicitly declare your intent to create a new anonymous type instance, whereas in Visual Basic the language syntax is lighter and hides the inner workings.

Group and *Into* Clauses

The *group* clause can be used to project a result grouped by a key. It can be used as an alter-native to the *from* clause and allows you to use single-value keys as well as multiple-value keys. Listing 2-9 shows a query that groups developers by programming language.

LISTING 2-9 A C# query expression to group developers by programming language

```csharp
Developer[] developers = new Developer[] {
    new Developer { Name = "Paolo", Language = "C#" },
    new Developer { Name = "Marco", Language = "C#" },
    new Developer { Name = "Frank", Language = "VB.NET" },
};

var developersGroupedByLanguage =
    from  d in developers
    group d by d.Language;

foreach (var group in developersGroupedByLanguage) {
    Console.WriteLine("Language: {0}", group.Key);
    foreach (var item in group) {
        Console.WriteLine("\t{0}", item.Name);
    }
}
```

The output of the code excerpt in Listing 2-9 is:

```
Language: C#
        Paolo
        Marco
Language: VB.NET
        Frank
```

As you can see, the result of the query is an enumeration of groups identified by a key and made up of inner items. The example enumerates each group in the query result, writing its *Key* property to the console and then iterating the items in each group to extract their values. As mentioned previously, you can group items by using a multiple-value key that makes use of anonymous types. Listing 2-10 shows an example that groups developers by language and an age cluster.

LISTING 2-10 A C# query expression to group developers by programming language and age

```csharp
Developer[] developers = new Developer[] {
    new Developer { Name = "Paolo", Language = "C#", Age = 32 },
    new Developer { Name = "Marco", Language = "C#", Age = 37},
    new Developer { Name = "Frank", Language = "VB.NET", Age = 48  },
};
```

```
var developersGroupedByLanguage =
    from  d in developers
    group d by new { d.Language, AgeCluster = (d.Age / 10) * 10 };

foreach (var group in developersGroupedByLanguage) {
    Console.WriteLine("Language: {0}", group.Key);
    foreach (var item in group) {
        Console.WriteLine("\t{0}", item.Name);
    }
}
```

This time, the output of the code excerpt in Listing 2-10 is:

```
Language: { Language = C#, AgeCluster = 30 }
        Paolo
        Marco
Language: { Language = VB.NET, AgeCluster = 40 }
        Frank
```

In this example, the *Key* for each group is an anonymous type defined by two properties: *Language* and *AgeCluster*.

Visual Basic also supports grouping results by using the *Group By* clause. Listing 2-11 shows a query that is equivalent to the one shown in Listing 2-9.

LISTING 2-11 A Visual Basic query expression to group developers by programming language

```
Dim developers As Developer() = {
    New Developer With {.Name = "Paolo", .Language = "C#", .Age = 32},
    New Developer With {.Name = "Marco", .Language = "C#", .Age = 37},
    New Developer With {.Name = "Frank", .Language = "VB.NET", .Age = 48}}

Dim developersGroupedByLanguage =
    From    d In developers
    Group   d By d.Language Into Group
    Select  Language, Group

For Each group In developersGroupedByLanguage
    Console.WriteLine("Language: {0}", group.Language)
    For Each item In group.Group
        Console.WriteLine("    {0}", item.Name)
    Next
Next
```

The Visual Basic syntax is a bit more complex than the corresponding C# syntax. In Visual Basic, you project the grouping by using the *into* clause to create a new *Group* object of items and then explicitly declare the selection pattern. However, the result of the grouping is easier to enumerate because the *Key* value keeps its name (*Language*).

C# also provides an *into* clause that is useful in conjunction with the *group* keyword, even if using it is not mandatory. You can use the *into* keyword to store the results of a *select*, *group*, or *join* statement in a temporary variable. You might use this construction when you need to execute additional queries over the results. Because of this behavior, this keyword is also called a *continuation* clause. Listing 2-12 shows an example of a C# query expression that uses the *into* clause.

LISTING 2-12 A C# query expression using the *into* clause

```
var developersGroupedByLanguage =
    from   d in developers
    group  d by d.Language into developersGrouped
    select new {
        Language = developersGrouped.Key,
        DevelopersCount = developersGrouped.Count()
    };

foreach (var group in developersGroupedByLanguage) {
    Console.WriteLine ("Language {0} contains {1} developers",
        group.Language, group.DevelopersCount);
}
```

Orderby Clause

The *orderby* clause, as you can assume from its name, lets you sort the result of a query in either ascending or descending order. The ordering can use one or more keys that combine different sorting directions. Listing 2-13 shows a query that extracts orders placed by customers, ordered by *EuroAmount*. (By default, when not explicitly defined, the *orderby* clause sorts values in ascending sequence.)

LISTING 2-13 A C# query expression with an *orderby* clause

```
var ordersSortedByEuroAmount =
    from   c in customers
    from   o in c.Orders
    orderby o.EuroAmount
    select  new { c.Name, o.IdOrder, o.EuroAmount };
```

Listing 2-14 shows a query that selects orders sorted by customer *Name* and *EuroAmount* in descending order.

LISTING 2-14 A C# query expression with an *orderby* clause with multiple ordering conditions

```
var ordersSortedByCustomerAndEuroAmount =
    from    c in customers
    from    o in c.Orders
    orderby c.Name, o.EuroAmount descending
    select  new { c.Name, o.IdOrder, o.EuroAmount };
```

Listing 2-15 shows the query from Listing 2-14 written in Visual Basic.

LISTING 2-15 A Visual Basic query expression with an *orderby* clause with multiple ordering conditions

```
Dim ordersSortedByCustomerAndEuroAmount =
    From    c In customers,
            o In c.Orders
    Order  By c.Name, o.EuroAmount Descending
    Select c.Name, o.IdOrder, o.EuroAmount
```

Here, both languages have very similar syntax.

Join Clause

The *join* keyword lets you associate different data sources on the basis of a member that can be compared for equivalency. It works similarly to a SQL equijoin statement. You cannot compare items to join by using comparisons such as "greater than," "less than," or "not equal to." You can define equality comparisons only by using a special *equals* keyword that behaves differently from the "==" operator, because the position of the operands is significant. With *equals*, the left key consumes the outer source sequence, and the right key consumes the inner source sequence. The outer source sequence is in scope only on the left side of *equals*, and the inner source sequence is in scope only on the right side. Here is this concept presented in pseudocode:

```
join-clause ::= join innerItem in innerSequence on outerKey equals innerKey
```

By using the *join* clause, you can define inner joins, group joins, and left outer joins. An inner join is a join that returns a flat result, mapping the outer data source elements with the corresponding inner data source. It skips outer data source elements that lack corresponding inner data source elements. Listing 2-16 presents a simple query with an inner join between product categories and related products.

LISTING 2-16 A C# query expression with an inner join

```csharp
public class Category {
    public Int32 IdCategory { get; set; }
    public String Name { get; set; }
}

public class Product {
    public String IdProduct { get; set; }
    public Int32 IdCategory { get; set; }
    public String Description { get; set; }
}

// ... code omitted ...

Category[] categories = new Category[] {
    new Category { IdCategory = 1, Name = "Pasta"},
    new Category { IdCategory = 2, Name = "Beverages"},
    new Category { IdCategory = 3, Name = "Other food"},
};

Product[] products = new Product[] {
    new Product { IdProduct = "PASTA01", IdCategory = 1, Description = "Tortellini" },
    new Product { IdProduct = "PASTA02", IdCategory = 1, Description = "Spaghetti" },
    new Product { IdProduct = "PASTA03", IdCategory = 1, Description = "Fusilli" },
    new Product { IdProduct = "BEV01", IdCategory = 2, Description = "Water" },
    new Product { IdProduct = "BEV02", IdCategory = 2, Description = "Orange Juice" },
};

var categoriesAndProducts =
    from   c in categories
    join   p in products on c.IdCategory equals p.IdCategory
    select new {
        c.IdCategory,
        CategoryName = c.Name,
        Product = p.Description
    };

foreach (var item in categoriesAndProducts) {
    Console.WriteLine(item);
}
```

The output of this code excerpt is similar to the following. Notice that the "Other food" category is missing from the output because no products are included in it:

```
{ IdCategory = 1, CategoryName = Pasta, Product = Tortellini }
{ IdCategory = 1, CategoryName = Pasta, Product = Spaghetti }
{ IdCategory = 1, CategoryName = Pasta, Product = Fusilli }
{ IdCategory = 2, CategoryName = Beverages, Product = Water }
{ IdCategory = 2, CategoryName = Beverages, Product = Orange Juice }
```

A group join defines a join that produces a hierarchical result set, grouping the inner sequence elements with their corresponding outer sequence elements. In cases in which an outer sequence element is missing its corresponding inner sequence elements, the outer element will be joined with an empty array. A group join does not have a relational counterpart in SQL syntax because of its hierarchical result. Listing 2-17 shows an example of such a query. (You will see an expanded form of this type of query in Chapter 3.)

LISTING 2-17 A C# query expression with a group join

```csharp
var categoriesAndProducts =
    from c in categories
    join p in products on c.IdCategory equals p.IdCategory
        into productsByCategory
    select new {
        c.IdCategory,
        CategoryName = c.Name,
        Products = productsByCategory
    };

foreach (var category in categoriesAndProducts) {
    Console.WriteLine("{0} - {1}", category.IdCategory, category.CategoryName);
    foreach (var product in category.Products) {
        Console.WriteLine("\t{0}", product.Description);
    }
}
```

The output of this code excerpt follows. Notice that this time the "Other food" category is present in the output, even though it is empty:

```
1 - Pasta
        Tortellini
        Spaghetti
        Fusilli
2 - Beverages
        Water
        Orange Juice
3 - Other food
```

Visual Basic provides a specific keyword called *Group Join* to define group joins in query expressions.

A left outer join returns a flat result set that includes any outer source element even if it is missing its corresponding inner source element. To produce this result, you need to use the *DefaultIfEmpty* extension method, which returns a default value in the case of an empty data source value. We will cover this and many other extension methods in more detail in Chapter 3. In Listing 2-18, you can see an example of this syntax.

LISTING 2-18 A C# query expression with a left outer join

```
var categoriesAndProducts =
    from c in categories
    join p in products on c.IdCategory equals p.IdCategory
        into productsByCategory
    from pc in productsByCategory.DefaultIfEmpty(
      new Product {
        IdProduct = String.Empty,
        Description = String.Empty,
        IdCategory = 0} )
    select new {
        c.IdCategory,
        CategoryName = c.Name,
        Product = pc.Description
    };

foreach (var item in categoriesAndProducts) {
    Console.WriteLine(item);
}
```

This example produces the following output:

```
{ IdCategory = 1, CategoryName = Pasta, Product = Tortellini }
{ IdCategory = 1, CategoryName = Pasta, Product = Spaghetti }
{ IdCategory = 1, CategoryName = Pasta, Product = Fusilli }
{ IdCategory = 2, CategoryName = Beverages, Product = Water }
{ IdCategory = 2, CategoryName = Beverages, Product = Orange Juice }
{ IdCategory = 3, CategoryName = Other food, Product =  }
```

Notice that the "Other food" category is present with an empty product, which is provided by the *DefaultIfEmpty* extension method.

One last point to emphasize about the *join* clause is that you can compare elements by using composite keys. You simply make use of anonymous types as shown with the *group* keyword. For example, if you had a composite key in *Category* made up of *IdCategory* and *Year*, you could write the following statement with an anonymous type used in the *equals* condition:

```
from c in categories
join p in products
    on new { c.IdCategory, c.Year } equals new { p.IdCategory, p.Year }
    into productsByCategory
```

As you have already seen in this chapter, you can also get the results of joins by using nested *from* clauses, which is a useful approach whenever you need to define non-equijoin queries.

Visual Basic has syntax quite similar to C#, but offers some shortcuts to define joins more quickly. You can define implicit *join* statements by using multiple *In* clauses in the *From* statement and defining the equality conditions with a *Where* clause. In Listing 2-19, you can see an example of this syntax.

LISTING 2-19 A Visual Basic implicit join statement

```
Dim categoriesAndProducts =
    From    c In categories, p In products
    Where   c.IdCategory = p.IdCategory
    Select c.IdCategory, CategoryName = c.Name, Product = p.Description

For Each item In categoriesAndProducts
    Console.WriteLine(item)
Next
```

In Listing 2-20, you can see the same query defined by using the standard explicit *join* syntax.

LISTING 2-20 A Visual Basic explicit join statement

```
Dim categoriesAndProducts =
    From    c In categories Join p In products
            On p.IdCategory Equals c.IdCategory
    Select c.IdCategory, CategoryName = c.Name, Product = p.Description
```

Notice that in Visual Basic the order of elements in the equality comparison does not matter because the compiler will arrange them on its own, making the query syntax more relaxed, as happens in classic relational SQL.

Let Clause

The *let* clause allows you to store the result of a subexpression in a variable that can be used somewhere else in the query. This clause is useful when you need to reuse the same expression many times in the same query, and you do not want to define it every single time you use it. Using the *let* clause, you can define a new range variable for that expression and subsequently reference it within the query. Once assigned, a range variable defined by a *let* clause cannot be changed. However, if the range variable holds a queryable type, it can be queried. In Listing 2-21, you can see an example of this clause applied to select the same product categories with the count of their products, sorted by the counter itself.

LISTING 2-21 A C# sample of usage of the *let* clause

```
var categoriesByProductsNumberQuery =
    from    c in categories
    join    p in products on c.IdCategory equals p.IdCategory
        into productsByCategory
    let     ProductsCount = productsByCategory.Count()
    orderby ProductsCount
    select  new { c.IdCategory, ProductsCount};

foreach (var item in categoriesByProductsNumberQuery) {
    Console.WriteLine(item);
}
```

Here is the output of the code excerpt in Listing 2-21:

```
{ IdCategory = 3, ProductsCount = 0 }
{ IdCategory = 2, ProductsCount = 2 }
{ IdCategory = 1, ProductsCount = 3 }
```

Visual Basic uses syntax very similar to C#, and also allows you to define multiple aliases, separated by commas, within the same *let* clause.

Additional Visual Basic Keywords

Visual Basic includes additional query expression keywords that are available in C# only by using extension methods. These keywords are described in the following list:

- ■ ***Aggregate***   Useful for applying an aggregate function to a data source. You can use *Aggregate* to begin a new query instead of a From clause.
- ■ ***Distinct***   Can be used to eliminate duplicate values in query results.
- ■ ***Skip***   Can be used to skip the first N elements of a query result.
- ■ ***Skip While***   Can be used to skip the first elements of a query result that satisfy a specified predicate.
- ■ ***Take***   Can be used to return the first N elements of a query result.
- ■ ***Take While***   Can be used to take the first elements of a query result that satisfy a specified predicate.

You can use *Skip* and *Take* (or *Skip While* and *Take While*) together to paginate query results. You will revisit this subject with some examples in Chapter 3.

> ### More About Query Syntax
>
> At this point, you have seen all the query keywords available through the programming languages. However, remember that each query expression is converted by the language compiler into an invocation of the corresponding extension methods. Whenever you need to query a data source by using LINQ and no keyword exists for a particular operation in a query expression, you can use native or custom extension methods directly in conjunction with query expression syntax. When you use extension methods only (as shown in Listing 2-3), the syntax is called method syntax. When you use query syntax in conjunction with extension methods (as shown in Listing 2-17), the result is known as mixed query syntax.

Deferred Query Evaluation and Extension Method Resolution

This section examines two query expression behaviors: *deferred query evaluation* and *extension method resolution*. Both concepts are important for all LINQ implementations.

Deferred Query Evaluation

A query expression is not evaluated when it is defined, but only when it is used. Consider the example in Listing 2-22.

LISTING 2-22 A sample LINQ query over a set of developers

```
List<Developer> developers = new List<Developer>(new Developer[] {
    new Developer { Name = "Paolo", Language = "C#", Age = 32 },
    new Developer { Name = "Marco", Language = "C#", Age = 37},
    new Developer { Name = "Frank", Language = "VB.NET", Age = 48  }
});

var query =
    from   d in developers
    where  d.Language == "C#"
    select new { d.Name, d.Age };

Console.WriteLine("There are {0} C# developers.", query.Count());
```

This code declares a very simple query that contains just two items, as you can see by reading the code that declares the list of developers or simply by checking the console output of the code that invokes the *Count* extension method:

```
There are 2 C# developers.
```

Now imagine that you want to change the content of the source sequence by adding a new *Developer* instance—after the *query* variable has been defined (as shown in Listing 2-23).

LISTING 2-23 Sample code to modify the set of developers that are being queried

```
developers.Add(new Developer {
    Name = "Roberto", Language = "C#", Age = 35 });

Console.WriteLine("There are {0} C# developers.", query.Count());
```

If you enumerate the *query* variable again or check its item count, as we do in Listing 2-23 after a new developer is added, the result is three. The added developer is included in the result even though he was added *after* the definition of *query*.

The reason for this behavior is that, from a logical point of view, a query expression describes a kind of "query plan." It is not actually executed until it is used, and it will be executed again and again every time you run it. Some LINQ implementations—such as LINQ to Objects—implement this behavior through delegates. Others—such as LINQ to SQL—might use expression trees that take advantage of the *IQueryable<T>* interface. This behavior is known as *deferred query evaluation*—and it is a fundamental concept in LINQ, regardless of which LINQ implementation you are using.

Deferred query evaluation is useful because you can define queries once and apply them several times: if the source sequence has been changed, the result will always reflect the most recent content. However, consider a situation in which you want a snapshot of the result at a particular "safe point" that you want to re-use many times, avoiding re-execution, either for performance reasons or to keep the snapshot independent of changes to the source sequence. To do that, you need to make a copy of the result, which you can do by using a set of operators called *conversion operators* (such as *ToArray*, *ToList*, *ToDictionary*, *ToLookup*), created specifically for this purpose.

> **More Info** Conversion operators are covered in detail in Chapter 3.

Extension Method Resolution

Extension method resolution is one of the most important concepts to understand if you want to master LINQ. Consider the code in Listing 2-24, which defines a custom list of type *Developer* (named *Developers*) and a class, *DevelopersExtension*, that provides an extension method named *Where* that applies specifically to instances of the *Developers* type.

LISTING 2-24 Sample code to modify the set of developers that are being queried

```
public sealed class Developers : List<Developer> {
    public Developers(IEnumerable<Developer> items) : base(items) { }
}

public static class DevelopersExtension {
    public static IEnumerable<Developer> Where(
        this Developers source, Func<Developer, bool> predicate) {

        Console.WriteLine("Invoked Where extension method for Developers");
        return (source.AsEnumerable().Where(predicate));
    }

    public static IEnumerable<Developer> Where(
        this Developers source,
        Func<Developer, int, bool> predicate) {
```

```
        Console.WriteLine("Invoked Where extension method for Developers");
        return (source.AsEnumerable().Where(predicate));
    }
}
```

The only special action the custom *Where* extension methods take is to write some output to the console, indicating that they have executed. After that, the methods pass the request to the *Where* extension methods defined for any standard instance of type *IEnumerable<T>*, converting the source with a method called *AsEnumerable*, which we will cover in Chapter 3.

Now, if you use the usual *developers* array, the behavior of the query in Listing 2-25 is quite interesting.

LISTING 2-25 A query expression over a custom list of type *Developers*

```
Developers developers = new Developers(new Developer[] {
    new Developer { Name = "Paolo", Language = "C#", Age = 32 },
    new Developer { Name = "Marco", Language = "C#", Age = 37 },
    new Developer { Name = "Frank", Language = "VB.NET", Age = 48  },
});

var query =
    from    d in developers
    where   d.Language == "C#"
    select d;

Console.WriteLine("There are {0} C# developers.", query.Count());
```

The query expression will be converted by the compiler into the following code, as you saw earlier in this chapter:

```
var query =
    developers
    .Where (d => d.Language == "C#")
    .Select(d => d);
```

As a result of the presence of the *DevelopersExtension* class, the extension method *Where* that executes is the one defined by *DevelopersExtension*, rather than the general-purpose one defined in *System.Linq.Enumerable*. (To be considered as an extension method container class, the *DevelopersExtension* class must be declared as *static* and defined in the current namespace or in any namespace included in active *using* directives.) The resulting code produced by the compiler resolving extension methods is the following:

```
var query =
    Enumerable.Select(
        DevelopersExtension.Where(
            developers,
            d => d.Language == "C#"),
        d => d );
```

In the end, you are always calling static methods of a static class, but the syntax required is lighter and more intuitive with extension methods than with the more verbose static method explicit calls.

At this point, you are beginning to experience the real power of LINQ. Using extension methods, you can define custom behaviors for specific types. In the following chapters, we will discuss LINQ to Entities, LINQ to SQL, LINQ to XML, and other implementations of LINQ. These implementations are just specific implementations of query operators, thanks to the extension method resolution realized by the compilers.

Now everything looks fine. But now imagine that you need to query the custom list of type *Developers* with the standard *Where* extension method rather than with the specialized one. To achieve that, you will need to convert the custom list to a more generalized type to divert the extension method resolution made by the compiler. This is another scenario that can benefit from conversion operators, which we will cover in Chapter 3.

Some Final Thoughts About LINQ Queries

In this section, we will cover a few more details about degenerate query expressions and exception handling.

Degenerate Query Expressions

Sometimes you need to iterate over the elements of a data source without any filtering, ordering, grouping, or custom projection. Consider for example the query presented in Listing 2-26.

LISTING 2-26 A degenerate query expression over a list of type *Developers*

```
Developer[] developers = new Developer[] {
    …
};

var query =
    from   d in developers
    select d;

foreach (var developer in query) {
    Console.WriteLine(developer.Name);
}
```

This code excerpt simply iterates over the data source, so you might wonder why the code does not simply use the data source directly, as in Listing 2-27.

LISTING 2-27 Iteration over a list of type *Developers*

```
Developer[] developers = new Developer[] {
...
};

foreach (var developer in developers) {
    Console.WriteLine(developer.Name);
}
```

Apparently, the results of both Listings 2-26 and 2-27 are the same. However, using the query expression in Listing 2-26 ensures that if a specific *Select* extension method for the data source exists, the custom method will be called and the result will be consistent as a result of the translation of the query expression into its corresponding method syntax.

A query that simply returns a result equal to the original data source (thus appearing trivial or useless) is called a *degenerate query expression*. On the other hand, iterating directly over the data source (as in Listing 2-27) skips the invocation of any custom *Select* extension method and does not guarantee the correct behavior (unless, of course, you explicitly want to iterate over the data source *without* using LINQ).

Exception Handling

Query expressions can refer to external methods within their definitions. Sometimes those methods can fail. Consider the query defined in Listing 2-28, which invokes the *DoSomething* method for each data source item.

LISTING 2-28 A C# query expression that references an external method that throws a fictitious exception

```
static Boolean DoSomething(Developer dev) {
    if (dev.Age > 40)
        throw new ArgumentOutOfRangeException("dev");

    return (dev.Language == "C#");
}

static void Main() {
    Developer[] developers = new Developer[] {
        new Developer { Name = "Frank", Language = "VB.NET", Age = 48  },
        // other initializations omitted for the sake of brevity
    };
```

```
    var query =
        from    d in developers
        let     SomethingResult = DoSomething(d)
        select new { d.Name, SomethingResult };

    foreach (var item in query) {
        Console.WriteLine(item);
    }
}
```

The *DoSomething* method throws a fictitious exception for any developer older than 40. We
call this method from inside the query. During query execution, when the query iterates over
the developer Frank, who is 48 years old, the custom method will throw an exception.

First, you should think carefully about calling custom methods in query definitions, because it
is a potentially dangerous habit, as you can see when executing this sample code. However, in
cases in which you do decide to call external methods, the best way to work with them is to
wrap the enumeration of the query result with a *try … catch* block. In fact, as you saw in the
section "Deferred Query Evaluation," a query expression is executed each time it is enumerated, and not when it is defined. Thus, the correct way of writing the code in Listing 2-28 is
presented in Listing 2-29.

LISTING 2-29 A C# query expression used with exception handling

```
Developer[] developers = new Developer[] {
    new Developer { Name = "Frank", Language = "VB.NET", Age = 48  },
    // other initializations omitted for the sake of brevity
};

var query =
    from    d in developers
    let     SomethingResult = DoSomething(d)
    select new { d.Name, SomethingResult };

try {
    foreach (var item in query) {
        Console.WriteLine(item);
    }
}
catch (ArgumentOutOfRangeException e) {
    Console.WriteLine(e.Message);
}
```

In general, it is useless to wrap a query expression definition with a *try … catch* block. Moreover, for the same reason, you should avoid using the results of methods or constructors
directly as data sources for a query expression and should instead assign their results to
instance variables, wrapping the variable assignment with a *try … catch* block as in Listing 2-30.

LISTING 2-30 A C# query expression with exception handling in a local variables declaration

```csharp
static void queryWithExceptionHandledInDataSourceDefinition() {
    Developer[] developers = null;

    try {
        developers = createDevelopersDataSource();
    }
    catch (InvalidOperationException e) {
        // Imagine that the createDevelopersDataSource
        // throws an InvalidOperationException in case of failure

        // Handle it somehow ...
        Console.WriteLine(e.Message);
    }

    if (developers != null)
    {
        var query =
            from    d in developers
            let     SomethingResult = DoSomething(d)
            select new { d.Name, SomethingResult };

        try {
            foreach (var item in query) {
                Console.WriteLine(item);
            }
        }
        catch (ArgumentOutOfRangeException e) {
            Console.WriteLine(e.Message);
        }
    }
}

private static Developer[] createDevelopersDataSource() {
    // Fictitious InvalidOperationException thrown
    throw new InvalidOperationException();
}
```

Summary

This chapter discussed the principles of query expressions and their different syntax flavors (query syntax, method syntax, and mixed syntax), as well as all the main query keywords available in C# and Visual Basic. You have seen two important LINQ features: deferred query evaluation and extension method resolution. You have also seen examples of degenerate query expression and how to handle exceptions while enumerating query expressions. In the next chapter, you will examine LINQ to Objects in detail.

Chapter 3
LINQ to Objects

Modern programming languages and software development architectures are based increasingly on object-oriented design and development. As a result, you often need to query and manage objects and collections rather than records and data tables. You also need tools and languages that work independently of specific data sources or persistence layers. LINQ to Objects is the main implementation of Microsoft Language Integrated Query (LINQ). You can use it to query in-memory collections of objects, entities, and items.

This chapter describes the main classes and operators on which LINQ is based, so you will understand its architecture and become familiar with its syntax. The examples in this chapter use LINQ to Objects so that the content can focus on queries and operators.

Sample Data for Examples

The data used in the examples in this chapter consists of a set of *customers*, each of which has ordered *products*. The following Microsoft Visual C# code defines these types.

```csharp
public enum Countries {
    USA,
    Italy,
}

public class Customer {
    public string Name;
    public string City;
    public Countries Country;
    public Order[] Orders;

    public override string ToString() {
        return String.Format("Name: {0} - City: {1} - Country: {2}",
        this.Name, this.City, this.Country );
    }
}

public class Order {
    public int IdOrder;
    public int Quantity;
    public bool Shipped;
    public string Month;
    public int IdProduct;
```

```
    public override string ToString() {
        return String.Format( "IdOrder: {0} - IdProduct: {1} - " +
                              "Quantity: {2} - Shipped: {3} - " +
                              "Month: {4}", this.IdOrder, this.IdProduct,
                              this.Quantity, this.Shipped, this.Month);
    }
}

public class Product {
    public int IdProduct;
    public decimal Price;

    public override string ToString() {
        return String.Format("IdProduct: {0} - Price: {1}", this.IdProduct,
          this.Price );
    }
}
```

The following code excerpt initializes some instances of these types.

```
// ---------------------------------------------------------
// Initialize a collection of customers with their orders:
// ---------------------------------------------------------
customers = new Customer[] {
  new Customer {Name = "Paolo", City = "Brescia",
          Country = Countries.Italy, Orders = new Order[] {
              new Order { IdOrder = 1, Quantity = 3, IdProduct = 1 ,
                          Shipped = false, Month = "January"},
              new Order { IdOrder = 2, Quantity = 5, IdProduct = 2 ,
                          Shipped = true, Month = "May"}}},
  new Customer {Name = "Marco", City = "Torino",
          Country = Countries.Italy, Orders = new Order[] {
              new Order { IdOrder = 3, Quantity = 10, IdProduct = 1 ,
                          Shipped = false, Month = "July"},
              new Order { IdOrder = 4, Quantity = 20, IdProduct = 3 ,
                          Shipped = true, Month = "December"}}},
  new Customer {Name = "James", City = "Dallas",
          Country = Countries.USA, Orders = new Order[] {
              new Order { IdOrder = 5, Quantity = 20, IdProduct = 3 ,
                          Shipped = true, Month = "December"}}},
  new Customer {Name = "Frank", City = "Seattle",
          Country = Countries.USA, Orders = new Order[] {
              new Order { IdOrder = 6, Quantity = 20, IdProduct = 5 ,
                          Shipped = false, Month = "July"}}}};
```

```
products = new Product[] {
    new Product {IdProduct = 1, Price = 10 },
    new Product {IdProduct = 2, Price = 20 },
    new Product {IdProduct = 3, Price = 30 },
    new Product {IdProduct = 4, Price = 40 },
    new Product {IdProduct = 5, Price = 50 },
    new Product {IdProduct = 6, Price = 60 }};
```

Here is the corresponding Microsoft Visual Basic type definition code.

```
Public Enum Countries
    USA
    Italy
End Enum

Public Class Customer
    Public Name As String
    Public City As String
    Public Country As Countries
    Public Orders As Order()
    Public Overrides Function ToString() As String
        Return String.Format("Name: {0} - City: {1} - Country: {2}",
            Me.Name, Me.City, Me.Country)
    End Function
End Class

Public Class Order
    Public IdOrder As Integer
    Public Quantity As Integer
    Public Shipped As Boolean
    Public Month As String
    Public IdProduct As Integer

    Public Overrides Function ToString() As String
        Return String.Format (
        "IdOrder: {0} - IdProduct: {1} - " &
        "Quantity: {2} - Shipped: {3} - " &
        "Month: {4}",  Me.IdOrder, Me.IdProduct,
        Me.Quantity, Me.Shipped, Me.Month)
    End Function
End Class

Public Class Product
    Public IdProduct As Integer
    Public Price As Decimal
```

```vb
    Public Overrides Function ToString() As String
        Return String.Format("IdProduct: {0} - Price: {1}", Me.IdProduct,
            Me.Price)
    End Function
End Class
```

And here is the corresponding Visual Basic initialization code.

```vb
' ----------------------------------------------------------
' Initialize a collection of customers with their orders:
' ----------------------------------------------------------
customers = New Customer() {
    New Customer With {.Name = "Paolo", .City = "Brescia",
        .Country = Countries.Italy, .Orders = New Order() {
            New Order With {.IdOrder = 1, .Quantity = 3, .IdProduct = 1,
                .Shipped = False, .Month = "January"},
            New Order With {.IdOrder = 2, .Quantity = 5, .IdProduct = 2,
                .Shipped = True, .Month = "May"}}},
    New Customer With {.Name = "Marco", .City = "Torino",
        .Country = Countries.Italy, .Orders = New Order() {
            New Order With {.IdOrder = 3, .Quantity = 10, .IdProduct = 1,
                .Shipped = False, .Month = "July"},
            New Order With {.IdOrder = 4, .Quantity = 20, .IdProduct = 3,
                .Shipped = True, .Month = "December"}}},
    New Customer With {.Name = "James", .City = "Dallas",
        .Country = Countries.USA, .Orders = New Order() {
            New Order With {.IdOrder = 5, .Quantity = 20, .IdProduct = 3,
                .Shipped = True, .Month = "December"}}},
    New Customer With {.Name = "Frank", .City = "Seattle",
        .Country = Countries.USA, .Orders = New Order() {
            New Order With {.IdOrder = 6, .Quantity = 20, .IdProduct = 5,
                .Shipped = False, .Month = "July"}}}}

products = New Product() {
    New Product With {.IdProduct = 1, .Price = 10},
    New Product With {.IdProduct = 2, .Price = 20},
    New Product With {.IdProduct = 3, .Price = 30},
    New Product With {.IdProduct = 4, .Price = 40},
    New Product With {.IdProduct = 5, .Price = 50},
    New Product With {.IdProduct = 6, .Price = 60}}
```

Query Operators

This section describes the main methods and generic delegates provided by the *System.Linq* namespace, which is hosted by System.Core.dll, for querying items with LINQ.

The *Where* Operator

Imagine that you need to list the names and cities of customers from Italy. To filter a set of items, you can use the *Where* operator, which is also called a *restriction operator* because it restricts a set of items. Listing 3-1 shows a simple example.

LISTING 3-1 A query with a restriction

```
var expr =
    from    c in customers
    where   c.Country == Countries.Italy
    select new { c.Name, c.City };
```

Here are the signatures of the *Where* operator:

```
public static IEnumerable<TSource> Where<TSource>(
    this IEnumerable<TSource> source,
    Func<TSource, Boolean> predicate);
public static IEnumerable<TSource> Where<TSource>(
    this IEnumerable<TSource> source,
    Func<TSource, Int32, Boolean> predicate);
```

As you can see, two signatures are available. Listing 3-1 uses the first one, which enumerates items of the *source* sequence and yields those that verify the predicate (*c.Country == Countries.Italy*). The second signature accepts an additional parameter of type *Int32* for the predicate, which is used as a zero-based index of the elements within the *source* sequence. Keep in mind that passing null arguments to the predicates results in an *ArgumentNullException* error. You can use the index parameter to start filtering by a particular index, as shown in Listing 3-2.

LISTING 3-2 A query with a restriction and an index-based filter

```
var expr =
    customers
    .Where((c, index) => (c.Country == Countries.Italy && index >= 1))
    .Select(c => c.Name);
```

> **Important** Listing 3-2 uses the method syntax because the version of *Where* that we want to call is not supported by an equivalent query expression clause. We will use both syntaxes from here onward.

The result of Listing 3-2 will be a list of Italian customers, skipping the first one. As you can see from the following console output, the *index*-based partitioning occurs over the data source already filtered by *Country*. The results show a single name:

```
Marco
```

The capability to filter items of the *source* sequence by using their positional index is useful when you want to extract a specific page of data from a large sequence of items. Listing 3-3 shows an example.

LISTING 3-3 A query with a paging restriction

```
int start = 5;
int end = 10;

var expr =
    customers
    .Where((c, index) => ((index >= start) && (index < end)))
    .Select(c => c.Name);
```

> **Note** Keep in mind that it is generally not a good practice to store large sequences of data loaded from a database persistence layer in memory; thus, in general, you should not have to paginate data in memory. Usually, it is better to page data at the persistence layer level.

Projection Operators

The following sections describe how to use *projection operators*. You use these operators to select (or "project") contents from the source enumeration into the result.

Select

In Listing 3-1, you saw an example of defining the result of the query by using the *Select* operator. The signatures for the *Select* operator are:

```
public static IEnumerable<TResult> Select<TSource, TResult>(
    this IEnumerable<TSource> source,
    Func<TSource, TResult> selector);
public static IEnumerable<TResult> Select<TSource, TResult>(
    this IEnumerable<TSource> source,
    Func<TSource, Int32, TResult> selector);
```

The *Select* operator is a projection operator because it projects the query results, making them available through an object that implements *IEnumerable<TResult>*. This object will enumerate items identified by the *selector* predicate. Like the *Where* operator, *Select* enumerates the *source* sequence and yields the result of the *selector* predicate. Consider the following predicate:

```
var expr = customers.Select(c => c.Name);
```

This predicate's result is a sequence of customer names (*IEnumerable<String>*). Now consider this example:

```
var expr = customers.Select(c => new { c.Name, c.City });
```

This predicate projects a sequence of instances of an anonymous type, defined as a tuple of *Name* and *City*, for each customer object. With this second *Select* overload, you can also provide an argument of type *Int32* for the predicate—a zero-based index used to define the positional index of each item inserted in the resulting sequence. Listing 3-4 shows an example.

LISTING 3-4 A projection with an *index* argument in the *selector* predicate

```
var expr =
    customers
    .Select((c, index) => new { index, c.Name, c.Country } );

foreach (var item in expr) {
    Console.WriteLine(item);
}
```

Running the query in Listing 3-4 produces this result:

```
{ index = 0, Name = Paolo, Country = Italy }
{ index = 1, Name = Marco, Country = Italy }
{ index = 2, Name = James, Country = USA }
{ index = 3, Name = Frank, Country = USA }
```

As with the *Where* operator, the *Select* operator's simple overload is available as a query expression keyword, while the more complex overload needs to be invoked explicitly as an extension method.

As you have already seen in Chapter 2, "LINQ Syntax Fundamentals," the query expression syntax of the *Select* operator changes slightly between C# and Visual Basic in respect to anonymous type projection. In Visual Basic, anonymous type creation is implicitly determined by the query syntax, whereas in C#, you must explicitly declare that you want a *new* anonymous type.

SelectMany

Imagine that you want to select all the orders of customers from Italy. You could write the query shown in Listing 3-5 using the verbose method.

LISTING 3-5 The list of orders made by Italian customers

```
var orders =
    customers
    .Where(c => c.Country == Countries.Italy)
    .Select(c => c.Orders);

foreach(var item in orders) { Console.WriteLine(item); }
```

Because of the behavior of the *Select* operator, the resulting type of this query will be *IEnumerable<Order[]>*, where each item in the resulting sequence represents the array of orders of a single customer. In fact, the *Orders* property of a *Customer* instance is of type *Order[]*. The output of the code in Listing 3-5 would be the following:

```
DevLeap.Linq.LinqToObjects.Operators.Order[]
DevLeap.Linq.LinqToObjects.Operators.Order[]
```

To have a "flat" *IEnumerable<Order>* result type, you need to use the *SelectMany* operator:

```
public static IEnumerable<TResult> SelectMany<TSource, TResult>(
    this IEnumerable<TSource> source,
    Func<TSource, IEnumerable<TResult>> selector);
public static IEnumerable<TResult> SelectMany<TSource, TResult>(
    this IEnumerable<TSource> source,
    Func<TSource, Int32, IEnumerable<TResult>> selector);
public static IEnumerable<TResult> SelectMany<TSource, TCollection, TResult>(
    this IEnumerable<TSource> source,
    Func<TSource, IEnumerable<TCollection>> collectionSelector,
    Func<TSource, TCollection, TResult> resultSelector);
public static IEnumerable<TResult> SelectMany<TSource, TCollection, TResult>(
    this IEnumerable<TSource> source,
    Func<TSource, Int32, IEnumerable<TCollection>> collectionSelector,
    Func<TSource, TCollection, TResult> resultSelector);
```

This operator enumerates the *source* sequence and merges the resulting items, providing them as a single enumerable sequence. The second overload available is analogous to the equivalent overload for *Select*, which allows a zero-based integer index for indexing purposes. Listing 3-6 shows an example.

LISTING 3-6 The flattened list of orders made by Italian customers

```
var orders =
    customers
    .Where(c => c.Country == Countries.Italy)
    .SelectMany(c => c.Orders);
```

Using the query expression syntax, the query in Listing 3-6 can be written with the code shown in Listing 3-7.

LISTING 3-7 The flattened list of orders made by Italian customers, written with a query expression

```
var orders =
    from    c in customers
    where   c.Country == Countries.Italy
        from    o in c.Orders
        select o;
```

Both Listing 3-6 and Listing 3-7 have the following output, where the *ToString* override of the *Order* type is used:

```
IdOrder: 1 - IdProduct: 1 - Quantity: 3 - Shipped: False - Month: January
IdOrder: 2 - IdProduct: 2 - Quantity: 5 - Shipped: True - Month: May
IdOrder: 3 - IdProduct: 1 - Quantity: 10 - Shipped: False - Month: July
IdOrder: 4 - IdProduct: 3 - Quantity: 20 - Shipped: True - Month: December
```

The *select* keyword in query expressions, for all but the initial *from* clause, is translated to invocations of *SelectMany*. In other words, every time you see a query expression with more than one *from* clause, you can apply this rule: the *select* over the first *from* clause is converted to an invocation of *Select*, and the other *select* commands are translated into a *SelectMany* call.

The third and fourth overloads of *SelectMany* are useful whenever you need to select a custom result from the source set of sequences instead of simply merging their items, as with the two previous overloads. These overloads invoke the *collectionSelector* projection over the *source* sequence and return the result of the *resultSelector* projection. The result is applied to each item in the collections selected by *collectionSelector* and eventually projects a zero-based integer index in the case of the last *SelectMany* overload shown. In Listing 3-8, you can see an example of the third method overload used to extract a new anonymous type made from the *Quantity* and *IdProduct* of each order by Italian customers.

LISTING 3-8 The list of *Quantity* and *IdProduct* of orders made by Italian customers

```
var items = customers
  .Where(c => c.Country == Countries.Italy)
  .SelectMany(c => c.Orders,
    (c, o) => new { o.Quantity, o.IdProduct });
```

You can write the same query as in Listing 3-8 with the query expression shown in Listing 3-9.

LISTING 3-9 The list of *Quantity* and *IdProduct* of orders made by Italian customers, written with a query expression

```
var items =
    from   c in customers
    where  c.Country == Countries.Italy
        from   o in c.Orders
        select new {o.Quantity, o.IdProduct};
```

Ordering Operators

Another useful set of operators is the ordering operators group. Ordering operators determine the ordering and direction of elements in output sequences.

OrderBy and *OrderByDescending*

Sometimes it is helpful to apply an ordering to the results of a database query. LINQ can order the results of queries, in ascending or descending order, using ordering operators, similar to SQL syntax. For example, if you need to select the *Name* and *City* of all Italian customers in descending order by *Name*, you can write the corresponding query expression shown in Listing 3-10.

LISTING 3-10 A query expression with a descending *orderby* clause

```
var expr =
    from   c in customers
    where  c.Country == Countries.Italy
    orderby c.Name descending
    select new { c.Name, c.City };
```

The query expression syntax will translate the *orderby* keyword into one of the following ordering extension methods:

```
public static IOrderedEnumerable<TSource> OrderBy<TSource, TKey>(
    this IEnumerable<TSource> source,
    Func<TSource, TKey> keySelector);
public static IOrderedEnumerable<TSource> OrderBy<TSource, TKey>(
    this IEnumerable<TSource> source,
    Func<TSource, TKey> keySelector,
    IComparer<TKey> comparer);
public static IOrderedEnumerable<TSource> OrderByDescending<TSource, TKey>(
    this IEnumerable<TSource> source,
    Func<TSource, TKey> keySelector);
public static IOrderedEnumerable<TSource> OrderByDescending<TSource, TKey>(
    this IEnumerable<TSource> source,
    Func<TSource, TKey> keySelector,
    IComparer<TKey> comparer);
```

As you can see, the two main extension methods, *OrderBy* and *OrderByDescending*, both have two overloads. The methods' names suggest their objective: *OrderBy* is for ascending order, and *OrderByDescending* is for descending order. The *keySelector* argument represents a function that extracts a key, of type *TKey*, from each item of type *TSource*, taken from the *source* sequence. The extracted key represents the typed content to be compared by the comparer while ordering, and the *TSource* type describes the type of each item of the *source* sequence. Both methods have an overload that allows you to provide a custom *comparer*. If no comparer is provided or the *comparer* argument is null, the *Default* property of the *Comparer<T>* generic type is used (*Comparer<TKey>.Default*).

> **Important** The default *Comparer* returned by *Comparer<T>.Default* uses the generic interface *IComparable<T>* to compare two objects. If type *T* does not implement the *System.IComparable<T>* generic interface, the *Default* property of *Comparer<T>* returns a *Comparer* that uses the *System.IComparable* interface. If the type of *T* does not implement either of these interfaces, the *Compare* method of the *Default* comparer will throw an exception.

It is important to emphasize that these ordering methods return not just *IEnumerable<TSource>* but *IOrderedEnumerable<TSource>*, which is an interface that extends *IEnumerable<T>*.

The query expression in Listing 3-10 will be translated to the following extension method calls:

```
var expr =
    customers
    .Where(c => c.Country == Countries.Italy)
    .OrderByDescending(c => c.Name)
    .Select(c => new { c.Name, c.City } );
```

As you can see from the previous code excerpt, the *OrderByDescending* method, as well as all the ordering methods, accepts a key selector lambda expression that selects the key value from the range variable (*c*) of the current context. The selector can extract any sorting field available in the range variable, even if it is not projected in the output by the *Select* method. For example, you can sort customers by *Country* and select their *Name* and *City* properties.

ThenBy and *ThenByDescending*

Whenever you need to order data by many different keys, you can take advantage of the *ThenBy* and *ThenByDescending* operators. Here are their signatures:

```
public static IOrderedEnumerable<TSource> ThenBy<TSource, TKey>(
    this IOrderedEnumerable<TSource> source,
    Func<TSource, TKey> keySelector);
public static IOrderedEnumerable<TSource> ThenBy<TSource, TKey>(
    this IOrderedEnumerable<TSource> source,
    Func<TSource, TKey> keySelector,
    IComparer<TKey> comparer);
```

```
public static IOrderedEnumerable<TSource> ThenByDescending<TSource, TKey>(
    this IOrderedEnumerable<TSource> source,
    Func<TSource, TKey> keySelector);
public static IOrderedEnumerable<TSource> ThenByDescending<TSource, TKey>(
    this IOrderedEnumerable<TSource> source,
    Func<TSource, TKey> keySelector,
    IComparer<TKey> comparer);
```

These operators have signatures similar to *OrderBy* and *OrderByDescending*. The difference is that *ThenBy* and *ThenByDescending* can be applied only to *IOrderedEnumerable<T>* and not to any *IEnumerable<T>*. Therefore, you can use the *ThenBy* or *ThenByDescending* operators just after the first use of *OrderBy* or *OrderByDescending*. Here is an example:

```
var expr = customers
    .Where(c => c.Country == Countries.Italy)
    .OrderByDescending(c => c.Name)
    .ThenBy(c => c.City)
    .Select(c => new { c.Name, c.City } );
```

In Listing 3-11, you can see the corresponding query expression.

LISTING 3-11 A query expression with *orderby* and *thenby*

```
var expr =
    from    c in customers
    where   c.Country == Countries.Italy
    orderby c.Name descending, c.City
    select  new { c.Name, c.City };
```

Important In the case of multiple occurrences of the same key within a sequence to be ordered, the result is not guaranteed to be "stable." In such conditions, the original ordering might not be preserved by the comparer.

A custom *comparer* might be useful when the items in your *source* sequence need to be ordered using custom logic. For example, imagine that you want to select all the orders of your customers ordered by month, shown in Listing 3-12.

LISTING 3-12 A query expression ordered using the comparer provided by *Comparer<T>.Default*

```
var expr =
    from c in customers
        from    o in c.Orders
        orderby o.Month
        select  o;
```

If you apply the default comparer to the *Month* property of the orders, you will get a result alphabetically ordered because of the behavior of *Comparer<T>.Default*, which was described earlier. The result is wrong because the *Month* property is just a string and not a number or a date:

```
IdOrder: 4 - IdProduct: 3 - Quantity: 20 - Shipped: True - Month: December
IdOrder: 5 - IdProduct: 3 - Quantity: 20 - Shipped: True - Month: December
IdOrder: 1 - IdProduct: 1 - Quantity: 3 - Shipped: False - Month: January
IdOrder: 3 - IdProduct: 1 - Quantity: 10 - Shipped: False - Month: July
IdOrder: 6 - IdProduct: 5 - Quantity: 20 - Shipped: False - Month: July
IdOrder: 2 - IdProduct: 2 - Quantity: 5 - Shipped: True - Month: May
```

You should use a custom *MonthComparer* that correctly compares months:

```
using System.Globalization;

class MonthComparer: IComparer<string> {
    public int Compare(string x, string y) {
        DateTime xDate = DateTime.ParseExact(x, "MMMM", new CultureInfo("en-US"));
        DateTime yDate = DateTime.ParseExact(y, "MMMM", new CultureInfo("en-US"));
        return(Comparer<DateTime>.Default.Compare(xDate, yDate));
    }
}
```

The newly defined custom *MonthComparer* could be passed as a parameter while invoking the *OrderBy* extension method, as in Listing 3-13.

LISTING 3-13 A custom *comparer* used with an *OrderBy* operator

```
var orders =
    customers
    .SelectMany(c => c.Orders)
    .OrderBy(o => o.Month, new MonthComparer());
```

Now the result of Listing 3-13 will be the following, correctly ordered by month:

```
IdOrder: 1 - IdProduct: 1 - Quantity: 3 - Shipped: False - Month: January
IdOrder: 2 - IdProduct: 2 - Quantity: 5 - Shipped: True - Month: May
IdOrder: 3 - IdProduct: 1 - Quantity: 10 - Shipped: False - Month: July
IdOrder: 6 - IdProduct: 5 - Quantity: 20 - Shipped: False - Month: July
IdOrder: 4 - IdProduct: 3 - Quantity: 20 - Shipped: True - Month: December
IdOrder: 5 - IdProduct: 3 - Quantity: 20 - Shipped: True - Month: December
```

Reverse Operator

Sometimes you need to reverse the result of a query, listing the last item in the result first. LINQ provides a last-ordering operator, called *Reverse*, which allows you to perform this operation:

```
public static IEnumerable<TSource> Reverse<TSource>(
    this IEnumerable<TSource> source);
```

The implementation of *Reverse* is quite simple. It just yields each item in the *source* sequence in reverse order. Listing 3-14 shows an example of its use.

LISTING 3-14 The *Reverse* operator applied

```
var expr =
    customers
    .Where(c => c.Country == Countries.Italy)
    .OrderByDescending(c => c.Name)
    .ThenBy(c => c.City)
    .Select(c => new { c.Name, c.City } )
    .Reverse();
```

The *Reverse* operator, like many other operators, does not have a corresponding keyword in query expressions. However, you can merge query expression syntax with operators (described in Chapter 2) as shown in Listing 3-15.

LISTING 3-15 The *Reverse* operator applied to a query expression with *orderby* and *thenby*

```
var expr =
    (from   c in customers
     where  c.Country == Countries.Italy
     orderby c.Name descending, c.City
     select  new { c.Name, c.City }
    ).Reverse();
```

As you can see, we apply the *Reverse* operator to the expression resulting from Listing 3-11. Under the covers, the inner query expression is first translated to the resulting list of extension methods, and then the *Reverse* method is applied at the end of the extension methods chain. It is just like Listing 3-14, but hopefully easier to write.

Grouping Operators

Now you have seen how to select, filter, and order sequences of items. Sometimes when querying contents, you also need to group results based on specific criteria. To realize content groupings, you use a grouping operator.

The *GroupBy* operator, also called a grouping operator, is the only operator of this family and provides a rich set of eight overloads. Here are the first four:

```
public static IEnumerable<IGrouping<TKey, TSource>> GroupBy<TSource, TKey>(
    this IEnumerable<TSource> source, Func<TSource, TKey> keySelector);
public static IEnumerable<IGrouping<TKey, TSource>> GroupBy<TSource, TKey>(
    this IEnumerable<TSource> source, Func<TSource, TKey> keySelector,
    IEqualityComparer<TKey> comparer);
```

```
public static IEnumerable<IGrouping<TKey, TElement>> GroupBy<TSource, TKey, TElement>(
    this IEnumerable<TSource> source, Func<TSource, TKey> keySelector,
    Func<TSource, TElement> elementSelector);
public static IEnumerable<IGrouping<TKey, TElement>> GroupBy<TSource, TKey, TElement>(
    this IEnumerable<TSource> source, Func<TSource, TKey> keySelector,
    Func<TSource, TElement> elementSelector,
    IEqualityComparer<TKey> comparer);
```

These *GroupBy* method overloads select pairs of keys and items for each item in *source*. They use the *keySelector* predicate to extract the *Key* value from each item to group results based on the different *Key* values. The *elementSelector* argument, if present, defines a function that maps the source element within the *source* sequence to the destination element of the resulting sequence. If you do not specify the *elementSelector*, elements are mapped directly from the source to the destination. (You will see an example of this later in the chapter, in Listing 3-18.) They then yield a sequence of *IGrouping<TKey, TElement>* objects, where each group consists of a sequence of items with a common *Key* value.

The *IGrouping<TKey, TElement>* generic interface is a specialized implementation of *IEnumerable<TElement>*. This implementation can return a specific *Key* of type *TKey* for each item within the enumeration:

```
public interface IGrouping<TKey, TElement> : IEnumerable<TElement> {
    TKey Key { get; }
}
```

From a practical point of view, a type that implements this generic interface is simply a typed enumeration with an identifying type *Key* for each item.

There are also four more signatures useful to shape a custom result projection:

```
public static IEnumerable<TResult> GroupBy<TSource, TKey, TResult>(
     this IEnumerable<TSource> source, Func<TSource, TKey> keySelector,
    Func<TKey, IEnumerable<TSource>, TResult> resultSelector);
public static IEnumerable<TResult> GroupBy<TSource, TKey, TElement, TResult>(
    this IEnumerable<TSource> source, Func<TSource, TKey> keySelector,
    Func<TSource, TElement> elementSelector,
    Func<TKey, IEnumerable<TSource>, TResult> resultSelector);
public static IEnumerable<TResult> GroupBy<TSource, TKey, TResult>(
    this IEnumerable<TSource> source, Func<TSource, TKey> keySelector,
    Func<TKey, IEnumerable<TSource>, TResult> resultSelector,
    IEqualityComparer<TKey> comparer);
public static IEnumerable<TResult> GroupBy<TSource, TKey, Telement, TResult>(
    this IEnumerable<TSource> source, Func<TSource, TKey> keySelector,
    Func<TSource, TElement> elementSelector,
    Func<TKey, IEnumerable<TSource>, TResult> resultSelector,
    IEqualityComparer<TKey> comparer);
```

With the *resultSelector* argument present in these last signatures, you can define a projection for the *GroupBy* operation, which lets you return an *IEnumerable<TResult>*. This last set of overloads is useful for selecting a flattened enumeration of items, based on aggregations over the grouping sets. You will see an example of this syntax later in this section.

One last optional argument you can pass to some of these methods is a custom *comparer*, which is useful when you need to compare key values and define group membership. If no custom *comparer* is provided, the *EqualityComparer<TKey>.Default* is used. The order of keys and items within each group corresponds to their occurrence within the *source*. Listing 3-16 shows an example of using the *GroupBy* operator.

LISTING 3-16 The *GroupBy* operator used to group customers by *Country*

```
var expr = customers.GroupBy(c => c.Country);

foreach(IGrouping<Countries, Customer> customerGroup in expr) {
    Console.WriteLine("Country: {0}", customerGroup.Key);
    foreach(var item in customerGroup) {
        Console.WriteLine("\t{0}", item);
    }
}
```

Here is the console output of Listing 3-16:

```
Country: Italy
        Name: Paolo - City: Brescia - Country: Italy
        Name: Marco - City: Torino - Country: Italy
Country: USA
        Name: James - City: Dallas - Country: USA
        Name: Frank - City: Seattle - Country: USA
```

As Listing 3-16 shows, you need to enumerate all group keys before iterating over the items contained within each group. Each group is an instance of a type that implements *IGrouping<Countries, Customer>*, because the code uses the default *elementSelector* that directly projects the source *Customer* instances into the result. In query expressions, the *GroupBy* operator can be defined using the *group … by …* syntax, which is shown in Listing 3-17.

LISTING 3-17 A query expression with a *group … by …* syntax

```
var expr =
    from  c in customers
    group c by c.Country;

foreach(IGrouping<Countries, Customer> customerGroup in expr) {
    Console.WriteLine("Country: {0}", customerGroup.Key);
    foreach(var item in customerGroup) {
        Console.WriteLine("\t{0}", item);
    }
}
```

The code defined in Listing 3-16 is semantically equivalent to that shown in Listing 3-17.

Listing 3-18 is another example of grouping, this time with a custom *elementSelector*.

LISTING 3-18 The *GroupBy* operator used to group customer names by *Country*

```
var expr =
    customers
    .GroupBy(c => c.Country, c => c.Name);
foreach(IGrouping<Countries, String> customerGroup in expr) {
    Console.WriteLine("Country: {0}", customerGroup.Key);
    foreach(var item in customerGroup) {
        Console.WriteLine("\t{0}", item);
    }
}
```

Here is the result of this code:

```
Country: Italy
  Paolo
  Marco
Country: USA
  James
  Frank
```

In this last example, the result is a class that implements *IGrouping<Countries, String>*, because the *elementSelector* predicate projects only the customers' names (of type *String*) into the output sequence.

In Listing 3-19, you can see an example of using the *GroupBy* operator with a *resultSelector* predicate argument.

LISTING 3-19 The *GroupBy* operator used to group customer names by *Country*

```
var expr = customers
  .GroupBy(c => c.Country,
    (k, c) => new { Key = k, Count = c.Count() });
foreach (var group in expr) {
    Console.WriteLine("Key: {0} - Count: {1}", group.Key, group.Count);
}
```

This last example projected the *Key* value of each group and the *Count* of elements for each group. In cases when you need them, there are also *GroupBy* overloads that allow you to define both a *resultSelector* and a custom *elementSelector*. They are useful whenever you need to project groups, calculating aggregations on each group of items, but also having the single items through a custom *elementSelector* predicate. Listing 3-20 shows an example.

LISTING 3-20 The *GroupBy* operator used to group customer names by *Country*, with a custom *resultSelector* and *elementSelector*

```
var expr = customers
    .GroupBy(
        c => c.Country, // keySelector
        c => new { OrdersCount = c.Orders.Count() }, // elementSelector
        (key, elements) => new { // resultSelector
            Key = key,
            Count = elements.Count(),
            OrdersCount = elements.Sum(item => item.OrdersCount) });

foreach (var group in expr) {
    Console.WriteLine("Key: {0} - Count: {1} - Orders Count: {2}",
        group.Key, group.Count , group.OrdersCount);
}
```

The code in Listing 3-20 shows an example of a query that returns a flat enumeration of items made of customers grouped by *Country*, the count of customers for each group, and the total count of orders executed by customers of each group. Notice that the result of the query is an *IEnumerable<TResult>* and not an *IGrouping<TKey, TElement>*. Here is the output of the code in Listing 3-20:

```
Key: Italy - Count: 2 - Orders Count: 4
Key: USA - Count: 2 - Orders Count: 2
```

Join Operators

Join operators define relationships within sequences in query expressions. From a SQL and relational point of view, almost every query requires joining one or more tables. In LINQ, a set of join operators implements this behavior.

Join

The first operator of this group is, of course, the *Join* method, defined by the following signatures:

```
public static IEnumerable<TResult> Join<TOuter, TInner, TKey, TResult>(
    this IEnumerable<TOuter> outer,
    IEnumerable<TInner> inner,
    Func<TOuter, TKey> outerKeySelector,
    Func<TInner, TKey> innerKeySelector,
    Func<TOuter, TInner, TResult> resultSelector);
public static IEnumerable<TResult> Join<TOuter, TInner, TKey, TResult>(
    this IEnumerable<TOuter> outer,
    IEnumerable<TInner> inner,
    Func<TOuter, TKey> outerKeySelector,
    Func<TInner, TKey> innerKeySelector,
    Func<TOuter, TInner, TResult> resultSelector,
    IEqualityComparer<TKey> comparer);
```

Join requires a set of four generic types. The *TOuter* type represents the type of the *outer* source sequence, and the *TInner* type describes the type of the *inner* source sequence. The predicates *outerKeySelector* and *innerKeySelector* define how to extract the identifying keys from the *outer* and *inner* source sequence items, respectively. These keys are both of type *TKey*, and their equivalence defines the join condition. The *resultSelector* predicate defines what to project into the result sequence, which will be an implementation of *IEnumerable<TResult>*. *TResult* is the last generic type needed by the operator, and it defines the type of each single item in the join result sequence. The second overload of the method has an additional custom equality comparer, used to compare the keys. If the *comparer* argument is null or if the first overload of the method is invoked, a default key comparer (*EqualityComparer<TKey>.Default*) will be used.

Here is an example that will make the use of *Join* clearer. Consider the sample customers, with their orders and products. In Listing 3-21, a query joins orders with their corresponding products.

LISTING 3-21 The *Join* operator used to map orders with products

```
var expr =
    customers
    .SelectMany(c => c.Orders)
    .Join( products,
            o => o.IdProduct,
            p => p.IdProduct,
            (o, p) => new {o.Month, o.Shipped, p.IdProduct, p.Price } );
```

The following is the result of the query:

```
{Month = January, Shipped = False, IdProduct = 1, Price = 10}
{Month = May, Shipped = True, IdProduct = 2, Price = 20}
{Month = July, Shipped = False, IdProduct = 1, Price = 10}
{Month = December, Shipped = True, IdProduct = 3, Price = 30}
{Month = December, Shipped = True, IdProduct = 3, Price = 30}
{Month = July, Shipped = False, IdProduct = 5, Price = 50}
```

In this example, *orders* represents the outer sequence and *products* is the inner sequence. The *o* and *p* used in lambda expressions are of type *Order* and *Product*, respectively. Internally, the operator collects the elements of the *inner* sequence into a hash table, using their keys extracted with *innerKeySelector*. It then enumerates the *outer* sequence and maps its elements, based on the *Key* value extracted with *outerKeySelector*, to the hash table of items. Because of its implementation, the *Join* operator result sequence keeps the order of the *outer* sequence first, and then uses the order of the *inner* sequence for each *outer* sequence element.

From a SQL point of view, the example in Listing 3-21 can be thought of as an inner equijoin somewhat like the following SQL query:

```
SELECT    o.Month, o.Shipped, p.IdProduct, p.Price
FROM      Orders AS o
INNER JOIN Products AS p
     ON   o.IdProduct = p.IdProduct
```

If you want to translate the SQL syntax into the *Join* operator syntax, you can think about the columns selection in SQL as the *resultSelector* predicate, while the equality condition on *IdProduct* columns (of orders and products) corresponds to the pair of *innerKeySelector* and *outerKeySelector* predicates.

The *Join* operator has a corresponding query expression syntax, which is shown in Listing 3-22.

LISTING 3-22 The *Join* operator query expression syntax

```
var expr =
    from c in customers
        from  o in c.Orders
        join  p in products
              on o.IdProduct equals p.IdProduct
        select new {o.Month, o.Shipped, p.IdProduct, p.Price };
```

Important As described in Chapter 2, the order of items to relate (*o.IdProduct equals p.IdProduct*) in query expression syntax *must* specify the outer sequence first and the inner sequence after; otherwise, the query expression will not compile. This requirement is different from standard SQL queries, in which item ordering does not matter.

In Listing 3-23, you can see the Visual Basic syntax corresponding to Listing 3-22. Take a look at the SQL-like selection syntax.

LISTING 3-23 The *Join* operator query expression syntax expressed in Visual Basic

```
Dim expr =
    From c In customers
    From o In c.Orders
    Join p In products
        On o.IdProduct Equals p.IdProduct
    Select o.Month, o.Shipped, p.IdProduct, p.Price
```

GroupJoin

In cases in which you need to define something similar to a SQL LEFT OUTER JOIN or a RIGHT OUTER JOIN, you need to use the *GroupJoin* operator. Its signatures are quite similar to the *Join* operator:

```
public static IEnumerable<TResult>
    GroupJoin<TOuter, TInner, TKey, TResult>(
        this IEnumerable<TOuter> outer,
        IEnumerable<TInner> inner,
        Func<TOuter, TKey> outerKeySelector,
        Func<TInner, TKey> innerKeySelector,
        Func<TOuter, IEnumerable<TInner>, TResult> resultSelector);
public static IEnumerable<TResult>
    GroupJoin<TOuter, TInner, TKey, TResult>(
        this IEnumerable<TOuter> outer,
        IEnumerable<TInner> inner,
        Func<TOuter, TKey> outerKeySelector,
        Func<TInner, TKey> innerKeySelector,
        Func<TOuter, IEnumerable<TInner>, TResult> resultSelector,
        IEqualityComparer<TKey> comparer);
```

The only difference is the definition of the *resultSelector* projector. It requires an instance of *IEnumerable<TInner>*, instead of a single object of type *TInner*, because it projects a hierarchical result of type *IEnumerable<TResult>*. Each item of type *TResult* consists of an item extracted from the *outer* sequence and a group of items, of type *TInner*, joined from the *inner* sequence.

As a result of this behavior, the output is not a flattened outer equijoin, which would be produced by using the *Join* operator, but a hierarchical sequence of items. Nevertheless, you can define queries using *GroupJoin* with results equivalent to the *Join* operator whenever the mapping is a one-to-one relationship. In cases in which a corresponding element group in the *inner* sequence is absent, the *GroupJoin* operator extracts the *outer* sequence element paired with an empty sequence (*Count = 0*). In Listing 3-24, you can see an example of this operator.

LISTING 3-24 The *GroupJoin* operator used to map products with orders, if present

```
var expr =
    products
    .GroupJoin(
        customers.SelectMany(c => c.Orders),
        p => p.IdProduct,
        o => o.IdProduct,
        (p, orders) => new { p.IdProduct, Orders = orders });

foreach(var item in expr) {
    Console.WriteLine("Product: {0}", item.IdProduct);
    foreach (var order in item.Orders) {
        Console.WriteLine("\t{0}", order); }}
```

The following is the result of Listing 3-24:

```
Product: 1
    IdOrder: 1 - IdProduct: 1 - Quantity: 3 - Shipped: False - Month: January
    IdOrder: 3 - IdProduct: 1 - Quantity: 10 - Shipped: False - Month: July
Product: 2
    IdOrder: 2 - IdProduct: 2 - Quantity: 5 - Shipped: True - Month: May
Product: 3
    IdOrder: 4 - IdProduct: 3 - Quantity: 20 - Shipped: True - Month: December
    IdOrder: 5 - IdProduct: 3 - Quantity: 20 - Shipped: True - Month: December
Product: 4
Product: 5
    IdOrder: 6 - IdProduct: 5 - Quantity: 20 - Shipped: False - Month: July
Product: 6
```

You can see that products 4 and 6 have no mapping orders, but the query returns them nonetheless. You can think about this operator like a SELECT ... FOR XML AUTO query in Transact-SQL. In fact, it returns results hierarchically grouped like a set of XML nodes nested within their parent nodes, similar to the default result of a FOR XML AUTO query.

In a query expression, the *GroupJoin* operator is defined as a *join ... into ...* clause. The query expression shown in Listing 3-24 is equivalent to Listing 3-25.

LISTING 3-25 A query expression with a *join ... into ...* clause

```
var customersOrders =
    from c in customers
        from o in c.Orders
        select o;

var expr =
    from   p in products
    join   o in customersOrders
                on p.IdProduct equals o.IdProduct
                into orders
    select new { p.IdProduct, Orders = orders };
```

In this example, we first define an expression called *customersOrders* to extract the flat list of orders. (This expression still uses the *SelectMany* operator because of the double *from* clause.) You could also define a single query expression, nesting the *customersOrders* expression within the main query. This approach is shown in Listing 3-26.

LISTING 3-26 The query expression of Listing 3-25 in its compact version

```
var expr =
    from   p in products
    join   o in (
        from c in customers
            from   o in c.Orders
            select o
        ) on p.IdProduct equals o.IdProduct
        into orders
    select new { p.IdProduct, Orders = orders };
```

Set Operators

Our journey through LINQ operators continues with a group of methods that handle sets of data, applying common set operations (*union*, *intersect*, and *except*) and selecting unique occurrences of items (*distinct*).

Distinct

Imagine that you want to extract all products that are mapped to orders, avoiding duplicates. This requirement could be solved in standard SQL by using a DISTINCT clause within a JOIN query. LINQ provides a *Distinct* operator too. Its signatures are quite simple. It requires only a *source* sequence, from which all the distinct occurrences of items will be yielded, and provides an overload with a custom *IEqualityComparer<TSource>*, which you will learn later:

```
public static IEnumerable<TSource> Distinct<TSource>(
    this IEnumerable<TSource> source);
public static IEnumerable<TSource> Distinct<TSource>(
    this IEnumerable<TSource> source,
    IEqualityComparer<TSource> comparer);
```

An example of the operator is shown in Listing 3-27.

LISTING 3-27 The *Distinct* operator applied to the list of products used in orders

```
var expr =
    customers
    .SelectMany(c => c.Orders)
    .Join(products,
        o => o.IdProduct,
        p => p.IdProduct,
        (o, p) => p)
    .Distinct();
```

Distinct does not have an equivalent query expression clause; therefore, just as in Listing 3-15, you can apply this operator to the result of a query expression, as shown in Listing 3-28.

LISTING 3-28 The *Distinct* operator applied to a query expression

```
var expr =
    (from c in customers
          from   o in c.Orders
          join   p in products
                 on o.IdProduct equals p.IdProduct
          select p
    ).Distinct();
```

By default, *Distinct* compares and identifies elements using their *GetHashCode* and *Equals* methods because internally it uses a default comparer of type *EqualityComparer<T>.Default*. You can, if necessary, override the type behavior to change the *Distinct* result, or you can just use the second overload of the *Distinct* method:

```
public static IEnumerable<TSource> Distinct<TSource>(
    this IEnumerable<TSource> source,
    IEqualityComparer<TSource> comparer);
```

This last overload accepts a *comparer* argument, available so you can provide a custom *comparer* for instances of type *TSource*.

> **Note** You will see an example of how to compare reference types in the *Union* operator in Listing 3-29.

Union, Intersect, and *Except*

The group of set operators contains three more operators that are useful for classic set operations: *Union*, *Intersect*, and *Except*, all of which share a similar definition:

```
public static IEnumerable<TSource> Union<TSource>(
    this IEnumerable<TSource> first,
    IEnumerable<TSource> second);
public static IEnumerable<TSource> Union<TSource>(
    this IEnumerable<TSource> first,
    IEnumerable<TSource> second,
    IEqualityComparer<TSource> comparer);
public static IEnumerable<TSource> Intersect<TSource>(
    this IEnumerable<TSource> first,
    IEnumerable<TSource> second);
public static IEnumerable<TSource> Intersect<TSource>(
    this IEnumerable<TSource> first,
    IEnumerable<TSource> second,
    IEqualityComparer<TSource> comparer);
```

```
public static IEnumerable<TSource> Except<TSource>(
    this IEnumerable<TSource> first,
    IEnumerable<TSource> second);
public static IEnumerable<TSource> Except<TSource>(
    this IEnumerable<TSource> first,
    IEnumerable<TSource> second,
    IEqualityComparer<TSource> comparer);
```

The *Union* operator enumerates the *first* sequence and the *second* sequence in that order and yields each element that has not already been yielded. For example, in Listing 3-29, you can see how to merge two sets of *Integer* numbers.

LISTING 3-29 The *Union* operator applied to sets of *Integer* numbers

```
Int32[] setOne = {1, 5, 6, 9};
Int32[] setTwo = {4, 5, 7, 11};

var union = setOne.Union(setTwo);
foreach (var i in union) {
    Console.Write(i + ", ");
}
```

The console output of Listing 3-29 is:

```
1, 5, 6, 9, 4, 7, 11,
```

As with the *Distinct* operator, *Union*, *Intersect*, and *Except* compare elements by using the *GetHashCode* and *Equals* methods (in the first overload), or by using a custom *comparer* in the second overload. Consider the code excerpt shown in Listing 3-30.

LISTING 3-30 The *Union* operator applied to a couple of sets of products

```
Product[] productSetOne = {
    new Product {IdProduct = 46, Price = 1000 },
    new Product {IdProduct = 27, Price = 2000 },
    new Product {IdProduct = 14, Price = 500 } };
Product[] productSetTwo = {
    new Product {IdProduct = 11, Price = 350 },
    new Product {IdProduct = 46, Price = 1000 } };

var productsUnion = productSetOne.Union(productSetTwo);

foreach (var item in productsUnion) {
    Console.WriteLine(item);
}
```

Here is the console output of this code:

```
IdProduct: 46 - Price: 1000
IdProduct: 27 - Price: 2000
IdProduct: 14 - Price: 500
IdProduct: 11 - Price: 350
IdProduct: 46 - Price: 1000
```

This result might seem unexpected because the first and the last rows appear to be identical. However, if you look at the initialization code used in Listing 3-30, each product is a different instance of the *Product* reference type. Even if the second product of *productSetTwo* is semantically equal to the first product of *productSetOne*, they are different objects that have two different hash codes.

The problem is that there is no value type semantic defined for the *Product* reference type. To get the expected result, you can implement a value type semantic by overriding the *GetHashCode* and *Equals* implementations of the type to be compared. In this situation, it might be useful to do that, as you can see in this new *Product* implementation:

```
public class Product {
    public int IdProduct;
    public decimal Price;

    public override string ToString(){
        return String.Format("IdProduct: {0} - Price: {1}",
            this.IdProduct, this.Price);
    }

    public override bool Equals(object obj) {
        if (!(obj is Product))
            return false;
        else {
            Product p = (Product)obj;
            return (p.IdProduct == this.IdProduct &&
                p.Price == this.Price);
        }
    }

    public override int GetHashCode(){
        return String.Format("{0}|{1}", this.IdProduct, this.Price)
            .GetHashCode();
    }
}
```

Another way to get the correct result is to use the second overload of the *Union* method, providing a custom *comparer* for the *Product* type. A final way to get the expected distinct behavior is to define the *Product* type as a value type, using *struct* instead of *class* in its declaration—however, keep in mind that it is not always possible to define a *struct*, because sometimes you need to implement an object-oriented infrastructure using type inheritance:

```
// Using struct instead of class, we get a value type
public struct Product {
    public int IdProduct;
    public decimal Price;
}
```

Remember that an anonymous type is defined as a reference type with a value type semantic. In other words, all anonymous types are defined as a class with an override of *GetHashCode* and *Equals* written by the compiler, using an implementation that leverages *GetHashCode* and *Equals* for each property of the anonymous type instance.

In Listing 3-31, you can find an example of using *Intersect* and *Except*.

LISTING 3-31 The *Intersect* and *Except* operators applied to the same products set used in Listing 3-30

```
var expr = productSetOne.Intersect(productSetTwo);
var expr = productSetOne.Except(productSetTwo);
```

The *Intersect* operator yields only the elements that occur in both sequences, whereas the *Except* operator yields all the elements in the *first* sequence that are not present in the *second* sequence. Once again, there are no compact clauses to define set operators in query expressions, but you can apply them to query expression results, as in Listing 3-32.

LISTING 3-32 Set operators applied to query expressions

```
var expr = (
    from c in customers
        from o in c.Orders
            join p in products on o.IdProduct equals p.IdProduct
    where c.Country == Countries.Italy
    select p)
    .Intersect(
    from c in customers
        from o in c.Orders
            join p in products on o.IdProduct equals p.IdProduct
    where c.Country == Countries.USA
    select p);
```

Value Type vs. Reference Type Semantic

Remember that all the considerations for *Union* and *Distinct* operators are also valid for *Intersect* and *Except*. In general, they are valid for each operation that involves a comparison of two items made by LINQ to Objects. The result of the *Intersect* operation illustrated in Listing 3-31 is an empty set whenever the *Product* type is a reference type with no override of the *GetHashCode* and *Equals* methods. If you define *Product* as a value type (using *struct* instead of *class*), you get a product (IdProduct: 46 - Price: 1000) as an *Intersection* result. Once again, we want to emphasize that when using LINQ, it is better to use types with a value type semantic, even if they are reference types, so that you get consistent behavior across all regular and anonymous types.

Zip

A new set operator introduced with Microsoft .NET Framework 4 is *Zip*. Here is the corresponding definition:

```
public static IEnumerable<TResult> Zip<TFirst, TSecond, TResult>(
    this IEnumerable<TFirst> first,
    IEnumerable<TSecond> second,
    Func<TFirst, TSecond, TResult> resultSelector);
```

The *Zip* operator merges each element of the first sequence with the corresponding element with the same index in the second sequence. It is called "Zip" because you can think of it like a zipper, connecting two separate lists into a single list, keeping the items in each list in the same sequence. You can see an example of its use in Listing 3-33.

LISTING 3-33 The *Zip* operator applied to sets of *Integer* numbers and the days of the week

```
Int32[] numbers = { 1, 2, 3, 4, 5, 6, 7, 8, 9, 10 };
DayOfWeek[] weekDays = {
    DayOfWeek.Sunday,
    DayOfWeek.Monday,
    DayOfWeek.Tuesday,
    DayOfWeek.Wednesday,
    DayOfWeek.Thursday,
    DayOfWeek.Friday,
    DayOfWeek.Saturday};

var weekDaysNumbers = numbers.Zip(weekDays,
    (first, second) => first + " - " + second);

foreach (var item in weekDaysNumbers)
    Console.WriteLine(item);
```

Here is the console output of Listing 3-33:

```
1 - Sunday
2 - Monday
3 - Tuesday
4 - Wednesday
5 - Thursday
6 - Friday
7 - Saturday
```

If the sequences do not have the same number of elements, the method merges sequences until it reaches the end of the shorter sequence. For example, in Listing 3-33 the *numbers* sequence had 10 elements, whereas the *weekDays* sequence had only 7; therefore, the result sequence has only 7 elements.

Aggregate Operators

At times, you need to aggregate sequences to make calculations on source items. To accomplish this, LINQ provides a family of aggregate operators that implement the most common aggregate functions, including *Count*, *LongCount*, *Sum*, *Min*, *Max*, *Average*, and *Aggregate*. Many of these operators are simple to use because their behavior is easy to understand. However, remember that LINQ to Objects works over in-memory instances of *IEnumerable<T>* types, thus the code working on this enumeration might have some performance issues in cases when you need to browse the query result multiple times.

Count and *LongCount*

Imagine that you want to list all customers, each one followed by the number of orders that customer has placed. In Listing 3-34, you can see one syntax, based on the *Count* operator.

LISTING 3-34 The *Count* operator applied to customer orders

```
var expr =
    from   c in customers
    select new { c.Name, c.Country, OrdersCount = c.Orders.Count() };
```

The *Count* operator provides a couple of signatures, as does the *LongCount* operator:

```
public static int Count<TSource>(
    this IEnumerable<TSource> source);
public static int Count<TSource>(
    this IEnumerable<TSource> source,
    Func<TSource, Boolean> predicate);
public static long LongCount<TSource>(
    this IEnumerable<TSource> source);
public static long LongCount<TSource>(
    this IEnumerable<TSource> source,
    Func<TSource, Boolean> predicate);
```

The signature shown in Listing 3-34 is the common and simpler one; it simply counts items in the *source* sequence. The second method overload accepts a *predicate* used to filter the items to count. The *LongCount* variations simply return a *long* instead of an *integer*.

Sum

The *Sum* operator requires more attention because it has multiple definitions:

```
public static Numeric Sum(
    this IEnumerable<Numeric> source);
public static Numeric Sum<TSource>(
    this IEnumerable<TSource> source,
    Func<TSource, Numeric> selector);
```

For simplicity, the preceding definitions use *Numeric* to generalize the return type of the *Sum* operator. In practice, *Sum* has many definitions, one for each of the main *Numeric* types: *Int32*, *Nullable<Int32>*, *Int64*, *Nullable<Int64>*, *Single*, *Nullable<Single>*, *Double*, *Nullable<Double>*, *Decimal*, and *Nullable<Decimal>*.

> **Important** Remember that in C#, the question mark that appears after a value type name (*T?*) is shorthand that defines a nullable type (*Nullable<T>*) of this type. For example, you can write *int?* instead of *Nullable<System.Int32>*.

The first implementation sums the *source* sequence items, assuming that the items are all of the same numeric type, and returns the result. In the case of an empty *source* sequence, zero is returned. This implementation can be used when the items can be summed directly. For example, you can sum an array of integers as in this code:

```
int[] values = { 1, 3, 9, 29 };
int   total  = values.Sum();
```

When the sequence is not made up of simple *Numeric* types, you must extract values to be summed from each item in the *source* sequence. To do that, you can use the second overload, which accepts a *selector* argument. You can see an example of this syntax in Listing 3-35.

LISTING 3-35 The *Sum* operator applied to customer orders

```
var customersOrders =
    from c in customers
        from  o in c.Orders
        join  p in products
            on o.IdProduct equals p.IdProduct
        select new { c.Name, OrderAmount = o.Quantity * p.Price };

foreach (var o in customersOrders) {
    Console.WriteLine(o);
}

Console.WriteLine();
```

```
var expr =
    from    c in customers
    join    o in customersOrders
            on c.Name equals o.Name
            into customersWithOrders
    select new { c.Name,
                 TotalAmount = customersWithOrders.Sum(o => o.OrderAmount) };

foreach (var item in expr) {
    Console.WriteLine(item);
}
```

The code in Listing 3-35 joins customers into the *customersOrders* sequence to get the list of the customer names associated with the total amount of orders placed. The query results in the following output:

```
{ Name = Paolo, OrderAmount = 30 }
{ Name = Paolo, OrderAmount = 100 }
{ Name = Marco, OrderAmount = 100 }
{ Name = Marco, OrderAmount = 600 }
{ Name = James, OrderAmount = 600 }
{ Name = Frank, OrderAmount = 1000 }
```

Next, another join is used for each customer to get the total value of that customer's orders, calculated with the *Sum* operator, with the following result:

```
{ Name = Paolo, TotalAmount = 130 }
{ Name = Marco, TotalAmount = 700 }
{ Name = James, TotalAmount = 600 }
{ Name = Frank, TotalAmount = 1000 }
```

As usual, you can collapse the previous code by using nested queries, as shown in Listing 3-36.

LISTING 3-36 The *Sum* operator applied to customer orders, with a nested query

```
var expr =
    from    c in customers
    join    o in (
            from c in customers
                from    o in c.Orders
                join    p in products
                        on o.IdProduct equals p.IdProduct
                select new { c.Name, OrderAmount = o.Quantity * p.Price }
            ) on c.Name equals o.Name
            into customersWithOrders
    select new { c.Name,
                 TotalAmount = customersWithOrders.Sum(o => o.OrderAmount) };
```

SQL vs. LINQ Query Expression Syntax

At this point, it is worth making a comparison with SQL syntax because there are similarities—but also important differences. Here is a SQL statement similar to the query expression in Listing 3-35, assuming that customer names are unique:

```
SELECT    c.Name, SUM(o.OrderAmount) AS OrderAmount
FROM      customers AS c
INNER JOIN (
    SELECT     c.Name, o.Quantity * p.Price AS OrderAmount
    FROM       customers AS c
    INNER JOIN orders AS o ON c.Name = o.Name
    INNER JOIN products AS p ON o.IdProduct = p.IdProduct
    ) AS o
ON        c.Name = o.Name
GROUP BY c.Name
```

You can see that this SQL syntax is redundant. In fact, you can obtain the same result with this simpler SQL query:

```
SELECT    c.Name, SUM(o.OrderAmount) AS OrderAmount
FROM      customers AS c
INNER JOIN (
    SELECT     o.Name, o.Quantity * p.Price AS OrderAmount
    FROM       orders AS o
    INNER JOIN products AS p ON o.IdProduct = p.IdProduct
    ) AS o
ON        c.Name = o.Name
GROUP BY c.Name
```

But it can be simpler and shorter still, as in the following SQL query:

```
SELECT    c.Name, SUM(o.Quantity * p.Price) AS OrderAmount
FROM      customers AS c
INNER JOIN orders AS o ON c.Name = o.Name
INNER JOIN products AS p ON o.IdProduct = p.IdProduct
GROUP BY  c.Name
```

If you started from this last SQL query and tried to write a corresponding query expression syntax using LINQ, you would probably encounter some difficulties. The reason is that SQL queries data through relationships, but all data is flat (in tables) until it is queried. On the other hand, LINQ handles data that can have native hierarchical relationships, as the Customer/Orders/Products data example does. This difference implies that sometimes one approach has advantages over the other; which is best depends on the specific query and data.

For these reasons, the best expression of a query can appear differently in SQL and in LINQ query expression syntax, even if the query obtains the same results from the same data.

Min and *Max*

Within the set of aggregate operators, *Min* and *Max* calculate the minimum and maximum values of the source sequence, respectively. Both extension methods provide a rich set of overloads:

```
public static Numeric Min/Max(
    this IEnumerable<Numeric> source);
public static TSource Min<TSource>/Max<TSource>(
    this IEnumerable<TSource> source);
public static Numeric Min<TSource>/Max<TSource>(
    this IEnumerable<TSource> source,
    Func<TSource, Numeric> selector);
public static TResult Min<TSource, TResult>/Max<TSource, TResult>(
    this IEnumerable<TSource> source,
    Func<TSource, TResult> selector);
```

The first signature, like the *Sum* operator, provides many definitions for the main numeric types (*Int32*, *Nullable<Int32>*, *Int64*, *Nullable<Int64>*, *Single*, *Nullable<Single>*, *Double*, *Nullable<Double>*, *Decimal*, and *Nullable<Decimal>*). It computes the minimum or maximum value on an arithmetic basis, using the elements of the *source* sequence. This signature is useful when the source elements are numbers by themselves, as in Listing 3-37.

LISTING 3-37 The *Min* operator applied to order quantities

```
var expr =
    (from c in customers
        from  o in c.Orders
        select o.Quantity
    ).Min();
```

The second signature computes the minimum or maximum value of the source elements, regardless of their type. The comparison is made using the *IComparable<TSource>* interface implementation, if supported by the source elements, or the nongeneric *IComparable* interface implementation. If the source type *TSource* does not implement either of these interfaces, an *ArgumentException* error will be thrown, with an *Exception.Message* equal to "At least one object must implement *IComparable*." To examine this situation, take a look at Listing 3-38, in which the resulting anonymous type does not implement either of the interfaces required by the *Min* operator.

LISTING 3-38 The *Min* operator applied to wrong types (thereby throwing an *ArgumentException*)

```
var expr =
    (from c in customers
        from o in c.Orders
        select new { o.IdProduct, o.Quantity }
    ).Min();
```

In the case of an empty source or null values in the source sequence, the result will be null whenever the *Numeric* type is a nullable type; otherwise, an *InvalidOperationException* will be thrown. The *selector* predicate, available in the last two signatures, defines the function with which to extract values from the *source* sequence elements. For example, you can use these overloads to avoid errors related to missing interface implementations (*IComparable<T>*/ *IComparable*), as in Listing 3-39.

LISTING 3-39 The *Max* operator applied to custom types, with a value selector

```
var expr =
    (from c in customers
         from o in c.Orders
         select new { o.IdProduct, o.Quantity }
    ).Min(o => o.Quantity);
```

Average

The *Average* operator calculates the arithmetic average of a set of values, extracted from a source sequence. Like the previous operators, this function works with the source elements themselves or with values extracted using a custom *selector*:

```
public static Result Average(
    this IEnumerable<Numeric> source);
public static Result Average<TSource>(
    this IEnumerable<TSource> source,
    Func<TSource, Numeric> selector);
```

The *Numeric* type can be *Int32, Nullable<Int32>, Int64, Nullable<Int64>, Single, Nullable<Single>, Double, Nullable<Double>, Decimal,* and *Nullable<Decimal>*. The *Result* type always reflects the "nullability" of the numeric type. When the *Numeric* type is *Int32* or *Int64*, the *Result* type is *Double*. When the *Numeric* type is *Nullable<Int32>* or *Nullable<Int64>*, the *Result* type is *Nullable<Double>*. Otherwise, the *Numeric* and *Result* types are the same.

When the sum of the values used to compute the arithmetic average is too large for the result type, an *OverflowException* error is thrown. Because of its definition, the *Average* operator's first signature can be invoked only on a *Numeric* sequence. If you want to invoke it on a source sequence of non-numeric type instances, you need to provide a custom *selector*. In Listing 3-40, you can see an example of both overloads.

LISTING 3-40 Both *Average* operator signatures applied to product prices

```
var expr =
    (from p in products
     select p.Price
     ).Average();
```

```
var expr =
    (from p in products
     select new { p.IdProduct, p.Price }
    ).Average(p => p.Price);
```

The second signature is useful when you are defining a query in which the average is just one of the results you want to extract. The example in Listing 3-41 extracts all customers and their average order amounts.

LISTING 3-41 Customers and their average order amounts

```
var expr =
    from   c in customers
    join   o in (
           from c in customers
               from   o in c.Orders
               join   p in products
                      on o.IdProduct equals p.IdProduct
               select new { c.Name, OrderAmount = o.Quantity * p.Price }
           ) on c.Name equals o.Name
           into customersWithOrders
    select new { c.Name,
                 AverageAmount = customersWithOrders.Average(o => o.OrderAmount) };
```

The results will be similar to the following:

```
{ Name = Paolo, AverageAmount = 65 }
{ Name = Marco, AverageAmount = 350 }
{ Name = James, AverageAmount = 600 }
{ Name = Frank, AverageAmount = 1000 }
```

Aggregate

The last operator in this set is *Aggregate*. Take a look at its definition:

```
public static T Aggregate<TSource>(
    this IEnumerable<TSource> source,
    Func<TSource, TSource, TSource> func);
public static TAccumulate Aggregate<TSource, TAccumulate>(
    this IEnumerable<TSource> source,
    TAccumulate seed,
    Func<TAccumulate, TSource, TAccumulate> func);
public static TResult Aggregate<TSource, TAccumulate, TResult>(
    this IEnumerable< TSource > source,
    TAccumulate seed,
    Func<TAccumulate, TSource, TAccumulate> func,
    Func<TAccumulate, TResult> resultSelector);
```

This operator repeatedly invokes the *func* function, storing the result in an accumulator. Every step calls the function with the current accumulator value as the first argument, starting from *seed*, and the current element within the *source* sequence as the second argument. At the end of the iteration, the operator returns the final accumulator value.

The only difference between the first two signatures is that the second requires an explicit value for the *seed* of type *TAccumulate*. The first signature uses the first element in the *source* sequence as the *seed* and infers the *seed* type from the *source* sequence itself. The third signature looks like the second, but it requires a *resultSelector* predicate to call when extracting the final result.

In Listing 3-42, we use the *Aggregate* operator to extract the most expensive order for each customer.

LISTING 3-42 Customers and their most expensive orders

```
var expr =
    from    c in customers
    join    o in (
            from c in customers
                from    o in c.Orders
                join    p in products
                        on o.IdProduct equals p.IdProduct
                select new { c.Name, o.IdProduct,
                                OrderAmount = o.Quantity * p.Price }
            ) on c.Name equals o.Name
            into orders
    select new { c.Name,
                MaxOrderAmount =
                    orders
                    .Aggregate((a, o) => a.OrderAmount > o.OrderAmount ?
                                        a : o)
                    .OrderAmount };
```

As you can see, the function called by the *Aggregate* operator compares the *OrderAmount* property of each order executed by the current customer and keeps track of the more expensive one in the accumulator variable (*a*). At the end of each customer aggregation, the accumulator will contain the most expensive order, and its *OrderAmount* property will be projected into the final result, coupled with the customer *Name* property. The following is the output from this query:

```
{ Name = Paolo, MaxOrderAmount = 100 }
{ Name = Marco, MaxOrderAmount = 600 }
{ Name = James, MaxOrderAmount = 600 }
{ Name = Frank, MaxOrderAmount = 1000 }
```

In Listing 3-43, you can see another sample of aggregation. This example calculates the total amount ordered for each product.

LISTING 3-43 Products and their ordered amounts

```
var expr =
    from   p in products
    join   o in (
           from c in customers
                from   o in c.Orders
                join   p in products
                       on o.IdProduct equals p.IdProduct
                select new { p.IdProduct, OrderAmount = o.Quantity * p.Price }
           ) on p.IdProduct equals o.IdProduct
           into orders
    select new { p.IdProduct,
                 TotalOrderedAmount =
                     orders
                     .Aggregate(0m, (a, o) => a += o.OrderAmount)};
```

Here is the output of this query:

```
{ IdProduct = 1, TotalOrderedAmount = 130 }
{ IdProduct = 2, TotalOrderedAmount = 100 }
{ IdProduct = 3, TotalOrderedAmount = 1200 }
{ IdProduct = 4, TotalOrderedAmount = 0 }
{ IdProduct = 5, TotalOrderedAmount = 1000 }
{ IdProduct = 6, TotalOrderedAmount = 0 }
```

In this second sample, the aggregate function uses an accumulator of *Decimal* type. It is initialized to zero (*seed = 0m*) and accumulates the *OrderAmount* values for every step. The result of this function will also be a *Decimal* type.

Both of the previous examples could also be defined by invoking the *Max* or *Sum* operators, respectively. They are shown in this section to help you learn about the *Aggregate* operator's behavior. In general, keep in mind that the *Aggregate* operator is useful whenever there are no specific aggregation operators available; otherwise, you should use a specific operator such as *Min*, *Max*, *Sum*, and so on. For example, consider the example in Listing 3-44.

LISTING 3-44 Customers and their most expensive orders paired with the month of execution

```
var expr =
    from   c in customers
    join   o in (
           from c in customers
                from   o in c.Orders
                join   p in products
                       on o.IdProduct equals p.IdProduct
                select new { c.Name, o.IdProduct, o.Month,
                             OrderAmount = o.Quantity * p.Price }
           ) on c.Name equals o.Name into orders
```

```
select new { c.Name,
             MaxOrder =
                 orders
                 .Aggregate( new { Amount = 0m, Month = String.Empty },
                             (a, s) => a.Amount > s.OrderAmount
                                       ? a
                                       : new { Amount = s.OrderAmount,
                                               Month = s.Month })};
```

The result of Listing 3-44 is:

```
{ Name = Paolo, MaxOrder = { Amount = 100, Month = May } }
{ Name = Marco, MaxOrder = { Amount = 600, Month = December } }
{ Name = James, MaxOrder = { Amount = 600, Month = December } }
{ Name = Frank, MaxOrder = { Amount = 1000, Month = July } }
```

In this example, the *Aggregate* operator returns a new anonymous type called *MaxOrder*: it is a tuple composed of the amount and month of the most expensive order made by each customer. The *Aggregate* operator used here cannot be replaced by any of the other predefined aggregate operators because of its specific behavior and result type.

The only way to produce a similar result using standard aggregate operators is to call two different aggregators. That would require two *source* sequence scannings: one to get the maximum amount and one to get its month. Be sure to pay attention to the *seed* definition, which declares the resulting anonymous type that will be used by the aggregation function as well.

Aggregate Operators in Visual Basic

Visual Basic introduces a set of new keywords and clauses in LINQ query expression syntax that supports easy aggregation over data items. In particular, the *Aggregate* clause lets you include aggregate functions in query expressions. Here is the syntax of this clause:

```
Aggregate element [As type] In collection
    [, element2 [As type2] In collection2, [...]]
    [ clause ]
    Into expressionList
```

In the preceding example, *element* is the item taken from an iteration over the source *collection* to use to execute the aggregation. The *clause* part of the syntax (which is optional) represents any query expression used to refine the items to aggregate. For example, it could be a *Where* clause. The *expressionList* part of the syntax is mandatory and defines one or more comma-delimited expressions that identify an aggregate function to be applied to the *collection*. The standard aggregate functions you can use are the *All, Any, Average, Count, LongCount, Max, Min,* and *Sum* functions.

Listing 3-45 shows an example of using the *Aggregate* clause to get the average price of products ordered by customers.

LISTING 3-45 Average price of products ordered by customers

```
Dim productsOrdered =
    From c In customers
    From o In c.Orders
        Join p In products
        On o.IdProduct Equals p.IdProduct
    Select p
 Dim expr = Aggregate p In productsOrdered
    Into Average(p.Price)
```

As you saw earlier in this chapter in examples written in C#, you can merge the previous code to write a single query expression, as in Listing 3-46.

LISTING 3-46 Average price of products ordered by customers, determined with a unique query expression

```
Dim expr = Aggregate p In (
    From c In customers
    From o In c.Orders
        Join p In products
        On o.IdProduct Equals p.IdProduct
    Select p)
    Into Average(p.Price)
```

The most interesting feature of the *Aggregate* clause lies in its ability to apply any kind of aggregate function, even custom ones that you define. Whenever you define a custom extension method that extends *IEnumerable<T>*, you can use it in the *expressionList* within the *Aggregate* clause. In Listing 3-47 you can see an example of a custom aggregate function that calculates the standard deviation of a set of values describing the price of products.

LISTING 3-47 Custom aggregate function to calculate the standard deviation of a set of *Double* values

```
<Extension()>
Function StandardDeviation(
    ByVal source As IEnumerable(Of Double)) As Double

    If source Is Nothing Then
        Throw New ArgumentNullException("source")
    End If

    If source.Count = 0 Then
        Throw New InvalidOperationException("Cannot compute Standard
        Deviation for an empty set.")
    End If
```

```vb
        Dim avg = Aggregate v In source Into Average(v)
        Dim accumulator As Double = 0

        For Each x In source
            accumulator += (x - avg) ^ 2
        Next

    Return Math.Sqrt(accumulator / (source.Count))

End Function

<Extension()>
Function StandardDeviation(Of TSource)(
        ByVal source As IEnumerable(Of TSource),
        ByVal selector As Func(Of TSource, Double)) As Double

    Return (From element In source Select
        selector(element)).StandardDeviation()

End Function

Sub Main()

    Dim expr = Aggregate p In products
                Into StandardDeviation(p.Price)

End Sub
```

Generation Operators

When working with data by applying aggregates, arithmetic operations, and mathematical functions, you sometimes need to iterate over numbers or item collections. For example, think about a query that needs to extract orders placed for a particular set of years, between 2005 and 2010, or a query that needs to repeat the same operation over the same data. The generation operators are useful for operations such as these.

Range

The first operator in this set is *Range*, which is a simple extension method that yields a set of *Integer* numbers, selected within a specified range of values, as shown in its signature:

```csharp
public static IEnumerable<Int32> Range(
    Int32 start,
    Int32 count);
```

The code in Listing 3-48 illustrates how to limit orders to the months between January and June.

> **Important** Please note that in the following example, a *where* condition would be more appro-
> priate because it iterates over *orders* many times. The example in Listing 3-48 is provided only for
> demonstration and is not the best solution for the specific query.

LISTING 3-48 A set of months generated by the *Range* operator, used to filter orders

```
var expr = Enumerable.Range(1, 6)
    .SelectMany(x => (
        from o in (
            from c in customers
            from o in c.Orders
            select o)
        where o.Month ==
            new CultureInfo("en-US").DateTimeFormat.GetMonthName(x)
        select new { o.Month, o.IdProduct }));
```

The *Range* operator can also be used to implement classic mathematical operations. Listing
3-49 shows an example of using *Range* and *Aggregate* to calculate the factorial of a number.

LISTING 3-49 A factorial of a number using the *Range* operator

```
static int Factorial(int number) {
    return (Enumerable.Range(0, number + 1)
        .Aggregate(0, (s, t) => t == 0 ? 1 : s *= t)); }
```

Repeat

Another generation operator is *Repeat*, which returns a set of *count* occurrences of *element*.
When the *element* is an instance of a reference type, each repetition returns a reference to the
same instance, not a copy of it:

```
public static IEnumerable<TResult> Repeat<TResult>(
    TResult element,
    int count);
```

The *Repeat* operator is useful for initializing enumerations (using the same element for
all instances) or for repeating the same query many times. Listing 3-50 repeats the customer name selection two times.

LISTING 3-50 The *Repeat* operator, used to repeat the same query many times

```
var expr =
    Enumerable.Repeat( ( from c in customers
                         select c.Name), 2)
    .SelectMany(x => x);
```

In this example, *Repeat* returns a sequence of sequences, formed by two lists of customer names. For this reason, we used *SelectMany* to get a flat list of names.

Empty

The last of the generation operators is *Empty*, which you can use to create an empty enumeration of a particular type *TResult*. This operation can be useful for initializing empty sequences:

```
public static IEnumerable<TResult> Empty<TResult>();
```

Listing 3-51 provides an example that uses *Empty* to fill an empty enumeration of *Customer*.

LISTING 3-51 The *Empty* operator used to initialize an empty set of customers

```
IEnumerable<Customer> customers = Enumerable.Empty<Customer>();
```

Quantifier Operators

Imagine that you need to check for the existence of elements within a sequence by using conditions or selection rules. First you select items with *Restriction* operators, and then you use aggregate operators such as *Count* to determine whether any item that verifies the condition exists. There is, however, a set of operators, called quantifiers, specifically designed to check for existence conditions over sequences.

Any

The first operator we will describe in this group is the *Any* method. It provides a couple of overloads:

```
public static Boolean Any<TSource>(
    this IEnumerable<TSource> source,
    Func<TSource, Boolean> predicate);
public static Boolean Any<TSource>(
    this IEnumerable<TSource> source);
```

As you can see from the method's signatures, the method has an overload accepting a predicate. This overload returns *true* whenever an item exists in the *source* sequence that verifies the predicate provided. There is also a second overload that requires only the *source* sequence, without a predicate. This method returns *true* when at least one element in the *source* sequence exists or *false* if the *source* sequence is empty. To optimize its execution, *Any* returns as soon as a result is available. Listing 3-52 checks whether any orders of product one (*IdProduct == 1*) exist within all customers' orders.

LISTING 3-52 The *Any* operator applied to all customer orders to check orders of *IdProduct == 1*

```
bool result =
    (from c in customers
         from   o in c.Orders
         select o)
    .Any(o => o.IdProduct == 1);

result = Enumerable.Empty<Order>().Any();
```

In the first example above, the operator evaluates items only until the first order matching the condition (*IdProduct == 1*) is found. The second example in Listing 3-52 illustrates a trivial use of the *Any* operator with a *false* result, using the *Empty* operator described earlier.

> **Important** The *Any* operator applied to an empty sequence will always return *false*. The internal operator implementation in LINQ to Objects enumerates all the *source* sequence items. It returns *true* as soon as it finds an element that verifies the *predicate*. When the sequence is empty, the *predicate* is never called and *Any* returns *false*.

All

When you want to determine whether all the items of a sequence verify a filtering condition, you can use the *All* operator. It returns a *true* result only if the condition is verified by all the elements in the *source* sequence:

```
public static Boolean All<TSource>(
    this IEnumerable<TSource> source,
    Func<TSource, Boolean> predicate);
```

For example, in Listing 3-53, we determine whether every order has a positive quantity.

LISTING 3-53 The *All* operator applied to all customer orders to check the quantity

```
bool result =
    (from c in customers
         from o in c.Orders
         select o)
    .All(o => o.Quantity > 0);

result = Enumerable.Empty<Order>().All(o => o.Quantity > 0);
```

> **Important** The *All* operator applied to an empty sequence will always return *true*. The internal operator implementation in LINQ to Objects enumerates all the *source* sequence items. It returns *false* as soon as it finds an element that does not verify the *predicate*. When the sequence is empty, the *predicate* is never called and *All* returns *true*.

Contains

The last quantifier operator is the *Contains* extension method, which determines whether a *source* sequence contains a specific item value:

```
public static Boolean Contains<TSource>(
    this IEnumerable<TSource> source,
    TSource value);
public static Boolean Contains<TSource>(
    this IEnumerable<TSource> source,
    TSource value,
    IEqualityComparer<TSource> comparer)
```

In the LINQ to Objects implementation, the method tries using the *Contains* method of *ICollection<T>* if the *source* sequence implements this interface. When *ICollection<T>* is not implemented, *Contains* enumerates all the items in *source*, comparing each one with the given *value* of type *TSource*. If you provide a custom *comparer, Contains* uses the second method overload; otherwise, it uses the *EqualityComparer<T>.Default*.

In Listing 3-54, you can see an example of the *Contains* method as it is used to check for the existence of a specific order within the collection of orders of a customer.

LISTING 3-54 The *Contains* operator applied to the first customer's orders

```
// the first customer has an order with the following values
var orderOfProductOne = new Order {IdOrder = 1, Quantity = 3, IdProduct =
    1 , Shipped = false, Month = "January"};
bool result = customers[0].Orders.Contains(orderOfProductOne);
```

Unlike what you would expect, at the end of Listing 3-54 the result will be *false* even though an order exists for the first customer that contains the same values for each field. The *Contains* method returns *true* only if you use the same object as the one to compare. Otherwise, you need a custom *comparer* or a value type semantic for *Order* type (a reference type that overloads the *GetHashCode* and *Equals* methods or a value type, as described earlier) to look for an equivalent order in the sequence.

Partitioning Operators

Selection and filtering operations sometimes need to be applied only to a subset of the elements of the source sequence. For example, you might need to extract only the first *n* elements that verify a condition. You can use the *Where* and *Select* operators with the zero-based index argument of their predicate, but this approach is not always useful and intuitive. It is better to have specific operators for these kinds of operations because they are performed quite frequently.

A set of partitioning operators is provided to satisfy these needs. *Take* and *TakeWhile* select the first *n* items or the first items that verify a predicate, respectively. *Skip* and *SkipWhile* complement the *Take* and *TakeWhile* operators, skipping the first *n* items or the first items that validate a predicate.

Take

Here is the definition for *Take*:

```
public static IEnumerable<TSource> Take<TSource>(
    this IEnumerable<TSource> source,
    Int32 count);
```

The *Take* operator requires a *count* argument that represents the number of items to take from the *source* sequence. Negative values of *count* determine an empty result; values larger than the sequence size return the full *source* sequence. This method is useful for all queries in which you need the top *n* items. For example, you could use this method to select the top *n* customers based on their order amount, as shown in Listing 3-55.

LISTING 3-55 The *Take* operator, applied to extract the two top customers ordered by order amount

```
var topTwoCustomers =
    (from    c in customers
     join    o in (
             from c in customers
                  from   o in c.Orders
                  join   p in products
                         on o.IdProduct equals p.IdProduct
                  select new { c.Name, OrderAmount = o.Quantity * p.Price }
             ) on c.Name equals o.Name
             into customersWithOrders
     let     TotalAmount = customersWithOrders.Sum(o => o.OrderAmount)
     orderby TotalAmount descending
     select  new { c.Name, TotalAmount }
    ).Take(2);
```

As you can see, the *Take* operator clause is quite simple, whereas the whole query is more articulated. The query contains several of the basic elements and operators discussed already. The *let* clause, in addition to *Take*, is the only clause that you have not already seen in action in a LINQ to Objects query. As discussed in Chapter 2, the *let* keyword is useful for defining an alias for a value or for a variable representing a formula. In this sample, we need to use the sum of all order amounts on a customer basis as a value to project into the resulting anonymous type. At the same time, the same value is used as a sorting condition. Therefore, we defined an alias named *TotalAmount* to avoid duplicate formulas.

TakeWhile

The *TakeWhile* operator works like the *Take* operator, but it checks a formula to extract items instead of using a counter. Here are the method's signatures:

```
public static IEnumerable<TSource> TakeWhile<TSource>(
    this IEnumerable<TSource> source,
    Func<TSource, Boolean> predicate);
public static IEnumerable<TSource> TakeWhile<TSource>(
    this IEnumerable<TSource> source,
    Func<TSource, Int32, Boolean> predicate);
```

There are two overloads of the method. The first requires a *predicate* that will be evaluated on each *source* sequence item. The method enumerates the *source* sequence and yields items if the *predicate* is *true*; it stops the enumeration when the *predicate* result becomes *false*, or when the end of the *source* is reached. The second overload also requires a zero-based index for the *predicate* to indicate where the query should start evaluating the *source* sequence.

Imagine that you want to identify your top customers, generating a list that makes up a minimum aggregate amount of orders. The problem looks similar to the one we solved with the *Take* operator in Listing 3-55, but we do not know how many customers we need to examine. *TakeWhile* can solve the problem by using a predicate that calculates the aggregate amount and uses that number to stop the enumeration when the target is reached. The resulting query is shown in Listing 3-56.

LISTING 3-56 The *TakeWhile* operator, applied to extract the top customers that form 80 percent of all orders

```
// globalAmount is the total amount for all the orders
var limitAmount = globalAmount * 0.8m;
var aggregated = 0m;
var topCustomers =
    (from    c in customers
     join    o in (
             from c in customers
                 from    o in c.Orders
                 join    p in products
                         on o.IdProduct equals p.IdProduct
                 select new { c.Name, OrderAmount = o.Quantity * p.Price }
             ) on c.Name equals o.Name
             into customersWithOrders
     let     TotalAmount = customersWithOrders.Sum(o => o.OrderAmount)
     orderby TotalAmount descending
     select  new { c.Name, TotalAmount }
    )
    .TakeWhile( X => {
                bool result = aggregated < limitAmount;
                aggregated += X.TotalAmount;
                return result;
            } );
```

Skip and SkipWhile

The *Skip* and *SkipWhile* signatures are very similar to those for *Take* and *TakeWhile*:

```
public static IEnumerable<TSource> Skip<TSource>(
    this IEnumerable<TSource> source,
    Int32 count);
public static IEnumerable<TSource> SkipWhile<TSource>(
    this IEnumerable<TSource> source,
    Func<TSource, Boolean> predicate);
public static IEnumerable<TSource> SkipWhile<TSource>(
    this IEnumerable<TSource> source,
    Func<TSource, Int32, Boolean> predicate);
```

As mentioned previously, these operators complement the *Take* and *TakeWhile* operators. In fact, the following code returns the full sequence of customers:

```
var result = customers.Take(3).Union(customers.Skip(3));
var result = customers.TakeWhile(p).Union(customers.SkipWhile(p));
```

The only point of interest is that *SkipWhile* skips the *source* sequence items while the *predicate* evaluates to *true* and starts yielding items as soon as the *predicate* result is *false*, suspending the *predicate* evaluation on all the remaining items.

Element Operators

Element operators work with individual items of a sequence. They are designed to extract a specific element either by position or by using a predicate, rather than by using a default value in case of missing elements.

First

The *First* method extracts the first element in the sequence by using a predicate or a positional rule:

```
public static TSource First<TSource>(
    this IEnumerable<TSource> source);
public static TSource First<TSource>(
    this IEnumerable<TSource> source,
    Func<TSource, Boolean> predicate);
```

The first overload returns the first element in the *source* sequence, and the second overload uses a *predicate* to identify the first element to return. If there are no elements that verify the *predicate* or the *source* sequence contains no elements, the operator will throw an *InvalidOperationException* error. Listing 3-57 shows an example of the *First* operator.

LISTING 3-57 The *First* operator, used to select the first US customer

```
var item = customers.First(c => c.Country == Countries.USA);
```

Of course, this example could be defined by using a *Where* and *Take* operator. However, the *First* method better demonstrates the intention of the query, and it also guarantees a single (partial) scan of the *source* sequence.

FirstOrDefault

If you need to find the first element only if it exists, without any exception in case of failure, you can use the *FirstOrDefault* method. This method works like *First*, but if there are no elements that verify the predicate or if the *source* sequence is empty, it returns a default value:

```
public static TSource FirstOrDefault<TSource>(
    this IEnumerable<TSource> source);
public static TSource FirstOrDefault<TSource>(
    this IEnumerable<TSource> source,
    Func<TSource, Boolean> predicate);
```

The default returned is *default(TSource)* in the case of an empty *source*, where *default(TSource)* returns *null* for reference types and nullable types. If no *predicate* argument is provided, the method returns the first element of the *source* if it exists. Examples are shown in Listing 3-58.

LISTING 3-58 Examples of the *FirstOrDefault* operator syntax

```
var item = customers.FirstOrDefault(c => c.City == "Las Vegas");
Console.WriteLine(item == null ? "null" : item.ToString()); // returns null

IEnumerable<Customer> emptyCustomers = Enumerable.Empty<Customer>();
item = emptyCustomers.FirstOrDefault(c => c.City == "Las Vegas");
Console.WriteLine(item == null ? "null" : item.ToString()); // returns null
```

Last and LastOrDefault

The *Last* and *LastOrDefault* operators are complements of *First* and *FirstOrDefault*. The former have signatures and behaviors that mirror the latter:

```
public static TSource Last<TSource>(
    this IEnumerable<TSource> source);
public static TSource Last<TSource>(
    this IEnumerable<TSource> source,
    Func<TSource, Boolean> predicate);
public static TSource LastOrDefault<TSource>(
    this IEnumerable<TSource> source);
public static TSource LastOrDefault<TSource>(
    this IEnumerable<TSource> source,
    Func<TSource, Boolean> predicate);
```

These methods work like *First* and *FirstOrDefault*. The only difference is that they select the last element in *source* instead of the first.

Single

Whenever you need to select a specific and unique item from a *source* sequence, you can use the operators *Single* or *SingleOrDefault*:

```
public static TSource Single<TSource>(
    this IEnumerable<TSource> source);
public static TSource Single<TSource>(
    this IEnumerable<TSource> source,
    Func<TSource, Boolean> predicate);
```

If no *predicate* is provided, *Single* extracts from the *source* sequence the first single element. Otherwise, it extracts the single element that verifies the *predicate*. If there is no predicate and the source sequence contains more than one item, the method throws an *InvalidOperation-Exception* error. The *Single* method also throws an *InvalidOperationException* error when there is a *predicate* and there are no matching elements or when the source contains more than one match. You can see some examples in Listing 3-59.

LISTING 3-59 Examples of the *Single* operator syntax

```
// returns Product 1
var item = products.Single(p => p.IdProduct == 1);
Console.WriteLine(item == null ? "null" : item.ToString());

// InvalidOperationException
item = products.Single();
Console.WriteLine(item == null ? "null" : item.ToString());

// InvalidOperationException
IEnumerable<Product> emptyProducts = Enumerable.Empty<Product>();
item = emptyProducts.Single(p => p.IdProduct == 1);
Console.WriteLine(item == null ? "null" : item.ToString());
```

SingleOrDefault

The *SingleOrDefault* operator provides a default result value in the case of an empty sequence or no matching elements in *source*. Its signatures are like those for *Single*:

```
public static TSource SingleOrDefault<TSource>(
    this IEnumerable<TSource> source);
public static TSource SingleOrDefault<TSource>(
    this IEnumerable<TSource> source,
    Func<TSource, Boolean> predicate);
```

The default value returned by this method is *default(TSource)*, as in the *FirstOrDefault* and *LastOrDefault* extension methods.

> **Important** The default value is returned only if no elements match the *predicate*. The method throws an *InvalidOperationException* error when the *source* sequence contains more than one matching item.

ElementAt and ElementAtOrDefault

Whenever you need to extract a specific item from a sequence based on its position, you can use the *ElementAt* or *ElementAtOrDefault* method:

```
public static TSource ElementAt<TSource>(
    this IEnumerable<TSource> source,
    Int32 index);
public static TSource ElementAtOrDefault<TSource>(
    this IEnumerable<TSource> source,
    Int32 index);
```

The *ElementAt* method requires an *index* argument that represents the position of the element to extract. The *index* is zero based; therefore, you need to provide a value of 2 to extract the third element. When the value of *index* is negative or greater than the size of the *source* sequence, the method throws an *ArgumentOutOfRangeException* error. The *ElementAtOrDefault* method differs from *ElementAt* because it returns a default value—*default(TSource)* for reference types and nullable types—in the case of a negative *index* or an *index* greater than the size of the *source* sequence. Listing 3-60 shows some examples of how to use these operators.

LISTING 3-60 Examples of the *ElementAt* and *ElementAtOrDefault* operator syntax

```
// returns Product at index 2
var item = products.ElementAt(2);
Console.WriteLine(item == null ? "null" : item.ToString());

// returns null
item = Enumerable.Empty<Product>().ElementAtOrDefault(6);
Console.WriteLine(item == null ? "null" : item.ToString());

// returns null
item = products.ElementAtOrDefault(6);
Console.WriteLine(item == null ? "null" : item.ToString());
```

DefaultIfEmpty

DefaultIfEmpty returns a default element for an empty sequence:

```
public static IEnumerable<TSource> DefaultIfEmpty<TSource>(
    this IEnumerable<TSource> source);
public static IEnumerable<TSource> DefaultIfEmpty<TSource>(
    this IEnumerable<TSource> source,
    TSource defaultValue);
```

By default, it returns the list of items of a *source* sequence. In the case of an empty source, it returns a default value that is *default(TSource)* in the first overload or *defaultValue* if you use the second overload of the method.

Defining a specific default value can be helpful in many circumstances. For example, imagine that you have a public static property named *Empty* that returns an empty instance of a *Customer*, as in the following code excerpt:

```
private static volatile Customer empty;
private static Object emptySyncLock = new Object();

public static Customer Empty {
    get {
        // Multithreaded singleton pattern
        if (empty == null) {
            lock (emptySyncLock) {
                if (empty == null) {
                    empty = new Customer();
                    empty.Name = String.Empty;
                    empty.Country = Countries.Italy;
                    empty.City = String.Empty;
                    empty.Orders = (new List<Order>(Enumerable.Empty<Order>())).ToArray();
                }
            }
        }
        return (empty);
    }
}
```

Sometimes this is useful, especially when unit-testing code. Another situation is when a query uses *GroupJoin* to realize a left outer join. The possible resulting nulls can be replaced by a default value chosen by the query author.

In Listing 3-61, you can see how to use *DefaultIfEmpty*, including a custom default value such as *Customer.Empty*.

LISTING 3-61 Example of the *DefaultIfEmpty* operator syntax, both with *default(T)* and a custom default value

```
var expr = customers.DefaultIfEmpty();

var customers = Enumerable.Empty<Customer>(); // Empty array
IEnumerable<Customer> customersEmpty =
    customers.DefaultIfEmpty(Customer.Empty);
```

Other Operators

To complete the coverage of LINQ to Objects query operators, this section describes a few final extension methods.

Concat

As the name suggests, the concatenation operator, named *Concat,* simply appends one sequence to another, as you can see from its signature:

```
public static IEnumerable<TSource> Concat<TSource>(
    this IEnumerable<TSource> first,
    IEnumerable<TSource> second);
```

The only requirement for *Concat* arguments is that they enumerate the same type *TSource*. You can use this method to append any *IEnumerable<T>* sequence to another of the same type. Listing 3-62 shows an example of customer concatenation.

LISTING 3-62 The *Concat* operator, used to concatenate Italian customers with US customers

```
var italianCustomers =
    from  c in customers
    where c.Country == Countries.Italy
    select c;

var americanCustomers =
    from  c in customers
    where c.Country == Countries.USA
    select c;

var expr = italianCustomers.Concat(americanCustomers);
```

SequenceEqual

Another useful operator is the equality operator, which corresponds to the *SequenceEqual* extension method:

```
public static Boolean SequenceEqual<TSource>(
    this IEnumerable<TSource> first,
    IEnumerable<TSource> second);
public static Boolean SequenceEqual<TSource>(
    this IEnumerable<TSource> first,
    IEnumerable<TSource> second,
    IEqualityComparer<TSource> comparer);
```

This method compares each item in the first sequence with each corresponding item in the second sequence. If the two sequences have exactly the same number of items and the items in every position are equal, the two sequences are considered equal. Remember the possible issues of reference type semantics in this kind of comparison. You can consider overriding *GetHashCode* and *Equals* on the *TSource* type to drive the result of this operator, or you can use the second method overload, providing a custom implementation of *IEqualityComparer<T>*.

Conversion Operators

The methods included in the set of conversion operators are *AsEnumerable*, *ToArray*, *ToList*, *ToDictionary*, *ToLookup*, *OfType*, and *Cast*. Conversion operators are defined primarily to solve problems and needs related to LINQ deferred query evaluation. (See Chapter 2 for more details on this topic.) Sometimes you might need a stable and immutable result from a query expression, or you might want to use a generic extension method operator instead of a more specialized one. The following sections describe the conversion operators in more detail.

 Note There is one other conversion operator, *AsQueryable*, which, because of its complexity, is covered separately in more detail in Chapter 15, "Extending LINQ."

AsEnumerable

Here is the signature for *AsEnumerable*:

```
public static IEnumerable<TSource> AsEnumerable<TSource>(
    this IEnumerable<TSource> source);
```

The *AsEnumerable* operator simply returns the *source* sequence as an object of type *IEnumerable<TSource>*. This kind of "conversion on the fly" makes it possible to call the general-purpose extension methods over *source*, even if its type has specific implementations of them.

Consider a custom *Where* extension method for a type *Customers*, such as the one defined in Listing 3-63.

LISTING 3-63 A custom *Where* extension method defined for the type *Customers*

```
public class Customers : List<Customer> {
    public Customers(IEnumerable<Customer> items): base(items) {
    }
}

public static class CustomersExtension {
    public static Customers Where(this Customers source,
        Func<Customer, Boolean> predicate) {
        Customers result = new Customers();

        Console.WriteLine("Custom Where extension method");
        foreach (var item in source) {
            if (predicate(item))
                result.Add(item);
        }
        return result;
    }
}
```

Notice the presence of the *Console.WriteLine* method call inside the sample code.

Important In real solutions, you would probably use a custom iterator rather than an explicit list to represent the result of this extension method, but for the sake of simplicity we decided not to do that in this quick example.

In Listing 3-64 you can see an example of a query expression executed over an instance of the type *Customers*.

LISTING 3-64 A query expression over a list of *Customers*

```
Customers customersList = new Customers(customers);

var expr =
    from    c in customersList
    where   c.Country == Countries.Italy
    select c;

foreach (var item in expr) {
    Console.WriteLine(item);
}
```

The output of this sample code will be the following:

```
Custom Where extension method
Name: Paolo - City: Brescia - Country: Italy - Orders Count: 2
Name: Marco - City: Torino - Country: Italy - Orders Count: 2
```

As you can see, the output starts with the *Console.WriteLine* invoked in our custom *Where* extension method. In fact, as described in Chapter 2, LINQ queries are translated into the corresponding extension methods, and for the *Customers* type, the *Where* extension method is the custom definition shown earlier.

Now imagine that you want to define a query over an instance of the *Customers* type *without* using the custom extension method; instead, you want to use the default *Where* operator defined for the *IEnumerable<T>* type. The *AsEnumerable* extension method accomplishes this requirement for you, as you can see in Listing 3-65.

LISTING 3-65 A query expression over a list of *Customers* converted with the *AsEnumerable* operator

```
Customers customersList = new Customers(customers);

var expr =
    from   c in customersList.AsEnumerable()
    where  c.City == "Brescia"
    select c;

foreach (var item in expr) {
    Console.WriteLine(item);
}
```

The code in Listing 3-65 will use the standard *Where* operator defined for *IEnumerable<T>* within *System.Linq.Enumerable*.

ToArray and *ToList*

Two other useful conversion operators are *ToArray* and *ToList*. They convert a source sequence of type *IEnumerable<TSource>* into an array of *TSource* (*TSource[]*) or into a generic list of *TSource* (*List<TSource>*), respectively:

```
public static TSource[] ToArray<TSource>(
    this IEnumerable<TSource> source);
public static List<TSource> ToList<TSource>(
    this IEnumerable<TSource> source);
```

The results of these operators are snapshots of the sequence. When they are applied inside a query expression, the result will be stable and unchanged, even if the *source* sequence changes. Listing 3-66 shows an example of using *ToList*.

LISTING 3-66 A query expression over an immutable list of *Customers* obtained by the *ToList* operator

```
List<Customer> customersList = new List<Customer>(customers);

var expr = (
    from   c in customersList
    where  c.Country == Countries.Italy
    select c).ToList();

foreach (var item in expr) {
    Console.WriteLine(item);
}
```

These methods are also useful whenever you need to enumerate the result of a query many times, but execute the query only once for performance reasons. Consider the example in Listing 3-67. It would probably be inefficient to refresh the list of products to join with orders every time. Therefore, you can create a "copy" of the products query.

LISTING 3-67 A query expression that uses *ToList* to copy the result of a query over products

```
var productsQuery =
    (from   p in products
     where  p.Price >= 30
     select p)
    .ToList();

var ordersWithProducts =
    from c in customers
        from   o in c.Orders
        join   p in productsQuery
               on o.IdProduct equals p.IdProduct
        select new { p.IdProduct, o.Quantity, p.Price,
                     TotalAmount = o.Quantity * p.Price};

foreach (var order in ordersWithProducts) {
    Console.WriteLine(order);
}
```

This way, you can avoid evaluating the *productsQuery* every time you enumerate the *ordersWithProducts* expression—such as in a *foreach* block.

ToDictionary

Another operator in this set is the *ToDictionary* extension method. It creates an instance of *Dictionary<TKey, TSource>*. The *keySelector* predicate identifies the key of each item. The *elementSelector*, if provided, is used to extract each single item. These predicates are defined through the available signatures:

```
public static Dictionary<TKey, TSource> ToDictionary<TSource, TKey>(
    this IEnumerable<TSource> source,
    Func<TSource, TKey> keySelector);
public static Dictionary<TKey, TSource> ToDictionary<TSource, TKey>(
    this IEnumerable<TSource> source,
    Func<TSource, TKey> keySelector,
    IEqualityComparer<TKey> comparer);
public static Dictionary<TKey, TElement> ToDictionary<TSource, TKey, TElement>(
    this IEnumerable<TSource> source,
    Func<TSource, TKey> keySelector,
    Func<TSource, TElement> elementSelector);
public static Dictionary<TKey, TElement> ToDictionary<TSource, TKey, TElement>(
    this IEnumerable<TSource> source,
    Func<TSource, TKey> keySelector,
    Func<TSource, TElement> elementSelector,
    IEqualityComparer<TKey> comparer);
```

When the method constructs the resulting dictionary, it assumes the uniqueness of each key extracted by invoking the *keySelector*. If duplicate keys exist, the method throws an *Argument-Exception* error. The method compares key values using the *comparer* argument if provided; otherwise, it uses *EqualityComparer<TKey>.Default*. Listing 3-68 uses the *ToDictionary* operator to create a dictionary of customers.

LISTING 3-68 An example of the *ToDictionary* operator, applied to customers

```
var customersDictionary =
    customers
    .ToDictionary(c => c.Name,
                  c => new {c.Name, c.City});
```

The first argument of the operator is the *keySelector* predicate, which extracts the customer *Name* as the key. The second argument is *elementSelector*, which creates an anonymous type that consists of customer *Name* and *City* properties. Here is the result of the query in Listing 3-68:

```
[Paolo, { Name = Paolo, City = Brescia }]
[Marco, { Name = Marco, City = Torino }]
[James, { Name = James, City = Dallas }]
[Frank, { Name = Frank, City = Seattle }]
```

Important Like the *ToList* and *ToArray* operators, *ToDictionary* references the *source* sequence items in case they are reference types. The *ToDictionary* method in Listing 3-67 effectively evaluates the query expression and creates the output dictionary. Therefore, *customersDictionary* does not have a deferred query evaluation behavior; it is the result produced by a statement execution.

ToLookup

Another conversion operator is *ToLookup*, which can be used to create enumerations of type *Lookup<K, T>*, whose definition follows:

```
public class Lookup<K, T> : IEnumerable<IGrouping<K, T>> {
    public int Count { get; }
    public IEnumerable<T> this[K key] { get; }
    public bool Contains(K key);
    public IEnumerator<IGrouping<K, T>> GetEnumerator();
}
```

Each object of this type represents a one-to-many dictionary, which defines a tuple of keys and sequences of items, somewhat like the result of a *GroupJoin* method. Here are the available signatures:

```
public static Lookup<TKey, TSource> ToLookup<TSource, TKey>(
    this IEnumerable<TSource> source,
    Func<TSource, TKey> keySelector);
public static Lookup<TKey, TSource> ToLookup<TSource, TKey>(
    this IEnumerable<TSource> source,
    Func<TSource, TKey> keySelector,
    IEqualityComparer<TKey> comparer);
public static Lookup<TKey, TElement> ToLookup<TSource, TKey, TElement>(
    this IEnumerable<TSource> source,
    Func<TSource, TKey> keySelector,
    Func<TSource, TElement> elementSelector);
public static Lookup<TKey, TElement> ToLookup<TSource, TKey, TElement>(
    this IEnumerable<TSource> source,
    Func<TSource, TKey> keySelector,
    Func<TSource, TElement> elementSelector,
    IEqualityComparer<TKey> comparer);
```

As in *ToDictionary*, there is a *keySelector* predicate, an *elementSelector* predicate, and a *comparer*. The sample in Listing 3-69 demonstrates how to use this method to extract all orders for each product.

LISTING 3-69 An example of the *ToLookup* operator, used to group orders by product

```
var ordersByProduct =
    (from c in customers
        from   o in c.Orders
        select o)
    .ToLookup(o => o.IdProduct);

Console.WriteLine( "\n\nNumber of orders for Product 1: {0}\n",
                   ordersByProduct[1].Count());
```

```
foreach (var product in ordersByProduct) {
    Console.WriteLine("Product: {0}", product.Key);
    foreach(var order in product) {
        Console.WriteLine("  {0}", order);
    }
}
```

As you can see, *Lookup<K, T>* is accessible through an item key (*ordersByProduct[1]*) or through enumeration (the *foreach* loop). The following is the output of this example:

```
Number of orders for Product 1: 2

Product: 1
  IdOrder: 1 - IdProduct: 1 - Quantity: 3 - Shipped: False - Month: January
  IdOrder: 3 - IdProduct: 1 - Quantity: 10 - Shipped: False - Month: July
Product: 2
  IdOrder: 2 - IdProduct: 2 - Quantity: 5 - Shipped: True - Month: May
Product: 3
  IdOrder: 4 - IdProduct: 3 - Quantity: 20 - Shipped: True - Month: December
  IdOrder: 5 - IdProduct: 3 - Quantity: 20 - Shipped: True - Month: December
Product: 5
  IdOrder: 6 - IdProduct: 5 - Quantity: 20 - Shipped: False - Month: July
```

OfType and *Cast*

The last two operators of this set are *OfType* and *Cast*. The first filters the source sequence, yielding only items of type *TResult*. It is useful in the case of sequences with items of different types. For example, working with an object-oriented approach, you might have an object with a common base class and particular specialization in derived classes:

```
public static IEnumerable<TResult> OfType<TResult>(
    this IEnumerable source);
```

If you provide a type *TResult* that is not supported by any of the source items, the operator will return an empty sequence.

The *Cast* operator enumerates the source sequence and tries to yield each item, cast to type *TResult*. In the case of failure, an *InvalidCastException* error will be thrown (see Listing 2-4 for a sample of this operator):

```
public static IEnumerable<TResult> Cast<TResult>(
    this IEnumerable source);
```

Because of their signatures, which accept any *IEnumerable* sequence, these two methods can be used to convert old nongeneric types to newer *IEnumerable<T>* types. This conversion makes it possible to query these types with LINQ even if the types are unaware of LINQ.

> **Important** Each item returned by *OfType* and *Cast* is a reference to the original object and not a copy. *OfType* does not create a snapshot of a source; instead, it evaluates the source every time you enumerate the operator's result. This behavior is different from other conversion operators.

Summary

This chapter explained the principles of LINQ query expressions and the syntax rules behind them, as well as query operators and conversion operators. The chapter used LINQ to Objects as a reference implementation—but all the concepts are valid for other LINQ implementations, which are covered in the following chapters.

Part II
LINQ to Relational

Chapter 4

Choosing Between LINQ to SQL and LINQ to Entities

In upcoming chapters, you will learn how to use LINQ to SQL and LINQ to Entities. You might wonder whether you need to learn both—and depending on your requirements, how to choose between them. In fact, you should study both before making a decision. To help you decide, this chapter provides solid comparisons and other information for you to consider. The chapter includes a "big picture" overview and guidelines that can help you choose, which might at least influence which technology you would want to learn first. This chapter does not mention features that are equivalent in both LINQ to SQL and LINQ to Entities because, of course, those have no influence on your choice.

Comparison Factors

Before starting any comparison, you have to figure out in which tier of your application's architecture you intend to use one of these Microsoft Language Integrated Query (LINQ) implementations. In the following sections, you will see a comparison of LINQ to SQL and LINQ to Entities in the context of an application's data layer, without considering the use of either of these LINQ providers for the business layer.

 More Info In Chapter 18, "LINQ in a Multitier Solution," you can find a deep discussion about the possible uses of LINQ in a distributed architecture.

From the title of this chapter, you might think that it compares LINQ to SQL directly with LINQ to Entities; in reality, the comparison is between LINQ to SQL and the Microsoft ADO. NET Entity Framework. LINQ to Entities is a LINQ provider that is based on the ADO.NET Entity Framework; the Entity Framework is an engine external to LINQ that provides Object Relational Mapping (ORM) features. In contrast, LINQ to SQL is a LINQ provider that includes ORM features in its own implementation. Thus, references to "Entity Framework" in this chapter refer to LINQ to Entities for the purpose of comparison.

Our choice for building a data layer is to use the Entity Framework with plain-old CLR object (POCO) entities. You will see the reasons for that choice in the following sections. However, because you might find scenarios in which LINQ to SQL would be a better choice, you will also see case descriptions that support using LINQ to SQL.

When to Choose LINQ to Entities and the Entity Framework

A decision to use an existing object model with an ORM could impact the object model itself. For example, the default code template used by the Entity Framework requires that entity classes inherit from the *EntityObject* base class. LINQ to SQL does not require inheriting from a particular base class, so at first glance, it would seem to be easier to use with an existing object model. However, choosing LINQ to SQL can also impact an existing object model. The new support for POCO in the Entity Framework in Microsoft .NET Framework 4 makes it the preferred choice in this scenario.

Consider this existing *Customer* entity class that contains an array of *Orders* for that *Customer*:

```
public class Customer {
    public string CustomerID;
    public string CompanyName;
    public Order[] Orders;
}
```

In the Entity Framework, the default code template inherits from *EntityObject* in this way:

```
public class Customer : EntityObject {
    public string CustomerID;
    public string CompanyName;
    public EntityCollection<Order> Orders;
}
```

In LINQ to SQL, you can avoid inheriting from a specific base class, but you still have to change the declaration of the *Orders* property. This property offers the orders list for a particular customer, returning an *EntitySet* of orders, such as in the following code:

```
public class Customer {
    public string CustomerID;
    public string CompanyName;
    public EntitySet<Order> Orders;
}
```

Thus, both LINQ to SQL and the Entity Framework by default require changing an existing object model so that it has properties to navigate relationships such as the *Orders* property in the *Customer* class.

As mentioned earlier, in Entity Framework 4, you also have the option to use existing classes (POCO) without modifying their inheritance hierarchy. So you could write the *Customer* class that supports POCO as follows:

```
public class Customer {
    public string CustomerID;
    public string CompanyName;
    public ICollection<Order> Orders;
}
```

This option required no more changes than the LINQ to SQL option. The *Orders* member type was changed from an array of *Order* to an *ICollection<Order>*; however, both this collection and the original array of *Order* return the same *ICollection<T>* interface using the POCO support, so you can iterate through such a property in the same way as before.

The Entity Framework has a conceptual model that supports many-to-many relationships between entities. Using LINQ to SQL, you can define entities that are directly mapped to physical tables. The Entity Framework uses a different concept, involving an entity model and physical binding. At the physical level, the Entity Framework automatically defines underlying database bridge tables that have two one-to-many relationships with the tables corresponding to two related entities. These relationships implement the many-to-many relationship that is defined between these two entities in the conceptual model. Thus, LINQ to Entities and the Entity Framework are preferable when you need a higher level of abstraction from the physical tables in the database, such as a many-to-many relationship between two entities in the conceptual model.

LINQ to Entities and the Entity Framework offer long-term support and the new Entity Data Model Designer. This designer has more advanced features than the Object Relational Designer (O/R Designer) used for LINQ to SQL, which is available in Microsoft Visual Studio. Although LINQ to SQL (part of the .NET Framework) will be supported for years to come, all new development efforts are now committed to the Entity Framework. Thus, if you are building a long-term plan, you might prefer the Entity Framework because it is likely to have better support and development efforts in future versions. If you evaluate the differences between the current designers, you can already see evidence of this shift.

> **More Info**   You can find more information about the O/R Designer for LINQ to SQL at *http://msdn.microsoft.com/en-us/library/bb384429.aspx*, and about the Entity Data Model Designer for the Entity Framework at *http://msdn.microsoft.com/en-us/library/cc716685.aspx*.

In Microsoft Visual Studio 2010, the O/R Designer for LINQ to SQL can reverse engineer an existing database, but if you want to design entity classes first, there is no integrated feature that generates a corresponding database (the "model-first" approach). When reverse engineering an existing database, the LINQ to SQL designer imports the definition of a table that you can modify in the designer itself; for example, you can change access or delay loading settings. However, if the table structure changes, you have to delete and regenerate the corresponding class in the designer to reflect the updated table structure in your class—meaning you lose the customized settings. There is a workaround: you can change the class definition in the designer manually to synchronize it with the existing table structure in the database. Alternatively, you can rely on third-party tools such as PLINQO (*http://www.plinqo.com*) or Huagati tools (*http://www.huagati.com/dbmltools/*), which provide ways to synchronize a LINQ to SQL model with an existing database whose structure has been changed.

In contrast, the Entity Data Model Designer for LINQ to Entities in Visual Studio 2010 is much more developed, and supports both forward engineering of an Entity Data Model (EDM) to a database and reverse engineering of an existing database into a new EDM. Moreover, you can update the EDM in the designer when the database structure changes. Still, there is no direct support for generating a SQL change script to apply changes to an existing database if you use the Entity Data Model Designer to design entity classes first and you want to automatically generate new or update existing database tables. Of course, you can generate the SQL statements for the whole database and then generate the update scripts using other Visual Studio tools. However, because the Database Generation feature in the Entity Data Model Designer is extensible, you can generate a migration T-SQL script using the Entity Data Model Designer Database Generation Power Pack Entity Framework, which offers additional features.

> **More Info** You can download the PowerPack from *http://visualstudiogallery.msdn.microsoft.com /en-us/df3541c3-d833-4b65-b942-989e7ec74c87*.

When to Choose LINQ to SQL

As you have seen, the Entity Framework has many arguments in its favor. However, there are still a few cases in which you might choose LINQ to SQL.

First, LINQ to SQL is simpler and has fewer internal layers than the Entity Framework. This results in better performance, and sometimes, more direct control over the generated SQL code. The performance differential was higher in .NET Framework 3.5; the Entity Framework is optimized in .NET Framework 4. Even though the Entity Framework will always be a little bit slower than LINQ to SQL, the performance today is very close—and in some cases even better. You can see an example of performance comparisons between several ORM tools that support LINQ at *http://ormbattle.net/*.

Moreover, you should consider the better performance and increased control of LINQ to SQL only when you are absolutely sure that you will never have to support a database other than Microsoft SQL Server or Microsoft SQL Server Compact Edition (CE). For example, you might consider using LINQ to SQL whenever you would have used the *SqlClient* class to directly access ADO.NET just to read data from SQL Server, such as during program configuration. (You might consider SQL Server CE in this case, because it runs in-process, and does not require an external database engine.) You might also use LINQ to SQL when extracting data in a batch process designed to work only on SQL Server. Lastly, you might consider LINQ to SQL whenever you must support .NET Framework 3.5 and cannot depend on .NET Framework 4.

The last consideration concerns concurrency. If you read an entity from the database, modify the entity in memory, and then try to save changes to the database, you might get an exception if someone else has modified the same entity from some other client in the meantime. Both LINQ to SQL and the Entity Framework handle optimistic concurrency access and throw an exception whenever such a conflict occurs. However, there is a difference in the level of detail provided to your code about the concurrency issue. In the Entity Framework, an *OptimisticConcurrencyException* instance provides the entities that failed the update operation, as you can see in the following code (which will be explained in more detail in Chapter 10, "LINQ to Entities: Managing Data"):

```
catch (OptimisticConcurrencyException ex) {
    foreach (var entry in ex.StateEntries) {
        Console.WriteLine(
            "The entity with EntityKey of {0} and an EntityState of {1} has a conflict",
            entry.EntityKey.EntityKeyValues[0],
            entry.State);
    }

    // Solve the conflict forcing client-side modifications
    context.Refresh(RefreshMode.ClientWins, c);

    Int32 result = context.SaveChanges();
    if (result > 0) {
        Console.WriteLine("Forcibly updated {0} entities!", result);
    }
}
```

The Entity Framework does not offer built-in support for locating the concurrency conflict at the member level. If you need to locate the members that caused the conflict during update, you have to compare all the members of the original and current in-memory values of the entity with the concurrency problem—and you still do not have the database values (that would require another round trip to the server to retrieve the current row values).

LINQ to SQL provides more granular information about which members caused the concurrency issue, as shown in the following code (this will be discussed in more detail in Chapter 6, "LINQ to SQL: Managing Data"):

```
catch (ChangeConflictException ex) {
    foreach (ObjectChangeConflict occ in db.ChangeConflicts) {
        MetaTable metatable = db.Mapping.GetTable(occ.Object.GetType());
        Customer entityInConflict = occ.Object as Customer;

        Console.WriteLine(
            "Table={0}, IsResolved={1}",
            metatable.TableName, occ.IsResolved);
        foreach (MemberChangeConflict mcc in occ.MemberConflicts) {
            object currVal = mcc.CurrentValue;
            object origVal = mcc.OriginalValue;
```

```
            object databaseVal = mcc.DatabaseValue;
            MemberInfo mi = mcc.Member;
            Console.WriteLine("Member: {0}", mi.Name);
            Console.WriteLine("current value: {0}", currVal);
            Console.WriteLine("original value: {0}", origVal);
            Console.WriteLine("database value: {0}", databaseVal);
        }
    }
    db2.Refresh(RefreshMode.KeepChanges,customer2);
}
```

LINQ to SQL also provides the current database value of each member when a concurrency issue occurs while updating an entity—without requiring another round trip to the server. Still, this single feature, although convenient, is hardly a reason that justifies the adoption of LINQ to SQL over the Entity Framework. However, it is important to highlight this difference, particularly if you are considering migrating existing LINQ to SQL code to the Entity Framework.

Other Considerations

The other considerations when comparing LINQ to SQL and the Entity Framework do not directly favor one or the other, but are important to know before making a decision.

When you write a query in LINQ to SQL, the LINQ query tree is converted directly into a SQL query. LINQ to Entities requires one extra step before creating the equivalent SQL query. The Entity Framework has its own query language, called *Entity SQL*, which is database-agnostic and queries the conceptual model of entities. A LINQ to Entities query is converted into an equivalent Entity SQL query tree, which is then converted into the SQL dialect of the database you are targeting. This last step is under the control of the database provider, so you can consider it external to the Entity Framework itself. It is true that these differences may impact performance, but another interesting impact occurs during dynamic query creation.

For example, suppose you need to add conditions to the predicate of a LINQ query that depend on choices made through the user interface. In LINQ, you cannot rely on string concatenation to build the query you want, adding conditions after the *WHERE* clause as you would in a regular SQL statement. Modifying the in-memory LINQ query is both possible and works as expected, as you will learn in Chapter 14, "Inside Expression Trees," but it requires that you understand how LINQ queries are represented in memory through an object model. In LINQ to SQL, you do not have alternatives to this approach, other than building regular SQL queries and using the *ExecuteQuery* method, which means you lose the ability to map the result to anonymous types. Most important, when you directly manipulate a SQL statement, you are accessing the physical layer directly (removing the abstraction level provided by LINQ to SQL), which introduces the possibility of SQL injection attacks. Security is an important consideration here: both LINQ to SQL and the Entity Framework build SQL code in a way that follows best practices and avoids SQL injection attacks. Conversely, when you create SQL code manually, you bypass all the sanity checks provided by these frameworks.

However, with the Entity Framework, you also have the option to create an Entity SQL statement using the string concatenation approach, without incurring the risk of SQL injection attacks. In fact, Entity SQL can be represented in a textual format similar to traditional ANSI SQL, but that operates on conceptual entities instead of physical tables. You can create such a query by using the *EntityCommand* class. The conversion to a SQL dialect is handled by the specific database provider, which should make all the sanity checks necessary to avoid possible SQL injection attacks. The code generated by the existing Microsoft providers grants the same level of protection offered by LINQ to SQL in this regard.

Lastly, LINQ to SQL offers support to directly use certain T-SQL statements (such as *LIKE* and *DATEDIFF*) in a LINQ query by using extension methods in the *SqlMethods* class. LINQ to Entities offers similar support through the *EntityFunctions* and *SqlFunctions* classes, which provide access to a broader range of SQL functions but do not include equivalent syntax for the *LIKE* statement. However, you can obtain that functionality for most common uses by using the *Contains*, *StartsWith*, and *EndsWith* methods of a string type in a LINQ to Entities query. Additionally, you can use the *LIKE* syntax in the Entity Framework by writing an Entity SQL statement in text form.

Summary

This chapter provided a comparison between LINQ to SQL and LINQ to Entities that should help you choose which LINQ provider to use for the data layer of your applications. By default, you should choose LINQ to Entities and the Entity Framework for any new project. You should limit the choice of LINQ to SQL to projects that demand migration of existing code, where a full conversion to LINQ to Entities may be unaffordable, or when requirements dictate that you use .NET Framework 3.5 for compatibility.

Chapter 5
LINQ to SQL: Querying Data

The first and most obvious application of Microsoft Language Integrated Query (LINQ) is in querying an external relational database. LINQ to SQL is a LINQ component that provides the capability to query a relational Microsoft SQL Server database, offering you an object model based on available entities. In other words, you can define a set of objects that represents a thin abstraction layer over the relational data, and you can query this object model by using LINQ queries that are automatically converted into corresponding SQL queries by the LINQ to SQL engine. LINQ to SQL supports Microsoft SQL Server 2008 through SQL Server 2000 and Microsoft SQL Server Compact 3.5.

Using LINQ to SQL, you can write a simple query such as the following:

```
var query =
    from    c in Customers
    where   c.Country == "USA"
            && c.State == "WA"
    select  new {c.CustomerID, c.CompanyName, c.City };
```

This query is converted into a SQL query that is sent to the relational database:

```
SELECT CustomerID, CompanyName, City
FROM    Customers
WHERE   Country = 'USA'
  AND   Region = 'WA'
```

> **Important** The SQL queries generated by LINQ that we show in this chapter are illustrative only. Microsoft reserves the right to independently define the SQL query that is generated by LINQ, and we sometimes use simplified queries in the text. Thus, you should not rely on the SQL query that is shown.

At this point, you might have a few questions, such as:

- How can you write a LINQ query using object names that are validated by the compiler?
- When is the SQL query generated from the LINQ query?
- When is the SQL query executed?

To understand the answers to these questions, you need to understand the entity model in LINQ to SQL, and then delve into deferred query evaluation.

Entities in LINQ to SQL

Any external data must be described with appropriate metadata bound to class definitions. Each table must have a corresponding class decorated with particular attributes. That class corresponds to a row of data and describes all columns in terms of data members of the defined type. The type can be a complete or partial description of an existing physical table, view, or stored procedure result. Only the described fields can be used inside a LINQ query for both projection and filtering. Listing 5-1 shows a simple entity definition.

> **Important** You need to include the *System.Data.Linq* assembly in your projects to use LINQ to SQL classes and attributes. The attributes used in Listing 5-1 are defined in the *System.Data.Linq. Mapping* namespace.

LISTING 5-1 Entity definition for LINQ to SQL

```
using System.Data.Linq.Mapping;

[Table(Name="Customers")]
public class Customer {
    [Column] public string CustomerID;
    [Column] public string CompanyName;
    [Column] public string City;
    [Column(Name="Region")] public string State;
    [Column] public string Country;
}
```

The *Customer* type defines the content of a row, and each field or property decorated with *Column* corresponds to a column in the relational table. The *Name* parameter can specify a column name that is different from the data member name. (In this example, the *State* member corresponds to the Region table column.) The *Table* attribute specifies that the class is an entity representing data from a database table; its *Name* property specifies a table name that could be different from the entity name. It is common to use the singular form for the class name (which represents a single row) and the plural form for the name of the table (a set of rows).

You need a *Customers* table to build a LINQ to SQL query over *Customers* data. The *Table<T>* generic class is the right way to create such a type:

```
Table<Customer> Customers = ...;
// ...
var query =
    from    c in Customers
    // ...
```

Note To build a LINQ query over *Customers*, you need a class that implements *IEnumerable<T>*, using the *Customer* type as *T*. However, LINQ to SQL needs to implement extension methods in a different way than the LINQ to Objects implementation used in Chapter 3, "LINQ to Objects." You must use an object that implements *IQueryable<T>* to build LINQ to SQL queries. The *Table<T>* class implements *IQueryable<T>*. To include the LINQ to SQL extension, the statement *using System.Data.Linq;* must be part of the source code.

The *Customers* table object has to be instantiated. To do that, you need an instance of the *DataContext* class, which defines the bridge between the LINQ world and the external relational database. The nearest concept to *DataContext* that comes to mind is a database connection—in fact, the database connection string or the *Connection* object is a mandatory parameter for creating a *DataContext* instance. *DataContext* exposes a *GetTable<T>* method that returns a corresponding *Table<T>* for the specified type:

```
DataContext db = new DataContext("Database=Northwind");
Table<Customer> Customers = db.GetTable<Customer>();
```

Note Internally, the *DataContext* class uses the *SqlConnection* class from Microsoft ADO.NET. You can pass an existing *SqlConnection* to the *DataContext* constructor, and you can also read the connection used by a *DataContext* instance through its *Connection* property. All services related to the database connection, such as connection pooling (which is turned on by default), are accessible at the *SqlConnection* class level and are not directly implemented in the *DataContext* class.

Listing 5-2 shows the resulting code when you put all the pieces together.

LISTING 5-2 Simple LINQ to SQL query

```
DataContext db = new DataContext( ConnectionString );
Table<Customer> Customers = db.GetTable<Customer>();

var query =
    from    c in Customers
    where   c.Country == "USA"
            && c.State == "WA"
    select  new {c.CustomerID, c.CompanyName, c.City };

foreach( var row in query ) {
    Console.WriteLine( row );
}
```

The *query* variable is initialized with a query expression that forms an expression tree. An expression tree maintains a representation of the expression in memory rather than pointing to a method through a delegate. When the *foreach* loop enumerates data selected by the query, the expression tree is used to generate the corresponding SQL query, using the metadata and information from the entity classes and the referenced *DataContext* instance.

> **Note** The *deferred execution* method used by LINQ to SQL converts the expression tree into a SQL query that is valid in the underlying relational database. The LINQ query is functionally equiv-alent to a string containing a SQL command, but with at least two important differences:
>
> ❑ The LINQ query is tied to the object model and not to the database structure.
>
> ❑ Its representation is semantically meaningful without requiring a SQL parser, and without being tied to a specific SQL dialect.
>
> The expression tree can be dynamically built in memory before its use, as you will learn in Chapter 14, "Inside Expression Trees."

The data returned from the SQL query accessing *row* and placed into the *foreach* loop is then used to fill the projected anonymous type following the *select* keyword. In this example, the *Customer* class is never instantiated, and LINQ uses it only to analyze its metadata.

To explore the generated SQL command, you can use the *GetCommand* method of the *Data-Context* class by accessing the *CommandText* property of the returned *DbCommand*, which contains the generated SQL query; for example:

```
Console.WriteLine( db.GetCommand( query ).CommandText );
```

A simpler way to examine the generated SQL is to call *ToString* on a LINQ to SQL query. The overridden *ToString* method produces the same result as the *GetCommand(query).Com-mandText* statement:

```
Console.WriteLine( query );
```

The simple LINQ to SQL query in Listing 5-2 generates the following SQL query:

```
SELECT [t0].[CustomerID], [t0].[CompanyName], [t0].[City]
FROM    [Customers] AS [t0]
WHERE   ([t0].[Country] = @p0) AND ([t0].[Region] = @p1)
```

To get a trace of all SQL statements that are sent to the database, you can assign a value to the *DataContext.Log* property, as shown here:

```
db.Log = Console.Out;
```

The next section provides more detail on how to generate entity classes for LINQ to SQL.

External Mapping

The mapping between LINQ to SQL entities and database structures has to be described through metadata information. In Listing 5-1, you saw attributes on an entity definition that fulfills this rule. However, you can also use an external XML mapping file to decorate entity classes instead of using attributes. An XML mapping file looks like this:

```
<Database Name="Northwind">
   <Table Name="Products">
      <Type Name="Product">
         <Column Name="ProductID" Member="ProductID"
                 Storage="_ProductID" DbType="Int NOT NULL IDENTITY"
                 IsPrimaryKey="True" IsDbGenerated="True" />
```

The *Type* tag defines the relationship with an entity class, and the *Member* attribute of the *Column* tag defines the corresponding member name of the class entity (in case it differs from the column name of the table). By default, *Member* is not required and if not present, is assumed to be the same as the *Name* attribute of *Column*. This XML file usually has a *.dbml* file name extension.

> **More Info**   You can produce a Database Markup Language (DBML) file automatically with some of the tools described in Chapter 7, "LINQ to SQL: Modeling Data and Tools."

To load the DBML file, you can use an *XmlMappingSource* instance, generated by calling its *FromXml* static method, and then pass that instance to the *DataContext* derived class constructor. The following example shows how to use such syntax:

```
string path = "Northwind.dbml";
XmlMappingSource prodMapping =
      XmlMappingSource.FromXml(File.ReadAllText(path));
Northwind db = new Northwind(
      "Database=Test_Northwind;Trusted_Connection=yes",
      prodMapping
   );
```

One use of this technique is in a scenario in which different databases must be mapped to a specific data model. Differences in databases might include table and field names (for example, localized versions of the database). In general, consider this option when you need to realize a light decoupling of mapping between entity classes and the physical data structure of the database.

> **More Info**   It is beyond the scope of this book to describe the details of the XML grammar for a DBML file, but you can find that syntax described in the LinqToSqlMapping.xsd and DbmlSchema.xsd files that reside in your Program Files\Microsoft Visual Studio 10.0\Xml\Schemas directory if you have installed Microsoft Visual Studio 2010. If you do not have either of these files, you can copy the code from the following product documentation pages: "External Mapping" at *http://msdn.microsoft.com/en-us/library/bb386907.aspx* and "Code Generation in LINQ to SQL" at *http://msdn.microsoft.com/en-us/library/bb399400.aspx*.

Data Modeling

The set of entity classes that LINQ to SQL requires is a thin abstraction layer over the relational model. Each entity class defines an accessible table of data, which can be queried and modified. Modified entity instances can apply their changes to the data contained in the relational database. In this section, you will learn how to build a data model for LINQ to SQL.

> **More Info** The options for data updates are described in Chapter 6, "LINQ to SQL: Managing Data."

DataContext

The *DataContext* class handles the communication between LINQ and external relational data sources. Each instance has a single *Connection* property that refers to a relational database. Its type is *IDbConnection*; therefore, it should not be specific to a particular database product. However, the LINQ to SQL implementation supports only SQL Server databases. Choosing between specific versions of SQL Server depends only on the connection string passed to the *DataContext* constructor.

> **Important** The architecture of LINQ to SQL supports many data providers so that it can map to different underlying relational databases. A provider is a class that implements the *System.Data. Linq.Provider.IProvider* interface. However, that interface is declared as internal and is not documented. Microsoft supports only a SQL Server provider. The Microsoft .NET Framework supports SQL Server since version 2000 for both 32-bit and 64-bit executables, as well as SQL Server Compact 3.5 SP2.

DataContext uses metadata to map the physical structure of the relational data so that LINQ to SQL can generate the appropriate SQL code. You also use *DataContext* to call a stored procedure and persist data changes in entity class instances in the relational database.

Classes that specialize access for a particular database can be derived from *DataContext*. Such classes offer an easier way to access relational data, including members that represent available tables. You can define fields that reference existing tables in the database simply by declaring them, without a specific initialization, as in the following code:

```
public class SampleDb : DataContext {
    public SampleDb(IDbConnection connection)
            : base( connection ) {}
    public SampleDb(string fileOrServerOrConnection)
            : base( fileOrServerOrConnection ) {}
    public SampleDb(IDbConnection connection, MappingSource mapping)
            : base( connection, mapping ) {}

    public Table<Customer> Customers;
}
```

Note Table members are initialized automatically by the *DataContext* base constructor, which examines the type at execution time through Reflection, finds those members, and initializes them based on the mapping metadata.

Entity Classes

An entity class has two roles. The first role is to provide metadata to the LINQ query engine; for this, the class itself suffices—it does not require instantiation of an entity instance. The second role is to provide storage for data read from the relational data source, as well as to track possible updates and support their submission back to the relational data source.

An entity class is any reference type definition decorated with the *Table* attribute. You cannot use a *struct* (which is a value type) for this. The *Table* attribute can have a *Name* parameter that defines the name of the corresponding table in the database. If *Name* is omitted, the name of the class is used as the default:

```
[Table(Name="Products")] public class Product { ... }
```

Note Although the term commonly used is *table*, nothing prevents you from using an updatable view in place of a table name in the *Name* parameter. Using a non-updatable view will also work— at least until you try to update data without using that entity class.

An entity class can have any number and type of members. Just remember that only those data members or properties decorated with the *Column* attribute are significant in defining the mapping between the entity class and the corresponding table in the database:

```
[Column] public int ProductID;
```

An entity class should have a unique key. This key is necessary to support unique identity (more on this later), to identify corresponding rows in database tables, and to generate SQL statements that update data. If you do not have a primary key, entity class instances can be created but are not modifiable. The Boolean *IsPrimaryKey* property of the *Column* attribute, when set to *true*, states that the column belongs to the primary key of the table. If the primary key used is a composite key, all the columns that form the primary key will have *IsPrimaryKey=true* in their parameters:

```
[Column(IsPrimaryKey=true)] public int ProductID;
```

By default, a column mapping uses the same name as the member to which the *Column* attribute is applied. You can specify a different name in the *Name* parameter. For example, the following *Price* member corresponds to the *UnitPrice* field in the database table:

```
[Column(Name="UnitPrice")] public decimal Price;
```

If you want to filter data access through member property accessors, you have to specify the underlying storage member using the *Storage* parameter. If you specify a *Storage* parameter, LINQ to SQL bypasses the public property accessor and interacts directly with the underlying value. Understanding this is particularly important if you want to track only the modifications made by your code and not the read/write operations made by the LINQ framework. In the following code, the *ProductName* property is accessed for each read/write operation made by your code:

```
[Column(Storage="_ProductName")]
public string ProductName {
    get { return this._ProductName; }
    set { this.OnPropertyChanging("ProductName");
        this._ProductName = value;
        this.OnPropertyChanged("ProductName");
    }
}
```

In contrast, LINQ to SQL performs a direct read/write operation on the *_ProductName* data member when it executes a LINQ operation.

The correspondence between relational type and .NET Framework type assumes a default relational type that corresponds to the .NET Framework type used. Whenever you need to define a different type, you can use the *DBType* parameter, specifying a valid type by using valid SQL syntax for your relational data source. You need to use this parameter only when you want to create a database schema starting from entity class definitions (a process described in Chapter 6). Here's an example of the *DBType* parameter in use:

```
[Column(DBType="NVARCHAR(20)")] public string QuantityPerUnit;
```

When the database automatically generates a column value (such as with the IDENTITY keyword in SQL Server), you might want to synchronize the entity class member with the generated value whenever you insert an entity instance into the database. To do that, you need to set the *IsDBGenerated* parameter for that member to *true*, and you also need to adapt the *DBType* accordingly—for example, by adding the *IDENTITY* modifier for SQL Server tables:

```
[Column(DBType="INT NOT NULL IDENTITY",
        IsPrimaryKey=true, IsDBGenerated=true)]
public int ProductID;
```

It is worth mentioning that a specific *CanBeNull* parameter exists. This parameter is used to specify that the value can contain the null value; however, it is important to note that the *NOT NULL* clause in *DBType* is still necessary if you want to create such a condition in a database created by LINQ to SQL:

```
[Column(DBType="INT NOT NULL IDENTITY", CanBeNull=false,
        IsPrimaryKey=true, IsDBGenerated=true)]
public int ProductID;
```

Other parameters that are relevant in updating data are *AutoSync*, *Expression*, *IsVersion*, and *UpdateCheck*.

> **More Info**   Chapter 6 provides a more detailed explanation of the parameters *IsVersion*, *Expression*, *UpdateCheck*, *AutoSync*, and *IsDBGenerated*.

Entity Inheritance

Sometimes a single table contains many types of entities. For example, imagine a list of contacts—some might be customers, others might be suppliers, and still others might be company employees. From a data point of view, each entity can have specific fields. (For example, a customer can have a discount field, which is not relevant for employees and suppliers.) From a business logic point of view, each entity can implement different business rules. The best way to model this kind of data in an object-oriented environment is by using inheritance to create a hierarchy of specialized classes. LINQ to SQL allows a set of classes derived from the same base class to map to the same relational table.

The *InheritanceMapping* attribute decorates the base class of a hierarchy, indicating the corresponding derived classes that are based on the value of a special *discriminator column*. The *Code* parameter defines a possible value, and the *Type* parameter defines the corresponding derived type. The discriminator column is defined by setting the *IsDiscriminator* argument to *true* in the *Column* attribute specification.

Listing 5-3 provides an example of a hierarchy based on the *Contacts* table of the *Northwind* sample database.

LISTING 5-3 Hierarchy of classes based on contacts

```
[Table(Name="Contacts")]
[InheritanceMapping(Code = "Customer", Type = typeof(CustomerContact))]
[InheritanceMapping(Code = "Supplier", Type = typeof(SupplierContact))]
[InheritanceMapping(Code = "Shipper", Type = typeof(ShipperContact))]
[InheritanceMapping(Code = "Employee", Type = typeof(Contact), IsDefault = true)]
public class Contact {
    [Column(IsPrimaryKey=true)] public int ContactID;
    [Column(Name="ContactName")] public string Name;
    [Column] public string Phone;
    [Column(IsDiscriminator = true)] public string ContactType;
}

public class CompanyContact : Contact {
    [Column(Name="CompanyName")] public string Company;
}
```

```
public class CustomerContact : CompanyContact {
}

public class SupplierContact : CompanyContact {
}

public class ShipperContact : CompanyContact {
    public string Shipper {
        get { return Company; }
        set { Company = value; }
    }
}
```

Contact is the base class of the hierarchy. If the contact is a *Customer, Supplier,* or *Shipper,* the corresponding classes derive from an intermediate *CompanyContact* type, which defines the *Company* field corresponding to the CompanyName column in the source table. The *CompanyContact* intermediate class is necessary because you cannot reference the same column (CompanyName) in more than one field, even if this happens in different classes in the same hierarchy. The *ShipperContact* class defines a *Shipper* property that exposes the same value of *Company* but with a different semantic meaning.

Important This approach requires that you flatten the union of all possible data columns for the whole hierarchy into a single table. If you have a normalized database, you might have data for different entities separated in different tables. You can define a view to use LINQ to SQL to support entity hierarchy, but to update data you must make the view updatable.

The level of abstraction offered by having different entity classes in the same hierarchy is well described by the sample queries shown in Listing 5-4. The *queryTyped* query uses the *OfType* operator, whereas *queryFiltered* query relies on a standard *where* condition to filter out contacts that are not customers.

LISTING 5-4 Queries using a hierarchy of entity classes

```
var queryTyped =
    from    c in contacts.OfType<CustomerContact>()
    select  c;

var queryFiltered =
    from    c in contacts
    where   c is CustomerContact
    select  c;
```

```
foreach( var row in queryTyped ) {
    Console.WriteLine( row.Company );
}

// We need an explicit cast to access the CustumerContact members
foreach( CustomerContact row in queryFiltered ) {
    Console.WriteLine( row.Company );
}
```

The SQL queries produced by these LINQ queries are functionally identical to the following (although the actual query is different because of generalization coding):

```
SELECT  [t0].[ContactType], [t0].[CompanyName] AS [Company],
        [t0].[ContactID], [t0].[ContactName] AS [Name],
        [t0].[Phone]
FROM    [Contacts] AS [t0]
WHERE   [t0].[ContactType] = 'Customer'
```

The difference between *queryTyped* and *queryFiltered* queries lies in the returned type. A *queryTyped* query returns a sequence of *CustomerContact* instances, whereas *queryFiltered* returns a sequence of the base class *Contact*. With *queryFiltered*, you need to explicitly cast the result into a *CustomerContact* type if you want to access the *Company* property.

Unique Object Identity

An instance of an entity class stores an in-memory representation of table row data. If you instantiate two different entities containing the same row from the same *DataContext*, both will reference the same in-memory object. In other words, object identity (same references) maintains data identity (same table row) using the entity unique key. The LINQ to SQL engine ensures that the same object reference is used when an entity instantiated from a query result coming from the same *DataContext* is already in memory. This check does not happen if you create an instance of an entity by yourself or in a different *DataContext* (regardless of the real data source). In Listing 5-5, you can see that *c1* and *c2* reference the same *Contact* instance, even if they originate from two different queries, whereas *c3* is a different object, even if its content is equivalent to the others.

> **Note** If you want to force data from the database to reload using the same *DataContext*, you must use the *Refresh* method of the *DataContext* class. Chapter 6 discusses this in more detail.

LISTING 5-5 Object identity

```
var queryTyped =
    from    c in contacts.OfType<CustomerContact>()
    orderby c.ContactID
    select  c;

var queryFiltered =
    from    c in contacts
    where   c is CustomerContact
    orderby c.ContactID
    select  c;

Contact c1 = null;
Contact c2 = null;
foreach( var row in queryTyped.Take(1) ) {
    c1 = row;
}
foreach( var row in queryFiltered.Take(1) ) {
    c2 = row;
}
Contact c3 = new Contact();
c3.ContactID = c1.ContactID;
c3.ContactType = c1.ContactType;
c3.Name = c1.Name;
c3.Phone = c1.Phone;
Debug.Assert( c1 == c2 ); // same instance
Debug.Assert( c1 != c3 ); // different objects
```

Entity Constraints

Entity classes support the maintenance of valid relationships between entities, just like the support offered by foreign keys in a standard relational environment. However, the entity classes cannot represent all possible check constraints of a relational table. No attributes are available to specify the same alternate keys (unique constraint), triggers, and check expressions that can be defined in a relational database. This fact is relevant when you start to manipulate data using entity classes because you cannot guarantee that an updated value will be accepted by the underlying database. (For example, it could have a duplicate unique key.) However, because you can load into entity instances only parts (rows) of the whole table, these kinds of checks are not possible without accessing the relational database anyway.

Associations Between Entities

Relationships between entities in a relational database are modeled on the concept of foreign keys in one table referring to primary keys of another table. Class entities can use the same concept through the *Association* attribute, which can describe both sides of a one-to-many relationship described by a foreign key.

EntityRef

Let's start with the concept of *lookup*, which is the typical operation used to get the customer related to one order. *Lookup* can be seen as the direct translation into the entity model of the foreign key relationship existing between the *CustomerID* column of the Orders table and the primary key of the Customers table. In the example entity model, the *Order* entity class will have a *Customer* property (of type *Customer*) that shows the customer data. This property is decorated with the *Association* attribute and stores its information in an *EntityRef<Customer>* member (named *_Customer*), which enables deferred loading of references (as you will see shortly). Listing 5-6 shows the definition of this association.

LISTING 5-6 Association *EntityRef*

```
[Table(Name="Orders")]
public class Order {
    [Column(IsPrimaryKey=true)] public int OrderID;
    [Column] private string CustomerID;
    [Column] public DateTime? OrderDate;

    [Association(Storage="_Customer", ThisKey="CustomerID", IsForeignKey=true)]
    public Customer Customer {
        get { return this._Customer.Entity; }
        set { this._Customer.Entity = value; }
    }

    private EntityRef<Customer> _Customer;
}
```

As you can see, the CustomerID column must be defined in *Order*; otherwise, it would not be possible to obtain the related *Customer*. The *IsForeignKey* argument specifies that *Order* is the child side of a parent-child relationship. The *ThisKey* argument of the *Association* attribute indicates the "foreign key" column (which would be a comma-separated list if more columns were involved for a composite key) that defines the relationship between entities. If you want to hide this detail in the entity properties, you can declare that column as private, just as in the *Order* class shown earlier.

Note There are two other arguments for the *Association* attribute. One is *IsUnique*, which must be *true* whenever the foreign key also has a uniqueness constraint. In that case, the relationship with the parent table is one-to-one instead of many-to-one. The other argument is *Name*, which is used only to define the name of the constraint for a database generated from the metadata by using the *DataContext.CreateDatabase* method, which will be described in Chapter 6.

Using the *Order* class in a LINQ query, you can specify a *Customer* property in a filter without writing a join between *Customer* and *Order* entities. In the following query, the *Country* member of the related *Customer* is used to filter orders that come from customers of a particular *Country*:

```
Table<Order> Orders = db.GetTable<Order>();
var query =
    from    o in Orders
    where   o.Customer.Country == "USA"
    select o.OrderID;
```

The previous query is translated into a SQL JOIN like the following one:

```
SELECT      [t0].[OrderID]
FROM        [Orders] AS [t0]
LEFT JOIN  [Customers] AS [t1]
        ON [t1].[CustomerID] = [t0].[CustomerID]
WHERE       [t1].[Country] = "USA"
```

Until now, we have used entity relationships only for their metadata in building LINQ queries. When an instance of an entity class is created, a reference to another entity (such as the previous *Customer* property) works with a technique called *deferred loading*. The related *Customer* entity is not instantiated and loaded into memory from the database until it is accessed either in read or write mode.

> **Note** *EntityRef<T>* is a wrapper class that is instantiated with the container object (a class derived from *DataContext*) to give a valid reference for any access to the referenced entity. Each read/write operation is filtered by a property *getter* and *setter*, which execute a query to load data from the database the first time this entity is accessed if it is not already in memory.

In other words, to generate a SQL query to populate the *Customer*-related entity when the *Country* property is accessed, you use the following code:

```
var query =
    from    o in Orders
    where   o.OrderID == 10528
    select o;

foreach( var row in query ) {
    Console.WriteLine( row.Customer.Country );
}
```

The process of accessing the *Customer* property involves determining whether the related *Customer* entity is already in memory for the current *DataContext*. If it is, that entity is accessed; otherwise, the following SQL query is executed and the corresponding *Customer* entity is loaded in memory and then accessed:

```
SELECT [t0].[Country], [t0].[CustomerID], [t0].[CompanyName]
FROM   [Customers] AS [t0]
WHERE  [t0].[CustomerID] = "GREAL"
```

The GREAL string is the *CustomerID* value for order 10528. As you can see, the SELECT statement queries all columns declared in the *Customer* entity, even if they are not used in the expression that accessed the *Customer* entity. (In this case, the executed code never referenced the *CompanyName* member.)

EntitySet

The other side of an association is a table that is referenced from another table through its primary key. Although this is an implicit consequence of the foreign key constraint in a relational model, you need to explicitly define this association in the entity model. If the Customers table is referenced from the Orders table, you can define an *Orders* property in the *Customer* class that represents the set of *Order* entities related to a given *Customer*. The relationship is implemented by an instance of *EntitySet<Order>*, which is a wrapper class over the sequence of related orders. You might want to directly expose this *EntitySet<T>* type, as in the code shown in Listing 5-7. In that code, the *OtherKey* argument of the *Association* attribute specifies the name of the member on the related type (*Order*) that defines the association between *Customer* and the set of *Order* entities.

LISTING 5-7 *Association EntitySet* (visible)

```
[Table(Name="Customers")]
public class Customer {
    [Column(IsPrimaryKey=true)] public string CustomerID;
    [Column] public string CompanyName;
    [Column] public string Country;

    [Association(OtherKey="CustomerID")]
    public EntitySet<Order> Orders;
}
```

You might also decide to expose *Orders* as a property, as in the declaration shown in Listing 5-8. In this case, the *Storage* argument of the *Association* attribute specifies the *EntitySet<T>* for physical storage. You could make only an *ICollection<Order>* visible outside the *Customer* class, instead of an *EntitySet<Order>*, but this is not a common practice.

LISTING 5-8 *Association EntitySet* (hidden)

```
public class Customer {
    [Column(IsPrimaryKey=true)] public string CustomerID;
    [Column] public string CompanyName;
    [Column] public string Country;

    private EntitySet<Order> _Orders;

    [Association(OtherKey="CustomerID", Storage="_Orders")]
    public EntitySet<Order> Orders {
        get { return this._Orders; }
        set { this._Orders.Assign(value); }
    }
    public Customer() {
        this._Orders = new EntitySet<Order>();
    }
}
```

With both models of association declaration, you can use the *Customer* class in a LINQ query, accessing the related *Order* entities without the need to write a join. You simply specify the *Orders* property. The next query returns the names of customers who placed more than 20 orders:

```
Table<Customer> Customers = db.GetTable<Customer>();
var query =
    from   c in Customers
    where  c.Orders.Count > 20
    select c.CompanyName;
```

The previous LINQ query is translated into a SQL query like the following one:

```
SELECT [t0].[CompanyName]
FROM   [Customers] AS [t0]
WHERE ( SELECT COUNT(*)
        FROM [Orders] AS [t1]
        WHERE [t1].[CustomerID] = [t0].[CustomerID]
      ) > 20
```

This example creates no *Order* entity instances. The *Orders* property serves only as a metadata source to generate the desired SQL query. If you return a *Customer* entity from a LINQ query, you can access the *Orders* of a customer on demand:

```
var query =
    from   c in Customers
    where  c.Orders.Count > 20
    select c;
```

```
foreach( var row in query ) {
    Console.WriteLine( row.CompanyName );
    foreach( var order in row.Orders ) {
        Console.WriteLine( order.OrderID );
    }
}
```

The preceding code uses deferred loading. Each time you access the *Orders* property of a customer for the first time (as indicated by the bold in the preceding code), a query like the following one (which uses the *@p0* parameter to filter *CustomerID*) is sent to the database:

```
SELECT [t0].[OrderID], [t0].[CustomerID]
FROM   [Orders] AS [t0]
WHERE  [t0].[CustomerID] = @p0
```

If you want to load all orders for all customers into memory using only one query to the database, you need to request *immediate loading* instead of deferred loading. To do that, you have two options. The first approach, which is demonstrated in Listing 5-9, is to force the inclusion of an *EntitySet* using a *DataLoadOptions* instance and the call to its *LoadWith<T>* method.

LISTING 5-9 Use of *DataLoadOptions* and *LoadWith<T>*

```
DataContext db = new DataContext( ConnectionString );
Table<Customer> Customers = db.GetTable<Customer>();

DataLoadOptions loadOptions = new DataLoadOptions();
loadOptions.LoadWith<Customer>( c => c.Orders );
db.LoadOptions = loadOptions;
var query =
    from   c in Customers
    where  c.Orders.Count > 20
    select c;
```

The second option is to return a new entity that explicitly includes the *Orders* property for the *Customer*:

```
var query =
    from   c in Customers
    where  c.Orders.Count > 20
    select new { c.CompanyName, c.Orders };
```

These LINQ queries send a SQL query to the database to get all customers who placed more than 20 orders, including the entire order list for each customer. That SQL query might be similar to the one shown in the following code:

```
SELECT [t0].[CompanyName], [t1].[OrderID], [t1].[CustomerID], (
    SELECT COUNT(*)
    FROM [Orders] AS [t3]
    WHERE [t3].[CustomerID] = [t0].[CustomerID]
```

```
    ) AS [value]
FROM [Customers] AS [t0]
LEFT OUTER JOIN [Orders] AS [t1] ON [t1].[CustomerID] = [t0].[CustomerID]
WHERE (
    SELECT COUNT(*)
    FROM [Orders] AS [t2]
    WHERE [t2].[CustomerID] = [t0].[CustomerID]
    ) > 20
ORDER BY [t0].[CustomerID], [t1].[OrderID]
```

> **Note** As you can see, a single SQL statement is here and the LINQ to SQL engine parses the result, extracting different entities (*Customers* and *Orders*). Keeping the result ordered by *CustomerID*, the engine can build in-memory entities and relationships in a faster way.

You can filter the subquery produced by relationship navigation. Suppose you want to see only customers who placed at least five orders in 1997, and you want to load only these orders. You can use the *AssociateWith<T>* method of the *DataLoadOptions* class to do that, as demonstrated in Listing 5-10.

LISTING 5-10 Use of *DataLoadOptions* and *AssociateWith<T>*

```
DataLoadOptions loadOptions = new DataLoadOptions();
loadOptions.AssociateWith<Customer>(
    c => from   o in c.Orders
         where  o.OrderDate.Value.Year == 1997
         select o);
db.LoadOptions = loadOptions;
var query =
      from   c in Customers
      where  c.Orders.Count > 5
      select c;
```

The Microsoft Visual C# filter condition (*o.OrderDate.Value.Year == 1997*) is translated into the following SQL expression:

```
(DATEPART(Year, [t2].[OrderDate]) = 1997)
```

AssociateWith<T> can also control the initial ordering of the collection. To do that, you can simply add an order condition to the query passed as an argument to *AssociateWith<T>*. For example, if you want to get the orders for each customer starting from the newest one, add the *orderby* line shown in bold in the following code:

```
loadOptions.AssociateWith<Customer>(
    c => from   o in c.Orders
         where  o.OrderDate.Value.Year == 1997
         orderby o.OrderDate descending
         select  o);
```

Using *AssociateWith<T>* alone does not apply the immediate loading behavior. If you want both immediate loading and filtering through a relationship, you have to call both the *LoadWith<T>* and *AssociateWith<T>* methods. The order of these calls is not relevant. For example, you can write the following code:

```
DataLoadOptions loadOptions = new DataLoadOptions();
loadOptions.AssociateWith<Customer>(
    c => from   o in c.Orders
         where  o.OrderDate.Value.Year == 1997
         select o);
loadOptions.LoadWith<Customer>( c => c.Orders );
db.LoadOptions = loadOptions;
```

Loading all data into memory using a single query might be a better approach if you are sure you will access all data that is loaded, because you will spend less time in round-trip latency. However, this technique will consume more memory and bandwidth when the typical access to a graph of entities is random. Think about these details when you decide how to query your data model.

Graph Consistency

Relationships are bidirectional between entities—when an update is made on one side, the other side should be kept synchronized. LINQ to SQL does not automatically manage this kind of synchronization, which has to be done by the class entity implementation. Instead, LINQ to SQL offers an implementation pattern that is also used by code-generation tools such as SQLMetal, a tool that is part of the Windows Software Development Kit (SDK) (and has been part of the .NET Framework SDK since Microsoft .NET Framework 3.5), or the LINQ to SQL class generator included with Visual Studio. Chapter 7 describes both these tools. This pattern is based on the *EntitySet<T>* class on one side and on the complex *setter* accessor on the other side. Take a look at the tools-generated code if you are interested in the implementation details of this pattern.

Change Notification

You will see in Chapter 6 that LINQ to SQL is able to track changes in entities, submitting equivalent changes to the database. This process is implemented by default through an algorithm that compares an object's content with its original values, requiring a copy of each tracked object. The memory consumption can be high, but it can be optimized if entities participate in the change tracking service by announcing when an object has been changed.

The implementation of change notification requires an entity to expose all its data through properties implementing the *System.ComponentModel.INotifyPropertyChanging* interface. Each property *setter* needs to call the *PropertyChanging* method of *DataContext*. Tools-generated code for entities (such as that emitted by SQLMetal and Visual Studio) already implement this pattern.

More Info For more information about change tracking, see the product documentation "Object States and Change-Tracking (LINQ to SQL)" at *http://msdn.microsoft.com/en-us/library /bb386982.aspx.*

Relational Model vs. Hierarchical Model

The entity model used by LINQ to SQL defines a set of objects that maps database tables into objects that can be used and manipulated by LINQ queries. The resulting model represents a paradigm shift that has been revealed in descriptions of associations between entities because it moves from a relational model (tables in a database) to a hierarchical or graph model (objects in memory).

A hierarchical/graph model is the natural way to manipulate objects in a program written in C# or Microsoft Visual Basic. When you try to consider how to translate an existing SQL query into a LINQ query, this is the major conceptual obstacle you encounter. In LINQ, you can write a query using joins between separate entities, just as you do in SQL. However, you can also write a query that uses the existing relationships between entities, as we did with *EntitySet* and *EntityRef* associations.

Important Remember that SQL does not make use of relationships between entities when querying data. Those relationships exist only to define the data integrity conditions. LINQ does not have the concept of *referential integrity*, but it makes use of relationships to define possible navigation paths in the data.

Data Querying

A LINQ to SQL query gets sent to the database only when the program needs to read data. For example, the following *foreach* loop iterates rows returned from a table:

```
var query =
    from    c in Customers
    where   c.Country == "USA"
    select  c.CompanyName;
```

```
foreach( var company in query ) {
    Console.WriteLine( company );
}
```

The code generated by the *foreach* statement is equivalent to the following code. The exact moment the query is executed corresponds to the *GetEnumerator* call:

```
// GetEnumerator sends the query to the database
IEnumerator<string> enumerator = query.GetEnumerator();
while (enumerator.MoveNext()) {
    Console.WriteLine( enumerator.Current );
}
```

Writing more *foreach* loops in the same query generates an equal number of calls to *GetEnumerator*, and thus an equal number of repeated executions of the same query. If you want to iterate the same data many times, you might prefer to cache data in memory. Using *ToList* or *ToArray*, you can convert the results of a query into a *List* or an *Array*, respectively. When you call these methods, the SQL query is sent to the database immediately:

```
// ToList() sends the query to the database
var companyNames = query.ToList();
```

You might want to send the query to the database several times when you manipulate the LINQ query between data iterations. For example, you might have an interactive user interface that allows the user to add a new filter condition for each iteration of data. In Listing 5-11, the *DisplayTop* method shows only the first few rows of the result; query manipulation between calls to *DisplayTop* simulates a user interaction that ends in a new filter condition each time.

> **More Info** Listing 5-11 shows a very simple technique for query manipulation, adding more restrictive filter conditions to an existing query represented by an *IQueryable<T>* object. Chapter 14 describes the techniques to dynamically build a query tree in a more flexible way.

LISTING 5-11 Query manipulation

```
static void QueryManipulation() {
    DataContext db = new DataContext( ConnectionString );
    Table<Customer> Customers = db.GetTable<Customer>();
    db.Log = Console.Out;

    // All Customers
    var query =
        from    c in Customers
        select  new {c.CompanyName, c.State, c.Country };
```

```
        DisplayTop( query, 10 );

        // User interaction adds a filter
        // to the previous query
        // Customers from USA
        query =
            from    c in query
            where   c.Country == "USA"
            select c;

        DisplayTop( query, 10 );

        // User interaction adds another
        // filter to the previous query
        // Customers from WA, USA
        query =
            from    c in query
            where   c.State == "WA"
            select c;

        DisplayTop( query, 10 );
    }

    static void DisplayTop<T>( IQueryable<T> query, int rows ) {
        foreach( var row in query.Take(rows)) {
            Console.WriteLine( row );
        }
    }
}
```

Important The previous example used *IQueryable<T>* as the *DisplayTop* parameter. If you pass *IEnumerable<T>* instead, the results would *appear* identical, but the query sent to the database would not contain the *TOP (rows)* clause to filter data directly on the database. Passing *IEnumerable<T>* uses a different set of extension methods to resolve the *Take* operator, which does not generate a new expression tree. Refer to Chapter 2, "LINQ Syntax Fundamentals," for an introduction to the differences between *IEnumerable<T>* and *IQueryable<T>*.

One common query reads a single row from a table, defining a condition that is guaranteed to be unique, such as a record key, shown in the following code:

```
var query =
    from    c in db.Customers
    where   c.CustomerID == "ANATR"
    select  c;

var enumerator = query.GetEnumerator();
if (enumerator.MoveNext()) {
    var customer = enumerator.Current;
    Console.WriteLine( "{0} {1}", customer.CustomerID, customer.CompanyName );
}
```

When you know a query will return a single row, use the *Single* operator to state your intention. Using this operator, you can write the previous code in a more compact way:

```
var customer = db.Customers.Single( c => c.CustomerID == "ANATR" );
Console.WriteLine( "{0} {1}", customer.CustomerID, customer.CompanyName );
```

However, it is important to note that calling *Single* has a different semantic than the previous equivalent *query*. Calling *Single* generates a query to the database only if the desired entity (in this case, the *Customer* with *ANATR* as *CustomerID*) is not already in memory. If you want to read the data from the database, you need to call the *DataContext.Refresh* method:

```
db.Refresh(RefreshMode.OverwriteCurrentValues, customer);
```

> **More Info** Chapter 6 contains more information about the entity life cycle.

Projections

The transformation from an expression tree to a SQL query requires the complete understanding of the query operations sent to the LINQ to SQL engine. This transformation affects the use of object initializers. You can use projections through the *select* keyword, as in the following example:

```
var query =
    from    c in Customers
    where   c.Country == "USA"
    select  new {c.CustomerID, Name = c.CompanyName.ToUpper()} into r
    orderby r.Name
    select  r;
```

The whole LINQ query is translated into this SQL statement:

```
SELECT [t1].[CustomerID], [t1].[value] AS [Name]
FROM ( SELECT [t0].[CustomerID],
            UPPER([t0].[CompanyName]) AS [value],
            [t0].[Country]
       FROM [Customers] AS [t0]
     ) AS [t1]
WHERE    [t1].[Country] = "USA"
ORDER BY [t1].[value]
```

As you can see, the *ToUpper* method has been translated into an UPPER T-SQL function call. To do that, the LINQ to SQL engine needs a deep knowledge of the meaning of any operation in the expression tree. Consider this query:

```
var queryBad =
    from    c in Customers
    where   c.Country == "USA"
    select  new CustomerData( c.CustomerID, c.CompanyName.ToUpper()) into r
    orderby r.Name
    select  r;
```

The preceding example calls a *CustomerData* constructor that can do anything a piece of Intermediate Language (IL) code can do. In other words, there is no semantic value in calling a constructor other than the initial assignment of the instance created. The consequence is that LINQ to SQL cannot correctly translate this syntax into equivalent SQL code, and it throws an exception if you try to execute the query. However, you can safely use a parameterized constructor in the final projection of a query, as in the following example:

```
var queryParamConstructor =
    from    c in Customers
    where   c.Country == "USA"
    orderby c.CompanyName
    select  new CustomerData( c.CustomerID, c.CompanyName.ToUpper() );
```

If you only need to initialize an object, use object initializers instead of a parameterized constructor call, as in the following query:

```
var queryGood =
    from    c in Customers
    where   c.Country == "USA"
    select  new CustomerData { CustomerID = c.CustomerID,
                               Name = c.CompanyName.ToUpper() } into r
    orderby r.Name
    select  r;
```

> **Important** Always use object initializers to encode projections in LINQ to SQL. Use parameterized constructors only in the final projection of a query.

Stored Procedures and User-Defined Functions

Accessing data through stored procedures and user-defined functions (UDFs) requires the definition of corresponding methods decorated with attributes. With this definition, you can write LINQ queries in a strongly typed form. From the point of view of LINQ, it makes no difference whether a stored procedure or UDF is written in T-SQL or SQLCLR, but there are some details you must know to handle differences between stored procedures and UDFs.

Stored Procedures

Consider this *Customers by City* stored procedure:

```
CREATE PROCEDURE [dbo].[Customers By City]( @param1 NVARCHAR(20) )
AS BEGIN
    SET NOCOUNT ON;
    SELECT CustomerID, ContactName, CompanyName, City
    FROM    Customers AS c
    WHERE   c.City = @param1
END
```

You can define a method decorated with a *Function* attribute that calls the stored procedure through the *DataContext.ExecuteMethodCall* method. Listing 5-12 defines *CustomersByCity* as a member of a class derived from *DataContext*.

LISTING 5-12 Stored procedure declaration

```
class SampleDb : DataContext {
    // ...
    [Function(Name = "Customers by City", IsComposable = false)]
    public ISingleResult<CustomerInfo> CustomersByCity(string param1) {
        IExecuteResult executeResult =
            this.ExecuteMethodCall(
                    this,
                    (MethodInfo) (MethodInfo.GetCurrentMethod()),
                    param1);
        ISingleResult<CustomerInfo> result =
            (ISingleResult<CustomerInfo>) executeResult.ReturnValue;
        return result;
    }
}
```

The *ExecuteMethodCall* is declared in this way:

```
IExecuteResult ExecuteMethodCall( object instance,
                                  MethodInfo methodInfo,
                                  params object[] parameters)
```

The method's first parameter is the instance, which is not required if you call a static method. The second parameter is a metadata description of the method to call, which could be obtained through Reflection, as shown in Listing 5-12. The third parameter is an array containing parameter values to pass to the method that is called.

CustomersByCity returns an instance of *ISingleResult<CustomerInfo>*, which implements *IEnumerable<CustomerInfo>* and can be enumerated in a *foreach* statement like this one:

```
SampleDb db = new SampleDb( ConnectionString );
foreach( var row in db.CustomersByCity( "London" )) {
    Console.WriteLine( "{0} {1}", row.CustomerID, row.CompanyName );
}
```

As you can see in Listing 5-12, you have to access the *IExecuteResult* interface returned by *ExecuteMethodCall* to get the desired result. This requires further explanation. You use the same *Function* attribute to decorate a method wrapping either a stored procedure or a UDF. The discrimination between these constructs is made by the *IsComposable* argument of the *Function* attribute: if it is *false*, the following method wraps a stored procedure; if it is *true*, the method wraps a user-defined function.

> **Note** The name *IsComposable* relates to the composability of user-defined functions in a query expression. You will see an example of this when the mapping of UDFs is described in the next section of this chapter.

The *IExecuteResult* interface has a simple definition:

```
public interface IExecuteResult : IDisposable {
    object GetParameterValue(int parameterIndex);
    object ReturnValue { get; }
}
```

The *GetParameterValue* method allows access to the output parameters of a stored procedure. You need to cast this result to the correct type, also passing the ordinal position of the output parameter in *parameterIndex*.

The *ReturnValue* read-only property is used to access the return value of a stored procedure or UDF. The scalar value returned is accessible with a cast to the correct type: a stored procedure always returns an integer, whereas the type of a UDF function can be different. However, when the results are tabular, you use *ISingleResult<T>* to access a single result set, or *IMultipleResults* to access multiple result sets.

You always need to know the metadata of all possible returned result sets, applying the right types to the generic interfaces used to return data. *ISingleResult<T>* is a simple wrapper of *IEnumerable<T>* that also implements *IFunctionResult*, which has a *ReturnValue* read-only property that acts as the *IExecuteResult.ReturnValue* property you have already seen:

```
public interface IFunctionResult {
    object ReturnValue { get; }
}
public interface ISingleResult<T> :
    IEnumerable<T>, IEnumerable, IFunctionResult, IDisposable { }
```

You saw an example of *ISingleResult<T>* in Listing 5-12. We wrote the *CustomersByCity* wrapper in a verbose way to better illustrate the internal steps necessary to access the returning data.

Whenever you have multiple result sets from a stored procedure, you call the *IMultipleResult. GetResult<T>* method for each result set sequentially and specify the correct *T* type for the expected result. *IMultipleResults* also implements *IFunctionResult*, thereby also offering a *ReturnValue* read-only property:

```
public interface IMultipleResults : IFunctionResult, IDisposable {
    IEnumerable<TElement> GetResult<TElement>();
}
```

Consider the following stored procedure that returns two result sets with different structures:

```
CREATE PROCEDURE TwoCustomerGroups
AS BEGIN
    SELECT  CustomerID, ContactName, CompanyName, City
    FROM    Customers AS c
    WHERE   c.City = 'London'

    SELECT  CustomerID, CompanyName, City
    FROM    Customers AS c
    WHERE   c.City = 'Torino'
END
```

The results returned from this stored procedure can be stored in the following *CustomerInfo* and *CustomerShortInfo* types, which do not require any attributes in their declarations:

```
public class CustomerInfo {
    public string CustomerID;
    public string CompanyName;
    public string City;
    public string ContactName;
}

public class CustomerShortInfo {
    public string CustomerID;
    public string CompanyName;
    public string City;
}
```

The declaration of the LINQ counterpart of the *TwoCustomerGroups* stored procedure should be like the one shown in Listing 5-13.

LISTING 5-13 Stored procedure with multiple results

```
class SampleDb : DataContext {
    // ...
    [Function(Name = "TwoCustomerGroups", IsComposable = false)]
    [ResultType(typeof(CustomerInfo))]
    [ResultType(typeof(CustomerShortInfo))]
    public IMultipleResults TwoCustomerGroups() {
        IExecuteResult executeResult =
                this.ExecuteMethodCall(
                    this,
                    (MethodInfo) (MethodInfo.GetCurrentMethod()));
        IMultipleResults result =
            (IMultipleResults) executeResult.ReturnValue;
        return result;
    }
}
```

Each result set has a different type. When calling each *GetResult<T>*, you need to specify the correct type, which needs at least a public member with the same name for each returned column. If you specify a type with more public members than available columns, the "missing" members will have a default value. Moreover, each returned type has to be declared by using a *ResultType* attribute that decorates the *TwoCustomerGroups* method, as you can see in Listing 5-13. In the next sample, the first result set must match the *CustomerInfo* type, and the second result set must correspond to the *CustomerShortInfo* type:

```
IMultipleResults results = db.TwoCustomerGroups();
foreach( var row in results.GetResult<CustomerInfo>()) {
    // Access to CustomerInfo instance
}
foreach( var row in results.GetResult<CustomerShortInfo>()) {
    // Access to CustomerShortInfo instance
}
```

Remember that the order of *ResultType* attributes is not relevant, but you have to pay attention to the order of the *GetResult<T>* calls. The first result set will be mapped from the first *GetResult<T>* call, and so on, regardless of the parameter type used. For example, if you invert the previous two calls, asking for *CustomerShortInfo* before *CustomerInfo*, you get no error, but you do get an empty string for the *ContactName* of the second result set mapped to *CustomerInfo*.

> **Important** The order of *GetResult<T>* calls is relevant and must correspond to the order of returned result sets. Conversely, the order of *ResultType* attributes applied to the method representing a stored procedure is not relevant.

Another use of *IMultipleResults* is the case in which a stored procedure can return different types based on parameters. For example, consider the following stored procedure:

```
CREATE PROCEDURE ChooseResultType( @resultType INT )
AS BEGIN
    IF @resultType = 1
        SELECT * FROM [Customers]
    ELSE IF @resultType = 2
        SELECT * FROM [Products]
END
```

Such a stored procedure will always return a single result, but its type might be different on each call. We do not like this use of stored procedures and prefer to avoid this situation. However, if you have to handle this case, by decorating the method with both possible *ResultType* attributes, you can handle both situations:

```
[Function(Name = "ChooseResultType", IsComposable = false)]
[ResultType(typeof(Customer))]
[ResultType(typeof(Product))]
public IMultipleResults ChooseResultType( int resultType ) {
    IExecuteResult executeResult =
            this.ExecuteMethodCall(
                    this,
                    (MethodInfo) (MethodInfo.GetCurrentMethod()),
                    resultType );
    IMultipleResults result =
        (IMultipleResults) executeResult.ReturnValue;
    return result;
}
```

In the single *GetResult<T>* call, you have to specify the type that correctly corresponds to what the stored procedure will return:

```
IMultipleResults results = db.ChooseResultType( 1 );
foreach( var row in results.GetResult<Customer>()) {
    // Access to Customer instance
}
```

If you have a similar scenario, it would be better to encapsulate the stored procedure call (*ChooseResultType* in this case) in several methods, one for each possible returned type. This way, you limit the risk of mismatching the relationship between parameter and result type:

```
public IEnumerable<Customer> ChooseCustomer() {
    IMultipleResults results = db.ChooseResultType( 1 );
    return results.GetResult<Customer>();
}

public IEnumerable<Product> ChooseProduct() {
    IMultipleResults results = db.ChooseResultType( 2 );
    return results.GetResult<Product>();
}
```

Before turning to user-defined functions, it is worth taking a look at what happens when you call a stored procedure in a LINQ query. Consider the following code:

```
var query =
    from   c in db.CustomersByCity("London")
    where  c.CompanyName.Length > 15
    select new { c.CustomerID, c.CompanyName };
```

Apparently, this query can be completely converted into a SQL query. However, all the data returned from *CustomersByCity* is passed from the SQL server to the client, as you can see from the generated SQL statement:

```
EXEC @RETURN_VALUE = [Customers by City] @param1 = 'London'
```

Both the filter (*where*) and projection (*select*) operations are made by LINQ to Objects, filtering data that has been transmitted to the client and enumerating only rows that have a *Company-Name* value longer than 15 characters. Thus, stored procedures are not composable into a single SQL query. To make this kind of composition, you need to use user-defined functions.

User-Defined Functions

To be used in LINQ, a user-defined function needs the same kind of declaration as a stored procedure. When you use a UDF inside a LINQ query, the LINQ to SQL engine must consider it in the construction of the SQL statement, adding a UDF call to the generated SQL. The capability of a UDF to be used in a LINQ query is what we mean by composability—the capability to compose different queries and/or operators into a single query. Because the same *Function* attribute is used for both stored procedures and UDFs, the *IsComposable* argument is set to *true* to map a UDF, and is set to *false* to map a stored procedure. Remember that there is no difference between a UDF written in T-SQL or SQLCLR.

Listing 5-14 provides an example of a LINQ declaration of the scalar-valued UDF *MinUnit-PriceByCategory* that is defined in the sample Northwind database.

LISTING 5-14 Scalar-valued UDF

```
class SampleDb : DataContext {
    // ...
    [Function(Name = "dbo.MinUnitPriceByCategory", IsComposable = true)]
    public decimal? MinUnitPriceByCategory( int? categoryID) {
        IExecuteResult executeResult =
            this.ExecuteMethodCall(
                this,
                ((MethodInfo) (MethodInfo.GetCurrentMethod())),
                categoryID);
        decimal? result = (decimal?) executeResult.ReturnValue;
        return result;
    }
}
```

The call to a UDF as an isolated expression generates a single SQL query invocation. You can also use a UDF in a LINQ query such as the following:

```
var query =
    from   c in Categories
    select new { c.CategoryID,
                 c.CategoryName,
                 MinPrice = db.MinUnitPriceByCategory( c.CategoryID )};
```

The generated SQL statement *composes* the LINQ query with the UDF that is called, resulting in a SQL query like this:

```
SELECT [t0].[CategoryID],
       [t0].[CategoryName],
       dbo.MinUnitPriceByCategory([t0].[CategoryID]) AS [value]
FROM   [Categories] AS [t0]
```

There are some differences in table-valued UDF wrappers. Consider the following UDF:

```
CREATE FUNCTION [dbo].[CustomersByCountry] ( @country NVARCHAR(15) )
RETURNS TABLE
AS RETURN
    SELECT  CustomerID,
            ContactName,
            CompanyName,
            City
    FROM    Customers c
    WHERE   c.Country = @country
```

To use this UDF in LINQ, you need to declare a *CustomersByCountry* method, as shown in Listing 5-15. A table-valued UDF always sets *IsComposable* to *true* in *Function* arguments, but it calls the *DataContext.CreateMethodCallQuery* instead of *DataContext.ExecuteMethodCall*.

LISTING 5-15 Table-valued UDF

```
class SampleDb : DataContext {
    // ...
    [Function(Name = "dbo.CustomersByCountry", IsComposable = true)]
    public IQueryable<Customer> CustomersByCountry(string country) {
        return this.CreateMethodCallQuery<Customer>(
            this,
            ((MethodInfo) (MethodInfo.GetCurrentMethod())),
            country);
    }
}
```

A table-valued UDF can be used like any other table in a LINQ query. For example, you can join customers returned by the previous UDF with the orders they placed, as in the following query:

```
Table<Order> Orders = db.GetTable<Order>();
var queryCustomers =
    from    c in db.CustomersByCountry( "USA" )
    join    o in Orders
            on c.CustomerID equals o.CustomerID
            into orders
    select new { c.CustomerID, c.CompanyName, orders };
```

The generated SQL query will be similar to this one:

```
SELECT [t0].[CustomerID], [t0].[CompanyName],
       [t1].[OrderID], [t1].[CustomerID] AS [CustomerID2],
       (SELECT COUNT(*)
        FROM [Orders] AS [t2]
        WHERE [t0].[CustomerID] = [t2].[CustomerID]
        ) AS [value]
FROM dbo.CustomersByCountry('USA') AS [t0]
LEFT OUTER JOIN [Orders] AS [t1] ON [t0].[CustomerID] = [t1].[CustomerID]
ORDER BY [t1].[OrderID]
```

Compiled Queries

If you need to repeat the same query many times, eventually with different argument values, you might be worried about the multiple query construction. Several databases, such as SQL Server, try to parameterize received SQL queries automatically to optimize the compilation of the query execution plan. However, the program that sends a parameterized query to SQL Server will get better performance because SQL Server does not have to spend time analyzing it if the query is similar to one already processed. LINQ already does a fine job of query optimization, but each time that the same query tree is evaluated, the LINQ to SQL engine parses the query tree to build the equivalent SQL code. You can optimize this behavior by using the *CompiledQuery* class.

More Info The built-in SQL Server provider sends parameterized queries to the database. Every time you see a constant value in the SQL code presented in this chapter, keep in mind that the real SQL query sent to the database has a parameter for each constant in the query. That constant can be the result of an expression that is independent of the query execution. This kind of expression is resolved by the host language (C# in this case). When you use the *CompiledQuery* class, it eliminates the need to parse the query tree and create the equivalent SQL code every time LINQ processes the same query. You might ask: What is the break-even point that justifies the use of the *CompiledQuery* class? Rico Mariani did a performance test that is described in a blog post at *http://blogs.msdn.com/b/ricom/archive/2008/01/14/performance-quiz-13-linq-to-sql-compiled-query-cost-solution.aspx*. The response from his benchmark is that, with at least two calls for the query, the use of the *CompiledQuery* class produces a performance advantage.

To compile a query, you can use one of the *CompiledQuery.Compile* static methods. This approach passes the LINQ query as a parameter in the form of an expression tree, and then obtains a delegate with arguments corresponding to both the *DataContext* on which you want to operate and the parameters of the query. Listing 5-16 illustrates the compiled query declaration and use.

LISTING 5-16 Compiled query in a local scope

```
static void CompiledQueriesLocal() {
    DataContext db = new DataContext( ConnectionString );
    Table<Customer> Customers = db.GetTable<Customer>();

    var query =
        CompiledQuery.Compile(
            ( DataContext context, string filterCountry ) =>
                from    c in Customers
                where   c.Country == filterCountry
                select new { c.CustomerID, c.CompanyName, c.City } );

    foreach (var row in query( db, "USA" )) {
        Console.WriteLine( row );
    }

    foreach (var row in query( db, "Italy" )) {
        Console.WriteLine( row );
    }
}
```

As you can see in Listing 5-16, the *Compile* method requires a lambda expression whose first argument is a *DataContext* instance. That argument defines the connection over which the query will be executed. In this case, we do not use that argument inside our lambda expression. Assigning the *CompiledQuery.Compile* result to a local variable is easy (because you declare that variable with *var*), but you will not encounter this situation very frequently. Chances are that you will need to store the delegate returned from *CompiledQuery.Compile* in an instance or a static member to easily reuse it several times. To do that, you need to know the correct declaration syntax.

A compiled query is stored in a *Func* delegate, where the first argument must be an instance of *DataContext* (or a class derived from *DataContext*) and the last argument must be the type returned from the query. You can define up to three arguments in the middle that will be arguments of the compiled query. You will need to specify these arguments for each compiled query invocation. Listing 5-17 shows the syntax you can use in this scenario to create the compiled query and then use it.

LISTING 5-17 Compiled query assigned to a static member

```
public static Func< SampleDb, string, IQueryable<Customer>>
    CustomerByCountry =
        CompiledQuery.Compile(
            ( nwind.Northwind db, string filterCountry ) =>
                from   c in db.Customers
                where  c.Country == filterCountry
                select c );

static void CompiledQueriesStatic() {
    nwind.Northwind db = new nwind.Northwind( ConnectionString );

    foreach (var row in CustomerByCountry( db, "USA" )) {
        Console.WriteLine( row.CustomerID );
    }

    foreach (var row in CustomerByCountry( db, "Italy" )) {
        Console.WriteLine( row.CustomerID );
    }
}
```

Because the *Func* delegate that holds the compiled query needs the result type in its declaration, you cannot use an anonymous type as the result type of a compiled query. This is possible only when the compiled query is stored in a local variable, as you saw in Listing 5-16.

Different Approaches to Querying Data

When using LINQ to SQL entities, you have two approaches for querying the same data. The classic way to navigate a relational schema is to write associative queries, just as you can do in SQL. The alternative way offered by LINQ to SQL is through graph traversal. Given the same query result, you might obtain different SQL queries and a different level of performance using different LINQ approaches.

Consider this SQL query that calculates the total quantity of orders for a product (in this case, Chocolade, which is a localized name in the Northwind database):

```
SELECT    SUM( od.Quantity ) AS TotalQuantity
FROM      [Products] p
LEFT JOIN [Order Details] od
     ON   od.[ProductID] = p.[ProductID]
WHERE     p.ProductName = 'Chocolade'
```

The natural conversion into a LINQ query is shown in Listing 5-18. The *Single* operator gets the first row and puts it into *quantityJoin*, which is used to display the result.

LISTING 5-18 Query using *Join*

```
var queryJoin =
    from   p in db.Products
    join   o in db.Order_Details
           on p.ProductID equals o.ProductID
           into OrdersProduct
    where  p.ProductName == "Chocolade"
    select OrdersProduct.Sum( o => o.Quantity );
var quantityJoin = queryJoin.Single();
Console.WriteLine( quantityJoin );
```

As you can see, the associative query in LINQ can explicitly require the join between *Products* and *Order_Details* through *ProductID* equivalency. By using entities, you can implicitly use the relationship between *Products* and *Order_Details* defined in the *Product* class, as shown in Listing 5-19.

LISTING 5-19 Query using *Association*

```
var queryAssociation =
    from   p in db.Products
    where  p.ProductName == "Chocolade"
    select p.Order_Details.Sum( o => o.Quantity );
var quantityAssociation = queryAssociation.Single();
Console.WriteLine( quantityAssociation );
```

The single SQL queries produced by both of these LINQ queries are identical. The LINQ query with *join* is more explicit about the access to data, whereas the query that uses the association between *Product* and *Order_Details* is more implicit in this regard. Using implicit associations results in shorter queries that are less error-prone (because you cannot be wrong about the join condition). At first, you might find that a shorter query is harder to read; that might be because you are accustomed to seeing lengthier queries. Your comfort level with shorter ones might change over time.

Note The SQL query produced by the LINQ queries in Listings 5-18 and 5-19 is different between SQL Server 2000 and SQL Server 2005 or later versions. With SQL Server 2005, the OUTER APPLY join is used. This is the result of an internal implementation of the provider, but the final result is the same.

Examining this further, you can observe that reading a single product does not require a query expression. You can apply the *Single* operator directly on the Products table, as shown in Listing 5-20. Although the results are the same, the internal process is much different because this kind of access generates instances of the *Product* and *Order_Details* entities in memory, even if you do not use them in your program.

LISTING 5-20 Access through *Entity*

```
var chocolade = db.Products.Single( p => p.ProductName == "Chocolade" );
var quantityValue = chocolade.Order_Details.Sum( o => o.Quantity );
Console.WriteLine( quantityValue );
```

This is a two-step operation that sends two SQL queries to the database. The first one retrieves the *Product* entity. The second one accesses the Order Details table to get *all* the Order Details rows for the required product and sums up the *Quantity* value in memory for the required product. The operation generates the following SQL statements:

```
SELECT [t0].[ProductID], [t0].[ProductName], [t0].[SupplierID],
       [t0].[CategoryID], [t0].[QuantityPerUnit], [t0].[UnitPrice],
       [t0].[UnitsInStock], [t0].[UnitsOnOrder], [t0].[ReorderLevel],
       [t0].[Discontinued]
FROM   [dbo].[Products] AS [t0]
WHERE  [t0].[ProductName] = "Chocolade"

SELECT [t0].[OrderID], [t0].[ProductID], [t0].[UnitPrice], [t0].[Quantity],
       [t0].[Discount]
FROM   [dbo].[Order Details] AS [t0]
WHERE  [t0].[ProductID] = "Chocolade"
```

Code that uses this kind of access is shorter to write compared to a query, but its performance is worse if you need to get only the total *Quantity* value, without needing to retrieve *Product* and *Order_Detail* entities in memory for further operations.

The queries in Listings 5-18 and 5-19 did not create *Product* or *Order_Details* instances because the output required only the product total. From this point of view, if you already had the required *Product* and *Order_Details* instances for Chocolade in memory, the performance of those queries would be worse because they unnecessarily access the database to get data that is already in memory. On the other hand, a second access to get the sum *Quantity* could be faster if you use the entity approach. Consider this code:

```
var chocolade = db.Products.Single( p => p.ProductName == "Chocolade" );
var quantityValue = chocolade.Order_Details.Sum( o => o.Quantity );
Console.WriteLine( quantityValue );
var repeatCalc = chocolade.Order_Details.Sum( o => o.Quantity );
Console.WriteLine( repeatCalc );
```

The *quantityValue* evaluation requires a database query to create *Order_Details* entities, whereas the *repeatCalc* evaluation is made on the in-memory entities without the need to read other data from SQL Server.

> **Note** A good way to understand how your code behaves is to analyze the SQL queries that are produced. In the previous examples, we wrote a *Sum* in a LINQ query. When the generated SQL query contains a SUM aggregation operation, you are not reading entities in memory; however, when the generated SQL query does not contain the requested aggregation operation, that aggregation will be made in memory on corresponding entities.

A final thought on the number of generated queries: You might think that we generated two queries when accessing data through the *Product* entity because we had two distinct statements—one to assign the *chocolade* variable, and the other to assign a value to *quantity-Entity*. This assumption is not completely true. Even if you write a single statement, the use of a *Product* entity (the results from the *Single* operator call) generates a separate query. Listing 5-21 produces the same results (in terms of memory objects and SQL queries) as Listing 5-20.

LISTING 5-21 Access through *Entity* with a single statement

```
var quantityChocolade = db.Products.Single( p => p.ProductName == "Chang" )
                          .Order_Details.Sum( o => o.Quantity );
Console.WriteLine( quantityChocolade );
```

Finding a better way to access data really depends on the entire set of operations performed by a program. If you extensively use entities in your code to store data in memory, access to data through graph traversal based on entity access might offer better performance. On the other hand, if you always transform query results in anonymous types and never manipulate entities in memory, you might prefer an approach based on LINQ queries. As usual, the right answer is, "It depends."

Direct Queries

Sometimes you might need access to database SQL features that are not available with LINQ. For example, imagine that you want to use Common Table Expressions (CTEs) or the PIVOT command with SQL Server. LINQ does not have an explicit constructor to do that, even if its SQL Server provider could use these features to optimize some queries. In such cases, you can use the *ExecuteQuery<T>* method of the *DataContext* class to send a query directly to the database. Listing 5-22 shows an example. (The *T* in *ExecuteQuery<T>* is an entity class that represents a returned row.)

LISTING 5-22 Direct query

```
var query = db.ExecuteQuery<EmployeeInfo>( @"
    WITH EmployeeHierarchy (EmployeeID, LastName, FirstName,
                            ReportsTo, HierarchyLevel) AS
    ( SELECT EmployeeID,LastName, FirstName,
             ReportsTo, 1 as HierarchyLevel
      FROM    Employees
      WHERE   ReportsTo IS NULL

      UNION ALL

      SELECT      e.EmployeeID, e.LastName, e.FirstName,
                  e.ReportsTo, eh.HierarchyLevel + 1 AS HierarchyLevel
      FROM        Employees e
      INNER JOIN  EmployeeHierarchy eh
              ON  e.ReportsTo = eh.EmployeeID
    )
    SELECT   *
    FROM     EmployeeHierarchy
    ORDER BY HierarchyLevel, LastName, FirstName" );
```

As you can see, you need a type to get direct query results. We used the *EmployeeInfo* type in
this example, which is declared as follows:

```
public class EmployeeInfo {
    public int EmployeeID;
    public string LastName;
    public string FirstName;
    public int? ReportsTo; // int? Corresponds to Nullable<int>
    public int HierarchyLevel;
}
```

The names and types of *EmployeeInfo* members must match the names and types of the columns returned by the executed query. Please note that if a column can return a NULL value,
you need to use a nullable type, as we did for the *ReportsTo* member declared as *int?* above
(which corresponds to *Nullable<int>*).

> **Warning** Columns in the resulting rows that do not match entity attributes are ignored. Entity
> members that do not have corresponding columns are initialized with the default value. If the
> *EmployeeInfo* class contains a mismatched column name, that member will not be assigned with-
> out an error. Be sure to check name correspondence in the result if you find missing column or
> member values.

The *ExecuteQuery* method can receive parameters using the same parameter placeholders notation (also known as *curly notation*) used by *Console.WriteLine* and *String.Format*, but with a different behavior. Parameters are not replaced in the string sent to the database; they are substituted with automatically generated parameter names such as (*@p0, @p1, @p2, ...*) and are sent to SQL Server as arguments of the parametric query.

The code in Listing 5-23 shows the call to *ExecuteQuery<T>* using a SQL statement with two parameters. The parameters are used to filter the customers who made their first order within a specified range of dates.

LISTING 5-23 Direct query with parameters

```
var query = db.ExecuteQuery<CompanyOrders>(@"
      SELECT    c.CompanyName,
                MIN( o.OrderDate ) AS FirstOrderDate,
                MAX( o.OrderDate ) AS LastOrderDate
      FROM      Customers c
      LEFT JOIN Orders o
            ON o.CustomerID = c.CustomerID
      GROUP BY  c.CustomerID, c.CompanyName
      HAVING    COUNT(o.OrderDate) > 0
        AND     MIN( o.OrderDate ) BETWEEN {0} AND {1}
      ORDER BY  FirstOrderDate ASC",
    new DateTime( 1997, 1, 1 ),
    new DateTime( 1997, 12, 31 ) );
```

The parameters in the preceding query are identified by the *{0}* and *{1}* format items. The generated SQL query simply substitutes them with *@p0* and *@p1*. The results are returned in instances of the *CompanyOrders* class, declared as follows:

```
public class CompanyOrders {
    public string CompanyName;
    public DateTime FirstOrderDate;
    public DateTime LastOrderDate;
}
```

Deferred Loading of Entities

You have seen that using graph traversal to query data is a very comfortable way to proceed. However, sometimes you might want to stop the LINQ to SQL provider from automatically deciding what entities have to be read from the database and when, thereby taking control over that part of the process. You can do this by using the *DeferredLoadingEnabled* and *Load-Options* properties of the *DataContext* class.

The code in Listing 5-24 makes the same *QueryOrder* call under three different conditions, driven by the code in the *DemoDeferredLoading* method.

LISTING 5-24 Deferred loading of entities

```
public static void DemoDeferredLoading() {
    Console.Write("DeferredLoadingEnabled=true  ");
    DemoDeferredLoading(true);
    Console.Write("DeferredLoadingEnabled=false ");
    DemoDeferredLoading(false);
    Console.Write("Using LoadOptions            ");
    DemoLoadWith();
}

static void DemoDeferredLoading(bool deferredLoadingEnabled) {
    nwDataContext db = new nwDataContext(Connections.ConnectionString);
    db.DeferredLoadingEnabled = deferredLoadingEnabled;

    QueryOrder(db);
}

static void DemoLoadWith() {
    nwDataContext db = new nwDataContext(Connections.ConnectionString);
    db.DeferredLoadingEnabled = false;

    DataLoadOptions loadOptions = new DataLoadOptions();
    loadOptions.LoadWith<Order>(o => o.Order_Details);
    db.LoadOptions = loadOptions;

    QueryOrder(db);
}

static void QueryOrder(nwDataContext db) {
    var order = db.Orders.Single((o) => o.OrderID == 10251);
    var orderValue = order.Order_Details.Sum(od => od.Quantity * od.UnitPrice);
    Console.WriteLine(orderValue);
}
```

The call to *DemoDeferredLoading(true)* sets the *DeferredLoadingEnabled* property to *true*, which is the default condition for a *DataContext* instance. The call to *DemoDeferredLoading(false)* disables the *DeferredLoadingEnabled* property. Any access to the related entities does not automatically load data from the database, and the sum of *Order_Details* entities shows a total of 0. Finally, the call to *DemoLoadWith* also disables *DeferredLoadingEnabled*, but it sets the *LoadOptions* property of the *DataContext*, requesting the loading of *Order_Details* entities related to an *Order* instance. The execution of the *DemoDeferredLoading* method in Listing 5-24 produces the following output:

```
DeferredLoadingEnabled=true  670,8000
DeferredLoadingEnabled=false 0
Using LoadOptions            670,8000
```

Remember that the use of *LoadOptions* is possible regardless of the state of *DeferredLoading-Enabled*, and it is useful for improving performance when early loading of related entities (rather than deferred loading) is an advantage for your application. Consider carefully before using *DeferredLoadingEnabled*—it does not produce any error, but it limits the navigability of your data model through graph traversal. However, you must remember that *DeferredLoading-Enabled* is automatically considered to be *false* whenever the *ObjectTrackingEnabled* property (discussed in the next section) is disabled too.

Deferred Loading of Properties

LINQ to SQL provides a deferred loading mechanism that acts at the property level, loading data only when that property is accessed for the first time. You can use this mechanism when you need to load a large number of entities in memory, which usually requires space to accommodate all the properties of the class that correspond to table columns of the database. If a certain field is very large and is not always accessed for every entity, you can delay the loading of that property.

To request the deferred loading of a property, you simply use the *Link<T>* type to declare the storage variable for the table column, as you can see in Listing 5-25.

LISTING 5-25 Deferred loading of properties

```
[Table(Name = "Customers")]
public class DelayCustomer {
    private Link<string> _Address;

    [Column(IsPrimaryKey = true)] public string CustomerID;
    [Column] public string CompanyName;
    [Column] public string Country;

    [Column(Storage = "_Address")]
    public string Address {
        get { return _Address.Value; }
        set { _Address.Value = value; }
    }
}

public static class DeferredLoading {
    public static void DelayLoadProperty() {
        DataContext db = new DataContext(Connections.ConnectionString);
        Table<DelayCustomer> Customers = db.GetTable<DelayCustomer>();
        db.Log = Console.Out;

        var query =
            from   c in Customers
            where  c.Country == "Italy"
            select c;
```

```
        foreach (var row in query) {
            Console.WriteLine(
                "{0} - {1}",
                row.CompanyName,
                row.Address);
        }
    }
}
```

The query that is sent to the database to get the list of Italian customers is functionally equivalent to the following one:

```
SELECT [t0].[CustomerID], [t0].[CompanyName], [t0].[Country]
FROM    [Customers] AS [t0]
WHERE   [t0].[Country] = "Italy"
```

This query does not retrieve the *Address* field. When the result of the query is iterated in the *foreach* loop, the *Address* property of the current *Customer* is accessed for each customer for the first time. This produces a query to the database like the following one to get the *Address* value:

```
SELECT [t0].[Address]
FROM    [Customers] AS [t0]
WHERE   [t0].[CustomerID] = @p0
```

You should use the *Link<T>* type only when the content of a field is very large (which should *not* be the case for the *Address* field example) or when that field is rarely accessed. A field defined with the SQL type *VARCHAR(MAX)* is generally a good candidate, as long as its value is displayed only in a detailed form visible on demand and not on the main grid that shows query results. Using the LINQ to SQL class generator included in Visual Studio, you can use *Link<T>* and set the *Delay Loaded* property of the desired member property to *true*.

> **Important** You need to use the *Link<T>* type on the storage variable for a property of type *T* mapped to the column, as shown in Listing 5-25. You cannot use the *Link<T>* type directly on a public data member mapped to a table column (like all the other fields); if you do, you will get an exception during execution. That run-time error is of type *VerificationException*. Future versions may have a more analytical exception.

Read-Only *DataContext* Access

If you need to access data exclusively as read-only, you might want to improve performance by disabling a *DataContext* service that supports data modification:

```
DataContext db = new DataContext( ConnectionString );
db.ObjectTrackingEnabled = false;
var query = ...
```

The *ObjectTrackingEnabled* property controls the change tracking service described in Chapter 6. By default, *ObjectTrackingEnabled* is set to *true*.

> **Important** Disabling object tracking also disables the deferred loading feature of the same *Data-Context* instance. If you want to optimize performance by disabling the object tracking feature, you must be aware of the side effects of disabling deferred loading too. Refer to the "Deferred Loading of Entities" section earlier in this chapter for further details.

Limitations of LINQ to SQL

LINQ to SQL has some limitations when converting a LINQ query to a corresponding SQL statement. For this reason, some valid LINQ to Objects statements are not supported in LINQ to SQL. In this section, we cover the most important operators that you cannot use in a LINQ to SQL query. However, you can use specific T-SQL commands by using the extension methods defined in the *SqlMethods* class, which you will find in the *System.Data.Linq.SqlClient* namespace.

> **More Info** A complete list of unsupported methods and types is available on the "Data Types and Functions (LINQ to SQL)" page of the product documentation, available at *http://msdn.microsoft.com /en-us/library/bb386970.aspx*.

Aggregate Operators

The general-purpose *Aggregate* operator is not supported. However, specialized aggregate operators such as *Count*, *LongCount*, *Sum*, *Min*, *Max*, and *Average* are fully supported.

Any aggregate operator other than *Count* and *LongCount* requires particular care to avoid an exception if the result is *null*. If the entity class has a member of a nonnullable type and you make an aggregation on it, a null result (for example when no rows are aggregated) throws an exception. To avoid the exception, you should cast the aggregated value to a nullable type before considering it in the aggregation function. Listing 5-26 shows an example of the necessary cast.

LISTING 5-26 Null handling with aggregate operators

```
decimal? totalFreight =
    (from   o in Orders
     where  o.CustomerID == "NOTEXIST"
     select o).Min( o => (decimal?) o.Freight );
```

This cast is necessary only if you declared the *Freight* property with *decimal*, as shown in the following code:

```
[Table(Name = "Orders")]
public class Order {
    [Column] public decimal Freight;
}
```

Another solution is to declare *Freight* as a nullable type, using *decimal?*—but it is not a good idea to have different nullable settings between entities and corresponding tables in the database.

> **More Info** You can find a more complete discussion about this issue in the post "LINQ to SQL, Aggregates, EntitySet, and Quantum Mechanics," written by Ian Griffiths and located at *http://www.interact-sw.co.uk/iangblog/2007/09/10/linq-aggregates*.

Partitioning Operators

The *TakeWhile* and *SkipWhile* operators are not supported. *Take* and *Skip* operators are supported, but be careful with *Skip* because the generated SQL query could be complex and not very efficient when skipping a large number of rows, especially when the target database is SQL Server 2000.

Element Operators

The following operators are not supported: *ElementAt*, *ElementAtOrDefault*, *Last*, and *LastOrDefault*.

String Methods

Many of the .NET Framework *String* type methods are supported in LINQ to SQL because T-SQL has a corresponding method. However, there is no support for methods that are culture-aware (those that receive arguments of type *CultureInfo*, *StringComparison*, and *IFormatProvider*) and for methods that receive or return a *char* array.

DateTime Methods

The *DateTime* type in the .NET Framework is different than the *DATETIME* and *SMALLDATE-TIME* types in SQL Server. The range of values and the precision is greater in the .NET Framework than in SQL Server, meaning the .NET Framework can correctly represent SQL Server types, but not the opposite. Check out the *SqlMethods* extension methods, which can take advantage of several *DateDiff* functions.

LIKE Operator

Although the *LIKE* T-SQL operator is used whenever a *StartsWith*, *EndsWith*, or *Contains* operator is called on a string property, you can use *LIKE* directly by calling the *SqlMethods.Like* method in a predicate.

Unsupported SQL Functionalities

LINQ to SQL does not have syntax to make use of the *STDDEV* aggregation.

Thinking in LINQ to SQL

When you start working with LINQ to SQL, you might have to rethink the ways in which you are accustomed to writing queries, especially if you try to find the equivalent LINQ syntax for a well-known SQL statement. Moreover, a verbose LINQ query might be reduced when the corresponding SQL query is produced. You need to be aware of this change, and you have to fully understand it to be productive in LINQ to SQL. The final part of this chapter introduces you to thinking in LINQ to SQL.

The *IN/EXISTS* Clause

One of the best examples of the syntactic differences between T-SQL and LINQ is the *NOT IN* clause that you can use in SQL. LINQ does not have such a clause, which makes you wonder whether there is any way to express the same concept in LINQ. In fact, there is not always a direct translation for each single SQL keyword, but you can get the same result with semantically equivalent statements, sometimes with equal or better performance.

Consider this SQL query, which returns all the customers who do not have an order in the Orders table:

```
SELECT *
FROM    [dbo].[Customers] AS [t0]
WHERE   [t0].[CustomerID] NOT IN (
    SELECT [t1].[CustomerID]
    FROM    [dbo].[Orders] AS [t1]
)
```

This is not the fastest way to get the desired result. (Using *NOT EXISTS* is our favorite way—more on this shortly.) LINQ does not have an operator directly equivalent to *IN* or *NOT IN*, but it offers a *Contains* operator that you can use to write the code in Listing 5-27. Pay attention to the *not* operator (*!*) applied to the *where* predicate, which negates the *Contains* condition that follows.

LISTING 5-27 Use of *Contains* to get an *EXISTS/IN* equivalent statement

```
public static void DemoContains() {
    nwDataContext db = new nwDataContext(Connections.ConnectionString);
    db.Log = Console.Out;

    var query =
        from c in db.Customers
        where !(from o in db.Orders
                select o.CustomerID)
               .Contains(c.CustomerID)
        select new { c.CustomerID, c.CompanyName };

    foreach (var c in query) {
        Console.WriteLine(c);
    }
}
```

The following code is the SQL query generated by LINQ to SQL:

```
SELECT [t0].[CustomerID], [t0].[CompanyName]
FROM   [dbo].[Customers] AS [t0]
WHERE  NOT (EXISTS(
    SELECT NULL AS [EMPTY]
    FROM   [dbo].[Orders] AS [t1]
    WHERE  [t1].[CustomerID] = [t0].[CustomerID]
    ))
```

Using this approach to generate SQL code is not only semantically equivalent, but it also executes faster. If you look at the input/output (I/O) operation made by SQL Server 2005, the first query (using *NOT IN*) executes 364 logical reads on the Orders table, whereas the second query (using *NOT EXISTS*) requests only 5 logical reads on the same Orders table. That is a big difference. In this case, LINQ to SQL is the best choice.

The same *Contains* operator might generate an *IN* operator in SQL, for example, if it is applied to a list of constants, as in Listing 5-28.

LISTING 5-28 Use of *Contains* with a list of constants

```
public static void DemoContainsConstants() {
    nwDataContext db = new nwDataContext(Connections.ConnectionString);

    var query =
        from    c in db.Customers
        where   (new string[] { "London", "Seattle" }).Contains(c.City)
        select new { c.CustomerID, c.CompanyName, c.City };

    Console.WriteLine(query);

    foreach (var c in query) {
        Console.WriteLine(c);
    }
}
```

The SQL code generated by LINQ to SQL is simpler to read than the original query:

```
SELECT [t0].[CustomerID], [t0].[CompanyName], [t0].[City]
FROM    [dbo].[Customers] AS [t0]
WHERE   [t0].[City] IN ("London", "Seattle")
```

The LINQ query is counterintuitive in that you must specify the *Contains* operator on the list of constants, passing the value to look for as an argument—exactly the opposite of what you need to do in SQL:

```
where (new string[] { "London", "Seattle" }).Contains(c.City)
```

After years of experience in SQL, it is more comfortable to imagine this hypothetical *IsIn* syntax:

```
where c.City.IsIn( new string[] { "London", "Seattle" } )
```

However, it is probably only a question of time before you get used to the new syntax. In fact, the semantics of *Contains* corresponds exactly to the argument's position. To make the code clearer, you could simply declare the list of constants outside the query declaration, in a *cities* array, for example:

```
var cities = new string[] { "London", "Seattle" };
var query =
    from    c in db.Customers
    where   cities.Contains(c.City)
    select new { c.CustomerID, c.CompanyName, c.City };
```

> **Note** Creating the *cities* array outside the query instead of putting it in the *where* predicate simply improves code readability, at least in LINQ to SQL. From a performance point of view, only one *string* array is created in both cases. The reason is that in LINQ to SQL, the query defines only an expression tree, and the array is created only once to produce the SQL statement. In LINQ to SQL, unless you execute the same query many times, performance is equivalent under either approach (object creation inside or outside a predicate). This is different in LINQ to Objects, in which the predicate condition in the *where* clause would be executed for each row of the data source.

SQL Query Reduction

Every LINQ to SQL query is initially represented in memory as an expression tree. The LINQ to SQL engine converts this tree into an equivalent SQL query, visiting the tree and generating the corresponding code. However, theoretically this translation can be made in many ways, all producing the same results, even if not all the translations are equally readable or perform as well. The actual implementation of LINQ to SQL generates good SQL code, favoring performance over query readability, although the readability of the generated code is often quite acceptable.

> **More Info** You can find more information about query reduction in a LINQ provider in the following post from Matt Warren: "LINQ: Building an IQueryable Provider - Part IX," located at *http://blogs.msdn.com/mattwar/archive/2008/01/16/linq-building-an-iqueryable-provider-part-ix.aspx*. Implementation of a query provider is covered in Chapter 15, "Extending LINQ."

We described this quality of LINQ to SQL because it is important to know that unnecessary parts of the query are removed before the query is sent to SQL Server. You can use this knowledge to compose LINQ queries in many ways—for example, by appending new predicates and projections to an originally large selection of rows and columns, without worrying too much about unnecessary elements left in the query.

The LINQ query in Listing 5-29 first makes a query on Customers, which filters those customers with a *CompanyName* longer than 10 characters. Those companies are then filtered by *Country*, operating on the anonymous type generated by the inner query.

LISTING 5-29 Example of query reduction

```
var query =
    from s in (
        from   c in db.Customers
        where  c.CompanyName.Length > 10
        select new { c.CustomerID, c.CompanyName, c.ContactName, c.City,
                    c.Country, c.ContactTitle, c.Address }
    )
    where s.Country == "UK"
    select new { s.CustomerID, s.CompanyName, s.City };
```

Despite the length of the LINQ query, here is the SQL query it generates:

```
SELECT [t0].[CustomerID], [t0].[CompanyName], [t0].[City]
FROM   [dbo].[Customers] AS [t0]
WHERE  ([t0].[Country] = @p0) AND (LEN([t0].[CompanyName]) > @p1)
```

The generated SQL query made two important reductions. First, the *FROM* operates on a single table instead of a *SELECT ... FROM (SELECT ... FROM ...)* composition that would normally be made when translating the original query tree. Second, unnecessary fields have been removed; only *CustomerID*, *CompanyName*, and *City* are part of the *SELECT* projection because they are the only fields necessary to the consumer of the LINQ query. The first reduction improves query readability; the second improves performance because it reduces the amount of data transferred from the database server to the client.

Mixing .NET Code with SQL Queries

As noted previously, LINQ to SQL has some known limitations with regard to using the full range of the .NET Framework features, not all of which can be entirely translated into corresponding T-SQL operations. This does not necessarily mean that you *cannot* write a query containing an unsupported method, but you should be aware that such a method cannot be translated into T-SQL and must be executed locally on the client. The side effect of this can be that sections of the query tree that depend on a .NET Framework method without a corresponding SQL translation will be executed completely as a LINQ to Objects operation, meaning that all the data must be transferred to the client to apply the required operators.

You can see this effect with some examples. Consider the LINQ query in Listing 5-30.

LISTING 5-30 LINQ query with a native string manipulation in the projection

```
var query1 =
    from   p in db.Products
    where  p.UnitPrice > 50
    select new {
        ProductName = "** " + p.ProductName + " **",
        p.UnitPrice };
```

The generated SQL query embodies the string manipulation of the *ProductName*:

```
SELECT ("** " + [t0].[ProductName]) + " **" AS [ProductName],
       [t0].[UnitPrice]
FROM [dbo].[Products] AS [t0]
WHERE [t0].[UnitPrice] > 50
```

Now suppose you move the string concatenation operation into a .NET Framework extension method, like that shown in Listing 5-31.

LISTING 5-31 String manipulation extension method

```
static public class Extensions {
    public static string Highlight(this string s) {
        return "** " + s + " **";
    }
}
```

Then you can modify the LINQ query using the *Highlight* method as in Listing 5-32.

LISTING 5-32 LINQ query calling a .NET Framework method in the projection

```
var query2 =
    from   p in db.Products
    where  p.UnitPrice > 50
    select new {
        ProductName = p.ProductName.Highlight(),
        p.UnitPrice };
```

The result produced by *query2* in Listing 5-32 is the same as the one produced by *query1* in Listing 5-30. However, the SQL query sent to the database is different because it lacks the string manipulation operation:

```
SELECT [t0].[ProductName] AS [s],
       [t0].[UnitPrice]
FROM   [dbo].[Products] AS [t0]
WHERE  [t0].[UnitPrice] > 50
```

The *ProductName* field is returned as *s* and will be used as an argument to the *Highlight* call. For each row, a call to the .NET Framework *Highlight* method will be made. This is not an issue when you are directly consuming the *query2* results. However, if you turn the same operation into a subquery, the dependent queries cannot be translated into a native SQL statement. For example, consider *query3* in Listing 5-33.

LISTING 5-33 LINQ query combining native and custom string manipulation

```
var query3 =
    from a in (
        from   p in db.Products
        where  p.UnitPrice > 50
        select new {
            ProductName = p.ProductName.Highlight(),
            p.UnitsInStock,
            p.UnitPrice
        }
    )
    select new {
        ProductName = a.ProductName.ToLower(),
        a.UnitPrice };
```

The SQL query produced by *query3* in Listing 5-33 is the same as the one produced by *query2* in Listing 5-32, despite the addition of another string manipulation (*ToLower*) to *ProductName*:

```
SELECT [t0].[ProductName] AS [s],
       [t0].[UnitPrice]
FROM   [dbo].[Products] AS [t0]
WHERE  [t0].[UnitPrice] > 50
```

If you remove the call to *Highlight* and restore the original string manipulation directly inside the LINQ query, you will get a complete native SQL query again, as shown in Listing 5-34.

LISTING 5-34 LINQ query using native string manipulation

```
var query4 =
    from a in (
            from   p in db.Products
            where  p.UnitPrice > 50
            select new {
                ProductName = "** " + p.ProductName + " **",
                p.UnitPrice
            }
    )
    select new {
        ProductName = a.ProductName.ToLower(),
        a.UnitPrice
    };
```

The *query4* in Listing 5-34 produces the following SQL query, which does not require further manipulations by .NET Framework code:

```
SELECT LOWER([t1].[value]) AS [ProductName], [t1].[UnitPrice]
FROM (
    SELECT ("** " + [t0].[ProductName]) + " **" AS [value],
           [t0].[UnitPrice]
    FROM [dbo].[Products] AS [t0]
    ) AS [t1]
WHERE [t1].[UnitPrice] > 50
```

Until now, we have seen that there is a possible performance implication only when using a .NET Framework method that does not have a corresponding SQL counterpart. However, there are situations that cannot be handled by the LINQ to SQL engine and which throw an exception at execution time—for example, if you try to use the result of the *Highlight* call in a *where* predicate as shown in Listing 5-35.

LISTING 5-35 LINQ query calling a .NET Framework method in a *where* predicate

```
var query5 =
    from   p in db.Products
    where  p.ProductName.Highlight().Length > 20
    select new {
        ProductName = p.ProductName.Highlight(),
        p.UnitPrice
    };
```

At execution time, trying to access to the *query5* result (or asking for the generated SQL query) will raise the following exception:

```
System.NotSupportedException
Method 'System.String Highlight(System.String)'
has no supported translation to SQL.
```

As you have seen, it is important to understand what operators are supported by LINQ to SQL, because the code could work or break at execution time, depending on the use of such operators. It is hard to define a rule of thumb other than to avoid the use of unsupported operators. If you think that a LINQ query is composable and can be used as a source to build another query, the only safe guideline is to use operators supported by LINQ to SQL.

Summary

This chapter covered LINQ to SQL features used to query data. With LINQ to SQL, you can query a relational structure stored in a SQL Server database so that you can convert LINQ queries into native SQL queries and access UDFs and stored procedures if required. LINQ to SQL handles entity classes that map an underlying physical database structure through attributes or external XML files. Stored procedures and UDFs can be mapped to methods of a class representing a SQL Server database. LINQ to SQL supports most of the basic LINQ features that you saw in Chapter 3.

Chapter 6
LINQ to SQL: Managing Data

The previous chapter primarily covered how you can *read* data with LINQ to SQL. The next step is understanding how to *modify* the data in a database using LINQ to SQL.

Luckily, by using entities, updating a column for a specific row in a table is as simple as changing a property of an entity instance. For example, the following code reads a product, increases its price by 5 percent by modifying the *UnitPrice* property, and then applies the in-memory changes to the database by calling *SubmitChanges*:

```
Product product = db.Products.Single(p => p.ProductID == 42);
product.UnitPrice *= 1.05M;
db.SubmitChanges();
```

In this chapter, you will see how to handle entity updates applied to the database, and investigate concurrency, transactions, exceptions, and entity serialization.

CRUD and CUD Operations

The acronym "CRUD" means Create, Read, Update, and Delete. These are the fundamental operations that a storage system provides. They correspond to the SQL statements *INSERT*, *SELECT*, *UPDATE*, and *DELETE*, respectively. Using LINQ to SQL, you usually perform read operations indirectly—by executing Microsoft Language Integrated Query (LINQ) queries or by accessing LINQ entities through their relationships without a direct call to a *SELECT* SQL statement. For this reason, LINQ to SQL documentation uses another acronym, CUD (Create, Update, and Delete), to describe all the operations that manipulate data through entities. This chapter focuses on CUD operations performed by operating on LINQ to SQL entities.

By default, LINQ to SQL tracks all entity instances through its *identity management service* to maintain a unique instance of a row of data. This service is guaranteed only for objects created or handled by a single *DataContext* instance. (This behavior has implications that you will see shortly.) Keeping a single instance of a row of data allows a *DataContext* instance to manipulate in-memory objects without concern for potential data inconsistencies or duplication in memory. You will see more about how to deal with concurrent operations in the "Concurrent Operations" section, later in this chapter.

 Important Remember that a class entity must have at least a column with the *IsPrimaryKey=true* setting in the *Column* attribute; otherwise, it cannot be tracked by the identity management service, and data manipulation is not allowed.

Entity Updates

Changing data members and properties of an entity instance is an operation tracked by the LINQ to SQL *change tracking service*. This service retains the original value of a modified entity. With this information, the service generates a corresponding list of SQL statements that make the same changes to the database. You can see the list of delete, update, and insert operations that will be applied to the relational database by calling the *GetChangeSet* method on the *DataContext*:

```
var customer = db.Customers.Single( c => c.CustomerID == "FRANS" );
customer.ContactName = "Marco Russo";
Helper.DumpChanges(db.GetChangeSet());
db.SubmitChanges();
```

The *Helper.DumpChanges* method shown in Listing 6-1 simply inspects the *ChangeSet* instance to display the planned operations. If you run the preceding code, you get the following output:

```
** UPDATES **
CustomerID=FRANS, CompanyName=Franchi S.p.A.
{Inserts: 0, Deletes: 0, Updates: 1}
```

At the end, the call to the *SubmitChanges* method sends a single UPDATE statement to the relational database:

```
UPDATE [Customers]
SET    [ContactName] = "Marco Russo"
FROM   [Customers]
WHERE  ...
```

We will discuss the *WHERE* condition later. Remember that no SQL statement gets sent to the database until you call *SubmitChanges*.

LISTING 6-1 Helper methods *DumpChanges* and *Dump*

```
public static void DumpChanges(ChangeSet changeSet) {
    if (changeSet.Deletes.Count > 0) {
        Console.WriteLine("** DELETES **");
        foreach (var del in changeSet.Deletes) {
            Console.WriteLine(Dump(del));
        }
    }
    if (changeSet.Updates.Count > 0) {
        Console.WriteLine("** UPDATES **");
        foreach (var upd in changeSet.Updates) {
            Console.WriteLine(Dump(upd));
        }
    }
```

```
    if (changeSet.Inserts.Count > 0) {
        Console.WriteLine("** INSERTS **");
        foreach (var ins in changeSet.Inserts) {
            Console.WriteLine(Dump(ins));
        }
    }
    Console.WriteLine(changeSet);
}

public static string Dump(this object data) {
    if (data is Customer) {
        Customer customer = (Customer) data;
        return String.Format(
            "CustomerID={0}, CompanyName={1}",
            customer.CustomerID, customer.CompanyName);
    }
    else {
        throw new NotSupportedException(
            String.Format(
                "Dump is not supported on {0}",
                data.GetType().FullName) );
    }
}
```

If you want to add a record to a table or remove a record from a table, creating or deleting an object in memory is not enough. The *DataContext* instance must also be notified. You can do this directly by calling *InsertOnSubmit* or *DeleteOnSubmit* on the corresponding *Table* collection. (These methods operate on the in-memory copy of the data; a subsequent *SubmitChanges* call will forward the SQL commands to the database.) The following code illustrates this process:

```
var newCustomer = new Customer {
                    CustomerID = "DLEAP",
                    CompanyName = "DevLeap",
                    Country = "Italy" };
db.Customers.InsertOnSubmit(newCustomer);

var oldDetail = db.Order_Details.Single(
            od => od.OrderID == 10422
                && od.ProductID == 26);
db.Order_Details.DeleteOnSubmit(oldDetail);
```

In the following code, you can see that the generated SQL statements contain single SQL *INSERT* and *DELETE* statements:

```
INSERT INTO [Customers](CustomerID, CompanyName, ...)
VALUES("DLEAP", "DevLeap", ...)

DELETE FROM [dbo].[Order Details]
WHERE [OrderID] = 10422 AND [ProductID] = 26 AND ...
```

Whenever a deleted entity is referenced by other entities, those references must be checked as well. You have to either remove related entities or change their relationship. You'll see more about this process later in this chapter, in the section "Cascading Deletes and Updates."

> **Note** Calling *InsertOnSubmit* or *DeleteOnSubmit* several times for the same object (entities have a unique identity) will not generate the same SQL statement multiple times. If you insert or delete the same entity many times, the change-tracking service ignores redundant calls.

Another way to notify the *DataContext* of a new entity is to attach the new entity to an existing object already tracked by *DataContext*:

```
var newCustomer = new Customer {
                    CustomerID = "DLEAP",
                    CompanyName = "DevLeap",
                    Country = "Italy" };
var order = db.Orders.Single( o => o.OrderID == 10248 );
order.Customer = newCustomer;
```

The examples just shown introduce the need to understand how relationships between entities work when updates are applied to the database. Relationships are bidirectional between entities, so when you update on one side, the other side should be kept synchronized. The class entity implementation must handle synchronization. Entity classes generated by code-generation tools, such as SQLMetal and Microsoft Visual Studio, usually offer this level of service.

> **More Info** SQLMetal and Visual Studio are covered in Chapter 7, "LINQ to SQL: Modeling Data and Tools."

The previous operation inserted a customer tied to order 10248. If you explore the *newCustomer* entity after the *order.Customer* assignment, you will see that its *Orders* properties contain order 10248. Executing the following code displays one row containing the order 10248:

```
foreach( var o in newCustomer.Orders ) {
    Console.WriteLine( "{0}-{1}", o.CustomerID, o.OrderID );
}
```

You can work in the opposite way, assigning an order to the *Orders* property of a customer. Consequently, the *Customer* property of the assigned order will be updated:

```
var oldCustomer = db.Customers.Single( c => c.CustomerID == "VINET" );
var newCustomer = new Customer {
                    CustomerID = "DLEAP",
                    CompanyName = "DevLeap",
                    Country = "Italy" };
```

```
db.Customers.Add( newCustomer );
var order = oldCustomer.Orders.Single( o => o.OrderID == 10248 );
oldCustomer.Orders.Remove( order );
newCustomer.Orders.Add( order );
```

Regardless of which way you modify the object model, the result is that you create a new *Customer* entity instance and modify an *Order* entity instance. Therefore, the generated SQL statements sent to the database on a *SubmitChanges* call are an *INSERT* followed by an *UPDATE*:

```
INSERT INTO [Customers](CustomerID, CompanyName, ...)
VALUES("DEVLEAP", "DevLeap", ...)

UPDATE [dbo].[Orders]
SET [CustomerID] = "DLEAP"
WHERE [OrderID] = 10248 AND ...
```

Even if a *Customer* is no longer referenced by other entities in memory, it is not automatically deleted by the change tracking service. You need to call *DeleteOnSubmit* on a *Table<T>* collection to delete a row in a database table.

Finally, there are dedicated methods to insert or delete a sequence of entities of the same type, called *InsertAllOnSubmit<T>* and *DeleteAllOnSubmit<T>*, respectively.

> **Important** As you saw in Chapter 5, "LINQ to SQL: Querying Data," you can disable the change-tracking service for a *DataContext* by specifying *false* on its *ObjectTrackingEnabled* property. Whenever you need to get data exclusively in a read-only mode—for example, to display a report or a web page in a noninteractive state—setting *ObjectTrackingEnabled* to *false* will improve overall performance.

Cascading Deletes and Updates

You have seen that there are two ways to add a record to a table (one direct and one indirect). However, you remove a row in a direct way, by calling the *DeleteOnSubmit* method on the corresponding *Table* collection. When you remove an object, you need to be sure that no other entities reference it; otherwise, calling *SubmitChanges* will throw an exception, because the SQL *DELETE* statement would violate some referential integrity constraint (such as *FOREIGN KEY* that is declared in the database). You can unbind related entities by setting their foreign key to NULL, but this might throw an exception if constraints do not allow NULL values. Another option is to remove the child objects from an object you want to remove by calling the *DeleteOnSubmit* method on them. You can do that by using the *DeleteAllOnSubmit* method:

```
var order = db.Orders.Single( o => o.OrderID == 10248 );
db.Orders.DeleteOnSubmit( order );
db.Order_Details.DeleteAllOnSubmit( order.Order_Details );
```

At the moment of calling *SubmitChanges*, this update generates SQL statements that respect the referential integrity constraints shown in the following statements:

```
DELETE FROM [Order Details] WHERE ([OrderID] = 10248) AND ([ProductID] = 11) AND ...
DELETE FROM [Order Details] WHERE ([OrderID] = 10248) AND ([ProductID] = 42) AND ...
DELETE FROM [Order Details] WHERE ([OrderID] = 10248) AND ([ProductID] = 72) AND ...
DELETE FROM [Orders] WHERE [OrderID] = 10248 AND ...
```

The order of *DeleteOnSubmit* and *DeleteAllOnSubmit* calls is not relevant. As you can see, the deletion of rows in the Order Details table precedes the deletion in the Orders table, despite the fact that the LINQ code specified the opposite order for deleting the LINQ entities. LINQ to SQL automatically creates SQL statements in a sequence that correctly respects referential integrity constraints during deletion.

 Note Even after a call to *SubmitChanges*, deleted entities are not removed from the *Table* collection and are still in memory, but they have a specific state, described in the next section, "Entity States."

Another possible cascading operation in a relational database is the cascading update. For example, changing the primary key of a *Customer* changes all the foreign keys in related entities referring to that *Customer*. However, LINQ to SQL does not let you change the primary key of an entity. Instead, you need to create a new *Customer*, change the references from the old *Customer* to the new one, and finally, remove the old *Customer*. This operation is shown in Listing 6-2.

LISTING 6-2 Replace a *Customer* on existing orders

```
var oldCustomer = db.Customers.Single(c => c.CustomerID == "FRANS");
Customer newCustomer = new Customer();
newCustomer.CustomerID = "CHNGE";
newCustomer.Address = oldCustomer.Address;
newCustomer.City = oldCustomer.City;
newCustomer.CompanyName = oldCustomer.CompanyName;
newCustomer.ContactName = oldCustomer.ContactName;
newCustomer.ContactTitle = oldCustomer.ContactTitle;
newCustomer.Country = oldCustomer.Country;
newCustomer.Fax = oldCustomer.Fax;
newCustomer.Orders = oldCustomer.Orders;
newCustomer.Phone = oldCustomer.Phone;
newCustomer.PostalCode = oldCustomer.PostalCode;
newCustomer.Region = oldCustomer.Region;
```

The code in Listing 6-2 shows how to substitute the customer that has the ID *FRANS* with a new customer that is identical to *FRANS*, except for the primary key, which the code sets to *CHNGE*. The code copies all the entity properties from the old entity to the new entity, but the most interesting part is the single-line assignment to the *Orders* property:

```
newCustomer.Orders = oldCustomer.Orders;
```

Assigning an *EntitySet<T>* property propagates the assignment to the *EntityRef* property of *T* entities, which corresponds to the foreign key of the related table. In other words, that one line changes all the entities in *Orders*, setting their *Customer* property to *newCustomer*. This synchronization is implemented by the *Customer* entity class generated by SQLMetal or Visual Studio, which contains the code necessary to make the synchronization work.

> **Warning** LINQ to SQL does not support cascading operations. If a foreign key in the relational database is declared with the *ON DELETE CASCADE* or *ON UPDATE CASCADE* option, and if the affected entities have already been loaded into memory, a cascading update to the database is not propagated into the object model of LINQ to SQL. That kind of update should be the result of a direct SQL statement and not of SQL code generated by LINQ to SQL. In the latter case, the LINQ to SQL entities are not declared with associations corresponding to existing foreign keys in the relational database.

Entity States

Each entity instance has a state in a *DataContext* that defines its synchronization state in relation to the relational database. Moreover, each operation on an entity modifies its state to reflect the operation necessary to synchronize the relational database with the in-memory entity instance. The possible states of an instance are represented in Figure 6-1.

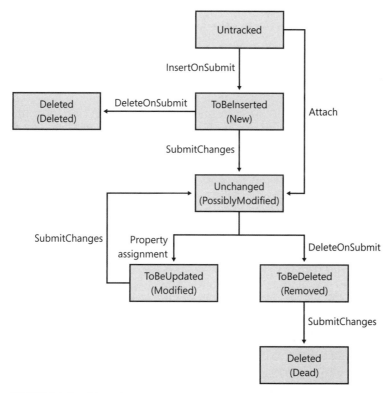

FIGURE 6-1 Possible entity states.

In Figure 6-1, the names in the boxes, outside the parentheses, show the state names used by the LINQ to SQL documentation, and the names within parentheses show the name of the *StandardChangeTracker.StandardTrackedObject.State* enumeration, which is an internal implementation mapped to LINQ to SQL. The following list shows the state definitions:

- **Untracked**   This is not a true state. It identifies an object that is not tracked by LINQ to SQL. A newly created object is always in this state until it is attached to a *DataContext*. Because this state reflects the relationship of an entity in a given *DataContext*, an entity created as a result of a *DataContext* instance query is *Untracked* by other *DataContext* instances. Finally, after deserialization, an entity instance is always *Untracked*.

- **Unchanged**   The initial state of an object retrieved by using the current *DataContext*.

- **PossiblyModified**   An object attached to a *DataContext*. Figure 6-1 represents the two states *Unchanged* and *PossiblyModified* within the same box (state).

- **ToBeInserted**   An object not retrieved by using the current *DataContext*. This is a newly created object that has been added with an *InsertOnSubmit* to a *Table<T>* collection, or that has been added to an *EntitySet<T>* of an existing entity instance.

- **ToBeUpdated**   An object that has been modified since it was retrieved. This state is set by changing any property value of an entity that was retrieved using the current *DataContext*.

- **ToBeDeleted**   An object marked for deletion by calling *DeleteOnSubmit*.

- **Deleted**   An object that has been deleted in the database. The entity instance for this object still exists in memory with this particular state. If you want to reuse the primary key of a *Deleted* entity, you need to define a new entity in a different *DataContext*.

You will see how to manipulate and customize entity classes in the "Customizing Insert, Update, and Delete" section, later in this chapter. At this stage, you just need to understand that the LINQ to SQL engine must track entity states to update the relational database correctly. You cannot directly access and manipulate the state of an entity.

Entity Synchronization

After you write an entity to the database by calling *SubmitChanges*, a change might be made directly to a column of the database table out of LINQ to SQL control. For example, an identity, trigger, or time stamp might write a value to the database. This value cannot be known in advance by the entity and must be read from the database after the *SubmitChanges* call. Therefore, before you use an entity you have written with a call to *SubmitChanges*, you probably need to update its values by re-reading the entity from the database. LINQ to SQL helps automate this process by providing the *AutoSync* parameter to the *Column* attribute that decorates entity properties. For each column, this parameter can have one of the following values provided by the *System.Data.Linq.Mapping.AutoSync* enumeration:

- **Default**   The entity update is automatically handled, based on known metadata of the column itself. For example, an IsDbGenerated column will be read after an *Insert* operation, and an IsVersion column will be updated after any *Update* or *Insert* operation.

- **Always**   The column is always updated from the database after any *SubmitChanges* call.

- **Never**   The column is never updated from the database.

- **OnInsert**   The column is updated from the database after the *SubmitChanges* call that inserts the entity.

- **OnUpdate**   The column is updated from the database after the *SubmitChanges* call that updates the entity.

The *AutoSync.Default* value should be a good choice most of the time because it defines a behavior that is consistent with the metadata defined for your entities. However, if you have triggers operating on a table that modify columns as part of their work, you might need to set the *AutoSync* property to a specific value. Remember that this synchronization system cannot automatically create and read new entities; it can only modify existing ones. For example, if you have a trigger that adds new rows to a table as a result of a database operation, you will need to read those new entities by executing a specific query to the database.

Database Updates

LINQ to SQL sends many SQL queries to the database in a transparent and implicit way. On the other hand, SQL commands that modify database state are sent only when you explicitly call *SubmitChanges* on the *DataContext* object (which is eventually derived in a more specialized class), as shown in Listing 6-3. The *Northwind* class here is derived from *DataContext*.

LISTING 6-3 Submit changes to the database

```
Northwind db = new Northwind( Connections.ConnectionString );
var customer = db.Customers.Single( c => c.CustomerID == "FRANS" );
customer.ContactName = "Marco Russo";
db.SubmitChanges();
```

The instance of *DataContext* (or the derived class) is similar to a database connection. It embeds all tracking information in addition to connection data. Despite its features, a *DataContext* instance is a lightweight object suitable for use in both client-server and n-tier applications. In the first case, you might create a *DataContext* object on the client side and keep it alive for the entire lifetime of the application. In an n-tier application, the data layer (where LINQ to SQL could be used) is typically a stateless intermediate layer. The *DataContext* class has been conceived with all these scenarios in mind. Its activation cost at run time has a small performance impact, so you can create new *DataContext* instances on demand without needing a complex cache system.

More Info You will find more information about the n-tier architecture in Chapter 18, "LINQ in a Multitier Solution."

The role of *SubmitChanges* is simply to send to the database a set of *INSERT*, *UPDATE*, and *DELETE* SQL statements, handling update conflicts at the database level. (Conflict handling will be discussed later in this chapter in the "Exceptions" section.) These statements are generated starting from the list of entities that need to be deleted, updated, and inserted. That list is accessible through a *ChangeSet* instance returned by the *DataContext.GetChangeSet* method, as you saw earlier in this chapter. This list of updated entities no longer provides the number and order of changes applied to the entities, but it does reflect the final result of all the modifications. We call this set of updated entities a *unit of work*.

More Info For a definition of the unit of work pattern, see "Unit of Work," by Martin Fowler, at *http://www.martinfowler.com/eaaCatalog/unitOfWork.html*.

The default implementation of *SubmitChanges* transforms the list of updated entities in a set of SQL statements and sends these commands in a particular order, following the requirements enforced by existing relationships between entities. For example, you can add and update *Order* and *Order_Detail* instances in any order in your object model. However, an Order_Details row will be inserted in the relational database only after the parent *Orders* row has been inserted, adhering to the foreign key relationship for *OrderID*. As noted earlier, the default *SubmitChanges* implementation produces the correct SQL statement order by analyzing these dependencies. However, *SubmitChanges* is a virtual method that you can override if you need to control this logic or change its behavior.

Overriding *SubmitChanges*

In some cases, you may need to override the *DataContext.SubmitChanges* instance method or simply intercept calls to it. For example, you might want to log updated entities, as shown in Listing 6-4. (The *Helper.DumpChanges* method called in Listing 6-4 was shown earlier in Listing 6-1.)

LISTING 6-4 Specialized *SubmitChanges* to log modified entities

```
public class CustomNorthwind : Northwind {
    public CustomNorthwind(string connectionString) :
        base(connectionString) { }

    public override void SubmitChanges(ConflictMode failureMode) {
        Helper.DumpChanges(this.GetChangeSet());
        base.SubmitChanges(failureMode);
    }
}
```

You might want to change the entities contained in the *ChangeSet* result returned by *GetChangeSet*. For example, the following code could be an interesting pattern to use to populate audit fields in an entity:

```
public partial class MyDataContext : DataContext {
    public override void SubmitChanges(ConflictMode failureMode) {
        ChangeSet cs = this.GetChangeSet();
        foreach(object entity in cs.Inserts) {
            if (entity is Employee) {
                Employee e = (Employee)entity;
                e.CreatedByUser = GetCurrentUser();
                e.CreationTime = DateTime.Now;
            }
        }
        base.SubmitChanges(failureMode);
    }
}
```

The previous code is applicable when the same action is used on entities of different types. Whenever you need to intercept a particular operation (insert, update, or delete) of a particular entity type (*Employee*, in this case), you can implement either the *UpdateTYPE*, *InsertTYPE*, or *DeleteTYPE* method, described in the "Stored Procedures" section later this chapter.

A more complex operation you can perform in *SubmitChanges* is to resolve circular references. The standard implementation of *SubmitChanges* throws an exception if it detects a circular reference when it evaluates the relationships between affected entities. For example, consider the following code that creates two instances of *Employee*:

```
Northwind db = new CustomNorthwind(Connections.ConnectionString);
Employee empMarco = new Employee();
db.Employees.InsertOnSubmit(empMarco);
empMarco.FirstName = "Marco";
empMarco.LastName = "Russo";
Employee empPaolo = new Employee();
empPaolo.FirstName = "Paolo";
empPaolo.LastName = "Pialorsi";
empPaolo.Employees.Add(empMarco);
empMarco.Employees.Add(empPaolo);
```

The preceding code describes a situation where *empMarco* reports to *empPaolo* and vice versa. This scenario might be nonsensical in the real world, but there are situations where circular references between entities could be meaningful. The well-known *Employees* table suffices for this example. If you try to call *SubmitChanges* for this code, the following exception will be thrown:

```
System.InvalidOperationException: A cycle was detected in the set of changes
```

If you want to build such a relationship, you need to break the cycle by using two *SubmitChanges*, as in the following code:

```
Northwind db = new CustomNorthwind(Connections.ConnectionString);
Employee empMarco = new Employee();
db.Employees.InsertOnSubmit(empMarco);
empMarco.FirstName = "Marco";
empMarco.LastName = "Russo";
Employee empPaolo = new Employee();
empPaolo.FirstName = "Paolo";
empPaolo.LastName = "Pialorsi";
empPaolo.Employees.Add(empMarco);
db.SubmitChanges();
empMarco.Employees.Add(empPaolo);
db.SubmitChanges();
```

You can build a custom *SubmitChanges* implementation that automatically handles your possible source of cycles. Please note that solving cycles properly requires you to make some assumptions about the kind of intermediate operations that are allowed. For this reason, there is no general-purpose solution to this kind of problem. Listing 6-5 shows a possible implementation of *SubmitChanges*.

LISTING 6-5 Specialized *SubmitChanges* to solve circular references of *Employee* entities

```
public class CircularReferenceNorthwind : Northwind {
    public CircularReferenceNorthwind(string connectionString) :
        base(connectionString) { }

    public override void SubmitChanges(ConflictMode failureMode) {
        Dictionary<Employee, Employee> employeeReferences;
        employeeReferences = new Dictionary<Employee, Employee>();

        // Remove and save references to other employees
        ChangeSet cs = this.GetChangeSet();
        foreach (object entity in cs.Inserts) {
            if (entity is Employee) {
                Employee e = (Employee) entity;
                employeeReferences.Add(e, e.Employee1);
                e.Employee1 = null;
            }
        }
        // Save Employees without references to other employees
        base.SubmitChanges(failureMode);

        // Restore references to other employees
        foreach (var item in employeeReferences) {
            item.Key.Employee1 = item.Value;
        }

        // Update Employees with references to other employees
        base.SubmitChanges(failureMode);
    }
}
```

This implementation makes an initial *SubmitChanges* call that inserts *Employee* entities. From this call, references to other employees have been removed (and saved in temporary objects). Then after inserting the employees, it restores the original employee references, and makes a second *SubmitChanges* call. The second call sends two *UPDATE* SQL statements that modify the two employees inserted with the first *SubmitChanges* call.

Customizing *Insert*, *Update*, and *Delete*

When submitting changes, you can override the default insert, update, and delete SQL statements generated by LINQ to SQL. To override these defaults, you can define one or more methods with specific signatures and pattern names. The following code is the syntax to use. Note that you need to replace *TYPE* in this syntax with the name of the modified type you are using:

```
public void UpdateTYPE(TYPE original, TYPE current) { ... }
public void InsertTYPE(TYPE inserted) { ... }
public void DeleteTYPE(TYPE deleted) { ... }
```

> **Important** The name of the method is important. The LINQ to SQL engine looks for a method with a matching signature and that has a name that starts with the word corresponding to the operation you are overriding (*Update*, *Insert*, or *Delete*), followed by the name of the modified type.

Stored Procedures

Usually, you use these specific overrides to call stored procedures rather than sending SQL statements that modify data in the database. You must define these methods on the *DataContext*-derived class. Because a derived class is already generated by a tool (such as SQLMetal or the Object Relational Designer in Visual Studio), which also creates partial methods with the correct signatures, you can add your methods using the *partial* class syntax, as shown in Listing 6-6. This example assumes that only changes in *UnitsInStock* properties need to be tracked, so it calls a stored procedure that updates only that value. The example also gets the original version of the *Product* entity using the *GetOriginalEntityState* method, which we will discuss in more detail in the "Concurrent Operations" section later in this chapter.

LISTING 6-6 Stored procedure to override an update

```
public partial class Northwind {
    partial void UpdateProduct(Product current) {
        Product original = ((Product) (Products.GetOriginalEntityState(current)));

        // Execute the stored procedure for UnitsInStock update
        if (original.UnitsInStock != current.UnitsInStock) {
            int rowCount = this.ExecuteCommand(
                            "exec UpdateProductStock " +
                            "@id={0}, @originalUnits={1}, @decrement={2}",
                            original.ProductID,
                            original.UnitsInStock,
                            (original.UnitsInStock - current.UnitsInStock));
            if (rowCount < 1) {
                throw new ChangeConflictException();
            }
        }
    }
}
```

 Important Conflict detection is your responsibility if you decide to override insert, update, and delete methods.

Intercepting *Insert*, *Update*, and *Delete* Operations

Implementing an *UpdateTYPE*, *InsertTYPE*, or *DeleteTYPE* method replaces the regular dynamic SQL statement generation. However, you can still make use of that behavior by calling *ExecuteDynamicUpdate*, *ExecuteDynamicInsert*, or *ExecuteDynamicDelete*, respectively. Using these methods, you can intercept the original process of an entity by placing your own code just before and after the dynamic SQL statement execution. For example, you can populate audit fields in an entity just as you did before overriding the *SubmitChanges* method; in this case, you have already filtered for only the desired entities. Here is an excerpt from a customized *InsertEmployee* method:

```
public partial class Northwind : DataContext {
    partial void InsertEmployee(Employee employee) {
        employee.CreatedByUser = GetCurrentUser();
        employee.CreationTime = DateTime.Now;
        base.ExecuteDynamicUpdate(employee);
    }
}
```

Database Interaction

Interaction with the database involves handling concurrent operations, transactions, and exceptions. This section examines what you need to know to write robust code using LINQ to SQL to interact with a database.

Concurrent Operations

Operating with in-memory entities in LINQ is a form of disconnected operations on data. In these cases, you always have to deal with concurrent operations made by other users or connections between the reading of data and its successive updates. Usually, you operate with optimistic concurrency. When a conflict occurs, a *ChangeConflictException* error is thrown by default. This exception contains a *ChangeConflicts* collection of *ObjectChangeConflict* instances that explains the reasons for the error. (Several conflicts can occur on different tables within a single *SubmitChanges* call.) Each *ObjectChangeConflict* instance describes the entity (a row of a table) conflict and contains a list of affected members in *MemberConflicts*. Listing 6-7 provides a demonstration, displaying information about a conflict by using the *Display-ChangeConflict* method.

LISTING 6-7 Retry loop for a concurrency conflict

```
public static void ConcurrentUpdates() {
    // ...
    Northwind db2 = new Northwind(Connections.ConnectionString);
    var customer2 = db2.Customers.Single(c => c.CustomerID == "FRANS");
    customer2.ContactName = "Paolo Pialorsi";

    for (int retry = 1; retry < 4; retry++) {
        Console.WriteLine("Retry loop {0}", retry);

        try {
            db2.SubmitChanges(); // Throws exception
            break;               // Exit from while if submit succeed
        }
        catch (ChangeConflictException ex) {
            Console.WriteLine(ex.Message);
            DisplayChangeConflict(db2);
            db2.Refresh(RefreshMode.KeepChanges,customer2);
        }
    }
    // ...
}

private static void DisplayChangeConflict(Northwind db) {
    foreach (ObjectChangeConflict occ in db.ChangeConflicts) {
        MetaTable metatable = db.Mapping.GetTable(occ.Object.GetType());
        Customer entityInConflict = occ.Object as Customer;
```

```
    Console.WriteLine(
        "Table={0}, IsResolved={1}",
        metatable.TableName, occ.IsResolved);
    foreach (MemberChangeConflict mcc in occ.MemberConflicts) {
        object currVal = mcc.CurrentValue;
        object origVal = mcc.OriginalValue;
        object databaseVal = mcc.DatabaseValue;
        MemberInfo mi = mcc.Member;
        Console.WriteLine("Member: {0}", mi.Name);
        Console.WriteLine("current value: {0}", currVal);
        Console.WriteLine("original value: {0}", origVal);
        Console.WriteLine("database value: {0}", databaseVal);
    }
  }
}
```

For each conflicting member, there are three values available, which are members of a *MemberChangeConflict* instance:

- **CurrentValue**   The value of the member in the entity instance that you wanted to write in the current *DataContext*.

- **OriginalValue**   The original value of the member when the entity was read from the database before its modification in the current *DataContext*.

- **DatabaseValue**   The value of the member that is currently stored in the database. The database has changed from *OriginalValue* to *DatabaseValue* since you read the entity, and you have to make a decision about which value you want to keep.

After a conflict, you might decide to re-read all the data, or rely on the *Refresh* method, as demonstrated in the previous code sample. The *Refresh* method updates data in memory according to the argument passed, which can have three possible values:

- **RefreshMode.KeepChanges**   Only the *CurrentValue* values that are different from *OriginalValue* are preserved. All other *CurrentValue* values are equal to *OriginalValue*, and they are both updated to *DatabaseValue*.

- **RefreshMode.KeepCurrentValues**   Keeps the *CurrentValue*, assigning the *DatabaseValue* to the *OriginalValue*. In other words, after *Refresh*, the original entity state is set to the current database values. Current entity values are unchanged after this *Refresh*; thus, a subsequent call to *SubmitChanges* attempts to save the *CurrentValue* to the database.

- **RefreshMode.OverwriteCurrentValues**   Discards any change made on the entity, replacing both *OriginalValue* and *CurrentValue* with the *DatabaseValue*.

KeepChanges and *KeepCurrentValues* are identical for changed values, but differ in how they handle unchanged values. *KeepCurrentValues* overwrites any database changes to the entity made since the original read, while *KeepChanges* merges the updates made to the entity with the updates made to the relational database.

For example, assume you are executing the code in Listing 6-7 in the following scenario. You read the *Customer* entity, which has a *ContactName* equal to Paolo Accorti and *City* equal to Torino. This is the *OriginalValue* of your entity, which you have modified by setting *ContactName* to Paolo Pialorsi. At this point, the entity in memory has a *CurrentValue* of *ContactName* set to Paolo Pialorsi, but the *City* property is still set to Torino. In the meantime, someone else modifies the database, setting *ContactName* to Marco Russo and *City* to Milano.

Table 6-1 describes this situation in the first row, which has a gray background. This row exemplifies a typical situation when you would get a *ChangeConflictException* when calling *SubmitChanges*. At this point, any *Refresh* call will change the *OriginalValue* of your entity, setting it to the current *DatabaseValue*, because this is the only way to successfully call *SubmitChanges* later. The different values of the *RefreshMode* enumeration passed to *Refresh* determine the final state of the *CurrentValue* of your entity, which will correspond to what will be saved to the database in an ensuing call to *SubmitChanges*. As you can see in Table 6-1, you can handle all possible combinations by choosing the appropriate value for this parameter.

TABLE 6-1 Effects of *RefreshMode* argument to *Refresh*

	CurrentValue	OriginalValue	DatabaseValue
ChangeConflictException	Paolo Pialorsi Torino	Paolo Accorti Torino	**Marco Russo Milano**
KeepChanges	Paolo Pialorsi **Milano**	Marco Russo Milano	Marco Russo Milano
KeepCurrentValues	Paolo Pialorsi Torino	Marco Russo Milano	Marco Russo Milano
OverwriteCurrentValues	**Marco Russo Milano**	Marco Russo Milano	Marco Russo Milano

Important Remember that *Refresh* just updates in-memory entity values. No matter which *RefreshMode* argument you use, your next call to *SubmitChanges* submits the *CurrentValue* values. Moreover, do not confuse the roles of *OverwriteCurrentValues* and *RefreshMode*. These can be easily misinterpreted as "overwrite the current database values" rather than "overwrite the current in-memory entity values," which is the real effect.

SubmitChanges accepts a parameter that specifies whether you want to stop at the first conflict or try all updates regardless of the conflict. The default is to stop at the first conflict:

```
db.SubmitChanges(ConflictMode.FailOnFirstConflict);

db.SubmitChanges(ConflictMode.ContinueOnConflict);
```

Column Attributes for Concurrency Control

You can control how a concurrency conflict is determined by using an entity class definition. Each *Column* attribute can have an *UpdateCheck* argument that can have one of the following three values:

- **Always**   Always use this column (which is the default) for conflict detection.
- **Never**   Never use this column for conflict detection.
- **WhenChanged**   Use this column only when the member has been changed by the application.

> **Note** LINQ to SQL generates shorter and faster SQL queries when a column is *not* considered for conflict detection when updating entities. However, remember that, by default, columns that are not checked for conflict detection are not updated in the entities when they are changed in the database after the initial read. Check the *AutoSync* column setting to get this kind of update; otherwise, you have to be sure that you do not use such columns after the *SubmitChanges* call, because those columns might not reflect the actual state of the database.

Other options for column definitions are represented by two Boolean flags: *IsDBGenerated* indicates that the value is autogenerated by the database, and *IsVersion* identifies a database time stamp or a version number. If a column has *IsVersion* set to *true*, the concurrency conflict is identified and only the entity's unique key and its time stamp/version column are compared. A typical use of *IsVersion* is for a *LastUpdate* column of the Microsoft SQL Server type *TIMESTAMP*. In this case, *IsDbGenerated* is set to *true* too, because a *TIMESTAMP* value is generated from SQL Server:

```
[Column(Storage="_lastUpdate", AutoSync=AutoSync.Always,
        CanBeNull=false, IsDbGenerated=true, IsVersion=true)]
public System.Data.Linq.Binary LastUpdate {
    get { return this._lastUpdate; }
}

private Binary _lastUpdate = default(Binary);
```

> **Note** Updates and deletes can have a long *WHERE* condition when no *IsVersion* column is speci-
> fied. Using *IsVersion* simplifies the query sent to the database to check concurrency conflicts. Only
> the column with *IsVersion* set to *true* is part of the *WHERE* condition that tries to match the record
> previously read. If that record has been changed in the meantime, a *ChangeConflictException* will
> be thrown.
>
> *IsDBGenerated* and *IsVersion* require LINQ to SQL to submit a *SELECT* statement after each
> *UPDATE* or *INSERT* operation. The relative advantages and disadvantages between having an
> *IsVersion* column and not having one depend on the number and complexity of table columns.

Transactions

A *SubmitChanges* call automatically starts a database-explicit transaction unless a
transaction is already active in the connection being used. *SubmitChanges* initially calls
IDbConnection.BeginTransaction and then applies all changes made in memory to the
database, inside the same transaction. Using the *TransactionScope* class contained in the
System.Transactions library since Microsoft .NET Framework 2.0, you can add any standard
command to the database or change any other transactional resource within the same transaction. Eventually, this transaction will be transparently promoted to a distributed transaction.
Listing 6-8 shows an example of a transaction controlled in this way.

LISTING 6-8 Transaction controlled by *TransactionScope*

```
Northwind db = new Northwind(Connections.ConnectionString);
Order_Detail orderDetail = db.Order_Details.Single(
                            o => o.OrderID == 10248
                                 && o.ProductID == 42);

if (orderDetail.Quantity >= 10) {
    orderDetail.Discount = 0.05F;
}

using (TransactionScope ts = new TransactionScope()) {
    db.SubmitChanges();
    ts.Complete();
}
```

When an exception occurs, the database transaction is canceled. If you do not call the *Complete*
method on the *TransactionScope* instance, the transaction automatically performs a rollback
when the *TransactionScope* instance is disposed of. (This happens when *ts* goes out of scope—
the *using* statement makes an automatic call to *Dispose*.)

If you have an existing Microsoft ADO.NET application that does not use *System.Transactions*, you can control database transactions by accessing the *DataContext.Transaction* property. For example, Listing 6-9 shows how to implement direct control of the transaction. In this case, the *Transaction.Commit* call is equivalent to the *TransactionScope.Complete* call made in Listing 6-8. However, you will usually use this technique when the connection (and the transaction) encloses direct ADO.NET calls.

LISTING 6-9 Transaction controlled through the *DataContext.Transaction* property

```
Northwind db = new Northwind(Connections.ConnectionString);
db.Connection.Open();
Order_Detail orderDetail = db.Order_Details.Single(
                            o => o.OrderID == 10248
                                 && o.ProductID == 42);

if (orderDetail.Quantity >= 10) {
    orderDetail.Discount = 0.05F;
}
using (db.Transaction = db.Connection.BeginTransaction()) {
    db.SubmitChanges();
    db.Transaction.Commit();
}
```

Exceptions

LINQ to SQL defines only the following exception classes:

- **System.Data.Linq.ChangeConflictException**   Thrown when change conflict is detected during updates (values have been updated since the client last read them).

- **System.Data.Linq.DuplicateKeyException**   Thrown when you attempt to add an object to the identity cache using a key that is already being used.

- **System.Data.Linq.ForeignKeyReferenceAlreadyHasValueException**   Thrown when an attempt is made to change a foreign key when the entity is already loaded.

However, you might need to handle exceptions of different types, thrown in different parts of your program. The following sections describe the most critical points.

DataContext Construction

When you call the constructor of a *DataContext*-derived class, errors in the attribute definitions of entities tied to the *DataContext* can cause a run-time exception. Usually, these kinds of errors cannot be recovered because you do not have a valid model to work with—as in, for example, the following incorrect storage definition:

```
private EntitySet<Order> _Orders;

[Association(OtherKey="CustomerID", Storage="_Wrong")]
public EntitySet<Order> Orders {
    get { return this._Orders; }
    set { this._Orders.Assign(value); }
}
```

This definition maps _Wrong instead of _Orders and produces the following exception:

```
System.InvalidOperationException: Bad Storage property: '_Order_Details1'
on member 'DevLeap.Linq.LinqToSql.Product.Order_Details'.
```

You won't get these kinds of errors if you generate the LINQ to SQL entities using a tool such as SQLMetal or Visual Studio. However, if you manually build your own queries, remember that the Microsoft Visual C# compiler cannot identify such errors at compile time.

Database Reads

Whenever you access the database, an exception is possible: SQL Server might not be active, data tables might have a different structure than you expected, and so on. Given the nature of LINQ to SQL, you might access the database in a very indirect way. For example, accessing a property might require reading an uncached entity from the database. The following code might throw an exception when accessing the *Customer* property of an *Order* for the first time because it might require access to the database:

```
public static void WriteOrderDestination(Order order) {
    Console.WriteLine(order.Customer.City);
}
```

The beauty of database access abstraction comes at a price: you cannot identify a specific point at which to access the database, as you can do in a data layer. If you distribute LINQ to SQL entities across the logical tiers of your application, you will have access to the database at several points. In a small application with a local database, this might not be an issue, but you might want to avoid such loss of control in a more complex application.

More Info You can be sure you have all required entities in memory by using *DataContext.Load-Options* and disabling deferred loading using its *DeferredLoadingEnabled* setting, as discussed in Chapter 4, "Choosing Between LINQ to SQL and LINQ to Entities."

Database Writes

Updated, inserted, and deleted LINQ to SQL entities are modified in the database at very specific and controlled points: only when you call *DataContext.SubmitChanges*. To highlight this behavior, *Table<T>* methods are named *InsertOnSubmit* and *DeleteOnSubmit*. However, remember that a *SubmitChanges* call can affect many more entities than those that were directly added, updated, or removed by calling these methods.

> **Warning** When you call *SubmitChanges*, in addition to the specific *ChangeConflictException* error discussed in the "Concurrent Operations" section earlier in this chapter, you might get an ADO.NET database access-related exception.

Entity Manipulation

Creating and manipulating entities might throw exceptions when there is an attempt to perform an operation not allowed by the change-tracking service. Two exceptions that might be thrown when accessing entity properties are the following:

- **DuplicateKeyException**   Thrown when an attempt is made to add an object to the identity cache using a key that is already in use—for example, when you try to add two different entities to a table that have the same primary key.

- **ForeignKeyReferenceAlreadyHasValueException**   Thrown when an attempt is made to change a foreign key but the entity is already loaded. This exception is thrown by the entity code generated by tools such as SQLMetal and Visual Studio.

Databases and Entities

Any update operation on the database made through LINQ to SQL requires the definition of proper entities mapping the underlying database structure. This final part of the chapter covers important details about entity definitions and manipulation that are useful in implementing a real-world application using LINQ to SQL.

Entity Attributes to Maintain Valid Relationships

Entity classes can have relationships with other entities, just as tables can in a relational database. Whereas a relational database declares the parent-child relationship only by declaring a foreign key on the child side, LINQ to SQL entities can show the relationship on both sides,

through the use of the *Association* attribute to decorate properties that define the relationships, as explained in Chapter 5. Implementing properties decorated with *Association* requires
code to establish the synchronization between in-memory entities when you manipulate
them. Thanks to this bidirectional synchronization, the programmer needs to update only one
side of the relationship; the entity code will synchronize the other side. Usually, you generate
that entity's code using a tool such as SQLMetal or Visual Studio.

For example, if you have two entities, *Product* and *Category*, these entities probably have a
one-to-many relationship. Each *Product* can belong to one *Category*, and each *Category* has a
set of related *Products*. The code generated by tools for the *Category* property in the *Product*
class will be like that shown in the following code. It updates the *Products* set in the *Category*-
related entities by removing the product from the old *Category* and then adding the product to the assigned *Category*. In other words, assigning the *Category* property to a *Product*
instance also updates the *Products* property of the referenced *Category* instance:

```
public partial class Product {
    [Association(Name = "Category_Product", Storage = "_Category",
                ThisKey = "CategoryID", IsForeignKey = true)]
    public Category Category {
        get { return this._Category.Entity; }
        set {
            Category previousValue = this._Category.Entity;
            if (((previousValue != value)
                || (this._Category.HasLoadedOrAssignedValue == false))) {
                this.SendPropertyChanging();
                if ((previousValue != null)) {
                    this._Category.Entity = null;
                    previousValue.Products.Remove(this);
                }
                this._Category.Entity = value;
                if ((value != null)) {
                    value.Products.Add(this);
                    this._CategoryID = value.CategoryID;
                }
                else {
                    this._CategoryID = default(Nullable<int>);
                }
                this.SendPropertyChanged("Category");
            }
        }
    }
}
```

The remaining part of the synchronization process sets the *Category* property of a *Product*
instance whenever that *Product* instance is added to the *Products* property of a *Category*
instance. This assignment is made through the *EntitySet<T>* type, which must be correctly initialized with the actions to be called to maintain the synchronization. The following example
shows the tool-generated code for the *Products* property of the *Category* class:

```
public partial class Category {
    private EntitySet<Product> _Products;

    public Category() {
        this._Products = new EntitySet<Product>(
                            new Action<Product>(this.attach_Products),
                            new Action<Product>(this.detach_Products));
        OnCreated();
    }

    [Association(Name="Category_Product", Storage="_Products",
                OtherKey="CategoryID")]
    public EntitySet<Product> Products {
        get { return this._Products; }
        set { this._Products.Assign(value); }
    }

    private void attach_Products(Product entity) {
        this.SendPropertyChanging();
        entity.Category = this;
    }

    private void detach_Products(Product entity) {
        this.SendPropertyChanging();
        entity.Category = null;
    }
}
```

If a programmer manually assigns both sides of a relationship, the second assignment will simply be redundant.

Deriving Entity Classes

In Chapter 5, you saw how to define an entity class derived from another one, as in the following code:

```
[Table(Name="Contacts")]
[InheritanceMapping(Code = "Customer", Type = typeof(CustomerContact))]
[InheritanceMapping(Code = "Supplier", Type = typeof(SupplierContact))]
[InheritanceMapping(Code = "Employee", Type = typeof(Employee), IsDefault = true)]
public class Contact {
    [Column(IsPrimaryKey=true)] public int ContactID;
    [Column(IsDiscriminator = true)] public string ContactType;
    // ...
}

public class CompanyContact : Contact {
    [Column(Name="CompanyName")] public string Company;
}
public class CustomerContact : CompanyContact {
}
```

```
public class SupplierContact : CompanyContact {
}

public class Employee : Contact {
    [Column] public string PhotoPath;
    [Column(UpdateChack=UpdateCheck.Never)] public Binary Photo;
}
```

These classes can be represented graphically with the hierarchy shown in Figure 6-2.

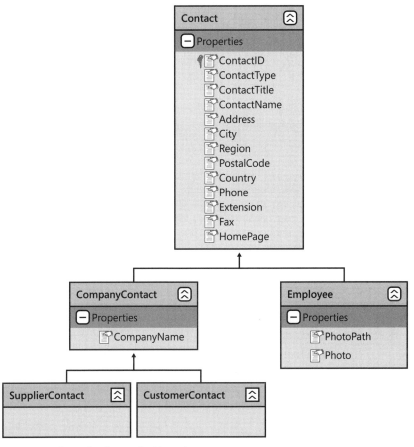

FIGURE 6-2 Example of an entity hierarchy.

This hierarchy has three different types used by your program: *SupplierContact*, *CustomerContact*, and *Employee*. There are also two classes, *Contact* and *CompanyContact*, which would be "abstract" from a C# point of view, even if a tool-generated class is always a type that can be instantiated. In reality, all these types are stored in the same table (Contact), with some columns used only by some types and not by others. The various types are differentiated via the *ContactType* column value (the discriminator field) in each row. The choice made by deriving specific types from the same table has several advantages:

- **Strong type check**   You create and manipulate entities of the right type corresponding to the discriminator field value.

- **Centralization of discrimination logic**   There is only one point (in the model) where the discriminating field is defined. You do not have dispatching logic potentially duplicated in your code.

- **Clear code**   You can write methods (and extension methods) that operate on fields specific to certain types of records, without writing conditional code to check the value of the discriminator field.

Whenever you have very similar entities stored in the same table, differentiated by some fields that are specific to a certain group of records, consider using entity inheritance in LINQ to SQL as a way to design your domain model.

Warning There are some issues related to applying entity inheritance to derived entities in a parent-child relationship. With the Object Relational Designer (O/R Designer) included in Microsoft Visual Studio 2008, you can create relationships only by using properties defined in the entities you are associating. The O/R Designer does not support inherited properties. However, you can still modify the Database Markup Language (DBML) file by hand and it will generate the right entity class code. After you create such an *Association*, it can be maintained through the O/R Designer, except for changing the participating properties.

Another important consideration about entity inheritance is that it has the capability to derive a class entity from an existing class. Tools such as SQLMetal and the O/R Designer build entity classes that do not derive from any other class. (Technically, they still derive from *System.Object*.) However, you can derive your entity classes from whatever base class you want. You can establish this definition by taking advantage of the *partial class* definition used by these tools. For example, say that you place the following declaration in your code:

```
public partial class Contact : EntityBase { }
```

The *Contact* class will derive from your own *EntityBase* class, and therefore all *Contact*-derived classes will also inherit the *EntityBase* behaviors. You can use the same partial declaration to add class attributes to an entity class. Unfortunately, there is no syntax sugar that you can use to add attributes at the member level, such as a property already decorated with *Column* in the tool-generated code. In fact, it is not possible to declare a partial property.

Attaching Entities

If you want to manipulate an entity in a disconnected way, you need to serialize the entities and attach them to a *DataContext* instance, possibly an instance different from the one that originally created the entities.

Entity Serialization

Entities used by LINQ to SQL can be serialized using particular attributes that are defined in the *System.Runtime.Serialization* namespace: *DataContract* and *DataMember*. These attributes are applied to the class and property definitions, respectively. By default, SQLMetal and Visual Studio do not generate serializable entity classes; thus, their generated classes and properties are not decorated with *DataContract* and *DataMember*. However, you can alter this behavior by invoking SQLMetal at a command line, using the */serialization:unidirectional* parameter. For the O/R Designer, you can set the *Serialization Mode* designer property of the *DataContext* class. That property is set to *None* by default, but by using *Unidirectional*, you get the same behavior as you do with the */serialization:unidirectional* parameter in SQLMetal.

The *Unidirectional* serialization setting means that an entity is serialized with only a one-way association property so as to avoid a cycle. Only the property on the parent side of a parent-child relationship is marked for serialization (the property of type *EntitySet<T>*), whereas the other side in a bidirectional association is not serialized (usually a property stored on a member of type *EntityRef<T>*). You can see an example of serialization in Listing 6-10.

LISTING 6-10 Entity serialization

```
Northwind db = new Northwind(Connections.ConnectionString);
var customer = db.Customers.Single(c => c.CustomerID == "WHITC");
DataContractSerializer dcs = new DataContractSerializer(typeof(Customer));
StringBuilder sb = new StringBuilder();
using (XmlWriter writer = XmlWriter.Create(sb)) {
    dcs.WriteObject(writer, customer);
}
string xml = sb.ToString();
Console.WriteLine(xml);
```

Serializing the entity results in the XML output shown in Listing 6-11.

LISTING 6-11 Serialized *Customer* entity

```xml
<?xml version="1.0" encoding="utf-16"?>
<Customer xmlns:i="http://www.w3.org/2001/XMLSchema-instance"
 xmlns="http://schemas.datacontract.org/2004/07/DevLeap.Linq.LinqToSql">
    <CustomerID>WHITC</CustomerID>
    <CompanyName>White Clover Markets</CompanyName>
    <ContactName>Karl Jablonski</ContactName>
    <ContactTitle>Owner</ContactTitle>
    <Address>305 - 14th Ave. S. Suite 3B</Address>
    <City>Seattle</City>
    <Region>WA</Region>
    <PostalCode>98128</PostalCode>
    <Country>USA</Country>
    <Phone>(206) 555-4112</Phone>
    <Fax>(206) 555-4115</Fax>
</Customer>
```

At this point, the serialized entity can be easily transmitted to an external tier of a distributed architecture. When it comes back, you will need to deserialize and attach it to a new *DataContext* instance, because the same *DataContext* cannot have two entities with the same key. You will see how to handle this in the following section.

Attach Operation

A typical scenario that involves entity serialization is one in which a service provides instances of an entity class on demand. Data consumers might update that entity and send it back to the service, asking for an update of the corresponding data source. If your service uses SQL Server as the data source and LINQ to SQL as the data access layer, you will need to create LINQ to SQL entity instances that will make the desired database updates.

To stay consistent with the scenario you have been working with in this chapter, this service sends a consumer a *Customer* entity serialized by the code you saw in Listing 6-10. You do not care how the consumer internally manipulates the *Customer* entity it receives; it could easily be code written for a different platform than the .NET Framework. But what is important is that eventually you receive an XML document representing the possibly modified *Customer* entity you originally sent. Listing 6-12 shows a possible example of such an XML document. The *ContactName* tag content is in bold because that is the changed part of the original entity shown in Listing 6-11. The *ContactName* has been changed from Karl Jablonski to John Smith.

LISTING 6-12 *Customer* entity modified

```xml
<?xml version="1.0" encoding="utf-16"?>
<Customer xmlns:i="http://www.w3.org/2001/XMLSchema-instance"
 xmlns="http://schemas.datacontract.org/2004/07/DevLeap.Linq.LinqToSql">
    <CustomerID>WHITC</CustomerID>
    <CompanyName>White Clover Markets</CompanyName>
    <ContactName>John Smith</ContactName>
    <ContactTitle>Owner</ContactTitle>
    <Address>305 - 14th Ave. S. Suite 3B</Address>
    <City>Seattle</City>
    <Region>WA</Region>
    <PostalCode>98128</PostalCode>
    <Country>USA</Country>
    <Phone>(206) 555-4112</Phone>
    <Fax>(206) 555-4115</Fax>
</Customer>
```

In Listing 6-13, you can see how to deserialize this incoming XML document into a new *Customer* instance. Using the *Attach* method, you add that instance to the *Customers* table in the *Northwind* data context. Note that this is a different instance of the *Northwind* class than the one you used to get the original *Customer* entity in Listing 6-11.

LISTING 6-13 Attach an entity to a *DataContext*, providing its original state for optimistic concurrency

```csharp
Northwind nw = new Northwind(Connections.ConnectionString);
nw.Log = Console.Out;

Customer deserializedCustomer;
using (XmlTextReader reader = new XmlTextReader(new StringReader(xml))) {
    deserializedCustomer = (Customer) dcs.ReadObject(reader, true);
}
nw.Customers.Attach(deserializedCustomer, customer);

Console.WriteLine(
    "ContactName Original={0}, Updated={1}\n",
    customer.ContactName,
    deserializedCustomer.ContactName );

nw.SubmitChanges();
```

You know that the instance you received might be changed, but you do not know what the changed fields are. In fact, the XML document you receive does not contain the original state of the *ContactName* tag content. As described earlier in this chapter, you have several ways to handle concurrency. If you want to use optimistic concurrency, you must provide the

DataContext with two versions of the same entity: the original version and the updated one. The example in Listing 6-13 uses the original customer instance cached by the original query made in Listing 6-10. Executing the code in Listing 6-13 provides the following result:

```
ContactName Original=Karl Jablonski, Updated=John Smith

UPDATE [dbo].[Customers]
SET     [ContactName] = 'John Smith'
WHERE   ([CustomerID] = 'WHITC')
AND     ([ContactName] = 'Karl Jablonski')
AND     ...
```

> **Important** The *DataContext* class is designed to be created and destroyed frequently. It is good practice to create a new *DataContext* instance for each service request.

Making a cache of all the entities provided by a service would make the service itself stateful. In the Service Oriented Architecture (SOA) world, a service should be stateless. However, note that the code in Listing 6-13 uses the *Customer* instance obtained from another *DataContext* as the original entity version calling the *Attach* method. The same approach is not possible for the updated entity. You can pass only a new (or deserialized) entity to the *Attach* method because using an entity obtained from a different *DataContext* results in a *NotSupportedException*.

If you do not want to use the *Attach* method with two *Customer* instances as arguments (for current and original entity values), you can pass a single entity instance to *Attach*, asking the change tracking service to ignore original values and to consider the object as modified. In this case, your entity must either have a field tagged with *IsVersion=true* on *Column* attributes, or it must have all its fields tagged with *UpdateCheck=Never* on *Column* attributes. In the latter case, a column with *IsPrimary=true* must also exist. In any of these cases, you call the *Attach* method with the following syntax (the second argument is the *asModified* setting):

```
nw.Customers.Attach(deserializedCustomer, true);
```

Finally, you can also attach an entity, assuming it is unmodified, and then modify that instance and leave the work of finding updated fields to the change-tracking service. Of course, even this case assumes you have the original entity available—and that might not be common with SOA. In these cases, you need to call *Attach* with either syntax shown here:

```
nw.Customers.Attach(customer, false);
```

```
nw.Customers.Attach(customer);
```

Whenever you have a sequence of entities of the same type to attach to a *DataContext*, you can use the *DataContext.AttachAll* method. Both the *Attach* and *AttachAll* methods work only if *ObjectTrackingEnabled* is *true*.

> **More Info** You can find more information about using LINQ in a multitier architecture in Chapter 18.

Binding Metadata

The mapping between LINQ to SQL entities and database structures has to be described through metadata information. Until now, you have seen this requirement fulfilled by attributes within entity definitions. There is an alternative way to do this (using an external XML mapping file), and there are tools and methods that automate the generation of entity classes starting from a database and vice versa.

External XML Mapping File

If you do not want to use attribute-based mapping information, you can put all binding metadata in an external XML file. For example, consider a *Customer* entity class like the one in Listing 6-14, used in the *Northwind* class derived by *DataContext*.

LISTING 6-14 Entity class with binding information saved in an external XML file

```
public class Customer {
    public string CustomerID;
    public string CompanyName;
    public string City;
    public string State;
    public string Country;
}

public class Northwind : DataContext {
    public Northwind(string connection) :
        this(connection, GetMapping()) { }

    public Northwind(string connection, MappingSource mapping) :
        base(connection, mapping) { }

    static MappingSource GetMapping() {
        using (StreamReader reader = new StreamReader("Northwind.xml")) {
            return XmlMappingSource.FromReader(new XmlTextReader(reader));
        }
    }

    public System.Data.Linq.Table<Customer> Customers {
        get { return this.GetTable<Customer>(); }
    }

}
```

The *Northwind* class can be used without specifying a mapping file, implicitly using the *GetMapping* static method, as shown in Listing 6-15.

LISTING 6-15 Entity class with binding information saved in an external XML file

```
public static void SimpleQuery() {
    Northwind db = new Northwind(Connections.ConnectionString);
    var query = from   c in db.Customers
                where  c.City == "Seattle"
                select c;

    foreach( var customer in query ) {
        Console.WriteLine(
            "Customer={0}, State={1}",
            customer.CompanyName,
            customer.State);
    }
}
```

Using a second argument in the *Northwind* constructor call, you can specify different mapping information. The *Northwind.GetMapping* static method returns an *XmlMappingSource* instance, which reads the binding information contained in the Northwind.xml file shown in Listing 6-16.

LISTING 6-16 Entity class with binding information saved in an external XML file

```
<?xml version="1.0" encoding="utf-8" ?>
<Database Name="Northwind"
  xmlns="http://schemas.microsoft.com/linqtosql/mapping/2007">
    <Table Name="dbo.Customers" Member="Customers">
        <Type Name="Customer">
            <Column Name="CustomerID" Member="CustomerID"
                    IsPrimaryKey="true" />
            <Column Name="CompanyName" Member="CompanyName"/>
            <Column Name="City" Member="City"/>
            <Column Name="Region" Member="State"/>
            <Column Name="Country" Member="Country"/>
        </Type>
    </Table>
</Database>
```

Decoupling the binding information by storing it in an external file enables you to map an entity to different database schemas, handling differences such as different naming conventions, translated table and column names, or versioning between database schemas. For example, an older version of the database might not have a newer column. In that case, you can use different mapping files to best match different versions of the database.

Creating a Database from Entities

An application that automatically installs itself on a computer might have a reason to create a database that can persist its object graph. This is a typical situation—you need to handle simple configurations represented by a graph of objects.

If you have a class derived from *DataContext* that contains entity definitions decorated with *Table* and *Column* attributes, you can create the corresponding database by calling the *CreateDatabase* method. This method sends the necessary CREATE DATABASE statement, as well as the subsequent CREATE TABLE and ALTER TABLE statements:

```
const string ConnectionString =
    "Database=Test_Northwind;Trusted_Connection=yes";
public static void Create() {
    Northwind db = new Northwind( ConnectionString );
    db.CreateDatabase();
}
```

You can also drop a database and check for its existence. The name of the database is inferred from the connection string. You can duplicate a database schema in several databases simply by changing the connection string:

```
if (db.DatabaseExists()) {
    db.DeleteDatabase();    // Send a DROP DATABASE
}
db.CreateDatabase();
```

Remember that the database is created based on the *Table* and *Column* attributes decorating entity classes and their properties. In fact, the following two parameters of the *Column* attribute exist only to keep definitions useful for database generation:

- **DbType**   This is the type definition for the column in the database. This setting overrides the type that would be automatically generated by the LINQ to SQL engine.

- **Expression**   This is the T-SQL expression that is used as an expression for a computed value in a table.

 Important Remember that the *DbType* and *Expression* parameters of the *Column* attribute contain a string that is not parsed or checked by either the compiler or the LINQ to SQL engine. An error in these definitions produces an error at execution time.

Creating Entities from a Database

When you are creating an application that will use an existing physical data layer, you might want to create a set of entity classes for that database. You can use two available tools: SQL-Metal and the O/R Designer integrated into Visual Studio.

> **More Info** The entire next chapter is dedicated to the use of SQLMetal and the O/R Designer. See Chapter 7 for further information.

Differences Between the .NET Framework and SQL Type Systems

The product documentation illustrates all differences in the type systems of the .NET Framework and LINQ to SQL. Many operators require a specific conversion, such as cast operations and the *ToString* method, which are converted to *CAST* or *CONVERT* operators during SQL generation. Some conversions can result in significant differences if your code is sensitive to rounding differences. (For example, the .NET Framework *Math.Round* method and the SQL *ROUND* operator use different logic. See the *MidpointRounding* enumeration used to control the behavior.) Date and time manipulation also have minor differences. Above all, you need to remember that SQL Server supports *DATETIME* but not *DATE*.

> **More Info** The most important differences between the .NET Framework and LINQ to SQL are covered in the "Limitations of LINQ to SQL" section in Chapter 5.

Summary

This chapter covered performing CUD (Create, Update, and Delete) operations on a relational database using LINQ to SQL entities. Handling entity updates involves concurrency and transactions; the *DataContext* class in LINQ to SQL offers the connection points to control the LINQ to SQL engine's behavior. Finally, LINQ to SQL entity serialization requires a good understanding of the change-tracking service offered by a *DataContext* instance. Because you cannot serialize and then deserialize an entity in the same *DataContext*, this chapter included a section describing how to attach entities from a *DataContext*.

Chapter 7

LINQ to SQL: Modeling Data and Tools

The best way to write queries using LINQ to SQL is by having a *DataContext*-derived class in your code that exposes all the tables, stored procedures, and user-defined functions you need as properties of a class instance. You also need entity classes mapped to the database objects. As you have seen in previous chapters, you can create this mapping by using attributes to decorate classes or via an external XML mapping file. However, writing mapping information by hand is both tedious and error-prone; fortunately, there are some tools that can help you accomplish this task.

This chapter covers the file types involved in mapping entity classes to database objects, and the tools available to generate this information automatically. These tools are a command-line tool named SQLMetal, included in the Microsoft .NET Framework 3.5 Software Development Kit (SDK), and the Object Relational Designer (O/R Designer), which is an integrated graphical tool included in Microsoft Visual Studio. You will examine both tools from a practical point of view.

Important Throughout the rest of this book, you will see references to files contained in the *MSVS* folder. We use MSVS as an abbreviation for the following paths: %ProgramFiles(x86)%\Microsoft Visual Studio 10.0\folder if you have installed Microsoft Visual Studio 2010, and %ProgramFiles(x86)%\Microsoft Visual Studio 9.0\ if you have installed Microsoft Visual Studio 2008.

This chapter uses the Northwind database, which is included in the Microsoft Visual C# samples provided with both Visual Studio 2010 and Visual Studio 2008. The samples are in the MSVS\Samples\1033\CSharpSamples.zip file. You can also download an updated version of these samples from the "Visual C# 2008 Samples" page, located at *http://code.msdn.microsoft.com/csharpsamples*.

File Types

There are three types of files involved in creating LINQ to SQL entities and their mapping definition:

- Database markup language (DBML)
- Source code (C# or Visual Basic)
- External mapping file (XML)

A common mistake is confusing XML mapping files and DBML. At first glance, these two files are similar, but they are very different both in use and in the generation process.

DBML—Database Markup Language

The DBML file contains a description of the LINQ to SQL entities in a database markup language. Visual Studio installs a DbmlSchema.xsd file, which contains the schema definition of that language and can be used to validate a DBML file. The namespace used for this file is *http://schemas.microsoft.com/linqtosql/dbml/2007* (which is different from the namespace used by the XSD for the XML external mapping file).

> **Note** You can find the DbmlSchema.xsd schema file in the MSVS\Xml\Schemas folder.

You can generate the DBML file automatically by extracting metadata from an existing Microsoft SQL Server database. However, the DBML file includes more information than can be inferred from database tables. For example, settings for synchronization and delayed loading are specific to the intended use of the entity. Moreover, DBML files include information that is used only by the code generator that generates Microsoft Visual Basic or C# source code, such as the base class and namespace for generated entity classes. Listing 7-1 shows an excerpt from a sample DBML file.

LISTING 7-1 Excerpt from a sample DBML file

```xml
<?xml version="1.0" encoding="utf-8"?>
<Database Name="Northwind" Class="nwDataContext"
          xmlns="http://schemas.microsoft.com/linqtosql/dbml/2007">
  <Connection Mode="AppSettings"
              ConnectionString="Data Source=..."
              SettingsObjectName="DevLeap.Linq.LinqToSql.Properties.Settings"
              SettingsPropertyName="NorthwindConnectionString"
              Provider="System.Data.SqlClient" />
  <Table Name="dbo.Orders" Member="Orders">
    <Type Name="Order">
      <Column Name="OrderID" Type="System.Int32"
              DbType="Int NOT NULL IDENTITY" IsPrimaryKey="true"
              IsDbGenerated="true" CanBeNull="false" />
      <Column Name="CustomerID" Type="System.String"
              DbType="NChar(5)" CanBeNull="true" />
      <Column Name="OrderDate" Type="System.DateTime"
              DbType="DateTime" CanBeNull="true" />

    ...
```

```
        <Association Name="Customer_Order" Member="Customer"
                     ThisKey="CustomerID" Type="Customer"
                     IsForeignKey="true" />
      </Type>
    </Table>
      ...
  </Database>
```

The DBML file is the richest container of metadata information for LINQ to SQL. Usually, it can be generated from a SQL Server database and then modified manually, adding information that cannot be inferred from the database. This would be the typical approach when using the SQLMetal command-line tool. The O/R Designer offers a more dynamic way of editing this file, because you can import entities from a database and modify them directly in the DBML file through a graphical editor. You can also use the O/R Designer to edit the DBML file generated by SQLMetal.

The DBML file can be used to generate C# or Visual Basic source code for entities and *DataContext*-derived classes. Optionally, it can also be used to generate an external XML mapping file.

More Info   It is beyond the scope of this book to provide a detailed description of the DBML syntax. You can find more information and the whole DbmlSchema.xsd content in the "Code Generation in LINQ to SQL" product documentation at *http://msdn2.microsoft.com/library/bb399400.aspx*.

C# and Visual Basic Source Code

The definition of LINQ to SQL entity classes can reside in source code in C#, Visual Basic, or any other .NET Framework language. This definition code can be decorated with attributes that define the mapping of entities and their properties to database tables and their columns. Alternatively, you can define the mapping using an external XML mapping file. However, you cannot mix the two—you have to choose only one place to define entity mappings. If you use both, the external XML mapping file takes precedence over attributes defined on class entities.

This source code for defining LINQ to SQL entity classes can be generated automatically by tools such as SQLMetal directly from a SQL Server database. The SQLMetal code-generation function can also translate a DBML file to C# or Visual Basic source code. When you ask SQLMetal to generate entity source code, internally it generates a DBML file that is then converted to the entity source code. Listing 7-2 shows an excerpt of the C# source code generated from the DBML sample shown in Listing 7-1 for LINQ to SQL entities.

LISTING 7-2 Excerpt from the class entity source code in C#

```csharp
[System.Data.Linq.Mapping.DatabaseAttribute(Name="Northwind")]
public partial class nwDataContext : System.Data.Linq.DataContext {

    // ...

    public System.Data.Linq.Table<Order> Orders {
        get { return this.GetTable<Order>(); }
    }
}

[Table(Name="dbo.Orders")]
public partial class Order : INotifyPropertyChanging, INotifyPropertyChanged {
    private int _OrderID;
    private string _CustomerID;
    private System.Nullable<System.DateTime> _OrderDate;

    [Column(Storage="_OrderID", AutoSync=AutoSync.OnInsert,
            DbType="Int NOT NULL IDENTITY", IsPrimaryKey=true,
            IsDbGenerated=true)]
    public int OrderID {
        get { return this._OrderID; }
        set {
            if ((this._OrderID != value)) {
                this.OnOrderIDChanging(value);
                this.SendPropertyChanging();
                this._OrderID = value;
                this.SendPropertyChanged("OrderID");
                this.OnOrderIDChanged();
            }
        }
    }

    [Column(Storage="_CustomerID", DbType="NChar(5)")]
    public string CustomerID {
        get { return this._CustomerID; }
        set {
            if ((this._CustomerID != value)) {
                if (this._Customer.HasLoadedOrAssignedValue) {
                    throw new ForeignKeyReferenceAlreadyHasValueException();
                }
                this.OnCustomerIDChanging(value);
                this.SendPropertyChanging();
                this._CustomerID = value;
                this.SendPropertyChanged("CustomerID");
                this.OnCustomerIDChanged();
            }
        }
    }
```

```
[Column(Storage="_OrderDate", DbType="DateTime")]
public System.Nullable<System.DateTime> OrderDate {
    get { return this._OrderDate; }
    set {
        if ((this._OrderDate != value)) {
            this.OnOrderDateChanging(value);
            this.SendPropertyChanging();
            this._OrderDate = value;
            this.SendPropertyChanged("OrderDate");
            this.OnOrderDateChanged();
        }
    }
}

[Association(Name="Customer_Order", Storage="_Customer",
            ThisKey="CustomerID", IsForeignKey=true)]
public Customer Customer {
    get { return this._Customer.Entity; }
    set {
        Customer previousValue = this._Customer.Entity;
        if ((previousValue != value)
            || (this._Customer.HasLoadedOrAssignedValue == false)) {
            this.SendPropertyChanging();
            if ((previousValue != null)) {
                this._Customer.Entity = null;
                previousValue.Orders.Remove(this);
            }
            this._Customer.Entity = value;
            if ((value != null)) {
                value.Orders.Add(this);
                this._CustomerID = value.CustomerID;
            }
            else {
                this._CustomerID = default(string);
            }
            this.SendPropertyChanged("Customer");
        }
    }
}

// ...
}
```

The attributes in bold in Listing 7-2 are *not* generated in the source code file when you have
SQLMetal generate both a source code file and an external XML mapping file; instead, the
XML mapping file will contain the mapping information.

> **More Info** Attributes that define the mapping between entities and database tables are
> discussed in Chapter 5, "LINQ to SQL: Querying Data," and in Chapter 6, "LINQ to SQL:
> Managing Data."

XML—External Mapping File

An external mapping file can contain binding metadata for LINQ to SQL entities as an alternative to storing them in code attributes. This file is XML with a schema that is a subset of the DBML file. The DBML file also contains information useful for code generators. Remember that attributes defined on class entities are ignored whenever they are included in the definitions of an external mapping file.

The namespace used for this file is *http://schemas.microsoft.com/linqtosql/mapping/2007*, which is different from the one used by the DBML XSD file.

> **Note** The LinqToSqlMapping.xsd schema file should be located in the MSVS\Schemas folder. If you do not have that file, you can create it by copying the code from the "External Mapping Reference (LINQ to SQL)" documentation page at *http://msdn2.microsoft.com/library/bb386907.aspx*.

Listing 7-3 contains an example of an external mapping file generated from the DBML file presented in Listing 7-1. The *Storage* attribute, shown in bold, defines the mapping between the table column and the data member in the entity class, which stores the value and exposes it through the member property defined by the *Member* attribute. The value assigned to *Storage* depends on the implementation generated by the code generator; for this reason, it is not included in the DBML file.

LISTING 7-3 Excerpt from a sample XML mapping file

```xml
<?xml version="1.0" encoding="utf-8"?>
<Database Name="northwind"
          xmlns="http://schemas.microsoft.com/linqtosql/mapping/2007">
  <Table Name="dbo.Orders" Member="Orders">
    <Type Name="Orders">
      <Column Name="OrderID" Member="OrderID" Storage="_OrderID"
              DbType="Int NOT NULL IDENTITY" IsPrimaryKey="true"
              IsDbGenerated="true" AutoSync="OnInsert" />
      <Column Name="CustomerID" Member="CustomerID" Storage="_CustomerID"
              DbType="NChar(5)" />
      <Column Name="OrderDate" Member="OrderDate" Storage="_OrderDate"
              DbType="DateTime" />

      ...

      <Association Name="FK_Orders_Customers" Member="Customers"
                   Storage="_Customers" ThisKey="CustomerID"
                   OtherKey="CustomerID" IsForeignKey="true" />
    </Type>
  </Table>
    ...
</Database>
```

More Info If a provider has custom definitions that extend existing ones, the extensions are available only through an external mapping file—but not with attribute-based mapping. For example, with an XML mapping file, you can specify different *DbType* values for Microsoft SQL Server 2008, SQL Server 2005, SQL Server 2000, and SQL Server Compact 3.5. External XML mapping files are discussed in detail in Chapter 6.

LINQ to SQL File Generation

Usually, you will use a tool to generate most of the files used in LINQ to SQL. The diagram in Figure 7-1 illustrates the relationships between the different file types and the relational database. In the remaining part of this section, you will see the most important patterns of code generation that you can use.

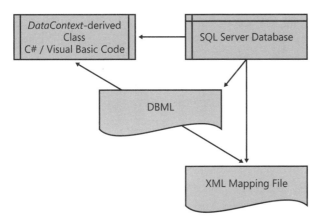

FIGURE 7-1 Relationships between file types and the relational database.

Generating a DBML File from an Existing Database

If you have a relational database, you can generate a DBML file that describes tables, views, stored procedures, and user-defined functions (UDFs), mapping them to class entities that can be created by a code generator. After generating the DBML file, you can edit it with any text editor or with the O/R Designer.

Generating an Entity's Source Code with Attribute-Based Mapping

You can choose to generate source code for class entities in C# or Visual Basic with attribute-based mapping. This code can be generated from a DBML file or directly from a SQL Server database.

If you start from a DBML file, you can modify that DBML file and then regenerate the source code. In this case, you should not modify the generated source code because it might be overwritten in future code regeneration cycles. Instead, if you need to modify the generated source to customize generated classes, you should use a separate source code file, using the *partial class* declaration of the generated class entities. This is the pattern you use when working with the O/R Designer.

On the other hand, if you generate code directly from a SQL Server database, you can still customize the resulting source code file using partial classes; however, if you need to modify the mapping settings, you will have to modify the generated source code. In this case, you probably will never regenerate this file and can therefore modify the generated source directly.

Generating an Entity's Source Code with an External XML Mapping File

Finally, you can choose to generate source code for class entities in C# or Visual Basic together with an external XML mapping file. The source code and the XML mapping file can both be generated from a DBML file or directly from a SQL Server database.

If you start from a DBML file, you can still modify that DBML file and then regenerate the source code and the mapping file. Again, in this case you do not want to modify the generated files directly; use partial classes instead. This is the pattern used when you work with the O/R Designer.

Similarly, if you generate code directly from a SQL Server database, you should also customize the resulting source code using partial classes. Because the mapping information is stored in a separate XML file, you will need to modify that file to customize mapping settings. Most likely, you will never regenerate these files and can therefore make modifications directly to the generated files.

Creating a DBML File from Scratch

Finally, you can write a DBML file from scratch. In this case, you probably would not have an existing database file; instead, you would probably generate the database from your DBML file by calling the *DataContext.CreateDatabase* method on an instance of the generated class inherited from *DataContext*. This approach is theoretically possible when you write the XML file yourself, but in practice, it is far more likely to be done using the O/R Designer.

Choosing this approach implies that entity classes are more important than the database design, and that the database design itself is simply a consequence of the object model you designed for your application. In other words, using this method, the relational database becomes a simple persistence layer (without stored procedures, triggers, and other database-specific features), which consumers not using the LINQ to SQL engine should not access directly. In the real world, this can be the case for applications that use the database either as the storage mechanism for complex configurations, or to persist very simple information, typically in a stand-alone application with a local database. Whenever a client-server or multitier architecture is involved, the chances are good that additional consumer applications—for example, a reporting tool such as Reporting Services—will access the same database. These scenarios tend to be more database-centric and require better control of the database design, often eliminating the DBML-first approach as a viable option. In these situations, the best way of working is to define the database schema and the domain model separately, and then map the entities of the domain model onto the database tables.

SQLMetal

SQLMetal is a code-generation command-line tool that you can use to:

- Generate a DBML file from a database.
- Generate an entity's source code (and optionally a mapping file) from a database.
- Generate an entity's source code (and optionally a mapping file) from a DBML file.

The command syntax for SQLMetal is simple:

```
sqlmetal [options] [<input file>]
```

In the following sections, you will see several examples that demonstrate how to use SQLMetal.

More Info   You can find complete documentation for the SQLMetal command-line options on the "SQLMetal.exe (Code Generation Tool)" page at *http://msdn2.microsoft.com/library/bb386987.aspx*.

Generating a DBML File from a Database

To generate a DBML file with SQLMetal, you need to specify the */dbml* option, followed by the file name you want to create. The syntax to specify which database to use depends on the type of the database. For example, you can specify a standard SQL Server database with the */server* and */database* options:

```
sqlmetal /server:localhost /database:Northwind /dbml:northwind.dbml
```

Windows authentication is used by default. If you want to use SQL Server authentication, you can use the */user* and */password* options. Alternatively, you can use the */conn* (connection) option, which takes a connection string, but cannot be used with */server, /database, /user*, or */password*. The following command line using */conn* is equivalent to the previous example, which used */server* and */database*:

```
sqlmetal /conn:"Server=localhost;Database=Northwind;Integrated Security=yes"
    /dbml:northwind.dbml
```

If you have the Northwind .mdf file in the current directory and are using Microsoft SQL Server Express, you can achieve the same result by using the following line, which uses the input file parameter:

```
sqlmetal /dbml:northwind.dbml Northwnd.mdf
```

Similarly, you can specify an .sdf file (the extension for SQL Server Compact 3.5 files), as in the following line:

```
sqlmetal /dbml:northwind.dbml Northwind.sdf
```

By default, the generation process extracts only tables from a database, but you can also extract views, user-defined functions, and stored procedures by using */views, /functions*, and */sprocs*, respectively, as shown here:

```
sqlmetal /server:localhost /database:Northwind /views /functions /sprocs
    /dbml:northwind.dbml
```

 Note Remember that database views are treated like tables by LINQ to SQL.

Generating Source Code and a Mapping File from a Database

To generate an entity's source code, you need to specify the */code* option, followed by the file name to create. The generator infers the appropriate language from the file name extension, using the .cs extension for C# and the .vb extension for Visual Basic. However, you can explicitly specify a language by using */language:csharp* or */language:vb* to get C# or Visual Basic code, respectively. The syntax to specify the database to use depends on the type of the database, and is the same as that described in the preceding section, "Generating a DBML File from a Database."

For example, the following line generates C# source code for entities extracted from the Northwind database:

```
sqlmetal /server:localhost /database:Northwind /code:Northwind.cs
```

If you want all the tables and the views in Visual Basic, you can use the following command line:

```
sqlmetal /server:localhost /database:Northwind /views /code:Northwind.vb
```

Optionally, you can add generation of an XML mapping file by using the */map* option, as in the following command line:

```
sqlmetal /server:localhost /database:Northwind /code:Northwind.cs /map:Northwind.xml
```

> **Important** When you request an XML mapping file, the generated source code does not contain any attribute-based mapping.

The following options control how the entity classes are generated:

- ■ ***/namespace***   Controls the namespace of the generated code. (By default, there is no namespace.)

- ■ ***/context***   Specifies the name of the class inherited from *DataContext* that will be generated. (By default, it is derived from the database name.)

- ■ ***/entitybase***   Allows you to define the base class of the generated entity classes. (By default, there is no base class.) For example, the following command line generates all the entities in a *LinqBook* namespace, deriving them from the *DevLeap.LinqBase* base class:

```
sqlmetal /server:localhost /database:Northwind /namespace:LinqBook
    /entitybase:DevLeap.LinqBase /code:Northwind.cs
```

> **Note** If you specify a base class, you have to be sure that the class exists when the generated source code is compiled. It is a good practice to specify the full name of the base class.

- ■ ***/serialization:unidirectional***   Specify in the command line if you want to generate serializable classes, as in the following example:

```
sqlmetal /server:localhost /database:Northwind /serialization:unidirectional
    /code:Northwind.cs
```

> **More Info** See the section "Entity Serialization" in Chapter 6 for further information about serialization of LINQ to SQL entities.

- ■ ***/pluralize***   Controls how the names of entities and properties are generated. When you specify this option, generated entity names are singular, but table names in the *DataContext*-derived class properties are plural, regardless of the table name's form. In other words, the presence of either a Customer (or Customers) table generates a *Customer* entity class and a *Customers* property in the *DataContext*-derived class.

Generating Source Code and a Mapping File from a DBML File

The syntax for generating source code and a mapping file from a DBML file is identical to the syntax required to generate the same results from a database except that, instead of specifying a database connection, you instead specify the DBML file name as an input file parameter. For example, the following command line generates the C# class code for the Northwind. DBML model description:

```
sqlmetal /code:Northwind.cs Northwind.dbml
```

> **Important** Remember to use the */dbml* option only to *generate* a DBML file. You do not have to specify */dbml* when you want to use a DBML file as input.

You can use all the options for generating source code and a mapping file that we described in the "Generating Source Code and a Mapping File from a Database" section.

Using the Object Relational Designer

The O/R Designer is a graphical editor integrated with Visual Studio. It is the standard visual editor for a DBML file. With it, you can create new entities, edit existing ones, and generate an entity starting from an object in a SQL Server database. (The O/R Designer provides support for tables, views, stored procedures, and user-defined functions.) You can create a DBML file by choosing the LINQ To SQL Classes template in the Add New Item dialog box, shown in Figure 7-2, or by adding an existing DBML file to a project (choosing Project | Add Existing Item in Visual Studio).

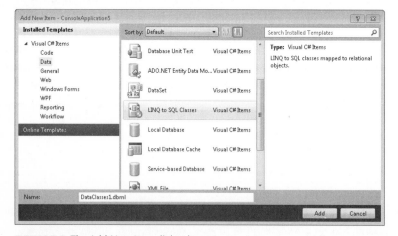

FIGURE 7-2 The Add New Item dialog box.

You can drag items from a connection opened in Server Explorer and drop them on a design surface. This results in the creation of a new entity that derives its content from the dropped object. Alternatively, you can create new entities by dragging items such as Class, Association, and Inheritance from the Toolbox. Figure 7-3 shows an empty DBML file opened in Visual Studio. On the left are the Toolbox and Server Explorer elements ready to be dragged onto the design surface.

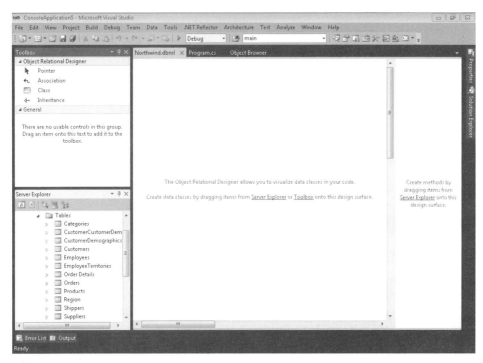

FIGURE 7-3 An empty DBML file opened with the O/R Designer.

As an example, dragging two tables, *Orders* and *Order Details*, from Server Explorer to the left pane of the DBML design surface results in a DBML file that contains two entity classes, *Order* and *Order_Detail*, as you can see in Figure 7-4. Because the database contains a foreign key constraint between the *Order Details* and *Orders* tables, the O/R Designer also generates an *Association* between the *Order* and *Order_Detail* entities.

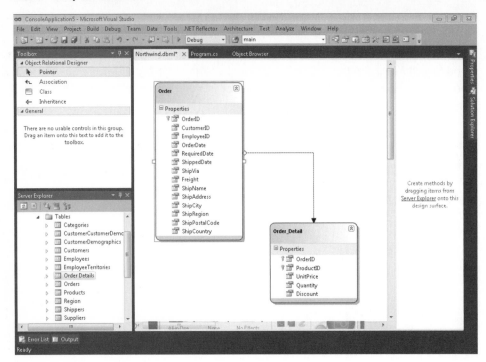

FIGURE 7-4 Two entities created from a server connection.

You can see that plural names (Orders and Order Details) have been translated into singular-name entity classes. However, the names of the *Table<T>* properties in the *NorthwindData-Context* class are plural (*Orders* and *Order_Details*), as you can see in the bottom part of the Class View shown in Figure 7-5.

Visual Studio updates the Class View each time you save the DBML file. In addition, every time you save this file, Visual Studio saves two other files: a *.layout* file, which is an XML file containing information about the current state of the design surface, and a *.cs/.vb* file, which is the source code generated for the entity classes. In other words, each time you save a DBML file from Visual Studio, the code generator is run on the DBML file and the source code for those entities gets updated. Figure 7-6, shows the files related to the *Northwind.dbml* (shown in the lower-right area of Figure 7-6) in Solution Explorer. Note that you now have both a *Northwind.dbml.layout* file and a *Northwind.designer.cs* file.

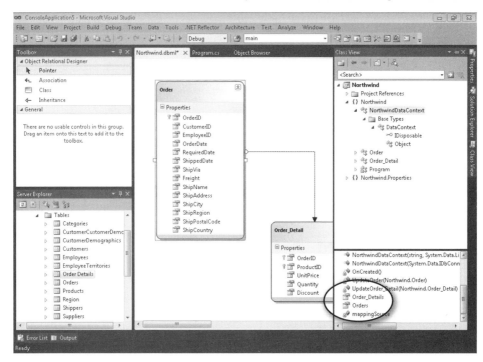

FIGURE 7-5 FPlural names for *Table<T>* properties in a *DataContext*-derived class.

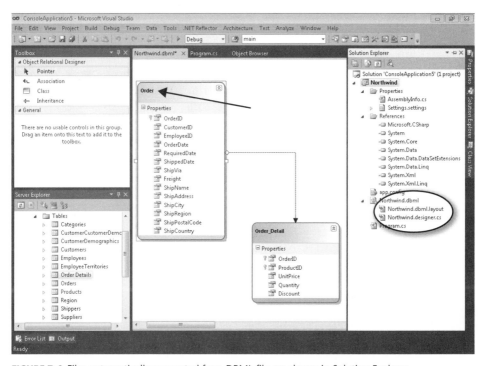

FIGURE 7-6 Files automatically generated for a DBML file are shown in Solution Explorer.

You should not modify the source code produced by the code generator. Instead, to customize generated classes, you should use corresponding partial classes contained in another file. For example, the *Northwind.cs* file shown in Figure 7-7 gets created the first time you select View | Code for a selected item in the O/R Designer. In this example, we chose View | Code from the context menu after selecting the Order entity on the design surface, shown in Figure 7-6.

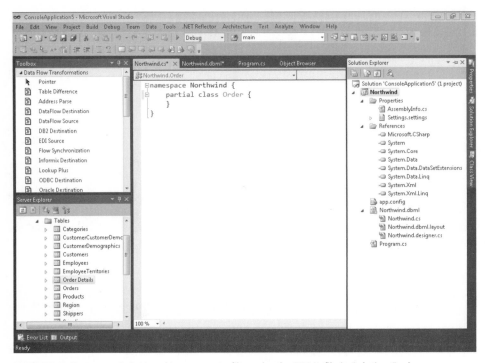

FIGURE 7-7 Custom code is stored in a separate file under the DBML file in Solution Explorer.

At this point, you will do most of the work in the Properties pane for each DBML item and in the source code. In the remaining part of this chapter, you will see the most important activities that you can perform with the DBML editor.

More Info This chapter does not cover how to extend an entity at the source-code level because that topic was covered in Chapter 5 and Chapter 6.

DataContext Properties

Each DBML file defines a class that inherits from *DataContext*. This class will have a *Table<T>* member for each entity defined in the DBML file. The class itself will be generated following the requirements specified in the Properties pane in the O/R Designer. Figure 7-8 shows the Properties pane for the *NorthwindDataContext* class.

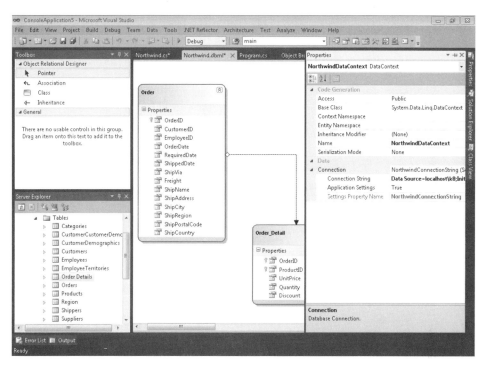

FIGURE 7-8 *DataContext* properties.

The properties for *DataContext* are separated into two groups. The simpler one is Data, which contains the default *Connection* for the *DataContext*; if you do not specify a connection when you create a *NorthwindDataContext* instance in your code, this connection will be used. You can use the *Application Settings* property to specify whether the *DataContext* should retrieve connection information from the application settings file. In that case, *Settings Property Name* will be the property retrieved from the application settings file.

The group of properties named *Code Generation* requires a more detailed explanation, which is provided in Table 7-1.

TABLE 7-1 Code-Generation Properties for *DataContext*

Property	Description
Access	Access modifier for the *DataContext*-derived class. It can be only *Public* or *Internal*. By default, it is *Public*.
Base Class	Base class for the data context specialized class. By default, it is *System.Data.Linq.DataContext*. You can define your own base class, which would probably be inherited by *DataContext*.
Context Namespace	Namespace of the generated *DataContext*-derived class only. It does not apply to the entity classes. Use the same value in *Context Namespace* and *Entity Namespace* if you want to generate *DataContext* and entity classes in the same namespace.
Entity Namespace	Namespace of the generated entities only. It does not apply to the *DataContext*-derived class. Use the same value in *Context Namespace* and *Entity Namespace* if you want to generate *DataContext* and entity classes in the same namespace.
Inheritance Modifier	Inheritance modifier to be used in the class declaration. It can be *(None)*, *abstract*, or *sealed*. By default, it is *(None)*.
Name	Name of the *DataContext*-derived class. By default, it is the name of the database with the suffix *DataContext*. For example, *NorthwindDataContext* is the default name for a *DataContext*-derived class generated for the Northwind database.
Serialization Mode	If this property is set to *Unidirectional*, the entity's source code is decorated with *DataContract* and *DataMember* for serialization purposes. By default, it is set to *None*.

Entity Class

When you select an entity class in the designer, you can change its properties in the Properties pane. In Figure 7-9, you can see the Properties pane for the selected *Order* entity class.

The properties for an entity class are separated into three groups: Data, Default Methods, and Code Generation.

The Data group contains only *Source*, which is the name of the table in the SQL Server database, including the owner or schema name. This property is filled in automatically when you generate an entity by dragging a table onto the designer surface.

The Default Methods group contains three read-only properties—*Delete*, *Insert*, and *Update*—that indicate the presence of custom Create, Update, and Delete (CUD) methods. These properties are disabled if the same DBML file contains no stored procedure definitions. If you have stored procedures that should be called for Insert, Update, and Delete operations on an entity, you must first import them into the DBML file (as described in the "Stored Procedures and User-Defined Functions" section later in this chapter). After importing the stored procedures, you can edit these properties by associating each of the CUD operations with the corresponding stored procedure.

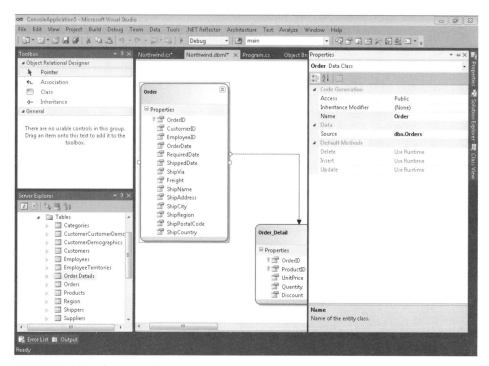

FIGURE 7-9 Entity class properties.

The Code Generation group properties are explained in Table 7-2.

TABLE 7-2 Code-Generation Properties for an Entity Class

Property	Description
Access	Access modifier for the entity class. It can be only *Public* or *Internal*. By default, it is *Public*.
Inheritance Modifier	Inheritance modifier to be used in the class declaration. It can be *(None)*, *abstract*, or *sealed*. By default, it is *(None)*.
Name	Name of the entity class. By default, it is the singular name of the table dragged from a database in Server Explorer. For example, *Order* is the default name for the Orders table in the Northwind database.
	Remember that the entity class will be defined in the namespace defined by the Entity Namespace of the related *DataContext* class.

Entity Members

An entity generated by dragging a table from Server Explorer has a set of predefined members that are created by reading table metadata from the relational database. Each of these members has its own settings in the Properties pane. You can add new members by clicking Add | Property on the contextual menu, or simply by pressing the Insert key. You can delete a member by pressing the Delete key or by clicking Delete on the contextual menu. Unfortunately, you cannot modify the sequence of the members in an entity through the O/R Designer; the sequence can be changed only by manually modifying the DBML file and moving the physical order of the *Column* tags within a *Type*.

> **Warning** You can open and modify the DBML file with a text editor such as Notepad. If you try to open the DBML file with Visual Studio, remember to use the Open With option from the drop-down list or the Open button in the Open File dialog box, picking the XML Editor choice to use the XML editor integrated in Visual Studio; otherwise, the O/R Designer will be used by default. You can also use the Open With command on a DBML file shown in Solution Explorer in Visual Studio.

When you select an entity member on the designer, you can change its properties in the Properties pane. In Figure 7-10, you can see the Properties pane for the selected *OrderID* member of the *Order* entity class.

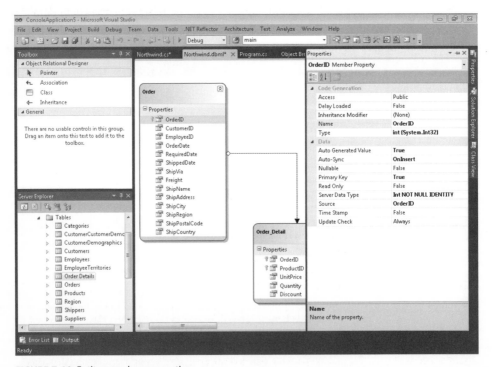

FIGURE 7-10 Entity member properties.

The properties for an entity member are separated into two groups: Code Generation and Data.

The Code Generation group controls the way member attributes are generated. Its properties are described in Table 7-3.

TABLE 7-3 **Code-Generation Properties for Data Members of an Entity**

Property	Description
Access	Access modifier for the entity class. It can be *Public*, *Protected*, *Protected Internal*, *Internal*, or *Private*. By default, it is *Public*.
Delay Loaded	If this property is set to *true*, the data member will not be loaded until its first access. This is implemented by declaring the member with the *Link<T>* class, which is explained in the "Deferred Loading of Properties" section in Chapter 5. By default, it is set to *false*.
Inheritance Modifier	Inheritance modifier to be used in the member declaration. It can be *(None)*, *new*, *new virtual*, *override*, or *virtual*. By default, it is *(None)*.
Name	Name of the member. By default, it is the same column name used in the *Source* property.
Type	Type of the data member. This type can be modified into a *Nullable<T>* according to the *Nullable* setting in the Data group or properties.

The Data group contains important mapping information between the entity data member and the table column in the database. The properties in this group are described in Table 7-4. Many of these properties correspond to settings of the *Column* attribute, which are described in Chapters 5 and 6.

TABLE 7-4 **Data Properties for Data Members of an Entity**

Property	Description
Auto Generated Value	Corresponds to the *IsDbGenerated* setting of the *Column* attribute.
Auto-Sync	Corresponds to the *AutoSync* setting of the *Column* attribute.
Nullable	If this property is set to *true*, the type of the data member is declared as *Nullable<T>*, where *T* is the type defined in the *Type* property. (See Table 7-3.)
Primary Key	Corresponds to the *IsPrimaryKey* setting of the *Column* attribute.
Read Only	If this property is set to *true*, only the *get* accessor is defined for the property that publicly exposes this member of the entity class. By default, it is set to *false*. Considering its behavior, this property could be part of the Code Generation group.
Server Data Type	Corresponds to the *DbType* setting of the *Column* attribute.
Source	The name of the column in the database table. Corresponds to the *Name* setting of the *Column* attribute.
Time Stamp	Corresponds to the *IsVersion* setting of the *Column* attribute.
Update Check	Corresponds to the *UpdateCheck* setting of the *Column* attribute.

Association Between Entities

An association represents a relationship between entities, which can be expressed through *EntitySet<T>*, *EntityRef<T>*, and the *Association* attribute we describe in Chapter 5. In Figure 7-4, you can see the association between the *Order* and *Order_Detail* entities expressed as an arrow that links these entities. In the O/R Designer, you can define associations between entities in two ways:

- When one or more entities are imported from a database, the existing foreign key constraints between tables, which are also entities of the designed model, are transformed into corresponding associations between entities.

- Selecting the Association item in the Toolbox, you can link two entities to define an association that might or might not have a corresponding foreign key in the relational database. To build the association, the two data members that define the relationship must be of the same type in the related entities. On the parent side of the relationship, the member must also have the *Primary Key* property set to *True*.

> **Note** An existing database might not have the foreign key relationship that corresponds to an association defined between LINQ to SQL entities. However, if you generate the relational database using the *DataContext.CreateDatabase* method of your model, the foreign keys are generated automatically for existing associations.

When you create an association, or double-click an existing one, the dialog box shown in Figure 7-11 appears. The two combo boxes, Parent Class and Child Class, are disabled when editing an existing association; they are enabled only when you create a new association by using the context menu and right-clicking an empty area of the design surface. Under Association Properties, you must select the members composing the primary key under the Parent Class, and then choose the appropriate corresponding members in the Child Class.

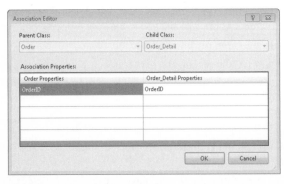

FIGURE 7-11 Association properties.

After creating an association, you can edit it in more detail by selecting the arrow in the graphical model and then editing it in the Properties pane, as shown in Figure 7-12.

By default, the *Association* is defined in a bidirectional manner. The child class gets a property with the same name as the parent class (*Order_Detail.Order* in our example), so it can get a typed reference to the parent itself. The parent class gets a property that represents the set of child elements (*Order.Order_Details* in our example).

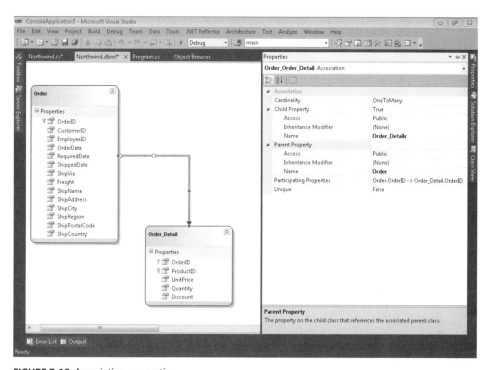

FIGURE 7-12 Association properties.

Table 7-5 provides an explanation of all the properties available in an association. As you will see, most of these settings can significantly change the output produced.

TABLE 7-5 Association Properties

Property	Description
Cardinality	Defines the cardinality of the association between parent and child nodes. This property has an impact only on the member defined in the parent class. Usually (and by default), it is set to *OneToMany*, which will generate a member in the parent class that will enumerate a sequence of child items. The only other possible value is *OneToOne*, which will generate a single property of the same type as the referenced child entity. See the sidebar "Understanding the Cardinality Property" later in this chapter for more information.
	By default, this property is set to *OneToMany*. Using the *OneToOne* setting is recommended, for example, when you split a logical entity that has many data members into more than one database table.
Child Property	If this property is set to *False*, the parent class will not contain a property with a collection or a reference of the child nodes. By default, it is set to *True*.
Child Property/Access	Access modifier for the member children in the parent class. It can be *Public* or *Internal*. By default, it is *Public*.
Child Property/Inheritance Modifier	Inheritance modifier to be used in the member children in the parent class. It can be *(None)*, *new*, *new virtual*, *override*, or *virtual*. By default, it is *(None)*.
Child Property/Name	Name of the member children in the parent class. By default, it has the plural name of the child entity class. If you set *Cardinality* to *OneToOne*, you would probably change this name to the singular form.
Parent Property/Access	Access modifier for the parent member in the child class. It can be *Public* or *Internal*. By default, it is *Public*.
Parent Property/Inheritance Modifier	Inheritance modifier to be used in the parent member in the child class. It can be *(None)*, *new*, *new virtual*, *override*, or *virtual*. By default, it is *(None)*.
Parent Property/Name	Name of the parent member in the child class. By default, it has the same singular name as the parent entity class.
Participating Properties	Displays the list of related properties that make the association work. Editing this property opens the Association Editor, which is shown in Figure 7-11.
Unique	Corresponds to the *IsUnique* setting of the *Association* attribute. It should be *True* when *Cardinality* is set to *OneToOne*. However, you are in charge of keeping these properties synchronized. *Cardinality* controls only the code generated for the *Child Property*, whereas *Unique* controls only the *Association* attribute, which is the only one used by the LINQ to SQL engine to compose SQL queries. By default, it is set to *False*.

If you have a parent-child relationship in the same table, the O/R Designer automatically detects it from the foreign key constraint in the relational table whenever you drag it into the model. It is recommended that you change the automatically generated name for *Child Property* and *Parent Property*. For example, importing the Employees table from Northwind results in *Employees* for the Child Property Name and *Employee1* for the Parent Property Name. You can rename these more appropriately as, for example, *DirectReports* and *Manager*, respectively.

> **Warning**   The Child Property and Parent Property of a parent-child *Association* referencing the same table cannot be used in a *DataLoadOptions.LoadWith<T>* call because it does not support cycles.

One-to-One Relationships

Most of the time, you create a one-to-many association between two entities, and the default values of the *Association* properties should be sufficient. However, it is easy to get lost with a one-to-one relationship. The first point to make is about when to use a one-to-one relationship. A one-to-one relationship should be intended as a one-to-zero-or-one relationship, where the related child entity might or might not exist. For example, you can define the simple model shown in Figure 7-13. For each *Contact*, you can have a related *Customer*, containing its amount of *Credit*. In the Properties pane, the properties of the association between *Contact* and *Customer* that have been changed from their default values are in bold.

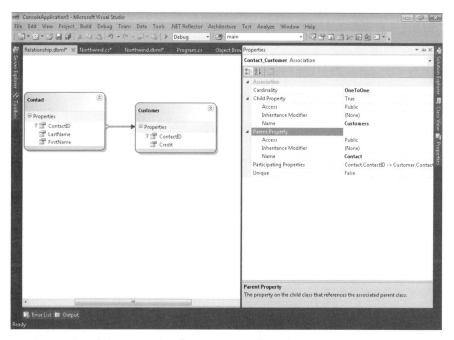

FIGURE 7-13 Association properties of a one-to-one relationship.

Cardinality should already be set to *OneToOne* when you create the *Association*. However, it is always better to check it. You also have to set the *Unique* property to *True* and change the *Child Name* property to the singular *Customer* value.

The *ContactID* member in the *Contact* entity is a primary key defined as *INT IDENTITY* in the database. Thus, it has the *Auto Generated Value* property set to *True* and *Auto-Sync* set to *OnInsert*. The *Customer* entity contains another member called *ContactID*, which is also a primary key, but is not generated from the database. In fact, you will use the key generated for a *Contact* to assign the *Customer.ContactID* value. Thanks to the *Contact.Customer* and *Customer.Contact* properties, you can simply assign the relationship by setting one of these properties, without worrying about the underlying *ContactID* field. In the following code, you can see an example of two *Contact* instances saved to the *DataContext*; one of them is associated with a *Customer* instance:

```
RelationshipDataContext db = new RelationshipDataContext();

Contact contactPaolo = new Contact();
contactPaolo.LastName = "Pialorsi";
contactPaolo.FirstName = "Paolo";

Contact contactMarco = new Contact();
Customer customer = new Customer();
contactMarco.LastName = "Russo";
contactMarco.FirstName = "Marco";
contactMarco.Customer = customer;
customer.Credit = 1000;

db.Contacts.InsertOnSubmit(contactPaolo);
db.Contacts.InsertOnSubmit(contactMarco);
db.SubmitChanges();
```

In this case the relationship was created by setting the *Contact.Customer* property, but you could obtain the same result by setting the *Customer.Contact* property. Take for example the following line of code:

```
contactMarco.Customer = customer;
```

Thanks to the synchronization code automatically produced by the code generator, the previous one-to-one relationship line of code produces the same result as writing the following:

```
customer.Contact = contactMarco;
```

However, you have to remember that the *Customer.Contact* member is mandatory if you create a *Contact* instance, whereas *Contact.Customer* can be left set to the default *null* value if no *Customer* is related to that *Contact*. At this point, it should be clear why the direction of the association is relevant even in a one-to-one relationship. As we said, it is not really a one-to-one relationship but a one-to-zero-or-one relationship, where the association stems from the parent that always exists to the child that may not exist.

Warning A common error made when defining a one-to-one association is using the wrong direction for the association. In the example, if the association went from *Customer* to *Contact*, it would not generate a compilation error; instead, the previous code would throw an exception when trying to submit changes to the database.

Understanding the *Cardinality* Property

To better understand the behavior of the *Cardinality* property, it is worth taking a look at the generated code. Here is an excerpt of the code generated with *Cardinality* set to *OneToMany*. The member is exposed with the plural name of *Customers*.

```
public partial class Contact {
    public Contact() {
        this._Customers = new EntitySet<Customer>(
                            new Action<Customer>(this.attach_Customers),
                            new Action<Customer>(this.detach_Customers));
    }

    private EntitySet<Customer> _Customers;

    [Association(Name="Contact_Customer", Storage="_Customers",
                ThisKey="ContactID", OtherKey="ContactID")]
    public EntitySet<Customer> Customers {
        get { return this._Customers; }
        set { this._Customers.Assign(value); }
    }
}
```

And this is the code generated when *Cardinality* is set to *OneToOne*. The member is exposed with the singular name of *Customer*. (You need to manually change the *Child Property Name* if you change the *Cardinality* property.)

```
public partial class Contact {
    public Contact() {
        this._Customer = default(EntityRef<Customer>);
    }

    private EntityRef<Customer> _Customer;

    [Association(Name="Contact_Customer", Storage="_Customer",
                ThisKey="ContactID", IsUnique=true, IsForeignKey=false)]
```

```
    public Customer Customer {
        get { return this._Customer.Entity; }
        set {
            Customer previousValue = this._Customer.Entity;
            if ((previousValue != value)
                || (this._Customer.HasLoadedOrAssignedValue == false)) {
                this.SendPropertyChanging();
                if ((previousValue != null)) {
                    this._Customer.Entity = null;
                    previousValue.Contact = null;
                }
                this._Customer.Entity = value;
                if ((value != null)) {
                    value.Contact = this;
                }
                this.SendPropertyChanged("Customer");
            }
        }
    }
}
```

As you can see, in the parent class, you get a *Contact.Customer* member of type *EntityRef<Customer>* when *Cardinality* is set to *OneToOne*. But with *Cardinality* set to *OneToMany*, you get a *Contact.Customers* member of type *EntitySet<Customer>*. Finally, the code generated for the *Customer* class does not depend on the *Cardinality* setting.

Entity Inheritance

LINQ to SQL supports the definition of a hierarchy of classes all bound to the same source table. The LINQ to SQL engine generates the right class in the hierarchy, based on the value of a specific row of that table. Each class is identified by a specific value in a column, following the *InheritanceMapping* attribute applied to the base class, as you saw in the section "Entity Inheritance" in Chapter 5.

Creating a hierarchy of classes in the O/R Designer, starting from an existing database, requires you to complete the following actions:

1. Create a Data class for each class of the hierarchy. You can drag the table for the base class from Server Explorer, and then create other empty classes by dragging a Class item from the Toolbox. Rename the classes you add according to their intended use.

2. Set the *Source* property for each added class equal to the *Source* property of the base class you dragged from the data source.

3. After you have at least a base class and a derived class, create the Inheritance relationship. Select the Inheritance item in the Toolbox, and draw a connection starting from the deriving class and ending with the base class. You can also define a multiple-level hierarchy.

4. If you have members in the base class that will be used only by some derived classes, you can cut and paste them in the designer. (Note that dragging and dropping members is not allowed.)

For example, in Figure 7-14 you can see the result of the following operations:

1. Drag the Contact table from Northwind.

2. Add the other empty Data classes (*Employee, CompanyContact, Customer, Shipper*, and *Supplier*).

3. Put the *dbo.Contacts* value into the *Source* property for all added Data classes. (Note that *dbo.Contacts* is already the *Source* value of the base class *Contact*.)

4. Define the *Inheritance* between *Employee* and *Contact* and between *CustomerContact* and *Contact*.

5. Define the *Inheritance* between *Customer* and *CompanyContact*, *Shipper* and *CompanyContact*, and *Supplier* and *CompanyContact*.

6. Cut the *CompanyName* member from *Contact*, and paste it into *CompanyContact*.

7. Set the Discriminator property of every *Inheritance* item to *ContactType*. (See Table 7-6 for further information about this property.)

8. Set the Inheritance Default Property of every *Inheritance* item to *Contact*.

9. Set the Base Class Discriminator Value of every *Inheritance* item to *Contact*.

10. Set the Derived Class Discriminator Value to *Employee, Customer, Shipper*, or *Supplier* for each corresponding *Inheritance* item.

This example uses an intermediate class (*CompanyContact*) to simplify the other derived classes (*Supplier, Shipper*, and *Customer*). We skipped the *CompanyContact* class that sets the Derived Class Discriminator Value because that intermediate class does not have concrete data in the database table.

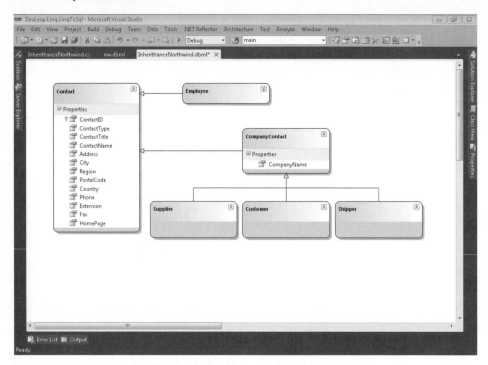

FIGURE 7-14 Design of a class hierarchy based on the Northwind.Contact table.

In Table 7-6, you can see an explanation of all the properties available for an Inheritance item. We used these properties to produce the design shown in Figure 7-14.

TABLE 7-6 Inheritance Properties

Property	Description
Inheritance Default	This is the type that will be used to create entities for rows that do not match any defined inheritance codes (which are the values defined for *Base Class Discriminator Value* and *Derived Class Discriminator Value*). This setting defines which of the generated *InheritanceMapping* attributes will have the *IsDefault=true* setting.
Base Class Discriminator Value	This is a value of the *Discriminator Property* that specifies the base class type. When you set this property for an *Inheritance* item, all *Inheritance* items originating from the same data class will assume the same value.
Derived Class Discriminator Value	This is a value of the *Discriminator Property* that specifies the derived class type. It corresponds to the *Code* setting of the *InheritanceMapping* attribute.
Discriminator Property	The column in the database that is used to discriminate between entities. When you set this property for an *Inheritance* item, all *Inheritance* items originating from the same data class will assume the same value. The selected data member in the base class will be decorated with the *IsDiscriminator=true* setting in the *Column* attribute.

Stored Procedures and User-Defined Functions

Dragging a stored procedure or a UDF from Server Explorer to the O/R Designer surface creates a method in the *DataContext* class corresponding to that stored procedure or UDF. In Figure 7-15, you can see an example of the *[Customers By City]* stored procedure dragged onto the Methods pane of the O/R Designer.

Note You can show and hide the Methods pane by using the context menu that opens when you right-click the design surface.

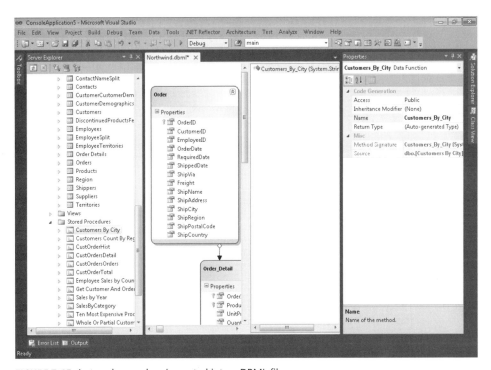

FIGURE 7-15 A stored procedure imported into a DBML file.

When you import either a stored procedure or a UDF, the O/R Designer creates a *Data Function* item in the *DataContext*-derived class. The properties of a *Data Function* are separated into two groups: Misc and Code Generation.

The Misc group contains two read-only properties, *Method Signature* and *Source*. The *Source* property contains the name of the stored procedure or UDF in the database. The value of the *Method Signature* property is constructed using the *Name* property (shown in Table 7-7) and the parameters of the stored procedure or UDF.

The Code Generation group of properties requires the more detailed explanation shown in Table 7-7.

TABLE 7-7 Code-Generation Properties for *Data Function*

Property	Description
Access	Access modifier for the generated method in the *DataContext*-derived class. It can be *Public, Protected, Protected Internal, Internal*, or *Private*. By default, it is *Public*.
Inheritance Modifier	Inheritance modifier to be used in the member declaration. It can be *(None), new, new virtual, override*, or *virtual*. By default, it is *(None)*.
Name	Name of the method representing a stored procedure or a UDF in the database. By default, the name is derived from the name of the stored procedure or the UDF, replacing invalid characters in C# or Visual Basic with an underscore (_). It corresponds to the *Name* setting of the *Function* attribute.
Return Type	Type returned by the method. It can be a common language runtime (CLR) type for scalar-valued UDFs, or *Class Data* for stored procedures and table-valued UDFs. In the latter case, by default it is *(Auto-generated Type)*. After it has been changed to an existing *Data Class* name, this property cannot be reverted to *(Auto-generated Type)*. See the next section, "Return Type of Data Function," for more information.

Return Type of Data Function

Usually a stored procedure or a table-valued UDF returns a number of rows, which in LINQ to SQL become a sequence of instances of an entity class (discussed in the "Stored Procedures and User-Defined Functions" section in Chapter 5). By default, the *Return Type* property is set to *(Auto-generated Type)*, which means that the code generator creates a class a member for each column returned by SQL Server. For example, the following code excerpt is part of the *Customers_By_CityResult* type automatically generated to handle the *Customer_By_City* result (the *get* and *set* accessors have been removed from the properties declaration for brevity):

```
public partial class Customers_By_CityResult {
    private string _CustomerID;
    private string _ContactName;
    private string _CompanyName;
    private string _City;

    public Customers_By_CityResult() { }

    [Column(Storage="_CustomerID", DbType="NChar(5) NOT NULL",
            CanBeNull=false)]
    public string CustomerID { ... }

    [Column(Storage="_ContactName", DbType="NVarChar(30)")]
    public string ContactName { ... }
```

```
    [Column(Storage="_CompanyName", DbType="NVarChar(40) NOT NULL",
            CanBeNull=false)]
    public string CompanyName { ... }

    [Column(Storage="_City", DbType="NVarChar(15)")]
    public string City { ... }
}
```

However, you can instruct the code generator to use an existing *Data Class* to store the data resulting from a stored procedure call, setting the *Return Type* property to the desired type. The combo box in the Properties pane presents all types defined in the *DataContext*. You should select a type compatible with the data returned by SQL Server.

> **Important** *Return Type* must have at least a public member with the same name as a returned column. If you specify a type with public members that do not correspond to returned columns, these "missing" members will have a default value.

You can create an entity class specifically to handle the result coming from a stored procedure or UDF call. In that case, you might want to define a class without specifying a *Source* property. In this way, you can control all the details of the returned type. You can also use a class corresponding to a database table. In this case, remember that you can modify the returned entity. However, to make the *SubmitChanges* work, you need to get the initial value for all required data members of the entity (at least those with the *UpdateCheck* constraint) to match the row at the moment of update. In other words, if the stored procedure or UDF does not return all the members for an entity, it is better to create an entity dedicated to this purpose, using only the returned columns and specifying the destination table as the *Source* property.

> **Note** To map *Return Type* to an entity during the method construction, you can drag the stored procedure or UDF and drop it on the entity class that you want to use as a return type. This way, the method is created only if the entity class has a corresponding column in the result for each of the entity members. If that condition is not satisfied, the O/R Designer displays an error message and cancels the operation.

Mapping to *Delete*, *Insert*, and *Update* Operations

You can use any imported stored procedures to customize the *Delete*, *Insert*, and *Update* operations of an entity class. To do that, after you import the stored procedures into *DataContext*, you need to bind them to the corresponding operation in the entity class. Figure 7-16 shows the Configure Behavior dialog box, which you can use to map stored procedure method arguments to the corresponding class properties.

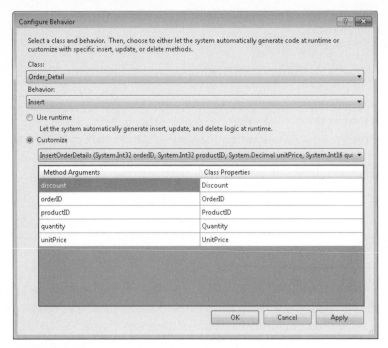

FIGURE 7-16 Use of a stored procedure to insert an *Order_Detail*.

More Info For more information, see the "Customizing Insert, Update, and Delete" section in Chapter 6.

Views and Schema Support

All views in a database can be used to generate an entity class in the DBML file. However, LINQ to SQL does not know whether a view is updatable, so it is your responsibility to use an entity derived from a view correctly, updating entity instances only if they come from an updatable view.

If the database has tables in different schemas, the O/R Designer does not consider them when creating the name of data classes or data functions. The schema is maintained as part of the *Source* value, but it does not participate in the name construction of generated objects. You can rename the objects, but they cannot be defined in different namespaces, because all the entity classes are defined in the same namespace, which is controlled by the *Entity Namespace* property of the generated *DataContext*-derived class.

More Info Other third-party code generators might support the use of namespaces, using SQL Server schemas to create entities in corresponding namespaces.

Summary

In this chapter, you have seen some of the available tools for generating LINQ to SQL entities and *DataContext* classes. The .NET Framework SDK includes the SQLMetal command-line tool. Visual Studio has a graphical editor known as the Object Relational Designer (O/R Designer). Both can create DBML files, generate source code in C# or Visual Basic, and create external XML mapping files. The O/R Designer also supports editing existing DBML files, and dynamically importing existing tables, views, stored procedures, and UDFs from an existing SQL Server database.

Chapter 8
LINQ to Entities: Modeling Data with Entity Framework

LINQ to Entities is the official Microsoft Language Integrated Query (LINQ) engine for querying Microsoft ADO.NET Entity Framework models. This chapter covers the main capabilities and features offered by the ADO.NET Entity Data Model Designer available in Microsoft Visual Studio 2010.

The Entity Data Model

The first and most important step in developing a solution based on the Entity Framework is creating the Entity Data Model (EDM) itself. To achieve this goal, you have two options in Visual Studio 2010:

- Start from an existing database schema.

- Start from scratch (an empty model) and generate the resulting database schema.

Both solutions have pros and cons, and this section covers them in detail. Although using the Entity Data Model Designer is straightforward, you can instead use the EdmGen.exe command-line tool—available in the Microsoft .NET Framework Software Development Kit (SDK)—to do essentially the same things the Entity Data Model Designer does.

Generating a Model from an Existing Database

If you already have a database for the persistence layer, you should start by generating your EDM from the database. This approach is called "database-first," because you start from the database.

 Note To start creating an EDM using the Visual Studio 2010 Entity Data Model Designer, refer to "How to: Create a New .edmx File (Entity Data Model Tools)" at *http://msdn.microsoft.com/en-us/library/cc716703.aspx*.

By choosing this option, you can use the Entity Data Model Designer to select the tables, views, and stored procedures that you want to include in the resulting model. Visual Studio provides a step-by-step wizard, named Entity Data Model Wizard, which by default supports the mapping of single tables or views to single entities, and of single stored procedures to corresponding methods. Figure 8-1 shows the main step of this wizard.

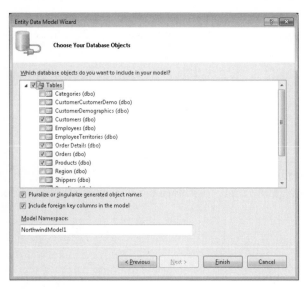

FIGURE 8-1 Selecting objects to model in the Entity Data Model Wizard.

In Figure 8-2, you can see the Entity Data Model Designer user interface (UI) that results from this modeling methodology, applied to some basic tables of the Northwind database.

As you can see in Figure 8-2, you have the opportunity to define entities that correspond in a one-to-one manner to the database's tables. Although it's not quite as apparent, you're not limited to one-to-one relationships, as you will see later in this chapter; you can shape your entities in a fashion more suitable to your needs. For example, you can aggregate multiple tables into a unique entity or group properties in complex types. When defining entities, you are free to give them whatever names you like. Sensibly, the wizard gives the generated entities names that correspond to their source table, pluralizing the names if you select that option (see Figure 8-1).

Every entity has a set of properties, each of which maps to the underlying columns in that entity's associated source data table or view. Through the Entity Data Model Designer, you can change the name, type, and modeling in general, of every column and/or property.

As you can see in Figure 8-2, the designer also infers relationships between tables, defining navigation properties and foreign keys between related tables. Relationships are described in more detail later in this chapter, in the section "Associations and Foreign Keys."

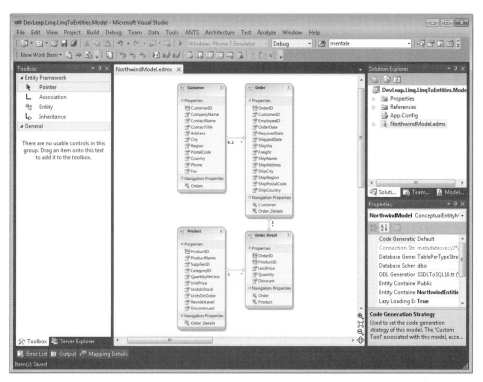

FIGURE 8-2 The Visual Studio Entity Data Model Designer.

If you change the database structure, or you later add additional tables, views, or stored procedures to the model, you can invoke the Update Model From Database feature from the designer's context menu. That feature prompts you with a wizard similar to the one used to generate the model the first time, letting you add, refresh, or remove tables, views, and stored procedures from your model.

Designing an EDM from an existing database is simple, but the result is tied very tightly to the physical database structure. Thus, it works only in situations where your database schema is known and largely fixed during your application's lifetime. In situations like this, you can think of an Object Relational Mapping (ORM) like the Entity Framework as essentially a data layer replacement, rather than a pure ORM approach. Nevertheless, this type of data model generation follows a well-supported path; you can take advantage of the capabilities of the Entity Framework to quickly define data access code, without having to worry about data access details.

Starting from an Empty Model

When you want to design your data model from scratch, independent of any existing persistence layer and concentrating solely on the model, you can begin with an empty model—the other option provided by the Visual Studio Entity Data Model Wizard. Using this option, you can design your entities, properties, constraints, relationships, and navigation properties freely on the designer surface. At some point (typically when you have finished the design process), you can generate a corresponding physical database structure by simply clicking Generate Database From Model on the designer's context menu. You can also use code to generate the database, invoking a specific method provided by the Entity Framework's class library.

Being able to generate a database from a model was a top feature request for the current version of the Entity Framework, because many .NET Framework developers like to design their data models without having to think about the physical persistence storage. This technique is also known as modeling with a "persistence ignorance" approach. You'll revisit the topic of data model persistence ignorance near the end of this chapter.

Figure 8-3 shows an Entity Framework domain model that was designed starting from an empty model.

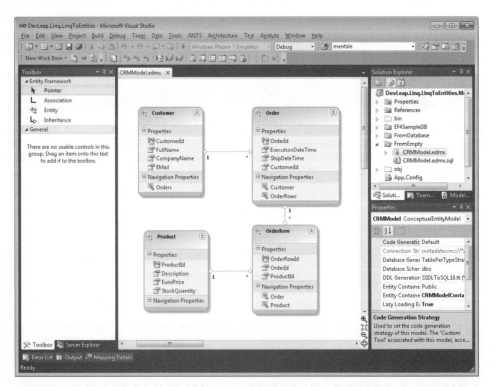

FIGURE 8-3 An EDM definition designed from scratch in the Visual Studio 2010 Entity Data Model Designer.

The result of this process is a Data Description Language (DDL) file ready to execute on a database. It is interesting to notice that the designer does *not* offer functionality to update the database schema after modifying the entity data model. Thus, whenever you change the entity model and need to update the persistence storage schema, you must recreate the target database from scratch. That can cause problems in a production environment; you might need a tool to compare the new database schema with the production schema so that you can synchronize them without losing any critical data. You can also download an Entity Designer Database Generation Power Pack from MSDN that provides you with some more generation workflows—most importantly, a database synchronization workflow that can per-form non-invasive *ALTER* commands and migrate data between different database versions.

> **Note** To download this package, go to *http://visualstudiogallery.msdn.microsoft.com/en-us /df3541c3-d833-4b65-b942-989e7ec74c87*.

The approach just described is called *model-first* and is very useful when building database-independent solutions. However, the result of this design technique is a physical database that must be analyzed and tuned to achieve an adequate level of performance. In fact, the DDL produced by the designer does not generate indexes or performance-tuning hints. To iden-tify the best indexes and tuning options, you should plan on using LINQ to Entities queries executed in a test environment to monitor and trace queries generated from the front-end to the back-end database.

> **More Info** Database generation is handled by a .NET Framework 4 Windows Workflow Foundation. You can customize this workflow, which is by default based on a file named TablePerTypeStrategy.xaml, located in the *MSVS*\common7\ide\extensions\microsoft\entity framework tools\dbgen folder. *MSVS* stands for the Microsoft Visual Studio installation folder. That same folder contains a file (SSDLToSQL10.tt) that describes the code template used to generate the DLL code.

Generated Code

Whether you chose the model-first or database-first approach, the designer generates an .edmx XML file that describes the entity model, as well as a code-behind file. This standard generated code defines a main class, inherited from the *ObjectContext* type, that represents the common and unique entry point for accessing the .edmx entities. In fact, it publishes the methods to access collections of entities, as well as to invoke stored procedures. Listing 8-1 shows an excerpt of the autogenerated *ObjectContext* for the sample model.

LISTING 8-1 Excerpt of the autogenerated code for the model-first entity data model, which inherits from *ObjectContext*

```
public partial class CRMModelContainer : ObjectContext {
    public CRMModelContainer() : base("name=CRMModelContainer", "CRMModelContainer") {
        // code omitted for simplicity ...
    }

    public CRMModelContainer(string connectionString) : base(connectionString,
    "CRMModelContainer") {
        // code omitted for simplicity ...
    }

    public CRMModelContainer(EntityConnection connection) : base(connection,
    "CRMModelContainer") {
        // code omitted for simplicity ...
    }

    partial void OnContextCreated();

    public ObjectSet<Customer> Customers {
        get {
            // code omitted for simplicity ...
        }
    }

    public ObjectSet<Order> Orders {
        get {
            // code omitted for simplicity ...
        }
    }

    public ObjectSet<Product> Products {
        get {
            // code omitted for simplicity ...
        }
    }

    public ObjectSet<OrderRow> OrderRows {
        get {
            // code omitted for simplicity ...
        }
    }

    // code omitted for simplicity ...
}
```

The *ObjectContext* class provides the basic behaviors for accessing the physical data through the entities of the EDM, as well as methods to handle objects' state and identity; data modifications; attaching and detaching of entities; execution of stored procedures; or running explicit SQL commands against the persistence store, and so on.

Moreover, the autogenerated code makes available a read-only property of type
ObjectSet<TEntity> for every entity defined in the EDM. This property is the entry point for
querying an entity by using LINQ queries.

The autogenerated code also defines a partial class for every entity in the model. Listing 8-2
contains an excerpt of the code that defines the model's *Customer* entity.

LISTING 8-2 A code excerpt representative of the autogenerated code for the *Customer* entity

```
[EdmEntityTypeAttribute(NamespaceName="CRMModel", Name="Customer")]
[Serializable()]
[DataContractAttribute(IsReference=true)]
public partial class Customer : EntityObject {
    public static Customer CreateCustomer(global::System.Int32 customerId,
            global::System.String fullName, global::System.String companyName,
            global::System.String eMail) {
        // Code omitted for simplicity ...
    }

    [EdmScalarPropertyAttribute(EntityKeyProperty=true, IsNullable=false)]
    [DataMemberAttribute()]
    public global::System.Int32 CustomerId {
        get; set;
    }
    partial void OnCustomerIdChanging(global::System.Int32 value);
    partial void OnCustomerIdChanged();

    [EdmScalarPropertyAttribute(EntityKeyProperty=false, IsNullable=false)]
    [DataMemberAttribute()]
    public global::System.String FullName {
        get; set;
    }
    partial void OnFullNameChanging(global::System.String value);
    partial void OnFullNameChanged();

    // Code omitted for simplicity ...

    [XmlIgnoreAttribute()]
    [SoapIgnoreAttribute()]
    [DataMemberAttribute()]
    [EdmRelationshipNavigationPropertyAttribute("CRMModel", "CustomerOrder", "Order")]
    public EntityCollection<Order> Orders {
        get; set;
    }
}
```

You can see that the entity type inherits by default from the *EntityObject* class; it provides a
public read/write property for each public property defined for an entity, and offers a couple
of partial methods for each property (*On[Property]Changing/Changed*) that you can use to
customize business logic while managing entity data.

You can see that the entity class itself, as well as its properties, is decorated with custom attributes that instruct the Entity Framework about that entity's behavior. For example, when the first attribute, *EdmEntityTypeAttribute*, is applied to the entity, it instructs the Entity Framework that this class represents an entity; when the attribute *EdmScalarPropertyAttribute* is applied to properties, it instructs the Entity Framework to manage the target property as a field of the custom entity.

> **Tip** In general, you should define a dedicated Visual Studio project to host .edmx files and their code-behind classes. In fact, you will probably need to share the generated code across multiple libraries, and having a dedicated assembly for the model simplifies managing chains of references.

In the "T4 Templates" section, later in this chapter, you will see how to customize the code template that generates the final code so that you can modify both the generated .NET Framework code and the XML inside the .edmx code.

Entity Data Model (.edmx) Files

The designer-generated .edmx file is an XML file based on a specific XML schema with the namespace *http://schemas.microsoft.com/ado/2008/10/edmx*. It consists of three main sections:

- **Storage Schema**   Defines the storage layer (the database) through a Storage Schema Definition Language (SSDL)

- **Conceptual Schema**   Describes the conceptual layer (the entity) through a Conceptual Schema Definition Language (CSDL)

- **Conceptual to Storage Mapping**   Defines the mappings between the conceptual schema and the storage schema

For multidatabase solutions, although the conceptual schema should remain exactly the same for each and every physical database, the storage schema and the mapping might change according to the specific physical database used.

In unusual situations, you may need to manually change some of the information described in the .edmx file, because the Entity Data Model Designer does not support every possible modification. However, for most common scenarios, designing the .edmx file through the UI will suffice.

The Entity Data Model Designer also has a Model Browser feature that you can use to navigate through the conceptual and storage models. Figure 8-4 shows the Model Browser for the Northwind model. Notice the tree view on the right, which presents the conceptual model (the NorthwindModel node) using entity types, complex types, and associations. Below the model is the entity container, which represents the *ObjectContext* specialized class, with entity sets, association sets, and eventually (although not shown in Figure 8-4), function imports (stored procedures). The other side of the screen holds the storage schema (the Northwind-Model.Store node in the tree view) with tables, views, stored procedures, and constraints. You can change the properties of all these items using the standard Visual Studio property grid toolbox.

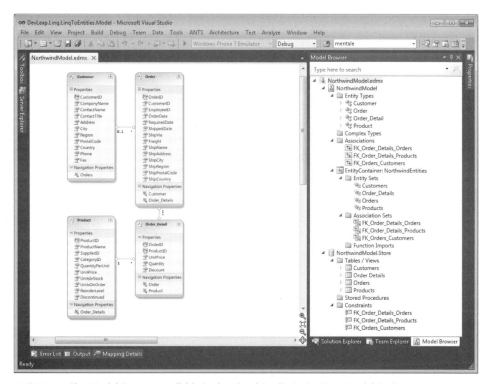

FIGURE 8-4 The Model Browser available in the Visual Studio Entity Data Model Designer.

Note The Model Browser opens when the Entity Data Model Designer is opened. If the Model Browser is not visible, right-click the main design surface and select Model Browser.

The .edmx file also contains a designer section that's specific to the Entity Data Model Designer, which holds information about shapes, connection paths, and so forth. You should not change this information manually.

Associations and Foreign Keys

One main feature of an Object Relational Mapper (ORM) is its ability to manage data as an in-memory graph of related entities, allowing you to navigate through entities based on relationships. However, one controversial factor in the definition of relationships between entities is the concept of *foreign keys*. In fact, from a database (storage) point of view, it is absolutely natural to have foreign keys in tables that are related to other tables, whereas in a conceptual model, foreign keys are, at best, a noisy form of plumbing. In the object oriented world, a relationship between two entities is a memory reference—not a foreign key property storing an ID value. With the Entity Framework in Microsoft .NET Framework 4, you can define relationships between entities in two ways: either with or without foreign keys. This section delves deeper into both these scenarios.

The first scenario, called *Independent Associations*, has been present since the first release of ADO.NET Entity Framework with Microsoft .NET Framework 3.5 Service Pack 1. Using this configuration, whenever you define a relationship between two entities, you also define a *navigation property* on both sides that corresponds to the related entity instances. For example, consider the association between *Customers* and *Orders* shown in Figure 8-5.

FIGURE 8-5 The Independent Association between *Customers* and *Orders*.

As you can see, the *Customer* entity has a navigation property to browse the *Orders* of the current *Customer*. The *Order* entity has a navigation property named *Customer* as well. If you need to access the *CustomerID* of the *Customer* instance related to an *Order* instance, you need to write code similar to that shown in Listing 8-3.

LISTING 8-3 An excerpt of code that works with Independent Associations between *Customers* and *Orders*

```
NorthwindEntities nw = new NorthwindEntities();

// Browse for orders of a specific customer
var query =
    from o in nw.Orders
    where o.Customer.CustomerID == "ALFKI"
    select new {
        o.OrderID,
        o.OrderDate,
        o.Customer.CustomerID
    };

// Add a new order to a specific customer
Order newOrder = new Order {
    OrderDate = DateTime.Now,
    Customer = nw.Customers.Single(c => c.CustomerID == "ANATR"),
    ShipCountry = "Italy",
};

nw.Orders.AddObject(newOrder);
nw.SaveChanges();
```

The code in bold demonstrates how the code works directly with the related entities. In fact, there is no foreign key property that represents the *CustomerID* inside the *Order* class. Thus, the only way to reference the properties of the *Customer* is to go through the object instance. Although this approach is "pure" from a conceptual viewpoint, it is extremely expensive because you have to materialize a *Customer* instance whenever you need to access the properties of the corresponding related *Order* instances.

The second scenario, called *Foreign Key Association*, is new in Entity Framework 4. In this case, the Entity Framework defines the scalar properties corresponding to the storage foreign key inside the related entities, without limiting you to navigation properties. Figure 8-6 shows the same relationship as Figure 8-5, but using a Foreign Key Association instead.

You can choose to work this way either through the model wizard or by editing the model inside the designer. In fact, if you double-click the association line between the entities, a dialog box appears that corresponds to the referential constraint of a Foreign Key Association or an Independent Association. With these dialog boxes (shown in Figure 8-7), you can edit or delete the referential constraint of the foreign key association. Moreover, when adding a new Association via the Entity Data Model Designer, you can select the option to Add Foreign Key Properties to the child entity.

FIGURE 8-6 The Foreign Key Association between *Customers* and *Orders*.

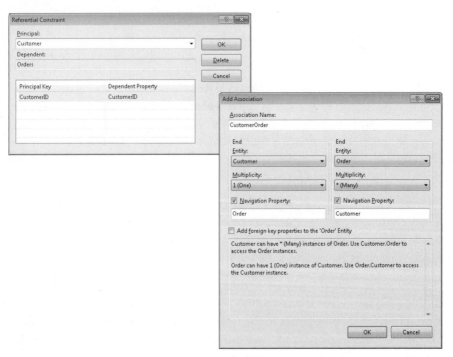

FIGURE 8-7 The Entity Data Model Designer dialog boxes for adding or managing the referential constraint of a Foreign Key Association (on the left) or an Independent Association (on the right).

Listing 8-4 shows a code excerpt that uses the foreign key association between *Customers* and *Orders* to achieve the same results as Listing 8-3.

LISTING 8-4 An excerpt of code working with Foreign Key Associations between *Customers* and *Orders*

```
NorthwindEntities nw = new NorthwindEntities();

// Browse for orders of a specific customer
var query =
    from o in nw.Orders
    where o.CustomerID == "ALFKI"
    select new {
        o.OrderID,
        o.OrderDate,
        o.CustomerID
    };

// Add a new order to a specific customer
Order newOrder = new Order {
    OrderDate = DateTime.Now,
    CustomerID = "ANATR",
    ShipCountry = "Italy",
};

nw.Orders.AddObject(newOrder);
nw.SaveChanges();
```

As you can see, the code in Listing 8-4 is simpler than in Listing 8-3 and you don't have to materialize a *Customer* instance to reference its *CustomerID*. This approach is particularly useful when you need to data-bind entities to Windows Presentation Foundation (WPF) or Windows Forms controls, as well as when developing Microsoft ASP.NET MVC solutions, just to provide a couple of examples.

> **Note** To keep foreign keys and references synchronized, the Entity Framework needs some supporting code. For standard autogenerated entities, the standard code generation template handles everything automatically. For custom entities, however, support for synchronizing foreign keys and references depends on the type of custom entities involved. For example, plain-old CLR objects (POCO) Proxy entities or entities that implement the *IEntityWithChangeTracker* interface will still support synchronization. (POCO is described in more detail in the "POCO Support" section, later in this chapter.)

You can mix association types within the same model, letting you choose the most appropriate solution for each of your associations. The only exception to this is if you have a join table that contains only foreign keys. In this situation, the Entity Framework always uses an independent association to define the many-to-many relationship.

While on the topic of associations, one last thing to notice is the cascade delete functionality provided by the Entity Framework and supported by the Entity Data Model Designer. In fact, when defining an association, you can choose either Cascade Delete, which deletes child records when a parent record is deleted, or None. Moreover, whenever the relationship between the entities is identifying (that is, the dependent entity cannot exist without the principal entity), the Entity Framework automatically enables the Cascade Delete behavior. Conversely, when the relationship is not identifying, the behavior can be None. In this case, when principal entity is deleted, a NULL value is assigned to the dependent entity's foreign key.

Complex Types

Another useful feature introduced in Entity Framework 4 is the concept of *complex type*. This is a set of properties that can be used as a group and shared by different entities. Alternatively, you can use it just to separate that group from other properties of a more complex entity. A complex type is not an independent entity; it's more like a reusable structure. In Figure 8-8, you can see the user interface of the Entity Data Model Designer with a set of scalar properties selected and ready to be converted into a complex type, by clicking Refactor Into New Complex Type on the contextual menu. In general, it is useful to refactor scalar properties into complex types whenever you can share them between different entity types. For example, the address is a complex type that belongs to a *Customer* entity, as well as to an *Employee* entity.

FIGURE 8-8 Part of the Entity Data Model Designer interface, used to refactor a set of properties into a complex type.

Figure 8-9 shows the result from a graphical point of view. The boxes surround the complex type, its definition, and its usage. Under the covers, the Entity Data Model Designer generates a custom .NET Framework type that describes the complex type, and defines a new property in the main entity, whose type corresponds to the autogenerated complex type.

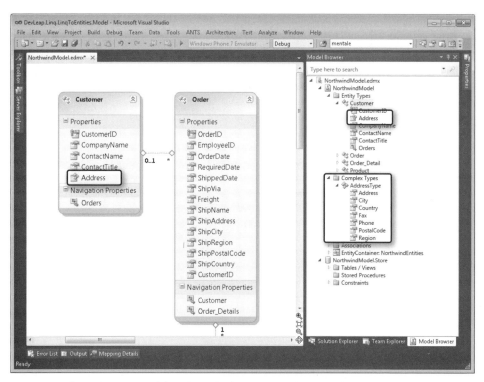

FIGURE 8-9 The Entity Data Model Designer displaying a complex property.

Listing 8-5 shows an excerpt of the autogenerated code that describes the *Address* complex property defined in Figures 8-8 and 8-9.

LISTING 8-5 The *Address* complex property defined in Figures 8-8 and 8-9

```
[EdmComplexTypeAttribute(NamespaceName="NorthwindModel", Name="AddressType")]
[DataContractAttribute(IsReference=true)]
[Serializable()]
public partial class AddressType : ComplexObject {

    [EdmScalarPropertyAttribute(EntityKeyProperty=false, IsNullable=true)]
    [DataMemberAttribute()]
```

```csharp
public global::System.String Address {
    get {
        return _Address;
    }
    set {
        OnAddressChanging(value);
        ReportPropertyChanging("Address");
        _Address = StructuralObject.SetValidValue(value, true);
        ReportPropertyChanged("Address");
        OnAddressChanged();
    }
}
private global::System.String _Address;
partial void OnAddressChanging(global::System.String value);
partial void OnAddressChanged();

[EdmScalarPropertyAttribute(EntityKeyProperty=false, IsNullable=true)]
[DataMemberAttribute()]
public global::System.String City {
    get {
        return _City;
    }
    set {
        OnCityChanging(value);
        ReportPropertyChanging("City");
        _City = StructuralObject.SetValidValue(value, true);
        ReportPropertyChanged("City");
        OnCityChanged();
    }
}
private global::System.String _City;
partial void OnCityChanging(global::System.String value);
partial void OnCityChanged();

// Code omitted for simplicity ...
}
```

As you can see, the *AddressType* class inherits from the *ComplexObject* type, which internally is inherited from the *StructuralObject* type, just as the *EntityObject* type does. This is significant, because it means that both entities and complex types share the same base type and the same underlying business logic. In fact, they are both capable of tracking changes and can attach/detach from the objects graph. Of course, you can change the generated code by customizing the T4 template file, just as you can with standard entities. The T4 template is discussed in more detail later in this chapter.

You can also use complex types as the result of stored procedures. With these complex types, you can publish some of your Database Management Systems (DBMS) stored procedures as methods of the *ObjectContext* class. You'll cover the modeling of stored procedures later in this chapter.

Inheritance and Conditional Mapping

When creating real entity models, you sometimes need to support inheritance between entities. Within Entity Framework 4, inheritance is fully supported, and can be defined and customized using the Visual Studio Entity Data Model Designer. Conceptual model inheritance is similar to object-oriented inheritance; however, in the conceptual model, a derived type inherits all scalar, complex, and navigation properties from its parent entity, and cannot override any inherited property. An inherited entity can also have custom properties and behaviors, just as in the object-oriented world. Lastly, the conceptual model has single inheritance; you cannot inherit one entity from more than one base entity. A typical example of entity inheritance is shown in Figure 8-10, which depicts a *Contact* entity, defined as an abstract type, along with a two specialized inherited entities (*Supplier* and *Customer*).

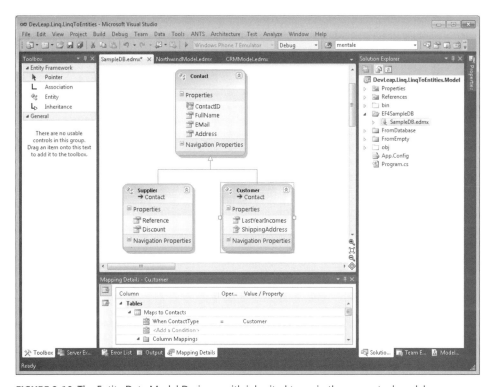

FIGURE 8-10 The Entity Data Model Designer with inherited types in the conceptual model.

The underlying persistence store has a table named *Contacts* with a *ContactType* field. This field can take a value of *Supplier* when the contact is a supplier or a value of *Customer* when the contact describes a customer instance. In addition to the main *Contacts* table, there are two tables that hold details about customers (table *CustomersDetails*) and suppliers (table *SuppliersDetails*). In Figure 8-11, you can see the database diagram used for this section.

The lower part of the designer shown in Figure 8-10 defines a mapping rule that instructs the Entity Framework to materialize a contact as a *Customer* type whenever the *ContactType* column has a value of *Customer*, or as a *Supplier* when the *ContactType* column has a value of *Supplier*. Notice that you cannot define multiple mapping conditions on a single field. The result of this mapping is a set of entities that are either of type *Customer* or *Supplier*.

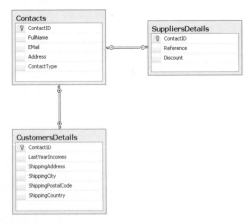

FIGURE 8-11 The database diagram of the entity inheritance sample.

You can see that the base abstract *Contact* type has properties (*ContactID*, *FullName*, *EMail*, and *Address*) that are common to both *Supplier* and *Customer* entities. Moreover, the *Supplier* type maps two scalar properties (*Reference* and *Discount*) to the corresponding columns in the *SuppliersDetails* table. Similarly, the *Customer* type has two specific properties, one scalar (*LastYearIncomes*) and one complex (*ShippingAddress*), defined by mapping the columns of the *CustomersDetails* table.

Listing 8-6 shows an excerpt of code working with inherited entities.

LISTING 8-6 A code excerpt using entity inheritance at the conceptual level

```
EF4SampleDBEntities ctx = new EF4SampleDBEntities();

// Browse all the contacts based on their type
foreach (var i in ctx.Contacts) {
    if (i is Supplier) {
        Supplier s = (Supplier)i;
        Console.WriteLine("Supplier {0} has ID {1}, and has a reference of {2}.",
            s.FullName, s.ContactID, s.Reference);
    }
    else if (i is Customer) {
        Customer c = (Customer)i;
        Console.WriteLine("Customer {0} has ID {1}, with an income of {2} last year",
            c.FullName, c.ContactID, c.LastYearIncomes);
    }
}
```

```
// Filter Customer entities only
var customers = from   c in ctx.Contacts.OfType<Customer>()
                select c;

foreach (var c in customers) {
    Console.WriteLine("Customer {0} has ID {1}, with an income of {2} last year",
        c.FullName, c.ContactID, c.LastYearIncomes);
}
```

Notice the usage of the *is* operator as a filter for contact types in the first code block. In the second code block of Listing 8-6, you can see the *OfType<T>* extension method, used to filter and extract only the entities of type *Customer*.

Modeling Stored Procedures

Physical databases often have stored procedures to manage direct access to data. In general, using stored procedures is a good choice for performance, maintainability, and security reasons. Nevertheless, using an ORM that directly makes Create, Read, Update, Delete, and Query (CRUDQ) operations against the physical data tables, skipping stored procedures, could be an issue for the original data access design policy. Fortunately, the Entity Framework, like many other ORMs, allows defining stored procedures for Create, Update, Delete (CUD) operations, as well as for executing specific commands to retrieve entities, complex type, or scalar values.

First of all, to be able to invoke a stored procedure from the Entity Framework, you must reference it in the storage schema, updating the model by clicking Update Model From Database on the context menu of the Entity Data Model Designer. After defining the reference at the storage level, you need to import the procedure at the conceptual level, defining a function that corresponds to the underlying stored procedure. This function becomes a method of the *ObjectContext* defined behind our model.

Non-CUD Stored Procedures

This section discusses those stored procedures that are not used for CUD operations. (Those that are used are covered in the next section.) Consider the database used in the previous section, with a table of *Contacts*. Imagine having a stored procedure named *GetCustomersByAddress*, which retrieves all the customers that have a specific search word in their address field. In Listing 8-7, you can see the DDL corresponding to this stored procedure.

LISTING 8-7 The DDL defining the *GetCustomersByAddress* stored procedure

```
CREATE PROCEDURE [dbo].[GetCustomersByAddress]
@Address nvarchar(100)
AS
BEGIN
    SELECT c.ContactID, c.FullName, c.EMail, c.[Address],
    cd.LastYearIncomes, cd.ShippingAddress, cd.ShippingCity,
    cd.ShippingPostalCode, cd.ShippingCountry
    FROM dbo.Contacts AS c
    INNER JOIN dbo.CustomersDetails AS cd ON c.ContactID = cd.ContactID
    WHERE c.ContactType = 'Customer'
    AND c.[Address] LIKE @Address
END
GO
```

As you can see, the stored procedure is very simple; it selects the results based on the *ContactType* field value and a *LIKE* comparison against the *Address* field. In Figure 8-12, you can see the designer Add Function Import form for importing the function into the model; this form appears after having defined the function in the storage schema.

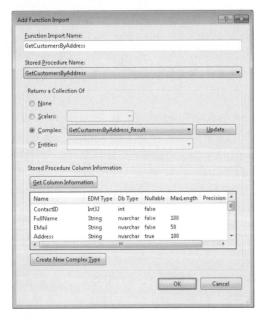

FIGURE 8-12 The dialog box used to import a stored procedure as a function into the conceptual model.

As you can see from Figure 8-12, you can choose how an imported stored procedure should return its results, if any. The options are as follows:

- **None**   This option is useful when the stored procedure does not return anything.

- **Scalars**   Select this option when the stored procedure returns a single scalar value. For example, a stored procedure that counts a set of records or retrieves a single field of a single record.

- **Complex**   Select this option whenever the result is a set of items with a complex structure. You've already seen how to define a Complex Type. (See the "Complex Types" section earlier in this chapter for further details.) Alternatively, you can define a new complex type by clicking the Get Column Information button, and then clicking the Create New Complex Type button.

- **Entities**   This option is useful when you want the stored procedure to return a collection of entities already defined in the conceptual model.

Using the previous example, the *GetCustomersByAddress* stored procedure retrieves a list of *Customer* types, made of the following fields: *ContactID*, *FullName*, *EMail*, *Address*, *LastYearIncomes*, *ShippingAddress*, *ShippingCity*, *ShippingPostalCode*, and *ShippingCountry*. It would be most useful to select a result of type *Entities* and then select an entity of type *Customer*. Unfortunately, the *Customer* type has a complex property to represent the *ShippingAddress* and the current version of the Entity Framework does not support entities with complex properties as results of a stored procedure. For these reasons, we defined the result as a new complex type (*GetCustomersByAddress_Result*) autogenerated by the designer; you can translate that type into a *Customer* instance using custom code.

The imported function is a method of the autogenerated *ObjectContext* derived class. In Listing 8-8 is an excerpt of code that invokes the method, as well as the definition of the method in the *ObjectContext*.

LISTING 8-8 An excerpt of code invoking the *GetCustomersByAddress* method and the method definition in the *ObjectContext*

```
public partial class EF4SampleDBEntities : ObjectContext {
    // Code omitted for simplicity ...

    public ObjectResult<GetCustomersByAddress_Result> GetCustomersByAddress(
            global::System.String address) {
        ObjectParameter addressParameter;
        if (address != null) {
            addressParameter = new ObjectParameter("Address", address);
        }
        else {
            addressParameter =
                new ObjectParameter("Address", typeof(global::System.String));
        }
```

```
        return base.ExecuteFunction<GetCustomersByAddress_Result>
("GetCustomersByAddress", addressParameter);
    }
    // Code omitted for simplicity ...
}

public class Program {
    static void InvokeStoredProcedure() {
        EF4SampleDBEntities ctx = new EF4SampleDBEntities();
        ObjectResult<GetCustomersByAddress_Result> result =
            ctx.GetCustomersByAddress("%Firenze%");

        foreach (var c in result) {
            Console.WriteLine(
                    "Customer {0} has ID {1}, with an income of {2} last year",
                    c.FullName, c.ContactID, c.LastYearIncomes);
        }
    }
}
```

The imported function internally invokes the *ExecuteFunction* of the base *ObjectContext* class, which accepts the stored procedure name and a dynamic array of parameters. The parameters are objects of type *ObjectParameter* and not (for example) of type *SqlParameter*, because they are an abstraction on top of the physical persistence storage. The result of the function is an object of type *ObjectResult<T>*, where *T* is a *GetCustomersByAddress_Result* type in our example.

CUD Stored Procedures

Another category of stored procedures are those defined to support data modification over entities of the conceptual model. These stored procedures are used in CUD operations. Consider the stored procedures defined in Listing 8-9. They allow adding, updating, and deleting a customer record.

LISTING 8-9 The DDL defining the CUD stored procedures to manage *Customers*

```
CREATE PROCEDURE [dbo].[AddCustomer]
@FullName nvarchar(100),
@EMail nvarchar(50),
@Address nvarchar(100),
@LastYearIncomes money,
@ShippingAddress nvarchar(100),
@ShippingCity nvarchar(100),
@ShippingPostalCode nvarchar(10),
@ShippingCountry nchar(2)
AS
```

```sql
BEGIN
    INSERT INTO Contacts (FullName, EMail, [Address], ContactType )
    VALUES (@FullName, @EMail, @Address, 'Customer')

    DECLARE @ContactID int
    SELECT @ContactID = SCOPE_IDENTITY()

    INSERT INTO CustomersDetails (ContactID, LastYearIncomes, ShippingAddress,
    ShippingCity, ShippingPostalCode, ShippingCountry)
    VALUES (@ContactID, @LastYearIncomes, @ShippingAddress, @ShippingCity,
    @ShippingPostalCode, @ShippingCountry)

    SELECT @ContactID AS ContactID
END
GO

CREATE PROCEDURE [dbo].[UpdateCustomer]
@ContactID int,
@FullName nvarchar(100),
@EMail nvarchar(50),
@Address nvarchar(100),
@LastYearIncomes money,
@ShippingAddress nvarchar(100),
@ShippingCity nvarchar(100),
@ShippingPostalCode nvarchar(10),
@ShippingCountry nchar(2)
AS
BEGIN
    UPDATE Contacts SET
    FullName = @FullName,
    EMail = @EMail,
    [Address] = @Address
    WHERE ContactID = @ContactID

    UPDATE CustomersDetails SET
    LastYearIncomes = @LastYearIncomes,
    ShippingAddress = @ShippingAddress,
    ShippingCity = @ShippingCity,
    ShippingPostalCode = @ShippingPostalCode,
    ShippingCountry = @ShippingCountry
    WHERE ContactID = @ContactID
END
GO

CREATE PROCEDURE [dbo].[DeleteCustomer]
    @ContactID int
AS
BEGIN
    DELETE FROM CustomersDetails WHERE ContactID = @ContactID
    DELETE FROM Contacts WHERE ContactID = @ContactID
END
GO
```

To use these stored procedures for CUD operations, you first need to reference them in the storage schema, updating the model from the database. Then, you need to map each CUD operation to the corresponding stored procedure.

To map stored procedures to CUD operations, you can use the Mapping Details panel of the designer, switching to the Map Entities To Functions view or clicking Stored Procedure Mapping on the entity context menu. This option is disabled for abstract types because you should not insert, update, or delete them directly.

Note With Entity Framework in .NET Framework 4, you can map just single operations of an entity type to a stored procedure, leaving other operations autogenerated by the environment. For example, you can map the update operation to a stored procedure and let the framework continue to map the delete and insert operations. However, bear in mind that CUD mapping to stored procedures is an "all or nothing" option in the case of entities in an inheritance chain. Thus, if you need to map a single operation to a custom stored procedure, and if the entity inherits from another entity, you will also have to map all the other CUD operations. For entities that belong to an inheritance hierarchy, the Entity Framework also requires that you define CUD mapping for every entity of the hierarchy. If you do not define a custom CUD mapping for every entity in the hierarchy, you will get a validation error such as: "Error 2028: If an *EntitySet* mapping includes a function binding, function bindings must be included for all types. The following types do not have function bindings: *[TypeName]*." The *[TypeName]* argument will include the name of every entity of the hierarchy that doesn't have a full CUD mapping. One last thing to consider is that CUD mapping, from the Entity Data Model Designer point of view, requires that every stored procedure parameter is mapped to a property of the entity. If you need to handle stored procedures differently, you can manually edit the .edmx file, using an XML editor, to replace the stored procedure invocation with an explicit T-SQL command that internally invokes the original stored procedure with your customizations.

For the sake of simplicity in this section, only Customer CUD operations are mapped, to avoid mapping the whole type hierarchy. In Figure 8-13, you can see the designer user interface. In the figure, notice that the Mapping Details panel shows details about the three CUD stored procedures. Listing 8-10 shows a sample method that uses these stored procedures to add, update, and delete a sample *Customer*.

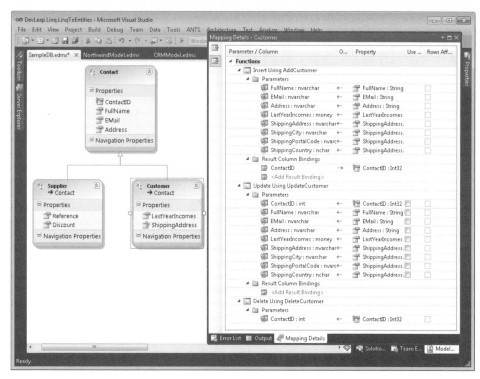

FIGURE 8-13 The interface to import a stored procedure as a function into the conceptual model.

LISTING 8-10 A code excerpt that under the cover uses custom CUD operations for *Contact* entity

```
EF4SampleDBEntities ctx = new EF4SampleDBEntities();

Customer customerToAdd = new Customer();
customerToAdd.FullName = "Frank White";
customerToAdd.EMail = "frank@email.com";
customerToAdd.Address = "USA - Redmond";
customerToAdd.LastYearIncomes = 300;
customerToAdd.ShippingAddress.ShippingAddress = "Microsoft Way, 1";
customerToAdd.ShippingAddress.ShippingCity = "Redmond, WA";
customerToAdd.ShippingAddress.ShippingPostalCode = "98052";
customerToAdd.ShippingAddress.ShippingCountry = "US";

ctx.AddToContacts(customerToAdd);
```

```
// Here it is executed the statement
// exec [dbo].[AddCustomer] @FullName=N'Frank White',@EMail=N'frank@email.com',
// @Address=N'USA - Redmond',@LastYearIncomes=300.0000,
// @ShippingAddress=N'Microsoft Way, 1', @ShippingCity=N'Redmond, WA',
// @ShippingPostalCode=N'98052',@ShippingCountry=N'US'
ctx.SaveChanges();

Int32 newId = customerToAdd.ContactID;
Customer customerToUpdate =
    (from   c in ctx.Contacts.OfType<Customer>()
     where  c.ContactID == newId
     select c).FirstOrDefault();

customerToUpdate.EMail = "frank@email.net";

// Here it is executed the statement
// exec [dbo].[UpdateCustomer] @ContactID=9,@FullName=N'Frank White',
// @EMail=N'frank@email.net',@Address=N'USA - Redmond',@LastYearIncomes=300.0000,
// @ShippingAddress=N'Microsoft Way, 1',@ShippingCity=N'Redmond, WA',
// @ShippingPostalCode=N'98052',@ShippingCountry=N'US'
ctx.SaveChanges();

ctx.Contacts.DeleteObject(customerToUpdate);

// Here it is executed the statement
// exec [dbo].[DeleteCustomer] @ContactID=9
ctx.SaveChanges();
```

Note that the *Insert* function reads the *ContactID* (the *IDENTITY* value) of the newly added *Customer* and automatically assigns that value to the *ContactID* property of the inserted item.

POCO Support

Certainly the most requested and awaited feature of Entity Framework 4 is full and true support for POCO. But what does POCO mean? Substantially, it is the idea of having an ORM able to map data coming from the DBMS into persistence-ignorant entities. A persistence ignorant entity is an entity that has no internal knowledge of where and how to persist itself from a storage point of view. If you think about the autogenerated entities we used in this chapter (see Listing 8-2 for reference), you'll see that the standard code generation template emits classes that inherit from the *EntityObject* type, provided by the Entity Framework class library. Moreover, the properties of these entities are tagged with attributes specific to the Entity Framework and EDM modeling. Lastly, the property setter methods contain infrastructural code to manage change tracking and notifications, as well as some fix-up methods to better support associations between entities. All this code means the autogenerated entities are "not ignorant" about their persistence, which leads to a dependency on Entity Framework libraries.

Although Entity Framework 1.0 supported IPOCO entities (entities that implement some specific interfaces to be persistence independent, but not completely ignorant), Entity Framework 4 is able to map conceptual model entities to completely independent and persistence-ignorant entities. To give that a try, you can revisit the conceptual model in the "Inheritance and Conditional Mapping" section earlier in this chapter. In the model's property grid, select the Code Generation Strategy property and change its value from Default to None. The result of this action is that the Entity Data Model Designer stops autogenerating code. Now define a set of custom classes, for example, in a dedicated assembly, like those in Listing 8-11.

LISTING 8-11 The definition of our POCO custom entities

```
namespace DevLeap.Linq.Entities {

    public abstract class Contact {
        public Int32 ContactID { get; set; }
        public String FullName { get; set; }
        public String EMail { get; set; }
        public String Address { get; set; }
    }

    public class Customer : Contact {
        public Decimal LastYearIncomes { get; set; }
        public ShippingAddressType ShippingAddress { get; set; }
    }

    public class ShippingAddressType {
        public String ShippingAddress { get; set; }
        public String ShippingCity { get; set; }
        public String ShippingPostalCode { get; set; }
        public String ShippingCountry { get; set; }
    }

    public class Supplier : Contact {
        public String Reference { get; set; }
        public Int32 Discount { get; set; }
    }
}
```

As you can see, these classes are completely independent from the Entity Framework and could be any class that you already have in your software architecture. The only requirement is that you must use types that have names and property names identical to those of the entities defined in the conceptual model. In fact, the Entity Framework works using the "pattern of convention," which matches the names in the conceptual model with the names in the entity model. To load collections of these entities with data coming from the DBMS through the Entity Framework, you must define a custom *ObjectContext* type that will bind the entities with the Entity Framework. In Listing 8-12, you can see a very simple example of such a class.

LISTING 8-12 A custom *ObjectContext* type to bind custom entities with the Entity Framework

```
public class EF4SampleDBEntities: ObjectContext {
    public EF4SampleDBEntities(String connectionString)
        : base(connectionString, "EF4SampleDBEntities") {
        this.Contacts = base.CreateObjectSet<Contact>();
    }

    public ObjectSet<Contact> Contacts { get; private set; }
}
```

As you can intuit from the code in Listing 8-12, the class must inherit from the standard Entity Framework *ObjectContext* type, and should offer all the entity sets as properties of type *ObjectSet<T>*. You also need to ensure that the property of type *ObjectSet<T>* was created before accessing it, so the code invokes the *CreateObjectSet<T>* method inside the custom *ObjectContext* constructor. When building this example, we defined this class in the same assembly as the EDM, to isolate the assembly containing the POCO entities. With that in place, Listing 8-13 shows code that uses these classes.

LISTING 8-13 Sample code using the custom *ObjectContext* with POCO entities

```
class Program {
    static void Main(string[] args) {
        EF4SampleDBEntities ctx = new EF4SampleDBEntities("here the connection
string");

        var customers =
            from c in ctx.Contacts.OfType<Customer>()
            select c;

        foreach (var c in customers) {
            Console.WriteLine("Customer {0} has ID {1}, with an income of {2} last
year",
                c.FullName, c.ContactID, c.LastYearIncomes);
        }
    }
}
```

Obviously, the developer experience is essentially the same as with autogenerated entities, but now uses custom entities that take advantage of a pure abstraction from the persistence storage.

However, it is not all magic. In fact, with this approach, you actually lose some capabilities. For example, you cannot use lazy loading to dynamically load entities in the graph through navigation properties. To better explain this concept, imagine that you also have a table of *Orders*, defined to store customers' orders. In the conceptual model, you can associate the *Order* entity with the *Customer* one, as you can see in Figure 8-14.

> **More Info** Lazy loading is described in Chapter 9, "LINQ to Entities: Querying Data."

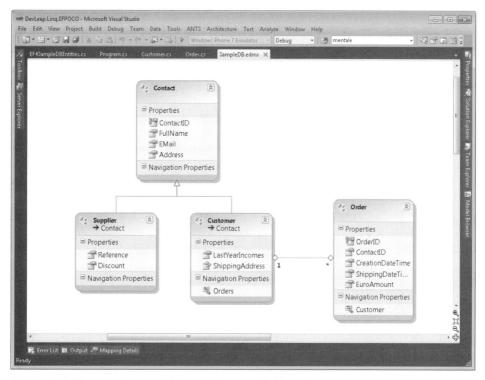

FIGURE 8-14 The conceptual model with Orders associated to customers.

Therefore, the Entity Framework conceptual model has a navigation property named *Orders* for each *Customer* instance; in addition, there's a *Customer* navigation property that returns the *Customer* for any single *Order* instance. With the standard autogenerated code, these properties, in their default configurations, automatically load their content upon user code access. This means that when you access the *Orders* property of a specific *Customer* instance, the Entity Framework infrastructure will load the list of all the orders of the current customer from the DBMS—unless they are already loaded. This behavior is called *lazy loading*, which is usually both useful and resource-friendly—although it can sometimes be the cause of inefficiency.

Listing 8-14 shows some slightly revised code for the custom entities that supports the new *Order* type and the navigation properties between *Customer* and *Order*. As you can see, the collection of orders provided by the *Customer* type is of type *ICollection<T>*, which is a requirement of the Entity Framework. It is not a terribly restrictive requirement because almost every collection in the .NET Framework inherits from *ICollection<T>*. Also note that the *Customer* constructor creates a new instance of the collection.

LISTING 8-14 The POCO custom entities modified to support navigation properties between *Customer* and *Order*

```
public class Order {
    public Guid OrderID { get; set; }
    public Int32 ContactID { get; set; }
    public DateTime CreationDateTime { get; set; }
    public DateTime ShippingDateTime { get; set; }
    public Decimal EuroAmount { get; set; }
    public Customer Customer { get; set; }
}

public class Customer : Contact {
    public Customer() {
        this.Orders = new List<Order>();
    }

    public Decimal LastYearIncomes { get; set; }
    public ShippingAddressType ShippingAddress { get; set; }
    public ICollection<Order> Orders { get; private set; }
}
```

Using this revised code, you can navigate from customers to their orders and vice versa. However, when using custom entities, it's your responsibility to instruct the Entity Framework to load the orders together with each customer. Otherwise, the standard behavior of the Entity Framework for POCO entities, is to *not* load any associated entity. To make the Entity Framework load data with associations, you can use the *Include* method of the *ObjectSet<T>* class, as shown in Listing 8-15.

LISTING 8-15 An excerpt of code that loads both customers and their orders

```
var customers =
    from   c in ctx.Contacts.OfType<Customer>().Include("Orders")
    select c;
```

> **More Info**   Chapter 9 goes into more detail about the *Include* function.

In this section's example, it will be executed as a single query against the DBMS that loads all the entities of type *Customer*, together with their orders. If you want to load orders for certain customers only, you could instead use lazy loading, changing the code of the custom entities and of the custom *ObjectContext* a little, as shown in Listing 8-16. In this example, you can see a new definition of the *ObjectContext* that adds a configuration directive in the class constructor that explicitly enables lazy loading.

LISTING 8-16 The custom *ObjectContext* type with lazy loading enabled

```
public class EF4SampleDBEntities: ObjectContext {
    public EF4SampleDBEntities(String connectionString)
        : base(connectionString, "EF4SampleDBEntities") {
        this.Contacts = base.CreateObjectSet<Contact>();
        this.ContextOptions.LazyLoadingEnabled = true;
    }

    public ObjectSet<Contact> Contacts { get; private set; }
}
```

However, this change isn't sufficient by itself. You also need to make the *ICollection<T>* navigation property of the *Customer* entity *virtual*. When you do that, the Entity Framework automatically creates a custom entity that inherits from the *Customer* type, overriding the virtual property and providing the implementation to support lazy loading of the property. From that point forward, when you access *Customer* entities in your code, in reality you'll be accessing a custom proxy dynamically created by the Entity Framework infrastructure that causes lazy loading to work as expected.

T4 Templates

Throughout this chapter, you've seen code autogenerated by the Entity Data Model Designer. However, the code is not generated by the designer itself. Instead, it uses a feature called the *Text Template Transformation Toolkit* (also called *T4 Templates*), which has been available since Visual Studio 2005. By default, the Entity Data Model Designer uses a T4 template of its own, which is a file with a .tt extension. However, you can change that to build custom entities by providing a customized T4 template. For example, suppose you want to generate POCO entities like those created in the previous section. To do that, you can define a custom T4 template to generate them from the .edmx file.

> **Note** Teaching you how to write custom T4 templates is out of scope for this book, but you can find a lot of information about it by referring to "Code Generation and Text Templates" on MSDN Online, located at *http://msdn.microsoft.com/en-us/library/bb126445.aspx*.

You should also know that Microsoft provides out-of-the-box T4 templates to implement specific behaviors in Entity Framework 4. To apply a custom T4 template to the code generated for an .edmx file, you can simply select Add Code Generation Item from the Entity Data Model Designer context menu. Visual Studio prompts you with a dialog box from which you can choose a T4 template to use. The following templates are available:

- **ADO.NET EntityObject Generator**   This is the default T4 template applied by the Entity Framework and generates a strongly typed *ObjectContext* class and persistence-aware classes.

- **ADO.NET POCO Entity Generator**   This template generates a strongly typed *Object-Context* class and entity classes with persistence ignorance. Unfortunately, these classes are not terribly lightweight, even if they are POCO. If you need to generate entities like those discussed in the previous section, you will probably need to handcraft a T4 template of your own by customizing this one.

- **ADO.NET Self-Tracking Entity Generator**   This template generates a strongly typed *ObjectContext* class and Self-Tracking entity classes. These entities are able to track their state autonomously, even when they are detached from the *ObjectContext*, shipped somewhere else (for example, through a Windows Communication Foundation service) and then later attached again to another *ObjectContext* instance.

> **More Info** The last T4 template is covered in more detail in Chapter 10 "LINQ to Entities: Managing Data."

Summary

This chapter covered the process of designing an entity model for Entity Framework 4. In particular, you learned how to define models starting from an already existing database or by designing a model from scratch (from empty), generating the database from the entity model. You've seen an overview of what an .edmx file is, and how the designer generates one. You've covered entity associations—both independent and foreign key associations—and you saw how to define complex properties. You also learned how to take advantage of inheritance and conditional mapping. You learned about the options for mapping stored procedures so you can extend the *ObjectContext* with custom functions, as well as how to customize the CUD operations for entities. Finally, you learned how Entity Framework 4 supports POCO, and reviewed the options for code generation via T4 templates.

Chapter 9
LINQ to Entities: Querying Data

The main reason to use an Object Relational Mapper (ORM) is so you can manage data at a conceptual level, querying the model independently from the underlying physical storage. Whereas the previous chapter focused on modeling the conceptual schema, this chapter dives into querying the model.

EntityClient Managed Providers

Microsoft ADO.NET Entity Framework is first of all another ADO.NET managed provider, which queries a repository of entities and entity sets, instead of a database made of records and tables. Thus, we can approach the Entity Framework the same way as with *SqlClient*, *OracleClient*, and any other ADO.NET managed provider.

 More Info For further details about ADO.NET Managed Providers, you can read the document "ADO.NET Architecture" on MSDN Online at *http://msdn.microsoft.com/en-us/library/27y4ybxw.aspx*.

The Entity Framework object model contains types to define a connection, a command, and a data reader. Those types are *EntityConnection*, *EntityCommand*, and *EntityDataReader*, and are also called *EntityClient* managed providers.

For example, suppose you are working with the Entity Data Model (EDM) defined in Chapter 8, "LINQ to Entities: Modeling Data with Entity Framework," for the Northwind database (see Figure 8-2 in Chapter 8). You could query its contents using the ADO.NET programming model and the *EntityClient* managed provider. You still need to create a connection, execute a command, and read the rows through a forward-only, read-only data reader. You can see an example of this approach in Listing 9-1.

LISTING 9-1 A code excerpt that reads entities through the Entity Framework as a list of records

```
EntityConnection cn = new EntityConnection(connectionString);
EntityCommand cmd = new EntityCommand(
                "SELECT VALUE c FROM NorthwindEntities.Customers AS c", cn);

cn.Open();
using (EntityDataReader dr = cmd.ExecuteReader(CommandBehavior.SequentialAccess)) {
    while (dr.Read()) {
        Console.WriteLine(dr["CustomerID"]);
    }
}
cn.Close();
```

The *EntityConnection* class is similar to any other class that inherits from *DbConnection*. You create it by providing a connection string, calling its *Open* method before invoking any commands, and then calling the *Close* method after reading any result data from the reader.

The *EntityCommand* class behaves much like any other class inheriting from *DbCommand*, although the SQL statement you provide to its constructor is not an ANSI SQL or a T-SQL statement. Instead, you write queries in a SQL-like syntax that you provide to the command. This syntax is called *Entity SQL syntax*.

More Info Entity SQL syntax is a SQL-like language specifically created to define queries against the conceptual model of an Entity Framework EDM. For those who already know the SQL language, Entity SQL is user-friendly and useful for querying entities and relationships of the conceptual model. This new query language introduced with the Entity Framework supports dynamic queries, similar to programming with dynamic SQL. The language provides the common primitive keywords typical of any query language. Full coverage of Entity SQL is out scope for this book, which focuses on LINQ, and not on Entity SQL.

Finally, the *EntityDataReader* is an implementation of *DbDataReader*. It supports reading data row by row. Nevertheless, the result of the query is not just a result set of rows, but a set of entities. In fact, the output of the query is a list of *DbDataRecord* objects, each one representing a *Customer* instance.

However, the main difference between the ADO.NET Entity Framework and standard ADO.NET data access is that the Entity Framework is based on the idea of *entity* rather than *record*. By making a few changes to the code, you can extract objects of type *Customer* directly rather than items of type *DbDataRecord*. You can see the new code in Listing 9-2.

LISTING 9-2 A code excerpt that reads entities through the Entity Framework as a list of typed objects

```
using (NorthwindEntities db = new NorthwindEntities()) {
    var customers = db.CreateQuery<Customer>(
        "SELECT VALUE c FROM NorthwindEntities.Customers AS c");

    foreach (Customer c in customers) {
        Console.WriteLine(c.Display());
    }
}
```

There are several subtle differences in this code and the code you saw in Listing 9-1. First, instead of using the *EntityConnection*, this code uses a class inherited from *ObjectContext* (*NorthwindEntities*), which internally uses an *EntityConnection* instance. It then calls the *CreateQuery* generic method of the *NorthwindEntities* class (the custom *ObjectContext*) to instruct the Entity Framework to query the repository, passing an Entity SQL query that will return the *VALUE* of each entity. The generic type provided to the *CreateQuery* method describes the resulting type that you can use in the consumer code. The result of this particular method invocation is an instance of the *ObjectQuery<Customer>* type, which internally implements *IQueryable<Customer>* for enumerating customers.

LINQ to Entities

Even if you could potentially query the conceptual model using the *EntityClient* programming model and Entity SQL queries only, that would be a dangerous thing to do in a runtime-interpreted language, because any issue in the Entity SQL code would become a runtime bug. Instead, it would be far safer (and easier) to write queries using Microsoft Language Integrated Query (LINQ) syntax, giving you the compile-time checking and the IntelliSense provided by Microsoft Visual Studio. That is exactly the logic behind LINQ to Entities, which is a LINQ query provider that works against the *ObjectQuery<T>* type. LINQ to Entities is specifically defined to query the entities of an EDM by using LINQ query syntax. The *ObjectQuery<T>* class is inherited by *ObjectSet<T>*, which is the type used by the Entity Framework to represent sets of entities (see Chapter 8). Thus, you can create queries against any set of entities defined in the conceptual model.

Listing 9-3 shows an example that retrieves Italian customers of the Northwind conceptual model, using LINQ to Entities.

LISTING 9-3 A code excerpt that queries entities by using LINQ to Entities

```
using (NorthwindEntities db = new NorthwindEntities()) {
    var query = from   c in db.Customers
                where  c.Country == "Italy"
                select c;

    foreach (var c in query) {
        Console.WriteLine(c.ContactName);
    }
}
```

As you can see, the code is similar to the code you used with LINQ to SQL, because from a LINQ syntax perspective, a query is always the same; it is the underlying query provider that makes the difference.

In Listing 9-3, the query provider visits the query expression and generates a command tree that is an abstract representation of the query, and is independent from the concrete underlying Database Management System (DBMS). Lastly, it converts the command tree into a concrete SQL query that targets the real DBMS in the back end. Just after generating the command tree—but before executing the final SQL query—the query provider evaluates any client-side argument, including variables, command parameters, and so on.

To gain a better understanding of client-side evaluation, consider the LINQ query used in Listing 9-3. In Listing 9-4, you can see the corresponding T-SQL code.

LISTING 9-4 The T-SQL code generated from the LINQ to Entities query used in Listing 9-3

```
SELECT
[Extent1].[CustomerID] AS [CustomerID],
[Extent1].[CompanyName] AS [CompanyName],
[Extent1].[ContactName] AS [ContactName],
[Extent1].[ContactTitle] AS [ContactTitle],
[Extent1].[Address] AS [Address],
[Extent1].[City] AS [City],
[Extent1].[Region] AS [Region],
[Extent1].[PostalCode] AS [PostalCode],
[Extent1].[Country] AS [Country],
[Extent1].[Phone] AS [Phone],
[Extent1].[Fax] AS [Fax]
FROM [dbo].[Customers] AS [Extent1]
WHERE N'Italy' = [Extent1].[Country]
```

As you can see, the query selects all the columns of all the Italian customers, defining the filter condition using the WHERE keyword and an explicit value of *Italy*. Now, consider the code in Listing 9-5.

LISTING 9-5 A LINQ to Entities query with a filtering variable in the query expression

```
String countryFilter = "Italy";

using (NorthwindEntities db = new NorthwindEntities()) {
    var query = from   c in db.Customers
                where  c.Country == countryFilter
                select c;

    foreach (var c in query) {
        Console.WriteLine(c.ContactName);
    }
}
```

The only difference between Listing 9-3 and Listing 9-5 is that the latter uses a variable to hold the filter for the *Country* property. However, this is a big difference for the Entity Framework, because from the client-side evaluation of the query, it argues that the filter on the country must be managed as a parameter. You can see the difference by reading the generated SQL code for this second query, as shown in Listing 9-6.

LISTING 9-6 The T-SQL code generated from the LINQ to Entities query used in Listing 9-5

```
exec sp_executesql N'SELECT
[Extent1].[CustomerID] AS [CustomerID],
[Extent1].[CompanyName] AS [CompanyName],
[Extent1].[ContactName] AS [ContactName],
[Extent1].[ContactTitle] AS [ContactTitle],
[Extent1].[Address] AS [Address],
[Extent1].[City] AS [City],
[Extent1].[Region] AS [Region],
[Extent1].[PostalCode] AS [PostalCode],
[Extent1].[Country] AS [Country],
[Extent1].[Phone] AS [Phone],
[Extent1].[Fax] AS [Fax]
FROM [dbo].[Customers] AS [Extent1]
WHERE [Extent1].[Country] = @p__linq__0',N'@p__linq__0
   nvarchar(4000)',@p__linq__0=N'Italy'
```

As you can see, the DBMS receives a *sp_executesql* command based on a parametric query.

Regardless the type of SQL query that gets sent to the DBMS, the final step in executing a LINQ query against an *ObjectQuery<T>* instance is materializing the resulting entities—or more generally, .NET types. In fact, the Entity Framework materializes any resulting rows into CLR types just after it executes the query.

Selecting Single Entities

In real code, you often need to select a single entity, for example, by providing its primary key. LINQ to Entities, like LINQ in general, provides specific methods to satisfy this need. For example, the *Single* method selects a single and unique entity that satisfies the filtering criteria provided as an expression, as described in Chapter 3, "LINQ to Objects." When no entity—or more than one entity—meets the filter requirements, the method throws an *InvalidOperationException*. The following example illustrates using this method to select a customer instance by its primary key, *CustomerID*:

```
Customer alfki = db.Customers.Single(c => c.CustomerID == "ALFKI");
```

If you are not sure that an entity satisfying the filter exists, and do not want to catch an exception in such cases, you can use the *SingleOrDefault* method, which returns a *default(TEntity)*— or *null* in the case of objects—result in such situations. A common pattern for using the *SingleOrDefault* method occurs when you need to either create an entity if one does not exist, or modify the existing one if it does. By using *SingleOrDefault*, you can create a new entity only if the result is *null*.

Two other methods similar to *Single* and *SingleOrDefault* are *First* and *FirstOrDefault*. The main difference is that *First* and *FirstOrDefault* return the *first* occurrence of an item satisfying a filter. These methods do not throw an exception when there are multiple results; they simply return the first target item, functioning much like a *SELECT TOP 1* SQL statement. The *First* method still throws an *InvalidOperationException* when no entities satisfy the filter, but *First-OrDefault* returns a value of *default(TEntity)* (again, *null*). Here is an example of using the *First* method:

```
Customer firstAmericanCustomer = db.Customers.First(c => c.Country == "USA");
```

Unsupported Methods and Keywords

The LINQ to Entities provider engine does not support the complete LINQ syntax because some client functions and methods as well as some LINQ query operators cannot be translated into SQL code. Some of these unsupported LINQ keywords and methods are *Reverse*, *Aggregate*, *ElementAt*, *ElementAtOrDefault*, *Last*, *LastOrDefault*, *SkipWhile*, and *TakeWhile*. In addition, some methods have overloads that are not supported. The interesting part of this discussion is not the list of supported or unsupported methods, but how LINQ to Entities behaves when a query uses these methods. Unfortunately, the language compiler cannot determine that the keywords or methods are not supported, so you do not get a compile-time exception; however, you do get a run-time exception stating that "this method cannot be translated into a store expression" (or similar text). Thus, to avoid run-time instability, it is important to know whether you can use a method. Listing 9-7 shows an example that uses the unsupported *Reverse* method.

LISTING 9-7 A LINQ to Entities query that compiles but does not run on the DBMS

```
var query = (from   c in db.Customers
             where  c.Country == countryFilter
             select c).Reverse();
```

Similarly, you can easily write queries that—even though they are perfectly OK with the client-side compiler—require functionality not available on the data-store side, so these will throw an exception as well. Listing 9-8 shows another example.

LISTING 9-8 Another LINQ to Entities query that compiles but does not run on the DBMS

```
var query = from   c in db.Customers
            from   o in c.Orders
            where  c.Country == countryFilter
                   && o.OrderDate > DateTime.Now.AddDays(-7)
            select o;
```

The preceding query attempts to select all the orders executed in the last seven days, by customers from the specified country (*countryFilter*). However, the *DataTime.Now.AddDays* function is not supported, and cannot be translated into a SQL expression.

It is easy to create examples that—like Listings 9-7 and 9-8—do not work. The goal here is simply to underline the issue, not create a comprehensive list of unsupported keywords/methods.

> **More Info** For a complete list of supported and unsupported LINQ methods, you can read the document "Supported and Unsupported LINQ Methods (LINQ to Entities)" on MSDN Online at *http://msdn.microsoft.com/en-us/library/bb738550.aspx.*

Canonical and Database Functions

Fortunately, instead of using unsupported syntax like you saw in the previous section, you can enrich your LINQ to Entities queries with custom functions that work on strings, dates, aggregations, mathematical functions, and so on, taking advantage of some specific functions provided by infrastructure classes of the Entity Framework.

The Entity Framework in Microsoft .NET Framework 4 provides two classes: *SqlFunctions* and *EntityFunctions*. You can invoke these inside of queries with the guarantee that they will be converted properly into the command tree, so the query will not fail during the translation from conceptual to storage model.

The methods defined in *EntityFunctions* are called *canonical functions*, whereas the methods defined in *SqlFunctions* are called *database functions*. The difference between canonical and database functions is that the former are translated to corresponding data source functions for the specific DBMS provider, and the latter are Microsoft SQL Server–specific and can be used only against a SQL Server DBMS. Furthermore, the canonical functions arguments and return types belong to the conceptual model, whereas the database functions in general work with primitive CLR types. There is no guarantee that any Entity Framework provider will offer full support for all the canonical functions; but every provider can implement and offer custom functions as Microsoft does with SQL Server and the *SqlFunctions* class.

Listing 9-9 shows a LINQ to Entities query example that has the same semantic meaning as the one shown in Listing 9-8. However, this time the query uses canonical functions, making it executable against any DBMS.

LISTING 9-9 A LINQ to Entities query that uses canonical functions

```
var query = from    c in db.Customers
            from    o in c.Orders
            where   c.Country == countryFilter
                    && EntityFunctions.DiffDays(o.OrderDate, DateTime.Now) <= 7
            select new { o.OrderID, o.OrderDate };
```

Executing Listing 9-9 against a SQL Server DBMS produces the SQL statement shown in Listing 9-10.

LISTING 9-10 The SQL code generated for the LINQ to Entities query of Listing 9-9

```
exec sp_executesql N'SELECT
[Extent2].[OrderID] AS [OrderID],
[Extent2].[OrderDate] AS [OrderDate]
FROM   [dbo].[Customers] AS [Extent1]
INNER JOIN [dbo].[Orders] AS [Extent2] ON [Extent1].[CustomerID] = [Extent2].[CustomerID]
WHERE ([Extent1].[Country] = @p__linq__0) AND ((DATEDIFF (day, [Extent2].[OrderDate],
SysDateTime())) <= 7)',N'@p__linq__0 nvarchar(4000)',@p__linq__0=N'Italy'
```

In this case, you can obtain the same result using a database function, as shown in Listing 9-11, which uses a SQL Server–specific function.

LISTING 9-11 The same LINQ to Entities query of Listing 9-9, using a database function

```
var query = from    c in db.Customers
            from    o in c.Orders
            where   c.Country == countryFilter
                    && SqlFunctions.DateAdd("day", 7, o.OrderDate) >=
                    SqlFunctions.GetDate()
            select new { o.OrderID, o.OrderDate };
```

For the sake of completeness, Listing 9-12 shows the SQL code generated for the query in Listing 9-11.

LISTING 9-12 The SQL code generated for the LINQ to Entities query of Listing 9-11

```
exec sp_executesql N'SELECT
[Extent2].[OrderID] AS [OrderID],
[Extent2].[OrderDate] AS [OrderDate]
FROM   [dbo].[Customers] AS [Extent1]
INNER JOIN [dbo].[Orders] AS [Extent2] ON [Extent1].[CustomerID] = [Extent2].[CustomerID]
WHERE ([Extent1].[Country] = @p__linq__0) AND ((DATEADD(day, cast(7 as float(53)),
[Extent2].[OrderDate])) >= (GETDATE()))',N'@p__linq__0
nvarchar(4000)',@p__linq__0=N'Italy'
```

Notice that even though the target is SQL Server in both cases, the output SQL code differs slightly, because *SqlFunctions* does not offer a *DiffDays* method.

> **Tip**   In general, always use canonical functions where possible, as conceptual schemas do, because they are DBMS independent. You should use database functions only when you do not have a valid alternative using canonical functions.

> **More Info**   You can find a full list of both canonical functions and database functions for SQL Server on MSDN at *http://msdn.microsoft.com/en-us/library/bb738626.aspx* and *http://msdn.microsoft.com /en-us/library/system.data.objects.sqlclient.sqlfunctions.aspx*.

User-Defined Functions

Sometimes you need to reference custom user defined functions (UDFs) when declaring LINQ to Entities queries. With the Entity Framework, you can define UDFs in the EDM, as described in Chapter 8. As soon as you import a UDF into the conceptual model, you can invoke it in LINQ queries. Consider the UDF defined in Listing 9-13, which calculates the total amount of orders for a specific Northwind customer.

LISTING 9-13 The SQL code to generate a custom UDF

```
USE [Northwind]
GO
SET ANSI_NULLS ON
GO
SET QUOTED_IDENTIFIER ON
GO
CREATE FUNCTION [dbo].[TotalOrdersAmount](@CustomerID nchar(5))
RETURNS MONEY
AS
    BEGIN
    DECLARE @total MONEY;
    SELECT @total = SUM(od.UnitPrice * od.Quantity)
        FROM Customers AS c
        INNER JOIN Orders AS o ON c.CustomerID = o.CustomerID
        INNER JOIN [Order Details] AS od ON od.OrderID = o.OrderID
        WHERE c.CustomerID = @CustomerID
        GROUP BY c.CustomerID
    RETURN @total;
    END
```

To make this UDF available in the model, you need to declare it explicitly as a static method of the inherited *ObjectContext* class. Listing 9-14 shows the method declaration.

LISTING 9-14 A UDF import statement in the inherited *ObjectContext*

```
[EdmFunction("NorthwindModel.Store", "TotalOrdersAmount")]
public static decimal TotalOrdersAmount(String CustomerID) {
    throw new NotSupportedException("You cannot call this method directly.");
}
```

After declaring the UDF, you can invoke it within a LINQ to Entities query. The query in Listing 9-15 selects the top five Northwind customers, arranged in descending order with total order amount.

LISTING 9-15 The LINQ to Entities query using the custom UDF

```
var query = (from    c in db.Customers
             orderby NorthwindEntities.TotalOrdersAmount(c.CustomerID) descending
             select  new { c.CustomerID, c.CompanyName }).Take(5);
```

As you can see, the function is invoked inside the LINQ query. However, the LINQ to Entities query engine does not invoke the CLR method; it directly calls the UDF on the server side. In fact, if you look back at the definition, the CLR method simply throws an exception if it is invoked directly. Nevertheless, the LINQ query expression referencing that method will be handled by translating the method into its corresponding *EdmFunction*, which is the *Total-OrdersAmount* function of the *NorthwindModel.Store*, that is, the UDF defined in Listing 9-13.

Looking at the SQL command sent to the DBMS, shown in Listing 9-16, you can see that LINQ to Entities invokes the UDF directly on the server side.

LISTING 9-16 The SQL code generated for the LINQ to Entities query of Listing 9-15

```
SELECT TOP (5)
[Project1].[C2] AS [C1],
[Project1].[CustomerID] AS [CustomerID],
[Project1].[CompanyName] AS [CompanyName]
FROM ( SELECT
    [dbo].[TotalOrdersAmount]([Extent1].[CustomerID]) AS [C1],
    [Extent1].[CustomerID] AS [CustomerID],
    [Extent1].[CompanyName] AS [CompanyName],
    1 AS [C2]
    FROM [dbo].[Customers] AS [Extent1]
) AS [Project1]
ORDER BY [Project1].[C1] DESC
```

Using this technique, you can define any custom function that is not directly available through the standard canonical and database functions. However, remember that working in this manner introduces dependencies on the physical storage schema.

Stored Procedures

As you saw in Chapter 8 in the section "Modeling Stored Procedures," you can import stored procedures into the model and make them available as methods of the *ObjectContext*. Every time you import a stored procedure, the Entity Framework internally calls the *ExecuteFunction* method of the base *ObjectContext* class to invoke the corresponding stored procedure. If necessary, you can do exactly the same thing, calling the *ExecuteFunction* method directly to invoke custom stored procedures. Just remember that before you can invoke a stored procedure using this method, you need to define it in the conceptual schema by importing its definition from the storage schema, as shown in Chapter 8. The *ExecuteFunction* method offers three different signatures:

```
public int ExecuteFunction(string functionName, params ObjectParameter[] parameters);

public ObjectResult<TElement> ExecuteFunction<TElement>(
    string functionName, params ObjectParameter[] parameters);

public ObjectResult<TElement> ExecuteFunction<TElement>(
    string functionName, MergeOption mergeOption, params ObjectParameter[] parameters);
```

The first signature supports invoking data modification stored procedures, which do not return rows. It accepts a stored procedure name, some optional parameters, and returns an *Int32* type containing the number of rows affected by the command. The other two generic method signatures are provided to invoke stored procedures that select data (of type *TElement*). When the resulting items are entities defined in the conceptual model, the last method signature lets you control how you want to manage object identities; this is explained in more detail in the "*MergeOption*" section later in this chapter.

Now consider the following stored procedure, defined in the standard Northwind database:

```
CREATE procedure [dbo].[Ten Most Expensive Products] AS
SET ROWCOUNT 10
SELECT Products.ProductName AS TenMostExpensiveProducts, Products.UnitPrice
FROM Products
ORDER BY Products.UnitPrice DESC
```

Listing 9-17 shows a code excerpt that calls this stored procedure using the *ExecuteFunction* method.

LISTING 9-17 Using the *ExecuteFunction* method to call a stored procedure

```
using (NorthwindEntities db = new NorthwindEntities()) {
    var top10ExpensiveProducts =
            db.ExecuteFunction<Ten_Most_Expensive_Products_Result>(
                "Ten_Most_Expensive_Products");

    foreach (var p in top10ExpensiveProducts) {
        Console.WriteLine("{0} - {1}",
            p.TenMostExpensiveProducts, p.UnitPrice);
    }
}
```

Basically, *ExecuteFunction* can return any kind of result, including conceptual model entities, complex types, custom objects, or scalar values. The preceding example defines a complex type named *Ten_Most_Expensive_Products_Result* to hold the rows that the stored procedure returns.

ObjectQuery<T> and *ObjectContext*

As you have seen, the Entity Framework querying engine is essentially based on the *ObjectQuery<T>* type. Whenever you query the conceptual model, the resulting object is either of type *ObjectQuery<T>* or inherits from *ObjectQuery<T>*. This section covers some details about this type, so you can better understand how the Entity Framework querying works.

Lazy Loading

Starting with .NET Framework 4, the Entity Framework natively and automatically offers "lazy loading" of entities. The term *lazy loading* means the capability to load object references dynamically, which supports navigating graphs of objects by code. Consider the code excerpt in Listing 9-18, which retrieves a list of customers and then navigates through the orders of each customer.

LISTING 9-18 A code excerpt using the lazy loading behavior of Entity Framework 4

```
using (NorthwindEntities db = new NorthwindEntities()) {
    var customers = from   c in db.Customers
                    select c;

    foreach (var c in customers) {
        Console.WriteLine("{0}", c.CustomerID);
        foreach (var o in c.Orders) {
            Console.WriteLine("{0} - {1}", o.OrderID, o.OrderDate);
        }
    }
}
```

As you can see, the query references only the customers, but when the code begins to enumerate the orders collection of a single customer, the Entity Framework will query the storage again to extract the orders for that customer. If you trace the SQL code sent to the DBMS, you will see that the Entity Framework sends the query in Listing 9-19 to the DBMS, which returns the list of customers only at the point the code begins enumerating the *customers* variable that represents the query result.

LISTING 9-19 The SQL code generated for the LINQ to Entities query of Listing 9-18

```
SELECT
[Extent1].[CustomerID] AS [CustomerID],
[Extent1].[CompanyName] AS [CompanyName],
[Extent1].[ContactName] AS [ContactName],
[Extent1].[ContactTitle] AS [ContactTitle],
[Extent1].[Address] AS [Address],
[Extent1].[City] AS [City],
[Extent1].[Region] AS [Region],
[Extent1].[PostalCode] AS [PostalCode],
[Extent1].[Country] AS [Country],
[Extent1].[Phone] AS [Phone],
[Extent1].[Fax] AS [Fax]
FROM [dbo].[Customers] AS [Extent1]
```

Similarly, as soon as the code begins to enumerate the orders of the first customer instance, the Entity Framework sends another query, shown in Listing 9-20, to the DBMS to get that customer's orders. This second query gets repeated for each and every customer in the query result.

LISTING 9-20 The SQL code generated by the Entity Framework to dynamically load the orders of a single customer from Listing 9-18

```
exec sp_executesql N'SELECT
[Extent1].[OrderID] AS [OrderID],
[Extent1].[CustomerID] AS [CustomerID],
[Extent1].[EmployeeID] AS [EmployeeID],
[Extent1].[OrderDate] AS [OrderDate],
[Extent1].[RequiredDate] AS [RequiredDate],
[Extent1].[ShippedDate] AS [ShippedDate],
[Extent1].[ShipVia] AS [ShipVia],
[Extent1].[Freight] AS [Freight],
[Extent1].[ShipName] AS [ShipName],
[Extent1].[ShipAddress] AS [ShipAddress],
[Extent1].[ShipCity] AS [ShipCity],
[Extent1].[ShipRegion] AS [ShipRegion],
[Extent1].[ShipPostalCode] AS [ShipPostalCode],
[Extent1].[ShipCountry] AS [ShipCountry]
FROM [dbo].[Orders] AS [Extent1]
WHERE [Extent1].[CustomerID] = @EntityKeyValue1',N'@EntityKeyValue1 nchar(5)',
@EntityKeyValue1=N'ALFKI'
```

Lazy loading is an automatic Entity Framework behavior that was introduced with .NET Framework 4. Although it is usually helpful, you can of course turn the feature off when you want to avoid it. To switch lazy loading off, set the *ContextOptions.LazyLoadingEnabled* property of your custom *ObjectContext* to *false*:

```
db.ContextOptions.LazyLoadingEnabled = false;
```

So when should you turn it off? When you need to dynamically load only some of the entities in the entire graph, lazy loading is a useful behavior—a "light operation" that can, for example, avoid loading millions of orders in memory at the same time. Conversely, when you know that you are going to end up loading all the objects in a graph anyhow (in this case, all the orders for a specific set of customers), lazy loading simply ends up stressing the DBMS by making a separate query for each single customer's orders. In this case, it would be better to initially select all of the customers together with their orders, thus executing only a single query against the DBMS. For example, to see the difference between lazy loading enabled and disabled, you can use SQL Server Profiler to trace SQL statements sent to the DBMS. As you will see in the following sections, turning off lazy loading is not always the only way to solve such a problem.

Include

Since its first version, the Entity Framework has offered an *Include* method, available in the *ObjectQuery<T>* type, to help avoid multiple repetitive queries. Using the *Include* method, you declare which entities will be loaded together with the main query result, as shown in Listing 9-21.

LISTING 9-21 Using the *ObjectQuery<T>.Include* method

```
using (NorthwindEntities db = new NorthwindEntities()) {
    var customers = from   c in db.Customers
                    select c;

    ObjectQuery<Customer> customersQuery =
        (customers as ObjectQuery<Customer>).Include("Orders");

    foreach (var c in customersQuery) {
        Console.WriteLine("{0}", c.CustomerID);
        foreach (var o in c.Orders) {
            Console.WriteLine("{0} - {1}", o.OrderID, o.OrderDate);
        }
    }
}
```

Note that the code casts the result to *ObjectQuery<T>* to get access to its specific methods; the *Include* method is not available through the standard *IQueryable<T>* interface. Listing 9-22 shows an excerpt of the query sent to the DBMS as a consequence of using the *Include* method.

LISTING 9-22 The SQL code generated by the Entity Framework loading the orders together with the customers

```
SELECT
[Project1].[C1] AS [C1],
[Project1].[CustomerID] AS [CustomerID],
[Project1].[CompanyName] AS [CompanyName],
[Project1].[ContactName] AS [ContactName],
[Project1].[ContactTitle] AS [ContactTitle],
/* ... code omitted ... */
[Project1].[C2] AS [C2],
[Project1].[OrderID] AS [OrderID],
[Project1].[CustomerID1] AS [CustomerID1],
[Project1].[EmployeeID] AS [EmployeeID],
[Project1].[OrderDate] AS [OrderDate],
/* ... code omitted ... */
[Project1].[ShipCountry] AS [ShipCountry]
FROM ( SELECT
    [Extent1].[CustomerID] AS [CustomerID],
    [Extent1].[CompanyName] AS [CompanyName],
    [Extent1].[ContactName] AS [ContactName],
    [Extent1].[ContactTitle] AS [ContactTitle],
    /* ... code omitted ... */
    1 AS [C1],
    [Extent2].[OrderID] AS [OrderID],
    [Extent2].[CustomerID] AS [CustomerID1],
    [Extent2].[EmployeeID] AS [EmployeeID],
    [Extent2].[OrderDate] AS [OrderDate],
    /* ... code omitted ... */
    [Extent2].[ShipCountry] AS [ShipCountry],
    CASE WHEN ([Extent2].[OrderID] IS NULL) THEN CAST(NULL AS int) ELSE 1 END AS [C2]
    FROM   [dbo].[Customers] AS [Extent1]
    LEFT OUTER JOIN [dbo].[Orders] AS [Extent2] ON [Extent1].[CustomerID] =
    [Extent2].[CustomerID])  AS [Project1]
ORDER BY [Project1].[CustomerID] ASC, [Project1].[C2] ASC
```

The SQL code in Listing 9-22 produces a flat and redundant result set that the Entity Framework engine materializes into the final object graph.

You can use as many *Include* method invocations as needed to include many different entity sets into the resulting query. You simply need to chain them one after the other, as follows:

```
Customers.Include("Orders").Include("Orders.Order_Details")
  .Include("Orders.Order_Details.Product");
```

> **Warning** The argument to the *Include* method is a string, so it is error-prone and fails only at run time rather than at compile time.

Load and IsLoaded

One last method provided by *ObjectQuery<T>* for dynamically loading graphs of objects is the *Load* method. *Load* is generally used together with the *IsLoaded* property. It supports explicitly loading an entity set if it has not been already loaded. Listing 9-23 shows an example of using this method.

LISTING 9-23 Using the *ObjectQuery<T>.Load* method

```
using (NorthwindEntities db = new NorthwindEntities()) {
    var customers = from   c in db.Customers
                    select c;

    foreach (var c in customers) {
        Console.WriteLine("{0}", c.CustomerID);
        if (c.Country == "Italy") {
            if (!c.Orders.IsLoaded)
                c.Orders.Load();

            foreach (var o in c.Orders) {
                Console.WriteLine("{0} - {1}", o.OrderID, o.OrderDate);
            }
        }
    }
}
```

This is a useful technique when your code needs to load just some of the entity sets in the object graph dynamically, because you can load them selectively.

The LoadProperty Method

You have now seen how to dynamically load entity sets that are related to a single entity object, but sometimes, you need to navigate a single entity reference rather than a full entity set. For example, consider an entity of type *Order* and its *Customer* property. To get the customer, you do not need to load an *ObjectQuery<T>*, just a single instance of *T*, where *T* is of type *Customer*.

The base abstract class *ObjectContext* provides a *LoadProperty* method that is specifically defined to load a single entity reference. LoadProperty has four overloads:

```
public void LoadProperty(object entity, string navigationProperty);

public void LoadProperty(object entity, string navigationProperty, MergeOption mergeOption);

public void LoadProperty<TEntity>(
  TEntity entity, Expression<Func<TEntity, object>> selector);

public void LoadProperty<TEntity>(
   TEntity entity, Expression<Func<TEntity, object>> selector, MergeOption mergeOption);
```

As you can see, two of the overloads accept an untyped *Object* entity and a navigation property of type *String*. These methods are evaluated at run time. The string navigation property can be any valid navigation path, just like the ones you would provide to the *ObjectQuery<T>.Include* method. As noted before, these methods can fail at run time if you provide an invalid navigation path. The only difference between the first and the second over-load is that the second takes a third parameter of type *MergeOption*, which instructs the Entity Framework how to behave when loading data from the data source. For further details, see the next section, "*MergeOption*."

LoadProperty also has two generic overloads that accept a *TEntity* generic type, which con-strains the type of the first method argument, and an *Expression<Func<TEntity, object>>*, which represents a lambda expression that describes the navigation path. These latter two methods are strongly typed and checked at compile time, so they are generally better and safer solutions that avoid unpredictable runtime errors. Like the first two overloads, one includes the *MergeOption* argument; the other uses a default value for *MergeOption*.

Listing 9-24 shows an example of using of this method, applied to the *Customer* property of each *Order* entity instance.

LISTING 9-24 Using the *ObjectContext.LoadProperty* method

```
using (NorthwindEntities db = new NorthwindEntities()) {
    db.ContextOptions.LazyLoadingEnabled = false;

    var orders = from   o in db.Orders
                 select o;

    foreach (var o in orders) {
        Console.WriteLine("{0} - {1}", o.OrderID, o.OrderDate);
        db.LoadProperty<Order>(o, oc => oc.Customer);
        if (o.Customer.Country == "Italy") {
            Console.WriteLine("\tCustomer: {0} - {1}",
                            o.Customer.CustomerID, o.Customer.ContactName);
        }
    }
}
```

By this time, you can probably anticipate the problem: each time you ask the custom *Object-Context* to explicitly load a property, it queries the data source. As with lazy loading and the *Load* method, when you know you will need to load every entity reference, it is better to instruct the Entity Framework to load them all at the same time rather than stressing the data source with multiple queries.

MergeOption

Every time you execute a query, the Entity Framework keeps a unique copy of each entity in memory, which maintains object identity and guarantees that every thread accessing entities will get a reference to the same shared instance of that entity. The goal of this behavior is to avoid data concurrency. As you will see later in this chapter, you can turn off this behavior, which is turned on by default. Whenever you query the conceptual model to select an entity that has already been loaded into memory, the Entity Framework has the option to either keep the in-memory instance or to override it with fresh data coming from the data source. You can control this behavior by configuring the *MergeOption* property of the *ObjectQuery<T>* object that represents the query you are planning to execute. *MergeOption* can assume one of the following values:

- **AppendOnly**   Objects already existing in the *ObjectContext* are not loaded from the data source. This is the default value.

- **NoTracking**   Objects are always loaded from the data source, and have a state of *Detached*, with no tracking or identity management.

- **OverwriteChanges**   Objects are always loaded from the data source; any property change made in memory is overridden.

- **PreserveChanges**   Objects are always loaded from the data source, but only unmodified properties in memory are overridden by data source values.

Listing 9-25 illustrates use of the *MergeOption* property to change the default Entity Framework behavior.

LISTING 9-25 Using the *ObjectQuery<T>.MergeOption* property

```
using (NorthwindEntities db = new NorthwindEntities()) {
    Customer alfki = db.Customers.FirstOrDefault(c => c.CustomerID == "ALFKI");
    alfki.ContactName = "Brian Johnson";

    var customers = from   c in db.Customers
                    select c;
```

```
    ObjectQuery<Customer> customersQuery = (customers as ObjectQuery<Customer>);
    customersQuery.MergeOption = MergeOption.AppendOnly;

    foreach (var c in customersQuery) {
        Console.WriteLine("{0} - {1}", c.CustomerID, c.ContactName);
    }
}
```

Using the default configuration, the output of Listing 9-24 would be the following:

```
ALFKI - Brian Johnson
ANATR - Ana Trujillo
ANTON - Antonio Moreno
AROUT - Thomas Hardy
BERGS - Christina Berglund
...
```

Notice that the first customer (the one with *CustomerID == "ALFKI"*) has a contact name value of *Brian Johnson* because the Entity Framework appends only entities not already in memory. The code in Listing 9-25 loaded the first customer and changed its name to *Brian Johnson* before executing the query. However, if you change the *MergeOption* property (the bold line in Listing 9-25) to a value of *NoTracking*, the output is:

```
ALFKI - Maria Anders
ANATR - Ana Trujillo
ANTON - Antonio Moreno
AROUT - Thomas Hardy
BERGS - Christina Berglund
...
```

This time, the query loads all the customers, overwriting any in-memory changes, so the first customer's *ContactName* property (the one with *CustomerID == "ALFKI"*) shows the data source value in the output instead of the value assigned by the code. As you can see, this option strongly influences the result of executed queries. Nevertheless, under the covers, the data source always returns all the selected data selected—including the *ContactName* field. The Entity Framework behavior determines whether it skips some rows and/or columns during object materialization.

This behavior applies only to queries that return full entity sets; it does not apply to a custom projected entity set. As an example, Listing 9-26 is almost identical to Listing 9-25, except that it projects only the *CustomerID* and *ContactName* properties of each customer entity.

LISTING 9-26 *MergeOption* behavior with custom projected result sets

```
using (NorthwindEntities db = new NorthwindEntities()) {
    Customer alfki = db.Customers.FirstOrDefault(c => c.CustomerID == "ALFKI");
    alfki.ContactName = "Brian Johnson";

    var customers = from   c in db.Customers
                    select new { c.CustomerID, c.ContactName };

    foreach (var c in customers) {
        Console.WriteLine("{0} - {1}", c.CustomerID, c.ContactName);
    }
}
```

The output of this code is like the one in Listing 9-25, even though it does not alter the default *MergeOption* value. That is because the Entity Framework identity manager tracks only *conceptual entities* and does not track anonymous types; anonymous types are read only, so it would be completely useless to track them.

The *ToTraceString* Method

One last *ObjectQuery<T>* property you will be glad to know about is the *ToTraceString* method, which shows you the SQL code sent to the data source that corresponds to a query executed with the Entity Framework. You will find it useful to track SQL code executed against the DBMS, because seeing the SQL code helps you tune queries, stored procedures, and indexes on the physical data storage. When using Microsoft Visual Studio 2010, you can also take advantage of IntelliTrace support, which is useful because it can manage and trace every Entity Framework activity. Listing 9-27 shows an example of using *ToTraceString*.

LISTING 9-27 Using the *ObjectQuery<T>.ToTraceString* method

```
using (NorthwindEntities db = new NorthwindEntities()) {
    var customers = from   c in db.Customers
                    where  c.Country == "Italy"
                    select new { c.CustomerID, c.ContactName };

    Console.WriteLine(((ObjectQuery)customers).ToTraceString());

    foreach (var c in customers) {
        Console.WriteLine("{0} - {1}", c.CustomerID, c.ContactName);
    }
}
```

The code in Listing 9-27 converts the type of the query variable to an *ObjectQuery* type rather than *ObjectQuery<T>*, because the query returns a set of anonymous types, so you cannot predict the resulting type.

ExecuteStoreCommand and *ExecuteStoreQuery*

Although you are working with an ORM to abstract the programming model from the persistence storage, sometimes you might want to execute a SQL statement against the DBMS directly. The *ObjectContext* type provides a method for this purpose called *ExecuteStoreCommand*. This method executes an arbitrary SQL command directly against the data source using the existing connection provided by the current *ObjectContext* instance. Listing 9-28 shows an example that uses the *ExecuteStoreCommand* method.

LISTING 9-28 A code excerpt using the *ExecuteStoreCommand* method of the *ObjectContext*

```
using (NorthwindEntities db = new NorthwindEntities()) {
    Int32 rowsAffected = db.ExecuteStoreCommand(
        "DELETE FROM Customers WHERE Country = @CountryToDelete",
        new DbParameter[] { new SqlParameter("CountryToDelete", "Australia") });
    Console.WriteLine("Deleted {0} rows", rowsAffected);
}
```

The example intentionally uses a parametric query to remind you that you should always execute parametric queries to avoid SQL injection issues. The arguments of this method are as follows:

- The statement to execute, which is a *String* containing the native language of the data store

- An array of objects of type *DbParameter* or an array of explicit values that the library will convert into an array of *DbParameter*

The result is an *Int32* value that represents the number of rows affected by the command. Because of its integer-only return type, the *ExecuteStoreCommand* method is most useful for executing data modification commands that do not return rows.

When you need to execute arbitrary commands that return rows, the *ObjectContext* instance provides the *ExecuteStoreQuery* method. This method is almost the same as the *ExecuteStoreCommand* method, but returns an *ObjectResult<T>* that represents the result set selected by the store query. The method has a couple of overloads:

```
public ObjectResult<TElement> ExecuteStoreQuery<TElement>(
    string commandText, params object[] parameters);

public ObjectResult<TEntity> ExecuteStoreQuery<TEntity>(
    string commandText, string entitySetName, MergeOption mergeOption,
    params object[] parameters);
```

As you can infer from the signatures, there is a subtle but substantial difference between these method overloads: both query the data source, but the former returns a sequence of objects of type *TElement*, whereas the latter returns a sequence of entities from the conceptual model of type *TEntity*. Thus, the generic type *TElement* represents any kind of typed result that it is not a conceptual entity, whereas *TEntity* is one of the conceptual entities of the EDM. Therefore, the second overload also accepts a *MergeOption* argument that instructs the Entity Framework how to manage entity identities.

Listing 9-29 shows a code excerpt that uses the *ExecuteStoreQuery* method.

LISTING 9-29 Using the *ObjectContext.ExecuteStoreQuery* method

```
using (NorthwindEntities db = new NorthwindEntities()) {
    ObjectResult<Customer> result = db.ExecuteStoreQuery<Customer>(
        "SELECT * FROM Customers WHERE Country = @Country",
        new DbParameter[] { new SqlParameter("Country", "USA") });

    foreach (var c in result) {
        Console.WriteLine("{0} - {1}", c.CustomerID, c.ContactName);
    }
}
```

It is important to underscore that these queries are executed when the methods are invoked. In contrast, LINQ query execution is delayed until you access the results. This contrast means there is a significant difference between executing a LINQ query and a store query against an *ObjectContext* type.

When executing these methods, if the existing connection provided by the current *ObjectContext* instance is not open, the Entity Framework will open it before executing the query, and will close it after query execution completes. When the *ObjectContext* is in the context of a current transaction, the store command is executed in that transaction context.

The *Translate<T>* Method

Sometimes, executing a standard ADO.NET query—a standard *DbCommand* type such as a *SqlCommand*—returns a *DbDataReader* type (such as a *SqlDataReader*). Whenever these commands return a result set of rows that contain typed entities or objects available in your conceptual model, you can use the *Translate<T>* method of the *ObjectContext* to translate these rows into typed objects. Listing 9-30 contains an example that selects all the customer rows and translates them into typed *Customer* entity instances.

LISTING 9-30 Using the *ObjectContext .Translate<T>* method

```
using (NorthwindEntities db = new NorthwindEntities()) {
    using (SqlConnection cn = new SqlConnection(
            "server=localhost;database=Northwind;integrated security=SSPI;")) {
        cn.Open();
```

```
SqlCommand cmd = new SqlCommand("SELECT * FROM Customers", cn);
using (SqlDataReader dr = cmd.ExecuteReader(CommandBehavior.CloseConnection)) {

    ObjectResult<Customer> result = db.Translate<Customer>(dr);

    foreach (var c in result) {
        Console.WriteLine("{0} - {1}", c.CustomerID, c.ContactName);
    }
  }
 }
}
```

The *Translate<T>* method has two overloads:

```
public ObjectResult<TElement> Translate<TElement>(DbDataReader reader);
```

```
public ObjectResult<TEntity> Translate<TEntity>(DbDataReader reader, string entitySetName,
MergeOption mergeOption)
```

The first overload translates each data row into the corresponding *TElement* type, where *TElement* could be an entity of the conceptual model, as you saw in Listing 9-30. *TElement* could also be a typed object where only some properties match the columns selected in the SQL query. Listing 9-31 shows an example of using the *Translate* method to load a set of objects of type *LightCustomer*, which is a lightweight version of the standard *Customer* type.

LISTING 9-31 Using the *ObjectContext .Translate<T>* method to load a custom type that is not defined in the EDM

```
using (NorthwindEntities db = new NorthwindEntities()) {
    using (SqlConnection cn = new SqlConnection(
            "server=localhost;database=Northwind;integrated security=SSPI;")) {
        cn.Open();

        SqlCommand cmd = new SqlCommand("SELECT * FROM Customers", cn);
        using (SqlDataReader dr = cmd.ExecuteReader(CommandBehavior.CloseConnection)) {

            ObjectResult<LightCustomer> result = db.Translate<LightCustomer>(dr);

            foreach (var c in result) {
                Console.WriteLine("{0} - {1}", c.CustomerID, c.ContactName);
            }
        }
    }
}
```

Here is the definition of *LightCustomer*:

```
private class LightCustomer {
    public String CustomerID { get; set; }
    public String ContactName { get; set; }
}
```

Listing 9-31 intentionally selected all the columns of the customers table (SELECT *) to make you aware that the *Translate* function maps the data columns into object properties only for those columns that have a corresponding property in the output type. The Entity Framework makes the association based on the type's property names. Thus, the *Translate* method reduces memory consumption, from an object oriented viewpoint, even if it does not reduce the network and DBMS load, unless you define queries that select exactly the same columns mapped into the conceptual model.

The second overload of the *Translate* method accepts only a generic type (*TEntity*) that corresponds to an entity in the conceptual model, so it also accepts an argument of type *String* that represents the name of the *entitySet* into which it loads the retrieved entities, and a final *MergeOption* argument that controls how the Entity Framework manages entities' identities.

Query Performance

Looking under the hood of LINQ to Entities, you can see that every time you execute a query, you have to pay a kind of "fee" for the query processing. The LINQ to Entities query provider has to visit the expression tree that describes the query so that it can produce the corresponding command tree. Next, the Entity Framework has to evaluate the command tree on both the client side and the DBMS side. Finally, it executes the translated SQL command against the DBMS and materializes the resulting rows into final output objects. Obviously, all this processing has an effect on query performance.

In this section, you will see techniques you can use to improve query execution time and achieve better overall performance for your applications.

Pre-Build Store Views

The first technique to improve query performance is to pre-generate store views. Every time you create an instance of the custom *ObjectContext* type and execute a query, the Entity Framework generates views for the store and maintains them in cache during the lifetime of that *ObjectContext* instance. Generating the store views is an expensive operation, so pre-generating them can significantly improve performance. To pre-generate store views, you can use the EdmGen.exe command-line tool, entering the command */mode:ViewGeneration* and providing the full set of CSDL, SSDL, and MSL files, along with an output source code file. The output will be a source code file that you can include in your project and build along with the EDM autogenerated classes. In general, store view generation is configured as a pre-build event that regenerates the class file before every single compilation.

EnablePlanCaching

Another technique that can improve query execution performance is to enable query execution plan caching. To do this, set the *ObjectQuery<T>.EnablePlanCaching* property to *true*. This option works on a single query or entity set basis, so you must set the value individually for each and every query you know will be executed many times during the lifetime of the application.

Pre-Compiled Queries

You can save a little more time (and improve performance) by pre-compiling queries. Listing 9-32 shows an excerpt of the syntax required to pre-compile a LINQ to Entities query.

LISTING 9-32 An example of pre-compiling a LINQ to Entities query

```
static readonly Func<NorthwindEntities, String, IQueryable<Customer>>
    compiledSearchCustomersByCountry =
        CompiledQuery.Compile<NorthwindEntities, String, IQueryable<Customer>>(
        (db, countryFilter) => from   c in db.Customers
                               where  c.Country == countryFilter
                               select c);

private static void LinqToEntitiesCompiledQuery() {
    using (NorthwindEntities db = new NorthwindEntities()) {
        IQueryable<Customer> italianCustomers =
            compiledSearchCustomersByCountry.Invoke(db, "Italy");

        foreach (var c in italianCustomers) {
            Console.WriteLine(c.CompanyName);
        }

        IQueryable<Customer> germanCustomers =
            compiledSearchCustomersByCountry.Invoke(db, "Germany");

        foreach (var c in germanCustomers) {
            Console.WriteLine(c.CompanyName);
        }
    }
}
```

To pre-compile a query, use the *Compile* static method of the *CompiledQuery* class. The *Compile* method represents a set of method overloads that accept various *Func<>* delegates. The first argument type of *Func<>* is usually the class inherited from *ObjectContext*. The last argument is an *IQueryable<T>*, where *T* is the type of the resulting items, if known. In between the *ObjectContext* and the *IQueryable<T>* result, you list the query's arguments. The result of compiling a query is a delegate to the just-compiled code, so you use the *Invoke* method to call it. As usual, you can also use one of the asynchronous patterns available in the .NET Framework to implement server-side asynchronous code to invoke such a query. In .NET Framework 4, you should use the *Task* class to do this; in .NET Framework 3.5, you have to rely on the *BeginInvoke/EndInvoke* asynchronous pattern.

Compiling queries is very useful, particularly when you need to execute the same query many times, changing only the filter parameters without changing the whole query definition. You can supply up to 16 parameters of primitive types to compiled queries, but you cannot replace parts of the originally compiled query. If you need more than 16 parameters, you can use custom structures to hold argument values.

A compiled query usually returns an *ObjectQuery<T>* as the *IQueryable<T>* result, so you can customize it just like any other LINQ to Entities query. If you define a query that returns an anonymous type, you cannot declare the result type as a generic *IQueryable<T>*, but you can use the *var* keyword and take advantage of the automatic type inference in the .NET Framework. Listing 9-33 shows an example that defines and executes a compiled query that returns an anonymous type.

LISTING 9-33 A code excerpt about pre-compiling LINQ to Entities queries returning anonymous types

```
var compiledSearchCustomersNamesByCountry =
        CompiledQuery.Compile((NorthwindEntities db, String countryFilter)
            => from   c in db.Customers
               where  c.Country == countryFilter
               select new { c.CompanyName, c.ContactName });

using (NorthwindEntities db = new NorthwindEntities()) {
    var italianCustomersNames =
        compiledSearchCustomersNamesByCountry.Invoke(db, "Italy");

    foreach (var c in italianCustomersNames) {
        Console.WriteLine(c);
    }
}
```

As you can see, the preceding code does not provide a type for the result; it simply lets the compiler infer the type from the current query context.

Tracking vs. No Tracking

One last improvement you can make when querying the conceptual model is to disable entity tracking. As you have already seen, the Entity Framework automatically keeps track of every entity selected from the persistence store and automatically merges in-memory entities with data rows coming out from the data store. However, this automatic behavior is expensive. Whenever you do not need to keep track of changes to the entities (for example, whenever you select them just for making read-only data binding), you could disable the object tracking, setting the *MergeOption* of the *ObjectQuery<T>* accordingly—and consequently running queries faster. *ObjectQuery<T>* entity materialization with tracking disabled is lighter, and executes faster.

Summary

This chapter showed how to query an Entity Framework conceptual model using both Entity SQL and LINQ to Entities. In particular, you explored how LINQ to Entities works, which methods it supports, how to call canonical functions, database functions, and UDFs. You also explored the *ObjectQuery<T>* type, and how you can customize its behavior for loading graphs of objects, automatic inclusion, and entity state management. Finally, you saw some techniques for improving query performance.

Chapter 10
LINQ to Entities: Managing Data

This last chapter on LINQ to Entities focuses on how to handle data changes, concurrent operations, transactions, and data management. As in Chapter 9, "LINQ to Entities: Querying Data," the examples will primarily use the Northwind database, accessing its data through the Entity Data Model (EDM) conceptual model that we defined in Chapter 8, "LINQ to Entities: Modeling Data with Entity Framework." (Refer to Figure 8-2 in Chapter 8 to see an example of an Entity Data Model definition.)

Managing Entities

When you develop software solutions, reading and querying data—as discussed in Chapter 9—is only one part of the story. You typically query a set of entities to manage them, changing some properties (such as data field value), adding items to collections, and so on. One huge advantage when working with a conceptual model through an Object Relational Mapper (ORM) instead of through the Database Management System (DBMS)—or more generally, the persistence store—is that you can approach data in terms of objects and properties, letting the ORM be responsible for handling low-level data access, generating SQL statements, performing concurrency checks, and so on.

Adding a New Entity

Listing 10-1 shows a code excerpt that adds a new entity (a *Customer*) to an *EntitySet<T>* of the Entity Framework in Microsoft .NET Framework 4.

LISTING 10-1 Code excerpt showing how to add a new *Customer* instance to the collection of *Customers*

```
using (NorthwindEntities context = new NorthwindEntities()) {
    Customer c = new Customer {
        CustomerID = "DEVLP",
        CompanyName = "DevLeap",
        ContactName = "Paolo Pialorsi",
        Country = "Italy",
        City = "Brescia",
    };

    context.Customers.AddObject(c);
    context.SaveChanges();
}
```

As you can see, you simply need to create a new instance of a *Customer* type, fill its properties, and then add it to the set of *Customers* using the *EntitySet<T>.AddObject* method. To confirm your action, you also need to invoke the *ObjectContext.SaveChanges* method (covered later in this chapter). Under the covers, the Entity Framework sends the following SQL statement to the DBMS:

```
exec sp_executesql N'insert [dbo].[Customers]([CustomerID], [CompanyName], [ContactName],
[ContactTitle], [Address], [City], [Region], [PostalCode], [Country], [Phone], [Fax])
values (@0, @1, @2, null, null, @3, null, null, @4, null, null)
',N'@0 nchar(5),@1 nvarchar(40),@2 nvarchar(30),@3 nvarchar(15),@4 nvarchar(15)',
@0=N'DEVLP',@1=N'DevLeap',@2=N'Paolo Pialorsi',@3=N'Brescia',@4=N'Italy'
```

This is just one of several ways you can add an object to an entity set. You can also use the following *ObjectContext* methods:

```
public void AddObject(string entitySetName, object entity);
public void AddToCustomers(Customer customer);
```

The *AddObject* method is available through the base abstract class *ObjectContext*. You can use this method to add any entity to a specific entity set that is referenced by name. The *AddObject* method is an untyped general-purpose method, suitable for dynamic utility code that needs to manage different kinds of entity sets and entities.

The *AddToCustomers* method is specific to the *Customers* entity set and is auto-generated by the standard code template (T4) used by the Entity Data Model Designer. The method's implementation is trivial; internally, it is based on the untyped *AddObject* method, as shown here:

```
public void AddToCustomers(Customer customer) {
    base.AddObject("Customers", customer);
}
```

The advantage of the *AddToCustomers* method is that it is fully typed, which helps to avoid run-time errors.

Note In general, we prefer the method available through the *EntitySet<T>*, as shown in Listing 10-1, because it is generic in name and definition, but fully typed to avoid run-time issues.

Updating an Entity

Updating an existing entity requires that you retrieve an instance of the entity from the *EntitySet<T>*, either by using an explicit Microsoft Language Integrated Query (LINQ) or by browsing the full entity set. When you have an instance of the entity to update, you can edit its properties and invoke the *ObjectContext.SaveChanges* method to apply the changes.

Listing 10-2 shows a code excerpt that illustrates the steps required to update an existing customer's *Country* field.

LISTING 10-2 Steps to update an existing *Customer* instance

```
using (NorthwindEntities context = new NorthwindEntities()) {
    Customer c = context.Customers.FirstOrDefault(i => i.CustomerID == "DEVLP");
    c.Country = "Germany";

    context.SaveChanges();
}
```

As you can see, the code is nearly identical to Listing 10-1; the only difference is that Listing 10-2 modifies an existing instance rather than creating a new one and adding it to the *Customers* table. For the preceding update, the SQL statement sent to the DBMS will be as follows:

```
exec sp_executesql N'update [dbo].[Customers]
set [Country] = @0
where ([CustomerID] = @1)',
N'@0 nvarchar(15),@1 nchar(5)',@0=N'Germany',@1=N'DEVLP'
```

Notice that the statement is based on parameters, to avoid SQL injections, and that the record to be updated is identified only by its primary key. You will revisit this topic later in this chapter, in the "Managing Concurrency Conflicts" section.

Deleting an Entity

Deleting an existing entity, like updating it, requires you to retrieve an instance of that entity from the corresponding *EntitySet<T>*. After you have a reference to the entity, you can delete it by invoking the *EntitySet<T>.DeleteObject* method, as shown in Listing 10-3.

LISTING 10-3 Deleting an existing *Customer* instance

```
using (NorthwindEntities context = new NorthwindEntities()) {
    Customer c = context.Customers.FirstOrDefault(i => i.CustomerID == "DEVLP");

    context.Customers.DeleteObject(c);

    context.SaveChanges();
}
```

As in Listings 10-1 and 10-2, you need to invoke the *ObjectContext.SaveChanges* method to make the cancellation effective. Here is the SQL statement sent to the DBMS:

```
exec sp_executesql N'delete [dbo].[Customers]
where ([CustomerID] = @0)',N'@0 nchar(5)',@0=N'DEVLP'
```

Another way to delete an object from an entity set is to call the *ObjectContext.DeleteObject* method:

```
public void DeleteObject(object entity);
```

This method is independent of the entity's type because it accepts an argument of type *Object*. Thus, it can be used in either generic or untyped utility code. The SQL statement sent to the DBMS does not change regardless of which *DeleteObject* method you use.

Using *SaveChanges*

In the previous sections, when you managed entities, you had to confirm your actions by invoking the *ObjectContext.SaveChanges* method. Calling *SaveChanges* is a requirement because the Entity Framework—like nearly every other ORM—works internally with in-memory instances of entities, which map to existing rows of data in the underlying data source. Whenever you change an in-memory entity, the *ObjectContext* changes an *EntityState* variable that marks the entity status appropriately for the specified action. *EntityState* is covered in more detail in the next section; for now, just remember that unless you call *SaveChanges*, your changes will be lost as soon as the *ObjectContext* instance variable leaves scope.

The *ObjectContext.SaveChanges* method has three different overloads:

```
public virtual int SaveChanges(SaveOptions options);
public int SaveChanges();
public int SaveChanges(bool acceptChangesDuringSave);
```

The first overload was introduced with Entity Framework 4. This overload saves changes to the in-memory entities, letting you determine the detailed behavior of the *ObjectContext* both before and after saving changes. In fact, the *SaveOptions* argument corresponds to a flag enumeration that can assume the following values:

- **AcceptAllChangesAfterSave**   After saving all changes to the persistence store, this value resets the *EntityState* of the affected entities.

- **DetectChangesBeforeSave**   Before saving changes, the *ObjectContext* checks the *EntityState* of attached entities against its own internal state manager, to detect changes that may have occurred to entities when they were out of the context (while the entities were detached).

- **None**   Changes are saved without any kind of pre-action or post-action.

Because the *SaveOptions* method enumerates a list of flags, you can combine the values. The second *SaveChanges* overload (the only one you have used so far) internally invokes the first overload, using a bitwise OR of *DetectChangesBeforeSave* and *AcceptAllChangesAfterSave*.

The third overload is provided solely for backward compatibility. Internally, it still invokes the first overload, passing it a *SaveOptions* value that depends on the *Boolean* argument you provide. However, this overload is obsolete and you should not use it except for compatibility with legacy code.

All these overloads return an integer result that represents the number of added, modified, and deleted entities affected by the method invocation.

When concurrency issues arise, the *SaveChanges* method throws an *OptimisticConcurrency-Exception* (covered later in this chapter). For other data-related issues, such as primary key violations, the *SaveChanges* method throws an *UpdateException*. Internally, the *SaveChanges* method operates within the context of a transaction. Thus, when any error occurs, the method rolls back the transaction and cancels all modifications. You will see more information about transaction management later in this chapter.

Lastly, consider that whenever you invoke *SaveChanges*, you can also use a *SavingChanges* event raised by the *ObjectContext* at the start of the *SaveChanges* process. Typically, you would use the event to validate changes and modify entities' states before saving them.

Cascade Add/Update/Delete

So far, you have seen how to add, update, and delete single entities. However, quite often an entity has a set of relationships—and you need to manage those, as well. Listing 10-4 shows a code excerpt that inserts a customer with orders.

LISTING 10-4 A code excerpt showing how to add a new *Customer* instance with related *Orders*

```
using (NorthwindEntities context = new NorthwindEntities()) {
    // Create a new customer
    Customer c = new Customer {
        CustomerID = "DEVLP",
        CompanyName = "DevLeap",
        ContactName = "Paolo Pialorsi",
        Country = "Italy",
        City = "Brescia",
    };

    // Add a first order
    c.Orders.Add(new Order {
        OrderDate = DateTime.Now,
        RequiredDate = DateTime.Now.AddDays(3),
        ShipAddress = "My Home Address",
        ShipCity = "Brescia",
        ShipCountry = "Italy",
    });
```

```
    // Add a second order
    c.Orders.Add(new Order {
        OrderDate = DateTime.Now,
        RequiredDate = DateTime.Now.AddDays(5),
        ShipAddress = "My Work Address",
        ShipCity = "Brescia",
        ShipCountry = "Italy",
    });

    // Add the new customer together with his orders
    context.Customers.AddObject(c);

    // Save changes
    context.SaveChanges();
}
```

As you can see, the code adds a new *Customer* instance along with related orders, and saves the changes, just as in Listing 10-1. Under the covers, the Entity Framework automatically adds both the customer and that customer's orders because the *EntitySet<T>.AddObject* method adds to the *ObjectContext*—the whole objects' graph—not just the single *Customer* instance. From your perspective, you do not have to handle every *Order* instance separately. You also do not need to set the *CustomerID* property for each *Order* instance, because the Entity Framework does that for you. Finally, just after the changes have been saved, the *Orders* entities fetch their newly assigned *OrderID* from the DBMS, which in this case is an identity column. This is a huge benefit because it lets you write simpler and "more relaxed" code. The SQL code sent to the DBMS to insert the *Customer* instance is similar to the following:

```
exec sp_executesql N'insert [dbo].[Customers]([CustomerID], [CompanyName], [ContactName],
[ContactTitle], [Address], [City], [Region], [PostalCode], [Country], [Phone], [Fax])
values (@0, @1, @2, null, null, @3, null, null, @4, null, null)',
N'@0 nchar(5),@1 nvarchar(40),@2 nvarchar(30),@3 nvarchar(15),@4 nvarchar(15)',
@0=N'DEVLP',@1=N'DevLeap',@2=N'Paolo Pialorsi',@3=N'Brescia',@4=N'Italy'
```

The SQL code to insert each single *Order* is similar to the following:

```
exec sp_executesql N'insert [dbo].[Orders]([CustomerID], [EmployeeID], [OrderDate],
[RequiredDate], [ShippedDate], [ShipVia], [Freight], [ShipName], [ShipAddress], [ShipCity],
[ShipRegion], [ShipPostalCode], [ShipCountry])
values (@0, null, @1, @2, null, null, null, null, @3, @4, null, null, @5)
select [OrderID]
from [dbo].[Orders]
where @@ROWCOUNT > 0 and [OrderID] = scope_identity()',N'@0 nchar(5),@1 datetime2(7),@2
datetime2(7),@3 nvarchar(60),@4 nvarchar(15),@5 nvarchar(15)',@0=N'DEVLP',@1='2010-08-10
16:24:22.3440961',@2='2010-08-13 16:24:22.3460962',@3=N'My Home Address',@4=N'Brescia',
@5=N'Italy'
```

The code in bold identifies the most significant parts of the SQL statements.

The Entity Framework behaves like this example for all data updates. In fact, Listing 10-5 shows the process of updating a *Customer* instance, changing some properties of the customer and other properties of that customer's already-existing orders. The code also adds a new order to the customer's collection of orders. Despite the breadth of modifications, you need only invoke the *ObjectContext.SaveChanges* method to save the changes.

LISTING 10-5 A code excerpt showing how to update a *Customer* instance with related *Orders*

```
using (NorthwindEntities context = new NorthwindEntities()) {
    // Retrieve the customer together with his orders
    Customer c = ((ObjectQuery<Customer>)context.Customers)
        .Include("Orders")
        .FirstOrDefault(i => i.CustomerID == "DEVLP");

    // Change the country of the Customer
    c.Country = "Germany";

    foreach (var o in c.Orders) {
        // Update the delivery country
        // of each existing order
        o.ShipCountry = "Germany";
    }

    // Add a new order
    c.Orders.Add(new Order {
        OrderDate = DateTime.Now,
        RequiredDate = DateTime.Now.AddDays(3),
        ShipAddress = "My New Address",
        ShipCity = "Munich",
        ShipCountry = "Germany",
    });

    // Save changes
    context.SaveChanges();
}
```

Note The auto-generated SQL code is trivial and does not need to be shown.

Deleting an entity that has related objects deserves a more detailed analysis. In fact, the behavior of the Entity Framework depends both on the type of relationship and on the cascade delete configuration you choose. If you have an identifying relationship—one where the primary key of the principal entity is also part of the primary key of the dependent entity—deleting the principal entity also causes the Entity Framework to delete the dependent entities (a cascade delete). For non-identifying relationships—those based only on foreign key associations—deleting the principal entity does not delete the dependent entities; instead, the

Entity Framework sets their foreign key values to *NULL*, if they are nullable. If it is not possible to set the foreign key value to *NULL*, you must delete the dependent entities or assign them to another principal entity before deleting the principal entity. Alternatively, you can manually set the cascade delete behavior in the Entity Data Model Designer, to make the Entity Framework automatically delete dependent entities for you.

In this example, orders are related to customers with a non-identifying relationship using a "zero or one-to-many" multiplicity. By default, if you delete a customer that has related orders, the Entity Framework will preserve the orders, setting their *CustomerID* property to *NULL*. Listing 10-6 shows a code excerpt that deletes a single *Customer*, which sets the *CustomerID* of its related orders to *NULL* in the persistence store.

LISTING 10-6 A code excerpt that deletes a *Customer* instance, setting the *CustomerID* of related *Orders* to *NULL*

```
using (NorthwindEntities context = new NorthwindEntities()) {
    // Retrieve the customer together with his orders
    Customer c = ((ObjectQuery<Customer>)context.Customers)
        .Include("Orders")
        .FirstOrDefault(i => i.CustomerID == "DEVLP");

    // Delete the customer
    context.Customers.DeleteObject(c);

    // Save changes
    context.SaveChanges();
}
```

You can use the same code to delete the customer and that customer's orders at the same time, by simply setting the cascade delete option in the Entity Data Model Designer. In Figure 10-1, you can see that configuration by looking at the association properties (in the lower right of the figure). Note the *End1 OnDelete* property configured with a value of *Cascade*.

More Info As you learned in Chapter 8, you can use custom stored procedures instead of auto-generated SQL code while adding, updating, and deleting entities. You simply need to import and map stored procedures in the Entity Data Model Designer.

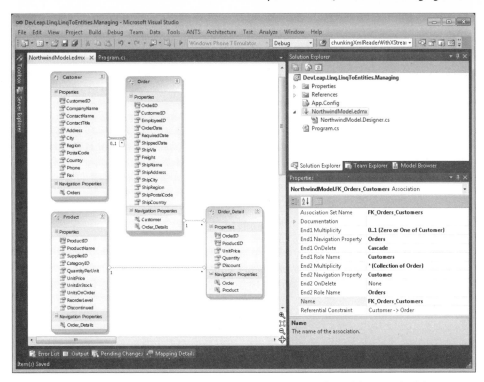

FIGURE 10-1 The Entity Data Model Designer with a relationship configured for cascade delete.

Managing Relationships

You can manage entity relationships programmatically. In fact, you can add, change, or remove relationships between entities. The first and easiest thing you can do is to associate an entity with another one. For example, you can assign an order to an existing customer; you saw an example of that in Listing 10-4. However, you can map one entity to another in several ways.

> **Note** This section discusses the behavior of entities generated using the default code template provided by the Entity Framework. If you change the code template, the results can be unpredictable.

For independent associations, you can assign an explicit object reference to the navigation property of the dependent entity, or to the mapping property of the principal entity. Here is an example of the former case:

```
order.Customer = customerInstance;
```

By default, setting the relationship between an already existing principal entity and a dependent entity by changing the navigation property automatically sets the corresponding foreign key, if there is one, and the *EntityReference* properties. Here is an example of the latter situation (already seen in Listing 10-4):

```
customer.Orders.Add(orderInstance);
```

As before, adding a dependent entity to the corresponding collection of the principal entity also synchronizes the navigation property, the foreign key—if it is configured—and the *EntityReference*. You can also use the foreign key properties to assign the relationship. Sticking with the customers and orders example, here is an example of such an assignment:

```
order.CustomerID = customerInstance.CustomerID;
context.Orders.AddObject(order);
```

In the previous example, you need to manually add the dependent entity to the containing collection to make the *ObjectContext* aware of its existence; simply assigning the appropriate CustomerID to the *Order.CustomerID* property does not affect the *ObjectContext* itself.

Here is an example of *disjunction*—disassociating an order from a customer:

```
order.CustomerID = null;
```

In the following situations, when you change existing relationships, the Entity Framework tracks the changes, and automatically synchronizes those changes between related entities:

- Entities automatically generated with the default code template (T4 template) used by the Entity Data Model Designer.

- Custom entities that implement the IPOCO interface *IEntityWithChangeTracker*.

- Plain-old CLR object (POCO) entities with automatically generated proxies. (See the "POCO Support" section in Chapter 8 for further details.)

In any other situation, you might have to manually synchronize relationships. For example, when working with POCO entities without proxies, you must manually invoke the *Object-Context.DetectChanges* method to synchronize related entities references. Luckily, the *ObjectContext.SaveChanges* method can invoke *DetectChanges* automatically when you use a *SaveOptions* value of *DetectChangesBeforeSave*, so you do not have to call *DetectChanges* explicitly unless you need immediate synchronization of the relationships. Later in this chapter, you will see an example where it is useful to manually invoke *DetectChanges* without calling the *SaveChanges* method.

Using *ObjectStateManager* and *EntityState*

You have seen how the Entity Framework automatically handles many data management operations for you. However, for management purposes, it is useful to see how all this works under the covers. Every instance of the class inherited from *ObjectContext* has an internal object state manager, which holds every single entity state, keeps its original and current properties' values, tracks any changes, and guarantees the uniqueness of references for every entity (that is, object identity). This state manager is called *ObjectStateManager;* you can access it through a property of the *ObjectContext*. In most common scenarios, you will not need to use it directly. However, in some cases, you will appreciate the ability to interact with it. For the sake of completeness, *ObjectContext* handles entities through objects of type *ObjectStateEntry*, which are managed by the *ObjectStateManager*. An *ObjectStateEntry* instance manages information about a single entity instance. For example, it handles the *EntityKey* that determines the unique identity of the managed entity.

> **More Info** To be identifiable by the *ObjectStateManager*, each entity should have a property or a set of properties that represent its *EntityKey*. Later in this section, you will see more about the structure of an *EntityKey* and how to use it.

An *ObjectStateEntry* instance also holds the *EntityState* property of the entity. This last property can assume the following values:

- **Added**   The entity is new; it was just added to the object graph managed by the *ObjectContext*, and the *SaveChanges* method has not yet been invoked.

- **Deleted**   The entity is marked for deletion, which means it was deleted from the *ObjectContext*, but the *SaveChanges* method has not yet been invoked. Just after saving changes, the *EntityState* becomes *Detached*.

- **Detached**   The entity was detached from the *ObjectContext,* was created and has not yet attached to an *ObjectContext*, or was definitely deleted from the *ObjectContext*. An entity with this *EntityState* is not tracked by the *ObjectStateManager* and consequently does not have an *ObjectStateEntry*.

- **Modified**   The entity was modified, and the *SaveChanges* method has not yet been invoked.

- **Unchanged**   The entity has not been modified since it was attached to the context or since the last time that the *SaveChanges* method was invoked.

The *ObjectStateEntry* also holds information about objects related to the current entity, the entity set name of the current entity, and sets of *CurrentValues* and *OriginalValues* of the entity's properties. Of course, entities with a state of *Added* do not have *OriginalValues*.

Every time you invoke the *ObjectContext.SaveChanges* method, the Entity Framework browses all the entities in the object graph and generates SQL statements corresponding to each entity state. Listing 10-7 shows both how you can manage the *ObjectStateManager* by your-self and how to read the *EntityState* of an entity instance.

LISTING 10-7 A code excerpt showing how to work with the *ObjectStateManager*

```
using (NorthwindEntities context = new NorthwindEntities()) {
    // Retrieve the customer together with his orders
    Customer c = context.Customers.FirstOrDefault(i => i.CustomerID == "ALFKI");

    // Get the ObjectStateEntry for the current entity
    ObjectStateEntry stateEntry = context.ObjectStateManager.GetObjectStateEntry(c);

    // Write the actual EntityState for the current entity
    Console.WriteLine("Current state for {0}: {1}", c.CustomerID, stateEntry.State);

    // Change a property of the entity
    c.Country = "Italy";

    // Write the actual EntityState for the current entity
    Console.WriteLine("Current state for {0}: {1}", c.CustomerID, stateEntry.State);

    // Compare the OriginalValues and the CurrentValues
    for (Int32 i = 0; i < stateEntry.CurrentValues.FieldCount; i++) {
        Console.WriteLine("Property: {0}\tOriginal:{1}\tCurrent:{2}",
            stateEntry.CurrentValues.DataRecordInfo.FieldMetadata[i].FieldType.Name,
            stateEntry.OriginalValues[i],
            stateEntry.CurrentValues[i]);
    }
}
```

Notice the code in bold; this code invokes the *GetObjectStateEntry* method, passing the current entity instance. There is also a *TryGetObjectStateEntry* method with the following signature:

```
public bool TryGetObjectStateEntry(EntityKey key, out ObjectStateEntry entry);
```

This last method is provided for those situations in which you are not sure about the existence of an *ObjectStateEntry* for the current entity instance. In fact, *GetObjectStateEntry* throws an *InvalidOperationException* if you invoke it against an untracked entity, whereas the *TryGetObjectStateEntry* method simply returns a value of *false*.

Moreover, in case you need to get the *ObjectStateEntry* objects for many entities based on the same *EntityState*, you can use the *ObjectStateManager.GetObjectStateEntries* method, which accepts a bit flag of type *EntityState* as an argument and returns an *IEnumerable<ObjectStateEntry>*.

Listing 10-7 also illustrates accessing the *State* property, which returns an *EntityState*, and the collections of *CurrentValues* and *OriginalValues*.

The console output of the code in Listing 10-7 is as follows:

```
Current state for ALFKI (before changing it): Unchanged
Current state for ALFKI (after changing it): Modified
Property: CustomerID    Original:ALFKI                 Current:ALFKI
Property: CompanyName    Original:Alfreds Futterkiste   Current:Alfreds Futterkiste
Property: ContactName    Original:Maria Anders          Current:Maria Anders
Property: ContactTitle   Original:Sales Representative   Current:Sales Representative
Property: Address        Original:Obere Str. 57         Current:Obere Str. 57
Property: City           Original:Munich                Current:Munich
Property: Region         Original:                      Current:
Property: PostalCode     Original:12201                 Current:12201
Property: Country        Original:Germany               Current:Italy
Property: Phone          Original:030-0074321           Current:030-0074321
Property: Fax            Original:030-0076545           Current:030-0076545
```

The bold text in the preceding listing shows the difference between the original and the current value of the *Country* property of the current *Customer* instance, as well as the *Modified* state after the *Country* property was modified. When you simply need to enumerate the modified properties of an entity, you can call the *ObjectStateEntry.GetModifiedProperties* method, which returns an *IEnumerable<String>* representing the names of the properties changed since the last invocation of the *ObjectContext.SaveChanges* method.

DetectChanges and *AcceptAllChanges*

ObjectContext provides two supporting methods that by default are invoked internally by *SaveChanges*, but that you can also call directly from code. The first method is *DetectChanges*, which ensures that the *ObjectStateEntry* for tracked entities is synchronized with the changes that happen to them. *SaveChanges* automatically invokes *DetectChanges* at the beginning of the save process. However, you can invoke it manually, which is useful when working with POCO entities without proxies.

 More Info For further details about POCO entities and change-tracking proxies, see Chapter 8.

For example, if you need to execute a LINQ query, configuring the *MergeOption* of the *ObjectQuery<T>* with a value of *PreserveChanges*, and you are working with POCO entities without proxy support, you should call *DetectChanges* before executing the query, to synchronize the entities and relationships before query execution.

In fact, internally, *DetectChanges* attaches any new unattached objects in the object graph to the current *ObjectContext*, and updates the *EntityState* of the entities in the *ObjectContext*, comparing current property values to the existing snapshot of original values. This behavior avoids overriding the in-memory entities with data retrieved from the persistence store.

Conversely, if you fail to invoke *DetectChanges* before enumerating the LINQ query results, you could miss some data, because the *ObjectContext* would not be aware of your in-memory changes.

The other method provided by *ObjectContext* (and by default invoked internally by *SaveChanges*) is *AcceptAllChanges*, which accepts any changes made to the entities tracked by the *ObjectStateManager*. Internally, *ObjectContext* simply iterates all the tracked entities and sets their *EntityState* to a value of *Unchanged* for added or modified entities, or to a value of *Detached* for deleted entities. You should not invoke this method before calling the *ObjectContext.SaveChanges* method because you would lose all in-memory changes. The *ObjectContext* method is provided for cases in which you need to invoke *SaveChanges* without specifying a *SaveOption* value of *AcceptAllChangesAfterSave*. That happens when you want to execute some intermediate code between the *SaveChanges* invocation and the *AcceptAllChanges* method call, for example if you want to retry your modifications under a user-controlled transaction.

ChangeObjectState and *ChangeRelationshipState*

Sometimes you need to handle the state of an entity manually. For example, when working with entities that are not automatically tracked by the *ObjectContext*, you want to manually set their *EntityState* value. Starting with Entity Framework 4, the *ObjectStateManager* provides the *ChangeObjectState* method to satisfy this need. Here is the method signature:

```
public ObjectStateEntry ChangeObjectState(Object entity, EntityState entityState);
```

As you can see, the method accepts an argument of type *Object*, representing the entity instance for which to update the status, and an argument of type *EntityState*, which is the state you want to set. Listing 10-8 shows an example.

LISTING 10-8 Using the *ChangeObjectState* method of the *ObjectStateManager*

```
using (NorthwindEntities context = new NorthwindEntities()) {
    Customer c = new Customer {
        CustomerID = "DEVLP",
        CompanyName = "DevLeap",
        ContactName = "Paolo Pialorsi",
        Country = "Italy",
        City = "Brescia",
    };

    context.AttachTo("Customers", c);

    context.ObjectStateManager.ChangeObjectState(c, EntityState.Added);

    context.SaveChanges();
}
```

Listing 10-8 adds a new customer to the *ObjectContext* and to the persistence store just after the *SaveChanges* method call. Of course, as you saw in Listing 10-1, there are easier ways for adding an entity to the *ObjectContext*. However, this technique is useful when working with detached entities, as you will see later in this chapter.

When you need to change the state of a relationship between entities, you can use the *ObjectStateManager.ChangeRelationshipState* method—unless you are not using foreign key associations, which are not supported by this method. Here are all the overload signatures:

```
public ObjectStateEntry ChangeRelationshipState<TEntity>(TEntity sourceEntity,
    Object targetEntity, Expression<Func<TEntity, Object>> navigationPropertySelector,
EntityState relationshipState)
    where TEntity : class;
public ObjectStateEntry ChangeRelationshipState(Object sourceEntity, Object targetEntity,
    string navigationProperty, EntityState relationshipState);
public ObjectStateEntry ChangeRelationshipState(Object sourceEntity, Object targetEntity,
    string relationshipName, string targetRoleName, EntityState relationshipState);
```

These three signatures behave similarly; the only difference is the way you select the relationship, using an *Expression<Func<TEntity, Object>>* in the first case, the name of the navigation property in the second overload, or the role name in the last overload.

Of course, it is up to you to use these methods appropriately; otherwise, you can get unpredictable results.

ObjectStateManagerChanged

The *ObjectStateManager* offers an *ObjectStateManagerChanged* event that is useful to monitor when adding or removing entities from the state manager. When this event is raised, it provides an argument of type *CollectionChangeEventArgs*, which has the following simplified definition:

```
public class CollectionChangeEventArgs : EventArgs {
    public virtual CollectionChangeAction Action { get; }
    public virtual object Element { get; }
}
```

The *Action* property is of type *CollectionChangeAction*, and has a value of *Add* when an entity has been added, or *Remove* when an entity has been removed. The *Element* property is of type *Object* and contains the entity that was added or removed from the *ObjectStateManager*.

EntityKey

Earlier in this section, you saw that an *ObjectStateEntry* holds a reference to the *EntityKey* of an entity. From an Entity Framework viewpoint, an *EntityKey* is a complex type made of the following set of information:

- **EntityContainerName**   Defines the container of the entity. It is defined in the conceptual model, using the Entity Data Model Designer.

- **EntitySetName**   The name of the entity set containing the entity with that *EntityKey*.

- **EntityKeyValues**   Represents a key/value pair of properties and values that together define the identifying key of an entity instance.

- **IsTemporary**   Identifies the type of the *EntityKey*. When you add a new entity to an entity set, the Entity Framework automatically creates a temporary *EntityKey* and sets this property to *true*. When you invoke the *ObjectContext.SaveChanges* method, the Entity Framework generates a permanent key, and sets the value of this property to *false*. The permanent key generation happens as the entity transitions from the *Added* state to the *Unchanged* state—when the *AcceptChanges* method is invoked. A temporary key should not have an assigned value for *EntitySetName* or *EntityKeyValues*. Temporary keys are constructed by the Entity Framework and cannot be constructed manually.

As you can see, an *EntityKey* represents a reference to an entity in the object graph managed by an *ObjectContext* instance. Each *EntityKey* is durable and immutable; it cannot be changed after construction, and it cannot be changed after having been assigned to an entity instance. The *EntityKey* is useful for comparing equality of entities through their identifying keys, and for uniquely identifying an entity, to retrieve it from the *ObjectContext*.

From an equality comparison point of view, *EntityKey* behavior changes based on the type of key. Temporary keys use *reference equality*, which means that two entities have the same key only when the keys reference the same *EntityKey* instance in memory. The equality of permanent keys is based on the values of *EntityKeyValues*, *EntitySetName*, and *EntityContainerName*.

To create an *EntityKey* instance, you can use one of these four constructors:

```
public EntityKey();
public EntityKey(string qualifiedEntitySetName, string keyName, object keyValue);
public EntityKey(string qualifiedEntitySetName,
    IEnumerable<EntityKeyMember> entityKeyValues);
public EntityKey(string qualifiedEntitySetName,
    IEnumerable<KeyValuePair<string, object>> entityKeyValues);
```

Internally, the overloads do almost the same things. The default constructor is provided in case you want to manually configure the *EntityKeyValues*, *EntitySetName*, and *EntityContainerName* properties. The second overload is provided to create an *EntityKey* for an entity that has a simple (single-property) primary key, so you can directly provide the qualified entity set name and the single and unique key/value pair of the primary key. For example, if you want to create the *EntityKey* for a Northwind *Customer* entity, using a primary key that corresponds to its *CustomerID* property, you can use the following syntax:

```
EntityKey keyALFKI = new EntityKey("NorthwindEntities.Customers", "CustomerID", "ALFKI");
```

With the third and fourth constructors, you can create *EntityKey* instances in which the corresponding entities have composite (multi-property) primary keys. You can pass these overloads an argument of type *IEnumerable<EntityKeyMember>*, where *EntityKeyMember* represents a set of typed key/value pairs provided by the Entity Framework for the purpose of describing members of entity keys. Lastly, you can use an argument of type *IEnumerable<KeyValuePair <string, object>>* if you do not want to build the collection of *EntityKeyMember* instances manually.

> **More Info** For store-generated keys, such as identity or GUID columns, you should be careful when handling *EntityKey* values of newly added entities. For further details about managing *EntityKey* values in these situations, read the MSDN Online article "Working with Entity Keys" at *http://msdn.microsoft.com/en-us/library/dd283139.aspx*.

GetObjectByKey and *TryGetObjectByKey*

To retrieve an entity from the *ObjectContext* by using its identifying *EntityKey*, you can use a couple of methods provided by the *ObjectContext* class. The first method is *GetObjectByKey*, which has the following signature:

```
public Object GetObjectByKey(EntityKey key);
```

It retrieves an entity from the current *ObjectContext* if that entity is already in memory. Otherwise, it tries to retrieve the entity from the persistence store by executing a direct query on the DBMS. If it fails to retrieve an entity with the *EntityKey* provided, it throws an *ObjectNotFoundException*. If it succeeds, it returns a variable of type *Object*; it is up to you to cast the result to the right type.

The other method is *TryGetObjectByKey*. Here you can see its signature:

```
public bool TryGetObjectByKey(EntityKey key, out Object value);
```

Like many other methods with a name like *Try[Something]*, it tries to retrieve the entity with the provided *EntityKey*. When that fails, instead of throwing an exception, it returns a *boolean* result of *false* and a NULL reference in the *out* argument with the name *value*. When the entity exists, this method returns *true* and an instance of the retrieved entity in the *out* argument with the name *value*.

Listing 10-9 shows both these methods.

LISTING 10-9 Using the *GetObjectByKey* and *TryGetObjectByKey* methods

```
using (NorthwindEntities context = new NorthwindEntities()) {

    // Create an EntityKey with one kind of constructor overload
    EntityKey keyALFKI = new EntityKey("NorthwindEntities.Customers",
                                "CustomerID", "ALFKI");

    // Try to retrieve the corresponding customer instance
    Object alfkiUntyped;
    Boolean found = context.TryGetObjectByKey(keyALFKI, out alfkiUntyped);

    // Cast the result, if found, to a Customer instance and use it
    if (found) {
        Customer alfki = alfkiUntyped as Customer;
        Console.WriteLine(alfki.ContactName);
    }

    // Create another EntityKey with another kind of constructor overload
    EntityKey keyALFKI2 = new EntityKey("NorthwindEntities.Customers",
        new EntityKeyMember[] { new EntityKeyMember("CustomerID", "ALFKI")});

    // Retrieve the corresponding customer instance
    try {
        Customer alfki2 = context.GetObjectByKey(keyALFKI2) as Customer;

        // Use it
        Console.WriteLine(alfki2.ContactName);
    }
    catch (ObjectNotFoundException) {
        Console.WriteLine(
            "Error retrieving the customer instance. Entity not found!");
    }
}
```

It is important to emphasize that both *GetObjectByKey* and *TryGetObjectByKey* automatically retrieve the requested entity from the persistence store when it is not already in memory; otherwise, they both use the in-memory instance. This behavior makes these methods very useful for retrieving an entity reference that optimizes the workload of the persistence store, because the store is queried only if needed. Conversely, when you define a LINQ query to retrieve an entity, for example using the *First*, *FirstOrDefault*, *Single*, or *SingleOrDefault* methods, the Entity Framework always queries the store, skipping some or all the data retrieved, based on the configured *MergeOption*.

> **More Info**   For further details about *MergeOption*, see Chapter 9.

Managing Concurrency Conflicts

As detailed in the previous section, the *ObjectStateManager* keeps track of *EntityState* so that the Entity Framework can save changes against the persistence store appropriately. Moreover, so that it can properly autogenerate SQL statements, the *ObjectStateManager* keeps track of both *CurrentValues* and *OriginalValues*. From a concurrency management viewpoint, the Entity Framework implements an optimistic concurrency model by default. Thus, when you update an entity in memory and save it to the data source, Entity Framework does not check for concurrency issues; it simply updates the record with the in-memory values. Therefore, when you are managing data that can be subject to concurrency issues, you need to explicitly define a concurrency policy. The first thing you can do is define a property at the conceptual level using a *Concurrency Mode* with a value of *Fixed* rather than the default value of *None*. Figure 10-2 shows the *Concurrency Mode* configuration as it looks in the Entity Data Model Designer. When you have a property with such a configuration, the Entity Framework uses the original value of that property in the update and delete statements as a filtering condition, together with the properties corresponding to the *EntityKey* of the entity.

For example, underlying tables with a row version or time stamp field are the best candidates for the corresponding conceptual level concurrency management property. For other tables, you could define a set of properties—still at the conceptual level—that are mainly involved in concurrency and promote their *Concurrency Mode* property to a value of *Fixed*. In extreme cases, you might configure all the properties of a conceptual entity with a *Fixed* value, forcing the Entity Framework to check for concurrency conflicts on every data field.

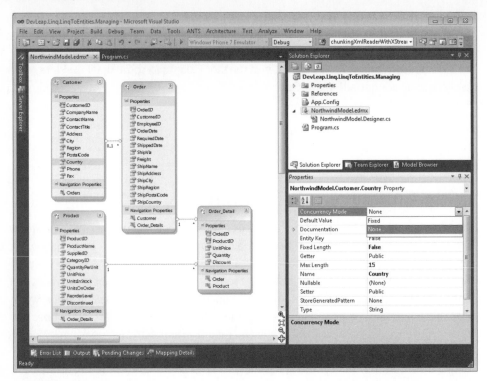

FIGURE 10-2 The Entity Data Model Designer with the *Concurrency Mode* property of a conceptual level property in evidence.

For example, imagine that the customers in the Northwind database are subject to concurrency, and that you want to use the *Country* conceptual property to discriminate concurrency. By default, the update statement sent to the DBMS is the one you already saw in Listing 10-2. However, setting the *Country* property to a *Concurrency Mode* value of *Fixed* will produce the following SQL statement for the code in Listing 10-2:

```
exec sp_executesql N'update [dbo].[Customers]
set [Country] = @0
where ((([CustomerID] = @1) and ([Country] = @2))',
N'@0 nvarchar(15),@1 nchar(5),@2 nvarchar(15)',@0=N'Germany',@1=N'DEVLP',@2=N'Italy'
```

The code in bold denotes the new selection criteria provided to the *UPDATE* statement, using the primary key (*CustomerID*) and the *Country* field with its original value (*@2 = Italy*). Thus, if the *Country* value changes while you are working with in-memory data, the *UPDATE* statement will fail, affecting zero records.

In such a case, the *ObjectContext.SaveChanges* method throws an exception of type *OptimisticConcurrencyException*, giving you the opportunity to solve the concurrency issue. The error message you get looks like this:

Store update, insert, or delete statement affected an unexpected number of rows (0).
Entities may have been **modified or deleted** since entities were loaded.
Refresh ObjectStateManager entries.

As you can see (highlighted in bold), the conflict can be the consequence of a concurrent
update or the target entity might have been deleted from the persistence store. Listing 10-10
shows a code excerpt that handles this situation.

LISTING 10-10 A code excerpt showing how to manage concurrency conflicts

```
// Update an existing customer instance
// raising a concurrency conflict
using (NorthwindEntities context = new NorthwindEntities()) {

    // Retrieve the customer instance
    Customer c = context.Customers.FirstOrDefault(i => i.CustomerID == "DEVLP");

    // Simulate an external concurrency conflict with another ObjectContext
    using (NorthwindEntities contextOther = new NorthwindEntities()) {
        Customer cOther = contextOther.Customers
                            .FirstOrDefault(i => i.CustomerID == "DEVLP");
        cOther.Country = "USA";
        contextOther.SaveChanges();
    }

    // Change the customer's country in the main ObjectContext
    c.Country = "Germany";

    // Update the persitence store checking concurrency issues
    try {
        Int32 result = context.SaveChanges();
        if (result > 0) {
            Console.WriteLine("Updated {0} entities!", result);
        }
    }
    catch (OptimisticConcurrencyException ex) {
        foreach (var entry in ex.StateEntries) {
            Console.WriteLine(
                "The entity with EntityKey of {0} and an EntityState of {1}
                    has a conflict",
                entry.EntityKey.EntityKeyValues[0],
                entry.State);
        }

        // Solve the conflict forcing client-side modifications
        context.Refresh(RefreshMode.ClientWins, c);

        Int32 result = context.SaveChanges();
        if (result > 0) {
            Console.WriteLine("Forcibly updated {0} entities!", result);
        }
    }
}
```

As you can see, the raised *OptimisticConcurrencyException* instance gives you a collection of *StateEntries* corresponding to the *ObjectStateEntry* instances of the entities with conflicts. You can enumerate this read-only collection to inspect the conflicts. For example, you might ask the end user how to solve the conflict. In this example, the code solves the conflict by first invoking the *ObjectContext.Refresh* method, which is provided expressly for this purpose, and then by invoking the *ObjectContext.SaveChanges* method one more time, to confirm the action.

The *Refresh* method has two signature overloads:

```
public void Refresh(RefreshMode refreshMode, IEnumerable collection);
public void Refresh(RefreshMode refreshMode, Object entity);
```

The former refreshes a collection of entities, whereas the latter refreshes a single entity. More-over, they both accept an argument of type *RefreshMode*, which states what to do with the provided entities. *RefreshMode* can assume the following values:

- **ClientWins**   Property changes made to the provided entities override current values in the persistence store. Thus, on the next call to *ObjectContext.SaveChanges* the changes made on the client side are forcibly sent to the data source. Internally, the refreshing process reloads the collection of *OriginalValues* with the current values in the persis-tence store.

- **StoreWins**   Property changes made to the provided entities are replaced with values coming from the data source. Thus, on the next call to *ObjectContext.SaveChanges*, the client-side changes are lost and the server-side (DBMS-side) values are kept. Internally, the refreshing process reloads both the collection of *OriginalValues* and *CurrentValues* with the current values in the persistence store.

You can argue from these definitions that the *Refresh* method is also useful for reloading an entity from the data store, even though its main purpose is solving concurrency conflicts.

Managing Transactions

By default the *ObjectContext.SaveChanges* method checks whether it is running under the context of a *TransactionScope* of the *System.Transactions* library, provided since Microsoft .NET Framework 2.0.

> **More Info**   *Complete coverage of the System.Transactions library provided since .NET Framework 2.0 is out of scope for this book. This book covers only a subset of functionalities provided by the library. To delve deeper into System.Transactions, read the MSDN online article "Introducing System. Transactions in the .NET Framework 2.0" at http://msdn.microsoft.com/en-us/library/ms973865.aspx.*

If the *Transaction.Current* object is not *NULL*, then the *SaveChanges* method will do its job, using that transaction. Otherwise, it creates a new transaction using the current data provider connection, invoking the *DbConnection.BeginTransaction* method and calling the *Commit* method of that transaction at the end. In fact, internally, the *ObjectContext* works with a Microsoft ADO.NET *DbConnection* object, provided by the currently configured data provider. As a result, every time you call *SaveChanges*, the changes are guaranteed to be applied transactionally on the persistence store. This behavior implies that all the changes you make in memory will be saved on the persistence store with an "all or nothing" policy.

One of the main features of the *TransactionScope* is its capability to create a promotable transaction. This transaction can be a locale transaction if you are using a unique transactional resource manager within the current transaction context, or a distributed transaction when you have more than one transactional resource involved. When you invoke *ObjectContext. SaveChanges* in a *TransactionScope* that is using a distributed transaction, you need to keep in mind that the final outcome of the transaction will not be driven only by the outcome of the *SaveChanges* method, but will depend on *all* the transactional resources involved in the transaction. For example, consider code that writes some changes to a DBMS by using Entity Framework, and also sends a message on a transactional queue using the Microsoft Message Queue (MSMQ) service. You can see an example of this in Listing 10-11, which for demonstration purposes uses an *INVALID QUEUE NAME* value for the queue name, to force the transaction to fail.

> **More Info** Complete coverage of working with MSMQ in the .NET Framework is out of scope for this book, which uses only a subset of functionalities provided by MSMQ. To explore *System.Messaging* more deeply, read the MSDN online article "MessageQueue Class" at *http://msdn.microsoft.com/en-us /library/system.messaging.messagequeue.aspx.*

LISTING 10-11 This example invokes *SaveChanges* under a *TransactionScope* in a distributed transaction, using an invalid configuration

```
// Prepare a MessageQueue
using (MessageQueue queue = new MessageQueue(@"INVALID QUEUE NAME")) {

    // Prepare a Message to enqueue
    Message msg = new Message();
    msg.Body = "This a message from LINQ";
    msg.Label = "LINQ Message";
    msg.Priority = MessagePriority.Normal;
    msg.Recoverable = true;

    // Change an existing customer instance
    using (NorthwindEntities context = new NorthwindEntities()) {
```

```
// Retrieve the customer instance
Customer c = context.Customers.FirstOrDefault(i => i.CustomerID == "ALFKI");

// Change the customer's country in the main ObjectContext
c.Country = "USA";

// Get the ObjectStateEntry for the current entity
ObjectStateEntry stateEntry = context.ObjectStateManager.GetObjectStateEntry(c);

// Update the persitence store checking concurrency issues
try {
    using (TransactionScope scope = new TransactionScope()) {
        Console.WriteLine("EntityState before SaveChanges: {0}",
            stateEntry.State);
        Int32 result = context.SaveChanges();

        Console.WriteLine("EntityState after SaveChanges: {0}",
            stateEntry.State);

        if (result > 0) {
            Console.WriteLine("Updated {0} entities!", result);
        }

        queue.Send(msg);

        scope.Complete();
    }
}
catch (Exception ex) {
    Console.WriteLine("Transaction aborted! Everything will be rolled back.");
    Console.WriteLine("Exception: {0}", ex.Message);
}

Console.WriteLine("EntityState after TransactionScope: {0}",
    stateEntry.State);
    }
}
```

To execute this code, you need to reference the *System.Transactions.dll* assembly, which by default is not referenced in standard .NET Framework projects. You also need to reference the *System.Messaging.dll* assembly to access the MSMQ classes. At first glance, this code looks fine, and it compiles without problems. However, it contains an error that you may occasionally experience at run time. When the transaction fails, both the DBMS and the queue are safe because the *TransactionScope* aborts any activity executed on the two transactional resource managers. Nevertheless, the *SaveChanges* overload that is used changes the *EntityState* of the entities from *Modified* to *Unchanged*—even though the transaction was rolled back. In fact, the transaction does not cover in-memory actions. The consequence of this behavior is data loss, because you cannot retry the operation later.

> **More Info** In reality the *System.Transactions* library can manage volatile transactions, as well as durable transactions. However, the Entity Framework autogenerated entities do not support volatile transaction enlistment. You can research volatile transactions by reading the MSDN Magazine article "Volatile Resource Managers in .NET Bring Transactions to the Common Type" at *http://msdn.microsoft.com/en-us/magazine/cc163688.aspx*.

Here is the console output of the sample code in Listing 10-11, after failure:

```
EntityState before SaveChanges: Modified
EntityState after SaveChanges: Unchanged
Updated 1 entities!
Transaction aborted! Everything will be rolled back.
Exception: Length cannot be less than zero.
Parameter name: length
EntityState after TransactionScope: Unchanged
```

The critical lines are shown in bold. As you can see, the transaction is rolled back because of the thrown exception. However, the *EntityState* of the *Customer* instance still gets set to *Unchanged*, just after the *SaveChanges* method invocation, and it is not rolled back to *Modified*.

To work around this issue, when using a *TransactionScope* context, you should always divide the saving-changes phase from the accepting-all-changes phase. As discussed earlier in this chapter, the *SaveChanges* method provides an overload that accepts a *SaveOptions* argument. You should use the *SaveOptions.None* or the *SaveOptions.DetectChangesBeforeSave* argument value, and avoid using the *SaveOptions.AcceptAllChangesAfterSave* option. After *TransactionScope* completion (that is, after the *TransactionScope.Complete* method invocation), you should manually call the *ObjectContext.AcceptAllChanges* method. This lets you preserve *EntityState* even if the transaction fails.

The code excerpt in Listing 10-12 shows the correct way of working with *TransactionScope* and the Entity Framework.

LISTING 10-12 An example invoking *SaveChanges* correctly under a *TransactionScope* in a distributed transaction

```
// Prepare a MessageQueue
using (MessageQueue queue = new MessageQueue(@".\private$\LinqDemoQueue")) {

    // Prepare a Message to enqueue
    Message msg = new Message();
    msg.Body = "This a message from LINQ";
    msg.Label = "LINQ Message";
    msg.Priority = MessagePriority.Normal;
    msg.Recoverable = true;
```

```
        Boolean success = false;

    // Change an existing customer instance
    using (NorthwindEntities context = new NorthwindEntities()) {

        // Retrieve the customer instance
        Customer c = context.Customers.FirstOrDefault(i => i.CustomerID == "ALFKI");

        // Change the customer's country in the main ObjectContext
        c.Country = "USA";

        // Get the ObjectStateEntry for the current entity
        ObjectStateEntry stateEntry = context.ObjectStateManager.GetObjectStateEntry(c);

        // Update the persitence store checking concurrency issues
        try {
            using (TransactionScope scope = new TransactionScope()) {
                Console.WriteLine("EntityState before SaveChanges: {0}",
                                stateEntry.State);

                Int32 result = context.SaveChanges(
                                    SaveOptions.DetectChangesBeforeSave);

                Console.WriteLine("EntityState after SaveChanges: {0}",
                                stateEntry.State);

                if (result > 0) {
                    Console.WriteLine("Updated {0} entities!", result);
                }

                queue.Send(msg);

                scope.Complete();
                success = true;
            }
        }
        catch (Exception ex) {
            Console.WriteLine("Transaction aborted! Everything will be rolled back.");
            Console.WriteLine(ex.Message);
        }

        if (success) {
            context.AcceptAllChanges();
        }

        Console.WriteLine("EntityState after TransactionScope: {0}",
                        stateEntry.State);
    }
}
```

Using the code in Listing 10-12, here is the console output when the transaction fails:

```
EntityState before SaveChanges: Modified
EntityState after SaveChanges: Modified
Updated 1 entities!
Transaction aborted! Everything will be rolled back.
Exception: Length cannot be less than zero.
Parameter name: length
EntityState after TransactionScope: Modified
```

As you can see, the *EntityState* of the modified customer does not change after invoking *SaveChanges*; at the end of the rolled-back transaction, it still has a value of *Modified*. Thus, you can retry the operation after solving the problem, and the *ObjectContext* will try again to update the persistence store.

Detaching, Attaching, and Serializing Entities

When working in applications with a distributed architecture, you sometimes need to transfer an entity from the application server to the presentation tier. In general, to satisfy this require-ment in the .NET Framework, you would use .NET Remoting, an .asmx Web Service, or a ser-vice made with Windows Communication Foundation (WCF). Whatever you use to transfer the entity from one layer of the application to another, you cannot transfer the *ObjectContext* and the *ObjectStateManager* together with the entity. Instead, you need to detach the entity from the *ObjectContext* and serialize it, sending the result "on the wire." This section covers detaching, attaching, and serializing entities managed by Entity Framework.

Detaching Entities

An entity detached from the *ObjectContext* is no longer referenced by the context itself, and is not tracked by the *ObjectStateManager*. To detach an entity, call the *ObjectContext.Detach* method, which accepts the entity to detach as its sole argument. The method has a void return value. Invoking it against an entity changes the *EntityState* of that entity to *Detached*, removing references to that entity from the current *ObjectContext*. Here is an example that detaches a *Customer* entity from the Northwind *ObjectContext*:

```
Customer c = context.Customers.FirstOrDefault(c => c.CustomerID == "ALFKI");
// work with the entity
// and at some point in time ... detach it
context.Detach(c);
```

Detach affects only the entity passed to the method; related objects are not detached. Thus, for independent associations, the relationship is lost, and when you have cascade delete set-tings on an identifying relationship, any detached entity is not involved. Moreover, because a detached entity is no longer referenced by the *ObjectStateManager*, any later property changes are lost, as well as such existing items as a temporary *EntityKey* (for new entities) and *OriginalValues* and *CurrentValues*. But the detached entity is not removed from the data source, so you will not lose real data.

Attaching Entities

On the application server, when you receive an entity from the presentation layer, you typically need to attach the entity to the *ObjectContext* and apply to the data source any changes made to it on the client side. Because the *ObjectContext* is a lightweight object, on the application server side, you should generally define a new unit of work for each request. (You will learn more about the "Unit of Work" in Chapter 18, "LINQ in a Multitier Solution".) Thus, when you re-attach the entity to the *ObjectContext*, you will have an *ObjectContext* instance that is different from the one from which you originally detached that entity.

To attach an entity to an *ObjectContext* you can use two different methods: *Attach* and *AttachTo*. Here are their signatures:

```
public void Attach(IEntityWithKey entity);
public void AttachTo(string entitySetName, object entity);
```

The *Attach* method attaches an entity with a valid *EntityKey* (one that implements *IEntityWithKey*). In this case, the Entity Framework infers the target *EntitySet* to attach the entity to from the *EntityKey*. However, if the entity does not have a valid *EntityKey*, you need to use the *AttachTo* method, providing an explicit target *entitySetName*. If you try to add an entity with an *EntityKey* that already exists in the *ObjectContext*, the operation will throw an *InvalidOperationException*.

As you saw in the "Detaching Entities" section, a detached entity loses *EntityState*, *OriginalValues*, and *CurrentValues*. Moreover, it gets attached to the *ObjectContext* in an *Unchanged* state. Therefore, to make the *ObjectContext* aware of any changes applied to the entity that you get back, you need to manually change the *EntityState*, using the methods shown in the "*ChangeObjectState* and *ChangeRelationshipState*" section earlier in this chapter.

Listing 10-13 shows an example that attaches an entity to a new instance of *ObjectContext*, using the *Attach* method.

LISTING 10-13   Detaching an entity and attaching it to a different *ObjectContext*

```
// Prepare a local variable to hold a customer instance
Customer c = null;

// Create a first ObjectContext
using (NorthwindEntities context = new NorthwindEntities()) {
```

```
    // Retrieve the customer instance
    c = context.Customers
        .FirstOrDefault(i => i.CustomerID == "ALFKI");

    // Detach the entity
    context.Detach(c);
}

// Here we are in the same method, but we have just closed the ObjectContext,
// due to the end of the using block and we simulate being on the presentation layer

// Write the current EntityState of the customer instance
Console.WriteLine("EntityState after Detach: {0}", c.EntityState);

// Change the customer instance while it is detached
c.Country = "USA";

// Create another ObjectContext (simulating two different "units of work")
using (NorthwindEntities context = new NorthwindEntities()) {

    // The customer instance has a valid EntityKey
    Console.WriteLine("EntityKey {0}.{1}: {2}",
        c.EntityKey.EntityContainerName,
        c.EntityKey.EntitySetName,
        c.EntityKey.EntityKeyValues[0]);

    // Attach the entity to the new ObjectContext
    context.Attach(c);

    // Write the current EntityState of the customer instance
    // after the Attach method invocation
    Console.WriteLine("EntityState after Attach: {0}", c.EntityState);

    // Change the EntityState of the customer instance to Modified
    context.ObjectStateManager.ChangeObjectState(c, EntityState.Modified);

    // Write the updated EntityState of the customer instance
    Console.WriteLine("EntityState after ChangeObjectState: {0}", c.EntityState);

    // Save changes made "offline" while the customer instance was detached
    context.SaveChanges();

    // Write the EntityState of the customer instance after invocation of SaveChanges
    Console.WriteLine("EntityState after SaveChanges: {0}", c.EntityState);
}
```

Here is the console output after running Listing 10-13:

```
EntityState after Detach: Detached
EntityKey NorthwindEntities.Customers: [CustomerID, ALFKI]
EntityState after Attach: Unchanged
EntityState after ChangeObjectState: Modified
EntityState after SaveChanges: Unchanged
```

Notice the different values assumed by the *EntityState* property of the entity, while moving across the code sample. The *UPDATE* statement sent to the persistence store updates all the columns because the *ObjectContext* does not have the *OriginalValues* of the entity available to determine which properties were changed while the entity was untracked.

Entities you attach to an *ObjectContext* are attached together with any related objects in the graph. Thus, if you have a *Customer* instance with a set of related *Orders*, attaching the customer also attaches that customer's orders.

> **Important** The information about attaching entities in this section applies to *existing* entities. If you simply want to attach a *new* entity to the *ObjectContext* and add it to the data source, you should use the methods shown at the beginning of this chapter, in the "Adding a New Entity" section. Otherwise, the new entity will be attached as *Unchanged*, as discussed here; therefore, the Entity Framework will not generate a corresponding *INSERT* statement when you invoke *Object-Context.SaveChanges*.

ApplyOriginalValues and *ApplyCurrentValues*

The example shown in Listing 10-13 works correctly as long as you keep the default optimistic concurrency behavior of the Entity Framework. However, if you configure one or more conceptual properties of the entities with a *Concurrency Mode* of *Fixed* (see the earlier section "Managing Concurrency Conflicts"), moving from an optimistic concurrency check to a more pessimistic model, the example above could stop working. In fact, if you update entities that have properties with a *Fixed* value for *Concurrency Mode*, the Entity Framework will generate an *UPDATE* statement that will keep track of the *OriginalValues* of those properties. But for modified entities attached to a fresh *ObjectContext*—the typical case in n-tier stateless applications— the *ObjectContext* does not have the *OriginalValues* for the modified entity, so it uses the *CurrentValues* as the *OriginalValues*, too. Thus, invoking *ObjectContext.SaveChanges* in this situation throws an *OptimisticConcurrencyException*, because in reality the *CurrentValues* and the *OriginalValues* of the entity should differ.

One solution to this issue is to query the persistence store to retrieve the real *OriginalValues*, merging client-side changes with persistence store values. To do that, you can call the *ObjectContext.Refresh* method, passing a *RefreshMode.ClientWins* value, just before calling *SaveChanges*, to avoid the problem.

Otherwise, you can use two methods that support reloading *OriginalValues* or *CurrentValues*, without the need to query the persistence store. These methods are exposed by the *Object-Context,* as well as by the *ObjectStateEntry* class, and work with an in-memory copy of the entity. Here are the signatures of the methods provided by *ObjectContext*:

```
public TEntity ApplyOriginalValues<TEntity>(string entitySetName, TEntity originalEntity)
    where TEntity: class;
public TEntity ApplyCurrentValues<TEntity>(string entitySetName, TEntity currentEntity)
    where TEntity: class;
```

The *ApplyOriginalValues* method accepts an *entitySetName* argument—the name of the target *EntitySet*—and an original instance of the entity to update. It copies the scalar proper- ties of the provided entity instance into the *OriginalValues* of the target entity in the *Object- Context*, using the *EntityKey* to identify the target entity. This method also compares the *OriginalValues* of the original entity with the *CurrentValues* of the actual entity instance, and automatically sets the *EntitySet* to a value of *Modified* when they differ. Thus, if you invoke this method prior to calling *ObjectContext.SaveChanges*, you do not need to explicitly call the *ChangeObjectState* method as shown in Listing 10-13.

The *ApplyCurrentValues* method does the same thing as the *ApplyOriginalValues* method, but copies the scalar properties of the provided entity instance into the *CurrentValues* of the target entity. It also compares the *OriginalValues* of the current entity with the *CurrentValues* of the provided entity, and automatically sets the *EntitySet* to a value of *Modified* when they differ.

In Listing 10-14, you can see a revised version of the code shown in Listing 10-13, using the *ApplyOriginalValues* method.

LISTING 10-14 A code excerpt that attaches an entity to the *ObjectContext*, and correctly handles the *EntityState* and its *OriginalValues*

```
// Prepare a local variable to hold a customer instance
Customer c = null;

// Create a first ObjectContext
using (NorthwindEntities context = new NorthwindEntities()) {

    // Retrieve the customer instance
    c = context.Customers
        .FirstOrDefault(i => i.CustomerID == "ALFKI");

    // Detach the entity
    context.Detach(c);
}

// Create a clone copy of the original Customer instance
Customer originalCustomer = CloneEntity(c);

// Here we are in the same method, but we have just closed the ObjectContext,
// due to the end of the using block and we simulate being on the presentation layer

// Write the current EntityState of the customer instance
Console.WriteLine("EntityState after Detach: {0}", c.EntityState);
```

```
// Change the customer instance while it is detached
c.Country = "USA";

// Create another ObjectContext (simulating two different "units of work")
using (NorthwindEntities context = new NorthwindEntities()) {

    // The customer instance has a valid EntityKey
    Console.WriteLine("EntityKey {0}.{1}: {2}",
        c.EntityKey.EntityContainerName,
        c.EntityKey.EntitySetName,
        c.EntityKey.EntityKeyValues[0]);

    // Attach the entity to the new ObjectContext
    context.Attach(c);

    // Write the current EntityState of the customer instance
    // after the Attach method invocation
    Console.WriteLine("EntityState after Attach: {0}", c.EntityState);

    // Refresh the OriginalValues of the current Entity
    context.ApplyOriginalValues("Customers", originalCustomer);

    // Write the current EntityState of the customer instance
    // after the Attach method invocation
    Console.WriteLine("EntityState after ApplyOriginalValues: {0}", c.EntityState);

    // Save changes made "offline" while the customer instance was detached
    context.SaveChanges();

    // Write the EntityState of the customer instance after invocation of SaveChanges
    Console.WriteLine("EntityState after SaveChanges: {0}", c.EntityState);
}
```

The console output of this example is as follows:

```
EntityState after Detach: Detached
EntityKey NorthwindEntities.Customers: [CustomerID, ALFKI]
EntityState after Attach: Unchanged
EntityState after ApplyOriginalValues: Modified
EntityState after SaveChanges: Unchanged
```

Notice that just after the invocation of *ApplyOriginalValues*, the *EntityState* has a value of *Modified*. The *UPDATE* statement sent to the persistence store updates only the modified columns, because the *ObjectContext* can compare the *OriginalValues* and the *CurrentValues*, determining the best statement. If you use custom Create, Update, and Delete (CUD) stored procedures, it is up to you to use both *CurrentValues* and *OriginalValues* when writing the commands against the persistence store.

More Info   For more information about using CUD stored procedures, see "CUD Stored Procedures" in Chapter 8.

These methods look like a good solution for the problem of refreshing the *EntityState* of detached entities, without having the need to query the persistence store to refresh data. Nevertheless, consider that both methods require that you keep a copy of the original entity somewhere in between detaching and re-attaching the entity. In a web-based solution, you could use the Microsoft ASP.NET Session object to store a copy of the original entity. In a distributed application, you could use the Caching services of Windows Server AppFabric. More generally, you need a repository that can be sharable across machines. However, to gain the best scalability for your solutions in an enterprise environment, you should develop stateless code, because the need to maintain per-user state, like the ASP.NET Session, reduces overall scalability and increases hardware requirements.

Serializing Entities

Whatever communication framework you use in your solutions, when you need to move an entity from the application server to the presentation tier, you need to transfer it across the wire.

If you use .NET Remoting as your communication framework, you use the runtime serialization engine of the .NET Framework, based on serializers that implement the *IFormatter* interface. For example, you can use the *BinaryFormatter*. The standard entities that are auto-generated by the Entity Data Model Designer's default T4 template support serialization with *BinaryFormatter*. Listing 10-15 shows an example of serialization, using the *BinaryFormatter*.

LISTING 10-15 Serializing a *Customer* instance using the *BinaryFormatter*

```
using (NorthwindEntities context = new NorthwindEntities()) {

    // Retrieve the customer instance
    Customer c = context.Customers
        .FirstOrDefault(i => i.CustomerID == "ALFKI");

    // Define an in memory store for the serialized entity
    MemoryStream mem = new MemoryStream();

    // Create a serializer and serialize the entity
    BinaryFormatter f = new BinaryFormatter();
    f.Serialize(mem, c);
}
```

You can also use the runtime binary serializer to clone an entity, for example, to store the original copy of an entity, as was shown in Listing 10-14, which used the utility method *CloneEntity<TEntity>*. Listing 10-16 shows the source code of this generic utility method.

LISTING 10-16 A generic utility method for cloning entities

```
// This is an utility method, which clones an entity
private static TEntity CloneEntity<TEntity>(TEntity originalEntity) {

    MemoryStream mem = new MemoryStream();
    BinaryFormatter f = new BinaryFormatter();
    f.Serialize(mem, originalEntity);
    mem.Position = 0;
    TEntity clonedEntity = (TEntity)f.Deserialize(mem);
    return clonedEntity;
}
```

Notice that the *BinaryFormatter* serializes the provided entity without visiting existing relationships, so the output loses related entities.

Another runtime serializer offered by the .NET Framework is the *SoapFormatter*, which is useful when working with .NET Remoting and Simple Object Access Protocol (SOAP) over HTTP(S). However, this serializer is *not* supported by the autogenerated entities of the Entity Framework, because they use generic types that are not supported by the internal *SoapFormatter* engine.

Instead, when you want to publish the autogenerated entities of the Entity Framework through an old-style .asmx Web Service, use the *XmlSerializer* class. Listing 10-17 shows how you can use this serializer with a *Customer* instance.

LISTING 10-17 Serializing a *Customer* instance using the *XmlSerializer*

```
using (NorthwindEntities context = new NorthwindEntities()) {

    // Retrieve the customer instance
    Customer c = context.Customers
        .FirstOrDefault(i => i.CustomerID == "ALFKI");

    StringWriter sw = new StringWriter();
    XmlWriter xw = XmlWriter.Create(sw, new XmlWriterSettings { Indent = true });

    XmlSerializer xs = new XmlSerializer(typeof(Customer));
    xs.Serialize(xw, c);

    xw.Flush();
    sw.Flush();

    Console.WriteLine(sw.ToString());
}
```

Here is the XML output produced by Listing 10-17:

```
<?xml version="1.0" encoding="utf-16"?>
<Customer xmlns:xsi="http://www.w3.org/2001/XMLSchema-instance"
    xmlns:xsd="http://www.w3.org/2001/XMLSchema">
    <EntityKey>
        <EntitySetName>Customers</EntitySetName>
        <EntityContainerName>NorthwindEntities</EntityContainerName>
        <EntityKeyValues>
            <EntityKeyMember>
                <Key>CustomerID</Key>
                <Value xsi:type="xsd:string">ALFKI</Value>
            </EntityKeyMember>
        </EntityKeyValues>
    </EntityKey>
    <CustomerID>ALFKI</CustomerID>
    <CompanyName>Alfreds Futterkiste</CompanyName>
    <ContactName>Maria Anders</ContactName>
    <ContactTitle>Sales Representative</ContactTitle>
    <Address>Obere Str. 57</Address>
    <City>Munich</City>
    <Region />
    <PostalCode>12201</PostalCode>
    <Country>Germany</Country>
    <Phone>030-0074321</Phone>
    <Fax>030-0076545</Fax>
</Customer>
```

As you can see, the *XmlSerializer* also handles only the entity itself, skipping any existing relationships. The resulting XML includes the *EntityKey* serialization, which you need to attach the entity to an *ObjectContext*.

Since .NET Framework 3.0 and WCF, you also have the option to use the so-called "DataContract serializers," which inherit from the *XmlObjectSerializer* abstract class. Autogenerated Entity Framework entities do support these types of serializers. Listing 10-18 shows how to serialize a *Customer* instance using the *DataContractSerializer*, which produces XML output.

LISTING 10-18 A code excerpt that serializes a *Customer* instance using the *DataContractSerializer*

```
using (NorthwindEntities context = new NorthwindEntities()) {

    context.ContextOptions.LazyLoadingEnabled = false;

    // Retrieve the customer instance
    Customer c = context.Customers
        .FirstOrDefault(i => i.CustomerID == "ALFKI");

    StringWriter sw = new StringWriter();
    XmlWriter xw = XmlWriter.Create(sw, new XmlWriterSettings { Indent = true });
```

```
        DataContractSerializer dc = new DataContractSerializer(typeof(Customer));
        dc.WriteObject(xw, c);

        xw.Flush();
        sw.Flush();

        Console.WriteLine(sw.ToString());
    }
```

In this last example, you need to disable lazy loading, otherwise the serialization engine will serialize the provided entity together with all its relationships, visiting the object graph in full depth. Here you can see the produced XML output:

```xml
<?xml version="1.0" encoding="utf-16"?>
<Customer xmlns:i="http://www.w3.org/2001/XMLSchema-instance"
    z:Id="i1" xmlns:z="http://schemas.microsoft.com/2003/10/Serialization/"
    xmlns="http://schemas.datacontract.org/2004/07/DevLeap.Linq.LinqToEntities.Managing">
    <EntityKey xmlns:d2p1="http://schemas.datacontract.org/2004/07/System.Data" z:Id="i2"
        xmlns="http://schemas.datacontract.org/2004/07/System.Data.Objects.DataClasses">
        <d2p1:EntityContainerName>NorthwindEntities</d2p1:EntityContainerName>
        <d2p1:EntityKeyValues>
            <d2p1:EntityKeyMember>
                <d2p1:Key>CustomerID</d2p1:Key>
                <d2p1:Value xmlns:d5p1="http://www.w3.org/2001/XMLSchema"
                    i:type="d5p1:string">ALFKI</d2p1:Value>
            </d2p1:EntityKeyMember>
        </d2p1:EntityKeyValues>
        <d2p1:EntitySetName>Customers</d2p1:EntitySetName>
    </EntityKey>
    <Address>Obere Str. 57</Address>
    <City>Munich</City>
    <CompanyName>Alfreds Futterkiste</CompanyName>
    <ContactName>Maria Anders</ContactName>
    <ContactTitle>Sales Representative</ContactTitle>
    <Country>Germany</Country>
    <CustomerID>ALFKI</CustomerID>
    <Fax>030-0076545</Fax>
    <Orders />
    <Phone>030-0074321</Phone>
    <PostalCode>12201</PostalCode>
    <Region></Region>
</Customer>
```

This XML is almost identical to the output of Listing 10-17 and, just like *XmlSerializer*, the *DataContractSerializer* output includes the *EntityKey*, which you need to attach the entity to an *ObjectContext*.

Caution All the information in this section about serialization of entities in the Entity Framework is relevant for autogenerated entities only. If you change the default T4 template to a custom code template (for example, to support POCO entities), the results could change unpredictably.

Using Self-Tracking Entities

One last topic to cover about managing entities in the Entity Framework is related to self-tracking entities, which can be generated through a custom T4 template offered by Microsoft as an Online Code Template. This generates entities that are able to track changes to their scalar properties, complex properties, and relationships—even when an *ObjectContext* is not available. The template produces a set of custom entities, a custom *ObjectContext*, and helper code that supports tracking logic and provides some extension methods.

These entities are defined primarily to support change tracking on the consumer side, where they are sent when using a communication framework such as WCF, even though you can use them even for server-side-only projects.

More Info This section discusses WCF (that is, DataContract serialization) only, because by default, self-tracking entities are intended to be serializable only with DataContract serializers. If you need to use them with ASMX Web Services or with .NET Remoting, you might want to change the T4 template manually, accordingly to your needs.

You will learn how to use self-tracking entities by walking through a sample related to this chapter. With Microsoft Visual Studio 2010, open the solution *DevLeap.Linq.LinqToEntities. SelfTracking* (provided with the downloadable sample code). The project publishes the *Customer* entities of Northwind through WCF as self-tracking entities.

To use these entities, you should define a project dedicated to host the Entity Data Model and the custom classes generated by the custom code template. It is good practice to keep the classes of this project separate from any other class, because you will share the resulting assembly on both the service-side and the consumer-side. In this example, the project containing the entities is named *DevLeap.Linq.LinqToEntities.SelfTracking.Model*. Listing 10-19 shows an excerpt of the *Customer* entity definition.

More Info You can find details about using a custom code template in Chapter 8, in the section "T4 Templates."

LISTING 10-19 A code excerpt of the self-tracking *Customer* entity

```
public partial class Customer : IObjectWithChangeTracker, INotifyPropertyChanged {

    [DataMember]
    public string CustomerID {
        get { return _customerID; }
        set {
            if (_customerID != value) {
                if (ChangeTracker.ChangeTrackingEnabled
                    && ChangeTracker.State != ObjectState.Added) {
                    throw new InvalidOperationException("The property 'CustomerID' is
part of the object's key and cannot be changed. Changes to key properties can only be
made when the object is not being tracked or is in the Added state.");
                }
                _customerID = value;
                OnPropertyChanged("CustomerID");
            }
        }
    }
    private string _customerID;

    [DataMember]
    public string CompanyName {
        get { return _companyName; }
        set {
            if (_companyName != value) {
                _companyName = value;
                OnPropertyChanged("CompanyName");
            }
        }
    }
    private string _companyName;

    // code omitted for the sake of simplicity ...

    [OnDeserialized]
    public void OnDeserializedMethod(StreamingContext context) {
        IsDeserializing = false;
        ChangeTracker.ChangeTrackingEnabled = true;
    }
}
```

As you can see, it is an IPOCO entity. In fact, it is a simple and lightweight class, without any specific base class, but that implements a couple of interfaces: *IObjectWithChangeTracker* and *INotifyPropertyChanged*. The latter is a .NET Framework native interface, which raises notifications just after changes to properties happen. The former is generated by the T4 template, so it does not inject any external dependencies. Its purpose is to reference an instance of an *ObjectChangeTracker* object, which handles the tracking of changes to the current entity. Here is the definition of the *IObjectWithChangeTracker* interface:

```
public interface IObjectWithChangeTracker {
    // Has all the change tracking information for the subgraph of a given object.
    ObjectChangeTracker ChangeTracker { get; }
}
```

As you can see from the code excerpt of Listing 10-19, whenever you change the value of a *Customer* instance property, the setter method of the property notifies the change using the *INotifyPropertyChanged.OnPropertyChanged* method. Internally, the *ObjectChangeTracker* instance related to the current entity intercepts the notification and changes the internal object state. Notice also the implementation of the *OnDeserializedMethod* method, auto-generated by the T4 template, which internally activates the *ObjectChangeTracker*, setting its *ChangeTrackingEnabled* property to *true* whenever you deserialize an entity. The purpose of this behavior is to automatically activate change tracking on entities when they are deserialized on the consumer side, just after a consumer application receives them from an external WCF service, and before the end user can start changing the entity.

To use these entities, you should define a WCF service to publish them. The example code defines one project for the contracts, another for the service implementation, and a web project to host the service and publish it through HTTP. Here is the service contract:

```
[ServiceContract(Namespace = "http://schemas.devleap.com/NorthwindService")]
public interface INorthwindService {
    [OperationContract]
    Customer GetCustomerByID(String customerID);

    [OperationContract]
    Customer UpdateCustomer(Customer customer);
}
```

As you can see, it offers two operations: *GetCustomerByID*, which returns a customer filtered by *CustomerID*, and *UpdateCustomer*, which receives a customer from a consumer and updates it in the persistence store.

Listing 10-20 shows the implementation of the contract in the *NorthwindService* class.

LISTING 10-20 A code excerpt from the self-tracking *Customer* entity

```
public class NorthwindService: INorthwindService {

    public Model.Customer GetCustomerByID(string customerID) {
        using (NorthwindEntities context = new NorthwindEntities()) {
            return (context.Customers
                        .FirstOrDefault(c => c.CustomerID == customerID));
        }
    }

    public Model.Customer UpdateCustomer(Model.Customer customer) {
        using (NorthwindEntities context = new NorthwindEntities()) {
            context.Customers.ApplyChanges(customer);
            context.SaveChanges();
        }

        return (customer);
    }
}
```

The *GetCustomerByID* method is trivial. In contrast, the *UpdateCustomer* method, although still simple, uses a custom extension method (generated by the T4 Self-Tracking entity template) that internally checks for off-line changes that occurred to entities and updates the *EntityState* in the *ObjectStateManager* of the current *ObjectContext* appropriately for those changes. When working with self-tracking entities, you should always invoke this method before calling the *ObjectContext.SaveChanges* method, to update any *EntityState* according to what happened to it on the consumer side. This extension method extends both the *ObjectSet<TEntity>* type and the *ObjectContext* type. Here are the available signatures:

```
public static void ApplyChanges<TEntity>(this ObjectSet<TEntity> objectSet, TEntity entity)
where TEntity : class, IObjectWithChangeTracker;
```

```
public static void ApplyChanges<TEntity>(this ObjectContext context, string entitySetName,
TEntity entity) where TEntity : IObjectWithChangeTracker;
```

As you can see, these extension methods extend self-tracking classes only, because of the constraint requiring the *IObjectWithChangeTracking* interface implementation. Thus, these methods, as well as the methods we will cover shortly, are available only in self-tracking scenarios.

The *ObjectChangeTracker* class is capable of tracking the state of entities, even without an *ObjectContext* instance, because internally it holds a *State* property, of custom autogenerated type *ObjectState*, for the current entity. Here you can see the definition of the *ObjectState* type:

```
[Flags]
public enum ObjectState {
    Unchanged = 0x1,
    Added = 0x2,
    Modified = 0x4,
    Deleted = 0x8
}
```

This is almost the same as the native *EntityState* provided by the Entity Framework. However, when serializing a self-tracking entity with DataContract serialization (that is, with a WCF service), the custom *State* property and the *ObjectChangeTracker* related to an entity are serialized together with the entity itself. Consequently, the change tracking logic will be available on the consumer side as well. Moreover, the self-tracking entities template offers a set of extension methods that target the entities so that you can manage the *State* of an entity manually. These methods are:

- **StartTracking**   Instructs the *ObjectChangeTracker* of an entity to start tracking changes.

- **StopTracking**   Instructs the *ObjectChangeTracker* of an entity to stop tracking changes.

- **AcceptChanges**   Clears any tracking information for the current entity and sets its *State* to *Unchanged*.

- **MarkAsDeleted**   Changes the state of the current entity to *Deleted*. When this method is called, the entity is removed from any collection containing it.

- **MarkAsAdded**   Changes the state of the current entity to *Added*.

- **MarkAsModified**   Changes the state of the current entity to *Modified*.

- **MarkAsUnchanged**   Changes the state of the current entity to *Unchanged*.

Notice that tracking is automatically turned on for newly created entities when they are related to a tracked entity, when you invoke any of the *MarkAs[State]* methods, or when you deserialize the entity.

Coming back to the sample solution, you can see that the consumer-side project (named *DevLeap.Linq.LinqToEntities.SelfTracking.ConsoleConsumer*) consumes the WCF service using a service reference explicitly configured to share types with the service side. In Listing 10-21, you can see a code excerpt from the console application's *Main* method.

LISTING 10-21 A code excerpt from the console consumer application

```
static void Main(string[] args) {

    // Create the service proxy
    using (NorthwindServiceClient nw = new NorthwindServiceClient()) {
        // Retrieve a Customer instance
        Model.Customer c = nw.GetCustomerByID("ALFKI");

        // Make some changes
        c.Country = "USA";

        // Update the customer through the service
        c = nw.UpdateCustomer(c);

        Console.WriteLine(c.Country);
    }
}
```

Notice that the consumer application can remain completely ignorant of the fact that the *Customer* instance is self-tracking enabled. It simply retrieves it, changes it, and sends it back to the service-side.

To achieve this goal, you need to create a service reference to the WCF service using the SvcUtil.exe command-line tool, specifying the */reference* attribute to reference the *DevLeap. Linq.LinqToEntities.SelfTracking.Model* assembly. Alternatively, you can simply reference the assembly containing the self-tracking entities in the consumer project, before adding the service reference. As you will see, the Visual Studio wizard for referencing a service will automatically reuse the *DevLeap.Linq.LinqToEntities.SelfTracking.Model* assembly, instead of recreating the entities on the consumer side.

Keep in mind that this particular type of solution is suitable only for .NET to .NET scenarios; the constraint to have the same .NET Framework assembly on both sides of the SOAP channel causes you to lose interoperability with other frameworks. However, in cases where you do not need to support interoperability, having self-tracking entities automatically built for you is still a great convenience, and reduces the development efforts required.

Summary

In this chapter, you learned how to add, update, and delete entities and graphs of entities that belong to an *ObjectContext*. You saw how the *ObjectContext* tracks *EntityState* using the *ObjectStateManager*, and how to manually manage the *EntityState* of an entity instance. You learned how to handle concurrency issues when saving data and how to resolve conflicts. You saw how to work in a transactional context, even with distributed transactions. Lastly, you learned how to detach, attach, and serialize entities in distributed software architectures, and how you can use self-tracking entities.

Chapter 11
LINQ to DataSet

The Microsoft .NET Framework native type *System.Data.DataSet* is an in-memory representation of a set of data. It is useful for getting a disconnected copy of data that comes from an external data source. Regardless of the data source, the internal representation of a *DataSet* follows the relational model, including tables, constraints, and relationships among the tables. In other words, you can consider the *DataSet* as a sort of in-memory relational database, which makes it a good target for a Microsoft Language Integrated Query (LINQ) implementation. In this chapter, you will see how LINQ can be used with a *DataSet*, to both query and populate it.

Introducing LINQ to DataSet

Because a *DataSet* is an in-memory set of objects, it is a target for LINQ to Objects. All the operations you learned about in Chapter 3, "LINQ to Objects," apply to querying a *DataSet*; however, you need a special operation to query a *DataTable* contained in a *DataSet*. The *DataTable* class does not implement *IEnumerable<T>*, so you need to create a wrapper object that implements *IEnumerable<T>* and allows LINQ queries. The *EnumerableRowCollection* class does this work. You can create it by simply calling the extension method *AsEnumerable* on a *DataTable*. This and other extension methods described later in this chapter, such as *AsDataView* and *CopyToDataTable*, are defined in the *DataTableExtensions* class, which is included in the *System.Data* namespace and is part of the *System.Data.DataSetExtensions* assembly.

To use LINQ to DataSet, you need to add a reference to the *System.Data.DataSetExtensions* assembly. You also might want to include the following statement in your code:

```
using System.Data;
```

Including the preceding statement makes extension methods declared in the *DataTableExtensions* class fully visible through Microsoft IntelliSense—as if they were native instance methods of the *DataSet* class.

Using LINQ to Load a *DataSet*

You can load a *DataSet* by querying a relational database. One way to do this is through a *DataAdapter*, as shown in Listing 11-1.

LISTING 11-1 Loading a *DataSet* by using a *DataAdapter*

```
const string QueryOrders = @"
SELECT  OrderID, OrderDate, Freight, ShipName,
        ShipAddress, ShipCity, ShipCountry
FROM    Orders
WHERE   CustomerID = @CustomerID

SELECT     od.OrderID, od.UnitPrice, od.Quantity, od.Discount,
           p.[ProductName]
FROM       [Order Details] od
INNER JOIN Orders o
      ON   o.[OrderID] = od.[OrderID]
LEFT JOIN  Products p
      ON   p.[ProductID] = od.[ProductID]
WHERE      o.CustomerID = @CustomerID";

DataSet ds = new DataSet("CustomerOrders");
SqlDataAdapter da = new SqlDataAdapter(QueryOrders, ConnectionString);
da.SelectCommand.Parameters.AddWithValue("@CustomerID", "QUICK");
da.TableMappings.Add("Table", "Orders");
da.TableMappings.Add("Table1", "OrderDetails");
da.Fill(ds);
```

The code in Listing 11-1 combines two *DataTable* instances into one *DataSet*, which corresponds to the orders placed by a specific customer.

Loading a *DataSet* with LINQ to SQL

To load a *DataSet* by using LINQ to SQL instead of a *DataAdapter*, you need to re-create the behavior of the *DataAdapter* because there is no generic method that populates a *DataTable* with an *IEnumerable<T>*. For this reason, we created the simple helper extension method named *CreateDataTable<T>*, which you can see in Listing 11-2. This method creates a *DataTable* instance and adds a new *DataRow* to the *DataTable* for each row returned by the *query* iteration.

LISTING 11-2 The helper *IEnumerable<T>* extension method *CreateDataTable<T>*

```
public static DataTable CreateDataTable<T>(
                        this IEnumerable<T> query,
                        string tableName) {
    DataTable table = new DataTable(tableName);
    var fields = typeof(T).GetProperties();

    // Create columns
    foreach (var field in fields) {
        DataColumn column = new DataColumn(field.Name);
        column.AllowDBNull =
            (typeof( T ).IsSubclassOf( typeof( ValueType ) ) ) ?
                IsNullableType( typeof( T ) ) :
                true;
        table.Columns.Add(column);
    }

    // Copy rows
    foreach (var row in query) {
        object[] values = new object[fields.Length];
        for( int i = 0; i < values.Length; i++ ) {
            values[i] = fields[i].GetValue(row, null);
        }
        table.Rows.Add(values);
    }
    return table;
}
```

More Info The MSDN documentation "How to: Implement CopyToDataTable<T> Where the Generic Type T Is Not a DataRow" contains a more complete implementation of a helper function similar to this *CreateDataTable<T>*. The implementation can also add rows to an existing table. You can find the source code for *ObjectShredder<T>* and the custom method *CopyToDataTable<T>* at *http://msdn.microsoft.com/library/bb669096.aspx*.

Using the *CreateDataTable<T>* method, you can populate a *DataTable* in the same way as you do using a *DataAdapter*. Listing 11-3 shows two LINQ to SQL queries used to populate two *DataTable* objects.

LISTING 11-3 Loading *DataSet* using LINQ to SQL queries

```
NorthwindDataContext db = new NorthwindDataContext(ConnectionString);
string filterCustomerID = "QUICK";

var customerOrders =
    from    o in db.Orders
    where   o.CustomerID == filterCustomerID
    select new {
        o.OrderID,
        o.OrderDate,
        o.Freight,
        o.ShipName,
        o.ShipAddress,
        o.ShipCity,
        o.ShipCountry
    };

var customerOrderDetails =
    from od in db.Order_Details
    join o in db.Orders
            on od.OrderID equals o.OrderID
    join p in db.Products
            on od.ProductID equals p.ProductID
    where o.CustomerID == filterCustomerID
    select new {
        od.UnitPrice,
        od.Quantity,
        od.Discount,
        p.ProductName
    };

DataSet ds = new DataSet("CustomerOrders");
ds.Tables.Add(customerOrders.CreateDataTable("Orders"));
ds.Tables.Add(customerOrderDetails.CreateDataTable("OrderDetails"));
```

From a performance point of view, using LINQ to SQL instead of the *DataAdapter* adds a layer to your code. Thus, response time is better using a *DataAdapter*, especially on the first call (when the LINQ to SQL engine initializes itself for the first time). However, LINQ to SQL avoids having unchecked SQL code in your source code, as shown in Listing 11-1.

Loading Data with LINQ to DataSet

If you need to populate a *DataTable* with the results of a query on another *DataTable*, you can use the *CopyToDataTable<T>* extension method, which is declared as follows:

```
public static DataTable CopyToDataTable<T>(this IEnumerable<T> source)
                where T: DataRow
```

As you can see, *CopyToDataTable<T>* is declared like the *CreateDataTable<T>* in Listing 11-2; however, it requires the generic *T* type to be a *DataRow* type. This constraint permits the *CopyToDataTable* implementation to handle original and modified values stored in the *DataRow* instances.

A simple use of *CopyToDataTable* is shown in Listing 11-4; the result of a LINQ query on one table is copied into a new table.

LISTING 11-4 Loading a *DataSet* using a LINQ query on another *DataTable*

```
DataSet ds = LoadDataSetUsingDataAdapter();

var highDiscountOrders =
    from  o in ds.Tables["OrderDetails"].AsEnumerable()
    where o.Field<float?>("Discount") > 0.2
    select o;

DataTable highDiscountOrdersTable = highDiscountOrders.CopyToDataTable();
highDiscountOrdersTable.TableName = "HighDiscountOrders";
ds.Tables.Add(highDiscountOrdersTable);
```

Note To query a *DataTable*, you need to use the *AsEnumerable* and *Field<T>* extension methods, which are explained in the next section, "Using LINQ to Query a *DataSet*."

Another option when using *CopyToDataTable* is to add data to or replace data in an existing table. In this case, you pass the existing table as the first argument, specifying the kind of overwrite of existing entities in the second argument. The following are two overrides of the *CopyToDataTable<T>* extension method:

```
public static DataTable CopyToDataTable<T>(this IEnumerable<T> source
                                    DataTable table,
                                    LoadOption options)
                where T: DataRow

public static DataTable CopyToDataTable<T>(this IEnumerable<T> source
                                    DataTable table,
                                    LoadOption options,
                                    FillErrorEventHandler errorHandler)
                where T: DataRow
```

The *LoadOption* enumeration used in the second argument has three possible values:

- **OverwriteChanges** Overwrites both the current and original value version of the data for each column.

- **PreserveChanges** Preserves the current value and changes only the original value version for each column. This is the default option value.

- **Upsert** A contraction meaning "update and insert," changes the current version of each column, leaving the original version unmodified.

In Listing 11-5, you can see an example of the *CopyToDataTable* call, which is not affected by the setting for *LoadOption* because the data is added to different rows.

LISTING 11-5 Loading data into an existing *DataTable* with *CopyToDataTable*

```
DataSet ds = LoadDataSetUsingDataAdapter();

var highDiscountOrders =
    from  o in ds.Tables["OrderDetails"].AsEnumerable()
    where o.Field<float?>("Discount") > 0.2
    select o;

DataTable selectionTable = highDiscountOrders.CopyToDataTable();

var lowDiscountOrders =
    from  o in ds.Tables["OrderDetails"].AsEnumerable()
    where o.Field<float?>("Discount") < 0.05
    select o;

lowDiscountOrders.CopyToDataTable( selectionTable,
                                   LoadOption.PreserveChanges);
```

The level of control provided by *LoadOptions* is useful when you receive a *DataTable* containing data that might have been modified since the data's original extraction and that you still have in the destination table. However, every time you project query results into an anonymous type, you need to use a technique like those described earlier, in the section "Loading a *DataSet* with LINQ to SQL."

Using LINQ to Query a *DataSet*

You can query a *DataTable* with LINQ just like any other *IEnumerable<T>* list.

> **Note** As mentioned previously, the *DataTable* class does not implement *IEnumerable<T>*. You have to call *AsEnumerable*, which is an extension method for *DataTable*, to obtain a wrapper that implements that interface.

A DataTable list is composed of *DataRow* objects, which means that you must access the *DataRow* member properties to get a field value. With this arrangement, you can call any *DataRow* member rather than use a query expression over a *DataTable*. You can use the *Field<T>* accessor method instead of using a direct cast on the result of the standard *DataRow* accessor (such as *o["OrderDate"]*). The query shown in Listing 11-6 gets the orders that show a date of 1998 or later.

LISTING 11-6 Querying a *DataTable* with LINQ

```
DataSet ds = LoadDataSetUsingDataAdapter();
DataTable orders = ds.Tables["Orders"];

var query =
    from   o in orders.AsEnumerable()
    where  o.Field<DateTime>( "OrderDate" ).Year >= 1998
    orderby o.Field<DateTime>( "OrderDate" ) descending
    select  o;
```

> **Note** *AsEnumerable* and *Field<T>* are two custom extension methods for *DataTable* and *DataRow* types. They are defined in *System.Data.DataTableExtensions* and *System.Data.DataRowExtensions*, respectively.

When you have several *DataTable* objects in a *DataSet*, you might want to use some type of join. The query shown in Listing 11-7 calculates the total order amount for each order from 1998 to the present.

LISTING 11-7 Joining two *DataTable* objects with LINQ

```
DataSet ds = LoadDataSetUsingDataAdapter();
DataTable orders = ds.Tables["Orders"];
DataTable orderDetails = ds.Tables["OrderDetails"];

var query =
    from   o in orders.AsEnumerable()
    join   od in orderDetails.AsEnumerable()
           on o.Field<int>( "OrderID" ) equals od.Field<int>( "OrderID" )
           into orderLines
    where  o.Field<DateTime>( "OrderDate" ).Year >= 1998
    orderby o.Field<DateTime>( "OrderDate" ) descending
    select  new { OrderID = o.Field<int>( "OrderID" ),
                  OrderDate = o.Field<DateTime>( "OrderDate" ),
                  Amount = orderLines.Sum(
                                  od => od.Field<decimal>( "UnitPrice" )
                                        * od.Field<short>( "Quantity" ) ) };
```

Listing 11-7 specifies the relationship between *orders* and *orderDetails* through the *join* syntax. If the *DataSet* contains information about existing relationships between entities, a LINQ query can take advantage of this. The code in Listing 11-8 uses *GetChildRows* to get the lines for the order details rather than explicitly joining the two tables.

LISTING 11-8 Using *DataSet* relationships in LINQ queries

```
DataSet ds = LoadDataSetUsingDataAdapter();
DataTable orders = ds.Tables["Orders"];
DataTable orderDetails = ds.Tables["OrderDetails"];
ds.Relations.Add( "OrderDetails",
                  orders.Columns["OrderID"],
                  orderDetails.Columns["OrderID"]);

var query =
    from   o in orders.AsEnumerable()
    where  o.Field<DateTime>( "OrderDate" ).Year >= 1998
    orderby o.Field<DateTime>( "OrderDate" ) descending
    select  new { OrderID = o.Field<int>( "OrderID" ),
                  OrderDate = o.Field<DateTime>( "OrderDate" ),
                  Amount = o.GetChildRows( "OrderDetails" ).Sum(
                              od => od.Field<decimal>( "UnitPrice" )
                                  * od.Field<short>( "Quantity" ) ) };
```

Understanding *DataTable.AsEnumerable*

You have seen that, by using the *AsEnumerable* extension method for *DataTable*, you can use a *DataTable* as a source in a LINQ query. It might be interesting to know exactly what *AsEnumerable* returns to better understand what happens when you make a LINQ query over a *DataTable*.

The *AsEnumerable* extension method is declared as follows:

```
public static EnumerableRowCollection<DataRow> AsEnumerable(
                                        this DataTable source);
```

The return type is a class named *EnumerableRowCollection,* which implements *IEnumerable<T>*. When you perform a LINQ query on that class, it uses specific extension methods for *EnumerableRowCollection<T>* that are defined in the *EnumerableRowCollection-Extensions* static class. The following LINQ operators have several overloaded versions:

- *Cast*
- *OrderBy*
- *OrderByDescending*
- *Select*
- *ThenBy*
- *ThenByDescending*
- *Where*

These methods are also used to support the creation of a *DataView* instance produced by LINQ queries, as explained in the next section.

Creating *DataView* Instances with LINQ

A *DataView* is a class that offers a view of a *DataTable* for sorting, filtering, searching, editing, and navigation. Usually, you would use a *DataView* when binding data to elements in a user interface. A *DataView* instance does not contain a copy of data; it contains only the rules to project the results, through properties such as *Sort* and *RowFilter*. In Listing 11-9, you can see a *DataView* that filters all the orders with a date of 1998 or later, sorting them by descending *OrderDate*.

LISTING 11-9 Creation of *DataView* in the traditional way

```
DataSet ds = LoadDataSetUsingDataAdapter();
DataTable orders = ds.Tables["Orders"];

string filter = String.Format("OrderDate >= #{0:d}#",
                              new DateTime(1998, 1, 1));
string sort = "OrderDate DESC";
DataView legacyView = new DataView( orders, filter, sort,
                                    DataViewRowState.CurrentRows);
```

You can also create a *DataView* from a LINQ query on a *DataTable* using the *AsDataView* extension method. Listing 11-10 creates the same *DataView* as Listing 11-9, but obtained with a LINQ query instead.

LISTING 11-10 Creation of *DataView* using a LINQ query over a *DataTable*

```
DataSet ds = LoadDataSetUsingDataAdapter();
DataTable orders = ds.Tables["Orders"];

var query =
    from    o in orders.AsEnumerable()
    where   o.Field<DateTime>("OrderDate").Year >= 1998
    orderby o.Field<DateTime>("OrderDate") descending
    select  o;

DataView view = query.AsDataView();
```

 Note The *DataView* class does not support projection on anonymous types. You always need a LINQ query over a *DataTable* to be able to call the *AsDataView* extension method.

The only supported operators in a LINQ query to create a *DataView* are those listed earlier in the "Understanding *DataTable.AsEnumerable*" section. Creating a *DataView* with LINQ offers a strongly typed way to define a *DataView*. The differences from the traditional way are apparent if you compare Listing 11-9 and Listing 11-10. Even though the traditional approach contains fewer lines, the *filter* and *sort* expression strings cannot be checked during compilation, which can be problematic because writing an expression that filters orders having an *OrderDate* greater than or equal to 1998 is both more difficult to write and more error-prone than the LINQ version in Listing 11-10.

When you create a *DataView* using a LINQ query, you get an instance of *LinqDataView*, which is a class that inherits *DataView*. Properties such as *RowFilter* and *Sort* are still available in *LinqDataView*, but you will not find the conversion of the filter or sort condition you defined in the LINQ query. However, if you set either of these conditions, you will change the behavior of that part of the *DataView*. For example, say you execute the following line after the code in Listing 11-10:

```
view.RowFilter = String.Format( "OrderDate < #{0:d}#",
                                new DateTime(1998, 1, 1));
```

You will replace the *where* condition of the LINQ query, but you will still have the behavior of the *orderby* condition. You can also remove a filter condition by setting the *RowFilter* property to *null*:

```
view.RowFilter = null;
```

After this assignment, there are no more filters on rows, but the results are still ordered by descending *OrderDate*, unless you also cancel the sorting clause with this statement:

```
view.Sort = null;
```

> **Note** Remember that reading *RowFilter* and *Sort* properties on a *DataView* do not show you whether a *where* predicate or an *orderby* condition is active from the originating LINQ query. However, by assigning them, you remove the corresponding behavior defined by the originating LINQ query.

Using LINQ to Query a Typed *DataSet*

A typed *DataSet* can be queried with a simpler syntax because it is not necessary to use the *Field<T>* accessor and the *AsEnumerable* method.

> **Note** If you create the typed *DataSet* with Microsoft Visual Studio, your typed *DataTable* classes will be derived from the *TypedTableBase<T>* class, which implements the *IEnumerable<T>* interface. Therefore, you do not have to call *AsEnumerable* to get a wrapper. Extension methods for *TypedTableBase<T>* are defined in the *TypedTableBaseExtensions* static class.

The query shown in Listing 11-10, which used the existing *DataSet* relationships, can be rewritten as shown in Listing 11-11, which uses a typed *DataSet*.

LISTING 11-11 Querying a typed *DataSet* with LINQ

```
var query =
    from    o in ds.Orders
    where   o.OrderDate.Year >= 1998
    orderby o.OrderDate descending
    select  new { o.OrderID, o.OrderDate,
                  Amount = o.GetOrder_DetailsRows().Sum(
                                od => od.UnitPrice * od.Quantity ) };
```

As you can see, the query syntax is much simpler, and similar to earlier queries on other entity types. However, you must use a predefined schema (the typed *DataSet*) to query a *DataSet* instance in this way, which prevents the use of this syntax with a *DataSet* containing a flexible schema defined at execution time. This does not mean that you should use an untyped *Data-Set*; it only emphasizes that untyped *DataSet*s can be queried only with the *Field<T>* accessor.

Accessing Untyped *DataSet* Data

Accessing data in an untyped *DataSet* requires the use of the *Field<T>* and *SetField<T>* accessors to get and set field values, respectively. These accessors are important because a null value in a *DataSet* is represented by the *IsNull* method returning *true*. You should check this condition each time you access a column just to avoid potential cast errors. *Field<T>* fully supports a nullable type for *T*. You can use these accessors for any *DataTable* or *DataRow* access—even outside a query expression. Listing 11-12 shows an example that uses a nullable type and tests its null value by querying the *HasValue* property of the nullable type.

LISTING 11-12 Querying an untyped *DataSet* with LINQ

```
foreach (DataRow r in orderDetails.Rows) {
    double? discount = r.Field<double?>("Discount");
    if (discount.HasValue && discount.Value > 0.10) {
        r.SetField<double?>("Discount", 0.10);
    }
}
```

Comparing *DataRow* Instances

Some LINQ operators need to compare *DataRow* instances. Although LINQ to SQL provides an object tracker that usually keeps the same reference for two requests of the same row from a table, *DataSet* offers no such mechanism. Thus, when comparing two *DataRow* instances, you need to compare their *content*, not just the instance references. The LINQ operators that you need for making the comparisons are:

- Distinct
- Except
- Intersect
- Union

The *DataRowComparer* class defined in the *System.Data* namespace provides a comparer that uses the *Equals* method to compare two *DataRow* instances. The comparison is made column by column, and returns true only if all corresponding columns are equal. You can use the singleton *DataRowComparer.Default* as the equality comparer for the LINQ operators that receive it as a parameter. In Listing 11-13, you can see an example of the *Intersect* operator, which internally compares *DataRow* instances.

LISTING 11-13 Use of *DefaultRowComparer.Default* as an equality comparer calling the *Intersect* operator

```
var queryOldOrders =
    from  o in ds.Orders
    where o.OrderDate.Year <= 1996
    select o;

var queryLowFreightOrders =
    from  o in ds.Orders
    where o.Freight < 50
    select o;

DataTable oldOrders = queryOldOrders.CopyToDataTable();
DataTable lowFreightOrders = queryLowFreightOrders.CopyToDataTable();

// Find the intersection of the two queries
var queryOrders= oldOrders.AsEnumerable().Intersect(
                    lowFreightOrders.AsEnumerable(),
                  DataRowComparer.Default);

DataTable orders = queryOrders.CopyToDataTable();
```

Important If you do not use *DataRowComparer.Default* as an equality comparer when *DataRow* comparison is involved, the comparison could be false even if the rows have the same content but a different instance reference. LINQ operators that should use this comparer are *Distinct*, *Except*, *Intersect*, and *Union*.

Summary

The *DataSet* class is a widely adopted model with which to get an in-memory set of data to use as a cache or to bind data to the user interface. LINQ supports both typed and untyped *DataSet* instances. You can use LINQ to populate a *DataSet* by querying a database with LINQ to SQL, or by using other LINQ implementations such as LINQ to XML. You can also use LINQ to query a *DataSet* by querying and joining *DataTable* instances, and eventually generating *DataView* instances from LINQ queries.

Part III
LINQ to XML

Chapter 12

LINQ to XML: Managing the XML Infoset

Since it became available on February 10, 1998, XML has been broadly supported and used. Today, every development framework supports XML and its related specifications, such as the following:

- **XML Schema Definition (XSD)** Defines the structure of XML documents.

- **Extensible Stylesheet Language for Transformations (XSLT)** Transforms XML documents from one schema to another.

- **XPath and XQuery** Searches and traverses XML contents.

- **Document Object Model (DOM)** Manages in-memory representations of XML documents.

- **Simple Object Access Protocol (SOAP) services** Achieves platform interoperability using well-defined and interoperable XML messages.

- **XML Infoset** Represents XML content as a set of information items, such as Document, Element, Attribute, Processing Instruction, and Comment. Each information item represents an abstract description of part of the XML content and includes a set of named properties.

Despite its widespread use, XML is still often an unwelcome technology for many developers because of its rigorous syntax. LINQ to XML provides a unified application programming interface (API) to define and manage XML contents using Microsoft .NET Framework code. The LINQ to XML programming framework is fully integrated with the .NET Framework type system and syntax. LINQ to XML uses Microsoft Language Integrated Query (LINQ) extension methods to read, create, search, query, and generally manage XML contents within applications that use .NET Framework code and a language-agnostic API, the same as with entities, database records, and collections of items.

Introducing LINQ to XML

LINQ to XML provides the power of the DOM and the expressiveness of XPath and XQuery through LINQ extension methods that you can use to manage and query in-memory XML nodes. It uses the latest enhancements to .NET Framework languages, such as anonymous methods, generics, and nullable types. Consider the following introductory sample XML document:

```xml
<?xml version="1.0" encoding="UTF-16" standalone="yes"?>
<customer id="C01">
  <firstName>Paolo</firstName>
  <lastName>Pialorsi</lastName>
  <addresses>
    <address type="email">paolo@devleap.it</address>
    <address type="url">http://www.devleap.it/</address>
    <address type="home">Brescia - Italy</address>
  </addresses>
</customer>
```

Listing 12-1 shows how you can build such a document with "old-style" DOM syntax, using Microsoft Visual C#.

LISTING 12-1 A sample of XML construction using DOM in C#

```csharp
// Create the XmlDocument
XmlDocument customerDocument = new XmlDocument();

// Define processing instruction and document element (root element)
customerDocument.AppendChild(customerDocument.CreateProcessingInstruction
  ("xml", "version='1.0' encoding='UTF-16' standalone='yes'"));
customerDocument.AppendChild(customerDocument.CreateElement("customer"));
customerDocument.DocumentElement.SetAttribute("id", "C01");

// Create and add "firstName" child element to the document element
XmlElement firstNameElement = customerDocument.CreateElement("firstName");
firstNameElement.InnerText = "Paolo";
customerDocument.DocumentElement.AppendChild(firstNameElement);

// Create and add "lastName" child element to the document element
XmlElement lastNameElement = customerDocument.CreateElement("lastName");
lastNameElement.InnerText = "Pialorsi";
customerDocument.DocumentElement.AppendChild(lastNameElement);

// Create "addresses" element
XmlElement addressesElement = customerDocument.CreateElement("addresses");

// Create and add "email address" child element to the "addresses" element
XmlElement emailAddressElement = customerDocument.CreateElement("address");
emailAddressElement.SetAttribute("type", "email");
emailAddressElement.InnerText = "paolo@devleap.it";
addressesElement.AppendChild(emailAddressElement);
```

```
// Create and add "url address" child element to the "addresses" element
XmlElement urlAddressElement = customerDocument.CreateElement("address");
urlAddressElement.SetAttribute("type", "url");
urlAddressElement.InnerText = "http://www.devleap.it/";
addressesElement.AppendChild(urlAddressElement);

// Create and add "home address" child element to the "addresses" element
XmlElement homeAddressElement = customerDocument.CreateElement("address");
homeAddressElement.SetAttribute("type", "home");
homeAddressElement.InnerText = "Brescia - Italy";
addressesElement.AppendChild(homeAddressElement);

// Add "addresses" child element to the document element
customerDocument.DocumentElement.AppendChild(addressesElement);
```

As you can see, the DOM syntax requires a lot of procedural code to define each single node (information item) and to append it to its parent node. It is also a verbose syntax, so it is not agile to write or read.

Now consider the Listing 12-2 code excerpt, which defines the same XML document but uses LINQ to XML in C#.

LISTING 12-2 A sample of XML functional construction

```
XDocument customer =
    new XDocument(
        new XDeclaration("1.0", "UTF-16", "yes"),
        new XElement("customer",
            new XAttribute("id", "C01"),
            new XElement("firstName", "Paolo"),
            new XElement("lastName", "Pialorsi"),
            new XElement("addresses",
                new XElement("address",
                    new XAttribute("type", "email"),
                        "paolo@devleap.it"),
                new XElement("address",
                    new XAttribute("type", "url"),
                        "http://www.devleap.it/"),
                new XElement("address",
                    new XAttribute("type", "home"),
                        "Brescia - Italy")))));
```

The preceding example is called *functional construction*. The code reveals how simple and intuitive it is to define an XML nodes hierarchy with LINQ to XML. As you can see, the code layout describes the final hierarchical structure by using nested constructors. The standard DOM approach shown in Listing 12-1 requires you to declare and collect many objects. This new syntax uses a single hierarchical statement to achieve this goal, allowing developers to focus on the structure of the final XML output rather than on DOM rules. From the perspective of XML Infoset, the functional construction approach defines each single item, each of which corresponds to one of the various XML nodes. For example, the *XDocument* type instance represents a Document information item of an XML Infoset. The example then defines many *XElement* instances , each of which describes an Element information item of the XML Infoset. Finally, the code creates *XAttribute* instances that map to XML attributes.

Microsoft Visual Basic has gone even further to make working with and defining XML simple. The language enhancements introduced with Microsoft Visual Basic 2008 offer a feature called *XML literals*, which you can use to place XML directly into the code. In fact, when the previous example is written in Visual Basic, it looks like the excerpt in Listing 12-3.

LISTING 12-3 A sample of Visual Basic XML literals

```
Dim customerXml As XDocument =
    <?xml version="1.0" encoding="UTF-16" standalone="yes"?>
        <customer id="C01">
            <firstName>Paolo</firstName>
            <lastName>Pialorsi</lastName>
            <addresses>
                <address type="email">paolo@devleap.it</address>
                <address type="url">http://www.devleap.it/</address>
                <address type="home">Brescia - Italy</address>
            </addresses>
        </customer>
```

The power and expressiveness of this syntax is truly evident. You write pure XML code directly inside your Visual Basic code. Querying XML with LINQ to XML is also simple. The following sample code enumerates all the *address* tags of a given customer in C#:

```
foreach(XElement a in customer.Descendants("addresses").Elements()) {
    Console.WriteLine(a);
}
```

Using Visual Basic, this query can be written using a more intuitive syntax, such as the following:

```
Dim address As XElement
For Each address In customerXml.<customer>.<addresses>.<address>
    Console.WriteLine(address.Value)
Next
```

You will see more about how to query XML in Chapter 13, "LINQ to XML: Querying Nodes." For now, just note that the example uses an XML-like syntax within Visual Basic code. The rest of this chapter covers all the features of LINQ to XML related to nodes and Infoset management.

LINQ to XML Programming

With the LINQ to XML programming framework, you can build and manage XML content. You can use LINQ to query XML content in a completely independent manner, and use LINQ to XML as a stand-alone API. This new API is built with World Wide Web Consortium (W3C) XML Infoset instances in mind, rather than an approach that relies just on manipulating XML 1.0 string documents full of brackets. In other words, the basic objective of this programming framework is to manipulate the in-memory tree of information items of an XML Infoset rather than focusing on basic handling of a plain XML text file.

Note W3C defines an XML Infoset as a set of information items that describes the structure of any well-formed XML document. You can think of an XML Infoset as the set of information items represented by an XML document instance; the information items are the in-memory node graph description corresponding to an XML document, which is separate from the physical nature of the document itself. For further details on XML Infoset, read the W3C Recommendation at *http://www.w3.org/TR/xml-infoset*.

The goal of the LINQ to XML API is to provide an object-oriented approach for XML construction and management, avoiding or solving many common issues related to XML manipulation through the W3C DOM. With LINQ to XML, the approach to XML is no longer document-centric, as it is in the W3C DOM, as you can see in Listing 12-1. Using LINQ to XML, you can create elements and elements can exist detached from any document. Namespace usage has been simplified as well, and traversing the in-memory tree is now much like scanning any other object graph. To make all this possible, the LINQ to XML framework is based on a set of classes, all with names prefixed by an *X* (which we will often refer to as *X* classes* in this chapter). These classes correspond to the main node types in an XML document. Figure 12-1 shows the object model hierarchy.

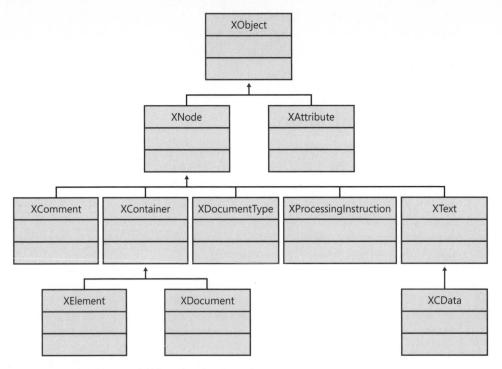

FIGURE 12-1 The object model hierarchy of main X* classes.

To start using this new API, you must reference the System.Xml.Linq assembly. The following sections describe the main types defined in the corresponding *System.Xml.Linq* namespace.

XDocument

The *XDocument* class represents an XML Infoset document instance, which is the root container of a set of information items. There is exactly one Document information item in each XML Infoset, as well as in LINQ to XML. You can create document instances using the type constructors or some factory methods. Here are the supported constructors:

```
public XDocument();
public XDocument(params object[] content);
public XDocument(XDeclaration declaration, params Object[] content);
public XDocument(XDocument other);
```

As you can see, the default constructor can be used to build an empty *XDocument* instance, but the most commonly used constructors are the second and third ones. They both accept a *params Object[]* list of objects that theoretically can be any kind of object. You should, however, use only *XElement*, *XProcessingInstruction*, *XDocumentType*, and *XComment* instances to keep the result well formed. (You will see more information about those X* classes later in this chapter.)

Consider again the code excerpt in Listing 12-2, which defines an *XDocument* instance, passing two parameters to the constructor: one *XDeclaration* instance and one *XElement* instance (the *customer* element). Those X* type instances represent the entire content of the *XDocument*.

With the last constructor of the *XDocument* type, you can create a document based on another *XDocument* instance.

If you're familiar with previous .NET Framework XML APIs, you may have noticed that *XDocument* does not have a constructor with a parameter of type *XmlReader*, *Stream*, or whatever describes a source file or Uniform Resource Identifier (URI). Instead, *XDocument*, like *XElement* (as you will see shortly), provides a set of static *Load* methods that act as factory methods. You can invoke these methods by passing a document URI as a *String* parameter, rather than passing an *XmlReader* or a *TextReader* argument, to access existing XML content directly. Another useful method provided by the *XDocument* type is the *Parse* static method, which you can use to parse a well-formed XML string and convert it into an *XDocument* instance.

To persist XML Infoset *XDocument* instances, use one of its *Save* method overloads. Generally, an *XDocument* instance is useful whenever you need to create processing instructions or document type declarations on top of the XML document; otherwise, *XElement* is a better choice and is easier to use.

> **Important** As you have already seen, Visual Basic XML literals are parsed by the Visual Basic compiler to generate standard LINQ to XML syntax. During this parsing phase, the compiler supports a subset of constructors provided by the various LINQ to XML types. For example, whenever you need to create an *XDocument* using Visual Basic XML literals, the only constructor supported is the one that requires an initial argument of type *XDeclaration* (for example, a processing instruction) on top of the document. Any other XML literal missing the trailing *XDeclaration* is assumed to be an *XElement* instance.

One last thing to notice is that the *XDocument* type inherits from the *XContainer* class, as you can see in Figure 12-1. The *XContainer* class defines all the real implementations of the code to handle nodes and the contents of the document itself.

XElement

XElement is one of the main LINQ to XML classes. As you can see in Figure 12-1, it has the same hierarchical level as the *XDocument* class and, like the *XDocument* type, is derived from the base *XNode* class through *XContainer*. As its name suggests, this class describes an XML element (a markup tag). It can be used as the container for any XML fragment (a well-formed excerpt of XML content) parented to a tag. *XElement* provides many constructors:

```
public XElement(XElement other);
public XElement(XName name);
public XElement(XStreamingElement other);
public XElement(XName name, object content);
public XElement(XName name, params object[] content);
```

The first constructor creates an *XElement* instance based on an already existing *XElement*. The second constructor overload lets you define an empty *XElement* with a specific element name. You will cover the third constructor later in this chapter during the discussion of the *XStreamingElement* class.

The last two constructors are the most useful because they support functional XML construction. The *Object content* or *params Object[] content* parameters of these constructors can be instances of simple content types (such as *String*, *Double*, *Single*, *Decimal*, *Boolean*, *DateTime*, *TimeSpan*, or *DateTimeOffset*), any type that implements *ToString*, or any type that implements *IEnumerable<T>*. The *params Object[]* list of objects can also include complex content, such as objects of type *XObject*, *XNode*, and *XAttribute*, discussed later in this chapter. These constructors handle any type of content you provide as a string value unless the content is an *X** type suitable as the content of an *XElement*. In fact, if you provide these constructors with an *XElement* instance that describes a tag, it will be added to the current element as a child. When you provide a simple content type, its string value will be used as the text content of the document element. Moreover, when you pass one of these two constructors an array of simple types, such as an array of *Boolean* or *Integer* variables, the constructor converts each value in the array to a string and appends it to the text content of the *XElement* instance.

Listing 12-4 shows the code to define an *XElement* named *customer*, with a child element named *firstName*.

LISTING 12-4 A sample *XElement* constructed using LINQ to XML

```
XElement customerTag = new XElement("customer",
    new XElement("firstName", "Paolo"));
```

Using a standard DOM approach, we would have to define an *XmlDocument* instance, explicitly create the elements, and then append each child node to its parent, losing expressiveness and readability in the process. The more complex DOM approach is shown in Listing 12-5.

LISTING 12-5 Definition of an XML element using DOM

```
XmlDocument customerDocument = new XmlDocument();
XmlElement customerElement = customerDocument.CreateElement("customer");
XmlElement firstNameElement = customerDocument.CreateElement("firstName");
firstNameElement.InnerText = "Paolo";
customerElement.AppendChild(firstNameElement);
customerDocument.AppendChild(customerElement);
```

The easiest way to define this customer element is to use Visual Basic XML literals, as demonstrated in Listing 12-6.

LISTING 12-6 Definition of an XML element using Visual Basic XML literals

```
Dim customerName As String = "Paolo"
Dim customerTag As XElement =
  <customer>
    <firstName><%= customerName %></firstName>
  </customer>
```

XElement also provides some static methods that act as factory methods. For example, you can use the *XElement.Load* method to load the element content from an existing *XmlReader* instance, so you can reuse existing code based on *System.Xml* classes. You can also invoke the *Load* method and pass it a *TextReader* or a file URI as a *String* parameter. When you read an XML document through the static *Load* method, the internal implementation reads the XML source using an *XmlReader*, which preserves efficiency. However, the entire XML document will be loaded in memory. Later in this chapter, you will see how to avoid loading the whole document into memory, delaying load operations by using a streamed approach.

Some *Load* method overloads accept a *LoadOptions* parameter. This parameter defines a flag enumeration of values that you can use to define how to handle white space (*Preserve-Whitespace*), line information (*SetLineInfo*), and base URI address (*SetBaseUri*) while reading the content of the *XElement* instance.

One last useful way to load content into an *XElement* type is the *Parse* static method. This method, similar to the corresponding *XDocument* method, parses a well-formed XML string and converts it into an *XElement* instance ready to be plugged into an XML tree.

Whenever you need to provide a textual representation of an *XElement* instance, you can use the various *Save* method overloads. The possible destinations are as follows:

- A file, providing its path as a *String*
- An *XmlWriter*
- A *TextWriter*
- A generic *Stream*

When you save an *XElement*, the default saving behavior is to ignore insignificant spaces. Alternatively, you can use overloads of the *Save* method that allow you to define specific behaviors for handling white space. Using the *SaveOptions* enumeration, you can instruct the *XElement* to serialize its content while preserving insignificant white spaces; it does this by calling *Save* with a value of *DisableFormatting* for the *SaveOptions* parameter.

You can also convert an *XElement* instance to a *String* simply by invoking the *ToString* method. Moreover, *XElement* provides direct casting of its content using a custom implementation of the *Explicit* operator. This custom operator is defined to obtain a typed version of the *Value* property of the *XElement*. Compared to classic *System.Xml.XmlElement*, direct casting is a great improvement because you can manage XML nodes typed from a .NET Framework point of view with a value-centric approach. To better understand this concept, consider the sample code in Listing 12-7.

LISTING 12-7 Sample of explicit type casting using *XElement* content

```
XElement order =
    new XElement("order",
        new XElement("quantity", 10),
        new XElement("price", 50),
            new XAttribute("idProduct", "P01"));

Decimal orderTotalAmount =
    (Decimal)order.Element("quantity") *
    (Decimal)order.Element("price");
Console.WriteLine("Order total amount: {0}", orderTotalAmount);
```

The code in Listing 12-7 uses an *XElement* that describes an order. Imagine that you received this instance of the order from an order management system rather than by constructing it explicitly in code. The code extracts the elements named *quantity* and *price,* and explicitly casts them to a *Decimal* type. The conversion returns the inner *Value* of each element node, trying to cast it to *Decimal*, but does not handle errors. To handle invalid content, you would need to catch a *FormatException* because the various *Explicit* operator overloads internally use *XmlConvert* from *System.Xml* or *Parse* methods of .NET Framework types. Be aware that *XElement* provides explicit conversions to the most common .NET Framework types and also to the corresponding nullable types.

Finally, note that the *XElement* constructor automatically handles XML encoding of text. Consider Listing 12-8.

LISTING 12-8 Sample of explicit escaping of XML text

```
XElement notes = new XElement("notes",
    "Some special characters like & > < <div/> etc.");
```

When you call *notes.ToString()* to get its textual representation, the result is encoded automatically through *XmlConvert* and looks like the following:

```
<notes>Some special characters like &amp; &gt; &lt; &lt;div/&gt; etc.</notes>
```

The class checks node names against XML naming rules, rejecting invalid names and throwing a *System.Xml.XmlException*. (For further details, see the information about the XSD types *Name* and *NMToken* on the W3C web site at *http://www.w3.org/TR/xmlschema-2/.)* This behavior is different from that of the old *XmlWriter*, where names were automatically encoded. You should be aware of syntactic rules rather than hide them under the covers. However, if you want to define "irregular" node names with LINQ to XML, you can just use the *XmlConvert* class by yourself, invoking its methods, *EncodeName* or *EncodeNmToken*, respectively. You can see an example of this approach in Listing 12-9.

LISTING 12-9 Sample of manual escaping of XML names

```
XElement notes = new XElement(XmlConvert.EncodeNmToken("strange name!",
    "My parent element has a strange name!");
```

This time, calling *notes.ToString()* will give you the following output:

```
<strange_x0020_name_x0021_>My parent element has a strange
name!</strange_x0020_name_x0021_>
```

As you can see, the name of the *XElement* has been encoded correctly.

XAttribute

This class represents an XML attribute instance. You can add it to any *XContainer* (for example, *XDocument* or *XElement*) using its constructor and LINQ to XML functional construction. Like the *XElement* class, *XAttribute* offers a rich set of conversion operators so it can provide its content already typed from a .NET Framework point of view. From a practical point of view, working with attributes is quite similar to working with elements. However, from an internal point of view, attributes are handled as a name/value pair mapped to the container element. Each *XAttribute* provides a couple of properties, called *NextAttribute* and *PreviousAttribute*, which are useful for browsing the sequence of attributes of an element.

In Listing 12-10, you can see an example of using the *XAttribute* type within a functional construction sentence.

LISTING 12-10 Sample of using *XAttribute*

```
XElement customerTag = new XElement(
    "customer",
    new XAttribute("id", "C01"), // The attribute added to customerTag
    "Paolo Pialorsi");
```

The result of this code is an element with the name *customer* that contains the text "Paolo Pialorsi," with an attribute named *id* and the value C01, as in the following XML fragment:

```
<customer id="C01">Paolo Pialorsi</customer>
```

XNode

XNode is the base class for many of the X* classes. It implements the entire tree-node management infrastructure, providing methods to add, move, remove, and replace nodes within the XML Infoset. For example, the *AddAfterSelf* and *AddBeforeSelf* methods are useful for inserting one or more nodes after or before the current node. Listing 12-11 provides an example of these methods; specifically, it shows how to use the *AddAfterSelf* method to insert two addresses for the customer in Listing 12-2, just after the first address.

LISTING 12-11 Sample usage of the *AddAfterSelf* method of *XNode*

```
XElement customer = XElement.Load(@"customer.xml");

// This sentence selects the first address element, child of addresses
XElement firstAddress =
    (customer.Descendants("addresses").Elements("address")).First();

firstAddress.AddAfterSelf(
    new XElement("address",
        new XAttribute("type", "IT-blog"),
            "http://blogs.devleap.com/"),
    new XElement("address",
        new XAttribute("type", "US-blog"),
            "http://weblogs.asp.net/PaoloPia/"));
```

As shown, you can add a set of nodes with one operation, because these methods provide several overloads, which are shown here:

```
public void AddAfterSelf(Object content);
public void AddBeforeSelf(Object content);
public void AddAfterSelf(params Object[] content);
public void AddBeforeSelf(params Object[] content);
```

The first two overloads in the preceding list require a single parameter of type *Object*, whereas the second two overloads accept a *params Object[]* variable list of parameters. You might be wondering why these methods, like many of the constructors described earlier, accept the type *Object* instead of *XNode* or any other X* class instance. The answer is quite simple but very interesting: Whenever you provide an object to methods and constructors of X* classes, LINQ to XML checks to determine whether the object is an X* type instance. When that is true, LINQ to XML hangs it in the node graph if this operation is allowed by the context node. Then it checks whether the object is an array or implements *IEnumerable* to recursively handle its contents. If the object is not an array, but can be converted to a *String* by calling its *ToString* method implementation, LINQ to XML appends the string representation to the current node's text content. NULL parameters are just ignored.

Using the functional construction syntax, you can load a set of nodes by using C# merged with LINQ queries. Listing 12-12 uses the customers sequence shown in Chapter 2, "LINQ Syntax Fundamentals," to build an XML document based on those customers.

LISTING 12-12 A LINQ to XML sentence merged with LINQ queries

```
XElement xmlCustomers = new XElement("customers",
    from   c in customers
    where  c.Country == Countries.Italy
    select new XElement("customer",
              new XAttribute("name", c.Name),
              new XAttribute("city", c.City),
              new XAttribute("country", c.Country)));
```

Note You can view results like those shown in Listing 12-12 by calling *xmlCustomers.Save(Console.Out);*.

The result looks like the following XML document:

```
<?xml version="1.0" encoding="utf-8"?>
<customers>
  <customer name="Paolo" city="Brescia" country="Italy" />
  <customer name="Marco" city="Torino" country="Italy" />
</customers>
```

You can achieve the same result by using Visual Basic XML literals, as shown in Listing 12-13.

LISTING 12-13 A LINQ to XML sentence merged with LINQ queries, using Visual Basic XML literals

```
Dim xmlCustomers As XElement =
  <customers>
    <%= From c In customers
        Where (c.Country = Countries.Italy)
        Select
        <customer>
          <firstName><%= c.FirstName %></firstName>
        </customer> %>
  </customers>
```

Another interesting method provided by *XNode* is *DeepEqual*. It is a static method that is useful for fully comparing two XML nodes for equality, as the name suggests. It works by comparing nodes through an internal abstract instance method also called *DeepEqual*. In this way, every type inherited from *XNode* implements its own *DeepEqual* behavior. For example, *XElement* compares element names, element content, and element attributes. The *XNode-EqualityComparer* class (which you will see later in this chapter during the coverage of LINQ to XML queries) is based on *DeepEqual*.

XName and *XNamespace*

When defining XML contents and node graphs, you usually need to map nodes to their XML namespace. Listing 12-14 shows the process of defining nodes with an XML namespace by using a classic DOM approach.

LISTING 12-14 XML namespace handling using classic DOM syntax

```
XmlDocument document = new XmlDocument();

XmlElement customer = document.CreateElement("c", "customer",
    "http://schemas.devleap.com/Customer");
document.AppendChild(customer);

XmlElement firstName = document.CreateElement("c", "firstName",
    "http://schemas.devleap.com/Customer");
firstName.InnerText = "Paolo Pialorsi";
customer.AppendChild(firstName);
```

The result of this code excerpt should be:

```
<?xml version="1.0" encoding="IBM437"?>
<c:customer xmlns:c="http://schemas.devleap.com/Customer">
  <c:firstName>Paolo Pialorsi</c:firstName>
</c:customer>
```

As you can see, the code uses an overload of the *CreateElement* method, which requires three parameters: a namespace prefix, a tag local name, and the full namespace URI. The same operation can be performed for XML attributes by using the *XmlDocument.CreateAttribute* method or the *XmlElement.SetAttribute* method. Truthfully, this older way of working is not all that difficult to understand and implement; nevertheless, developers often get confused when using this approach and complain that XML namespaces are difficult to manage. The real issue probably derives from namespace prefixes, which are aliases to the real XML namespaces. Theoretically, prefixes are supposed to simplify namespace references; in reality, they can cause confusion. To address feedback from developers, LINQ to XML was designed to provide an easier way of working with XML namespaces that avoids explicit use of prefixes. Every node name is an instance of the *XName* class, which can be defined either by a *String* or by a pairing of an *XNamespace* and a *String*. In Listing 12-15, you can see how to define XML content using a single default XML namespace.

LISTING 12-15 LINQ to XML namespace declaration

```
XNamespace ns = "http://schemas.devleap.com/Customer";
XElement customer = new XElement(ns + "customer",
    new XAttribute("id", "C01"),
    new XElement(ns + "firstName", "Paolo"),
    new XElement(ns + "lastName", "Pialorsi"));
```

The *XNamespace* definition looks like a *String*, but it is not. Internally, every *XNamespace* has a more complex behavior. Here is the output of the preceding code:

```
<?xml version="1.0" encoding="utf-8"?>
<customer id="C01" xmlns="http://schemas.devleap.com/Customer">
  <firstName>Paolo</firstName>
  <lastName>Pialorsi</lastName>
</customer>
```

Using Visual Basic syntax, you can define the namespace directly inside the XML content, as Listing 12-16 shows.

LISTING 12-16 Visual Basic XML literals used to declare XML content with a default XML namespace

```
Dim customer As XDocument =
  <?xml version="1.0" encoding="utf-8"?>
  <customer id="C01" xmlns="http://schemas.devleap.com/Customer">
    <firstName>Paolo</firstName>
    <lastName>Pialorsi</lastName>
  </customer>
```

Now consider Listing 12-17, which uses two XML namespaces.

LISTING 12-17 Multiple XML namespaces within a single *XElement* declaration

```
XNamespace nsCustomer = "http://schemas.devleap.com/Customer";
XNamespace nsAddress = "http://schemas.devleap.com/Address";

XElement customer = new XElement(nsCustomer + "customer",
    new XAttribute("id", "C01"),
    new XElement(nsCustomer + "firstName", "Paolo"),
    new XElement(nsCustomer + "lastName", "Pialorsi"),
    new XElement(nsAddress + "addresses",
        new XElement(nsAddress + "address",
            new XAttribute("type", "email"),
                "paolo@devleap.it"),
        new XElement(nsAddress + "address",
            new XAttribute("type", "home"),
                "Brescia - Italy")));
```

Again, the output is a document with all qualified XML nodes:

```
<?xml version="1.0" encoding="utf-8"?>
<customer id="C01" xmlns="http://schemas.devleap.com/Customer">
  <firstName>Paolo</firstName>
  <lastName>Pialorsi</lastName>
  <addresses xmlns="http://schemas.devleap.com/Address">
    <address type="email">paolo@devleap.it</address>
    <address type="home">Brescia - Italy</address>
  </addresses>
</customer>
```

At this point, you have seen that *XNamespace* is quite simple to use and that LINQ to XML automatically handles namespace declaration, avoiding the explicit use of prefixes. You are probably curious, however, about what happens when you define an *XName* as a concatenation of an *XNamespace* instance and a *String* to represent the local name of the node. Each *XName* instance can be represented as a *String* by using its *ToString* method:

```
Console.WriteLine(customer.Name.ToString());
```

Here is the result of the preceding line of code:

```
{http://schemas.devleap.com/Customer}customer
```

Let's try to use this resolved text instead of the concatenation (an *XNamespace* instance plus local name) used previously:

```
XElement testCustomer = new XElement("{http://schemas.devleap.com/Customer}customer");
Console.WriteLine(testCustomer.Name);
```

In the *System.Xml.Linq* framework, the resolved text *{namespace}local-name* is called the *expanded name* and is semantically equivalent to defining the *XNamespace* separately. The concatenation of an *XNamespace* and a *String* produces a new *XName* that is equivalent to the expanded name. By the way, writing node names by using the expanded name notation requires more processing power than using an explicitly declared *XNamespace* instance.

Writing the full namespace names is not always the best option; at this point, you are missing the XML namespace prefixes. You have seen how LINQ to XML handles namespace declaration; however, you might want to control node serialization, representing namespaces by overriding the default behavior of LINQ to XML. To do that, you can explicitly define the prefixes to use for namespaces by using *xmlns* attributes within your elements, as shown in Listing 12-18.

LISTING 12-18 LINQ to XML declaration of an XML namespace with a custom prefix

```
XNamespace ns = "http://schemas.devleap.com/Customer";
XElement customer = new XElement(ns + "customer",
    new XAttribute(XNamespace.Xmlns + "c", ns),
    new XAttribute("id", "C01"),
    new XElement(ns + "firstName", "Paolo"),
    new XElement(ns + "lastName", "Pialorsi"));
```

The output looks like the following:

```
<?xml version="1.0" encoding="utf-8"?>
<c:customer xmlns:c="http://schemas.devleap.com/Customer" id="C01">
  <c:firstName>Paolo</c:firstName>
  <c:lastName>Pialorsi</c:lastName>
</c:customer>
```

As you can see, the code defines *c* as the prefix for nodes associated with the *XNamespace* instance named *ns* (that is, *http://schemas.devleap.com/Customer*). The namespace declaration uses the *XAttribute* type; you will always be able to query the attributes of an *XElement* instance to search for namespace declarations. You perform such a query by checking the *IsNamespaceDeclaration* property of the attributes to see whether they are effectively namespace attributes or just attributes. You can see an example in Listing 12-19, which queries the customer *XElement* defined in Listing 12-18.

LISTING 12-19 LINQ to XML query for namespace against an *XElement* instance

```
var namespaces =
    from  n in customer.Attributes()
    where  n.IsNamespaceDeclaration == true
    select n;
foreach (var nsItem in namespaces) {
    Console.WriteLine("Value: {0}\nToString: {1}\nName: {2}",
        nsItem.Value,
        nsItem.ToString(),
        nsItem.Name);
}
```

The output of this code excerpt is the following:

```
Value: http://schemas.devleap.com/Customer
ToString: xmlns:c="http://schemas.devleap.com/Customer"
Name: {http://www.w3.org/2000/xmlns/}c
```

Listing 12-20 shows the corresponding (and easier) Visual Basic syntax.

LISTING 12-20 Visual Basic XML literals used to declare an XML namespace with a custom prefix

```
Dim customer As XDocument =
<?xml version="1.0" encoding="utf-8"?>
<c:customer xmlns:c="http://schemas.devleap.com/Customer" id="C01">
  <c:firstName>Paolo</c:firstName>
  <c:lastName>Pialorsi</c:lastName>
</c:customer>
```

You might think that starting from LINQ to XML, namespaces are simpler to handle and prefixes are transparently taken out of your control. On the other hand, you might now have the impression that if you need to influence prefixes, you need to do a little more work, at least when using C#. In fact, Visual Basic XML literals also simplify namespace declaration, using a feature called *global XML namespaces*. With this new feature, you can globally declare an XML namespace URI with its corresponding prefix within a Visual Basic code file so that you can reuse it many times in code. In Listing 12-21, you can see an example.

LISTING 12-21 Visual Basic XML literals and global XML namespaces

```vb
Imports System.Xml.Linq
Imports System.Linq
Imports <xmlns:c="http://schemas.devleap.com/Customer">
Public Class Program
  Private Shared Sub GlobalXmlNamespaceSample()

    Dim xmlCustomers As XDocument =
      <?xml version="1.0" encoding="utf-8"?>
        <c:customers>
            <c:customer name="Paolo" city="Brescia" country="Italy"/>
            <c:customer name="Marco" city="Torino" country="Italy"/>
            <c:customer name="James" city="Dallas" country="USA"/>
            <c:customer name="Frank" city="Seattle" country="USA"/>
        </c:customers>

    End Sub
End Class
```

The key point of this sample is the *Imports* statement, which declares the global namespace prefix *c* for namespace *http://schemas.devleap.com/Customer*. This particular kind of *Imports* syntax can be used to declare only an XML namespace *with its prefix*; you cannot use it to declare a default XML namespace *without* a prefix.

Listing 12-22 shows a final example that uses C# to define both a default namespace and a custom prefixed namespace.

LISTING 12-22 C# syntax used to define a default namespace and a custom prefix for a namespace

```csharp
XNamespace nsCustomer = "http://schemas.devleap.com/Customer";
XNamespace nsAddress = "http://schemas.devleap.com/Address";
XElement customer = new XElement(nsCustomer + "customer",
    new XAttribute("id", "C01"),
    new XElement(nsCustomer + "firstName", "Paolo"),
    new XElement(nsCustomer + "lastName", "Pialorsi"),
    new XElement(nsAddress + "address", "Brescia - Italy",
        new XAttribute(XNamespace.Xmlns + "a", nsAddress)));
```

The code in Listing 12-22 produces an XML fragment like the following one:

```xml
<?xml version="1.0" encoding="utf-8"?>
<customer id="C01">
  <firstName>Paolo</firstName>
  <lastName>Pialorsi</lastName>
  <a:address xmlns:a="http://schemas.devleap.com/Address">Brescia - Italy</a:address>
</customer>
```

To query the previous XML content for the purpose of extracting the *lastName* node, you can write a line of code like the following:

```
XElement lastNameElement = customer.Elements(nsCustomer + "lastName");
```

Using Visual Basic and global XML namespaces, we can use code like this:

```
Dim lastNameElement As XElement = customer.<c:lastName>
```

Chapter 13 examines in detail querying XML content by using LINQ to XML, using both C# and Visual Basic syntax.

Other X* Classes

This new framework has other available classes that define XML declarations (*XDeclaration*), processing instructions (*XProcessingInstruction*), document types (*XDocumentType*), comments (*XComment*), and text nodes (*XText*). These classes are all derived from *XNode* except for *XDeclaration,* which is not considered a node. All these types are typically used to build *XDocument* instances, as you have already seen in the description of *XDocument* constructors. *XText,* however, is not allowed to be a child of an *XDocument* unless you define it as empty or with nonsignificant characters. Notice that LINQ to XML nodes in the document's graph of nodes are not normalized, as in many other XML APIs. For example, if you add two *XText* nodes to an *XElement* node, they will not be merged into a single *XText* node. However, if you add two or more *String* variables to the content of an *XElement* node, their values will be merged into a unique *XText* node instance. Moreover, in LINQ to XML, empty ("") text nodes are valid and keep their existence in the XML tree. If you want to serialize an empty tag explicitly opened and closed (*<customer></customer>*), even if it has empty text content, you can simply add an empty *XText* child to it.

XStreamingElement

Sometimes you need to create XML node graphs starting from content read from a sequence of entities or objects. You can do this by using LINQ queries. You have already seen in Chapter 2 that LINQ queries support deferred evaluation. Now consider the following code excerpt:

```
XElement xmlOrders = new XElement("orders",
  from   c in customers
  from   o in c.Orders
  select new XElement("order",
    new XElement("id", o.IdProduct),
    new XElement("quantity", o.Quantity)));
```

The code defines a set of *<order/>* elements that are children of an *<orders/>* root element. Each child order element contains a couple of children, named *id* and *quantity*. These elements contain, respectively, the *IdProduct* and *Quantity* values of each *Order* instance. Using the previous syntax, the query expression, which was defined to create the list of order tags, is evaluated during the functional construction of the XML node graph. At the end of the statement, the XML output is ready and represents a point-in-time snapshot of the source values. Whenever you need to defer the LINQ query expression evaluation to its effective usage, you can use the *XStreamingElement* class. This class represents a tree of *IEnumerable<T>* that will be resolved only when effectively accessed, thus deferring the XML construction as well as the evaluation of any LINQ query that is contained. Consider the sample in Listing 12-23.

LISTING 12-23 Sample code showing usage of *XStreamingElement*

```
XStreamingElement xmlOrders = new XStreamingElement("orders",
    from   c in customers
    from   o in c.Orders
    select new XStreamingElement("order",
        new XStreamingElement("id", o.IdProduct),
        new XStreamingElement("quantity", o.Quantity)));
```

The query expression is evaluated only when saving or accessing the content of the *xmlOrders* variable. This behavior also becomes useful whenever you need to read a large source stream by using an *XmlReader*. You can use this behavior to write down the source stream, eventually applying a transformation to it by using an *XmlWriter*. Even though the result is equivalent to what you can get from an *XElement*, using an *XStreamingElement* maintains a small memory footprint, using *XmlReader/XmlWriter* instances while reading the source and writing to the destination.

In Listing 12-24 you can see an example of using *XStreamingElement* together with a chunking *XmlReader*, which loads the source XML file and chunks it, yielding each single *customer* element.

LISTING 12-24 Sample code showing usage of *XStreamingElement* together with a chunking *XmlReader*

```
static void chunkingXmlReaderWithXStreamingElement() {

    var customers = ChunkCustomers("CustomersWithOrders.xml");
    XStreamingElement xmlCustomers = new XStreamingElement("customers", customers);
    xmlCustomers.Save("CustomersWithOrdersOutput.xml");
}

static IEnumerable<XElement> ChunkCustomers(String uri) {

    XmlReaderSettings settings = new XmlReaderSettings();
    // Notice the max document size (4MB) setting
    settings.MaxCharactersInDocument = (1024 * 1024) * 4; // MAX 4MB
    XmlReader xr = XmlReader.Create(uri, settings);
```

```
    while (xr.Read()){
        if ((xr.NodeType == XmlNodeType.Element)
            && (xr.Name == "customer")) {
                yield return XElement.ReadFrom(xr) as XElement;
        }
    }
}
```

The final behavior of an *XStreamingElement* relates to the query you are going to execute. For example, if you define a source query for the *XStreamingElement* content that uses a clause that requires iterating the entire data source before providing any kind of result (such as a LINQ to Objects *ToList()* method over an *IEnumerable<T>* data source), the entire source will be loaded into memory anyway, so you lose the benefits of using an *XStreamingElement*. For example, in Listing 12-25, *XStreamingElement* is completely useless because the *ToList* method loads the entire *customers* collection anyhow.

LISTING 12-25 Sample code showing a bad usage of *XStreamingElement*

```
static void chunkingXmlReaderWithXStreamingElement() {

    var customers = ChunkCustomers("CustomersWithOrders.xml");

    XStreamingElement xmlCustomers = new XStreamingElement("customers",
        customers.ToList()); // This is a wrong usage of XStreamingElement

    xmlCustomers.Save("CustomersWithOrdersOutput.xml");
}
```

XObject and Annotations

XObject represents the base class of the entire LINQ to XML class framework. It mainly provides methods and properties to work with annotations on nodes. Annotations map metadata to XML nodes. For example, you can add custom user information to your nodes, as shown in Listing 12-26.

LISTING 12-26 Annotations applied to an *XElement* instance

```
XElement customer = XElement.Load(@"..\..\customer.xml");

CustomerAnnotation annotation = new CustomerAnnotation();
annotation.Notes = "This is a good customer!";
customer.AddAnnotation(annotation);
```

CustomerAnnotation is a custom type and can be any .NET Framework type. You can then retrieve annotations from XML nodes by using one of the two generic methods, *Annotation<T>* or *Annotations<T>*. These generic methods search for an annotation of type *T* (or one that is derived from *T*) in the current node. If an annotation exists, *Annotation<T>* returns the first one. *Annotations<T>* returns the full set of annotations:

```
annotation = customer.Annotation<CustomerAnnotation>();
```

Because *XObject* is the base class for every X* class type used to describe an XML node, you can add annotations to any node. Usually, you would use annotations to keep state information, such as a mapping to source entities or documents used to build the XML, whereas the code handles real XML content.

> **Note** Annotations are not part of the XML Infoset; they are neither serialized nor deserialized with XML content.

Another feature common to all types inherited from *XObject* are LINQ to XML events. These are an easy and common way of handling events related to changes applied to the node tree. The available events are *Changing* and *Changed*, which notify you about modifications that are going to happen and modifications that have already happened, respectively. The .NET Framework event handler receives an instance of an *XObjectChangeEventArgs* type, which provides an *ObjectChange* property of type *XObjectChange*. *XObjectChange* is an enumeration that assumes values of *Add* for node additions, *Name* for node name modifications, *Remove* for node removals, and *Value* for node value modifications. These events can be used to monitor modifications to one node and all its descendants. Only a modification of a tree raises an event; construction of an XML tree by using functional construction does not notify events. Because the event handling infrastructure is available for any X* class inheriting from *XObject*, you can subscribe to the events for one node to catch events of all its descendants, rather than subscribing to the same event for all the nodes of the subtree. In Listing 12-27, you can see an example of how to use these events.

LISTING 12-27 Example of XML tree modification events handling

```
XElement customer = XElement.Load(@"..\..\customer.xml");

// Subscribe to the changing event using a Lambda Expression
customer.Changing += (sender, e) => {
    Console.WriteLine("=> Changing event raised");
    Console.WriteLine("\tChanging of type: {0}", e.ObjectChange);

    XObject x = sender as XObject;
    Console.WriteLine("\tChanging node of type: {0}", x.NodeType);
```

```
    XElement element = sender as XElement;
    if (element != null) {
        Console.WriteLine("\tCurrent value: {0}", element.Value);
    }

    XAttribute attribute = sender as XAttribute;
    if (attribute != null) {
        Console.WriteLine("\tCurrent value: {0}", attribute.Value);
    }
};

// Subscribe to the changed event using a Lambda Expression
customer.Changed += (sender, e) => {
    Console.WriteLine("=> Changed event raised");
    Console.WriteLine("\tChanged of type: {0}", e.ObjectChange);

    XObject x = sender as XObject;
    Console.WriteLine("\tChanged node of type: {0}", x.NodeType);

    XElement element = sender as XElement;
    if (element != null) {
        Console.WriteLine("\tCurrent value: {0}", element.Value);
    }

    XAttribute attribute = sender as XAttribute;
    if (attribute != null) {
        Console.WriteLine("\tCurrent value: {0}", attribute.Value);
    }
};

// Look for the first address in customer
XElement emailAddress = customer
    .Descendants("address")
    .First(a => a.Attribute("type").Value == "email");
// Change the text content of the XML node
emailAddress.Value = "paolo@devleap.com";
// Change the value of the type attribute
emailAddress.Attribute("type").Value = "externalEmail";
```

It is interesting to observe the results of the sample shown in Listing 12-25, because changing the text content of an element raises four events: two *Changing/Changed* events to notify you of the removal of the original text content, and two *Changing/Changed* events to notify you of the addition of the new text content. Moreover, changing the value of an attribute node raises only a set of value *Changing/Changed* events. Here is the output of Listing 12-27:

```
=> Changing event raised
    Changing of type: Remove
    Changing node of type: Text
=> Changed event raised
    Changed of type: Remove
    Changed node of type: Text
```

```
=> Changing event raised
      Changing of type: Add
      Changing node of type: Text
=> Changed event raised
      Changed of type: Add
      Changed node of type: Text
=> Changing event raised
      Changing of type: Value
      Changing node of type: Attribute
      Current value: email
=> Changed event raised
      Changed of type: Value
      Changed node of type: Attribute
      Current value: externalEmail
```

You should not change the XML source tree while handling tree modification events because the result could be unpredictable and unstable. You should also know that *XObject* internally adds a specific annotation of type *XObjectChangeAnnotation* on top of nodes with an active modification-event subscription, which can be useful for finding nodes with active event handling.

Reading, Traversing, and Modifying XML

In the previous sections, you saw how to create and annotate XML content using LINQ to XML. Whenever you have XML available in memory, you can also navigate and eventually modify it. To navigate XML content, you can use the methods and properties of X* classes, or you can rely on LINQ queries over an X* object. In this section, you will look at the former way of working, and the latter in the next chapter.

Every *XNode* provides some methods and properties by which to navigate its hierarchy. For example, you can use the *IsAfter* or *IsBefore* method to compare ordinal positioning of nodes in a document. These methods internally use the *CompareDocumentOrder* static method of the *XNode* class and return a numeric index, of type *Integer*, which represents the "distance" between two *XNode* instances in the containing *XDocument*. It is also used by *XNodeDocument-OrderComparer*, and it is useful when ordering nodes in LINQ to XML queries.

Every *XNode* also provides a couple of properties, called *NextNode* and *PreviousNode*, which map to the next and previous nodes in the graph, as their names indicate. Pay attention to the relative cost of these properties. *NextNode* returns a reference to an internal field and is relatively cheap; *PreviousNode* requires a partial scan of the tree branch containing the current node and is a bit more expensive, so forward navigation is preferable in terms of resources. *XContainer* also provides *LastNode* and *FirstNode* properties.

Finally, every *XObject* offers a *Parent* property of type *XElement* that returns a reference to the parent element of the current node in the graph (although not all nodes have a value for their *Parent* property). For example, the children of an *XDocument* node have a *Parent* with a null value because *XDocument* is not an *XElement*.

Whenever you find a node while traversing the document by using one of these techniques and you want to modify it, you can use methods such as *Remove* or *ReplaceWith*. These methods are available for any *XNode*, to remove the node itself from the graph or to replace it with a new fragment. There are also *RemoveAttributes*, *ReplaceAttributes*, and *ReplaceAll* methods for objects of type *XElement*. These methods work with their respective attributes or with the full set of child nodes. Finally, *XElement* offers *SetAttributeValue*, *SetElementValue*, and *SetValue* to change the value of an attribute, a child element, or the entire current element, respectively.

In Listing 12-28, you can see how to replace one element with another.

LISTING 12-28 Example of tag replacement using the *XElement ReplaceWith* method

```
XElement customer = new XElement("customer",
    new XAttribute("id", "C01"),
    new XElement("firstName", "Paolo"),
    new XElement("lastName", "Pialorsi"));

// Do something in the meantime ...

customer.LastNode.ReplaceWith(
    new XElement("nickName", "PaoloPia"));
```

The preceding code block changes this XML:

```
<?xml version="1.0" encoding="utf-8"?>
<customer id="C01">
  <firstName>Paolo</firstName>
  <lastName>Pialorsi</lastName>
</customer>
```

into this XML:

```
<?xml version="1.0" encoding="utf-8"?>
<customer id="C01">
  <firstName>Paolo</firstName>
  <nickName>PaoloPia</nickName>
</customer>
```

Listing 12-29 shows you how to change attribute and element values.

LISTING 12-29 Example of attribute and child element management using *XElement* methods

```
customer.SetAttributeValue("id", "C02");
customer.SetElementValue("notes", "Notes about this customer");
```

By calling these methods, the LINQ to XML programming framework creates attributes or elements that do not yet exist or changes the values of those that already exist. When the value provided to these methods is null and the nodes already exist, they are removed.

While traversing an XML tree, keep in mind that the navigation technique you use influences the result. The methods and properties shown up to this point in the chapter work directly in memory and determine their results at the time that you invoke them. If you remove or replace an in-memory node, the action is taken instantly. In contrast, when you use queries over XML based on the LINQ to XML query engine, modification methods are applied to query expression results that will be evaluated only when they are effectively used, such as those you saw in Chapter 2.

Summary

In this chapter, you have seen how to define an XML Infoset using the LINQ to XML programming framework—by means of both functional construction and Visual Basic XML literals. You have learned how to use the main classes of the LINQ to XML programming framework to work with documents, elements, attributes, and all the information items of XML Infoset. Finally, you saw how to manage LINQ to XML events and annotations and navigate through, remove, and modify nodes using node properties and methods.

Chapter 13
LINQ to XML: Querying Nodes

Starting with the XML Infoset you learned about in Chapter 12, "LINQ to XML: Managing the XML Infoset," you can think of every node set as a sequence of nodes that you can
query using Microsoft Language Integrated Query (LINQ)—just like any sequence of type
IEnumerable<T>. From that perspective, you can make the case that every concept you have
already seen applied to other sequences of items in the LINQ query fields (such as LINQ to
Objects, LINQ to SQL, and so forth) can also be used with XML nodes. In fact, LINQ to XML
exposes every collection of nodes as an *IEnumerable<T>* instance.

Querying XML

You can use the standard query extension methods described in Chapter 3, "LINQ to Objects,"
to query XML nodes, but there are also a group of custom extension methods, declared
in the *System.Xml.Linq.Extensions* class, specifically defined to be applied to sequences of
IEnumerable<X>*. This section covers these methods.

Attribute, Attributes

Each instance of *XElement* supports a set of methods to access its attributes, as shown here:

```
public XAttribute Attribute(XName name);
public IEnumerable<XAttribute> Attributes();
public IEnumerable<XAttribute> Attributes(XName name);
```

As you can see, the first method returns a single *XAttribute* instance retrieved by name if it
exists. If it does not exist, the method returns *null*. The second method returns all the attributes of an *XElement* as an *IEnumerable<XAttribute>*, which is a useful type for LINQ queries.
The last method returns a sequence of type *IEnumerable<XAttribute>* that contains either no
items or one item, whose name matches the item provided as the value of the *name* parameter. Because attributes of one element are a collection of uniquely named nodes, an element
with multiple occurrences of the same attribute name cannot exist. Consider the following
XML document, also used in Chapter 12:

```
<?xml version="1.0" encoding="UTF-16" standalone="yes"?>
<customer id="C01">
  <firstName>Paolo</firstName>
  <lastName>Pialorsi</lastName>
  <addresses>
    <address type="email">paolo@devleap.it</address>
```

```
    <address type="url">http://www.devleap.it/</address>
    <address type="home">Brescia - Italy</address>
  </addresses>
</customer>
```

Listing 13-1 shows an example of the *Attribute* and *Attributes* extension methods within a LINQ query expression in Microsoft Visual C#.

LISTING 13-1 A sample LINQ to XML query based on the *Attribute* and *Attributes* extension methods

```
XElement xmlCustomer = XElement.Load(@"..\..\customer.xml");

Console.WriteLine("Attributes with name \"id\" count: {0}",
    xmlCustomer.Attributes().Where(a => a.Name == "id").Count());
Console.WriteLine("\"id\" attribute value: {0}",
    xmlCustomer.Attribute("id").Value);
```

The console output of this code excerpt is as follows:

```
Attributes with name "id" count: 1
"id" attribute value: C01
```

As you can see, there is only one *id* attribute, in the *customer* element, and it has a value of *C01*.

Element, Elements

Every *XContainer* instance (for example, *XDocument* and *XElement*) provides methods to return a single element by name or to select sequences of elements that are eventually filtered by their name (of type *XName*). Here are their signatures:

```
public XElement Element(XName name);
public IEnumerable<XElement> Elements();
public IEnumerable<XElement> Elements(XName name);
```

The *Element* method iterates over the child nodes of the current *XContainer* and returns the first *XElement*, whose name corresponds to the argument provided for the *XName* parameter. Because of the argument type (*XName*), you must provide a valid node name, and if you are looking for a qualified element, you need to include its XML namespace URI, as shown in Listing 13-2.

LISTING 13-2 A sample LINQ to XML query based on the *Element* extension method

```
XNamespace ns = "http://schemas.devleap.com/Customers";
XElement xmlCustomers = new XElement(ns + "customers",
    from   c in customers
    where  c.Country == Countries.Italy
    select new XElement(ns + "customer",
```

```
            new XAttribute("name", c.Name),
            new XAttribute("city", c.City),
            new XAttribute("country", c.Country)));
XElement element = xmlCustomers.Element(ns + "customer");
```

To get all the *customer* elements, you can use the *Elements* method, as shown in Listing 13-3.

LISTING 13-3 Another sample LINQ to XML query based on the *Elements* extension method

```
var elements = xmlCustomers.Elements();
foreach (XElement e in elements) {
    Console.WriteLine(e);
}
```

Here is the result:

```
<customer name="Paolo" city="Brescia" country="Italy" />
<customer name="Marco" city="Torino" country="Italy" />
```

The last overload of the *Elements* method supports filtering child elements by name. Using the *Element* or *Elements* method, there is no way, to get a single *XElement* child of the current *XContainer* without providing a filtering name, given that there is more than one child element. However, you can use the *First* extension method of LINQ to Objects to achieve that goal. Here is an example:

```
XElement firstElement = xmlCustomers.Elements().First();
```

Because the argument of the *Element* method is an *XName* type instance, you can also use the *XNamespace* class to select elements using their fully qualified name. Listing 13-4 shows an example.

LISTING 13-4 A sample LINQ to XML query based on *Elements* using a namespace

```
XNamespace ns = "http://schemas.devleap.com/Customers";
XElement xmlCustomers = new XElement(ns + "customers",
    from   c in customers
    where  c.Country == Countries.Italy
    select new XElement(ns + "customer",
        new XAttribute("name", c.Name),
        new XAttribute("city", c.City),
        new XAttribute("country", c.Country)));

XElement element = xmlCustomers.Element(ns + "customer");
```

XPath Axes "Like" Extension Methods

Some of the extension methods that are defined in the *Extensions* class of the namespace *System.Xml.Linq* are similar to XPath Axes functions. The first two methods described here are *Ancestors* and *Descendants*, which return an *IEnumerable<XElement>* sequence of elements. The *Ancestors* method extends any *IEnumerable<XNode>* instance, whereas *Descendants* extends any *IEnumerable<XContainer>* instance. *Descendants* returns all the elements after the current node in the document graph, regardless of their depth in the graph. *Ancestors* is somewhat complementary to *Descendants*; it returns all the elements before the current node in the document graph. The signatures of both methods are shown here:

```
public static IEnumerable<XElement> Ancestors<T>
  (this IEnumerable<T> source)
    where T: XNode;
public static IEnumerable<XElement> Ancestors<T>
  (this IEnumerable<T> source, XName name)
    where T: XNode;
public static IEnumerable<XElement> Descendants<T>
  (this IEnumerable<T> source)
    where T: XContainer;
public static IEnumerable<XElement> Descendants<T>
  (this IEnumerable<T> source, XName name)
    where T: XContainer;
```

These methods are useful for querying an XML source to find a particular element before or after the current one, regardless of its position in the graph. The *Descendants* method has a counterpart instance method, available for each *XContainer* instance (document or element). Here are the available signatures for this instance method:

```
public IEnumerable<XElement> Descendants();
public IEnumerable<XElement> Descendants(XName name);
```

Consider the XML document in Listing 13-5.

LISTING 13-5 Sample XML document used to illustrate searching with LINQ to XML

```xml
<?xml version="1.0" encoding="UTF-8"?>
<customers>
  <customer>
    <name>Paolo</name>
    <city>Brescia</city>
    <country>Italy</country>
  </customer>
  <customer>
    <name>Marco</name>
    <city>Torino</city>
    <country>Italy</country>
  </customer>
</customers>
```

The following line of code returns *8* as the number of descendant elements of an XML document like the one in Listing 13-5:

```
Console.WriteLine(xmlCustomers.Descendants().Count());
```

The descendant elements, grouped by name, are as follows:

- Two *<customer />* elements

- Two *<name />* elements

- Two *<city />* elements

- Two *<country />* elements

The code in Listing 13-6 uses the *Descendants* method to show the nodes together with their XML content.

LISTING 13-6 Code excerpt showing how to browse the results of a *Descendants* method invocation

```
XElement xmlCustomers = XElement.Load(@"..\..\Customers.xml");

foreach (var descendant in xmlCustomers.Descendants()) {
    Console.WriteLine("=> Element: {0}\n{1}",
        descendant.Name, descendant);
}
```

Executing this code, you get the following output:

```
=> Element: customer
<customer>
  <name>Paolo</name>
  <city>Brescia</city>
  <country>Italy</country>
</customer>
=> Element: name
<name>Paolo</name>
=> Element: city
<city>Brescia</city>
=> Element: country
<country>Italy</country>
=> Element: customer
<customer>
  <name>Marco</name>
  <city>Torino</city>
  <country>Italy</country>
</customer>
=> Element: name
<name>Marco</name>
=> Element: city
<city>Torino</city>
=> Element: country
<country>Italy</country>
```

As you can see, the list of descendant elements references them in the same order as they appear in the source XML document.

Two other extension methods that work like the previous ones are *AncestorsAndSelf* and *DescendantsAndSelf*. Here are their signatures:

```
public static IEnumerable<XElement> AncestorsAndSelf(
    this IEnumerable<XElement> source);
public static IEnumerable<XElement> AncestorsAndSelf(
    this IEnumerable<XElement> source, XName name);
public static IEnumerable<XElement> DescendantsAndSelf(
    this IEnumerable<XElement> source);
public static IEnumerable<XElement> DescendantsAndSelf(
    this IEnumerable<XElement> source, XName name);
```

These methods act like the previous methods, but they also return the current element. As with XPath Axes, you can retrieve all the elements of an XML source just by specifying the union of the results of *Ancestors* and *DescendantsAndSelf* or *AncestorsAndSelf* and *Descendants*.

The *XElement* type also provides *AncestorsAndSelf* and *DescendantsAndSelf*, which are the counterparts of the previously seen extension methods.

If you need to select all the descendant nodes rather than only the descendant elements, you can use methods such as *DescendantNodes*, which is suitable for *IEnumerable<XContainer>*, or *DescendantNodesAndSelf*, which extends *IEnumerable<XElement>*. Both methods return all descendant nodes, regardless of their node types, including the *XElement* node itself for the *DescendantNodesAndSelf* method. Again, the *DescendantNodes* extension method also exists as an instance method for the *XContainer* type, whereas the *DescendantNodesAndSelf* method has its counterpart instance method for the *XElement* type.

Consider this XML document shown previously in Chapter 12:

```
<?xml version="1.0" encoding="UTF-16" standalone="yes"?>
<customer id="C01">
  <firstName>Paolo</firstName>
  <lastName>Pialorsi</lastName>
  <addresses>
    <address type="email">paolo@devleap.it</address>
    <address type="url">http://www.devleap.it/</address>
    <address type="home">Brescia - Italy</address>
  </addresses>
</customer>
```

In Listing 13-7 you can see an example of how to use the *DescendantNodes* instance method.

LISTING 13-7 Code excerpt showing the *DescendantNodes* method invocation

```
XElement customer = XElement.Load(@"..\..\Customer.xml");

var descendantNodes = customer.DescendantNodes();
Console.WriteLine("There are {0} descendant nodes",
    descendantNodes.Count());

foreach (var descendant in descendantNodes) {
    Console.WriteLine("=> Node Type: {0}\n{1}",
        descendant.NodeType, descendant);
}
```

The console output of this code excerpt is the list of all nodes descending from the root *XElement* of the sample document. Here is the output:

```
There are 11 descendant nodes
=> Node Type: Element
<firstName>Paolo</firstName>
=> Node Type: Text
Paolo
=> Node Type: Element
<lastName>Pialorsi</lastName>
=> Node Type: Text
Pialorsi
=> Node Type: Element
<addresses>
  <address type="email">paolo@devleap.it</address>
  <address type="url">http://www.devleap.it/</address>
  <address type="home">Brescia - Italy</address>
</addresses>
=> Node Type: Element
<address type="email">paolo@devleap.it</address>
=> Node Type: Text
paolo@devleap.it
=> Node Type: Element
<address type="url">http://www.devleap.it/</address>
=> Node Type: Text
http://www.devleap.it/
=> Node Type: Element
<address type="home">Brescia - Italy</address>
=> Node Type: Text
Brescia - Italy
```

The preceding result contains Element and Text nodes, but it does not contain attributes because they are *not considered to be nodes* in LINQ to XML. In fact, the *XAttribute* type does not inherit from *XNode*; it inherits directly from the *XObject* base class.

There is also a *Nodes* extension method that extends *IEnumerable<XContainer>* and returns all the child nodes of that collection of *XContainer* instances—once again, regardless of their node types, excluding attributes (which are not nodes). The *XContainer* type offers the corresponding *Nodes* instance method.

XNode Selection Methods

The *XNode* class provides several methods that are useful for retrieving elements and nodes related to the current node itself. For example, both the *ElementsBeforeSelf* and *Elements-AfterSelf* methods return a sequence of type *IEnumerable<XElement>* that contains the elements before or after the current node, respectively. Both methods provide an overload with a parameter of type *XName* that you can use to filter elements by name, as shown in the following code:

```
public IEnumerable<XElement> ElementsBeforeSelf();
public IEnumerable<XElement> ElementsBeforeSelf(XName name);
public IEnumerable<XElement> ElementsAfterSelf();
public IEnumerable<XElement> ElementsAfterSelf(XName name);
```

In addition, the *NodesBeforeSelf* and *NodesAfterSelf* methods return a sequence of type *IEnumerable<XNode>* that contains all the nodes, regardless of their node type, that occur either before or after the current node. For example:

```
public IEnumerable<XNode> NodesAfterSelf();
public IEnumerable<XNode> NodesBeforeSelf();
```

Both these methods return any node (*XNode*), excluding attributes, as usual. Listing 13-8 shows an example of using *NodesBeforeSelf* and *NodesAfterSelf* applied to the *address* elements of the single-customer XML example you saw earlier, just before Listing 13-7.

LISTING 13-8 Code excerpt showing the use of *NodesBeforeSelf* and *NodesAfterSelf*

```
XElement customer = XElement.Load(@"..\..\customer.xml");

var firstAddress = customer.Element("addresses").FirstNode;
var nodesAfterSelf = firstAddress.NodesAfterSelf();

Console.WriteLine("Here is the first address:\n\t{0}",
    firstAddress);
Console.WriteLine("There are {0} addresses after the first address",
    nodesAfterSelf.Count());
foreach (var addressNode in nodesAfterSelf) {
    Console.WriteLine("\t{0}", addressNode);
}

Console.WriteLine();
```

```
var lastAddress = customer.Element("addresses").LastNode;
var nodesBeforeSelf = lastAddress.NodesBeforeSelf();

Console.WriteLine("Here is the last address:\n\t{0}",
    lastAddress);
Console.WriteLine("There are {0} addresses before the last address",
    nodesBeforeSelf.Count());
foreach (var addressNode in nodesBeforeSelf) {
    Console.WriteLine("\t{0}", addressNode);
}
```

The result of running this code is as follows:

```
Here is the first address:
        <address type="email">paolo@devleap.it</address>
There are 2 addresses after the first address
        <address type="url">http://www.devleap.it/</address>
        <address type="home">Brescia - Italy</address>

Here is the last address:
        <address type="home">Brescia - Italy</address>
There are 2 addresses before the last address
        <address type="email">paolo@devleap.it</address>
        <address type="url">http://www.devleap.it/</address>
```

Notice that the results are in document order, regardless of the direction (before or after) of the node retrieval method.

InDocumentOrder

One last extension method that needs to be explained is the *InDocumentOrder* method. It orders an *IEnumerable<XNode>* sequence of nodes related to the same *XDocument* by using an *XNodeDocumentOrderComparer* class, which bases its behavior on the *CompareDocumentOrder* method. This extension method is very useful when you want to select nodes that are ordered as they appear in a document.

 More Info For more information about the inner workings of node comparison, see Chapter 12.

Here is a brief example:

```
foreach (XNode a in xmlCustomers.DescendantsAndSelf().InDocumentOrder()) {
    Console.WriteLine("+ " + a);
}
```

The result of this sample code is the full list of nodes declared within the *xmlCustomers* document defined in Listing 13-5, in document order.

Understanding Deferred Query Evaluation

Under the covers, many of the extension methods described in the previous section work with deferred query evaluation, like every other LINQ query. Consequently, each time you call these methods, the results can change if the source XML to which they are applied changes. Consider the example in Listing 13-9, which displays all the *city* nodes of the customers located in Italy to the console window.

LISTING 13-9 A LINQ to XML query to extract all *city* nodes from a list of customers

```
XElement xmlCustomers = new XElement("customers",
    from   c in customers
    where  c.Country == Countries.Italy
    select new XElement("customer",
               new XElement("name", c.Name),
               new XElement("city", c.City),
               new XElement("country", c.Country)));

var cities = xmlCustomers.DescendantsAndSelf("city");

Console.WriteLine("\nBefore XML source modification");
foreach (var city in cities) {
    Console.WriteLine(city);
}
```

The result of running the query is as follows:

```
Before XML source modification
<city>Brescia</city>
<city>Torino</city>
```

Now try changing the source of the *xmlCustomers* object, adding customers who are not located in Italy. Then repeat the iteration over the *cities* query variable, which represents the LINQ query over *XElements* with the XML name of *city*. The code is shown in Listing 13-10.

LISTING 13-10 A LINQ to XML query that extracts all *city* nodes from a list of customers after adding some customers

```
xmlCustomers.Add(
    from   c in customers
    where  c.Country != Countries.Italy
    select new XElement("customer",
               new XElement("name", c.Name),
               new XElement("city", c.City),
               new XElement("country", c.Country)));

Console.WriteLine("\nAfter XML source modification");

// the query defined in cities is executed another time on the updated
// source because the foreach construct retrieves the enumerator as you
```

```
    // have already seen for the usual LINQ queries
    foreach (var city in cities) {
        Console.WriteLine(city);
    }
```

This time, the result includes the new cities, which are outside Italy:

```
After XML source modification
<city>Brescia</city>
<city>Torino</city>
<city>Dallas</city>
<city>Seattle</city>
```

To get a static result, you can invoke one of the conversion operators described in Chapter 3—*ToList*, *ToArray*, *ToDictionary*, or *ToLookup*—on the *cities* variable before the source is updated.

Using LINQ Queries over XML

You have already seen that many of the LINQ to XML methods navigate XML content and return instances of type *IEnumerable<XNode>* or *IEnumerable<XElement>*. Because LINQ queries can be applied to sequences of *IEnumerable<T>*, you can also use them to query XML content. Some of the previous examples used LINQ query expressions to create new XML content.

Now consider a situation in which you want to create sequences of items (for example, objects or entities) whose values are taken from XML content. You can use LINQ query expressions over XML nodes through LINQ to XML syntax to do that.

Listing 13-11 is an example of a query expression applied to the by-now-familiar XML list of customers. It filters the list of *customer* elements to extract the *name* element and the *city* attribute of each customer located in Italy, ordering the result by the *name* element value.

LISTING 13-11 Using LINQ to XML and query expressions to query XML content

```
var customersFromXml =
    from   c in xmlCustomers.Elements("customer")
    where  (String)c.Attribute("country") == "Italy"
    orderby (String)c.Element("name")
    select new {
               Name = (String)c.Element("name"),
               City = (String)c.Attribute("city")
    };

foreach (var customer in customersFromXml) {
    Console.WriteLine(customer);
}
```

The result is shown in the following output block:

```
{ Name = Marco, City = Torino }
{ Name = Paolo, City = Brescia }
```

This result is interesting, even if it is not all that exciting. To make the example more challenging, suppose you have the same XML list of customers, but also a sequence of orders, defined using the following LINQ query:

```
var orders =
    from  c in customers
    from  o in c.Orders
    select new {c.Name, o.IdProduct, o.Quantity};
```

Imagine that the orders were loaded via LINQ to SQL from a Microsoft SQL Server database. You can write a complex query that joins XML nodes with entities to extract a sequence of new objects, as shown in Listing 13-12.

LISTING 13-12 A LINQ query that merges LINQ to XML and LINQ to Objects

```
var ordersWithCustomersFromXml =
    from    c in xmlCustomers.Elements("customer")
    join    o in orders
    on      (String)c.Element("name") equals o.Name
    orderby (String)c.Element("name")
    select  new {
                Name = (String)c.Element("name"),
                City = (String)c.Attribute("city"),
                IdProduct = o.IdProduct,
                Quantity = o.Quantity };
```

This is a new and truly powerful feature of LINQ through which you can define queries over mixed contents by using a unique language and programming environment.

If you dislike the repetition of explicit casting of XML nodes inside the LINQ query, remember that you can use the *let* clause to define a more maintainable alias, as shown in Listing 13-13.

LISTING 13-13 A LINQ query that merges LINQ to XML and LINQ to Objects, simplified by using the *let* clause

```
var ordersWithCustomersFromXml =
    from    c in xmlCustomers.Elements("customer")
    let     xName = (String)c.Element("name")
    let     xCity = (String)c.Attribute("city")
    join    o in orders
    on      xName equals o.Name
    orderby xName
    select  new {
                Name = xName,
                City = xCity,
                IdProduct = o.IdProduct,
                Quantity = o.Quantity };
```

Both previous examples return a sequence that looks like the following when printed to the console window:

```
{ Name = Frank, City = Seattle, IdProduct = 5, Quantity = 20 }
{ Name = James, City = Dallas, IdProduct = 3, Quantity = 20 }
{ Name = Marco, City = Torino, IdProduct = 1, Quantity = 10 }
{ Name = Marco, City = Torino, IdProduct = 3, Quantity = 20 }
{ Name = Paolo, City = Brescia, IdProduct = 1, Quantity = 3 }
{ Name = Paolo, City = Brescia, IdProduct = 2, Quantity = 5 }
```

Using a LINQ query expression, you can also create a new XML graph, merging XML nodes and entities. Be careful when mixing LINQ to XML query expressions and LINQ to XML declarations over the same XML tree. In general, it is a good habit to avoid mixing declarative syntax and imperative syntax over the same node graph, whereas it is absolutely allowed and sometimes useful to generate new XML trees that query existing ones with LINQ to XML.

Querying XML Efficiently to Build Entities

Now imagine that you need to read a list of customers and their orders from an existing XML persistence layer, using a set of custom entities taken from your domain model. See Listing 13-14 for the definition of the *Customer* and *Order* types.

LISTING 13-14 Example *Customer* and *Order* type definitions

```csharp
public class Customer {
    public string Name;
    public string City;
    public Countries Country;
    public Order[] Orders;

    public override string ToString(){
        return String.Format("Name: {0} - City: {1} - Country: {2}",
            this.Name, this.City, this.Country);
    }
}

public class Order {
    public int IdOrder;
    public int Quantity;
    public bool Shipped;
    public string Month;
    public int IdProduct;

    public override string ToString() {
        return String.Format("IdOrder: {0} - IdProduct: {1} - Quantity:
            {2} - Shipped: {3} - Month: {4}",
            this.IdOrder, this.IdProduct, this.Quantity, this.Shipped,
            this.Month);
    }
}
```

The XML source document, representing the hypothetical data source, could be similar to the following:

```xml
<?xml version="1.0" encoding="utf-8"?>
<customers>
  <customer name="Paolo" city="Brescia" country="Italy">
    <orders>
      <order id="1" idProduct="1" quantity="3" shipped="false" month="January" />
      <order id="2" idProduct="2" quantity="5" shipped="true" month="May" />
    </orders>
  </customer>
  <customer name="Marco" city="Torino" country="Italy">
    <orders>
      <order id="3" idProduct="1" quantity="10" shipped="false" month="July" />
      <order id="4" idProduct="3" quantity="20" shipped="true" month="December" />
    </orders>
  </customer>
</customers>
```

Now you can load the XML content with LINQ to XML using an *XElement* object, and then query its nodes to build an in-memory list of *Customer* and *Order* instances. Listing 13-15 shows an example.

LISTING 13-15 Loading *Customer* and *Order* instances from an XML data source via LINQ to XML

```csharp
XElement xmlCustomers = XElement.Load("customersWithOrdersDataSource.xml");

var customersWithOrders =
    from c in xmlCustomers.Elements("customer")
    select new Customer {
        Name = (String)c.Attribute("name"),
        City = (String)c.Attribute("city"),
        Country = (Countries)Enum.Parse(typeof(Countries),
            (String)c.Attribute("country"), true),
        Orders = (
            from    o in c.Descendants("order")
            select new Order {
                IdOrder = (Int32)o.Attribute("id"),
                IdProduct = (Int32)o.Attribute("idProduct"),
                Quantity = (Int32)o.Attribute("quantity"),
                Month = (String)o.Attribute("month"),
                Shipped = (Boolean)o.Attribute("shipped")
            }
        ).ToArray()
    };

foreach (Customer c in customersWithOrders) {
    Console.WriteLine(c);
    foreach (Order o in c.Orders) {
        Console.WriteLine("  {0}", o);
    }
}
```

The bold text in the preceding code shows the invoked LINQ to XML methods (instance or extension). First, it retrieves the list of all the *customer* elements by using the *Elements* instance method of the *XElement* object, which represents the document root. Then it enumerates each of these *customer* elements to retrieve their attributes, using the *Attributes* instance method. Finally it builds the list of orders for each *Customer* type instance calling the *Descendants* instance method of the *XElement* type for each *customer* element previously selected. Notice that the code again uses the explicit type-casting feature offered by the *XAttribute* type to extract the typed values of the attributes.

Even if the code in Listing 13-15 is already completely functional and syntactically correct, it could be written more efficiently. In fact, the code you have seen loads the entire set of XML nodes into memory and then produces the output object model. With a small data source, doing that is not a problem, but for a large or remote data source, that approach could affect the overall performance of a solution. In such situations, it is preferable to use a chunking reader based on an *XmlReader* instance, like the one you saw in Listing 12-24 in Chapter 12.

Listing 13-16 shows an example equivalent to the one presented in Listing 13-15 but it uses a chunking reader instead.

LISTING 13-16 Loading *Customer* and *Order* instances from an XML data source by using a chunking reader

```
static IEnumerable<XElement>
ChunkedDataSourceReader(String uri, String chunkElement) {
    XmlReaderSettings settings = new XmlReaderSettings();
    XmlReader xr = XmlReader.Create(uri, settings);

    while (xr.Read()) {
        if ((xr.NodeType == XmlNodeType.Element)
            && (xr.Name == chunkElement)) {
            // For debugging and demo purposes only
            Console.WriteLine("Reading a chunk element from data source");
            yield return XElement.ReadFrom(xr) as XElement;
        }
    }
}

static void createEntitiesFromXmlUsingChunkingReader() {
    var xmlCustomers =
        ChunkedDataSourceReader("customersWithOrdersDataSource.xml",
            "customer");

    Console.WriteLine("Variable xmlCustomers defined");

    var customersWithOrders =
        from c in xmlCustomers
        select new Customer {
            Name = (String)c.Attribute("name"),
            City = (String)c.Attribute("city"),
```

```
            Country = (Countries)Enum.Parse(typeof(Countries),
                (String)c.Attribute("country"), true),
            Orders = (
                from o in c.Descendants("order")
                select new Order {
                    IdOrder = (Int32)o.Attribute("id"),
                    IdProduct = (Int32)o.Attribute("idProduct"),
                    Quantity = (Int32)o.Attribute("quantity"),
                    Month = (String)o.Attribute("month"),
                    Shipped = (Boolean)o.Attribute("shipped")
                }
            ).ToArray()
        };

    Console.WriteLine("LINQ query expression defined");

    foreach (Customer c in customersWithOrders) {
        Console.WriteLine(c);
        foreach (Order o in c.Orders) {
            Console.WriteLine("  {0}", o);
        }
    }
}
```

The key point of this sample is the definition of the XML data source variable named *xml-Customer* through the *ChunkedDataSourceReader* method. In fact, the query is the same as before, with the exception of the first *from* clause, which directly selects the chunks returned by the custom *ChunkedDataSourceReader* function. That function accepts two arguments: one that defines the XML data source Uniform Resource Identifier (URI), and a second that supplies the XPath rule, used to read each element chunk from the data source. The example reads the data source on a per-customer basis; thus, it uses an XPath rule with a *customer* value. The chunking reader reads the data source using an *XmlReader* and yields every occurrence of the requested element (*customer),* parsing it as an *XElement* by using the *ReadFrom* method of the *XNode* type. For debugging purposes, you can write a log message to the console every single time a chunking reader retrieves a new chunk.

Here is the console output of Listing 13-16:

```
Variable xmlCustomers defined
LINQ query expression defined
Reading a chunk element from data source
Name: Paolo - City: Brescia - Country: Italy
  IdOrder: 1 - IdProduct: 1 - Quantity: 3 - Shipped: False - Month: January
  IdOrder: 2 - IdProduct: 2 - Quantity: 5 - Shipped: True - Month: May
    Reading a chunk element from data source
Name: Marco - City: Torino - Country: Italy
  IdOrder: 3 - IdProduct: 1 - Quantity: 10 - Shipped: False - Month: July
  IdOrder: 4 - IdProduct: 3 - Quantity: 20 - Shipped: True - Month: December
```

Notice that the log output for each chunk occurs just before the effective enumeration of the corresponding *Customer* instance. The solution in Listing 13-16 is definitely more efficient than the one in Listing 13-15, particularly when working with large or remote XML data sources.

Transforming XML with LINQ to XML

Here is an example that applies the LINQ query information you have just seen. Imagine that you need to transform a source document into a new schema. Listing 13-17 shows the source document.

LISTING 13-17 Source XML with a list of customers

```xml
<?xml version="1.0" encoding="utf-8"?>
<customers>
  <customer name="Paolo" city="Brescia" country="Italy" />
  <customer name="Marco" city="Torino" country="Italy" />
  <customer name="James" city="Dallas" country="USA" />
  <customer name="Frank" city="Seattle" country="USA" />
</customers>
```

Listing 13-18 shows the output you want, in which the namespace of the elements has been changed, and that filters *customer* elements on the value of their *country* attribute.

LISTING 13-18 Output XML, with a transformed list of customers

```xml
<?xml version="1.0" encoding="utf-8"?>
<c:customers xmlns:c="http://schemas.devleap.com/Customers">
  <c:customer>
    <c:name>Paolo</c:name>
    <c:city>Brescia</c:city>
  </c:customer>
  <c:customer>
    <c:name>Marco</c:name>
    <c:city>Torino</c:city>
  </c:customer>
</c:customers>
```

Of course, you could use XSLT code to transform the source into the output. Listing 13-19 provides a simple XSLT that would do that.

LISTING 13-19 The XSLT used to transform XML from Listing 13-17 to Listing 13-18

```xml
<?xml version="1.0" encoding="UTF-8" ?>
<xsl:stylesheet version="1.0"
  xmlns:xsl="http://www.w3.org/1999/XSL/Transform"
  xmlns:c="http://schemas.devleap.com/Customers">
  <xsl:template match="customers">
    <c:customers>
      <xsl:for-each select="customer[@country = 'Italy']">
        <c:customer>
          <c:name><xsl:value-of select="@name"/></c:name>
          <c:city><xsl:value-of select="@city"/></c:city>
        </c:customer>
      </xsl:for-each>
    </c:customers>
  </xsl:template>
</xsl:stylesheet>
```

However, if you are already working with .NET Framework code, you can avoid leaving that context and instead use a simple LINQ query such as the one shown in Listing 13-20.

LISTING 13-20 A functional construction used to transform XML from Listing 13-17 to Listing 13-18

```csharp
XNamespace ns = "http://schemas.devleap.com/Customers";
XElement destinationXmlCustomers =
    new XElement(ns + "customers",
        new XAttribute(XNamespace.Xmlns + "c", ns),
        from   c in sourceXmlCustomers.Elements("customer")
        where  c.Attribute("country").Value == "Italy"
        select new XElement(ns + "customer",
                    new XElement(ns + "name", c.Attribute("name")),
                    new XElement(ns + "city", c.Attribute("city"))));
```

Note We personally like and appreciate the features of XSLT and their strong syntax, but using them requires learning another query language. We know and clearly understand that many developers are not familiar with XSLT syntax, and probably will prefer the LINQ solution, because it is easier for a .NET Framework developer to write—and because it is also checkable by the compiler and typed.

Listing 13-21 shows a Microsoft Visual Basic version of this transformation code.

LISTING 13-21 A Visual Basic XML literal used to transform XML from Listing 13-17 to Listing 13-18

```
Dim destinationXmlCustomers =
    <c:customers xmlns:c="http://schemas.devleap.com/Customers">
        <%= From c In sourceXmlCustomers.<customers>.<customer>
            Where (c.@country = "Italy")
            Select
            <c:customer xmlns:c="http://schemas.devleap.com/Customers">
                <c:name><%= c.@name %></c:name>
                <c:city><%= c.@city %></c:city>
            </c:customer> %>
    </c:customers>
```

The Visual Basic approach is probably the quickest to write and the easiest to understand, because you can think about the output XML directly. You can make it even easier by using global XML namespaces. Note that the syntax used to select elements and attributes from the source XML document uses a special Visual Basic syntax that allows you to reference nodes in an XPath-like way. The code first selects all the *customer* elements, which are children of the *customers* element within the *sourceXmlCustomer*, by using the following syntax:

```
sourceXmlCustomers.<customers>.<customer>
```

The Visual Basic compiler, as with XML literals, converts the syntax into a standard LINQ to XML invocation of *Elements* methods. In the same way, the syntax used to select the *name* and *city* attributes (*c.@name* and *c.@city*) recalls XPath attribute selection rules, and those get converted into calls to the *Attribute* method of the *XElement* type.

Here is one last thought about dynamic construction and transformation of XML contents: Sometimes XML schemas support optional elements or optional attributes. When you define transformations using LINQ to XML, you work at a higher level, using object instances rather than nodes. In cases where you define an *XElement* using functional construction and assign it a *null* value, the result is an empty closed element, like the one shown in the following example:

```
// Where c.City == null
XElement city = new XElement("customer",
    new XAttribute("id", c.IdCustomer),
    new XElement("city", c.City));
```

The result is an empty tag (*<city />*), as shown in the following line of code:

```
<customer id="10"><city /></customer>
```

For cases in which you need to omit the element declaration when it is empty (*null*), you can use the conditional operator, as shown in the following sample:

```
// Where c.City == null
XElement city = new XElement("customer",
    new XAttribute("id", c.IdCustomer), c.City != null ? new XElement(
        "city", c.City), null);
```

When you add *null* content to an *XContainer*, it is skipped without throwing any kind of exception.

Support for XSD and Validation of Typed Nodes

Many of the previous examples used explicit casting and accessed nodes through their names as quoted strings. Unfortunately, those casts and quotes are not type safe, and cannot be checked at compile time. However, XML document structure is often defined using an XML Schema Definition (XSD). There is a "strongly typed LINQ to XML" project, also known as *LINQ to XSD*, that allows access to XML nodes using a typed and self-describing approach and supports Microsoft IntelliSense. Using the LINQ to XSD project, the query you saw in Listing 13-13 would be written like the one in Listing 13-22.

LISTING 13-22 A LINQ query over XML, based on an XSD typed approach

```
var ordersWithCustomersFromXml =
    from    c in xmlCustomers.customerCollection
    join    o in orders
    on      c.Name equals o.Name
    orderby c.Name
    select  new {
                Name = c.Name,
                City = c.City,
                IdProduct = o.IdProduct,
                Quantity = o.Quantity };
```

As you can see, when you use this approach, the XML node graphs look like any other object graphs—regardless of whether they are made of elements, attributes, or nodes instead of objects. Keep in mind that at the time of this book's writing (September 2010), the LINQ to XSD project was still in beta. You can download the project from the Codeplex website at *http://linqtoxsd.codeplex.com/*.

Two of the extension methods defined in the *System.Xml.Schema.Extensions* class of the *System.Xml.Linq* assembly also offer XML schema support. The methods are *GetSchemaInfo*, which extends any *XElement* or *XAttribute* instance, and *Validate*, which extends *XDocument*, *XElement*, and *XAttribute*. Both these methods are available with a few overloads. The *GetSchemaInfo* method returns an annotation of type *System.Xml.Schema.IXmlSchemaInfo*, taken from the current node, if present. It retrieves a schema definition mapped to the current node by using LINQ to XML annotations. The *Validate* method, as you can figure out from its name, validates the source XML node by using an *XmlSchemaSet* containing the schemas to use. Consider the XML schema shown in Listing 13-23.

LISTING 13-23 An XML schema definition for the sample list of customers

```xml
<?xml version="1.0" encoding="utf-8" ?>
<xsd:schema id="Customer"
    targetNamespace="http://schemas.devleap.com/Customer"
    elementFormDefault="qualified"
    xmlns="http://schemas.devleap.com/Customer"
    xmlns:xsd="http://www.w3.org/2001/XMLSchema">
  <xsd:element name="customers">
    <xsd:complexType>
      <xsd:sequence>
        <xsd:element name="customer" minOccurs="0" maxOccurs="unbounded">
          <xsd:complexType>
            <xsd:attribute name="name" type="xsd:string" use="required" />
            <xsd:attribute name="city" type="xsd:string" use="required" />
            <xsd:attribute name="country">
              <xsd:simpleType>
                <xsd:restriction base="xsd:string">
                  <xsd:enumeration value="Italy" />
                  <xsd:enumeration value="USA" />
                </xsd:restriction>
              </xsd:simpleType>
            </xsd:attribute>
          </xsd:complexType>
        </xsd:element>
      </xsd:sequence>
    </xsd:complexType>
  </xsd:element>
</xsd:schema>
```

You can define an XML graph with this structure using LINQ to XML as usual, and map the nodes to the previous schema by using an *XNamespace* instance, as shown in Listing 13-24.

LISTING 13-24 An XML document with the schema in Listing 13-23, built using the LINQ to XML API

```
XNamespace ns = "http://schemas.devleap.com/Customer";
XDocument xmlCustomers = new XDocument(
    new XElement(ns + "customers",
        from   c in customers
        select new XElement(ns + "customer",
                   new XAttribute("city", c.City),
                   new XAttribute("name", c.Name),
                   new XAttribute("country", c.Country))));
```

At this point, the *xmlCustomers* variable represents an XML Infoset instance related to the schema in Listing 13-23 that uses its corresponding XML namespace.

Listing 13-25 shows how you can validate this *XDocument* by calling the *Validate* extension method.

LISTING 13-25 XML validation using the *Validate* extension method

```
static void validateXDocument() {

    // . . .

    XmlSchemaSet schemas = new XmlSchemaSet();
    schemas.Add(XmlSchema.Read(new StreamReader(@"..\..\customer.xsd"), null));
    xmlCustomers.Validate(schemas, xmlCustomers_validation);
}

static void xmlCustomers_validation(Object source, ValidationEventArgs args) {
    // In case of validation messages
    Console.WriteLine(args.Message);
}
```

Internally, the *Validate* method uses all the standard and common classes and tools of the *System.Xml.Schema* namespace.

You can merge the validation engine with LINQ to XML events to achieve an automatic validation behavior while changing XML tree content. Listing 13-26 shows an example implementation of this idea.

LISTING 13-26 XML validation using the *Validate* extension method within the *Changed* event

```
XNamespace ns = "http://schemas.devleap.com/Customer";
XDocument xmlCustomers = new XDocument(
    new XElement(ns + "customers",
        from   c in customers
        select new XElement(ns + "customer",
            new XAttribute("city", c.City),
            new XAttribute("name", c.Name),
            new XAttribute("country", c.Country))));
xmlCustomers.Save(Console.Out);
Console.WriteLine();

XmlSchemaSet schemas = new XmlSchemaSet();
schemas.Add(XmlSchema.Read(new StreamReader(@"..\..\customer.xsd"), null));

// Subscribe to Changed event on the root element
xmlCustomers.Changed += (sender, e) => {
    xmlCustomers.Validate(schemas, (source, args) => {
```

```
        if (args.Exception != null)
            throw new InvalidOperationException("Operation on XML
            inconsistent with associated schema.", args.Exception);
    });
};

// Removes the city attribute from the first customer
// (modification not allowed by the schema)
xmlCustomers.Element(ns + "customers")
    .Elements(ns + "customer").First()
    .SetAttributeValue("city", null);
}
```

Whenever you change the content of the XML tree, the *Changed* event occurs and invokes the code defined in the lambda expression provided in its definition. When a modification would make the document invalid with respect to the assigned XML schema, the validation callback defined by the inner lambda expression throws an *InvalidOperationException*, keeping track of the inner validation exception and, indeed, blocking modifications.

> **Note** The example shown in Listing 13-26 is purely for demonstration purposes, and you should not use it in large documents or in situations that require massive changes. On the contrary, in such situations, you should delay validation until the changes are complete, to avoid performance issues.

Support for XPath and *System.Xml.XPath*

One last group of extension methods offered by LINQ to XML is related to *System.Xml.XPath* integration. The *System.Xml.XPath.Extensions* class provides a few extension methods that are useful for managing *XNode* contents via XPath. The first method is *CreateNavigator*, which returns an *XPathNavigator*, as shown in the following code:

```
public static XPathNavigator CreateNavigator(this XNode node);
public static XPathNavigator CreateNavigator(this XNode node, XmlNameTable nameTable);
```

Internally, *CreateNavigator* creates an instance of an *XNodeNavigator* class, which is derived from *XPathNavigator* and is specifically defined to navigate X* class graphs. The main goal of this method is to make it possible to transform an *XNode* using standard *System.Xml.Xsl* classes. *XslCompiledTransform* can work with classes derived from *XPathNavigator* used as input. Listing 13-27 provides sample code that transforms the list of customers by using the XSLT defined earlier in Listing 13-19.

LISTING 13-27 XSLT transformation using *XslCompiledTransform* and the *CreateNavigator* extension method

```
XslCompiledTransform xslt = new XslCompiledTransform();
xslt.Load(@"..\..\customerFromSourceToDestination.xslt"); xslt.
Transform(sourceXmlCustomers.CreateNavigator(), null, Console.Out);
```

Another interesting method is *XPathEvaluate*, which evaluates an XPath rule against the current *XNode*, returning its value by using the internal class *XPathEvaluator*. The code in Listing 13-28 selects all *name* attributes from all the customers located in Italy.

LISTING 13-28 Example of using the *XPathEvaluate* extension method

```
XElement xmlCustomers = new XElement("customers",
    from   c in customers
    select new XElement("customer",
                new XAttribute("name", c.Name),
                new XAttribute("city", c.City),
                new XAttribute("country", c.Country)));

var result = (IEnumerable<Object>)xmlCustomers.XPathEvaluate(
    "/customer[@country = 'Italy']/@name");

foreach (var item in result) {
    Console.WriteLine(item);
}
```

Consider that the *XPathEvaluate* method cannot determine the result of the XPath query. Therefore, it always returns a value of type *Object*. It is your responsibility to know and correctly cast the result type.

The last two methods to discuss are *XPathSelectElement* and *XPathSelectElements*. The former returns the first element that matches the XPath expression provided as an argument, and the latter returns all the elements that match the expression. Internally, both use the *XPathEvaluator* class. The following example selects all the *customer* elements located in Italy:

```
var result = xmlCustomers.XPathSelectElements(
    "/customer[@country = 'Italy']");
```

This method can be useful for defining LINQ queries that work on a subset of nodes of the source XML graph—such as filtering *customer* elements by their *country* attribute value. An example is shown in Listing 13-29.

LISTING 13-29 Sample LINQ query over the result of the *XPathSelectElements* extension method

```
var ordersOfItalianCustomersFromXml =
    from    c in xmlCustomers.XPathSelectElements(
                    "/customer[@country = 'Italy']")
    let     xName = (String)c.Element("name")
    let     xCity = (String)c.Attribute("city")
    join    o in orders
    on      xName equals o.Name
    orderby xName
    select  new {
                Name = xName,
                City = xCity,
                IdProduct = o.IdProduct,
                Quantity = o.Quantity };
```

Remember that XPath rules are checked at run time, not at compile time. Therefore, you should be careful when defining them within LINQ queries. Consider also that—like many other LINQ extension methods—the XPath methods just discussed also support deferred query evaluation, so keep in mind that whenever you access results from queries that use these methods, the result is refreshed by rescanning the source XML graph, unless you copy it by using the LINQ conversion operators already discussed, such as *ToList*, *ToArray*, *ToDictionary*, or *ToLookup*.

Securing LINQ to XML

LINQ to XML was designed to handle trusted XML documents; therefore, you should avoid using LINQ to XML to manage contents received from unknown senders across the Internet. If you need to read, traverse, or modify XML trees received from outside your environment or from untrusted people, it is better to load the nodes through an *XmlReader* class that is properly configured for security and sandboxing, creating a LINQ to XML tree from the *XmlReader* instance. If necessary, you can also create a LINQ to XML nodes tree from an *XmlReader* instance using a predefined memory footprint. You do this by using custom code to read single groups of elements from the source XML and handling them with *XElement* objects (as you saw earlier in the chunking readers example). You can see a brief example of this in Listing 13-30.

LISTING 13-30 Chunked reading of an XML tree using a secured *XmlReader*

```
static void secureChunkReaderSample () {
    var customers = ChunkCustomers(@"..\..\CustomersWithOrders.xml");
    foreach (var c in customers) {
        Console.WriteLine(c);
    }
}
```

```
static IEnumerable<XElement> ChunkCustomers(String uri) {
    XmlReaderSettings settings = new XmlReaderSettings();
    settings.XmlResolver = new XmlSecureResolver(new XmlUrlResolver(), "c:\\sources");
    settings.MaxCharactersInDocument = 1024 * 1024 * 4; // Max 4MB
    XmlReader xr = XmlReader.Create(uri, settings);
    while (xr.Read())
    {
        if ((xr.NodeType == XmlNodeType.Element)
            && (xr.Name == "customer")) {
                yield return XElement.ReadFrom(xr) as XElement;
        }
    }
}
```

As you can see, the core part of Listing 13-30 is the enumerator method named *Chunk-Customers*. This method looks like the chunking methods you saw earlier in this chapter. It reads an assumably large customers XML file by using an *XmlReader* instance, chunking the nodes on a per customer basis. The difference in this sample is the configuration of the *XmlReaderSettings* instance; this example uses an *XmlSecureResolver* instance as the *Xml-Resolver* property, and a predefined maximum size of 4 MB for the whole document. With the *XmlSecureResolver* class, you can restrict the URIs accessible from the *XmlReader* instance that uses the resolver, avoiding, for example, cross-site scripting attacks. When working with LINQ to XML, you should always consider that, regardless of what you do (such as reading contents, transforming nodes with XSLT, validating with XSD, navigating trees with XPath), security checks are absent. Because of this, you must be very aware of the potential for denial of services realized through XSLT scripting, XSD and/or XPath processing overhead, and so on. Finally, consider that—for security reasons—LINQ to XML turns off Document Type Definition (DTD) validation to avoid possible denial-of-service attacks made possible because of too-heavy DTDs or DTD external references.

One last thing to note about LINQ to XML security is that *XObject* annotations are visible to any assembly loaded in an XML processing pipeline. Therefore, any annotation you make on an X* type instance can be read and modified from any piece of code in your application domain, which exposes the annotation to security issues.

Serializing LINQ to XML

The *XElement* type is serializable using the *XmlSerializer* engine or *DataContractSerializer*, so it is suitable for Microsoft ASP.NET Web Services and Windows Communication Foundation (WCF) service contracts and implementations. This book focuses only on the serialization part of the discussion. In Listing 13-31, you can see an example of the code used to serialize an *XElement* that uses a *DataContractSerializer* instance.

LISTING 13-31 *XElement* serialization using a *DataContractSerializer*

```
XElement xmlCustomers = new XElement("customers",
    from   c in listCustomers
    select new XElement("customer",
        new XElement("name", c.Name),
        new XAttribute("city", c.City),
        new XAttribute("country", c.Country)));

MemoryStream mem = new MemoryStream();
DataContractSerializer dc = new DataContractSerializer(typeof(XElement));
dc.WriteObject(mem, xmlCustomers);
```

The result of Listing 13-31 looks like the following XML excerpt:

```
<customers><customer city="Brescia"
country="Italy"><name>Paolo</name></customer><customer city="Torino"
country="Italy"><name>Marco</name></customer><customer city="Dallas"
country="USA"><name>James</name></customer><customer city="Seattle"
country="USA"><name>Frank</name></customer></customers>
```

As you can see, the output is simply the streamed representation of XML nodes. The interesting part of this section becomes apparent when you think about using *XElement* instances as the content of Simple Object Access Protocol (SOAP) service messages. For example, you can use a type like the one shown in Listing 13-32 as the argument of a WCF service contract.

LISTING 13-32 Sample type using *XElement*, serializable with *DataContractSerializer*

```
[DataContract(Namespace = "http://schemas.devleap.com/CustomerWithXml")]
public class CustomerWithXmlData {
    [DataMember]
    public XElement XmlData { get; set; }

    [DataMember]
    public String Name { get; set; }
}
```

The *XElement* type is the only serializable type in LINQ to XML because it implements the interface *IXmlSerializable* (as do a few other .NET Framework types), to define a customized serialization behavior. In particular, although the type is serializable, it does not provide any information about the schema of its node tree; in fact, it is configured to be exported as an *xsd:any* element section. No other LINQ to XML types are serializable, so that makes them unsuitable for use with ASP.NET Web Services or WCF.

Summary

In this chapter, you learned how to query, traverse, and transform XML node graphs using LINQ to XML query extensions. You discovered how to read XML contents to build in-memory entity models efficiently. You evaluated the support offered by *System.Xml.Linq* for XPath, XSD, and XSLT. Finally, you saw how to secure your code when working with LINQ to XML, and how to serialize XML nodes defined as *XElement* instances to use them within SOAP services.

Part IV

Advanced LINQ

Chapter 14
Inside Expression Trees

Handling and manipulating expression trees is an important skill to have because it enables you to use Microsoft Language Integrated Query (LINQ) in an advanced way. If you want to build a dynamic filter condition, you need to be able to construct an expression tree in memory without using the easy-to-use but lightweight lambda expression syntax assigned to *Expression<T>* variables. If you want to write your own LINQ provider (a topic covered in Chapter 15, "Extending LINQ"), you need to know how to navigate the nodes of an expression tree to correctly interpret its content, translating it into the operation required by your provider. Whether you want to build a dynamic filter condition, write your own LINQ provider, or simply understand what happens under the hood when the *IQueryable* interface is involved (as it is for any LINQ to SQL query), this chapter will definitely be interesting for you.

This chapter starts with an introduction to the characteristics of expression trees and the lambda expression syntax. Next, it dissects an expression tree, analyzing the more common and important node types. Then you learn about techniques for navigating (or *visiting*) and modifying an expression tree. The chapter closes with a discussion about generating expression trees dynamically.

 Note In this chapter, the term *visit* means navigating through an expression tree structure. This term stems from the algorithms used, which are generally called *expression tree visitors*.

Lambda Expressions

Lambda expressions are part of the Microsoft Visual C# syntax. The compiler can generate an expression tree starting from lambda expression syntax. This section simply recaps some concepts before moving on to a more advanced analysis of lambda expressions that will enable you to better analyze expression trees.

Lambda expression syntax in C# supports a more concise syntax that you can use to define an anonymous method. For example, the code in Listing 14-1 is based on a delegate.

LISTING 14-1 Declaration of *Inc* as an anonymous method

```
delegate int IncDelegate(int x);
static void TestDelegate() {
    IncDelegate Inc = delegate(int x) { return x + 1; };
    Console.WriteLine(Inc(2));
}
```

The code in Listing 14-2 is equivalent to Listing 14-1, but it uses the lambda expression syntax.

LISTING 14-2 Declaration of *Inc* as a lambda expression

```
delegate int IncDelegate(int x);
static void TestLambda() {
    IncDelegate Inc = x => x + 1;
    Console.WriteLine(Inc(2));
}
```

Both the previous examples define the delegate type *IncDelegate*; however, lambda expressions are typically declared using one of the following *Func* delegate declarations defined in the *System* namespace as part of the *System.Core* assembly (as you saw in Chapter 2, "LINQ Syntax Fundamentals"):

```
public delegate T Func<TResult>();
public delegate T Func<A0, TResult >( A0 arg0 );
public delegate T Func<A0, A1, TResult > ( A0 arg0, A1 arg1 );
public delegate T Func<A0, A1, A2, TResult >( A0 arg0, A1 arg1, A2 arg2 );
public delegate T Func<A0, A1, A2, A3, TResult >
                    ( A0 arg0, A1 arg1, A2 arg2, A3 arg3 );
public delegate T Func<A0, A1, A2, A3, A4, TResult >
                    ( A0 arg0, A1 arg1, A2 arg2, A3 arg3, A4 arg4 );
```

These *Func* declarations are simple delegates and can be used for both delegate and lambda expression syntax—because in the end you always get a delegate. Listing 14-3 shows *IncDelegate* and *IncLambda* declarations that are perfectly equivalent except that they are declared with different syntaxes.

LISTING 14-3 Comparison between delegate and lambda expression syntaxes

```
static void TestRecursive() {
    // Typical lambda expression using Func delegate
    Func<int, int> IncDelegate = delegate(int x) { return x + 1; };
    Func<int, int> IncLambda = x => x + 1;

    Console.WriteLine(IncDelegate(2));
    Console.WriteLine(IncLambda(2));
}
```

Lambda expressions might include several statements, but here the interest is only in those that consist of an expression body, which is a single *return* statement followed by an expression. (These lambda expressions can omit the *return* statement, as shown in Listings 14-2 and 14-3.) As you will see shortly, you can use lambda expressions defined as an expression body to generate an expression tree.

> **Important** Increment (++) and decrement (--) operators are not supported as part of an expression tree in C#. The reason is that their presence implies an assignment to modify the incremented/decremented variable, and assignment operators are not supported in an expression tree in C#. Nevertheless, Microsoft .NET Framework 4 also supports expression trees containing assignments, statements, and other operations. The reason is that the expression tree is also used by Dynamic Language Runtime (DLR), which requires a broader set of operations.

Recursive Lambda Expressions

Apparently, you cannot define a recursive lambda expression. For example, to define a lambda expression for factorial evaluation, you might want to write the following:

```
fac => x => x == 0 ? 1 : x * fac(x-1)
```

However, you cannot directly call the lambda expression you are defining from inside its definition. To make this syntax work, you need to define a fixed-point operator, as shown in the following *Fix* fixed-point generator:

```
static Func<T, T> Fix<T>(Func<Func<T, T>, Func<T, T>> F) {
    return t => F(Fix(F))(t);
}
```

Using *Fix*, you can obtain the recursion for the initial lambda expression:

```
Func<int, int> factorial =
    Fix<int>( fac => x => (x == 0) ? 1 : x * fac(x - 1) );
```

> **More Info** If you are interested in a more detailed explanation of recursive lambda expressions, you can find an excellent post by Mads Torgersen at *http://blogs.msdn.com/madst /archive/2007/05/11/recursive-lambda-expressions.aspx.*

For the discussion in this chapter, the important point is that you cannot directly write a recursive lambda and, hence, you cannot encode it as a lambda expression. You need a helper function such as *Fix*, and you need everyone who consumes the expression tree to understand its special significance.

What Is an Expression Tree?

An expression tree is a data structure that represents an expression using nodes as operands and operators. An operand can be an expression by itself, forming a recursive structure. For example, consider the following expression:

```
9 + (5 + 6) * 3
```

This expression can be represented by an expression tree like the one represented in Figure 14-1.

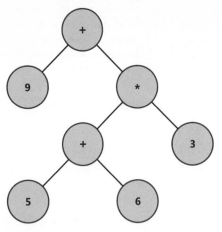

FIGURE 14-1 The graphical representation of an expression tree.

There is a large body of literature about expression tree libraries and algorithms. Starting with version 3.5, the .NET Framework includes a library for handling expression trees, formed by classes defined in the *System.Linq.Expressions* namespace in the *System.Core* assembly. You can use these classes directly to create expression trees. Using these same classes, compilers such as those for C# and Microsoft Visual Basic can translate expressions written in C# or Visual Basic into an expression tree created at run time.

Creating Expression Trees

The easiest way to create an expression tree is by using higher-language features. However, because an expression tree made up only of constants (such as the one in Figure 14-1) would be automatically converted into the result (a single constant value) at compile time, you need to build parametric expressions, such as the formula to calculate the area of a triangle:

```
b * h / 2
```

The corresponding lambda expression in C# is:

```
(b, h) => b * h / 2
```

In a real C# program, you need to assign that lambda expression to some variable. At this point, you also need to define the type on which the lambda expression is defined:

```
Func<double, double, double> TriangleArea = (b, h) => b * h / 2;
```

Now you have a delegate instance, *TriangleArea*, that is no different from a regular function. However, you can get an expression tree instead of the delegate simply by declaring *Triangle-Area* as an *Expression<TDelegate>* instead of a delegate (such as the *Func<A0, A1, TResult>* you used before):

```
Expression<Func<double, double, double>> TriangleAreaExp =
    (b, h) => b * h / 2;
```

Using this declaration, *TriangleAreaExp* is not a delegate; instead, it is a reference to the root node of an expression tree. You can see the difference by looking at the sample code in Listing 14-4.

LISTING 14-4 Difference between lambda expression and expression tree declarations

```
static void DemoTriangleArea() {
    Func<double, double, double> TriangleArea = (b, h) => b * h / 2;
    Console.WriteLine("*** Delegate ***");
    Console.WriteLine("ToString: {0}", TriangleArea.ToString());
    Console.WriteLine("Value: {0}", TriangleArea(7, 12));

    Expression<Func<double, double, double>> TriangleAreaExp =
        (b, h) => b * h / 2;
    Console.WriteLine("*** Expression tree ***");
    Console.WriteLine("ToString: {0}", TriangleAreaExp.ToString());
    Console.WriteLine("Value: {0}", TriangleAreaExp.Compile()(7, 12));
}
```

Here is the output produced by executing the code in Listing 14-4:

```
*** Delegate ***
ToString: System.Func`3[System.Double,System.Double,System.Double]
Value: 42
*** Expression tree ***
ToString: (b, h) => ((b * h) / 2)
Value: 42
```

TriangleArea.ToString displays the type name of the delegate class that encloses the *Triangle-Area* lambda expression. *TriangleAreaExp.ToString*, on the other hand, displays the lambda expression defined for *TriangleAreaExp* in a textual form. This is possible because the *ToString* method is overridden by the *Expression<TDelegate>* class, which *TriangleAreaExp* is an instance of. That method visits the expression tree, displaying it in human-readable form.

> **Note** Parentheses that explicitly state operator priorities have been added with respect to the original definition of the *TriangleAreaExp* expression. These parentheses are generated by the overridden *ToString* implementation.

As shown in Listing 14-4, you can execute an expression tree by calling the *Compile* method, which returns a delegate that is callable, just as it was in the original lambda expression assigned to *TriangleAreaExp*. This method performs work that is similar to *ToString,* visiting the entire expression tree (represented in Figure 14-2). However, instead of printing out the operands and operators found, it generates the necessary Intermediate Language (IL) code to implement the behavior described by the visited nodes, returning a reference to a delegate instance that contains that code.

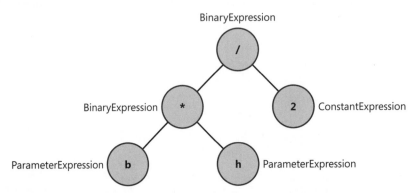

FIGURE 14-2 Expression tree with class names for node implementation.

Figure 14-2 shows a graphical representation of the expression tree contained in *TriangleAreaExp,* in which each node is named for the class that implements it in the *System.Linq.Expressions* namespace. You will explore the details and internals of expression trees later in this chapter.

> **Important** In the first part of this chapter, the graphical representations show only the *Body* part of a lambda expression. You will cover the entire expression tree that originates with a node of type *LambdaExpression* in the section "Dissecting Expression Trees" later in this chapter.

Encapsulation

Most likely, many of the expressions you use will contain calls to external methods. For example, consider the code in Listing 14-5.

LISTING 14-5 Call to external methods from an expression tree

```
static int Double(int n) {
    return n * 2;
}
static void CallInExpression() {
    Expression<Func<int, int>> CallExp = (x) => Double(x) + 1;
    Console.WriteLine("ToString: {0}", CallExp.ToString());
}
```

The *Double* static method contains a simple expression that could be encapsulated into an expression tree, but because it is a method, it is opaque to the expression tree. You can see in Figure 14-3 the expression tree assigned to *CallExp*, which contains the addition of *1* to the result of a method call to *Double* using *x* as an argument.

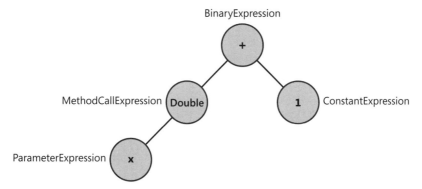

FIGURE 14-3 Expression tree containing a method call.

You might be tempted to "merge" an expression into an existing expression tree. Although this is possible, it is not an operation you can do by using the code generated by the compiler for lambda expressions assigned to *Expression<T>*. To accomplish such a merge, you could use a delegate obtained from a lambda expression instead of a function and write code like that shown in Listing 14-6.

LISTING 14-6 Call to a lambda expression from an expression tree

```
static void DelegateInExpression() {
    Func<int,int> Double = (n) => n * 2;
    Expression<Func<int, int>> CallExp = (x) => Double(x) + 1;
    Console.WriteLine("ToString: {0}", CallExp.ToString());
}
```

This produces an expression tree similar to the one represented in Figure 14-3 except that it uses an *InvocationExpression* node instead of *MethodCallExpression*.

Suppose you want to try declaring *Double* as an *Expression<T>*. Unfortunately, the following code does not compile:

```
Expression<Func<int, int>> Double = (n) => n * 2;
Expression<Func<int, int>> CallExp = (x) => Double(x) + 1;
```

The intention is to create an expression tree like the one shown in Figure 14-4, where the dark gray nodes are those of the *Double* expression tree, substituting the call to *Double* in the original expression tree assigned to *CallExp*. However, doing this requires an expression tree manipulation, as you will see shortly.

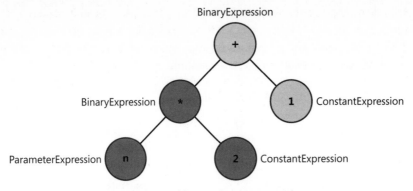

FIGURE 14-4 Expression tree obtained by merging two expression trees.

Using the C# syntax of a lambda expression to build an expression tree, you cannot combine an existing expression tree with a new one. In a lambda expression, an expression tree must be compiled before it can be used. Thus, you can try to merge two expression trees using the lambda expression syntax only by writing something like in the code contained in Listing 14-7.

LISTING 14-7 Call to a lambda expression from an expression tree

```
static void ExpressionInExpression () {
    Expression<Func<int, int>> Double = (n) => n * 2;
    Expression<Func<int, int>> CallExp = (x) => Double.Compile()(x) + 1;
    Console.WriteLine("ToString: {0}", CallExp.ToString());
}
```

Unfortunately, this produces an expression tree assigned to *CallExp* that is still like the one shown in Figure 14-3; the only difference is that it uses an *InvocationExpression* node instead of *MethodCallExpression*. The *Compile* call in Listing 14-7 generates the delegate for *Double*, but after that, you get the same syntax and behavior as demonstrated by Listing 14-6.

 Important The compiler generates an expression tree only when a lambda expression with an expression body is assigned to an *Expression<T>* type instance. The compiler is not able to combine one expression tree with another. You can write the code to do that, but you will probably make some additional assumptions that the compiler might not make—in particular, you might make an assumption to solve the replacement of expression arguments.

Immutability and Modification

The nodes of an expression tree are immutable. You can change an expression tree only by creating another one, which can be made of nodes (more precisely, subtrees) of an existing tree that are tied together using newly created nodes with properties different from those in the original tree.

To help you better understand this concept, consider this analogy comparing an expression tree and a string. Both classes produce instances that are read-only. To make a modification, you need to create a new instance. In the case of an expression tree, the implications are wider, because if you want to change a part of the tree, you need to change all the nodes, from the top-level node to the one that actually needs to be modified.

As an example, consider the following expression:

```
Expression<Func<int, int>> Double = (n) => (n * 2 + 1) * 4;
```

> **Note** The preceding example anticipates some of the concepts that you will see later, in the section "Dissecting Expression Trees."

Figure 14-5 shows a representation of the equivalent expression tree. A *BinaryExpression* type is a node that has two child nodes, identified by its *Left* and *Right* properties, used to navigate the tree.

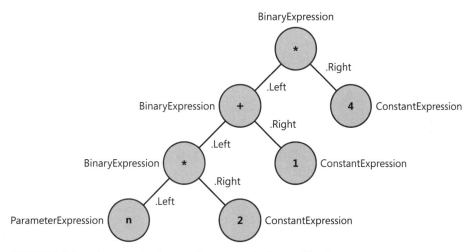

FIGURE 14-5 Sample expression tree used as an exercise for modifications.

If you wanted to replace the constant *4* with *5*, you would be tempted to write the code in Listing 14-8. First, you save in the *top* variable the top-level node of the tree; its right node is the constant *4*. Then, you try to assign its *Value* property to *5*, but that line of code does not compile, because the *Value* property is read-only and cannot be changed.

LISTING 14-8 Code that tries to modify an expression tree node that does not compile

```
class Program {
    static void Immutability() {
        Expression<Func<int, int>> Formula = (n) => (n * 2 + 1) * 4;

        Console.WriteLine(Formula.ToString());

        Expression top = Formula.Body;
        ConstantExpression constant = top.Right() as ConstantExpression;
        Console.WriteLine(constant.Value);

        constant.Value = 5; // Compiler error - Value is a read-only property
    }

    // Other code (like Main) omitted ...
}

// Helper extension methods to simplify the code
// These helper methods are not safe - they throw exceptions
// whenever applied on nodes that are not of type BinaryExpression
public static class TreeHelper {
    public static Expression Left(this Expression exp) {
        return (exp as BinaryExpression).Left;
    }

    public static Expression Right(this Expression exp) {
        return (exp as BinaryExpression).Right;
    }
}
```

Note Listing 14-8 includes two helper extension methods of the *Expression* class (*Left* and *Right*) that are also used in the following example of expression tree modification. The purpose of these *Left* and *Right* helper methods is only to make the navigation code simpler to read. They are not intended to be used in real-world code because they throw exceptions if applied to nodes of types other than *BinaryExpression*.

At this point, you have two options. You can create a completely new expression tree with the desired nodes, or you can create new nodes only for the changed part of the tree, recycling existing nodes that are not touched by your modification. The code in Listing 14-9 implements this second option, replacing the constant node *4* with a new constant node having a value of *5*.

LISTING 14-9 Substitution in an expression tree: replace *4* with *5*

```
static void ReplaceLevel2() {
    Expression<Func<int, int>> Formula = (n) => (n * 2 + 1) * 4;

    // Replace 4 with 5
    // Results in
    //      (n * 2 + 1) * 5
    Expression top = Formula.Body;
    ConstantExpression newRight = Expression.Constant(5);
    Expression newTree = Expression.MakeBinary(
                            top.NodeType,
                            top.Left(),
                            newRight );
    Console.WriteLine("Original tree: {0}", top.ToString());
    Console.WriteLine("Modified tree: {0}", newTree.ToString());
}
```

The *Expression* class has static methods that are used as class factories to get new instances of expression tree nodes. Listing 14-9 creates a new constant node with the value of *5*, attaches that node to the *Right* branch of a new top-level node, which is of type *BinaryExpression*, and copies the existing *Left* branch from the original expression tree. Here is the output produced by executing the code in Listing 14-9:

```
Original tree: (((n * 2) + 1) * 4)
Modified tree: (((n * 2) + 1) * 5)
```

Figure 14-6 shows the replaced nodes highlighted in dark gray. As you can see, in reality the example did not change the existing tree; instead, it created a new one, which links to the existing subtree and is identical in the new tree. (See the light gray nodes in Figure 14-6.)

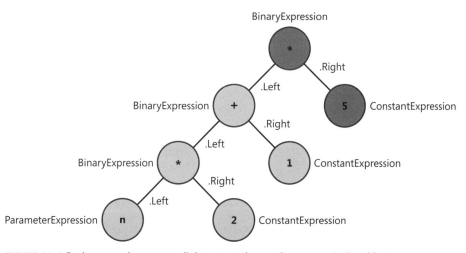

FIGURE 14-6 Dark gray nodes are new; light gray nodes are the same as in the older tree.

The deeper you go down the tree to make changes, the more nodes you will need to change. You always have to replace the nodes starting from the top-level node of the subtree containing the node you want to replace. So to replace the constant *4* with *5*, you must replace the top-level node (the *BinaryExpression* that performs multiplication). Similarly, to replace the constant *1* with a value of *3*, you need to replace three nodes, highlighted in dark gray in Figure 14-7.

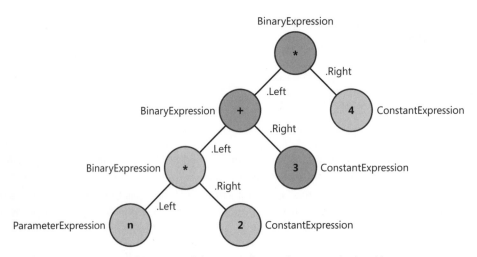

FIGURE 14-7 Dark gray nodes are new; light gray nodes are the same as in the older tree.

Listing 14-10 shows the code required to replace the constant *1* with the constant *3*.

LISTING 14-10 Substitution in an expression tree: replace *1* with *3*

```
static void ReplaceLevel3() {
    Expression<Func<int, int>> Formula = (n) => (n * 2 + 1) * 4;

    // Replace 1 with 3
    // Results in
    //      (n * 2 + 3) * 4
    Expression top = Formula.Body;
    ConstantExpression newConstantSum = Expression.Constant(3);
    Expression newSum = Expression.MakeBinary(
                        top.Left().NodeType,
                        top.Left().Left(),
                        newConstantSum );
    Expression newTree = Expression.MakeBinary(
                        top.NodeType,
                        newSum,
                        top.Right() );
    Console.WriteLine("Original tree: {0}", top.ToString());
    Console.WriteLine("Modified tree: {0}", newTree.ToString());
}
```

The output produced by executing the code in Listing 14-10 is:

```
Original tree: (((n * 2) + 1) * 4)
Modified tree: (((n * 2) + 3) * 4)
```

> **Note** Having immutable nodes that can be created only by referencing child nodes makes it impossible to create circular references in an expression tree.

It should be clear now that modifying an expression tree requires more than a few lines of code. In fact, these short samples were possible only because we made many assumptions about the expression tree, knew the tree's structure exactly, and knew the position of the nodes we wanted to change. In the real world, you would often need to interpret an expression without knowing its structure in advance. You might need to replace some parameters, remove some conditions, or simply combine two or more expressions together. In any case, there is a need for a more sophisticated expression tree analysis that requires a deeper knowledge of the expression tree structure.

The remaining part of this chapter introduces the most important concepts for understanding the elements from which expression trees are composed, and some of the techniques to navigate and manipulate them.

Dissecting Expression Trees

An expression tree always starts from a single top-level node—which is also the last part of the expression to be executed. Properties of this node link to other nodes. Every other node might have one or more child nodes that constitute arguments to the operation that the node represents. For example, one node might be an operator that sums two operands. In turn, each operand might be another node in the expression tree that encloses other operations. The leaves of the tree are nodes that have no children, such as (but not limited to) constants and parameters.

When you build an expression tree from a lambda expression, the first node is always an *Expression<T>* instance, which has a *Body* property containing another node and a *Parameters* property with an array of the parameters used in the expression tree. These parameters correspond to the parameters of the lambda expression. The previous part of this chapter did not show representations of this first node in the graphical illustrations of expression trees. Consider the following expression (shown earlier in Listing 14-4):

```
Expression<Func<double, double, double>> TriangleAreaExp =
        (b, h) => b * h / 2;
```

Figure 14-8 shows a more accurate graphical representation of this tree.

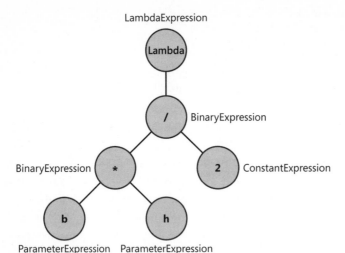

FIGURE 14-8 Expression tree with class names for node implementation.

The top-level node corresponds to a *TriangleAreaExp* instance. This node is of the generic type *Expression<T>*, where the constructed type is *Expression<Func<double, double,double>>*. *Expression<T>* is a class that inherits from *LambdaExpression*, which inherits from the abstract class *Expression*. Any node of the expression tree is of a class that specializes *Expression*. A class such as this can have its own properties that, when the properties are of type *Expression*, define other nodes tied to the tree. To illustrate this, Figure 14-9 shows an example of a more complex expression tree that corresponds to the following expression:

```
Expression<Func<int, int>> Formula =
    (n) => 1 + Double(n * (n % 2 == 0 ? -1 : 1));
```

An expression tree can have nodes with 0, 1, 2, or even more child nodes. Most of the time, you will find some *BinaryExpression* instances, but the resulting tree is not always a binary tree. For example, Figure 14-9 contains a conditional operator (*IIF*) with three child nodes: the condition (*Test* property) and the possible return values (*IfTrue* and *IfFalse* properties).

 Note Different node types might have a different structure for navigation, and the common base class (*Expression*) does not expose public properties to navigate the child nodes, regardless of the effective instantiated class. This implies that a complete navigation of an expression tree needs a correct interpretation of all the types that might be part of the visited expression tree.

Thus, the dissection starts with the *Expression* class, defined in *System.Linq.Expressions* as part of the *System.Core* assembly.

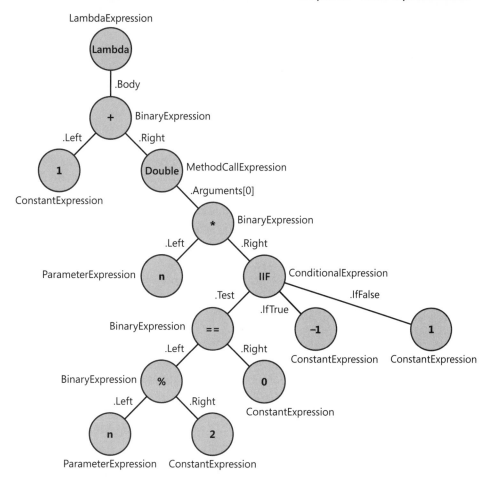

FIGURE 14-9 Complex expression tree.

The *Expression* Class

The *Expression* class has two roles. First, it is an abstract class inherited by all the node types. Second, it is a container for many public static methods that create tree nodes or offer helper functions. As an abstract class, its definition is very simple:

```
public abstract class Expression {
    protected Expression( ExpressionType nodeType, Type type );
    internal virtual void BuildString(StringBuilder builder);
    public override string ToString();

    // Properties
    public ExpressionType NodeType { get; }
    public Type Type { get; }

    // Static members omitted
}
```

There are no public instance methods or public constructors. The only way to get an instance of a node is to call one of the public static methods of *Expression*, which creates one instance of an *Expression* derived type. The *ToString* override internally calls the virtual *BuildString* method (which is typically overridden in derived classes) to return a correct representation of the expression tree segment represented by the node itself. The important parts are the two public properties:

- **NodeType** This is an instance of the *ExpressionType* enumeration. It defines which operator the node in the expression tree represents. Some *Expression*-derived classes always have the same value for *NodeType*, although others set this property to specify the operation that the node represents. For example, a *ConstantExpression* always sets this property to *ExpressionType.Constant*, whereas *BinaryExpression* needs to specify which operator the node defines, such as *Add*, *And*, or many others.

- **Type** This is the type of the object that results from evaluating the node's subtree.

Classes derived from *Expression* have few constraints imposed by the base class. However, these classes are already defined in the *System.Linq.Expressions* namespace. Understanding the role and the behavior of the most important node types of an expression tree is more interesting.

The static methods that are part of the *Expression* class are used as factory methods to create the various node types. There is at least one factory method for each possible *ExpressionType* value. At this level, you do not need to know the type that implements the desired operator (for example, *BinaryExpression*); however, it is important to know what the *ExpressionType* value is that corresponds to the desired operator (for example, *Add*). Typically, the name of the static method corresponds to the name of the member in the *ExpressionType* enumeration. For example, to create a *BinaryExpression* representing a multiplication of two expressions, you can call one of the *Expression.Multiply* factory methods (there are some overloads) that return a *BinaryExpression* instance with a *NodeType* value of *ExpressionType.Multiply*.

You are forced to use factory methods of the *Expression* class because the constructors of classes derived from *Expression* are declared as *internal*. Factory methods in the *Expression* class also conduct a sanity check of arguments before creating the node instance, throwing an exception in case of an error. You will see some examples of using factory methods in the section "Dynamically Building an Expression Tree" later in this chapter.

 Note Another important action of the factory methods is the search for the implementation of custom operators. This book does not include detailed examples, but expression trees support operator overloading.

Expression Tree Node Types

There are 25 public classes derived from *Expression* in the *System.Linq.Expressions* namespace. Each class can represent one or more operands through the *NodeType* property, and 85 different operands are available (the number of members of the *ExpressionType* enumeration).

ExpressionType Enumeration

The *ExpressionType* enumeration defines all the possible node types of an expression tree. Each value corresponds to one or more factory methods in the *Expression* class, typically with the same name as the enumeration member. The only exception is *MemberAccess*, which has more specific factory methods, such as *Expression.Field* and *Expression.Property*. Table 14-1 shows a complete list of *ExpressionType* members, each with a short description. Please note that members preceded by an asterisk (*) cannot be generated directly by a C# expression body and are required to support dynamic languages.

TABLE 14-1 *ExpressionType* **Enumeration Members**

ExpressionType	Description
Add	Performs an arithmetic addition without overflow checking.
* *AddAssign*	Performs an addition compound assignment without overflow checking.
* *AddAssignChecked*	Performs an addition compound assignment with overflow checking.
AddChecked	Performs an arithmetic addition with overflow checking.
And	Performs a bitwise or logical AND operation.
AndAlso	Performs a short-circuit conditional AND operation.
* *AndAssign*	Performs a bitwise or logical AND compound assignment operation.
ArrayIndex	Indexes an item into a one-dimensional array.
ArrayLength	Gets the length of a one-dimensional array.
* *Assign*	Performs an assignment operation.
* *Block*	A block of expressions.
Call	Performs a method call.
Coalesce	Performs a null coalescing operation.
Conditional	Performs a conditional operation. C# 3.0: *condition ? expression : expression* Visual Basic 2008: *IF(condition, expression, expression)*
Constant	Expression that has a constant value.
Convert	Performs a cast or conversion operation. If the operation is a numeric conversion, and if the converted value does not fit the target type, it overflows silently.
ConvertChecked	Performs a cast or conversion operation. If the operation is a numeric conversion, and if the converted value does not fit the target type, an exception is thrown.
* *DebugInfo*	Debugging information.

ExpressionType	Description
* Decrement	Performs a unary decrement operation. The object should not be modified in place.
* Default	Default value.
Divide	Performs an arithmetic division.
* DivideAssign	Performs a division compound assignment.
* Dynamic	Dynamic operation.
Equal	Performs an equality comparison.
ExclusiveOr	Performs a bitwise or logical XOR operation.
* ExclusiveOrAssign	Performs a bitwise or logical XOR compound assignment operation.
* Extension	An extension expression.
* Goto	A "go to" expression, such as goto Label in C#.
GreaterThan	Performs a "greater than" numeric comparison.
GreaterThanOrEqual	Performs a "greater than or equal to" numeric comparison.
* Increment	Performs a unary increment operation. The object should not be modified in place.
* Index	An index operation or an operation that accesses a property that takes arguments.
Invoke	Applies a delegate or lambda expression to a list of argument expressions.
* IsFalse	A false condition value.
* IsTrue	A true condition value.
* Label	A label (used for Goto).
Lambda	Lambda expression.
LeftShift	Performs a bitwise left-shift operation.
* LeftShiftAssign	Performs a bitwise left-shift compound assignment operation.
LessThan	Performs a "less than" numeric comparison.
LessThanOrEqual	Performs a "less than or equal to" numeric comparison.
ListInit	Creates a new IEnumerable object, initializing it from a list of elements.
* Loop	A loop, such as for or while.
MemberAccess	Reads from a field or property.
MemberInit	Creates a new object, initializing one or more of its members.
Modulo	Performs an arithmetic remainder operation.
* ModuloAssign	Performs an arithmetic remainder compound assignment operation.
Multiply	Performs an arithmetic multiplication without overflow checking.
* MultiplyAssign	Performs a multiplication compound assignment operation without overflow checking.
* MultiplyAssignChecked	Performs a multiplication compound assignment operation with overflow checking.

ExpressionType	Description
MultiplyChecked	Performs an arithmetic multiplication with overflow checking.
Negate	Performs an arithmetic negation operation without overflow checking.
NegateChecked	Performs an arithmetic negation operation with overflow checking.
New	Calls a constructor to create a new object.
NewArrayBounds	Creates a new array where the bounds for each dimension are specified.
NewArrayInit	Creates a new one-dimensional array, initializing it from a list of elements.
Not	Performs a bitwise or logical complement operation.
NotEqual	Performs an inequality comparison.
OnesComplement	Performs a ones complement operation.
Or	Performs a bitwise or logical OR operation.
* *OrAssign*	Performs a bitwise or logical OR compound assignment operation.
OrElse	Performs a short-circuit conditional OR operation.
Parameter	References a parameter defined in the context of the expression.
* *PostDecrementAssign*	Performs a unary postfix decrement operation. The object should be modified in place.
* *PostIncrementAssign*	Performs a unary postfix increment operation. The object should be modified in place.
Power	Raises a number to a power.
* *PowerAssign*	A compound assignment operation that raises a number to a power.
* *PreDecrementAssign*	Performs a unary prefix decrement operation. The object should be modified in place.
* *PreIncrementAssign*	Performs a unary prefix increment operation. The object should be modified in place.
Quote	Expression that has a constant value of type *Expression*. A *Quote* node can contain references to parameters defined in the context of the expression it represents.
RightShift	Performs a bitwise right-shift operation.
* *RightShiftAssign*	Performs a bitwise right-shift compound assignment operation.
* *RuntimeVariables*	A list of run-time variables.
Subtract	Performs an arithmetic subtraction without overflow checking.
* *SubtractAssign*	Performs a subtraction compound assignment without overflow checking.
* *SubtractAssignChecked*	Performs a subtraction compound assignment with overflow checking.
SubtractChecked	Performs an arithmetic subtraction with overflow checking.
* *Switch*	A switch operation, such as switch in C#.
* *Throw*	An operation that throws an exception.
* *Try*	A try-catch expression.

ExpressionType	Description
TypeAs	Provides an explicit reference or boxing conversion where null is supplied if the conversion fails.
* *TypeEqual*	Performs an exact type test.
TypeIs	Performs a type test.
UnaryPlus	Performs a unary plus operation. The result of a predefined unary plus operation is simply the value of the operand, but user-defined implementations might have nontrivial results.
* *Unbox*	Performs an unbox value type operation.

Classes Derived from *Expression*

Table 14-2 illustrates all the node types that can be part of an expression tree. The table has three columns, as described in the following list:

- **Type** This column shows the name of the class that implements the node of the element types listed in the second column. That class is defined in the *System.Linq.Expressions* namespace of the *System.Core* assembly and inherits the *Expression* abstract class. Note that types preceded by an asterisk (*) cannot be directly used by a C# expression body and are required to support dynamic languages.

- **NodeType** This column lists the values of the *ExpressionType* enumeration that are supported by the *NodeType* property of the class specified in the first column, Type. Some types implement only one *ExpressionType* (such as *ConstantExpression*), although others implement many different elements (such as *BinaryExpression*).

- **Expression Properties** This column is a list of the properties of type *Expressions* that the type exposes. These properties have to be iterated to continue the visit of a tree to the nodes related to the instance of the visited *Type*.

TABLE 14-2 Classes Derived from *Expression*

Type	NodeType	Expression Properties
BinaryExpression	*Add; AddAssign; AddAssignChecked; AddChecked; And; AndAlso; AndAssign; Assign; ArrayIndex; Coalesce; Divide; DivideAssign; Equal; ExclusiveOr; ExclusiveOrAssign; GreaterThan; GreaterThanOrEqual; LeftShift; LeftShiftAssign; LessThan; LessThanOrEqual; Modulo; ModuloAssign; Multiply; MultiplyAssign; MultiplyAssignChecked; MultiplyChecked; NotEqual; Or; OrAssign; OrElse; Power; PowerAssign; RightShift; RightShiftAssign; Subtract; SubtractAssign; SubtractAssignChecked; SubtractChecked*	*Left* *Right*
* *BlockExpression*	*Block*	

Type	NodeType	Expression Properties
ConditionalExpression	*Conditional*	*Test*
		IfTrue
		IfFalse
ConstantExpression	*Constant*	*-*
* DebugInfoExpression	*DebugInfo*	
* DefaultExpression	*Default*	
* DynamicExpression	*Dynamic*	
Expression<T> **Note: derives from** **LambdaExpression**	*Lambda*	*Body* *Parameters*
* GotoExpression	*Goto*	
* IndexExpression	*Index*	
InvocationExpression	*Invoke*	*Expression* *Arguments*
* LabelExpression	*Label*	
LambdaExpression	*Lambda*	*Body* *Parameters*
ListInitExpression	*ListInit*	*NewExpression*
* LoopExpression	*Loop*	
MemberExpression	*MemberAccess*	*Expression*
MemberInitExpression	*MemberInit*	*NewExpression*
MethodCallExpression	*Call*	*Object Arguments*
NewArrayExpression	*NewArrayBounds; NewArrayInit*	*Expressions*
NewExpression	*New*	*Arguments*
ParameterExpression	*Parameter*	*-*
* RuntimeVariablesExpression	*RuntimeVariables*	
* SwitchExpression	*Switch*	
* TryExpression	*Try*	
TypeBinaryExpression	*TypeIs*	*Expression*
UnaryExpression	*ArrayLength; Convert; ConvertChecked; Decrement; Increment; IsFalse; IsTrue; Negate; NegateChecked; Not; OnesComplement; PostDecrementAssign; PostIncrementAssign; PreDecrementAssign; PreIncrementAssign; Quote; TypeAs; Throw; UnaryPlus; Unbox*	*Operand*

Practical Nodes Guide

The previous two tables provide a quick reference to the node types and *Expression* implementation classes that you can include in an expression tree. For more detailed explanations, see the product documentation located at *http://msdn.microsoft.com/library /system.linq.expressions.expression.aspx*. This book provides only a guided tour of the most common and important nodes of an expression tree, introducing you to the skills necessary to handle and manipulate an expression tree. This tour uses the following expression, which you already saw in Figure 14-9:

```
Expression<Func<int, int>> Formula =
    (n) => 1 + Double(n * (n % 2 == 0 ? -1 : 1));
```

> **Note** If you want a tool that you can use to see a hierarchical representation of an expression tree from inside a Microsoft Visual Studio debugger or in your own application, take a look at the *LinqSamples\ExpressionTreeVisualizer* project that is part of the sample code included with Microsoft Visual Studio 2008. Look for a CSharpSamples.zip package in the Samples\1033 subdirectory under the Visual Studio 2008 installation folder.

LambdaExpression and *ParameterExpression*

Earlier, you saw that the first node of any expression tree generated from the C# lambda expression syntax is an instance of *LambdaExpression*. In reality, it is an instance of a constructed *Expression<T>* type derived from *LambdaExpression*, and does not add other members of type *Expression* to those inherited from the base *LambdaExpression* class. A *LambdaExpression* node has two properties that are of particular interest for visiting an expression tree:

```
public class LambdaExpression : Expression {
    // Other code omitted...
    public Expression Body { get; }
    public ReadOnlyCollection<ParameterExpression> Parameters { get; }
}
```

Body is the first node of the expression defined in the lambda expression. *Parameters* is a collection of *ParameterExpression*, which is derived from *Expression* and has the special purpose of referencing a parameter defined in the context of the lambda expression. These same nodes will be referenced again inside the expression tree whenever the parameter is used as an argument for an operation:

```
public class ParameterExpression : Expression {
    // Other code omitted...
    public string Name { get; }
}
```

The *ParameterExpression* class does not contain references to other nodes. It is always a leaf in an expression tree. Knowing the parameters of a lambda expression is necessary for building the corresponding delegate when the expression tree is compiled because the parameters specify the number and types of required arguments.

BinaryExpression

In the example, the *Body* property of the *LambdaExpression* references a *BinaryExpression* instance having a *NodeType* property equal to *Add*. This node defines the sum between the constant *1* and the result of a call to *Double*. The *BinaryExpression* class has the following public properties that are interesting for visiting an expression tree:

```
public class BinaryExpression : Expression {
    // Other code omitted...

    public LambdaExpression Conversion { get; }
    public bool IsLifted { get; }
    public bool IsLiftedToNull { get; }
    public override bool CanReduce { get; }

    public Expression Left { get; }
    public MethodInfo Method { get; }
    public Expression Right { get; }
}
```

Any binary operator has two child nodes, pointed to by the *Left* and *Right* properties of the *BinaryExpression* instance. Another important property is *Method*, which points to a custom implementation of the operator. (Whenever *Method* is null, the predefined operator is used.) In our sample expression tree (shown in Figure 14-9 earlier in the chapter), the *Left* property points to the constant of *1* and the *Right* property references the *Double* method call through an instance of the *MethodCallExpression* class.

> **Note** Refer to the product documentation for a deeper explanation of *Conversion*, *CanReduce*, *IsLifted*, and *IsLiftedToNull*. These properties are useful only for some node types and in some scenarios.

ConstantExpression

ConstantExpression instances are always leaves in the expression tree. This type provides only a *Value* property and exposes no property that can point to child nodes:

```
public sealed class ConstantExpression : Expression {
    // Other code omitted...
    public object Value { get; }
}
```

The C# compiler creates a single *ConstantExpression* whenever an expression made by constants can be resolved at compile time. For example, the expression *8 / 2 + 1* produces a single *ConstantExpression* with a value of *5*.

MethodCallExpression

The call to the *Double* static method of our expression tree is represented by an instance of *MethodCallExpression*:

```
public sealed class MethodCallExpression : Expression {
    // Other code omitted...
    public ReadOnlyCollection<Expression> Arguments { get; }
    public MethodInfo Method { get; }
    public Expression Object { get; }
}
```

This class has a *Method* property pointing to the code to execute. The *Object* property represents the instance to be used as the *this* parameter and a collection of *Arguments* to be passed for the rest of the parameters to the called method.

In this example, the remaining part of the expression tree is stored in *Argument[0]*. In fact, the argument for *Double* is another expression tree that has a *Multiplication* as its first node:

```
Double(n * (n % 2 == 0 ? -1 : 1))
```

Keep in mind that the *Object* property of the *MethodCallExpression* class returns an *Expression*, because the instance to be used as the *this* parameter might also be the result of an expression, as in the following code:

```
string[] s = { "Linq", "Programming", "Book" };
Expression<Func<int,string>> Get = (i) => s[i].ToUpper();
```

In the preceding *Get* expression, the corresponding instance of *MethodCallExpression* references a *MethodInfo* object wrapping the *String.ToUpper* method in its *Method* property. The instance on which that method operates is defined by the expression *s[i]* stored in the *Object* property—or an equivalent expression if *s* is a local variable (see the following Note). As always, any *Expression* might have a whole subtree to evaluate before obtaining the desired value.

> **Note** A local variable used in a lambda expression that is converted into an expression tree needs to reference a member of the object that is automatically generated by the compiler when an anonymous delegate is compiled. Because the lambda expression is an anonymous delegate, the string representation of a local variable (like *s* in our example) appears with a name that might seem different from the local variable specified in the original expression. That is why we used the language "an equivalent expression if *s* is a local variable" in the paragraph that precedes this note.

ConditionalExpression

The last type to consider in the example expression tree is *ConditionalExpression*. C# has a conditional expression through the *? :* syntax, although Visual Basic uses the new *IF()*

statement (which is different from the legacy *IIF()* function). The *Test* expression must be evaluated. If it is true, only the *IfTrue* expression is evaluated and returned as the result; otherwise, only the *IfFalse* expression is evaluated and returned as the result:

```
public sealed class ConditionalExpression : Expression {
    // Other code omitted...
    public Expression IfFalse { get; }
    public Expression IfTrue { get; }
    public Expression Test { get; }
}
```

Navigating an expression tree containing a *Conditional* node requires that you consider all three subtrees that can be tied to that operator.

InvocationExpression

Another important node type is *InvocationExpression*, which is created when a node *ExpressionType.Invoke* is requested. With this node, you can reference an external expression tree. The public properties are pretty simple:

```
public sealed class InvocationExpression : Expression {
    // Other code omitted...
    public ReadOnlyCollection<Expression> Arguments { get; }
    public Expression Expression { get; }
}
```

There is an *Expression* property with a collection of *Arguments*. When an expression tree contains such a node, you have a tree that is nested in another tree. However, the trees are still separate, because moving from one to another requires a remapping of the expression tree parameters. To combine two expression trees, you need to call the *Expression.Invoke* method. You will see an example of using this method later in this chapter, in the "Combining Existing Expression Trees" section.

Visiting an Expression Tree

In the first part of this chapter, you examined the content of an expression tree, assuming that you knew the type of the nodes that the tree contains. In the real world, you will probably need to analyze and manipulate an expression tree without knowing its content in advance. You need to be able to adapt to any expression tree, looking for particular nodes, inserting new conditions, and altering the expression tree. To do any of these operations, you need to know how to *visit* an expression tree, enumerating all its nodes just as you would if you had a linear collection of nodes.

Visiting a tree is a well-covered topic, and you can use several algorithms to do it. As mentioned earlier, a peculiarity of expression trees is that they have several types of nodes, each one with different properties that affect the navigation of the tree. This peculiarity requires that, to be able to visit all the nodes of the tree, you must use an algorithm that knows the structure of all node types.

To begin, consider the pattern used by inheriting the *ExpressionVisitor* class available in the *System.Linq.Expressions* namespace since .NET Framework 4.

> **Note** In .NET Framework 3.5, a similar class was published in the product documentation (specifically, in the "How to: Implement an Expression Tree Visitor" topic in the Online Help) and further developed by Matt Warren on his blog (*http://blogs.msdn.com/mattwar/archive/2007/07/31 /linq-building-an-iqueryable-provider-part-ii.aspx*). You can refer to that class (included in sample code) if you are targeting .NET Framework 3.5.

The pattern consists of an abstract class, *ExpressionVisitor*, that exposes a method to visit a node and calls itself recursively for all child nodes, visiting the entire tree in this way. The specialization of this class implements particular actions as a result of the nodes' analysis. The customized *ExpressionVisitor* class used in Listing 14-11 has a virtual method called *Visit*, which receives an *Expression* and returns an *Expression*. Later, you will see how to use the return value to create a new expression tree that visits an existing one. The *Visit* method simply analyzes the top-level node of the tree and dispatches it to a more specialized method, according to the node type it finds. Despite its length, the *Visit* method shown in Listing 14-11 is pretty simple.

> ### *ExpressionVisitor* Differences Between .NET Framework 4 and .NET Framework 3.5
>
> The *ExpressionVisitor* class used in the Listings in this chapter is an implementation available in the sample code. Since .NET Framework 4, an *ExpressionVisitor* class is available in the *System.Core* assembly, in the *System.Linq.Expressions* namespace. The .NET Framework 4 implementation of *ExpressionVisitor* is functionally equivalent to the custom implementation code shown in this chapter, and you can derive from both implementations in the same way. The custom implementation shown in Listing 14-11 is used because the .NET Framework 4 code is more complex, and is based on virtual methods available in the classes that represent the nodes of the expression tree. For educational purposes, this book uses the custom implementation from .NET Framework 3.5 because it is both simpler to understand and functionally equivalent.

LISTING 14-11 *Visit* method in the *ExpressionVisitor* class

```
public abstract class ExpressionVisitor {
    protected ExpressionVisitor() {}

    protected virtual Expression Visit(Expression exp) {
        if (exp == null)
            return exp;
        switch (exp.NodeType) {
            case ExpressionType.Negate:
            case ExpressionType.NegateChecked:
            case ExpressionType.Not:
            case ExpressionType.Convert:
            case ExpressionType.ConvertChecked:
            case ExpressionType.ArrayLength:
            case ExpressionType.Quote:
            case ExpressionType.TypeAs:
            case ExpressionType.UnaryPlus:
                return this.VisitUnary((UnaryExpression) exp);
            case ExpressionType.Add:
            case ExpressionType.AddChecked:
            case ExpressionType.Subtract:
            case ExpressionType.SubtractChecked:
            case ExpressionType.Multiply:
            case ExpressionType.MultiplyChecked:
            case ExpressionType.Divide:
            case ExpressionType.Modulo:
            case ExpressionType.And:
            case ExpressionType.AndAlso:
            case ExpressionType.Or:
            case ExpressionType.OrElse:
            case ExpressionType.LessThan:
            case ExpressionType.LessThanOrEqual:
            case ExpressionType.GreaterThan:
            case ExpressionType.GreaterThanOrEqual:
            case ExpressionType.Equal:
            case ExpressionType.NotEqual:
            case ExpressionType.Coalesce:
            case ExpressionType.ArrayIndex:
            case ExpressionType.RightShift:
            case ExpressionType.LeftShift:
            case ExpressionType.ExclusiveOr:
            case ExpressionType.Power:
                return this.VisitBinary((BinaryExpression) exp);
            case ExpressionType.TypeIs:
                return this.VisitTypeIs((TypeBinaryExpression) exp);
            case ExpressionType.Conditional:
                return this.VisitConditional((ConditionalExpression) exp);
            case ExpressionType.Constant:
                return this.VisitConstant((ConstantExpression) exp);
            case ExpressionType.Parameter:
                return this.VisitParameter((ParameterExpression) exp);
            case ExpressionType.MemberAccess:
                return this.VisitMemberAccess((MemberExpression) exp);
```

```
                    case ExpressionType.Call:
                        return this.VisitMethodCall((MethodCallExpression) exp);
                    case ExpressionType.Lambda:
                        return this.VisitLambda((LambdaExpression) exp);
                    case ExpressionType.New:
                        return this.VisitNew((NewExpression) exp);
                    case ExpressionType.NewArrayInit:
                    case ExpressionType.NewArrayBounds:
                        return this.VisitNewArray((NewArrayExpression) exp);
                    case ExpressionType.Invoke:
                        return this.VisitInvocation((InvocationExpression) exp);
                    case ExpressionType.MemberInit:
                        return this.VisitMemberInit((MemberInitExpression) exp);
                    case ExpressionType.ListInit:
                        return this.VisitListInit((ListInitExpression) exp);
                    default:
                        throw new Exception(
                                    string.Format(
                                        "Unhandled expression type: '{0}'",
                                        exp.NodeType));
                }
            }
            // Other code omitted...
    }
```

As you can see, there is a specific method for visiting each type of node, based on the available properties provided by the corresponding *Expression*-derived class. As described in the sidebar "*ExpressionVisitor* Differences Between .NET Framework 4 and .NET Framework 3.5," in .NET Framework 4, a virtual method (*VisitExtension*) of the base *Expression* class is called for each node of the expression tree. In both cases, for each node type, the code might have to visit properties that reference other expressions, calling their *Visit* method recursively. In Listing 14-12, you can see sample code for the *VisitBinary* method: it calls *Visit* on the *Left*, *Right*, and *Conversion* properties. If any of these internal nodes have been changed during the visit, the code returns a new *BinaryExpression* instance with the new properties; otherwise, the original node is returned.

Note Remember, node instances are immutable after their creation. The call to *Visit* returns a node different from the one passed as the argument only as a result of a change at any level of the visited subtree. For this reason, we have to create a new node storing the new subtree.

LISTING 14-12 *VisitBinary* method in the *ExpressionVisitor* class

```
public abstract class ExpressionVisitor {
    protected virtual Expression VisitBinary(BinaryExpression b) {
        Expression left = this.Visit(b.Left);
        Expression right = this.Visit(b.Right);
        Expression conversion = this.Visit(b.Conversion);
        if (left != b.Left || right != b.Right
            || conversion != b.Conversion) {
            if (b.NodeType == ExpressionType.Coalesce
                && b.Conversion != null)
                return Expression.Coalesce(
                            left, right,
                            conversion as LambdaExpression);
            else
                return Expression.MakeBinary(
                            b.NodeType,
                            left, right,
                            b.IsLiftedToNull, b.Method);
        }
        return b;
    }
    // Other code omitted...
}
```

Leaf nodes are those that cannot have other child nodes. They do not require another instance of *Visit* or code to check whether an internal node has been changed. This is the case for *VisitConstant* and *VisitParameter*, as you can see in Listing 14-13.

LISTING 14-13 *VisitConstant* and *VisitParameter* methods in the *ExpressionVisitor* class

```
public abstract class ExpressionVisitor {
    protected virtual Expression VisitConstant(ConstantExpression c) {
        return c;
    }

    protected virtual Expression VisitParameter(ParameterExpression p) {
        return p;
    }
    // Other code omitted...
}
```

To complete the tree navigation, some node types make it necessary to visit a list of expressions, such as the list of arguments in the case of the *MethodCallExpression* and *InvocationExpression* nodes, as you can see in Listing 14-14. The *VisitExpressionList* implementation iterates the collection of expressions and calls *Visit* for each node. (The source code for *VisitExpressionList* is not included here but is part of this book's sample code.)

LISTING 14-14 *VisitMethodCall* and *VisitInvocation* methods in the *ExpressionVisitor* class

```
public abstract class ExpressionVisitor {
    protected virtual Expression VisitMethodCall(MethodCallExpression m) {
        Expression obj = this.Visit(m.Object);
        IEnumerable<Expression> args =
                this.VisitExpressionList(m.Arguments);
        if (obj != m.Object || args != m.Arguments) {
            return Expression.Call(obj, m.Method, args);
        }
        return m;
    }
    protected virtual Expression VisitInvocation(InvocationExpression iv) {
        IEnumerable<Expression> args =
                this.VisitExpressionList(iv.Arguments);
        Expression expr = this.Visit(iv.Expression);
        if (args != iv.Arguments || expr != iv.Expression) {
            return Expression.Invoke(expr, args);
        }
        return iv;
    }
    // Other code omitted...
}
```

Typically, you should always start from a lambda expression node, which is visited by the *VisitLambda* method that simply pays a visit to its *Body* property. The source code for *VisitLambda* is shown in Listing 14-15.

LISTING 14-15 *VisitLambda* method in the *ExpressionVisitor* class

```
public abstract class ExpressionVisitor {
    protected virtual Expression VisitLambda(LambdaExpression lambda) {
        Expression body = this.Visit(lambda.Body);
        if (body != lambda.Body) {
            return Expression.Lambda(lambda.Type, body, lambda.Parameters);
        }
        return lambda;
    }
    // Other code omitted...
}
```

The other node types are not discussed in this chapter because the logic should be clear enough at this point. Even though all the nodes derive from a common base class (*Expression*), they must be evaluated type by type to be able to make a complete visit of an expression tree. The *ExpressionVisitor* class is an abstract class that implements a *Visit* algorithm that can be specialized in a derived class for many purposes, such as the following:

■ To traverse the entire tree to translate the expression tree into another form. This is what the LINQ to SQL provider does to convert an in-memory expression tree into a corresponding SQL query.

■ To modify the properties of a node in an expression tree. Because all the nodes are immutable, this requires replacing the modified node and all its parent nodes. The replacement of parent nodes is automatically done by the *ExpressionVisitor* implementation that was just introduced.

■ To add and remove nodes from a tree or combine different expression trees. These are variations of the tree modification presented in the preceding bullet point.

> **Note** The methods specialized for each type of node return a new node if any of the child nodes have been changed. Classes derived from *ExpressionVisitor* can simply specialize the behavior for a single type of node, returning a new node instance cloned from the existing one but with some differences in one or more of its properties. All the upper-level nodes referencing the new subtree are automatically built by the standard implementation of *ExpressionVisitor*.

Here is an example of a simple derived class that displays an expression tree's content without modifying it. To do that, it intercepts the *Visit* call and displays the content of each node, indenting the node according to its depth level in the tree. Listing 14-16 shows the code for such an implementation.

LISTING 14-16 *DisplayVisitor* specialization of the *ExpressionVisitor* class

```
class DisplayVisitor : ExpressionVisitor {
    private int level = 0;
    protected override Expression Visit(Expression exp) {
        if (exp != null) {
            for (int i = 0; i < level; i++) {
                Console.Write("   ");
            }
            Console.WriteLine( "{0}  -  {1}",
                exp.NodeType, exp.GetType().Name );
        }
        level++;
        Expression result = base.Visit(exp);
        level--;
        return result;
    }

    public void Display(Expression exp) {
        Console.WriteLine("===== DisplayVisitor.Display =====");
        this.Visit(exp);
    }
}
```

The code in Listing 14-17 tests the *DisplayVisitor* class, using the same expression represented in Figure 14-9.

LISTING 14-17 Code to test the *DisplayVisitor* class

```
static int Double(int n) {
    return n * 2;
}

static void DemoExpressionVisitor() {
    Expression<Func<int, int>> Formula =
        (n) => 1 + Double(n * (n % 2 == 0 ? -1 : 1));
    Console.WriteLine( Formula.ToString() );
    DisplayVisitor visitor = new DisplayVisitor();
    visitor.Display(Formula);
}
```

Here is the output produced by executing the *DemoExpressionVisitor* method in Listing 14-17:

```
n => (1 + Double((n * IIF(((n % 2) == 0), -1, 1))))
===== DisplayVisitor.Display =====
Lambda   -   Expression`1
  Add   -   SimpleBinaryExpression
     Constant   -   ConstantExpression
     Call   -   MethodCallExpressionN
        Multiply   -   SimpleBinaryExpression
           Parameter   -   PrimitiveParameterExpression`1
           Conditional   -   FullConditionalExpression
              Equal   -   LogicalBinaryExpression
                 Modulo   -   SimpleBinaryExpression
                    Parameter   -   PrimitiveParameterExpression`1
                    Constant   -   ConstantExpression
                 Constant   -   ConstantExpression
              Constant   -   ConstantExpression
              Constant   -   ConstantExpression
  Parameter   -   PrimitiveParameterExpression`1
```

A further specialization of the various base class methods could support output of more detailed information for each node. You will see a more complex specialization of the *ExpressionVisitor* to manipulate the expression tree in the section "Dynamically Building an Expression Tree" later in this chapter.

You have seen one implementation for visiting an expression tree. This implementation will probably be used most often because it is based on a class of the .NET Framework and on a classic object-oriented approach. However, other implementations might be more appropriate. For example, if you want to frequently change a small piece of logic in expression tree analysis but do not want to (or cannot) create a derived class for each case, you might consider an approach based more on "functional-style" programming, illustrated in the following sidebar "An Alternative Visitor Pattern." The key point here is that you are not forced to use a specific pattern to visit an expression tree.

An Alternative Visitor Pattern

As stated earlier, you can implement an algorithm to visit an expression tree in many ways. We cannot show all the possible alternatives, but want to introduce another implementation that differs from the previous approach, both for educational purposes and because it might be preferable in some circumstances.

In Listing 14-18, you can see an excerpt of the source code for the *Visit* lambda expression that has been published by Jomo Fisher on his blog "Dealing with Linq's Immutable Expression Trees" at *http://blogs.msdn.com/jomo_fisher/archive/2007/05/23/dealing-with-linq-s-immutable-expression-trees.aspx*.

LISTING 14-18 Implementation of an *Expression* visitor algorithm through a lambda expression

```
public static class ExprOp {
    static public Func<Expression, Expression> Visit =
        FuncOp.Create<Expression, Expression>(
            (self, expr) => {
            if (expr == null) {
                return expr;
            }
            switch (expr.NodeType) {
                case ExpressionType.Coalesce:
                    var c = (BinaryExpression) expr;
                    var left = self(c.Left);
                    var right = self(c.Right);
                    var conv = self(c.Conversion);
                    return (left == c.Left
                            && right == c.Right
                            && conv == c.Conversion)
                            ? expr
                            : Expression.Coalesce(
                                    left,
                                    right,
                                    (LambdaExpression) conv);
                case ExpressionType.Conditional:
                    var ce = (ConditionalExpression) expr;
                    var t = self(ce.Test);
                    var it = self(ce.IfTrue);
                    var @if = self(ce.IfFalse);
                    return (t == ce.Test
                            && it == ce.IfTrue
                            && @if == ce.IfFalse)
                        ? expr
                        : Expression.Condition(t, it, @if);
                // Code for other cases has been omitted
                // handled cases are:
                //   ExpressionType.TypeIs
```

```
//    ExpressionType.MemberAccess
//    ExpressionType.Call
//    ExpressionType.Lambda
//    ExpressionType.New
//    ExpressionType.NewArrayInit
//    ExpressionType.NewArrayBounds
//    ExpressionType.Invoke
//    ExpressionType.MemberInit
//    ExpressionType.ListInit
// There is no default handling, thus all the other
// node types are not handled by this switch statement
// but are intercepted by the if statements after
// the switch statement
}
if (expr.IsBinary()) {
    var b = (BinaryExpression) expr;
    var left = self(b.Left);
    var right = self(b.Right);
    return (left == b.Left && right == b.Right)
            ? expr
            : Expression.MakeBinary(
                    expr.NodeType,
                    left,
                    right);
}
else if (expr.IsUnary()) {
    var u = (UnaryExpression) expr;
    var op = self(u.Operand);
    return (u.Operand == op)
            ? expr
            : Expression.MakeUnary(
                    u.NodeType,
                    op,
                    expr.Type);
}
return expr;
    }
);
public static bool IsBinary(this Expression expr) {
    return expr is BinaryExpression;
}
public static bool IsUnary(this Expression expr) {
    return expr is UnaryExpression;
}
// Other code omitted...
}
```

You can see some similarities between this approach and the approach used with the *ExpressionVisitor* class shown in Listing 14-11. The *Visit* lambda expression iterates the tree nodes using a recursive approach. One major difference is that instead of having a *switch* statement with a *case* for each node type, this visitor implementation handles the two classes *BinaryExpression* and *UnaryExpression* separately. These classes enclose the majority of node types; the others should be implemented in the previous *switch* statement. We commented out some *case* statements in the *switch* statement because we were not interested in further navigating those corresponding nodes.

> **Note** Comparing the type of the expression node with an *is* condition, as the *IsBinary* and *IsUnary* methods do, results in worse performance than a *switch* condition. Implementing them as done in the *ExpressionVisitor* class shown in Listing 14-11 might increase the execution time of the entire visit by up to 10 percent. (The exact number strictly depends on the nodes contained in the visited expression tree.)
>
> However, this approach is immune from the addition of new node types in a future release of these classes because they will not break existing code. This algorithm will not visit subtrees originating from unsupported nodes, and it will handle the new nodes itself as leaf nodes, but the tree navigation will be completed without errors. For example, near the end of the .NET Framework 3.5 development cycle, two node types were added: *Power* (for *BinaryExpression*) and *UnaryPlus* (for *UnaryExpression*). These were handled in Listing 14-11, but they were not handled in the online help original source code included with the release-to-market (RTM) version of .NET Framework 3.5. Listing 14-18 does not have to be fixed if a new node type is added to a future release of the .NET Framework.
>
> You should also consider that, beginning with .NET Framework 4, the *ExpressionVisitor* class is part of the .NET Framework Base Class Library, so it will be updated to support new node types that might be added to the .NET Framework in the future. Thus, deriving from *ExpressionVisitor* class is the suggested way to implement your own pattern: it is faster and it is more supported.

A more interesting characteristic of the *Visit* lambda expression in Listing 14-18 is that you do not have to define a derived class to visit (and possibly modify) an expression tree. You can use lambda expressions to "inject" code inside the visitor algorithm, as shown in Listing 14-19, to visit the expression tree represented in Figure 14-9 using the lambda expression approach.

LISTING 14-19 Expression tree visit based on a lambda expression approach

```
static void DemoVisitLambda() {
    Expression<Func<int, int>> Formula =
        (n) => 1 + Double(n * (n % 2 == 0 ? -1 : 1));
    Console.WriteLine(Formula.ToString());

    int level = 0;
    var visitFormula = ExprOp.Visit.Chain(
        (self, last, expr) => {
```

```
        if (expr != null) {
            for (int i = 0; i < level; i++) {
                Console.Write("    ");
            }
            Console.WriteLine(
                "{0}  -  {1}",
                expr.NodeType,
                expr.GetType().Name);
        }
        level++;
        var result = last(expr);
        level--;
        return result;
    }
);

    visitFormula(Formula);
}
```

Each node of the tree is processed by the lambda expression passed as a parameter to the *Chain* extension method applied to the *ExprOp.Visit* lambda expression. Each node is simply displayed with the right indentation and further processed to continue the visit by calling *last(expr)*, which calls the original *Visit* lambda expression on the *expr* node.

The output produced by the execution of the *DemoVisitLambda* method in Listing 14-19 is almost identical to the output obtained when executing the *DemoExpression-Visitor* method in Listing 14-17:

```
n => (1 + Double((n * IIF(((n % 2) == 0), -1, 1))))
===== DemoVisitLambda =====
Lambda  -  Expression`1
   Add  -  SimpleBinaryExpression
      Constant  -  ConstantExpression
      Call  -  MethodCallExpressionN
         Multiply  -  SimpleBinaryExpression
            Parameter  -  PrimitiveParameterExpression`1
            Conditional  -  FullConditionalExpression
               Equal  -  LogicalBinaryExpression
                  Modulo  -  SimpleBinaryExpression
                     Parameter  -  PrimitiveParameterExpression`1
                     Constant  -  ConstantExpression
                  Constant  -  ConstantExpression
               Constant  -  ConstantExpression
               Constant  -  ConstantExpression
```

The code here makes use of some helper extension methods contained in a static class named *FuncOp*. For example, the illusion of having a *self* keyword that calls the same lambda expression that you are defining is the result of some helper classes and methods that are part of the *FuncOp* static class.

> **More Info** For brevity, the source code of *FuncOp* is not included here. However, the methods are included in the book's sample code. You can find a detailed explanation of them in Jomo Fisher's blog post at *http://blogs.msdn.com/jomo_fisher/archive/2007/05/07 /visitor-revisitted-linq-function-composablity-and-chain-of-responsibility.aspx*.

The alternative *Visitor* approach just described is particularly useful when you have very little code to "inject" into a visitor because it does not require you to define a new class but rather to apply a simple transformation or examination on an existing expression tree. However, when the operation you want to perform becomes more complex, it is better to use the previous approach of inheriting from the *ExpressionVisitor* class because you would probably have to write a dedicated class anyway.

Dynamically Building an Expression Tree

The final part of this chapter explores how you can build an expression tree dynamically. First, you will see how the compiler performs this job when it encounters an assignment of an *Expression<T>* variable. Then you will see some typical operations you might want to perform when building an expression tree.

How the Compiler Generates an Expression Tree

One of the best ways to learn how to build an expression tree is by first understanding the way the compiler performs the job. Consider Listing 14-20, which uses the lambda expression *(n) => n + 1*. That gets assigned, respectively, to a *Func<int,int>* variable and an *Expression<Func<int,int>>* variable.

LISTING 14-20 Lambda expression and expression tree assignments

```
static void TreeConstruction() {
    Func<int, int> lambdaInc = (n) => n + 1;
    Expression<Func<int, int>> exprInc;
    exprInc = (n) => n + 1;

    Console.WriteLine("lambdaInc : {0}", lambdaInc.ToString());
    Console.WriteLine("exprInc   : {0}", exprInc.ToString());
}
```

Here is the output produced by executing the *TreeConstruction* method in Listing 14-20:

```
lambdaInc : System.Func`2[System.Int32,System.Int32]
exprInc   : n => (n + 1)
```

If you have read this chapter carefully up to this point, you should be ready to explain the difference between *lambdaInc* and *exprInc*. However, even a novice can understand that, for some reason, *lambdaInc* is a reference to an instance of a type probably constructed by the compiler (because we did not declare such a type), while *exprInc* is a structure that contains the definition of the expression in a readable form. But what happens under the hood when the compiler processes the *TreeConstruction* method? You will examine *lambdaInc* and *exprInc* separately.

The lambda expression is a syntax that is understood by the compiler to generate an anonymous delegate. You can declare *lambdaInc* as:

```
Func<int, int> lambdaInc = delegate(int n) { return n + 1; };
```

This is the shorter form for defining a delegate. Therefore, *lambdaInc* can be written as shown in Listing 14-21, producing a result equivalent to Listing 14-20 for *lambdaInc*. The only difference is that this time the compiler does not have to create a delegate.

LISTING 14-21 Lambda expression assignment

```
static int IncOperation(int n) {
    return n + 1;
}

static void LambdaDelegate() {
    Func<int, int> lambdaInc = new Func<int,int>(IncOperation);
    Console.WriteLine("lambdaInc : {0}", lambdaInc.ToString());
}
```

In the end, a lambda expression is a delegate that points to a piece of code in your program. Now, if you analyze what happens when the compiler interprets the *exprInc* assignment in Listing 14-20, you will discover that the generated code is not a delegate. The goal is to get the expression tree represented in Figure 14-10.

In Listing 14-22, you can see an *exprInc* assignment that is equivalent to the one generated by the compiler for the code in Listing 14-20, which generates the execution tree shown in Figure 14-10.

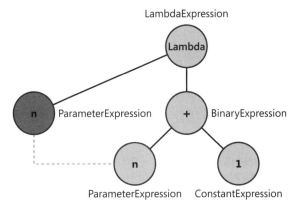

FIGURE 14-10 The expression tree for *(n) => n + 1*.

LISTING 14-22 Expression tree assignment

```
static void ExpressionAssignment() {
    Expression<Func<int, int>> exprInc;
    ConstantExpression constant = Expression.Constant(1, typeof(int));
    ParameterExpression parameter =
        Expression.Parameter(typeof(int), "n");
    BinaryExpression add = Expression.Add( parameter, constant );
    exprInc = Expression.Lambda<Func<int, int>>(
                add,
                new ParameterExpression[] { parameter } );
    Console.WriteLine("exprInc   : {0}", exprInc.ToString());
}
```

As you can see, the code builds the expression tree starting from leaves (constant *1* and parameter *n*) and then goes up to the *Add* operation, which is the *Body* of the lambda expression assigned to *exprInc*. That lambda needs an array of parameters made by the same nodes (in this case, there is only one) used as parameters in the expression tree. The dotted line between the two *ParameterExpression* nodes in Figure 14-10 indicates that those nodes are physically represented by the same instance of *ParameterExpression*. Notice that the bold-faced code in Listing 14-22 is the expansion of this single line of Listing 14-20:

```
exprInc = (n) => n + 1;
```

The lambda expression syntax is commonly called "syntactic sugar," because it is a language addition used only to make it "sweeter" for humans to use. However, when lambda expressions are transformed into expression trees by the compiler, this sugar becomes important to us much like it is for a hypoglycemic person! Unfortunately, when you have to create an expression tree dynamically, you probably need to build each node of the tree as shown in Listing 14-22.

Finally, remember that when you assign an *Expression<T>* variable with a lambda expression, the code that creates the expression tree is executed when the assignment is performed. Generated nodes are immutable, and the tree can be modified only by creating new nodes, as you saw earlier in this chapter.

Combining Existing Expression Trees

You have just seen how to create an expression tree starting from scratch. You can design the expression tree on a chart and then manually define all the nodes you need. However, often you might want to alter an existing tree, encapsulating it in a larger expression. As an example, consider the following lambda expression:

```
(b, h) => b * h
```

This expression can represent the formula to calculate the area of a rectangle. Imagine that you assign this lambda to an *Expression<T>* like this:

```
Expression<Func<double, double, double>> rectArea = (b, h) => b * h;
```

You end up with an expression tree like the one represented in Figure 14-11.

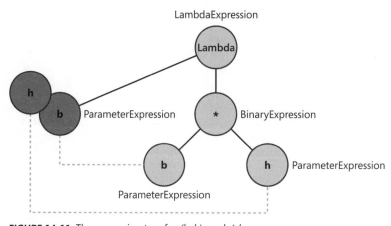

FIGURE 14-11 The expression tree for *(b, h) => b * h*.

If you want to calculate a volume, you might write the following lambda expression:

```
(x, y, z) => x * y * z
```

If you let the compiler generate an expression tree for this lambda, you obtain the tree represented in Figure 14-12.

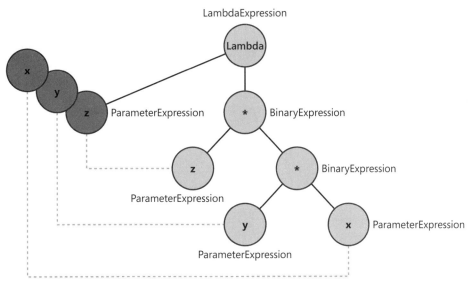

FIGURE 14-12 The expression tree for *(x, y, z) => x * y * z*.

However, you might want to recycle the *rectArea* formula in this way to get the same result:

```
(x, y, z) => rectArea(x, y) * z
```

Unfortunately, that code does not compile. But if it did compile, you would obtain the expression tree represented in Figure 14-13. Even though they produce the same result, it is clear that Figures 14-12 and 14-13 represent different expression trees.

The difference is important, because you might want to generate the expression trees represented in both Figures 14-12 and 14-13, starting from the *rectArea* expression tree represented in Figure 14-11. However, obtaining the result that "hides" the inner expression, as in Figure 14-12, is much harder than building the tree represented in Figure 14-13, because you need to completely rebuild the encapsulated tree to substitute its parameters with those of the resulting expression tree.

The simplest method incorporates the parameters of the encapsulated expression tree into those of the resulting expression tree, and then adds possible new parameters required by the added nodes. You can see this implementation in Listing 14-23. The node type that links to another expression tree is *Invoke*. To begin, add a *Multiply* node, and make a parameter mapping only from *x* to *b* and from *y* to *h*. As stated earlier, Figure 14-13 shows the resulting expression tree.

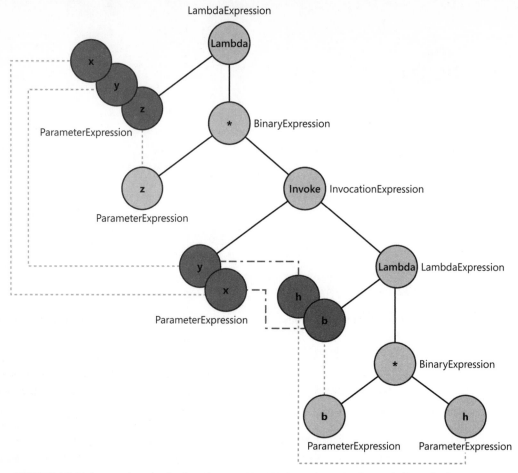

FIGURE 14-13 The expression tree for *(x, y, z) => rectArea(x, y) * z* where *rectArea = (b, h) => b * h.*

LISTING 14-23 Expression tree combination

```
static void TreeCombination() {
    Expression<Func<double, double, double>> rectArea = (b, h) => b * h;

    ParameterExpression x = Expression.Parameter(typeof(double), "x" );
    ParameterExpression y = Expression.Parameter(typeof(double), "y");
    ParameterExpression z = Expression.Parameter(typeof(double), "z");
    Expression area = Expression.Invoke(rectArea, new Expression[] { x, y });
    Expression multiply = Expression.Multiply(z, area);
    Expression<Func<double,double,double,double>> volume =
        Expression.Lambda<Func<double,double,double,double>>(
            multiply,
            new ParameterExpression[] { x, y, z });
```

```
    Console.WriteLine("Area    = {0}", rectArea.ToString());
    Console.WriteLine("Volume = {0}", volume.ToString());
    Console.WriteLine("Area value    = {0}", rectArea.Compile()(20, 10));
    Console.WriteLine("Volume value = {0}", volume.Compile()(20, 10, 8));
}
```

The output produced by executing the *TreeCombination* method in Listing 14-23 is:

```
Area    = (b, h) => (b * h)
Volume = (x, y, z) => (z * Invoke((b, h) => (b * h),x,y))
Area value    = 200
Volume value = 1600
```

> **Important** Be sure you understand the role of the *Invoke* node type. To help you do this, we pro-
> vided this example, which might seem useless by itself but is the simplest way to explain how to
> handle the *Invoke* node. In a complex expression tree, the node's behavior might appear obscure
> and be difficult to understand.

The second step is to obtain the expression tree shown in Figure 14-12, starting from the
one we obtained in Listing 14-23 and that corresponds to the graphical representation
shown in Figure 14-13. To perform the removal of *Invoke* and the parameter substitution,
you need to visit the expression tree using the classes derived by *ExpressionVisitor* shown in
Listing 14-24. The *RemoveInvokeVisitor<T>.VisitInvocation* method calls *ReplaceParameters-
Visitors.Visit* to replace lambda expression parameters in the visited expression tree. The
RemoveInvokeVisitor<T> class is the main *ExpressionVisitor*-derived class that you will use
to visit the tree and produce the required result.

LISTING 14-24 Classes to remove *Invoke* and make the parameter substitution

```
class RemoveInvokeVisitor<T> : ExpressionVisitor {
    private ReadOnlyCollection<ParameterExpression> lambdaParameters;

    public RemoveInvokeVisitor(
                ReadOnlyCollection<ParameterExpression> parameters) {
        this.lambdaParameters = parameters;
    }

    protected override Expression VisitInvocation(InvocationExpression iv) {
        var newPars = iv.Arguments;
        LambdaExpression lambda = (iv.Expression) as LambdaExpression;
        if (lambda != null) {
            var oldPars = lambda.Parameters;
            ReplaceParametersVisitors replace =
                new ReplaceParametersVisitors(oldPars, newPars);
            return this.Visit( replace.ReplaceVisit(lambda.Body) );
        }
```

```
            else {
                return base.VisitInvocation(iv);
            }
        }

    public Expression<T> RemoveInvokeVisit(Expression<T> exp) {
        return (Expression<T>) Visit(exp);
    }
}

class ReplaceParametersVisitors : ExpressionVisitor {
    private ReadOnlyCollection<Expression> newParameters;
    private ReadOnlyCollection<ParameterExpression> oldParameters;
    public ReplaceParametersVisitors(
        ReadOnlyCollection<ParameterExpression> oldParameters,
        ReadOnlyCollection<Expression> newParameters) {

        this.newParameters = newParameters;
        this.oldParameters = oldParameters;
    }

    protected override Expression  VisitParameter(ParameterExpression p) {
        if (oldParameters != null
            && newParameters != null) {
            if (oldParameters.Contains(p)) {
                return newParameters[oldParameters.IndexOf(p)];
            }
        }
        return base.VisitParameter(p);
    }

    public Expression ReplaceVisit(Expression exp) {
        return Visit(exp);
    }
}
```

This is similar to the code of the *TreeCombination* method you saw previously in Listing 14-23, but with some added lines. The excerpt in Listing 14-25 shows only the added lines, which eliminate the *Invoke* node from the expression tree and make the necessary parameter substitution.

LISTING 14-25 Expression tree combination

```
static void TreeCombination() {
    // Omitted code...
    var cleaner =
        new RemoveInvokeVisitor<
                Func<double, double, double, double>>(volume.Parameters);
    var cleanVolume= cleaner.RemoveInvokeVisit(volume);
    Console.WriteLine("CleanVolume = {0}", cleanVolume.ToString());
    Console.WriteLine("CleanVolume value = {0}", cleanVolume.Compile()(20, 10, 8));
}
```

The following is the complete output produced by the execution of the new *TreeCombination* method in Listing 14-25:

```
Area    = (b, h) => (b * h)
Volume = (x, y, z) => (z * Invoke((b, h) => (b * h),x,y))
Area value   = 200
Volume value = 1600
CleanVolume = (x, y, z) => (z * (x * y))
CleanVolume value = 1600
```

As you can see, the *CleanVolume* expression tree is in the form that is graphically represented in Figure 14-12.

Dynamic Composition of an Expression Tree

Often, you need to create an expression tree based on conditions that occur during program execution. For example, a user makes some choices through the user interface to filter data to be queried. You might want to translate this set of conditions to an expression tree that will be passed as the predicate of a *Where* condition to a LINQ query. In this case, you know that a predicate is a lambda expression that returns a *bool*. Having some constraints for the query expression to create can simplify your code because you can make some assumptions and base your code on that.

Here is an example that queries the currently running processes, using the *System.Diagnostic. Process* class. In Listing 14-26, you can see the structure of the query executed by the *Display* method, which receives a *filterExpression* expression tree to be used as a parameter for the *Where* condition. If that argument is passed as *null*, the code uses a dummy filter that always returns *true*.

LISTING 14-26 Query of current processes filtered by *filterExpression*

```
static void Display(Expression<Func<Process, bool>> filterExpression) {
    // If not defined, use a dummy filter
    if (filterExpression == null) {
        filterExpression = (p) => true;
    }

    Console.WriteLine("Filter : {0}", filterExpression.ToString());

    var query =
        Process.GetProcesses().AsQueryable()
        .Where(filterExpression)
        .Select(p => p.ProcessName);

    // Dump filtered processes
    foreach (var row in query) Console.WriteLine(row);
}
```

We wanted to call the *Display* method, defining its *filterExpression* parameter in a dynamic way. You can see in Listing 14-27 the *FilterSelection* method, which uses the *ProcessFilters* class (described shortly) to combine different filters. *ProcessFilters* includes an *Add* method that adds a condition that operates on a *System.Diagnostic.Process* property. It executes a specific comparison with a defined constant value. In this example, the interest is only in listing processes that are responding and that have a base priority greater than *8*. However, instead of hard coding filters such as these, you can build a user interface to provide more choices among properties, operators, and constant values before passing them to a more flexible *FilterSelection* method.

LISTING 14-27 Use of the *ProcessFilters* class

```
static Expression<Func<Process, bool>> FilterSelection() {
    ProcessFilters pf = new ProcessFilters();

    // Set dynamic filters
    pf.Add("Responding", ExpressionType.Equal, true );
    pf.Add("BasePriority", ExpressionType.GreaterThan, 8);

    return pf.GetExpression();
}

static void Main(string[] args) {
    Expression<Func<Process, bool>> filterExpression = FilterSelection();
    Display(filterExpression);
}
```

The very last operation involved in building the expression tree is creating the top-level node of the tree itself. In this case, the node corresponds to a lambda expression that contains the dynamically created expression tree (*bodyFilter*) and a single parameter of type *Process*. This lambda expression is created when the *GetExpression* method is called by the *FilterSelection* method, shown earlier.

Listing 14-28 shows the code for the *ProcessFilters* class used in the *FilterSelection* method.

LISTING 14-28 Implementation of the *ProcessFilters* class

```
public class ProcessFilters {
    ParameterExpression paramExp;
    Expression bodyFilter;
    public ProcessFilters() {
        paramExp = Expression.Parameter(typeof(Process), "p");
        bodyFilter = null;
    }

    // Create a lambda expression - we always have one single parameter
    // of type Process that is declared as paramExp by the constructor
```

```
public Expression<Func<Process, bool>> GetExpression() {
    if (bodyFilter == null) {
        return null;
    }
    Expression<Func<Process, bool>> filter;
    filter = Expression.Lambda<Func<Process, bool>>(
    bodyFilter,
    new ParameterExpression[] { paramExp });
    return filter;
}

// Add an AND with a filter on fieldName compared
// with comparisonValue with the required operator
public void Add( string fieldName,
                ExpressionType comparisonOperator,
                object comparisonValue) {

    switch (comparisonOperator) {
        case ExpressionType.Equal:
        case ExpressionType.NotEqual:
        case ExpressionType.LessThan:
        case ExpressionType.LessThanOrEqual:
        case ExpressionType.GreaterThan:
        case ExpressionType.GreaterThanOrEqual:
            // Supported operations
            break;
        default:
            throw new NotSupportedException(
                String.Format(
                    "Operator {0} is not supported in ProcessFilters.Add",
                    comparisonOperator.ToString()));
    } // end switch (check comparisonOperator)

    ConstantExpression comparisonConstant =
        Expression.Constant( comparisonValue,
                            comparisonValue.GetType());
    MemberExpression fieldAccess =
        Expression.Property( paramExp,
                            fieldName);
    BinaryExpression comparison =
        Expression.MakeBinary( comparisonOperator,
                            fieldAccess,
                            comparisonConstant );
    if (bodyFilter == null) {
        bodyFilter = comparison;
    }
    else {
        bodyFilter = Expression.AndAlso(bodyFilter, comparison);
    }
}
}
```

The *ProcessFilter* class holds an expression tree that saves the "current" body of the expression in the private member *bodyFilter*. The resulting expression tree is a lambda expression with a single parameter of type *System.Diagnostic.Process*. The *ProcessFilters* constructor creates this parameter, which is then used to read the requested properties. (See the *fieldAccess* assignment in the *Add* method.)

The *Add* method of the *ProcessFilters* class simply creates a *BinaryExpression* between the property specified in *fieldName* and the constant specified in *comparisonValue*, using the operator specified by *comparisonOperator*. If the *bodyFilter* member already contains at least one other node, the new top-level node is an *AndAlso* between the new comparison and the existing expression tree. (This example always inserts an *AND* operator for each condition added to a *ProcessFilters* instance. Most of the time, that is the only action required, but you could implement a more sophisticated system that allows specifying *OR* conditions too.)

Figure 14-14 shows a representation of the final execution tree created dynamically by the example. Nodes created at the same time have the same background color. The more recent nodes (Lambda) have darker backgrounds; older nodes have a lighter background. The *&&* *BinaryExpression* performs the *AND* operation between the >= and == nodes.

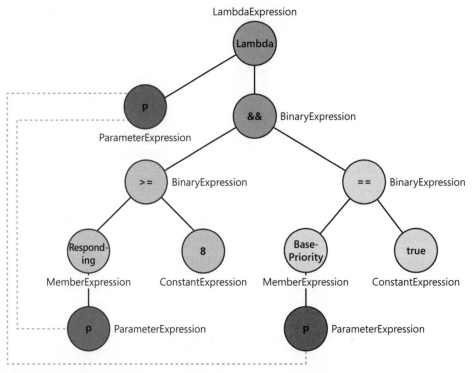

FIGURE 14-14 Dynamically created expression tree.

Executing the *Main* method in Listing 14-27 produces a result similar to the following one (noting that the effective result depends on the processes currently executed on the testing machine):

```
Filter : p => ((p.Responding == True) AndAlso (p.BasePriority > 8))
smss
csrss
wininit
winlogon
csrss
dwm
lsass
msvsmon
services
```

To experiment, try creating a custom query against the running processes on your machine by changing the *Add* calls in the *FilterSelection* method shown in Listing 14-27. More importantly, the goal is for you to be able to apply the techniques you have seen in this chapter to handle and manipulate expression trees in your programs.

> **Note** There is an interesting free library named LINQKit that contains a class named *Predicate-Builder*, whose purpose is to dynamically compose expression predicates by writing fewer lines of code. You can download LINQKit from *http://www.albahari.com/nutshell/linqkit.aspx*.

Summary

This chapter showed the internal behavior of lambda expressions and expression trees and how they relate to each other. You saw how to encapsulate and modify expression trees, and how to handle their immutability. You saw an analysis of the classes contained in the *System.Linq.Expressions* namespace that support expression trees, exploring in detail the implementation of the most common and important node types. After that, you analyzed some algorithms that are used to visit expression trees. Finally, you examined how the compiler generates expression trees from lambda expression syntax and how you can create and manipulate an expression tree dynamically.

Chapter 15

Extending LINQ

One interesting aspect of Microsoft Language Integrated Query (LINQ) is its extensibility: you can extend LINQ by adding new operators, by writing your own implementation of standard query operators (for example, *Where*, *OrderBy*, and *Distinct*), and by implementing the *IQueryable* interface to access any kind of external data.

The first two options (adding new query operators or replacing existing ones) is fundamentally a way to customize LINQ to Objects. Working with objects in memory provides for a simple replacement or extension without the need to know very much about the existing implementation of LINQ to Objects. A different scenario is involved when you use LINQ to access data that does not consist of in-memory objects—for example, when you use LINQ to SQL. In that case, you need to implement all the operators from scratch because you will usually need to convert the expression tree into another query language.

This chapter explores these three extensibility options for LINQ, describing how to create new custom operators, showing an example of customizing an existing operator, and describing how to create a custom LINQ provider by implementing the *IQueryable* interface.

Custom Operators

LINQ offers a full set of operators that cover most of the possible operations on a set of entities. However, you might require some other operator to add a particular semantic meaning to your query—especially if you can reuse that same operator several times in your code. As an example, you will implement a custom operator that returns, for a given collection, the element with the lowest value for a particular property.

Consider the *Stock* and *Quote* entities defined in Listing 15-1. A *Stock* instance contains a list of *Quote* instances, each with a price and time of collection.

LISTING 15-1 Entities used in the custom operator example

```
public class Quote {
    public Stock Stock { get; set; }
    public decimal Price { get; set; }
    public DateTime Time { get; set; }
}
```

```
public class Stock {
    public string Ticker { get; set; }
    public string Name { get; set; }
    public decimal Shares { get; set; }
    public List<Quote> Quotes { get; set; }

    public override string ToString() {
        return String.Format(
            "{0}: {1}  MIN {2} - MAX {3}",
            Ticker,
            Shares,
            Quotes.Min(q => q.Price),
            Quotes.Max(q => q.Price));
    }
}
```

The *ToString* override in *Stock* displays the minimum and maximum price contained in the *Quotes* list. To do that, it uses the *Min* and *Max* aggregation operators. Listing 15-2 shows how to use these classes.

LISTING 15-2 Quotes collection initialization

```
Stock stock = new Stock { Name = "Stock Demo", Ticker = "AGHQ", Shares = 100000M };
stock.Quotes = new List<Quote> {
    new Quote { Stock = stock, Time = new DateTime(2007, 12, 5, 11, 8, 45 ),
                Price = 57.63M },
    new Quote { Stock = stock, Time = new DateTime(2007, 12, 5, 11, 8, 56 ),
                Price = 56.92M },
    new Quote { Stock = stock, Time = new DateTime(2007, 12, 5, 11, 9, 08 ),
                Price = 57.05M },
    new Quote { Stock = stock, Time = new DateTime(2007, 12, 5, 11, 9, 23 ),
                Price = 56.87M }
};

Console.WriteLine( "Stock: {0}", stock);
```

The execution of the code in Listing 15-2 produces the following output:

```
Stock: AGHQ: 100000  MIN 56,87 - MAX 57,63
```

As you can see, it does not display the time when the minimum and maximum prices have been collected.

Now consider the calculation of the minimum value. The *Min* aggregate operator used is defined in this way:

```
public static TResult Min<TSource, TResult> (
    this IEnumerable<TSource> source,
    Func<TSource, TResult> selector);
```

The *Min* operator returns the same type used in the comparison. However, you want to compare the *Price* property of the *Quote* class but also want to get back the instance of *Quote*
that has the minimum *Price*, not just the minimum *Price* itself. If the *Quote* class implemented
the *IComparable* interface, you could have called the *Min* operator directly on the *Quotes*
collection:

```
Quotes.Min()
```

This would have returned a single *Quote* instance following the comparison rules defined in
the *IComparable* implementation. However, you do not want to follow this approach because
the *IComparable* interface implementation could also be used for sorting quotes, and a *Quote*
could be sorted by stock name, price, and time. Thus, in our scenario, it is preferred not to
define a semantic of automatic comparison between two *Quote* instances. Instead, you explicitly define the value to be compared (*Price*) in the *Min* call:

```
Quotes.Min(q => q.Price)
```

Because the *Min* operator returns the same type used to make the comparison, the result
of the *Min* operator is a value of the same type of *Price*. However, to get the whole *Quote*
instance, you need to use another approach. One solution is to use the *Aggregate* operator,
as you can see in Listing 15-3.

> **Note** If several quotes have the same price, *Min* will return only the first one. This example does
> not consider the need to get all the quotes with the minimum price.

LISTING 15-3 Get the item with the minimum price using *Aggregate*

```
Quote minQuote;

// Get the item with the minimum price using Aggregate operator
minQuote = stock.Quotes.Aggregate( (t, s) => t.Price < s.Price ? t : s );
Console.WriteLine(
    "Min item using Aggregate - {0} : {1}",
    minQuote.Time,
    minQuote.Price);
```

The use of *Aggregate* produces code that is compact and gets the job done, producing the
required result:

```
Min item using Aggregate - 12/5/2007 11:09:23 AM : 56.87
```

However, the code is not easy to read. If you do not include an explicit comment, you need to read the code very carefully to understand what it is going to do. Moreover, that code is more error prone and not intuitive to write. To simplify the code, you need a custom operator that behaves similarly to *Min* but returns the object from the sequence and not the expression value used to make the comparison. You can see the definition of this new operator, named *MinPrice,* in Listing 15-4.

LISTING 15-4 Definition of the *MinPrice* operator for the *Quote* class

```
static class Extensions {
    public static Quote MinPrice( this IEnumerable<Quote> source) {
        return source.Aggregate( (t, s) => t.Price < s.Price ? t : s );
    }
}
```

The *MinPrice* operator returns the *Quote* instance, which simply wraps the call to the *Aggregate* operator that compares two quotes by explicitly comparing their *Price* property. Listing 15-5 shows how to use this new LINQ extension operator.

LISTING 15-5 Use of the *MinPrice* operator

```
// Get the item with the minimum price using a specific custom operator
Quote minQuote = stock.Quotes.MinPrice();
Console.WriteLine(
    "Min item using MinPrice  - {0} : {1}",
    minQuote.Time,
    minQuote.Price);
```

The code in Listing 15-5 produces the required result:

```
Min item using MinPrice  - 12/5/2007 11:09:23 AM : 56.87
```

> **Note** *MinPrice* is an extension method applied only to sequences of *Quote* instances because it extends the *IEnumerable<Quote>* interface, which is an instantiation of the generic *IEnumerable<T>* interface.

Unfortunately, this approach requires you to define a new operator every time you want to apply it to a type other than *Quote,* or if you want to change the property to be compared. A more generic approach requires the use of more verbose code that includes a more complex overload of the *Aggregate* operator. Listing 15-6 shows an implementation of such an operator, named *MinItem.*

LISTING 15-6 Definition of a generic version of the *MinItem* operator

```
static class Extensions {
  public static TSource MinItem<TSource, TCompareValue>(
        this IEnumerable<TSource> source,
        Func<TSource, TCompareValue> comparerExpression) {

        // We get a constructed Comparer<T> instance
        // for the type to be compared
        Comparer<TCompareValue> comparer = Comparer<TCompareValue>.Default;
        // indexElement is used to execute two different pieces of code
        // in the lambda expression for Aggregate: one for the very
        // first iteration, the other for the following iterations
        int indexElement = 0;
        // The Aggregate will execute the lambda expression
        // for each element in the source sequence
        return source.Aggregate(
            default(TSource),
            (minValue, item) =>
                    (indexElement++ == 0 ?
                        // First iteration - no comparison,
                        // returns item as initial minValue
                        item :
                        // Second or later  iteration: does the comparison
                        // and returns item if it is lower than the
                        // previous minValue; otherwise, returns minValue
                        (comparer.Compare( comparerExpression(item),
                                        comparerExpression(minValue)) < 0 ?
                            item :
                            minValue)));
    }
}
```

Using a generic *TSource* type, you must specify its comparer by calling the *Aggregate* operator. You also need to handle the special case for the first element in the sequence; we used
indexElement to do that.

> **Note** You might wonder why you simply cannot use a Boolean variable instead of an *int* to han-
> dle the special case for the first element. The reason is that, in a lambda expression, you have to
> write a single expression. By using the post-increment operator on *indexElement*, you can change
> its value without the need to define (and call) another function simply to change the state of the
> variable. Of course, this implementation assumes that the sequence has fewer than 2^31 elements.

The *MinItem* operator code in Listing 15-6 can now be applied to any type, using any expression to apply the comparison. The call to *MinItem* can specify any expression, as you can see
in Listing 15-7, which first retrieves the *Quote* instance with the lowest price and then retrieves
the *Quote* instance with the earliest time.

LISTING 15-7 Use of the *MinItem* operator

```
// Get the item with the minimum price using a generic custom operator
Quote minQuote = stock.Quotes.MinItem(x => x.Price);
Console.WriteLine(
    "Min item using MinItem(price) - {0} : {1}",
    minQuote.Time,
    minQuote.Price);

// Get the item with the minimum time using a generic custom operator
minQuote = stock.Quotes.MinItem(x => x.Time);
Console.WriteLine(
    "Min item using MinItem(time)  - {0} : {1}",
    minQuote.Time,
    minQuote.Price);
```

Here is the result produced by executing the code in Listing 15-7:

```
Min item using MinItem(price) - 12/5/2007 11:09:23 AM : 56.87
Min item using MinItem(time)  - 12/5/2007 11:08:45 AM : 57.63
```

Adding new operators to LINQ is a way to extend its capabilities. Beyond adding new features, you can also improve code readability by wrapping existing operators into more specialized and meaningful ones.

Specialization of Existing Operators

Existing LINQ operators can be specialized for use with particular types. For example, you might want to apply a particular operator to a specific constructed type. This practice is not terribly common, because you usually need to implement *IQueryable* to perform complex customizations.

Here is an example of a meaningful specialization of the *Where* operator. Imagine that you have an *IVisible* interface with a *Visible* property that defines the visibility of an item in a collection. You could implement that interface in the *Customer* class, as you can see in Listing 15-8.

LISTING 15-8 Definition of the *IVisible* interface and *Customer* class

```
public interface IVisible {
    bool Visible { get; set; }
}

public class Customer : IVisible {
    public Customer() {
        this.Visible = true;
    }

    public string Name { get; set; }
```

```
    public int Age { get; set; }
    public bool Visible { get; set; }

    public override string  ToString() {
        return String.Format("{0} is {1} years old", Name, Age);
    }
}
```

You want to skip any customer with *Visible* set to *false* when a query expression makes use of the *Where* operator—but without having to check the *Visible* property in the predicate expression. Listing 15-9 shows a *Where* specialization that works in this way when applied to types that implement the *IVisible* interface.

LISTING 15-9 Specialization of the *Where* standard query operator

```
static class Extensions {
    public static IEnumerable<TSource> Where<TSource>(
            this IEnumerable<TSource> source,
            Func<TSource, Boolean> predicate)
        where TSource : IVisible {

        foreach (TSource item in source) {
            if (item.Visible && predicate(item)) {
                yield return item;
            }
        }
    }
}
```

Listing 15-10 shows the use of the customized *Where* operator by initializing a simple array of customers, filtering them through a query expression that explicitly returns only for customers with an age lower than 40. Moreover, customers with the *Visible* property set to *false* will be implicitly skipped by the custom *Where* operator.

LISTING 15-10 Use of a specialized *Where* for types implementing the *IVisible* interface

```
Customer[] customers =
    { new Customer { Name = "John", Age = 24, Visible = false },
      new Customer { Name = "Allison", Age = 45 },
      new Customer { Name = "Brad", Age = 33 } };

var query =
    from   c in customers
    where  c.Age < 40
    select c;

foreach (var row in query) {
    Console.WriteLine(row);
}
```

The output produced by the code in Listing 15-10 is the following:

```
Brad is 33 years old
```

The other two customers have been skipped either because they do not satisfy the condition in the *Where* predicate (Allison is more than 40 years old) or are not visible (John).

The previous example implements an implicit filter based on the *Visible* state of an object implementing the *IVisible* interface. However, this filter is active only with the presence of a *Where* condition. An alternative (and probably simpler) way to skip objects that do not have *Visible* set to *true*, is to write another operator to be applied to the source sequence just before the query expression itself. Instead of querying a sequence of *Customer* instances, you can query the sequence filtered by the *OnlyVisible* method defined in Listing 15-11, which filters for visible customers (*Visible* set to *true*) before applying any other LINQ standard operator.

LISTING 15-11 An alternative way to filter a sequence for only *Visible* customers

```
static class Extensions {
    public static IEnumerable<TSource> OnlyVisible<TSource>(
            this IEnumerable<TSource> source)
        where TSource : IVisible {

        foreach (TSource item in source) {
            if (item.Visible) {
                yield return item;
            }
        }
    }
}
```

This approach requires the query to be made on the result of a call to the *OnlyVisible* method. Listing 15-12 shows a query expression that uses this syntax.

LISTING 15-12 Use of an *OnlyVisible* operator to get only *Visible* customers

```
var query =
    from   c in customers.OnlyVisible()
    where  c.Age < 40
    select c;
```

The result produced by Listing 15-12 is the same as for Listing 15-10.

As you can see, there is an important difference in terms of semantics. If you specialize the *Where* operator, you also hide the internal behavior from the query. In contrast, using the *OnlyVisible* operator makes this filter more explicit, but requires an explicit call to it in the query expression. You might have many options for implementing a similar behavior, but there are subtle differences that will likely make one option more desirable than others, depending on your requirements. In this example, if you can choose to query for invisible customers, the *OnlyVisible* implementation is probably better. Otherwise, it would be preferable to use the *Where* operator or gain complete control of the *Customers* collection by wrapping it in a method that also calls *OnlyVisible*.

Dangerous Practices

This section shows an example of a dangerous use of operator specialization. It uses the *MinItem* custom operator defined earlier in this chapter to hijack calls to the standard *Min* operator made on a sequence of *Quote* instances. Listing 15-13 shows an implementation of such a *Min* operator specialization.

LISTING 15-13 Specialization of the *Min* operator for *Quote* instances

```
static class Extensions {
    public static TSource Min<TSource, TCompareValue>(
            this IEnumerable<TSource> source,
            Func<TSource, TCompareValue> comparerExpression)
        where TSource : Quote {
        return source.MinItem(comparerExpression);
    }
}
```

This *Min* specialization applies only to types compatible with *Quote*, so it does not change the semantics for every type on which *Min* is applied—that could break existing code if recompiled. (You cannot break already-compiled code because the Microsoft Visual C# compiler resolves extension methods during compilation.) This method allows you to write the code in Listing 15-14.

LISTING 15-14 Use of the specialized *Min* operator on sequences of *Quote* instances

```
// Get item with the minimum price using a generic custom operator
Quote minQuote = stock.Quotes.Min(x => x.Price);
Console.WriteLine(
    "Min item using Min(price) - {0} : {1}",
    minQuote.Time,
    minQuote.Price);

// Get item with the minimum time using a generic custom operator
minQuote = stock.Quotes.Min(x => x.Time);
Console.WriteLine(
    "Min item using Min(time)  - {0} : {1}",
    minQuote.Time, -
    minQuote.Price);
```

As stated earlier, specializing a standard operator by changing its semantics is a dangerous practice. This example changes the semantics of the *Min* operator. Here is the original:

```
public static TCompareValue Min<TSource, TCompareValue> (
    this IEnumerable<TSource> source,
    Func<TSource, TCompareValue> selector);
```

And here is what it changes to:

```
public static TSource Min<TSource, TCompareValue> (
    this IEnumerable<TSource> source,
    Func<TSource, TCompareValue> selector);
```

In other words, the *Min* operator returns the source object that has the minimum value for a specified expression instead of returning the minimum value of the expression itself. This is an important semantic difference that could confuse whoever writes LINQ queries.

More generally, if you create your own version of a standard operator and do not limit the types on which it is applied, you can hide the "original" standard method in your code. That might be your intent, but if you are including code written by someone else, you have to be sure that there are no side effects caused by your changes. Be careful when overriding the behavior of existing standard operators!

> **Important** When you specialize a standard operator, use semantics, a pattern of use for parameters, and a return type that are all compatible with the existing operator you are overriding. If you need to change the semantics, consider defining a new custom operator, and assigning it a specific name.

Limits of Specialization

Extending LINQ through operator specialization has some limitations. For example, you cannot change the syntax and semantics of standard operators used in query expressions. As an example, imagine the access to a sorted dictionary by filtering only one or more keys in the *Where* condition of a query expression, as in the following pseudocode:

```
SortedDictionary<string, string> list;

var query =
    from   l in list
    where  l.Key == "M"
    select l.Value;
```

Using a specialization of the standard *Where* operator might not be enough to improve the performance of the whole query resolution because LINQ evaluates the *Boolean* condition (*l.Key == "M"*) in a "black box," which makes it impossible to understand how to optimize the access through the sorted keys collection. As mentioned, adding a new operator is a better solution for this, and the next part of this chapter shows how to implement the *IQueryable* interface to achieve a similar outcome, but with more flexibility. However, let us try to analyze the predicate expression from a specialized *Where* operator. Listings 15-15 through 15-20 illustrate one implementation of a faster *Where* operator for a *SortedDictionary*.

LISTING 15-15 LINQ queries on a *SortedDictionary*

```
static void DemoSortedList() {
    SortedDictionary<string, string> list = new SortedDictionary<string, string>();
    for (char ch = 'Z'; ch >= 'A'; ch--) {
        list.Add(ch.ToString(), "Letter " + ch.ToString());
    }

    Console.WriteLine("-- queryStandard --");
    var queryStandard =
        from   l in list
        where  l.Key == "M"
        select l.Value;
    Dump(queryStandard);

    Console.WriteLine("-- queryFast --");
    var queryFast = list.WhereKey("M");
    Dump(queryFast);
}

static void Dump<T>(IEnumerable<T> sequence) {
    foreach (T item in sequence) {
        Console.WriteLine(item);
    }
}
```

Listing 15-15 creates and populates a *SortedDictionary*. The code includes two queries: *queryStandard* and *queryFast*. The first, *queryStandard*, iterates through all the items in the list and returns only the one with "M" as the key, filtering each item of the sequence through the standard *Where* operator. Conversely, *queryFast* does not perform a complete list iteration; instead, it retrieves the single desired value by using the *WhereKey* operator, whose implementation is shown in Listing 15-16.

LISTING 15-16 Implementation of the *WhereKey* operator

```
static class Extensions {
    public static IEnumerable<TSource> WhereKey<TSource,TKey>(
            this  SortedDictionary<TKey, TSource> source,
            TKey key) {

        yield return source[key];
    }
}
```

The *WhereKey* operator differs from the standard *Where* operator because it does not get a generic *Boolean* condition to be evaluated on each item. Its semantics assume that a key value is passed to the operator and that the caller wants to receive a sequence of items that have this same key. Observing the implementation, you can see that only a single item is returned, but the *IEnumerable<T>* return type allows the projection of the results by writing code like the following:

```
var query =
    from    l in list.WhereKey("M")
    select new { Value = l, Length = l.Length };
```

The *WhereKey* implementation is faster than a regular *Where* operator because it reduces the number of comparisons needed to find the required element. To demonstrate this, Listing 15-17 defines a class (*KeyWrapper*) to be used as a key type in the *SortedDictionary* collection. The *KeyWrapper* class simply writes a marker each time its *Value* property is read and displays the items compared when the *CompareTo* method is called.

LISTING 15-17 Implementation of the *KeyWrapper* class

```
class KeyWrapper : IComparable {
    private string _s;
    public string Value {
        get {
            Console.Write("(" + _s + ") ");
            return _s;
        }
        set { _s = value; }
    }
    public override string ToString() {
        //Console.Write("+");
        return _s;
    }
    public KeyWrapper(string value) {
        _s = value;
    }

    public int CompareTo(object obj) {
        string operand = obj.ToString();
        Console.Write("[{0}<->{1}] ", this._s, operand);
        return _s.CompareTo(operand);
    }
}
```

To use the *KeyWrapper*, the code needs slight adjustments, as shown in Listing 15-18.

LISTING 15-18 LINQ queries on a *SortedDictionary*

```
static class Extensions {
    public static IEnumerable<TSource> WhereKey<TSource >(
            this SortedDictionary<KeyWrapper, TSource> source,
            string key) {

        yield return source[new KeyWrapper(key)];
    }
}

static void DemoSortedListTrace() {
    SortedDictionary<KeyWrapper, string> list = new
        SortedDictionary<KeyWrapper, string>();

    for (char ch = 'Z'; ch >= 'A'; ch--) {
        list.Add(new KeyWrapper(ch.ToString()), "Letter " + ch.ToString());
    }

    Console.WriteLine("-- queryStandard --");
    var queryStandard =
        from  l in list
        where l.Key.Value == "M"
        select l.Value;
    Dump(queryStandard);

    Console.WriteLine("-- queryFast --");
    var queryFast = list.WhereKey("M");
    Dump(queryFast);
}
```

Listing 15-18 is an adaptation of the code in Listings 15-15 and 15-16 that uses the new *KeyWrapper* as the key type. The following is the output:

```
... (other output is produced by previous operations)
-- queryStandard --
(A) (B) (C) (D) (E) (F) (G) (H) (I) (J) (K) (L) (M) Letter M
(N) (O) (P) (Q) (R) (S) (T) (U) (V) (W) (X) (Y) (Z)
-- queryFast --
[M<->S] [M<->K] [M<->O] [M<->M] Letter M
```

The output shows that the *queryStandard* case iterates the whole sequence, even after having found the desired value. The less frequent instances of access in the *queryFast* case (which calls *CompareTo*) produce a faster execution.

Now that you know why a new custom operator can provide faster execution, it is worth showing how you can specialize the standard *Where* operator to improve its performance in accessing a *SortedDictionary* class, filtering with a single key value (as in the *queryStandard* case). Here is the definition of the standard *Where* operator:

```
public static IEnumerable<TSource> Where<TSource>(
    this IEnumerable<TSource> source,
    Func<TSource, Boolean> predicate);
```

The *predicate* is applied to each item of the *source* sequence. A standard *Where* implementation could be similar to the following:

```
public static IEnumerable<TSource> Where<TSource>(
        this IEnumerable<TSource> source,
        Func<TSource, Boolean> predicate) {
    foreach (TSource item in source) {
        if (predicate(item)) {
            yield return item;
        }
    }
}
```

If you could use a constant instead of the *Boolean* predicate, you could define something like the following pseudocode, where *MoveFirstKey* refers to a method that returns an iterator that starts from the first instance of the key passed as an argument:

```
public static IEnumerable<TSource> Where<TKey, TSource>(
        this SortedDictionary<TKey, TSource> source,
        TKey key ) {
    IEnumerator<KeyValuePair<TKey,TSource>> fastScan = source.MoveFirstKey( key );
    if (fastScan.Current.Key != null) {
        while (fastScan.Current.Key.Equals(key)) {
            yield return fastScan.Current.Value;
            fastScan.MoveNext();
        }
    }
}
```

Note that the *SortedDictionary* collection does not have the required *MoveFirstKey* method used in the previous code snippet. Moreover, a *SortedDictionary* instance cannot have two items with the same key. The conditions used to look for possible duplicates of the same key are purely illustrative of the code required to implement that behavior in another class containing sorted objects.

However, replacing the predicate with a constant does not produce an operator that can be used through query expression syntax. In other words, you cannot write the following code:

```
var query =
    from    l in list
    where   "M"        // this produces an error
    select l.Value;
```

You still have to use it with a regular syntax:

```
var query =
    from   l in list.Where("M") // this does work
    select l.Value;
```

Nevertheless, you have already seen that specializing standard operators by changing their semantics is a dangerous practice. Therefore, it is better to analyze the expression contained in the predicate of the standard *Where* operator, catching the pattern of a comparison with the *Key* value to find an element in the dictionary. If such a pattern appears, you can substitute it with a *WhereKey* call or simply add a *WhereKey* call before the *Where* call, just to maintain full compatibility with the complete predicate. To do that, here is a *Where* operator with the following signature:

```
public static IEnumerable<TSource> Where<TSource>(
        this IEnumerable<TSource> source,
        Expression<Func<TSource, Boolean>> predicate);
```

In the previous code, you get the *predicate* as an expression tree. (You can read more about expression tree analysis in Chapter 14, "Inside Expression Trees.") Because the goal is to make an optimization specifically for *SortedDictionary*, here is a more specialized signature:

```
public static IEnumerable<KeyValuePair<TKey, TValue>> Where<TKey, TValue>(
        this SortedDictionary<TKey, TValue> source,
        Expression<Func<KeyValuePair<TKey, TValue>, Boolean>> predicate)
            where TKey : class;
```

Listing 15-19 shows the complete code for the *Where* operator, optimized for *SortedDictionary*. This code visits the filter expression tree to infer whether a constant comparison of the key can be optimized by taking advantage of the *SortedDictionary* implementation, as shown with the *WhereKey* operator.

LISTING 15-19 Specialization of a standard *Where* operator optimized for *SortedDictionary*

```
public static IEnumerable<KeyValuePair<TKey, TValue>> Where<TKey, TValue>(
        this SortedDictionary<TKey, TValue> source,
        Expression<Func<KeyValuePair<TKey, TValue>, Boolean>> predicate)
            where TKey : class {
    // This is for trace only: we display the predicate we've found
    Trace.WriteLine("** Where predicate **");
    Trace.WriteLine(predicate.ToString());
    Trace.WriteLine("** -------------- **");

    // After visiting the expression tree for the predicate, we need to
    //know if a standard or an optimized Where has to be performed
    bool replaceWithWhereKey = false;
    TKey keyToSearch = null;
```

```
        // The following expression results in a delegate that returns a copy
        // of the expression tree, eliminating an expression like
        //    <item>.Key == <constant>
        // where <item> is an instance of KeyValuePair<TKey,TValue> (an element
        // of our SortedDictionary) and <constant> is a constant value (we
        // tested only strings)
        var ReplaceEqual = ExprOp.Visit.Chain(
            (self, last, expr) => {
                if (expr == null) return null;
                // Visiting the expression tree, stop at a BinaryExpression
                // with an Equal comparison
                switch (expr.NodeType) {
                    case ExpressionType.Equal:
                        var b = (BinaryExpression) expr;
                        TKey _key = null;
                        MemberExpression memberAccess = null;
                        // Get MemberAccess and Constant regardless of their position
                        switch (b.Left.NodeType) {
                            case ExpressionType.MemberAccess:
                                memberAccess = b.Left as MemberExpression;
                                break;
                            case ExpressionType.Constant:
                                _key = (b.Left as ConstantExpression).Value as TKey;
                                break;
                        }
                        switch (b.Right.NodeType) {
                            case ExpressionType.MemberAccess:
                                memberAccess = b.Right as MemberExpression;
                                break;
                            case ExpressionType.Constant:
                                _key = (b.Right as ConstantExpression).Value as TKey;
                                break;
                        }
                        // Stops here without modifications if either
                        // memberAccess or _key have not been found
                        if ((memberAccess == null) || (_key == null)) {
                            return b;
                        }
                        // If we access the Key property of a
                        // KeyValuePair<TKey,TValue> type, we can do
                        // the substitution - our BinaryExpression is
                        // replaced with a constant value equal to true
                        if ((memberAccess.Member.ReflectedType ==
                                typeof(KeyValuePair<TKey, TValue>))
                                && (memberAccess.Member.Name == "Key")) {
                            // Set flag to replace the where condition in
                            // the caller (the Where operator)
                            replaceWithWhereKey = true;
                            keyToSearch = _key;
                            return Expression.Constant(true);
                        }
```

```
                    Console.WriteLine(b.Left.ToString());
                    return b;
            default:
                    return last(expr);
         } // end switch (expr.NodeType)
      } // end anonymous delegate
   );

   // The following call eliminates an
   //    <item>.Key == <constant>
   // comparison and makes a direct access to the Dictionary
   // using the <constant> found (saved in keyToSearch) if that
   // comparison has been found and removed
   var querySubstitution = ReplaceEqual(predicate);
   if (replaceWithWhereKey) {
      Trace.WriteLine("--- REPLACED WHERE ---");
      // Directly get the value associated with the given key
      // thanks to the SortedDictionary implementation
      var value = source[keyToSearch];
      var item = new KeyValuePair<TKey, TValue>(keyToSearch, value);
      if (predicate.Compile()(item)) {
         yield return item;
      }
   }
   else {
      // The traditional Where iteration takes place
      // if an optimized access has not been requested
      Trace.WriteLine("--- STANDARD WHERE ---");
      foreach (var item in source) {
         if (predicate.Compile()(item)) {
            yield return item;
         }
      }
   }
}
```

Despite its length, this implementation has several limitations: it supports only reference types for *TKey*, it supports one and only one *Key* comparison with a constant, and it does not support OR conditions around the *Key* comparison. There are probably other limitations, but the purpose of this sample is to illustrate the technique used to analyze and eventually change a predicate inside a *Where* operator.

> **Note** The code in Listing 15-19 makes use of an *ExprOp* class that is not included here; however it is in the sample code, and was originally written by Jomo Fisher and published on his blog at *http://blogs.msdn.com/jomo_fisher/archive/2007/05/07/visitor-revisitted-linq-function-composablity-and-chain-of-responsibility.aspx* and *http://blogs.msdn.com/jomo_fisher/archive/2007/05/23/dealing-with-linq-s-immutable-expression-trees.aspx*. See Chapter 14 for further information about expression tree analysis and manipulation.

Listing 15-20 shows an example of using the custom *Where* method optimized for *SortedDictionary*.

LISTING 15-20 Demo of queries on *SortedDictionary* using the optimized *Where* operator

```
static void DemoOptimization() {
    Trace.Listeners.Add(new TextWriterTraceListener(Console.Out));
    SortedDictionary<string, string> list = new SortedDictionary<string, string>();
    for (char ch = 'Z'; ch >= 'A'; ch--) {
        list.Add(ch.ToString(), "Letter " + ch.ToString());
    }

    Console.WriteLine("-- queryOptimized --");
    var queryOptimized =
        from   l in list
        where  l.Key == "M" && l.Value.Length > 1
        select l.Value;
    Dump(queryOptimized);
    Console.WriteLine("");

    Console.WriteLine("-- queryNotOptimized --");
    var queryNotOptimized =
        from   l in list
        where  l.Value == "Letter M" && l.Value.Length > 1
        select l.Value;
    Dump(queryNotOptimized);
    Console.WriteLine("");
}
```

As you may have noticed, the *Where* operator code in Listing 15-19 contains a trace. The trace results produced by executing Listing 15-20 show that the specialized *Where* operator has intercepted and optimized the *queryOptimized* method, whereas *queryNotOptimized* does not satisfy the requested condition (a comparison between *Key* and a constant—in this case, the code compared the *Value* property) and executes in a standard way (you can see the "STANDARD WHERE" trace message in that case) in the following output:

```
-- queryOptimized --
** Where predicate **
l => ((l.Key = "M") && (l.Value.Length > 1))
** --------------- **
--- REPLACED WHERE ---
Letter M

-- queryNotOptimized --
** Where predicate **
l => ((l.Value = "Letter M") && (l.Value.Length > 1))
** --------------- **
l.Value
--- STANDARD WHERE ---
Letter M
```

This section only touched the surface of the optimizations that are possible using custom operators. The *SortedDictionary* example showed a potentially deeper integration of LINQ with existing indexed structures.

> **Tip** If you want to improve LINQ queries on existing objects without having to worry too much about implementation details and which collections are used, you can look for alternative commercial and free libraries that make LINQ to Objects queries faster by creating indexes on data.

Creating a Custom LINQ Provider

Writing a specialized version of a standard LINQ operator is useful only when you want to operate with in-memory objects and when the intended customization does not require a comprehensive view of the query. But often, you need to transmit a query to a remote service, where "remote" is anything outside the application domain, and probably requires a specific syntax, such as SQL, XML, or simply a parameter list. In these cases, you need to analyze the query expression without executing it locally, to convert it to an appropriate form for the service requirements. The previous section showed that by specializing *Where*, you can analyze the predicate expression tree. However, this specialization is not enough if you want to comply with another operator, such as *Take*—which is not part of the *Where* predicate (although it could be part of an expression tree such as the one that was discussed and manipulated earlier in Chapter 14). You need a complete query tree for the entire query, and that requires a LINQ provider implementation, which typically means an implementation of the *IQueryable* interface.

> **Note** We say "typically" because you could also implement your own LINQ provider by writing a class with a definition for all the standard operators, just as the *Queryable* and *Enumerable* classes do. Nevertheless, this approach is not very common because *Queryable* already generates an expression tree that encloses the other expression trees used in the query, such as the one in the predicate of a *Where* operator. This makes it impractical to build another LINQ implementation that generates different structures to represent the query that—in the end—should always mix with expression trees. Having the query tree in the form of an expression tree is the best and fastest way to get the complete representation of the query. For this reason, most LINQ providers are simply implementations of the *IQueryable* interface that use the existing set of extension methods defined in the *Queryable* class.

In the next section, you will first see a description of the differences between *IEnumerable* and *IQueryable* in LINQ, and then you will see how to build a custom LINQ provider for a service that provides real-time flight status information.

The *IQueryable* Interface

The namespace *System.Linq* contains two important static classes. One is *Enumerable*, which contains all the LINQ standard operators that are collectively called LINQ to Objects. The other is *Queryable*, which contains an alternative implementation of the LINQ standard operators in which each method simply adds a node in an expression tree representing the desired operation. The final result is still an expression tree that represents the whole query tree. Given that both the *Enumerable* and *Queryable* classes are defined in the same namespace and that both contain the same set of extension methods, how does the compiler choose the implementation to use between these classes? It turns out that the distinction lies in the first parameter of these methods, which defines the type that the method extends. For example, consider the following definitions:

```
public static class Enumerable {
    public static IEnumerable<T> Where<T>(
        this IEnumerable<T> source,
        Func<T, bool> predicate);
    // ...
}

public static class Queryable {
    public static IQueryable<T> Where<T>(
        this IQueryable<T> source,
        Expression<Func<T, bool>> predicate);
    // ...
}
```

These definitions show two distinct differences between *Enumerable.Where<T>* and *Queryable.Where<T>*. The first is the type of the *source* parameter, which is respectively *IEnumerable<T>* and *IQueryable<T>*. The *Enumerable.Where<T>* statement extends all the classes implementing the *IEnumerable<T>* interface, whereas *Queryable.Where<T>* extends all the classes implementing the *IQueryable<T>* interface. To make this clear, it is helpful to quickly recall *IEnumerable<T>* and review the *IQueryable/IQueryable<T>* interfaces:

```
public interface IEnumerable {
    IEnumerator GetEnumerator();
}
public interface IEnumerable<T> : IEnumerable {
    IEnumerator<T> GetEnumerator();
}

public interface IQueryable : IEnumerable {
    Type ElementType { get; }
    Expression Expression { get; }
    IQueryProvider Provider { get; }
}
public interface IQueryable<T> : IEnumerable<T>, IQueryable, IEnumerable {
}
```

Because *IQueryable<T>* implements *IEnumerable<T>*, the resolution of the methods in *Queryable* takes precedence over those in *Enumerable* whenever the extended class implements *IQueryable<T>*. The precedence happens because the compiler favors the more specialized interface when resolving the overload between these extension methods. (The rule applied is that an implicit conversion exists from *IQueryable<T>* to *IEnumerable<T>*—see §7.4.3.4 in the C# 3.0 Language Specification for more details.)

> **Note** This chapter does not cover the *IOrderedQueryable* or *IOrderedQueryable<T>* interfaces. Those are simply specializations of *IQueryable/IQueryable<T>* that do not add new methods; they simply describe that the sort order of the extracted items is significant (generally resulting from an ordering operator such as *OrderBy*, *OrderByDescending*, *ThenBy*, or *ThenByDescending*).

The second difference between the preceding *Where* declarations is that the predicate parameter is passed to *Enumerable.Where<T>* as a lambda expression, but *Queryable.Where<T>* gets an expression tree of type *Expression<Func<T, bool>>* instead. The *Expression<T>* (in this case *Expression<Func<T, bool>>*) type instructs the compiler to build an expression tree for the enclosed lambda expression, just as you saw earlier in the *Where* operator optimized for *SortedDictionary* in Listing 12-19. At run time, the call to *Queryable.Where<T>* produces a node in the expression tree that includes the predicate expression tree. The following code shows the implementation of *Queryable.Where<T>*:

```
public static IQueryable<T> Where<T>(
    this IQueryable<T> source,
    Expression<Func<T, bool>> predicate) {
        MethodInfo currentMethod = (MethodInfo) MethodBase.GetCurrentMethod();
        return source.Provider.CreateQuery<T>(
            Expression.Call(
                null,
                currentMethod.MakeGenericMethod(
                    new Type[] { typeof(T) }),
                    new Expression[] {
                        source.Expression,
                        Expression.Quote(predicate)
                    }
                )
            );
}
```

The *CreateQuery<T>* call creates a node for an expression tree corresponding to the call to the *Where<T>* method. That call is made by a particular class that called *Provider*. You will see more about this class later in this chapter; for now, assume that the *Provider* class is directly related to the concrete type of *source* that implements *IQueryable<T>*. It is the role of the *IQueryable<T>.Provider* property to return an instance of the provider type that knows how to handle queries that return *IQueryable<T>*.

At this point, you know that *IQueryable* and *IEnumerable* influence the set of extension meth-ods the compiler chooses when it compiles a query expression. As a simplification, you also know that the compiler generates an execution tree only for lambda expressions declared with an *Expression<T>* type, whereas it generates method calls for LINQ operators. But how do they differ here?

The standard operators defined in the *Enumerable* class return an iterator that gets executed only when an enumerator is retrieved from the query—for example, in a *foreach* loop. (For this reason, query expressions execute only when you iterate over the results, not when the query is defined.) The operators defined in the *Queryable* class build nodes in an expression tree that correspond to the calls of the same operators. If the expression tree is executed, it returns the original expression tree—but typically, it is not executed. Instead, the expression tree generated from *Queryable* operators is visited by the linked *IQueryable* provider, which generates the actions corresponding to the desired operators. For example, a LINQ to SQL provider generates a corresponding SQL query. Therefore, the role of a LINQ *IQueryable* pro-vider (often called simply a LINQ provider) is to visit a query tree (that is, a particular execu-tion tree) and to generate the necessary corresponding actions.

> **Important** A method that returns an instance of *IQueryable* cannot contain a *yield* instruction. Such a method must explicitly return only an *IEnumerable* or *IEnumerator* interface. Although this book does not show specific sample code for this situation, you need to remember this limitation when defining your own extension methods for LINQ.

From *IEnumerable* to *IQueryable* and Back

What are the differences between *IEnumerable* and *IQueryable*? Is it possible to convert an *IEnumerable* into an *IQueryable*? And is it possible to convert an *IQueryable* into an *IEnumer-able*? Knowing the answers to these questions is important for using LINQ effectively, and it is fundamental if you are writing a LINQ provider. To understand the answer, you need some preliminary definitions.

Any query expression implements *IEnumerable*. Any instance of a type implementing *IEnumerable* can be converted into an *IQueryable* instance by calling *AsQueryable*. This call produces an expression tree made up of a single node that calls the original *IEnumerable* instance. This relationship is important for understanding why a complete *IQueryable* query has to be defined starting from an *IQueryable* sequence and cannot be obtained simply by applying *AsQueryable* on an existing *IEnumerable* query. Listing 15-21 shows the effects of using *AsQueryable*.

LISTING 15-21 Effects of using *AsQueryable*

```
int[] numbers = { 1, 2, 3, 5, 8, 13, 21 };
IQueryable<int> query1 =
    from  n in numbers.AsQueryable()  // Typically correct use
    where  n % 2 == 0
    select n;
IQueryable<int> query2 =
    (from  n in numbers
     where  n % 2 == 0
     select n).AsQueryable();          // Typically wrong use
Console.WriteLine(query1.ToString());
Console.WriteLine(query2.ToString());
```

Important The call to *AsQueryable* produces a complete query tree only when you build the query by applying *AsQueryable* to the data source (see *query1* in Listing 15-21), and not by applying *AsQueryable* to an already-defined query as *IEnumerable* (see *query2* in Listing 15-21). Usually you want to get a complete query tree, as in the first case (*query1*).

Executing the code in Listing 15-21 produces the following results:

```
System.Int32[].Where(n => ((n % 2) = 0))
System.Linq.Enumerable+<WhereIterator>d__0'1[System.Int32]
```

The preceding example has a complete query tree for *query1*, because it makes the call to *AsQueryable* on the *numbers* sequence. In this case, the call to the *Where* method is part of the expression tree displayed in the first row of the output. However, when applied to a whole query, as for *query2*, the resulting query tree only wraps the call to the *Where* iterator, as you can see in the second row of the output. Executing *query1* and *query2* provides identical results, but only *query1* can be correctly interpreted by a LINQ provider that visits that query tree. The content of *query2* is opaque, and will not be interpreted correctly by a LINQ provider that, for example, has to produce an equivalent SQL query. Once again, the reason for this behavior is related to the resolution of extension method calls: the compiler uses the *IQueryable* interface (and hence the *Queryable* extension methods) for all LINQ operators when the *AsQueryable* call is in the *from* clause, which defines the source for the query.

Note The *IQueryable* interface by itself does not imply that the *ToString* overload returns the query tree in a readable way. That is the province of the LINQ provider, which should (but is not required to) implement a way to do that. For example, LINQ to SQL shows the corresponding query in SQL form. In contrast, LINQ to Objects, which is the provider used in Listing 15-22, makes use of the existing *ToString* capabilities of the expression tree.

The *AsQueryable* method returns an instance of *EnumerableQuery<T>*, which is a class defined in the *System.Linq* namespace that implements *IQueryable* and *IEnumerable*. This class also overrides *ToString*, calling the corresponding *ToString* method of the expression tree when created from an expression or the name of the type implementing *IEnumerable* whose instance is wrapped.

You can also convert any instance of *IQueryable* into an *IEnumerable*, although this reverse conversion is not really necessary because *IQueryable* implements *IEnumerable* and there is an implicit conversion between those two. However, the presence of *AsEnumerable* in a query expression clearly states that using the *IEnumerable* interface is the programmer's choice and not a mistake.

Whether or not you call *AsEnumerable*, iterating an *IQueryable* requires the interpretation of the query tree and the preparation of some locally executable code. This work is done by the *GetEnumerator* method of the *IEnumerable* class: to be able to interpret the query tree, you need to know the concrete implementation of that *IEnumerable*. In the case of a LINQ to Objects query such as *query1* in Listing 15-21, the call is made to *EnumerableQuery<T>. GetEnumerator*, which then visits the expression tree, transforming *IQueryable* to *IEnumerable*, compiles the resulting expression tree in Intermediate Language (IL) code, and then executes it.

These inner details should give you a more precise understanding of what really happens under the covers. Although this is a high-level overview that did not cover all the details, keep these internals in mind when you write a new LINQ provider. If you do not need to write one, it is sufficient to remember that all *IEnumerable* instances are delegates, all *IQueryable* instances are query trees, and that, with some magic, you can convert each into the other.

Inside *IQueryable* and *IQueryProvider*

Now that you have had a quick look at the whole process, you can start to see more details about the internals of *IQueryable*. First, you will examine the *IQueryable* interface declaration (shown in the following code) member by member:

```
public interface IQueryable : IEnumerable {
    Type ElementType { get; }
    Expression Expression { get; }
    IQueryProvider Provider { get; }
}
```

The *IQueryable* interface is a wrapper around an *Expression*. As we never tire of saying, a query tree is just an expression tree. The difference is made explicit by the *IQueryable* wrapper, which contains two other members. One is *Provider*, which points to the LINQ provider that can interpret and execute the query tree (this is the *Provider* class referred to previously). The other is *ElementType*, which defines the type of the result produced by the iteration over the expression tree. With the code in Listing 15-22, you can compare the different *IQueryable* implementations obtained by using *AsQueryable* in two different queries on the same array.

LISTING 15-22 *IQueryable* content obtained from using *AsQueryable*

```
int[] numbers = { 1, 2, 3, 5, 8, 13, 21 };
IQueryable<int> queryEven =
    from   n in numbers.AsQueryable()
    where  n % 2 == 0
    select n;
Console.WriteLine("** queryEven **");
Console.WriteLine("Provider Type = {0}", queryEven.Provider.GetType());
Console.WriteLine("ElementType   = {0}", queryEven.ElementType);
Console.WriteLine("Expression    = {0}", queryEven.Expression);

IQueryable<int> queryNumbers = numbers.AsQueryable();
Console.WriteLine("** queryNumbers **");
Console.WriteLine("Provider Type = {0}", queryNumbers.Provider.GetType());
Console.WriteLine("ElementType   = {0}", queryNumbers.ElementType);
Console.WriteLine("Expression    = {0}", queryNumbers.Expression);
```

When you run this code, you can see the following result:

```
** queryEven **
Provider Type = System.Linq.EnumerableQuery'1[System.Int32]
ElementType   = System.Int32
Expression    = System.Int32[].Where(n => ((n % 2) = 0))
** queryNumbers **
Provider Type = System.Linq.EnumerableQuery'1[System.Int32]
ElementType   = System.Int32
Expression    = System.Int32[]
```

Notice that both queries have the same provider (*EnumerableQuery<Int32>*) and the same element type (*ElementType (Int32)*). This is not surprising, because both queries originate from a call to *numbers.AsQueryable*. The two queries differ only in their expression trees. Also keep in mind that a type that implements *IQueryable* also implements *IEnumerable*, which means that any *IQueryable* implementation must define a *GetEnumerator* method.

Up to this point, this book has discussed *IQueryable* without distinguishing it from *IQueryable<T>*. Take a look at the latter's declaration:

```
public interface IQueryable<T> : IEnumerable<T>, IQueryable, IEnumerable {
}
```

The *IQueryable<T>* version adds support only to the *IEnumerable<T>* class. Most of the time, you are really using *IEnumerable<T>* and *IQueryable<T>*; their nongeneric counterparts, *IEnumerable* and *IQueryable,* are used only when the code is not strongly typed (which can be useful when you handle legacy classes or when the data type cannot be specified for whatever reason). Usually, an implementation *IQueryable* is made on *IQueryable<T>*, implicitly supporting *IQueryable* as well.

If you want to implement *IQueryable*, you need to write a class that implements *IQueryProvider*, too. Its declaration is as follows:

```
public interface IQueryProvider {
    IQueryable CreateQuery(Expression expression);
    IQueryable<T> CreateQuery<T>(Expression expression);
    object Execute(Expression expression);
    TResult Execute<TResult>(Expression expression);
}
```

In this case, the generic and nongeneric versions of the methods are part of the same interface. A typical *IQueryProvider* implementation redirects the generic methods to the corresponding nongeneric version and casts the result. In this case, *typical* means common cases in which one provider does not have a behavior that depends on the *Execute* result type expected by the caller. Listing 15-23 shows a possible abstract class that implements this behavior. This section implements the custom provider by deriving from this *BaseQueryProvider* class.

LISTING 15-23 *IQueryProvider* implemented in a *BaseQueryProvider* abstract class

```
public abstract class BaseQueryProvider : IQueryProvider {
    public IQueryable<T> CreateQuery<T>(Expression expression) {
        if (expression == null) {
            throw new ArgumentNullException("expression");
        }
        if (!typeof(IQueryable<T>).IsAssignableFrom(expression.Type)) {
            throw new ArgumentException("Argument expression is not valid");
        }
        return (IQueryable<T>) this.CreateQuery(expression);
    }

    public TResult Execute<TResult>(Expression expression) {
        if (expression == null) {
            throw new ArgumentNullException("expression");
        }
        if (!typeof(IQueryable<TResult>).IsAssignableFrom(expression.Type)) {
            throw new ArgumentException("Argument expression is not valid");
        }
        return (TResult) this.Execute(expression);
    }

    public abstract IQueryable CreateQuery(Expression expression);
    public abstract object Execute(Expression expression);
}
```

Note The *EnumerableQuery<T>* class implements the LINQ standard *IQueryable* provider described previously. The implementation of *CreateQuery* and *Execute* here differs between generic and nongeneric versions, but their semantic meaning is the same. Therefore, the subsequent description of the *CreateQuery* and *Execute* requirements does not make a distinction between the generic and nongeneric versions.

The *CreateQuery* method has to create an *IQueryable* object that can evaluate the query represented by the expression tree passed as a parameter. In other words, it creates an instance of a class that implements *IQueryable*, setting its properties. The *Expression* property is set by the parameter received by *CreateQuery*. The *Provider* property is always set to *this* because the *CreateQuery* code is in the provider class implementation. (However, in another implementation, you could have a separate class for the provider implementation.) Finally, the *ElementType* property is the query return type, which should correspond to the *T* in *CreateQuery<T>*. The following fictitious code explains this behavior better than words (you will see code for a real provider later):

```
public IQueryable<T> CreateQuery<T>(Expression expression) {
    IQueryable<T> result = new QueryObject();
    result.Expression = expression;
    result.ElementType = typeof(T);
    result.Provider = this;
}
```

The *Execute* method's role is to interpret the stored query expression into actions related to the nature of the provider. For example, the LINQ to SQL provider translates the expression into SQL statements. This is typically the most complex part of an *IQueryProvider* implementation, and its behavior is strictly related to the nature of the provider. The *EnumerableQuery<T>* provider that *AsQueryable* uses simply compiles the expression tree in a delegate, using the same engine that compiles lambda expressions in IL code. The *EnumerableQuery<T>.GetEnumerator* method calls the *Execute* operation, and it also implements the replacement of *IQueryable* with *IEnumerable* in the expression tree before its compilation.

At this point, you are ready to write a real LINQ provider. Most of the discussion focuses on implementing the code needed to visit and interpret the query tree according to the provider requirements. Be sure to read Chapter 14 because you need to understand how to visit and manipulate an expression tree. The following section concentrates on the high-level operations, without covering too many details of the expression tree navigation.

Writing the *FlightQueryProvider*

Conceptually, any data manipulation or request that can be expressed in a declarative, standardized way is a good candidate for a LINQ provider, such as that offered by LINQ syntax. The most obvious providers are those that convert LINQ queries into existing query languages (such as SQL and CAML). However, those providers are too complex to be good candidates for a basic example. Moreover, any existing, widespread query language probably already has a provider, so you should not need to write another provider for it. More interesting (and more common) is a situation in which you have an existing service that queries data, and you want to standardize its access with LINQ. This scenario might be a web service, a custom TCP/IP format, a queue-based communications system, and so on. LINQ offers the advantage of syntax normalization to such data sources. Of course, the quality of the normalization depends on your provider's implementation and its level of abstraction.

As you can see, this discussion could be very long and—after a certain point—it might be very subjective. The goal here is simply to introduce you to a working LINQ provider that addresses a common scenario for your code.

> **Important** You will see a description of the existing service, and then examine the most impor-
> tant implementation details. To keep the sample easy to understand and (eventually) customizable
> by you, this example uses a library internal to our code as the service. In the real world, this service
> would probably be on a remote server, available through a communication protocol. However, the
> communication layer does not have a direct influence on the LINQ provider other than possible
> constraints on data serialization. If the service already exists, we assume that you have already
> solved these kinds of issues by writing Microsoft .NET Framework types that abstract from the
> communication details.
>
> If you are writing your own communication layer and want to take full advantage of LINQ and
> other .NET Framework features, read Chapter 18, "LINQ in a Multitier Solution."

The *FlightStatusService* Class

The existing service used for this example describes real-time information about flight status. It exposes an application programming interface (API) that you can query for flights that meet specific conditions. These kinds of services are typically not persisted in a relational database; when they are, there is latency on data updates, and even in that case, the database might not be accessible remotely. Hence, the constraint is to keep the existing service interface to retrieve the flight status information. Listing 15-24 shows the entry point of this service, the *FlightSearch* methods in the *FlightStatusService* class.

LISTING 15-24 *FlightSearch* methods as the entry points in *FlightStatusService*

```
public partial class FlightStatusService {

    public List<Flight> FlightSearch(QueryFilter pars) {
        return FlightSearch(pars, -1);
    }

    /// <summary>
    /// API to query flights status - parameters are constraints to filter
    /// only desired flights
    /// </summary>
    /// <param name="pars">Parameters for flights status search</param>
    /// <param name="maxFlights">Maximum numbers of flights in the result
    /// (-1 for all, 0 for empty result)</param>
    /// <returns>List of flights matching search parameters</returns>
```

```
public List<Flight> FlightSearch(QueryFilter pars, int maxFlights) {
    Console.WriteLine("---- FlightQuery execution ----");
    if (maxFlights >= 0) {
        Console.WriteLine("Maximum returned flights: {0}", maxFlights);
    }
    Console.WriteLine(pars);

    // ... Implementation details ...
    }
}
```

The main *FlightSearch* implementation has two parameters: the first (*pars*) is a *QueryFilter* instance that contains the conditions for the query; the second (*maxFlights*) is the maximum number of flights desired in the result (if set to *–1*, it means unlimited and returns all the flights matching the *pars* conditions). There is also a simplified version of *FlightSearch* that has only one parameter, which defaults *maxFlights* to unlimited. The return type of these methods is a generic list of *Flight* instances. You can see the code for the *Flight* class in Listing 15-25.

LISTING 15-25 *Flight* class definition, including the related *AirportInformation* class

```
public class Flight {
    public string Airline { get; set; }
    public string FlightNumber { get; set; }
    public string Aircraft { get; set; }
    public AirportInformation Departure { get; set; }
    public AirportInformation Arrival { get; set; }
    public TimeSpan TimeToArrival { get; set; }
    public int GroundSpeed { get; set; }
    public int Altitude { get; set; }

    public override string ToString() {
            return String.Format(
                "Flight {0}{1} ({2})\n"
                +"FROM: {3} Scheduled: {4}  Actual:    {5}\n"
                +"TO:    {6} Scheduled: {7}  Estimated: {8}\n"
                +"Time to arrival: {9}\n"
                +"Ground speed/Altitude: {10} KTS / {11} feet",
                Airline, FlightNumber, Aircraft,
                Departure.Airport, Departure.ScheduledTime, Departure.ActualTime,
                Arrival.Airport, Arrival.ScheduledTime, Arrival.ActualTime,
                TimeToArrival,
                GroundSpeed,
                Altitude);
    }
}

public class AirportInformation {
    public string Airport { get; set; }
    public DateTime ScheduledTime { get; set; }
    public DateTime ActualTime { get; set; }
}
```

Each flight has an *Airline* code, a *FlightNumber*, and an *Aircraft* type. A flight departs from an airport and arrives at another one: *Departure* and *Arrival* properties describe respective airport information such as *Airport* code, *ScheduledTime*, and actual/expected time. (The *ActualTime* property has to be interpreted as estimated time when the departure/arrival has yet to occur.) *ScheduledTime* and *ActualTime* values are in the local time for the corresponding airports. *TimeToArrival* provides information about estimated time to arrival, and *GroundSpeed* and *Altitude* provide other information about the actual status of the flight. The code for the *QueryFilter* class is somewhat similar to the *Flight* content, but it uses different types and names, as you can see in Listing 15-26.

LISTING 15-26 *QueryFilter* class definition

```csharp
public partial class FlightStatusService {
    public class QueryFilter {
        public string Airline = null;
        public string FlightNumber = null;
        public string Aircraft = null;
        public string DepartureAirport = null;
        public string ArrivalAirport = null;
        public int MinMinutesToArrival = -1;
        public int MaxMinutesToArrival = -1;
        public int MinGroundSpeed = -1;
        public int MaxGroundSpeed = -1;
        public int MinAltitude = -1;
        public int MaxAltitude = -1;

        public override string ToString() {
            StringBuilder sb = new StringBuilder();
            sb.AppendLine("FlightStatus.QueryFilters Dump");
            DumpEqualCondition(sb, "Airline", this.Airline);
            DumpEqualCondition(sb, "FlightNumber", this.FlightNumber);
            DumpEqualCondition(sb, "DepartureAirport", this.DepartureAirport);
            DumpEqualCondition(sb, "ArrivalAirport", this.ArrivalAirport);
            DumpBetweenCondition(sb, "MinutesToArrival",
                                     this.MinMinutesToArrival,
                                     this.MaxMinutesToArrival);
            DumpBetweenCondition(sb, "GroundSpeed",
                                     this.MinGroundSpeed,
                                     this.MaxGroundSpeed);
            DumpBetweenCondition(sb, "Altitude",
                                     this.MinAltitude,
                                     this.MaxAltitude);
            sb.AppendLine("-----------------------");
            return sb.ToString();
        }
```

```
internal void DumpEqualCondition( StringBuilder sb,
                                  string fieldName, string value) {
    if (value != null) {
        sb.Append(fieldName);
        sb.Append(" = ");
        sb.AppendLine(value.ToString());
    }
}
internal void DumpBetweenCondition( StringBuilder sb,
                                    string fieldName,
                                    int limitMin, int limitMax) {
    if ((limitMin >= 0) && (limitMax >= 0)) {
        sb.Append(fieldName);
        sb.Append(" BETWEEN ");
        sb.Append(limitMin.ToString());
        sb.Append(" AND ");
        sb.AppendLine(limitMax.ToString());
    }
    else if (limitMin >= 0) {
        sb.Append(fieldName);
        sb.Append(" >= ");
        sb.AppendLine(limitMin.ToString());
    }
    else if (limitMax >= 0) {
        sb.Append(fieldName);
        sb.Append(" <= ");
        sb.AppendLine(limitMax.ToString());
    }
}
```

Both the *Flight* and *QueryFilter* classes have a *ToString* override that displays their content in a readable form. The *QueryFilter* class uses some of the same names—those that match string properties contained in the *Flight* class. Actually, the service does not support filters on scheduled or actual times of departure and arrival, but there are two string properties for filtering the departure and arrival airport codes. For each numeric property exposed by *Flight*, there are two properties in *QueryFilter*—one for the minimum value and one for the maximum value—which support defining a range of values. Finally, *QueryFilter* has a range of minutes to filter the *TimeToArrival* of a flight (*MinMinutesToArrival/MaxMinutesToArrival*), both of type *int*. In contrast *Flight.TimeToArrival* is a *TimeSpan* instance. You will come back to these differences later.

Here are some calls to the *FlightSearch* method of the *FlightStatusService* class. Listing 15-27 illustrates the "old-style" technique that uses only Microsoft Visual C# 2.0 syntax.

LISTING 15-27 Sample calls to *FlightSearch* using C# 2.0

```
static void SearchFlightsOldWay() {
    FlightStatusService flightStatus = new FlightStatusService();

    FlightStatusService.QueryFilter filterTimeSpeed =
        new FlightStatusService.QueryFilter();
    filterTimeSpeed.MaxGroundSpeed = 400;
    filterTimeSpeed.MaxMinutesToArrival = 30;

    List<Flight> flightsNearLanding =
        flightStatus.FlightSearch(filterTimeSpeed);
    Dump(flightsNearLanding);

    FlightStatusService.QueryFilter filterAltitudeAirline =
        new FlightStatusService.QueryFilter();
    filterAltitudeAirline.MinAltitude = 20000;
    filterAltitudeAirline.MaxAltitude = 30000;
    filterAltitudeAirline.Airline = "WN";

    List<Flight> flightsMediumAltitude =
        flightStatus.FlightSearch(filterAltitudeAirline);
    Dump(flightsMediumAltitude);

    string airportCode = "NRT"; // Tokyo
    FlightStatusService.QueryFilter filterTokyo =
        new flightStatusService.QueryFilter();
    filterTokyo.ArrivalAirport = airportCode;

    // Filter only 1 output rows
    List<Flight> flightsTokyo =
        flightStatus.FlightSearch(filterAltitudeAirline, 1);
    Dump(flightsMediumAltitude);
}
```

In the following output produced by the execution of the code in Listing 15-27, each query has a "FlightQuery execution" header followed by a dump of the *QueryFilter* instance passed to the *FlightSearch* method. Each query exposes different challenges for the LINQ provider implementation that you will explore later:

```
---- FlightQuery execution ----
FlightStatusService.QueryFilter Dump
MinutesToArrival <= 30
GroundSpeed <= 400
-----------------------

Flight NK117 (Airbus A319)
FROM: DTW Scheduled: 25/12/2007 13.09.00  Actual:    25/12/2007 13.48.00
TO:   MCO Scheduled: 25/12/2007 15.43.00  Estimated: 25/12/2007 16.01.00
Time to arrival: 00:12:00
Ground speed/Altitude: 359 KTS / 22400 feet
-------------------
```

```
---- FlightQuery execution ----
FlightStatusService.QueryFilter Dump
Airline = WN
Altitude BETWEEN 20000 AND 30000
-----------------------


Flight WN1002 (Boeing 737-700)
FROM: RNO Scheduled: 25/12/2007 12.15.00  Actual:    25/12/2007 12.24.00
TO:   SJC Scheduled: 25/12/2007 13.15.00  Estimated: 25/12/2007 13.02.00
Time to arrival: 00:18:00
Ground speed/Altitude: 447 KTS / 22000 feet
--------------------
---- FlightQuery execution ----
Maximum returned flights: 1
FlightStatusService.QueryFilter Dump
Airline = WN
Altitude BETWEEN 20000 AND 30000
-----------------------


Flight WN1002 (Boeing 737-700)
FROM: RNO Scheduled: 25/12/2007 12.15.00  Actual:    25/12/2007 12.24.00
TO:   SJC Scheduled: 25/12/2007 13.15.00  Estimated: 25/12/2007 13.02.00
Time to arrival: 00:18:00
Ground speed/Altitude: 447 KTS / 22000 feet
--------------------
```

There is nothing truly "wrong" with the code in Listing 15-27, but it is not sufficiently self-documenting, it is boring to write, and it is verbose to read. You need a C# statement for each query condition. Sometimes you need to know the corresponding property of *QueryFilter* to apply a filter on a *Flight* property, because (for the reasons mentioned before) they do not always have the same name. You can improve the syntax a little by switching to the C# 3.0 syntax, as in Listing 15-28.

LISTING 15-28 Sample calls to *FlightSearch* using C# 3.0

```csharp
static void SearchFlightsCS30() {
    FlightStatusService flightStatus = new FlightStatusService();

    var flightsNearLanding =
        flightStatus.FlightSearch(
            new FlightStatusService.QueryFilter {
                MaxGroundSpeed = 400,
                MaxMinutesToArrival = 30
            });
    Dump(flightsNearLanding);
```

```
        var flightsMediumAltitude =
            flightStatus.FlightSearch(
                new FlightStatusService.QueryFilter {
                    MinAltitude = 20000,
                    MaxAltitude = 30000,
                    Airline = "WN"
                });
        Dump(flightsMediumAltitude);

        string airportCode = "NRT"; // Tokyo
        var flightsTokyo =
            flightStatus.FlightSearch(
                new FlightStatusService.QueryFilter {
                    ArrivalAirport = airportCode
                },
                1); // Filter only 1 output rows
        Dump(flightsTokyo);
    }
```

Listing 15-28 contains just as many lines as Listing 15-27, but the code looks nicer and is easier to read. However, to train a new developer, you would still need to document how to use the *QueryFilter* class to specify the filter conditions. It would be much nicer to give developers the ability to query a *Flight* collection just as they might query any other collection—even if that collection is not local but is hosted remotely by a service. In the end, the goal is to be able to write the code such as that in Listing 15-29, which uses LINQ query syntax.

LISTING 15-29 Sample calls to *FlightSearch* using LINQ

```
static void SearchFlightsLinq() {
    FlightStatusService flightStatus = new FlightStatusService();

    var flightsNearLanding =
        from   f in flightStatus.AsQueryable()
        where  f.GroundSpeed <= 400
               && f.TimeToArrival.TotalMinutes <= 30
        select f;
    Dump(flightsNearLanding);

    var flightsMediumAltitude =
        from   f in flightStatus.AsQueryable()

        where f.Altitude >= 20000
              && f.Altitude <= 30000
              && f.Airline == "WN"
        select f;
    Dump(flightsMediumAltitude);
```

```
    string airportCode = "NRT"; // Tokyo
    var filterTokyo =
        (from   f in flightStatus.AsQueryable()
         where  f.Arrival.Airport == airportCode
         select f)
        .Take(1); // Filter only 1 output rows
    Dump(filterTokyo);
}
```

The LINQ query syntax uses marginally fewer lines of code, but the important point is the declarative way that you can use it to query a remote service without having any knowledge of the *QueryFilter* class. You can use the well-known semantics of C# expressions in *Where* conditions that act on properties of the *Flight* class. The custom provider will make the conversion to a corresponding *QueryFilter* instance to get the same results as in the previous listings. To accomplish this, you "only" need to write an ad-hoc LINQ provider implementing *IQueryable* and *IQueryProvider*. That provider will analyze the query tree and, for example, interpret the *f.Arrival.Airport == airportCode* condition as an assignment of the *airportCode* value to the *ArrivalAirport* property of a *QueryFilter* instance. You must also write an *AsQueryable* implementation that extends the *FlightStatusService* class.

One important aspect of this scenario is the presence of the *Take* operator. (See the *filterTokyo* query in Listing 15-29.) You need to convert the *Take* operator in the *maxFlights* parameter of the *FlightSearch* call, to have flights filtered by the service rather than by the client. This single requirement makes it impossible to limit the implementation to a specialization of the *Where* operator, as shown in Listing 15-19 for the *SortedDictionary* class, which visited the *Where* predicate by receiving it as an expression tree. This time, you need to write a real *IQueryable* implementation.

Implementing *IQueryable* in *FlightQuery*

The first step in implementing a LINQ provider is to define a class that represents the query and implements *IQueryable<T>*. This provider needs to return data for only a single type— the *Flight* class—so you can define the *FlightQuery* class as a constructed type that implements *IQueryable<Flight>* instead of the generic *IQueryable<T>*, as you can see in Listing 15-30.

LISTING 15-30 *FlightQuery* class implementing *IQueryable<Flight>*

```
public class FlightQuery : IQueryable<Flight> {
    FlightQueryProvider provider;
    Expression expression;

    public FlightQuery(FlightQueryProvider provider) {
        if (provider == null) {
            throw new ArgumentNullException("provider");
        }
```

```
            this.provider = provider;
            this.expression = Expression.Constant(this);
    }

    public FlightQuery(FlightQueryProvider provider, Expression expression) {
        if (provider == null) {
            throw new ArgumentNullException("provider");
        }
        if (expression == null) {
            throw new ArgumentNullException("expression");
        }
        if (!typeof(IQueryable<Flight>).IsAssignableFrom(expression.Type)) {
            throw new ArgumentOutOfRangeException("expression");
        }
        this.provider = provider;
        this.expression = expression;
    }

    #region IQueryable implementation
    Expression IQueryable.Expression { get { return this.expression; } }
    Type IQueryable.ElementType { get { return typeof(Flight); } }
    IQueryProvider IQueryable.Provider { get { return this.provider; } }
    #endregion IQueryable implementation

    #region IEnumerable<T> implementation
    public IEnumerator<Flight> GetEnumerator() {
        return ((IEnumerable<Flight>)
            this.provider.Execute(this.expression)).GetEnumerator();
    }
    #endregion IEnumerable<T> implementation

    #region IEnumerable implementation
    IEnumerator IEnumerable.GetEnumerator() {
        return ((IEnumerable)
            this.provider.Execute(this.expression)).GetEnumerator();
    }
    #endregion IEnumerable implementation

    public override string ToString() {
        return this.provider.GetQueryText(this.expression);
    }
}
```

The *FlightQuery* class is relatively easy to create because it delegates most of the work to the *FlightQueryProvider* class that you still have to write. The two constructors check the parameters and save the values for the *Expression* and *Provider* properties implemented as part of the *IQueryable* interface. The third property defined by the *IQueryable* interface, *ElementType*, always returns *typeof(Flight)* because this provider supports only that class as a result.

You might wonder what the difference is between the first and the second *FlightQuery* constructor. Suppose you write something like this:

```
var query =  flightStatus.AsQueryable();
```

For the preceding code, the *AsQueryable* implementation has to return an instance of *FlightQuery* without having an expression tree (because *flightStatus* by itself is not an expression tree). The first constructor handles this situation. Because you always need a valid *Expression* in an *IQueryable* object, it creates an expression tree made of a single *ConstantExpression* node, which points to the *FlightQuery* instance itself (the one represented by *flightStatus* in our *AsQueryable* call). In other cases, you will have a query tree that uses the *IQueryable* implementation, for example:

```
var query2 = query.Where( (f) => f.GroundSpeed <= 400 );
```

The preceding example needs the second constructor, which has two parameters, *provider* and *expression*. The *CreateQuery* methods that are part of the *IQueryProvider* implementation typically invoke this second constructor. Specifically, the invocation is made by the implementation of the *Where<T>* operator defined in *Queryable.Where<T>* that builds the query tree for *query2*.

Remember that you are not forced to build exactly the same constructors in another *IQueryable* implementation, but most *IQueryable* implementations will probably have a similar structure because there is a common need for both constructors.

At this point, you can examine the *IEnumerable/IEnumerable<T>* implementations, which are mandatory because a class that implements *IQueryable<T>* also implements *IEnumerable* and *IEnumerable<T>*. The corresponding *GetEnumerator()* methods are functionally identical; the only difference is the return value type: *IEnumerator* or *IEnumerator<T>*. Both *GetEnumerator()* methods call the *Execute* method on the *provider* member (of type *FlightQueryProvider*), passing the stored *Expression* as a parameter, and they both call *GetEnumerator()* on the result (which should always be an *IEnumerable<Flight>*). Internally, the *FlightQueryProvider* has to call the *FlightSearch* method, passing the right parameters. This will be the core part of the provider implementation.

A final note on the *ToString* override: that method returns a textual representation of the query tree. The goal is to use the existing *ToString* implementation of the *FlightStatusService. QueryFilter* class, wrapped in the *GetQueryText* method of our provider. The hard part is to convert the query tree into a corresponding *FlightStatusService.QueryFilter* instance, but this is the same work required to implement the *Execute* method. The example provider implementation shares the code for these two operations.

Implementing *IQueryProvider* in *FlightQueryProvider*

The core of this custom provider is the *IQueryProvider* implementation. This implementation requires a fair amount of code, so it is split into several classes here. First, look at the *Flight-QueryProvider* implementation in Listing 15-31, which extends the *BaseQueryProvider* defined earlier in Listing 15-23.

LISTING 15-31 *FlightQueryProvider* class implementing *IQueryProvider*

```
public class FlightQueryProvider : BaseQueryProvider {
    // Force developers to pass a FlightStatusService in the constructor
    protected FlightQueryProvider() {}

    private FlightStatusService flightStatus;

    public FlightQueryProvider(FlightStatusService flightStatus) {
        if (flightStatus == null) {
            throw new ArgumentNullException("flightStatus");
        }
        this.flightStatus = flightStatus;
    }

    #region BaseQueryProvider abstract methods implementation
    public override object Execute(Expression expression) {
        FlightQueryParameters parameters = this.Translate(expression);
        return flightStatus.FlightSearch(
            parameters.Filter,
            parameters.MaxFlights);
    }

    public override IQueryable CreateQuery(Expression expression) {
        return new FlightQuery(this, expression);
    }
    #endregion BaseQueryProvider abstract methods implementation

    public string GetQueryText(Expression expression) {
        FlightQueryParameters parameters = this.Translate(expression);
        return parameters.ToString();
    }

    private FlightQueryParameters Translate(Expression expression) {
        expression = Evaluator.PartialEval(expression);
        return new FlightQueryTranslator().Translate(expression);
    }
}
```

The methods required by the abstract class *BaseQueryProvider* are *CreateQuery* and *Execute*. The *CreateQuery* method simply creates an instance of *FlightQuery*. The *Execute* method uses the private *Translate* method, which converts the query tree into an instance of *FlightQuery-Parameters* and executes the *FlightSearch* invocation, passing the parameters obtained by the query translation. The *Translate* method shares its behavior with the *GetQueryText* public method, which returns a textual representation of the query by making the same translation of the query tree into a *FlightQueryParameters* instance and then calling its *ToString* method. You can see the *FlightQueryParameters* definition in Listing 15-32. This class is simply a wrapper for all the possible parameters of the *FlightSearch* class.

LISTING 15-32 *FlightQueryParameters* class definition

```
internal class FlightQueryParameters {
    public FlightStatusService.QueryFilter Filter { get; set; }
    public int MaxFlights { get; set; }

    public FlightQueryParameters() {
        this.Filter = new FlightStatusService.QueryFilter();
        this.MaxFlights = -1;
    }

    public override string ToString() {
        if (MaxFlights >= 0) {
            return String.Format(
                "{0}Maximum returned flights: {1}",
                Filter.ToString(),
                MaxFlights);
        }
        else {
            return Filter.ToString();
        }
    }
}
```

Implementing an *ExpressionVisitor* in *FlightQueryTranslator*

The most important part of our provider is the *Translate* implementation, defined within the *FlightQueryTranslator* class, which derives from the base class *ExpressionVisitor*.

> **More Info**   The *ExpressionVisitor* class used in the example Flight Status LINQ provider is the implementation of an expression tree visitor published by Matt Warren on his blog at *http: //blogs.msdn.com/mattwar/archive/2007/07/31/linq-building-an-iqueryable-provider-part-ii.aspx*. Refer to Chapter 14 for further information about expression tree analysis and manipulation.

Because the *FlightQueryTranslator* is a long class, this explanation covers only the relevant code, starting with an overview of the member declarations in Listing 15-33, which shows the implementations of only two methods: the constructor and *Translate*. Listing 15-33 includes only the declaration of the other methods in the class.

LISTING 15-33 *FlightQueryTranslator* member declarations

```
public class FlightQueryTranslator : ExpressionVisitor {
    FlightQueryParameters queryParameters;

    internal FlightQueryTranslator() {}
    internal FlightQueryParameters Translate(Expression expression) {
        this.queryParameters = new FlightQueryParameters();
        this.Visit(expression);
        return this.queryParameters;
    }

    // ExpressionVisitor specialization
    protected override Expression VisitMethodCall(MethodCallExpression m);
    protected override Expression VisitUnary(UnaryExpression u);
    protected override Expression VisitBinary(BinaryExpression b);
    protected override Expression VisitConstant(ConstantExpression c);
    protected override Expression VisitMemberAccess(MemberExpression m);

    // Helper methods
    private void TranslateStandardComparisons(
        ExpressionType nodeType,
        ConstantExpression constant,
        MemberExpression memberAccess);

    private void TranslateAirportInformationComparison(
        ConstantExpression constant,
        MemberExpression memberAccess);

    private void TranslateTimeSpanComparison(
        ExpressionType nodeType,
        ConstantExpression constant,
        MemberExpression memberAccess);

    private static Expression StripQuotes(Expression e);
    internal static void SetIntParameter(
        int limit,
        ref int MinValue, ref int MaxValue,
        ExpressionType comparison);

    internal static int GetIntConstant(ConstantExpression constant);
    internal static double GetDoubleConstant(ConstantExpression constant);
}
```

The *Translate* method initializes the *queryParameters* member, which is compiled by the inspection of the query tree made by the *Visit* call. The method *Visit* is defined in the *ExpressionVisitor* base class. Other methods are overridden because *Translate* needs to intercept only some nodes—those of interest to the provider.

The example *FlightStatusService* implementation supports only two LINQ operators: *Where*, which defines the content of a *FlightStatus.QueryFilter* instance, and *Take*, which influences the *maxFlights* parameter of a *FlightSearch* call. Listing 15-34 shows the *VisitMethodCall* implementation that handles these operators. It throws a *NotSupportedException* if any other operator is used in the query.

> **Note** Listing 15-34 also includes the *StripQuotes* implementation. An *ExpressionType.Quote* node refers to a *UnaryExpression* instance that has a constant value of type *Expression*. Visiting the expression tree, a *MethodCallExpression* node can refer to any method. If one of the method's arguments is a lambda expression, it becomes a "quoted" expression (it is enclosed in an *ExpressionType.Quote* node type). The *Where* condition in an expression tree is represented as a *MethodCallExpression* node that stores the predicate as a quoted lambda expression. The *Where* predicate will not need to handle any further indirect processing. The call to *StripQuotes* returns a pure lambda expression as a predicate for the *Where* condition.

LISTING 15-34 *FlightQueryTranslator.VisitMethodCall* implementation

```
/// <summary>
/// These are the only supported extension methods (Where and Take)
/// We simply visit the Where condition and the Take parameter
/// and translate them into a FlightStatus.QueryParameters instance
/// </summary>
protected override Expression VisitMethodCall(MethodCallExpression m) {
    if (m.Method.DeclaringType == typeof(Queryable)) {
        switch (m.Method.Name) {
            case "Where":
                this.Visit(m.Arguments[0]);
                LambdaExpression lambda =
                    (LambdaExpression) StripQuotes(m.Arguments[1]);
                this.Visit(lambda.Body);
                return m;
            case "Take":
                this.Visit(m.Arguments[0]);
                ConstantExpression constant =
                    m.Arguments[1] as ConstantExpression;
                if (constant == null) {
                    throw new NotImplementedException(
                        "Take supported only for constant values");
                }
                queryParameters.MaxFlights = GetIntConstant(constant);
                return m;
        }
    }
    throw new NotSupportedException(
        string.Format("The method '{0}' is not supported", m.Method.Name));
}

private static Expression StripQuotes(Expression e) {
    while (e.NodeType == ExpressionType.Quote) {
        e = ((UnaryExpression) e).Operand;
    }
    return e;
}
```

Both *Take* and *Where* operators are applied to an *IQueryable* expression; for this reason, the first common step is to continue the visit on the first parameter of these methods, which is the instance of the class that these methods are extending. In this case, that first parameter should always be an expression tree that returns *IQueryable<FlightQuery>*. Subsequently, the implementation of these two operators differs.

Handling the *Take* operator is simple: the implementation supports only a constant value, so it simply tries to interpret the argument of the method call expression in *m.Arguments[1]*, saving its value in the *MaxFlights* property of the *queryParameters* instance.

To handle the *Where* condition, you need to visit its predicate, which is another expression tree, available in the second parameter of the *Where* call in *m.Arguments[1]*.

 Important Because this implementation supports only *Where* and *Take*, the code does not need to remember that it is inside a *Where* condition when making the call to *Visit (lambda.Body)*. In a more complex provider, you would probably need to keep track of the context in which an expression tree is visited.

A predicate in a *Where* condition is an expression that returns a *Boolean*. A query to the provider can have a meaningful predicate only by using comparison operators. If more than one comparison operator is present, this implementation supports only the AND between different conditions: the service does not have semantics that can support an OR between filter conditions. All these comparisons and logical operators are instances of *BinaryExpression* in our expression tree. The override for *VisitBinary* in Listing 15-35 filters the unsupported operations, continuing the visit of the query tree for the left and right parts of an AND condition. In other words, an AND has no effect other than continuing the expression tree visit.

LISTING 15-35 *FlightQueryTranslator.VisitBinary* implementation

```
/// <summary>
/// The AND condition simply continues the visit to the left and right parts
/// If there is a binary operation other than a supported comparison,
/// a NotSupportedException is thrown
/// </summary>
protected override Expression VisitBinary(BinaryExpression b) {
    switch (b.NodeType) {
        case ExpressionType.And:
        case ExpressionType.AndAlso:
            // Compare only other binary operators - we default to AND,
            // so this is not an error and does not produce other effects
            this.Visit(b.Left);
            this.Visit(b.Right);
            // We EXIT here, we do not process the condition further
            return b;
        case ExpressionType.Equal:
```

```
        case ExpressionType.LessThanOrEqual:
        case ExpressionType.GreaterThanOrEqual:
        case ExpressionType.LessThan:
        case ExpressionType.GreaterThan:
            return VisitBinaryComparison(b);
        default:
            // We DO NOT support:
            // - NotEqual
            // - Or
            throw new NotSupportedException(string.Format(
                "The binary operator '{0}' is not supported", b.NodeType));
    }
}
```

The *VisitBinaryComparison* implementation shown in Listing 15-36 has three steps. First, it evaluates the constant and the member to be compared. Comparisons between *Flight* members and/or between constants or other expressions are unsupported simply because there are no semantics to transfer similar constraints to the *FlightStatusService*. For this reason, the code assumes that a binary comparison must have a constant and a member access expression (in whatever position), and must throw an exception in all other cases.

LISTING 15-36 *FlightQueryTranslator.VisitBinaryComparison* implementation

```
/// <summary>
/// Performs a sanity check of constant and memberAccess
/// Then it performs a different translation according to
/// the type of the member to be compared with
/// </summary>
private Expression VisitBinaryComparison(BinaryExpression b) {
    // FIRST STEP
    // We support only a comparison between constant
    // and a possible flight query parameter
    ConstantExpression constant =
        (b.Left as ConstantExpression ?? b.Right as ConstantExpression);
    MemberExpression memberAccess =
        (b.Left as MemberExpression ?? b.Right as MemberExpression);

    // SECOND STEP
    // Sanity check of parameters
    if ((memberAccess == null) || (constant == null)) {
        throw new NotSupportedException(
            string.Format(
                "The binary operator '{0}' must compare a valid "
                +"flight attribute with a constant",
                b.NodeType));
    }
```

```
            // We need to get the constant value
            if (constant.Value == null) {
                throw new NotSupportedException(
                    string.Format(
                        "NULL constant is not supported in binary operator {0}",
                        b.ToString()));
            }
            switch (Type.GetTypeCode(constant.Value.GetType())) {
                case TypeCode.String:
                case TypeCode.Int16:
                case TypeCode.Int32:
                case TypeCode.Double:
                    break;
                default:
                    throw new NotSupportedException(
                        string.Format(
                            "Constant {0} is of an unsupported type ({1})",
                            constant.ToString(),
                            constant.Value.GetType().Name));
            }

            // THIRD STEP
            // Look for member name through Reflection
            // We assume that string properties in Flight have the same name
            // in QueryParameters
            // We have a special check for Flight members of complex types
            if (memberAccess.Member.ReflectedType == typeof(TimeSpan)) {
                TranslateTimeSpanComparison(b.NodeType, constant, memberAccess);
                return b;
            }
            else if (memberAccess.Member.ReflectedType == typeof(AirportInformation)) {
                TranslateAirportInformationComparison(constant, memberAccess);
                return b;
            }
            else if (memberAccess.Member.ReflectedType != typeof(Flight)) {
                throw new NotSupportedException(
                    string.Format(
                        "Member {0} is not of type Flight",
                        memberAccess.ToString()));
            }
            TranslateStandardComparisons(b.NodeType, constant, memberAccess);
            return b;
        }
```

The second step is simply a sanity check of the *memberAccess* and *constant* expressions. Something more complex happens during the third step. The simplest case is the comparison of a *Flight* member with a primitive type, such as *string* or *int*. Here is an example of such a query:

```
var query =
    from   f in flightStatus.AsQueryable()
    where  f.Airline == "UA" && f.Altitude >= 10000
    select f;
```

This standard case is handled by the *TranslateStandardComparisons* shown in Listing 15-37. Then there are special cases that compare the *Departure*, *Arrival*, or *TimeToArrival* members of the *Flight* class with some constant values, as in the following query:

```
var query =
    from    f in flightStatus.AsQueryable()
    where   f.Arrival.Airport == "NRT"
            && f.TimeToArrival.TotalHours >= 2
    select f;
```

The code in Listing 15-36 intercepts these cases (in the third step) by analyzing the type of the member access expression. There are two different methods for handling these cases, *TranslateAirportInformationComparison* and *TranslateTimeSpanComparison*, whose implementations are included in Listing 15-38.

LISTING 15-37 *FlightQueryTranslator.TranslateStandardComparisons* implementation

```
/// <summary>
/// The standard case supports an equal condition for strings
/// and other comparisons for GroundSpeed and Altitude integers
/// </summary>
private void TranslateStandardComparisons(
    ExpressionType nodeType,
    ConstantExpression constant,
    MemberExpression memberAccess) {

    string stringFieldName =
        (from field in typeof(Flight).GetProperties()
         where Type.GetTypeCode(field.PropertyType) == TypeCode.String
             && field.Name == memberAccess.Member.Name
         select field.Name).FirstOrDefault();

    // Loop for all strings (Airline, FlightNumber and Aircraft)
    if (stringFieldName != null) {
        if (nodeType != ExpressionType.Equal) {
            throw new NotSupportedException(
                string.Format(
                    "The binary operator '{0}' is not supported on {1} member",
                    nodeType,
                    memberAccess.Member.Name));
        }
        queryParameters.Filter.GetType()
            .GetField(stringFieldName)
            .SetValue(queryParameters.Filter, constant.Value);
    }
    else {
        // String not found
        switch (memberAccess.Member.Name) {
            case "GroundSpeed":
```

```
                    SetIntParameter(
                        GetIntConstant(constant),
                        ref queryParameters.Filter.MinGroundSpeed,
                        ref queryParameters.Filter.MaxGroundSpeed,
                        nodeType);
                    break;
                case "Altitude":
                    SetIntParameter(
                        GetIntConstant(constant),
                        ref queryParameters.Filter.MinAltitude,
                        ref queryParameters.Filter.MaxAltitude,
                        nodeType);
                    break;
                default:
                    throw new NotSupportedException(
                        string.Format("Condition on member {0} is not supported",
                        memberAccess.ToString()));
            }
        }
    }

    internal static void SetIntParameter(
        int limit,
        ref int minValue,
        ref int maxValue,
        ExpressionType comparison) {

        switch (comparison) {
            case ExpressionType.Equal:
                minValue = limit;
                maxValue = limit;
                break;
            case ExpressionType.LessThan:
                maxValue = limit - 1;
                break;
            case ExpressionType.LessThanOrEqual:
                maxValue = limit;
                break;
            case ExpressionType.GreaterThan:
                minValue = limit + 1;
                break;
            case ExpressionType.GreaterThanOrEqual:
                minValue = limit;
                break;
            default:
                throw new NotSupportedException(
                    string.Format(
                        "The binary operator '{0}' is not supported",
                        comparison));
        }
    }
}
```

At this point, the code speaks for itself. Sometimes it uses reflection to find members in the *FlightStatus.QueryFilter* structure or to explore the types of the member access expression being visited.

LISTING 15-38 *TranslateAirportInformationComparison* and *TranslateTimeSpanComparison* implementation

```
/// <summary>
/// We currently support only the filter on the Airport code
/// </summary>
private void TranslateAirportInformationComparison(
    ConstantExpression constant,
    MemberExpression memberAccess) {

    MemberExpression parent = memberAccess.Expression as MemberExpression;
    if (parent.Member.ReflectedType != typeof(Flight)) {
        throw new NotSupportedException(
            string.Format(
                "Member {0} is not of type Flight",
                memberAccess.ToString()));
    }
    // We support only Airport ...
    if (memberAccess.Member.Name == "Airport") {
        switch (parent.Member.Name) {
            case "Departure":
                queryParameters.Filter.DepartureAirport =
                    constant.Value.ToString();
                break;
            case "Arrival":
                queryParameters.Filter.ArrivalAirport =
                    constant.Value.ToString();
                break;
        }
    }
}


/// <summary>
/// We support only a TotalMinutes and TotalHours comparison
/// </summary>
private void TranslateTimeSpanComparison(
    ExpressionType nodeType,
    ConstantExpression constant,
    MemberExpression memberAccess) {

    MemberExpression parent = memberAccess.Expression as MemberExpression;
    if (parent.Member.ReflectedType != typeof(Flight)) {
        throw new NotSupportedException(
            string.Format(
                "Member {0} is not of type Flight",
                memberAccess.ToString()));
    }
```

```
        // We support only TotalMinutes for this simple provider
        if ((memberAccess.Member.Name == "TotalMinutes")
            && (parent.Member.Name == "TimeToArrival")) {
            SetIntParameter(
                (int) GetDoubleConstant(constant),
                ref queryParameters.Filter.MinMinutesToArrival,
                ref queryParameters.Filter.MaxMinutesToArrival,
                nodeType);
        }
        else if ((memberAccess.Member.Name == "TotalHours")
            && (parent.Member.Name == "TimeToArrival")) {
            SetIntParameter(
                (int) GetDoubleConstant(constant) * 60,
                ref queryParameters.Filter.MinMinutesToArrival,
                ref queryParameters.Filter.MaxMinutesToArrival,
                nodeType);
        }
        else {
            throw new NotSupportedException(
                string.Format(
                    "Query on {0} expression is not supported",
                    memberAccess.ToString()));
        }
    }
```

Finally, the implementation does not support expression trees that do not match the pattern of supported predicates. For that reason, the implementations of *VisitUnary*, *VisitConstant*, and *VisitMemberAccess* (all included in Listing 15-39) throw an exception—these expressions are already handled by the helper methods called inside the *VisitBinary* method.

LISTING 15-39 *VisitUnary*, *VisitConstant*, and *VisitMemberAccess* implementations in *FlightQueryTranslator*

```
protected override Expression VisitUnary(UnaryExpression u) {
    throw new NotSupportedException(
        string.Format(
            "The unary operator '{0}' is not supported",
            u.NodeType));
}

protected override Expression VisitConstant(ConstantExpression c) {
    if (c.Value is IQueryable) {
        // Assumes constant nodes implementing IQueryable
        // are flight sequences
        return c;
    }
    throw new NotSupportedException(
        string.Format(
            "The constant for '{0}' is not supported",
            c.ToString()));
}
```

```
protected override Expression VisitMemberAccess(MemberExpression m) {
    throw new NotSupportedException(
        string.Format(
            "The member '{0}' is not supported",
            m.Member.Name));
}
```

Working with the *FlightQueryProvider*

At this point, the LINQ provider is almost ready. You need only extend the *FlightStatusService* with the *AsQueryable* operator. For this example, assume that you do not own the code for the *FlightStatusService* class, so to extend it, you must use the extension method syntax shown in Listing 15-40.

LISTING 15-40 *AsQueryable* definition as an extension method of *FlightStatusService*

```
public static class FlightStatusExtension {
    public static IQueryable<Flight> AsQueryable(
        this FlightStatusService flightStatus ) {

        FlightQueryProvider context =
            new FlightQueryProvider(flightStatus);
        return new FlightQuery(context);
    }
}
```

The *AsQueryable* operator creates an instance of *FlightQueryProvider* bound to a *flightStatus* instance, and it returns a new instance of the *FlightQuery* class. Each call to *AsQueryable* creates a new instance for both the *FlightQueryProvider* and *FlightQuery* classes. Note that this approach is specific to this particular implementation; another provider could implement some caching techniques on the *IQueryProvider* implementation. However, the cost of objects implementing *IQueryProvider* is usually very light, such as the *DataContext* in LINQ to SQL. The *AsQueryable* operator itself is not mandatory; you can always get a *FlightQuery* instance by calling the *IQueryProvider.CreateQuery* method.

With that code in place, you can finally execute LINQ queries against the *FlightStatusService*. The code you originally saw in Listing 15-29 can now execute successfully. In addition, you can get the query translated from a LINQ implementation to a textual representation, as shown in Listing 15-41.

LISTING 15-41 Samples of LINQ queries applied to *FlightStatusService*

```
FlightStatusService flightStatus = new FlightStatusService();

var query1 =
    from   f in flightStatus.AsQueryable()
    where  f.Airline == "UA" && f.Altitude >= 10000
    select f;
Console.WriteLine("** query1 **");
Console.WriteLine(query1);

var query2 =
    (from   f in flightStatus.AsQueryable()
     where  f.Arrival.Airport == "NRT"
            && f.TimeToArrival.TotalHours >= 2
     select f).Take(2);
Console.WriteLine("** query2 **");
Console.WriteLine(query2);
```

The execution of Listing 15-41 produces the following results:

```
** query1 **
FlightStatusService.QueryFilter Dump
Airline = UA
Altitude >= 10000
-----------------------

** query2 **
FlightStatusService.QueryFilter Dump
ArrivalAirport = NRT
MinutesToArrival >= 120
-----------------------
Maximum returned flights: 2
```

Having a textual representation of a query expression is extremely useful when debugging, and also helps when building unit tests. The example *FlightQueryProvider* implementation provides this feature essentially for free, because most of the work is done by the *Translate* method shared between the *GetQueryText* and *Execute* methods.

Cost-Benefit Balance of a Custom LINQ Provider

Implementing a LINQ provider is not an easy task. You need a deep understanding of how to interpret the expression tree that represents the query. Moreover, it is easy for subtle bugs to remain hidden for years—and when they explode, you need to understand what is happening on many different levels of abstraction just to isolate the bug. Consider the possible errors in a query passed to a custom LINQ provider. These kinds of errors (just think of all our examples of *NotImplementedException*) can be checked only at execution time and not at compile time. Therefore, using the *IQueryable* interface somewhat exposes your code to errors that can be intercepted only during query execution.

> **Important** *IQueryable* query expressions cannot be completely checked at compile time, especially when they use unsupported operators and/or expressions.

Thus, a new LINQ provider definitely has a high cost. But what are the benefits?

Generally speaking, having LINQ queries is a good thing, because programmers express their will in a declarative form instead of an iterative one. LINQ abstracts the code from the data source's internal implementation, providing a more affordable abstraction from any specific data layer. Finally, LINQ is a standard and an increasingly important part of the .NET Framework; you probably already understand that, in a few years, reading and writing LINQ queries will be part of the standard skill set for the majority of .NET Framework programmers.

But is the cost of implementing a LINQ provider justified by its benefits?

Obviously, the answer is "that depends." A LINQ provider used only by one or a few programmers who are using a service could be very expensive. On the other hand, if hundreds of developers use a library, or if that library is used over several different data layers, the presence of a LINQ provider can lower the learning curve and produce a solid return on investment. These improvements become more important as the complexity of the underlying data model increases, because the simplification, readability, and maintainability of LINQ queries help amortize the cost of writing a custom LINQ provider.

> **Note** We did not mention the performance implications of using LINQ. Adding a layer to the software usually does not improve performance, unless it provides a sort of cache service, for example, like that provided by the LINQ to SQL provider through *DataContext* entities. It is a developer's responsibility to evaluate whether the performance cost involved in using LINQ is affordable. Typically, calling a remote service has other bottlenecks, such as latency in communication, so using LINQ should not be an issue. However, each scenario deserves a dedicated analysis.

Summary

In this chapter, you saw how to build custom operators, how to specialize existing operators, and finally, how to build a custom LINQ provider. Creating new LINQ operators or specializing one or more of the existing ones does not require complete control over query expressions. However, defining a custom LINQ provider that implements *IQueryable* and *IQueryProvider* requires many more resources. A custom LINQ provider is useful whenever you want to implement an external service whose API cannot be changed. To establish whether a LINQ provider is worth the time required to build it, you have to evaluate the cost-benefit balance for your own scenario.

Chapter 16

Parallelism and Asynchronous Processing

The expressiveness of Microsoft Language Integrated Query (LINQ) can be useful when approaching complex problems, such as parallelizing operations and processing events asynchronously. Because a LINQ expression is a declarative form that describes what the result should be, and not how it should be obtained, you can delegate the implementation of the algorithm to the underlying runtime. This is exactly what you do using LINQ to Objects when querying in-memory structures. Microsoft .NET Framework 4 integrates Parallel LINQ (PLINQ), which can scale out former LINQ to Objects operations over multiple cores, using the parallelism features offered by the Task Parallel Library, also part of .NET Framework 4.

 Note The Task Parallel Library and PLINQ are not available in Microsoft .NET Framework 3.5.

LINQ can also be useful whenever you want to describe events you are interested in. Because of their very nature, events are usually asynchronous, so you typically write considerable plumbing code just to look at events you are not really interested in. The Reactive Extensions for .NET (Rx) is a library for composing asynchronous and event-based programs using observable collections, which is particularly useful for programming in Microsoft Silverlight and JavaScript.

 Note The Reactive Extensions for .NET (Rx) library is available as a separate download for both .NET Framework 3.5 and .NET Framework 4.

This chapter provides an introduction to the Task Parallel Library and a complete guide to PLINQ. The final part of the chapter includes an overview of the Reactive Extensions for .NET.

Task Parallel Library

The Task Parallel Library (TPL) offers a set of types and application programming interfaces (APIs) that simplify the process of adding parallelism and concurrency to an application. The goal of the TPL is to scale the degree of concurrency dynamically in a way that uses all the available processors, if possible.

The TPL is the preferred way for .NET Framework developers to write multithreaded and parallel code. It is also used by Parallel LINQ, which is described later in this chapter. Although the TPL simplifies the code required to parallelize an algorithm and to take advantage of multithreading, you still need an understanding of basic multithreading concepts such as locks, deadlocks, and race conditions, which are not covered in this chapter.

Note You can find several learning resources for multithreading concepts on the Parallel Computing Developer Center on MSDN at *http://msdn.microsoft.com/concurrency*.

The *Parallel.For* and *Parallel.ForEach* Methods

The TPL provides classes and methods that simplify the parallelization of code, without requiring you to deal with details concerning threads, thread pools, and synchronization. The first example, shown in Listing 16-1, is the *For* method of the *Parallel* class included in the *System.Threading.Tasks* namespace.

LISTING 16-1 *Parallel.For* statement

```
static void SequentialFor() {
    Stopwatch sw = Stopwatch.StartNew();
    for (int index = 0; index < 100; index++) {
        ProcessData(index);
    }
    long elapsed = sw.ElapsedMilliseconds;
    Console.WriteLine("Sequential for: {0} milliseconds", elapsed);
}

static void ParallelFor() {
    Stopwatch sw = Stopwatch.StartNew();
    Parallel.For(0, 100, (index) => {
        ProcessData(index);
    } );
    long elapsed = sw.ElapsedMilliseconds;
    Console.WriteLine("Parallel for: {0} milliseconds", elapsed);
}
```

The *Parallel.For* call in the *ParallelFor* method replaces the *for* statement of the *SequentialFor* method. Running this code on a quad-processor machine results in the following:

```
Sequential for: 2837 milliseconds
Parallel for: 754 milliseconds
```

As you can see, the implementation based on *Parallel.For* uses different threads to run the code inside the original *for* loop, which calls the *ProcessData* method. In a multicore machine, this results in faster execution. In a single-core machine, the overhead required for parallelism would actually make the *Parallel.For* call slower than the original *for* statement if it actually used multiple threads. Therefore, *Parallel.For* creates multiple threads only if other execution cores are available, which also reduces possible overhead for single-core machines. However, in Listing 16-1, the *ProcessData* method simulates a heavy processing operation. If that process operation executes operations that involve suspending threads, such as any input/output (I/O) operations, the resulting *Parallel.For* execution time could be better than *for* even on a single-core machine.

> **Note** If the processor has to wait for an external resource or for synchronizing with another thread, the current thread is suspended. In this case, another thread can be served by the same processor that was serving the suspended thread.

The *Parallel.ForEach* method implements a parallel execution for what would normally be a simple *foreach* statement, as you can see in Listing 16-2.

LISTING 16-2 *Parallel.ForEach* statement

```
static void SequentialForEach(int[] data) {
    Stopwatch sw = Stopwatch.StartNew();
    foreach (int value in data) {
        ProcessData(value);
    }
    long elapsed = sw.ElapsedMilliseconds;
    Console.WriteLine("Sequential foreach: {0} milliseconds", elapsed);
}

static void ParallelForEach(int[] data) {
    Stopwatch sw = Stopwatch.StartNew();
    Parallel.ForEach(data, (value) => {
        ProcessData(value);
    } );
    long elapsed = sw.ElapsedMilliseconds;
    Console.WriteLine("Parallel foreach: {0} milliseconds", elapsed);
}
```

The *Parallel.ForEach* method is similar to the *Parallel.For* method. Both methods execute the delegate passed as the last argument on possibly different threads, which results in a faster response time for the entire loop when the code is executed on a multicore machine or when the loop contains operations that can suspend the thread. Here is the result obtained by running the code on a quad-core workstation:

```
Sequential for: 2846 milliseconds
Parallel for: 727 milliseconds
```

The *Parallel.For* and *Parallel.ForEach* methods both require that the operation for each cycle be independent from the others. In other words, you cannot assume that *ProcessData* will be called and receive *2* as an argument after it has been called receiving the argument *1*.

More importantly, if the executed code has to store results in a shared object, such as an *int* or a *List<T>* or any other shared object type, you must ensure that access to such shared objects is protected against concurrency. You can read more about the important considerations concerning such issues in the sidebar "Safe Programming in a Multithreaded Environment" later in this chapter.

The *Parallel.Invoke* Method

The *Parallel.Invoke* method receives an array of delegates that can be executed in any order and possibly in parallel on different threads. Decisions about order and threads are made automatically by the runtime, based on the available resources and the duration of each delegate. Thanks to the lambda expression syntax, you can use *Parallel.Invoke* by writing code such as that shown in Listing 16-3.

LISTING 16-3 *Parallel.Invoke* statement

```
static int Operation(int index) {
    DataCalculation(index);
    Console.WriteLine("Operation {0}", index);
    return index * 10;
}

static void DemoInvoke_Sequential() {
    Console.WriteLine("=== Sequential calls ===");
    Operation(1);
    Operation(2);
    Operation(3);
    Operation(4);
}

static void DemoInvoke_Parallel() {
    Console.WriteLine("=== Parallel.Invoke calls ===");
    Parallel.Invoke(
        () => Operation(1),
        () => Operation(2),
        () => Operation(3),
        () => Operation(4));
}
```

 Note In this example, the values returned by calls to *Operation* are not used, but they will be used in an example later in the chapter.

The calls to *Operation* made inside *DemoInvoke_Parallel* can be called in different threads and in a nondeterministic order. In fact, as you can see in the following result, the output produced by calling *DemoInvoke_Sequential* and then *DemoInvoke_Parallel* demonstrates that in the latter case the calls were made using different threads:

```
=== Sequential calls ===
Operation 1
Operation 2
Operation 3
Operation 4
=== Parallel.Invoke calls ===
Operation 2
Operation 1
Operation 3
Operation 4
```

The implementation of *Parallel.Invoke* creates several instances of the *Task* class, without exposing them to the control of the programmer.

The *Task* Class

The *System.Threading.Tasks.Task* class represents an asynchronous operation. It is a wrapper for a delegate that includes information such as the end of execution (*IsCompleted*, *IsCanceled*, *IsFaulted*), methods to control execution (*Start*, *Wait*), and patterns to stop *Task* execution. (You will see how to use the *CancellationToken* in the "Controlling Task Execution" section later in this chapter.) You could rewrite the code that uses *DemoInvoke_Parallel* in Listing 16-3 by instantiating *Task* objects, as shown in Listing 16-4.

LISTING 16-4 Use of the *Task* class

```
static void DemoTask() {
    Console.WriteLine("=== Task calls ===");
    Task t1 = Task.Factory.StartNew( delegate { Operation(1); } );
    Task t2 = Task.Factory.StartNew( delegate { Operation(2); } );
    Task t3 = Task.Factory.StartNew( delegate { Operation(3); } );
    Task t4 = Task.Factory.StartNew( delegate { Operation(4); } );
    Task.WaitAll(new Task[] { t1, t2, t3, t4 });
}
```

Listing 16-4 creates each *Task* instance by calling the *StartNew* method of the default *TaskFactory* instance, which is provided by the *Factory* static property of the *Task* class. This is the common way to create a default *Task*. The *Task.WaitAll* method accepts an array of *Task* instances, and waits until all the tasks have completed. Each *Task* may be executed in a different thread. One result of executing the *DemoTask* method in Listing 16-4 is the following (although this output might be different for each execution):

```
=== Task calls ===
Operation 3
Operation 4
Operation 2
Operation 1
```

The *Task* class is useful when you want to control asynchronous operations and maintain the ability to cancel one or more of them, without having to implement a custom handling of that scenario.

The *Task<TResult>* Class

The *Task<TResult>* class inherits from the *Task* class. It adds semantics to read a result value from an asynchronous operation without having to write synchronization code.

Neither Listing 16-3 nor Listing 16-4 bothered handling the result of the *Operation* method call. To do that, you would need to store the result of the *Operation* call in the *Task* instance (and to do *that*, you need to create a custom class that inherits *Task*). Then you would need to read that value from the *Task* object consumer. Fortunately, the *Task<TResult>* class already implements all these operations, making it easy to write code like that shown in Listing 16-5.

LISTING 16-5 Use of the *Task<TResult>* class

```
static void DemoTaskResult() {
    Console.WriteLine("=== Task<TResult> calls ===");
    var f1 = Task.Factory.StartNew( () => Operation(1) );
    var f2 = Task.Factory.StartNew( () => Operation(2) );
    var f3 = Task.Factory.StartNew( () => Operation(3) );
    var f4 = Task.Factory.StartNew( () => Operation(4) );

    int result = f1.Result + f2.Result + f3.Result + f4.Result;
    Console.WriteLine("Task result is {0}", result);
}
```

The process to create a *Task<TResult>* is identical to that of creating a *Task* instance. Which overload of the *Task.Factory.StartNew* method gets called depends on the lambda expression you pass as a parameter. In this case, the lambda expression returns a value, so *Task.Factory* calls the *Task<TResult>* version of *StartNew*. The *T* type is inferred from the delegate passed as an argument. In Listing 16-5, *Operation* is a method that returns an *int*; so calling *StartNew* generates instances of *Task<int>*. Attempting to access the *Task<TResult>.Result* property executes a *Task.Wait* call if the task is still not complete. This means that accessing several *Result* properties, as in Listing 16-5, might execute a series of *Wait* calls rather than a single *WaitAll* call. Because *Task<TResult>* inherits *Task*, you can always call *WaitAll* before accessing the *Result* property. For example, the following two lines guarantee a single wait operation:

```
TaskCoordinator.WaitAll(new Task[] { f1, f2, f3, f4 });
int result = f1.Value + f2.Value + f3.Value + f4.Value;
```

Regardless of the read order of the *Result* properties, the call to *Operation* can execute and complete in any order. The following output is a possible result of the execution of Listing 16-5:

```
=== Task<TResult> calls ===
Operation 3
Operation 2
Operation 4
Operation 1
```

Using *Task<TResult>* hides most of the details of thread synchronization that are necessary when an asynchronous operation needs to return data to another thread.

Controlling Task Execution

You have seen how to start a *Task* immediately after creating it. However, executing a *Task* is often useless until another *Task* has completed its job. This is a situation commonly known as *synchronization*, but in TPL, rather than synchronizing function execution, you can define the relationships that exist between tasks in terms of precedence and order of execution.

The simplest concept is the one of continuation. Each task instance has a *ContinueWith* method that can define a sequential execution relationship between a task and another one. The *ContinueWith* method gets the action used to define the corresponding new *Task*, which executes only after the task instance on which *ContinueWith* is called has completed. For example, imagine that you have to load a file from the network, and, when the loading is completed, you have to process the file content that has been loaded into memory. You might have two functions for that job: the first called *jobLoad*, which loads the file into memory, and a second called *jobProcess*, which makes a calculation over the data loaded from a previous call to *jobLoad*. The standard sequential code would be:

```
jobLoad();
jobProcess();
```

To make these execute in parallel, you might write:

```
Task taskLoad = Task.Factory.StartNew( () => { jobLoad(); } );
Task taskProcess = Task.Factory.StartNew( () => { taskLoad.Wait(); jobProcess(); } );
```

However, that solution is not very good because *taskProcess* would start before it is necessary, and its first operation would have to be a wait for *taskLoad* completion, suspending the task just after it started. It is much better to start *taskLoad* immediately after *taskProcess* completes. That is the behavior you obtain by calling the *ContinueWith* method:

```
Task taskLoad = Task.Factory.StartNew( () => { jobLoad(); } );
Task taskProcess = taskLoad.ContinueWith( (prevTask) => { jobProcess(); };
```

The *prevTask* parameter of the lambda expression corresponds to *taskLoad* in this case; this is useful whenever you do not save the previous task in *taskLoad*, for example, writing code that saves just the *taskProcess* returned by the *ContinueWith* call:

```
Task taskProcess = Task.Factory.StartNew( () => { jobLoad(); } )
    .ContinueWith( (prevTask) => { jobProcess(); };
```

The example in Listing 16-6 makes four calls to *Operation* that will be executed in sequential order, passing as a parameter *1*, *2*, *3*, and then *4*. Each *ContinueWith* call passes an *Action* as a parameter, which operates with a parameter containing a reference to the previous task. (It might be useful to get information from the preceding task, called *prevTask* in the lambda expression, although this example does not do that.)

LISTING 16-6 Use of the *ContinueWith* method

```
static void DemoContinuation() {
    Console.WriteLine("=== Task calls ===");
    Task tLast = Task.Factory.StartNew( () => { Operation(1); } )
        .ContinueWith( (prevTask) => { Operation(2); } )
        .ContinueWith( (prevTask) => { Operation(3); } )
        .ContinueWith( (prevTask) => { Operation(4); } );
    tLast.Wait(); // waits for Operation(4), which started after other operations
}
```

That code will always produce this result:

```
=== Task calls ===
Operation 1
Operation 2
Operation 3
Operation 4
```

You might wonder why someone should create four different tasks instead of just one that makes the four calls to *Operation* in a traditional iterative way. The reason is that each *Task* might have different parameters, with a particular regard to the synchronization context. This is covered in more detail in the section "*Task* Synchronization" later in this chapter.

The *ContinueWith* method illustrated in Listing 16-6 is not so useful when you have a task that must start after two or more other tasks (that do not depend on each other) have been completed. In this case, instead of creating the last task with *StartNew*, you can call the *ContinueWhenAll* method of the default *TaskFactory* provided by the *Factory* static property of the *Task* class. This way, you can pass a collection of *Task* objects that you want to be complete before the new *Task* starts. The action of the new *Task* receives a parameter (*prevTasks* in Listing 16-7) that contains the collection of tasks that you want to wait for.

LISTING 16-7 Use of the *ContinueWhenAll* method

```
static void DemoContinuationWhenAll() {
    Console.WriteLine("=== Task calls ===");
    Task t1 = Task.Factory.StartNew( () => { Operation(1); } );
    Task t2 = Task.Factory.StartNew( () => { Operation(2); } );
    Task t3 = Task.Factory.StartNew( () => { Operation(3); } );
    Task tLast = Task.Factory.ContinueWhenAll(
        new Task[] { t1, t2, t3 },
        (prevTasks) => {
            Console.WriteLine("----");
            Operation(4); } );

    tLast.Wait();
}
```

The only guaranteed result is that the *Operation 4* row will always be last, after the other three tasks have completed, as shown here. The execution order of the first three operations might vary in each run of the same code:

```
=== Task calls ===
Operation 3
Operation 2
Operation 1
----
Operation 4
```

In case you only need to wait for one task in a group of tasks to complete before starting the execution of a new *Task*, you can use the *ContinueWhenAny* method. Using *Continue-WhenAny* is similar to using *ContinueWhenAll*.

So far, you have created unrelated tasks that have been put into a relationship after their creation by using a continuation method. However, you can create a new *Task* instance inside the code of another *Task* instance, an operation called *creating a nested task*. A regular nested task is no different from any other task, and behaves in the same way: if you need any form of coordination between such tasks, you must use an implicit or explicit wait call or a continuation method. Listing 16-8 creates a *nestedTask* instance within the code of the *outerTask* instance, which waits for the end of *nestedTask* only because, at that point, it makes a call to the *Result* property of *nestedTask*.

LISTING 16-8 Creation of a nested task

```
static void DemoNestedTask() {
    Console.WriteLine("=== Task calls ===");
    Task outerTask = Task.Factory.StartNew( () => {
        Console.WriteLine("Outer task start");
        var nestedTask = Task.Factory.StartNew( () => {
            Console.WriteLine("Nested task start");
            Console.WriteLine("Nested task complete");
            return 42;
        } );
        // If there was no call on nestedTask.Result, outerTask might end
        // before nestedTask completion
        Console.WriteLine("Nested result={0}", nestedTask.Result);
        Console.WriteLine("Outer task complete");
    } );
    outerTask.Wait();
}
```

This is the result:

```
=== Task calls ===
Outer task start
Nested task start
Nested task complete
Nested result=42
Outer task complete
```

You can create a nested task using a parameter that defines a stronger relationship, creating a task called a *child task*, which is closely synchronized with the parent task. Listing 16-9 creates a child task using the same syntax that created the nested task in the preceding example, but with the addition of a *TaskCreationOptions.AttachedToParent* value as the second parameter to the *StartNew* call.

LISTING 16-9 Creation of a child task

```
static void DemoChildTask() {
    Console.WriteLine("=== Task calls ===");
    Task parentTask = Task.Factory.StartNew( () => {
        Console.WriteLine("Parent task start");
        var childTask = Task.Factory.StartNew(
            () => {
                Console.WriteLine("Child task start");
                Thread.Sleep(100);
                Console.WriteLine("Child task complete");
            },
            TaskCreationOptions.AttachedToParent);
        Console.WriteLine("Parent task complete");
    } );
```

```
    Console.WriteLine("Wait for outer task");
    parentTask.Wait();
    Console.WriteLine("Wait passed");
}
```

Executing the code in Listing 16-9 results in the following:

```
=== Task calls ===
Wait for outer task
Parent task start
Parent task complete
Child task start
Child task complete
Wait passed
```

A child task differs from a nested task (which is also called a *detached nested task*) because it offers these services:

- The parent task automatically waits for all child tasks to complete: the call *parentTask.Wait* in Listing 16-9 waits for both *parentTask* and *childTask* to complete because *parentTask* is completed only after all its child tasks are also completed.

- Any exception thrown in a child task is automatically propagated to parent tasks. (You will see an example of this later in Listing 16-12.)

- The status of the parent task (that is, its *IsCompleted* property state) depends on the status of its child tasks.

As you can see, using child tasks to automatically define synchronization behavior and exception propagation between related tasks is interesting. If you have ever tried to achieve the same behavior using delegates, asynchronous calls, and threads, you will appreciate the simplification that the *Task* class semantics offer.

The ability to cancel an operation in progress is also important. The TPL offers a cooperative model that cancels tasks based on a pattern that uses the *CancellationTokenSource* and *CancellationToken* classes. This pattern requires a task to poll periodically for a *CancellationToken* during task execution. Listing 16-10 shows an example that checks the *IsCancellationRequested* property of the *CancellationToken* instance to see if a cancellation has been requested. This test is required if you want to add some cleanup code before calling the *ThrowIfCancellationRequested* method, which tests the same property and throws a *TaskCanceledException* exception, which is caught by the *try/catch* block containing the *task.Wait*. Note that you always get an *AggregateException*, which contains at least a *TaskCanceledException* in its *InnerExceptions* but might also contain other exceptions from other tasks running concurrently. (You have just seen that the task you are waiting for may have executed other child tasks.)

LISTING 16-10 Use of *CancellationToken* to cancel a task

```
static void DemoCancelTask() {
    var tokenSource = new CancellationTokenSource();
    CancellationToken ct = tokenSource.Token;

    var task = Task.Factory.StartNew( () => {
        // Stop task if there is a pending cancellation request
        ct.ThrowIfCancellationRequested();

        bool moreToDo = true;
        while (moreToDo) {
            // Check pending cancellation request
            // (not necessary if cleanup code was not required)
            if (ct.IsCancellationRequested) {
                // Add cleanup code before stopping task
                // Stop task (there is surely a cancellation request at this point)
                ct.ThrowIfCancellationRequested();
            }

            Thread.Sleep(100);
            Console.Write(".");
        }
    }, tokenSource.Token);

    // Wait for ENTER, then cancel execution
    Console.ReadLine();
    tokenSource.Cancel();

    // Just continue on this thread, or Wait/WaitAll with try-catch:
    try {
        task.Wait();
    }
    catch (AggregateException e) {
        foreach (var v in e.InnerExceptions) {
            Console.WriteLine("{0}: {1}", e.Message, v.Message);
        }
    }
}
```

This is the result obtained by pressing Enter just after execution starts:

```
........
.One or more errors occurred.: A task was cancelled.
```

Note To bind code that will be executed when the *CancellationToken* is canceled by calling *ThrowIfCancellationRequested*, you can call the *Register* method on a *CancellationToken* instance. This is important because you gain the ability to move cleanup code to the bound method rather than put it directly in the polling code. This becomes even more important if you test the *IsCancellationRequested* property in more than one place in your code.

You have just seen the *AggregateException*, which is a special exception that aggregates all the exceptions thrown in parallel tasks. For example, consider the *Parallel* class methods you saw at the beginning of this chapter. A *Parallel.For* or a *Parallel.Invoke* call implicitly calls *Wait* for all the tasks that have been started to execute the required code in parallel. An exception in a running task does not exclude the possibility that other running tasks might throw other exceptions as well. Therefore, these exceptions are always grouped in an *AggregateException* instance. The original exceptions are accessible through the *AggregateException.InnerExceptions* property. In Listing 16-11, you can see an example of two tasks called by *Parallel.Invoke*.

LISTING 16-11 Handling exceptions from tasks

```
static void DemoExceptionTasks() {
    try {
        Parallel.Invoke(
            () => { throw new ArgumentException(); },
            () => { throw new NullReferenceException(); }
        );
    }
    catch (AggregateException ex) {
        foreach (var v in ex.InnerExceptions) {
            Console.WriteLine("Exception: " + v.Message);
        }
    }
}
```

These tasks throw two different exceptions. Executing that code produces the following result:

```
Exception: Object reference not set to an instance of an object.
Exception: Value does not fall within the expected range.
```

When a child task throws an exception, the exception is propagated to the parent task. In such cases, you catch an *AggregateException* instance thrown by the parent task, which contains another *AggregateException* instance that contains the exceptions thrown by its child task. In other words, child task exceptions are nested in an *AggregateException* instance tree.

Listing 16-12 shows an example of a child task that throws an *ArgumentException*. The *catch* block first intercepts an *AggregateException*, then iterates its *InnerExceptions* property, which shows another *AggregateException* that, iterating *InnerExceptions* again, finally shows the *ArgumentException* that was originally thrown by your code.

LISTING 16-12 Handling exceptions from child tasks

```
static void DemoExceptionChildTasks() {
    Console.WriteLine("=== Task calls ===");
    Task parentTask = Task.Factory.StartNew(() => {
        Console.WriteLine("Parent task start");
        var childTask = Task.Factory.StartNew(
            () => {
                Console.WriteLine("Child task start");
                Thread.Sleep(100);
                Console.WriteLine("Child task complete");
                throw new ArgumentException();
            },
            TaskCreationOptions.AttachedToParent);
        Console.WriteLine("Parent task complete");
    });
    Console.WriteLine("Wait for outer task");

    try {
        parentTask.Wait();
        Console.WriteLine("Wait passed");

        Thread.Sleep(200);
    }
    catch (AggregateException ex) {
        foreach (var v in ex.InnerExceptions) {
            Console.WriteLine("{0}: {1}", v.GetType().Name, v.Message);
            // Exceptions from child tasks are in another AggregateException
            if (v is AggregateException) {
                foreach (var childEx in (v as AggregateException).InnerExceptions) {
                    Console.WriteLine( "Child {0}: {1}",
                                        childEx.GetType().Name,
                                        childEx.Message);
                }
            }
        }
    }
}
```

Executing that code produces the following result:

```
=== Task calls ===
Wait for outer task
Parent task start
Parent task complete
Child task start
Child task complete
AggregateException: One or more errors occurred.
Child ArgumentException: Value does not fall within the expected range.
```

> **More Info** You have seen the basic techniques for controlling execution of tasks, handling exceptions, and implementing cancellation patterns in the TPL. You can explore the .NET Framework 4 documentation at *http://msdn.microsoft.com/en-us/library/dd537609.aspx* to get a more complete description of all the options available to control *Task* behavior.

Using Tasks for Asynchronous Operations

The .NET Framework has two standard patterns for asynchronous operations:

- **Asynchronous Programming Model (APM)**   The operation is represented by a pair of *Begin/End* methods, such as *BeginRead* and *EndRead* in many *Stream* derived classes.

- **Event-based asynchronous pattern (EAP)**   The operation is represented by a method/event pair named *OperationNameAsync* and *OperationNameCompleted*, such as *DownloadFileAsync* and *DownloadFileCompleted* in the *WebClient* class.

You can use TPL to both encapsulate these patterns and implement and expose them in your classes. The *FromAsync* method available in a *TaskFactory* instance class receives the two *Begin/End* methods as parameters and returns a *Task* or a *Task<TResult>* instance, depending on the result returned by the *End* call.

Listing 16-13 shows an example of encapsulating a simple copy file operation that uses *Begin-Read/EndRead* and *BeginWrite/EndWrite* to copy the SampleData.txt file into CopyData.txt.

LISTING 16-13 Encapsulating APM calls into *Task* instances

```
static void DemoApmCall() {
    // We create two tasks to copy file. The first read the file,
    // the second write the content in another file
    string pathRead = "SampleData.txt";
    string pathWrite = "CopyData.txt";
    FileInfo fi = new FileInfo(pathRead);
    byte[] buffer = new byte[fi.Length];

    FileStream fr = new FileStream(pathRead, FileMode.Open, FileAccess.Read,
                            FileShare.Read, buffer.Length, true);

    // taskRead will return the number of bytes read (same type returned by EndRead)
    Task<int> taskRead = Task<int>.Factory.FromAsync(fr.BeginRead, fr.EndRead,
                                            buffer, 0, buffer.Length, null);
    Task taskCopy = taskRead.ContinueWith((tr) => {
        // Close source file
        fr.Close();
```

```
        // Check if read length is correct
        if (tr.Result != buffer.Length) {
            throw new Exception("Error reading source file");
        }

        FileStream fw = new FileStream(pathWrite, FileMode.Create, FileAccess.Write,
                                FileShare.None, buffer.Length, true);
        // EndWrite is void - so Task is required
        Task taskWrite = Task.Factory.FromAsync(fw.BeginWrite, fw.EndWrite, buffer, 0,
                                        buffer.Length,
                                        TaskCreationOptions.AttachedToParent)
                    .ContinueWith((tw) => {
                        // Close dest file
                        fw.Close();
                    }, TaskContinuationOptions.AttachedToParent);
    });

    try {
        taskCopy.Wait();
    }
    catch (AggregateException ex) {
        foreach (var v in ex.InnerExceptions) {
            Console.WriteLine("{0}:{1}", v.GetType().Name, v.Message);
        }
    }
}
```

The *taskRead* instance reads the file into the buffer and continues with the *taskCopy* instance, which first closes the source file and then creates a child task named *taskWrite*, which writes the buffer into the new file. It then closes the destination file using a second child task. If an error occurs in any of the four tasks created to conclude the operation, the *taskCopy.Wait* call will catch an *AggregationException*.

Note You may have observed that creating four tasks to complete one copy operation is not very efficient; a single task with two synchronous operations on the source and destination files would have been better. However, this example is purely for educational purposes, because it lets you observe the way child tasks are attached to a parent, and recognize the need to close the file in a continuation task.

You can also use a *Task* or *Task<TResult>* instance to define your own implementation of the APM pattern in your class. For example, in Listing 16-14, you can see how to implement the *BeginCalculate* and *EndCalculate* methods of a *Calculator* class, which is supposed to make long and complex calculations over your data. Using tasks, you might interact with the running code in a more standard way (that is, using the *CancellationToken* class you saw previously in this chapter). However, you cannot cancel a task returned by *FromAsync*, because the underlying .NET Framework APIs do not support in-progress cancellation of file or network I/O. Thus, the only cancellation that might happen is on continuation tasks that are not created directly by *FromAsync* calls.

As you can see in Listing 16-4, the *Task* class implements *IAsyncResult*, which will be returned as the result of *BeginCalculate*. For this reason, there is no need to store the *Task* instance in the *Calculator* class. In fact, this specific implementation of *Calculator* might be a static class too, but in the real world, it might be necessary to store some data in each instance to support a more complex calculation.

LISTING 16-14 Implementation of APM using *Task*

```
class Calculator {
    public IAsyncResult BeginCalculate(int calcParameter,
            AsyncCallback ac, object state) {
        Task<int> f = Task<int>.Factory.StartNew(
                          (s) => Compute(calcParameter), state);
        if (ac != null) f.ContinueWith((res) => ac(f));
        return f;
    }

    public int Compute(int parameter) {
        return parameter * 42;
    }

    public int EndCalculate(IAsyncResult ar) {
        return ((Task<int>)ar).Result;
    }
}
```

The second pattern, initially introduced by Microsoft .NET Framework 2.0, is the event-based asynchronous pattern (EAP). The TPL does not have a method similar to *FromAsync* to embed an asynchronous call into a *Task*. However, you can use the *TaskCompletionSource<TResult>* class to represent any arbitrary set of operations as a *Task<TResult>*. You can use that class to expose asynchronous operations implemented using EAP, as shown in Listing 16-15.

LISTING 16-15 Encapsulating EAP calls into a *Task*

```
static Task<long[]> PingTask(string url, int packets, CancellationToken token) {
    TaskCompletionSource<long[]> tcs = new TaskCompletionSource<long[]>();
    Ping[] pings = new Ping[packets];
    long[] timings = new long[packets];
    int count = 0;
```

```
        // In case of cancellation, send cancel to all active pings
        token.Register(() => {
            foreach (var ping in pings) {
                if (ping != null) {
                    ping.SendAsyncCancel();
                }
            }
        });

        for (int i = 0; i < packets; i++) {
            // Saves i in currentPing for the PingCompleted asynchronous event handler
            int currentPing = i;
            pings[currentPing] = new Ping();
            Ping ping = pings[currentPing];
            ping.PingCompleted += new PingCompletedEventHandler((obj, args) => {
                timings[currentPing] = (args.Reply != null) ?
                                       args.Reply.RoundtripTime : -1;

                // Check if it is the last operation
                if (Interlocked.Increment(ref count) == packets) {
                    // if last ping completed, set Result on underlying task
                    tcs.TrySetResult(timings);
                }
            });
            ping.SendAsync(url, null);
        }
        return tcs.Task;
    }

    static void DemoEap() {
        string url = "www.bing.com";
        CancellationTokenSource ts = new CancellationTokenSource();
        var pingsTask = PingTask(url, 5, ts.Token);

        // Call ts.Cancel() if you want to cancel the pingsTask

        long[] timings = pingsTask.Result;
        foreach (long t in timings) {
            Console.WriteLine("Time: {0}", t);
        }
    }
}
```

Listing 16-15 shows an example of asynchronous ping calls made using EAP. These calls are embedded into a *Task* using an instance of *TaskCompletionSource<TResult>*. The *PingTask* static function starts a given number of *Ping.SendAsync* calls to a remote URL. Each *Ping.SendAsync* call makes an asynchronous call to the *PingCompleted* event. It is important to consider that the order of these calls is not deterministic; therefore, the code increments a counter using *Interlocked.Increment* to find the last completed operation, calling the *TrySetResult* method of *TaskCompletionSource* instance at that point.

Safe Programming in a Multithreaded Environment

The example in Listing 16-15 illustrates a number of interesting techniques required to program in a multithreaded environment. The *count* variable is incremented using *Interlocked.Increment* so that an explicit *lock* is not required (making the code more efficient).

Moreover, the loop saves the index counter (*i*) into a *currentPing* local variable so that each instance of the anonymous method passed as a *PingCompletedEventHandler* instance will have the right value. If the anonymous method, which is called in a different thread, used the counter variable directly, it would be accessing a shared value of *i*, which would both probably be different than expected at the time of execution, and might also be outside the range of the *pings* array elements.

For example, consider the following code:

```
for (int i = 0; i < array.length; i++) {
    Task.Factory.StartNew( () => Calc( array[i] ) );
}
```

The *array[i]* expression will be evaluated in a thread other than the one for the *foreach* loop. The problem is that the *i* variable changes after the task begins executing, producing a bad calculation and possibly an out-of-range exception. (The final value of *i* will be the length of *array*, but *array* is accessible only from zero to its length minus one.)

To avoid this mistake, you have to be very careful whenever you create a *Task* inside a loop (or in general when you provide anonymous methods that will be called in different threads). You need to save the variable used to iterate the loop in a local variable, to maintain its value for use by the anonymous method, which is called later in another thread. The following example saves a pointer to the item contained in the array, which is an equivalent way to write safe multithreaded code:

```
for (int i = 0; i < array.length; i++) {
    var item = array[i];
    Task.Factory.StartNew( () => Calc( item ) );
}
```

These concepts are important when you operate with the TPL and PLINQ, because you are writing code that often will be executed in different concurrent threads.

Concurrency Considerations

Writing multithreaded code exposes programmers to a much wider range of possible errors than single-threaded code. A program that correctly runs in a single thread might be affected by any sort of concurrency issues when moved into a multithreaded environment. In this section, you will see a number of important concurrency considerations when using the TPL and PLINQ.

Race Conditions

The most common issue in a multithreaded environment is concurrent write access to a shared object. A piece of code is thread-safe if it functions correctly during simultaneous execution by multiple threads. Unfortunately, very few classes in the .NET Framework are thread-safe by design (and performance is one of the reasons for that). Therefore, when using the Parallel Extensions to the .NET Framework, you still need to synchronize access to most classes. However, thread synchronization is an expensive operation that also limits scalability. A better approach is to write code that does not share data—but it is not always possible to do that, because you might have an algorithm that imposes the need for data sharing.

Consider the code in Listing 16-16, which implements a simple sum of the results returned from the *Operation* method called inside a *Parallel.For* call.

LISTING 16-16 Example of a race condition in a parallel operation

```
static void DemoConcurrency_RaceCondition() {
    Console.WriteLine("=== DemoConcurrency_RaceCondition ===");
    int sum = 0;
    Parallel.For(1, 10, (index) => {
        int local = sum;
        local += Operation(index);
        sum = local;
    });
    Console.WriteLine("Final sum: {0}", sum);
}
```

As you can see, *sum* is a local variable in the *DemoConcurrency* method. However, it is used by concurrent methods (the delegate that implements the cycle of the *For* method), and can be accessed by several threads at the same time. The code in Listing 16-16 should produce a final sum of 450. (*Operation* returns the value received as the argument multiplied by 10.) However, running the code in Listing 16-16 on a multicore machine should produce a final result lower than the expected value, as in the following output, where the final sum is 170:

```
=== DemoConcurrency_RaceCondition ===
Operation 4
Operation 3
Operation 2
Operation 5
Operation 6
Operation 7
Operation 9
Operation 1
Operation 8
Final sum: 170
```

There are several approaches to solve this issue. The most common approach is to use some synchronization statements that protect data from concurrent access (for example, using the *lock* statement in Microsoft Visual C#):

```
object sync = new object();
// ...
Parallel.For(0, 10, (index) => {
    lock (sync) {
        int local = sum;
        local += Operation(index);
        sum = local;
    }
});
```

However, using synchronization between concurrent threads can limit scalability. An alternative and more scalable approach is to avoid the concurrent access entirely. This approach does not require the use of a particular API, but it affects the way the code is designed. It is important to think about this kind of issue before writing code because refactoring a design issue after it has occurred is much more expensive than adding synchronization code. In Listing 16-17, you can see an implementation of the code in Listing 16-16 that uses parallel execution without concurrency issues.

LISTING 16-17 Safe code without race condition

```
static void DemoConcurrency_Safe() {
    Console.WriteLine("=== DemoConcurrency_Safe ===");
    int sum = 0;
    int[] results = new int[10];
    Parallel.For(1, 10, (index) => {
        results[index] = Operation(index);
    });
    sum = results.Sum();
    Console.WriteLine("Final sum: {0}", sum);
}
```

Each cycle of the *Parallel.For* stores the result of the call to *Operation* in a different memory zone. When the loop completes, the *results* array contains all the values returned from each *Operation* call, and only at this point are these values summed together, executing the *Sum* method in a single thread.

The truly difficult part about using parallelization techniques is finding the right balance between scalability and resource consumption. The solution shown in Listing 16-17 is more scalable, but it works by allocating an array of *int* that is not necessary with the synchronization approach. A dedicated analysis is required to find the best solution on a case-by-case basis.

More Info A valuable source of information for multithreaded programming in the .NET Framework is Jeffrey Richter's book *CLR via C#, Third Edition* (Microsoft Press, 2010).

Concurrent Collections

As you have seen, it is usually better to avoid sharing data at all, so that you will not have concurrency issues to handle. However, when you cannot avoid that, you have to reduce the number of locks required to access shared data to a minimum. Whenever you use traditional collection classes, like those contained in *System.Collections* and *System.Collections.Generic* namespaces, you have to implement your own protection against race conditions. Usually, this ends up in a wrapper that uses locking techniques to synchronize access to collections. However, .NET Framework 4 provides a new set of thread-safe collection classes in the namespace *System.Collections.Concurrent* that you should use whenever multiple threads might access the collection concurrently. These classes are:

- *BlockingCollection<T>*
- *ConcurrentBag<T>*
- *ConcurrentDictionary<TKey,TValue>*
- *ConcurrentQueue<T>*
- *ConcurrentStack<T>*

As you can see, not every standard collection class from *System.Collections* and *System.Collections.Generic* has a corresponding thread-safe class, but you should try using these classes whenever you cannot avoid concurrent access, because the scalability granted by *System.Collections.Concurrent* classes is likely higher than the one provided by implementing your own synchronization techniques with the standard collection classes.

The *System.Collections.Concurrent* namespace contains other classes that are useful for partitioning data; these classes are also used by PLINQ. The classes are *OrderablePartitioner<TSource>*, *Partitioner*, and *Partitioner<TSource>*.

Task Synchronization

You have seen that each *Task* is a sort of *single unit of work* in a multithreaded environment. You might split a complex operation into different tasks both to take advantage of multicore processing and I/O-bound asynchronous operations. Instead of dealing with low-level issues of synchronization between threads, you move the problem to a higher level of abstraction, defining relationship and synchronization between tasks. The best way to avoid locks is to completely avoid the sharing of data between different tasks. When you cannot avoid this, you can try to synchronize tasks so that a task is not executed until another task accessing shared data completes its job. This operation can be made using the continuation techniques you used before, by calling the *ContinueWith* and *ContinueWhenAll* methods. However, sometimes the shared data is external to the TPL tasks and requires more complex synchronization work. A typical example is the interaction with user interface (UI) elements in Windows Forms, in Windows Presentation Forms (WPF), or in Silverlight.

The execution of tasks in the TPL is coordinated by the *TaskScheduler* class. Each time a *Task* starts, it receives a reference to a *TaskScheduler*. By default, the default *TaskScheduler* is provided by the *TaskFactory* class, but you can both change the *TaskFactory* or provide a specialized *TaskScheduler* derived class to each single *Task* instance. In reality, the *TaskScheduler* class is abstract and the TPL provides two derived classes: *ThreadPoolTaskScheduler*, which is used by default, and *SynchronizationContextTaskScheduler*, which can execute in a synchronization context such as those of the UI elements mentioned before.

> **Note** You can find a more complete description of the .NET Framework 4 *TaskScheduler* implementations at *http://blogs.msdn.com/b/pfxteam/archive/2009/09/22/9898090.aspx*. You can also implement your own custom *TaskScheduler* derived class or use one of the classes provided in the documentation "Samples for Parallel Programming with the .NET Framework 4," available at *http://code.msdn.microsoft.com/ParExtSamples*.

The static *FromCurrentSynchronizationContext* method of the *TaskScheduler* class returns an instance of the *SynchronizationContextTaskScheduler*, which provides synchronization with the current synchronization context. In this way, you can create code that can be executed in any UI (without requiring synchronization code) without worrying about what your code has to do to correctly synchronize with the UI. The following example shows code attached to a button click event, which asynchronously loads an image and, at the end of the operation, assigns it to the *Image* property of a *PictureBox* item in a window:

```
public void Button1_Click( ... ) {
    Task.Factory.StartNew(() => {
        return LoadAndProcessImage(); // compute the image
    }).ContinueWith(t => {
        pictureBox1.Image = t.Result; // display it
    }, TaskScheduler.FromCurrentSynchronizationContext() );
}
```

Only the line of code containing the *Image* assignment has to be executed by synchronizing its execution with the UI thread, which occurs by simply passing the *FromCurrentSynchronizationContext* result to the second parameter of the *ContinueWith* call. The first task loads the image and the second task, which synchronizes with the UI, displays the image to the user. This approach is scalable and requires less code than traditional synchronization methods based on specific calls to the UI library.

PLINQ

Parallel LINQ (PLINQ) is an implementation of LINQ to Objects that executes queries in parallel using the TPL classes described in the preceding section.

Getting started with PLINQ is very simple. Consider this code:

```
int[] numbers = ...
var oddNumbers =
    from    i in numbers
    where   i % 2 == 1
    select i;
```

The *oddNumbers* query returns all the odd integers contained in the *numbers* array. To do that, it performs a sequential scan of *numbers*, and the result maintains the same order as the original source. This operation is executed in a single thread.

To use PLINQ, you simply call the *AsParallel* extension method on the data source, which in this case is the *numbers* array:

```
var oddNumbers =
    from    i in numbers.AsParallel()
    where   i % 2 == 1
    select i;
```

At this point, the scan of *numbers* is no longer implemented as a single sequential scan. Instead, the array scan can be split into several threads, using multiple available CPU cores. Most of the syntax-related explanation of PLINQ ends here, but because the syntax is simple, the *implications* of using such implicit parallelization techniques require much more information, which is described in the following sections. (Additional details about *AsParallel* arguments are covered in the following sections.)

Threads Used by PLINQ

A better way to understand PLINQ is by analyzing how many threads are involved when a PLINQ query executes. You can start by analyzing the behavior of a query consumer that does not make use of PLINQ; it uses a standard LINQ to Objects query, as in Listing 16-18.

LISTING 16-18 A simple LINQ to Object query

```
static void StandardLinq() {
    Console.WriteLine("=== StandardLinq ===");
    int[] data = LoadData(100000000);
    var query =
        from    i in data
        where   i % 12345678 == 0
        select new { Value = i, ThreadID = Thread.CurrentThread.ManagedThreadId };
```

```
    Stopwatch sw = Stopwatch.StartNew();
    foreach (var number in query) {
        Console.WriteLine("{0} - from ThreadId={1}",
                          number,
                          Thread.CurrentThread.ManagedThreadId);
    }
    long elapsed = sw.ElapsedMilliseconds;
    Console.WriteLine("Elapsed time   : {0} milliseconds", elapsed);
    Console.WriteLine("CurrentThreadId: {0}", Thread.CurrentThread.ManagedThreadId);
}
```

The code initializes a huge array of type *int* and looks for the few members that can be divided by 12345678. On a quad-core workstation used for tests, this was the result:

```
=== StandardLinq ===
{ Value = 0, ThreadID = 1 } - from ThreadId=1
{ Value = 12345678, ThreadID = 1 } - from ThreadId=1
{ Value = 24691356, ThreadID = 1 } - from ThreadId=1
{ Value = 37037034, ThreadID = 1 } - from ThreadId=1
{ Value = 49382712, ThreadID = 1 } - from ThreadId=1
{ Value = 61728390, ThreadID = 1 } - from ThreadId=1
{ Value = 74074068, ThreadID = 1 } - from ThreadId=1
{ Value = 86419746, ThreadID = 1 } - from ThreadId=1
{ Value = 98765424, ThreadID = 1 } - from ThreadId=1
Elapsed time   : 904 milliseconds
CurrentThreadId: 1
```

It is interesting to compare the elapsed time with the parallelized version. Look at the two places in the code that capture the managed thread ID. The query projection creates an anonymous type, which saves the number found and the thread used to execute the code to generate the anonymous type itself. The *CurrentThreadId* property provides the thread ID used by the *foreach* loop that enumerates the query. As you can see, this same ID appears after the output of each found number in the preceding output. Obviously, this sample executes all the code on the same thread.

Now, make a simple change to the query, adding *AsParallel* to the *data* source in the LINQ query, as shown in Listing 16-19.

LISTING 16-19 A simple PLINQ query

```
static void SamplePLinq() {
    Console.WriteLine("=== SamplePLinq ===");
    int[] data = LoadData(100000000);
    var query =
        from  i in data.AsParallel()
        where i % 12345678 == 0
        select new { Value = i, ThreadID = Thread.CurrentThread.ManagedThreadId };
```

```
Stopwatch sw = Stopwatch.StartNew();
foreach (var number in query) {
    Console.WriteLine("{0} - from ThreadId={1}",
                      number,
                      Thread.CurrentThread.ManagedThreadId);
}
long elapsed = sw.ElapsedMilliseconds;
Console.WriteLine("Elapsed time   : {0} milliseconds", elapsed);
Console.WriteLine("CurrentThreadId: {0}", Thread.CurrentThread.ManagedThreadId);
}
```

Executing this code produces a different result. The following output was obtained using the same quad-core hardware used to execute the sequential query in Listing 16-19:

```
=== SamplePLinq ===
{ Value = 37037034, ThreadID = 3 } - from ThreadId=1
{ Value = 49382712, ThreadID = 6 } - from ThreadId=1
{ Value = 0, ThreadID = 9 } - from ThreadId=1
{ Value = 12345678, ThreadID = 9 } - from ThreadId=1
{ Value = 74074068, ThreadID = 10 } - from ThreadId=1
{ Value = 24691356, ThreadID = 4 } - from ThreadId=1
{ Value = 98765424, ThreadID = 5 } - from ThreadId=1
{ Value = 61728390, ThreadID = 7 } - from ThreadId=1
{ Value = 86419746, ThreadID = 8 } - from ThreadId=1
Elapsed time   : 370 milliseconds
CurrentThreadId: 1
```

The thread used to execute the *foreach* loop and, consequently, the *WriteLine* (*ThreadID = 1*) is different from the threads used to execute the PLINQ query; those *ThreadID* values range from *3* to *10*). The PLINQ query partitions the original *data* array and assigns each data partition to a different thread. The result is that any given thread might return no result or more than one result. For example, *ThreadID = 9* returned two results, whereas other partitions and threads returned different results.

Having multiple running threads might incur a performance penalty caused by communication between threads, which introduces a new cost that is not present in the traditional LINQ version. However, this cost is dampened by using the multiple cores available that truly parallelize the execution of the LINQ query. (Considering Hyper-Threading, the operating system offers eight execution cores to the application.) Parallelizing the query reduced the overall execution time from 904 milliseconds to 370 milliseconds. That is already a good result, considering that the theoretical limit would have been a quarter of the original time (226 milliseconds); there will be always some overhead involving multithreading.

However, you may not always be so lucky. Do not assume that *AsParallel* always improves response time. Usually, the computation necessary to return at least one row is not nearly as long as it is in this case, which returns only 9 members out of an array of 100 million elements.

If the query had returned more rows, the sequential operation required to show the results would make the parallelization of this algorithm useless from an overall performance point of view.

Now that the differences between LINQ and PLINQ in terms of thread usage are clear, you can start to dig into PLINQ in more detail.

Implementing PLINQ

Adding the *AsParallel* call to the data source in the query simply calls the *AsParallel* extension method defined in *ParallelEnumerable*, which is included in the *System.Linq* namespace:

```
namespace System.Linq {
public static class ParallelEnumerable {
    public static ParallelQuery<TSource> AsParallel<TSource>(
            this Partitioner<TSource> source);
    public static ParallelQuery<TSource> AsParallel<TSource>(
            this IEnumerable<TSource> source);
    public static ParallelQuery AsParallel(this IEnumerable source);

    // ...
}
}
```

The first version of *AsParallel* gets a *Partitioner<TSource>* as a parameter.

> **More Info** To see how to use custom partitioning in PLINQ queries, see the "Partitioner(Of TSource) Class" documentation at *http://msdn.microsoft.com/en-us/library/dd381768.aspx*.

The type returned from *AsParallel* can be either *ParallelQuery* or its derived *ParallelQuery<TSource>*, which are defined as follows:

```
public class ParallelQuery : IEnumerable {
    // ...
}

public class ParallelQuery<TSource> : ParallelQuery, IEnumerable<TSource>, IEnumerable {
    // ...
}
```

ParallelQuery<TSource> implements *IEnumerable<TSource>* and *IEnumerable*. From the consumer point of view, the presence of the *ParallelQuery<TSource>* type simply enables extension methods to call the implementation defined in the *ParallelEnumerable* class. This class is defined in the System.Core.dll assembly and is similar to the *Enumerable* class defined in the same assembly. Both classes implement LINQ operators as extension methods and are defined in the *System.Linq* namespace. However, *Enumerable* extends *IEnumerable<TSource>* whereas *ParallelEnumerable* extends *ParallelQuery<TSource>*.

At this point, it is clear that a single data source in a query directly defines which extension method is called (LINQ or PLINQ, for example). But what happens when a query joins two sources? In this case, the left-most data source is the one that defines the implementation to use. In other words, if a data source that implements *ParallelQuery<TSource>* is used on the outer side of a join, even if the inner side implements only *IEnumerable<TSource>*, the run-time uses the *ParallelQuery* implementation and PLINQ handles the query instead of LINQ to Objects.

The *ParallelEnumerable* class contains all operators supported by PLINQ plus a few other extension methods that can be applied to a *ParallelQuery* to control the behavior or the result of the execution. In the next section, you will see how to use the methods shown in the following declarations:

```
namespace System.Linq {
public static class ParallelEnumerable {
    // ...
    public static IEnumerable<TSource> AsEnumerable<TSource>(
            this ParallelQuery<TSource> source);
    public static ParallelQuery<TSource> AsOrdered<TSource>(
            this ParallelQuery<TSource> source);
    public static ParallelQuery AsOrdered(this ParallelQuery source);
    public static IEnumerable<TSource> AsSequential<TSource>(
            this ParallelQuery<TSource> source);
    public static ParallelQuery<TSource> AsUnordered<TSource>(
            this ParallelQuery<TSource> source);

    public static ParallelQuery<TSource> WithCancellation<TSource>(
            this ParallelQuery<TSource> source, CancellationToken cancellationToken);
    public static ParallelQuery<TSource> WithDegreeOfParallelism<TSource>(
            this ParallelQuery<TSource> source, int degreeOfParallelism);
    public static ParallelQuery<TSource> WithExecutionMode<TSource>(
            this ParallelQuery<TSource> source, ParallelExecutionMode executionMode);
    public static ParallelQuery<TSource> WithMergeOptions<TSource>(
            this ParallelQuery<TSource> source, ParallelMergeOptions mergeOptions);
    internal static ParallelQuery<TSource> WithTaskScheduler<TSource>(
            this ParallelQuery<TSource> source, TaskScheduler taskScheduler);
}
}
```

Consuming the Result of a PLINQ Query

Just as with LINQ to Objects, execution of a PLINQ query begins only when the program starts to process the output of the query. The section "Threads Used by PLINQ" discussed the difference between the thread that processes the output of the query (the one executing the *foreach* statement in the example) and the threads that produce this output, implementing all the requested operations on the original data source. However, that example showed only one of the three modes of query processing offered by PLINQ.

Pipelined Processing

Pipelined processing is the default processing model that you saw earlier in Listing 16-19. In this model, a set of worker threads executes the query and a separate thread consumes the query result. The consumer thread processes data as soon as the worker threads start to produce results. This is the behavior obtained using the well-known *foreach* statement. Internally, there might be an output buffer that accumulates results and then passes them to the consumer of the query. You can control this buffer using the *WithMergeOptions* method, which can receive a *ParallelMergeOptions* enumeration value:

- **NotBuffered**   Output buffers are not used. Each element is available to the consumer of the query as soon as result elements have been computed. This option has the lowest latency but the higher overhead that might impact performance.

- **AutoBuffered**   Use output buffers of a size chosen by the system. The consumer of the query starts receiving data after buffers have been started to accumulate results. There is latency in consuming data, but overhead of passing data between threads might be reduced. This is a balance between latency and performance.

- **FullyBuffered**   The output buffers contain the full results. The consumer of the query starts receiving data only after query execution has been completed. This solution offers best performance but the worst latency, because the consumer does not receive any partial result during query execution.

By default, PLINQ queries use the *AutoBuffered* value. If you want to reduce the latency, you might write the query as shown in Listing 16-20.

LISTING 16-20 PLINQ query with the lowest latency offered by using *ParallelMergeOptions.NotBuffered*

```
static void SamplePLinq_NoLatency() {
    Console.WriteLine("=== SamplePLinq_NoLatency ===");
    int[] data = LoadData(100000000);
    var query =
        from   i in data.AsParallel().WithMergeOptions(ParallelMergeOptions.NotBuffered)
        where  i % 12345678 == 0
        select new { Value = i, ThreadID = Thread.CurrentThread.ManagedThreadId,
                     Timestamp = Stopwatch.GetTimestamp() };
```

```
Stopwatch sw = Stopwatch.StartNew();
foreach (var number in query) {
    long latency = Stopwatch.GetTimestamp() - number.Timestamp;
    Console.WriteLine("{0} - latency={1} Th={2}",
                      number, latency, Thread.CurrentThread.ManagedThreadId );
}
long elapsed = sw.ElapsedMilliseconds;
Console.WriteLine("Elapsed time    : {0} milliseconds", elapsed);
Console.WriteLine("CurrentThreadId: {0}", Thread.CurrentThread.ManagedThreadId);
}
```

The following is the result of an execution:

```
=== SamplePLinq_NoLatency ===
{ Value = 0, ThreadID = 4, Timestamp = 12913386989 } - latency=16 Th=1
{ Value = 12345678, ThreadID = 4, Timestamp = 12914011955 } - latency=54 Th=1
{ Value = 24691356, ThreadID = 6, Timestamp = 12914251481 } - latency=53 Th=1
{ Value = 49382712, ThreadID = 3, Timestamp = 12914328641 } - latency=23257 Th=1
{ Value = 61728390, ThreadID = 7, Timestamp = 12914340184 } - latency=40 Th=1
{ Value = 86419746, ThreadID = 8, Timestamp = 12914353581 } - latency=45 Th=1
{ Value = 74074068, ThreadID = 10, Timestamp = 12914370891 } - latency=26 Th=1
{ Value = 98765424, ThreadID = 9, Timestamp = 12914399154 } - latency=47 Th=1
{ Value = 37037034, ThreadID = 5, Timestamp = 12914437764 } - latency=42 Th=1
Elapsed time    : 429 milliseconds
CurrentThreadId: 1
```

The latency is expressed in microseconds and it is usually under 100 microseconds, with possible spikes at some tenths of milliseconds.

As you can see in Listing 16-20, the *WithMergeOptions* call follows the *AsParallel* one and specifies the merge options desired in its parameter. The *NotBuffered* value produces the lowest latency but an overall performance (see the *Elapsed time* value) that might be worse than the default *AutoBuffered* setting. In this case, the performance is close. In fact, consider the following result produced using the *AutoBuffered* value instead of *NotBuffered* (which is the same as removing the *WithMergeOptions* call):

```
=== SamplePLinq_NoLatency ===
{ Value = 74074068, ThreadID = 4, Timestamp = 13985635431 } - l=73857 Th=1
{ Value = 24691356, ThreadID = 10, Timestamp = 13985682794 } - l=29455 Th=1
{ Value = 0, ThreadID = 6, Timestamp = 13984967010 } - l=881290 Th=1
{ Value = 12345678, ThreadID = 6, Timestamp = 13985836104 } - l=12993 Th=1
{ Value = 98765424, ThreadID = 3, Timestamp = 13985847724 } - l=58275 Th=1
{ Value = 49382712, ThreadID = 8, Timestamp = 13985865589 } - l=41262 Th=1
{ Value = 61728390, ThreadID = 9, Timestamp = 13985902121 } - l=29349 Th=1
{ Value = 37037034, ThreadID = 7, Timestamp = 13986020375 } - l=18418 Th=1
{ Value = 86419746, ThreadID = 5, Timestamp = 13986043594 } - l=40673 Th=1
Elapsed time    : 422 milliseconds
CurrentThreadId: 1
```

This second execution using *AutoBuffered* has a latency that, at its minimum, is three orders of a degree higher than using the *NotBuffered* merge option. Instead of tens of microseconds, the latency is on the order of tens of milliseconds. So this case does not produce much improvement in the elapsed time (other tests produced worse performances), but strictly depends on the number of rows returned by the query. The higher the number of rows returned, the higher the gain in overall performance using *AutoBuffered*. The *FullyBuffered* merge option is explained in the following section.

Stop-and-Go Processing

With stop-and-go processing, the consumer waits for all the worker threads to finish their work before consuming data. In this way, the consumer thread does not contend for CPU resources with worker threads, and this often results in better execution time for getting all the results—even if the time to get the first element from the query is the same as the time to execute the entire query. Because the consumer does not need to use the CPU, the consumer thread can be used as a worker thread during query execution. This is clearly visible in Listing 16-21.

LISTING 16-21 A PLINQ query using the stop-and-go processing model

```
static void SamplePLinq_NoLatency() {
    Console.WriteLine("=== SamplePLinq_StopAndGo ===");
    int[] data = LoadData(100000000);
    var query =
        from   i in data.AsParallel().WithMergeOptions(
                         ParallelMergeOptions.FullyBuffered )
        where  i % 12345678 == 0
        select new { Value = i, ThreadID = Thread.CurrentThread.ManagedThreadId,
                     Timestamp = Stopwatch.GetTimestamp() };

    Stopwatch sw = Stopwatch.StartNew();
    foreach (var number in query) {
        long latency = Stopwatch.GetTimestamp() - number.Timestamp;
        Console.WriteLine("{0} - latency={1} Th={2}",
                         number, latency, Thread.CurrentThread.ManagedThreadId );
    }
    long elapsed = sw.ElapsedMilliseconds;
    Console.WriteLine("Elapsed time   : {0} milliseconds", elapsed);
    Console.WriteLine("CurrentThreadId: {0}", Thread.CurrentThread.ManagedThreadId);
}
```

The only significant difference between Listing 16-20 and Listing 16-21 is the *WithMerge-Options* parameter, which is *FullyBuffered* to get the stop-and-go behavior. Here is the output produced by executing the code:

```
=== SamplePLinq_StopAndGo ===
{ Value = 0, ThreadID = 9, Timestamp = 15633454497 } - l=1111349 Th=1
{ Value = 12345678, ThreadID = 9, Timestamp = 15634125532 } - l=440988 Th=1
{ Value = 24691356, ThreadID = 6, Timestamp = 15634391293 } - l=176607 Th=1
{ Value = 37037034, ThreadID = 5, Timestamp = 15634431322 } - l=137576 Th=1
{ Value = 49382712, ThreadID = 7, Timestamp = 15634436100 } - l=133900 Th=1
{ Value = 61728390, ThreadID = 10, Timestamp = 15634096308 } - l=474718 Th=1
{ Value = 74074068, ThreadID = 8, Timestamp = 15634312471 } - l=259550 Th=1
{ Value = 86419746, ThreadID = 4, Timestamp = 15634525082 } - l=48010 Th=1
{ Value = 98765424, ThreadID = 1, Timestamp = 15634332863 } - l=241228 Th=1
Elapsed time   : 420 milliseconds
CurrentThreadId: 1
```

The thread with ID 1 has been used for both the consumer loop and to produce part of the query result. In this example, there is a delay before the first row appears on the console, but after it arrives, the query completes almost immediately. If the query had returned a higher number of rows, there might have been an improvement in overall performance, which is not relevant in this case. Obviously, the latency is the worst here compared with the other *With-MergeOptions* described in the pipelined processing.

The stop-and-go processing model is automatically used by PLINQ when you call *ToArray* or *ToList*. Also, a sort in the query (using *OrderBy* or *OrderByDescending*) forces the use of a stop-and-go operation.

> **Note** The automatic use of the stop-and-go processing model when calling *ToArray* or *ToList* explains why you can observe a performance gain by calling one of these methods and then iterating the resulting collection, instead of iterating the result of a PLINQ query. However, remember that the stop-and-go processing model does not return any item until all the items have been processed.

Inverted Enumeration

Until now, the code that consumes the query results has always executed on a specific thread. In some circumstances (but not in our simple example), this thread might become a real bottleneck in your architecture. You can gain a higher degree of parallelism by invoking the consumer code in the same thread that produced an item during the query execution. You cannot do this using the standard C# syntax, but you can with an extension method named *ForAll*, declared in the *ParallelEnumerable* class. This extension method gets a single argument of type *Action<TSource>*. This argument usually represents a delegate that will be executed for each row of the result. Listing 16-22 shows an example of using the *ForAll* syntax.

LISTING 16-22 A PLINQ query using an inverted processing model

```
static void SamplePLinq_Inverted() {
    Console.WriteLine("=== SamplePLinq_Inverted ===");
    int[] data = LoadData(100000000);
    var query =
        from   i in data.AsParallel()
        where  i % 12345678 == 0
        select new { Value = i, ThreadID = Thread.CurrentThread.ManagedThreadId };

    Stopwatch sw = Stopwatch.StartNew();
    query.ForAll((number) => {
        Console.WriteLine("{0} - from ThreadId={1}",
                          number, Thread.CurrentThread.ManagedThreadId);
    } );
    long elapsed = sw.ElapsedMilliseconds;
    Console.WriteLine("Elapsed time   : {0} milliseconds", elapsed);
    Console.WriteLine("CurrentThreadId: {0}", Thread.CurrentThread.ManagedThreadId);
}
```

Looking at the output produced by executing the code in Listing 16-22, you can see that the *Console.WriteLine* calls are not executed in a single "consumer" thread; they now execute in the same thread used to produce the output row. Obviously, the code inside a *ForAll* should be thread-safe:

```
=== SamplePLinq_Inverted ===
{ Value = 0, ThreadID = 11 } - from ThreadId=11
{ Value = 61728390, ThreadID = 10 } - from ThreadId=10
{ Value = 74074068, ThreadID = 7 } - from ThreadId=7
{ Value = 37037034, ThreadID = 8 } - from ThreadId=8
{ Value = 49382712, ThreadID = 9 } - from ThreadId=9
{ Value = 86419746, ThreadID = 5 } - from ThreadId=5
{ Value = 98765424, ThreadID = 1 } - from ThreadId=1
{ Value = 24691356, ThreadID = 4 } - from ThreadId=4
{ Value = 12345678, ThreadID = 11 } - from ThreadId=11
Elapsed time   : 430 milliseconds
CurrentThreadId: 1
```

The overall result shows that the performance has not improved, but the result is very similar to the one obtained with the pipelined processing, using a standard sequential *foreach* iteration of the results. The inverted enumeration does not pay the overhead of the context switch between threads to execute consumer code. However, that might vary for each execution. In fact, the *Console.WriteLine* method called here uses some synchronization techniques to protect against concurrent execution. Having code in the consumer part that does not require synchronization should result in a more predictable gain in performance.

> **Note** You should consider using inverted enumeration when the cost for context switching between worker threads and consumer threads is high, or when using a single consumer thread becomes the performance bottleneck. Both of these conditions will likely be more frequent with a query that returns a large number of elements. Another reason to use inverted enumeration might be the lower latency between the generation of an element and its processing (that is, no context switching, even when the query returns a small number of elements).

Controlling Result Order in PLINQ

You can see in previous examples that, using PLINQ, the order of results does not correspond to the order of source data, even for simple filter operations. This is conformant to LINQ concepts: if you depend on a particular order of results, you have to explicitly make such a declaration in the LINQ query, by using operators like *OrderBy* and *OrderByDescending*. This behavior is similar to that of LINQ to SQL or LINQ to Entities, but is different from that of LINQ to Objects, which preserves original data source order in results. To get the LINQ to Objects behavior in PLINQ, you can add the *AsOrdered* operator on the source sequence, which enables order preservation in a PLINQ expression, as shown in Listing 16-23.

LISTING 16-23 A PLINQ query with order preservation

```
static void SamplePLinq_Ordered() {
    Console.WriteLine("=== SamplePLinq_Ordered ===");
    int[] data = LoadData(100000000);
    var query =
        from  i in data.AsParallel().AsOrdered()
        where  i % 12345678 == 0
        select new { Value = i, ThreadID = Thread.CurrentThread.ManagedThreadId };

    Stopwatch sw = Stopwatch.StartNew();
    foreach (var number in query) {
        Console.WriteLine("{0} - ThreadId={1}",
                          number, Thread.CurrentThread.ManagedThreadId);
    }
    long elapsed = sw.ElapsedMilliseconds;
    Console.WriteLine("Elapsed time   : {0} milliseconds", elapsed);
    Console.WriteLine("CurrentThreadId: {0}", Thread.CurrentThread.ManagedThreadId);
}
```

Listing 16-23 adds the *AsOrdered* operator after the *AsParallel* call. The result produced by code execution shows that the result maintains the source order, despite the fact that the data processing operation uses different threads:

```
=== SamplePLinq_Ordered ===
{ Value = 0, ThreadID = 10 } - ThreadId=1
{ Value = 12345678, ThreadID = 10 } - ThreadId=1
{ Value = 24691356, ThreadID = 5 } - ThreadId=1
```

```
{ Value = 37037034, ThreadID = 3 } - ThreadId=1
{ Value = 49382712, ThreadID = 4 } - ThreadId=1
{ Value = 61728390, ThreadID = 9 } - ThreadId=1
{ Value = 74074068, ThreadID = 6 } - ThreadId=1
{ Value = 86419746, ThreadID = 8 } - ThreadId=1
{ Value = 98765424, ThreadID = 7 } - ThreadId=1
Elapsed time    : 432 milliseconds
CurrentThreadId: 1
```

The use of *AsOrdered* has an impact on performance, so you should use it only when strictly necessary. When a part of a LINQ query depends on *AsOrdered*, but only for one subexpression, you should use *AsUnordered* to remove the constraint as soon as it is no longer required, writing nested LINQ queries. You can see an example in Listing 16-24, where both *AsOrdered* and *AsUnordered* are used in nested queries.

LISTING 16-24 A PLINQ query adding and then removing order-preservation condition

```
static void SamplePLinq_Unordered() {
    Console.WriteLine("=== SamplePLinq_Unordered ===");
    int[] data = LoadData(100000000);
    var queryEven =
        from   i in data.AsParallel().AsOrdered()
        where  i % 2 == 0
        select new { Value = i, ThreadID = Thread.CurrentThread.ManagedThreadId };

    var queryTop20Even = queryEven.Take(20);

    var queryFinal = from r in queryTop20Even.AsUnordered()
                     join s in queryTop20Even.AsUnordered()
                           on r.Value equals s.Value
                     where  r.Value > 30
                     select r;

    Stopwatch sw = Stopwatch.StartNew();
    foreach (var number in queryFinal) {
        Console.WriteLine("{0} - ThreadId={1}",
                          number, Thread.CurrentThread.ManagedThreadId);
    }
    long elapsed = sw.ElapsedMilliseconds;
    Console.WriteLine("Elapsed time    : {0} milliseconds", elapsed);
    Console.WriteLine("CurrentThreadId: {0}", Thread.CurrentThread.ManagedThreadId);
}
```

The *AsOrdered* is used in *queryEven* because *queryTop20Even* takes the first 20 even numbers. After the *Take* operation, *queryFinal* makes a join between two *queryTop20Even* results and no longer has any dependencies on source order. Therefore, the join is made by using *query-Top20Even* transformed by *AsUnordered*, which removes any dependency from source order. The execution result might appear similar to the following result, which depends on the order for the first part of the query (returns the first 20 even numbers in *data*) but does not force order preserving in the final result of *queryFinal*, returning the even numbers greater than 30 in any order:

```
=== SamplePLinq_Unordered ===
{ Value = 36, ThreadID = 10 } - ThreadId=1
{ Value = 38, ThreadID = 10 } - ThreadId=1
{ Value = 32, ThreadID = 8 } - ThreadId=1
{ Value = 34, ThreadID = 8 } - ThreadId=1
Elapsed time    : 68 milliseconds
CurrentThreadId: 1
```

Of course, you can always use the *OrderBy* operator to get the same result. The *OrderBy* effect is automatically limited to the query in which it is used and does not propagate its effects to outer queries when queries are nested, as *AsOrdered* does. However, if the data is already sorted in the data source, you might consider both options, by creating some performance tests, especially if you estimate that the cost involved in sorting is high.

Processing Query Results

Instance members of most .NET Framework classes are not thread safe. For example, filling data in a collection class such as *List<T>* requires you to call the *List<T>* instance members in a safe way. When you use PLINQ, you have to be careful about these kinds of issues.

For example, this is a safe way to load a list:

```
List<int> result = new List<int>();
var query =
    from   i in data.AsParallel()
    where  i % 2 == 0
    select i;
foreach (var number in query) {
    result.Add(number);
}
```

The preceding code uses pipelined processing. The calls to *List<T>.Add* in the *foreach* loop are always made from the same thread that creates the *List<T>* instance itself. You might be tempted to use code such as the following, which is faster but uses the *result* instance of *List<T>* in an unsafe manner:

```
List<int> result = new List<int>();
var query =
    from   i in data.AsParallel()
    where  i % 2 == 0
    select i;
query.ForAll((number) => {
    result.Add(number);
});
```

Because *ForAll* executes the code in several threads, it can cause a race condition resulting from calling the *List<T>.Add* method from different threads at the same moment. To avoid this risk and to get the minimum overhead in performance for synchronization, you can call the *ToList<T>* extension method on any PLINQ query, as in the following code:

```
var query =
    from    i in data.AsParallel()
    where   i % 2 == 0
    select i;
List<int> result = query.ToList();
```

This is both the fastest and safest way to populate a *List<T>* from a PLINQ result. Other similar extension methods available are *ToArray<T>*, *ToDictionary<T>*, and *ToLookup<T>*.

> **Note** You can use *ForAll* to populate thread-safe collections included in the *System.Collections.Concurrent* namespace, which were mentioned in the "Concurrent Collections" section previously in this chapter.

Handling Exceptions with PLINQ

Throwing an exception during a PLINQ query execution does not immediately stop all PLINQ query activities. Processing of a PLINQ query usually involves several threads. When an exception is thrown in one of those threads, the system tries to stop all other threads in execution serving the PLINQ query. However, in the meantime, other threads can throw other exceptions. In the end, more than one exception might be thrown from a PLINQ query before you can catch the first one. For this reason, all exceptions thrown inside a PLINQ query are gathered into a single instance of *AggregateException*, which gets thrown after the PLINQ query has been stopped. An *AggregateException* contains a list of all the exceptions thrown in the PLINQ query in its *InnerExceptions* property. (The *AggregateException* is also described in the "Controlling Task Execution" section earlier in this chapter.) PLINQ internally uses the TPL and inherits all its behaviors, including those regarding exception handling. Listing 16-25 shows an example of a PLINQ query that throws several divide-by-zero exceptions during its execution.

LISTING 16-25 Exception handling for a PLINQ query

```
static void SamplePLinq_ExceptionHandling() {
    int[] data = LoadData(100);
    var query =
        from    i in data.AsParallel()
        where   i % 5 == 0
        select new { Value = i * 2 / (i % 10),
                    ThreadID = Thread.CurrentThread.ManagedThreadId };
```

```
    try {
        foreach (var number in query) {
            Console.WriteLine("{0} - from ThreadId={1}",
                            number,
                            Thread.CurrentThread.ManagedThreadId);
        }
    }
    catch (AggregateException ex) {
        Console.WriteLine(ex.Message);
        Console.WriteLine(
            String.Format( "AggregateException with {0} inner exceptions",
                        ex.InnerExceptions.Count ) );
        int counter = 0;
        foreach (var innerException in ex.InnerExceptions) {
            Console.WriteLine("({0})--> {1} : {2}",
                            ++counter,
                            innerException.GetType().Name,
                            innerException.Message);
        }
    }
}
```

The following output was produced on a quad-core machine:

```
One or more errors occurred.
AggregateException with 4 inner exceptions
(1)--> DivideByZeroException : Attempted to divide by zero.
(2)--> DivideByZeroException : Attempted to divide by zero.
(3)--> DivideByZeroException : Attempted to divide by zero.
(4)--> DivideByZeroException : Attempted to divide by zero.
```

A traditional execution in LINQ to Objects would have produced only one *DivideByZero-Exception*. In PLINQ, you always have an *AggregateException*, even when the PLINQ query throws only one exception.

Canceling a PLINQ Query

The cancellation of a PLINQ query has the same requirements as the cancellation of a TPL task, which is discussed in the section "Controlling Task Execution" earlier in this chapter. In the case of a PLINQ query, you must pass the *CancellationToken* instance when calling the *WithCancellation* method after *AsParallel*, as you can see in Listing 16-26. This operation transfers the *CancellationToken* to the underlying task that executes the query using the PLINQ engine.

LISTING 16-26 Cancellation of a PLINQ query

```
static void SamplePLinq_Cancellation() {
    Console.WriteLine("=== SamplePLinq_Cancellation ===");
    int[] data = LoadData(100000000);
    CancellationTokenSource cs = new CancellationTokenSource();

    // Requests an async cancellation in 100 milliseconds
    Task.Factory.StartNew(() => {
        Thread.Sleep(100);
        cs.Cancel();
    });

    var query =
        from  i in data.AsParallel().WithCancellation( cs.Token )
        where i % 12345678 == 0
        select new { Value = i, ThreadID = Thread.CurrentThread.ManagedThreadId };

    try {
        foreach (var number in query) {
            Console.WriteLine("{0} - from ThreadId={1}",
                            number, Thread.CurrentThread.ManagedThreadId);
        }
        Console.WriteLine("CurrentThreadId: {0}",
            Thread.CurrentThread.ManagedThreadId);
    }
    catch (OperationCanceledException ex) {
        Console.WriteLine("Operation canceled: {0}", ex.Message);
    }
    catch (AggregateException ex) {
        if (ex.InnerExceptions != null) {
            foreach (Exception e in ex.InnerExceptions) {
                Console.WriteLine("AggregateException - {0}", e.Message);
            }
        }
    }
}
```

In Listing 16-26, you call the *Cancel* method on the *CancellationTokenSource* instance through a task that waits 100 milliseconds (it has to wait for the PLINQ query start of execution). The exception thrown in this case is an *OperationCanceledException* that is not included in an *AggregateException* (which is handled in a different catch in the previous example). Executing the example produces the following result:

```
=== SamplePLinq_Cancellation ===
Operation canceled: The query has been canceled via the token supplied to WithCancellation.
```

Controlling Execution of a PLINQ Query

PLINQ makes a few decisions about parallelization based on analyzing the query before executing it. However, you might want to change its default behavior, or interact with the underlying TPL affecting *Task* instances created by PLINQ.

For example, you might want to force query execution in a parallel mode, regardless of the results of the query analysis made by PLINQ, which might favor a standard sequential execution in some conditions. To do that, you call *WithExecutionMode* after *AsParallel*, passing the *ForceParallelism* value as a parameter:

```
var query = from c in customers.AsParallel()
                    .WithExecutionMode(ParallelExecutionMode.ForceParallelism)
      ...
```

PLINQ defines the exact number of concurrently executing tasks that will be used to process the query. This number is called the *degree of parallelism* of the query. By default, the degree of parallelism is equal to the number of processors available on the machine. You can change this number by calling *WithDegreeOfParallelism* after *AsParallel*, passing the number of processors to use (*degreeOfParallelism*) as a parameter:

```
var query = from c in customers.AsParallel().WithDegreeOfParallelism(16)
      ...
```

Usually, you would not change this property, but you might use it to reduce the number of processors used in a PLINQ query, to avoid CPU harvesting against other services running on the same machine.

Finally, you might want to wait for the end of the parallel execution of a nested query by calling *AsSequential* or *AsEnumerable*. These calls are identical in PLINQ, because the *AsEnumerable* implementation calls *AsSequential*. From a semantic point of view, *AsSequential* expresses the programmer's intent more clearly. Any methods called after *AsSequential* or *AsEnumerable* are executed by LINQ to Objects instead of PLINQ. In the following example, *queryParallel* executes on parallel threads, but its result (which is ordered) is used by *querySequential* calling *AsSequential*:

```
var queryParallel = from    i in data.AsParallel()
                    where   i % 12345678 == 0
                    orderby i
                    select  i;

var querySequential = from   n in queryParallel.AsSequential().Take(3)
                      select n;
```

Note You might wonder whether *AsSequential* is the same as *AsOrdered*. Although the results might be similar, in this case they are different. *AsOrdered* applies conditions to the PLINQ execution engine and still returns a PLINQ query, whereas *AsSequential* does not execute PLINQ at all; it invokes LINQ to Objects execution.

Changes in Data During Execution

Working in a multithreading context requires that you pay more attention to any possible race condition you might create in your program. Usually, you write a query assuming that the data source does not change its content during query execution. If a query uses only pure functions, your only concerns are about possible external modifications during query execution. A *pure function* is a function that has no side effects and does not depend on any state beyond its local scope. For example, a projection or predicate expression that contains code that modifies a shared resource might be a source of race conditions. Consider the following code:

```
int accumulator = 0;
var query =
    from  i in data.AsParallel()
    select new { Aggregated = accumulator += i, Value = i };
```

As you can see, this query should produce a column named *Aggregated*, which contains the aggregate of *Value* up until the displayed row. However, with PLINQ there are two issues here. First, when splitting the order of execution into several threads, the *accumulator* is not incremented in the right order. Second, the write access to *accumulator* has the same kind of race condition described earlier in the discussion of Listing 16-16, resulting in an incorrect value after query execution.

Important Code in a PLINQ query must not change data that can be shared across different threads. This includes expressions written inside the query, methods called by these expressions, and code for custom operators. Review the section "Race Conditions" earlier in this chapter to get a broader discussion of this type of issue.

PLINQ and Other LINQ Implementations

When you use PLINQ with other LINQ providers, you have to make sure that those providers operate in a compatible way. In general, data sources that implement *IEnumerable<TSource>* can operate as data sources for a PLINQ query. For example, you can parallelize a LINQ to XML query, as you can see in Listing 16-27.

LISTING 16-27 PLINQ used with a LINQ to XML query

```
static void XmlPLinq() {
    XElement doc = XElement.Load("NorthwindCustomersWithOrders.xml");
    var query =
        from   c in doc.Elements("customer").AsParallel()
        where  c.Element("country").Value == "Italy"
        select new {
            CompanyName = c.Element("companyName").Value,
            ThreadID = Thread.CurrentThread.ManagedThreadId
        };

    foreach (var item in query) {
        Console.WriteLine("{0} - from ThreadId={1}",
                          item,
                          Thread.CurrentThread.ManagedThreadId);
    }
}
```

The result produced by executing the code in Listing 16-27 might be similar to these, which were executed on a quad-core machine:

```
{ CompanyName = Franchi S.p.A., ThreadID = 3 } - from ThreadId=1
{ CompanyName = Reggiani Caseifici, ThreadID = 10 } - from ThreadId=1
{ CompanyName = Magazzini Alimentari Riuniti, ThreadID = 8 } - from ThreadId=1
```

You need to consider different issues when you use a provider that operates with *IQueryable*, such as LINQ to SQL. For these providers, you need to materialize the query result by calling *AsEnumerable*, and only then can you call *AsParallel*. If you do not take this step and apply *AsParallel* to the data source, you will end up loading all the table rows in memory and the query will be executed using PLINQ. For example, consider the following LINQ to SQL query:

```
var query =
    from   c in db.GetTable<Customer>()
    where  c.Country == "Italy"
    select new { c.CompanyName };
```

This query produces the following SQL code, which is sent to the Microsoft SQL Server database:

```
SELECT [t0].[CompanyName]
FROM   [Customers] AS [t0]
WHERE  [t0].[Country] = "Italy"
```

If you apply *AsParallel* to the data source, the whole query becomes a PLINQ query, so it queries the entire *Customers* table (all columns and all rows) from the SQL Server database. In other words, imagine writing this LINQ query:

```
var query =
    from   c in db.GetTable<Customer>().AsParallel()
    where  c.Country == "Italy"
    select new { c.CompanyName };
```

The SQL query sent to the database will be:

```
SELECT [t0].[CustomerID], [t0].[CompanyName], [t0].[City],
       [t0].[Region] AS [State], [t0].[Country]
FROM   [Customers] AS [t0]
```

If you want to send an optimized query to SQL Server and process its result in a parallel way, you can call *AsParallel* on the entire LINQ to SQL query:

```
var query =
    from row in
        (from   c in db.GetTable<Customer>()
         where  c.Country == "Italy"
         select new { c.CompanyName }
        ).AsParallel()
    select new {
        row.CompanyName,
        ThreadID = Thread.CurrentThread.ManagedThreadId
    };
```

Applying parallelism to the result of a LINQ to SQL query (or to any other *IQueryable* provider) should not be a very frequent occurrence. Only if the processing of data coming from these queries is particularly heavy does it make sense to parallelize it. Usually, the *IQueryable* provider is in charge of query optimization. However, one scenario in which this technique could be useful is when you have a query that combines data coming from SQL Server with data coming from other sources, such as LINQ to XML or LINQ to Objects.

Reactive Extensions for .NET

LINQ to Objects is based on *IEnumerable<T>* and *IEnumerator<T>* interfaces. It defines a pull-based model, which requests data only when the code asks for it:

```
interface IEnumerable<out T> {
    IEnumerator<T> GetEnumerator();
}

interface IEnumerator<out T> {
    bool MoveNext();
    T Current { get; }
}
```

The .NET Framework 4 introduced two new interfaces, *IObservable<T>* and *IObserver<T>*, which are the foundation of push-based data access models:

```
interface IObservable<out T> {
    IDisposable Subscribe (IObserver<T> observer);
}

interface IObserver<in T> {
    void OnNext(T value);
    void OnCompleted();
    void OnError(Exception e);
}
```

The Reactive Extensions for .NET (Rx) is a superset of the standard LINQ sequence operators and is based on the interfaces *IObservable<T>* and *IObserver<T>*. The concept is that, instead of querying for data in a pull-based model, a collection is "observed" until there is an interesting event. At that point, the code that handles data is executed asynchronously. This model is good for event-based computations, such as streams of data coming from the network, UI events, and similar activities. A common example of Rx use is to define a query over streaming of stock prices that are observed in real time, executing code only for stock prices that match certain conditions, and ignoring the others.

> **Important**   Rx is available as a Microsoft DevLabs project download. It is a prototype and not a Microsoft product. At the time of writing, it is not officially supported by Microsoft. You can find the download and more information about it at *http://msdn.microsoft.com/en-us/devlabs/ee794896.aspx*.

A complete discussion about Rx is outside the scope of this book. However, it is interesting to take a look at some of the services it provides. You can define LINQ queries to intercept events, filtering only those of interest. For example, the following code intercepts *KeyDown* events for characters between A and Z. The *goodKeys* contains a query that can be subscribed and unsubscribed:

```
IObservable<IEvent<KeyEventArgs>> keypresses = Observable.FromEvent<KeyEventArgs>(
    txt, "KeyDown");
IObservable<String> goodKeys = keypresses
                                .Select(IKP => IKP.EventArgs.Key)
                                .Where(key => key >= Key.A && key <= Key.Z)
                                .Select(key => key.ToString());
```

You can subscribe to the *goodKeys* query, associating it with code that will be called when one of the filtered events occurs. In this case, the code inserts the character pressed on the keyboard into an *InputKeys* buffer:

```
IDisposable unsub = goodKeys.Subscribe(key => InputKeys.Insert(0, key));
```

When the event is no longer relevant, you can unsubscribe by disposing of the *unsub* object returned by the previous *Subscribe* call:

```
unsub.Dispose();
```

> **More Info** Rx also offers patterns, classes, and methods to embed APM calls. To learn more, take a look at the documentation and samples available at *http://rxwiki.wikidot.com/101samples*.

Summary

This chapter showed how to use PLINQ to take advantage of multithreaded processing of in-memory data that otherwise would have been queried using LINQ to Objects. You have seen the types of issues that concurrency might cause when working with parallelization. Because PLINQ internally uses the TPL, you saw the features offered by the *Parallel* class, and the capabilities of the *Task* class. It is important to understand that all the concurrency considerations for TPL are equally valid for PLINQ. You saw a comprehensive discussion of specific PLINQ features for handling cancellation, controlling execution, and handling exceptions, and explored the possible interactions between PLINQ and other LINQ providers, such as LINQ to XML and LINQ to SQL. Finally, you saw a short introduction to Reactive Extensions for .NET, which uses a push-based model that builds on LINQ, and is useful for processing events asynchronously.

Chapter 17
Other LINQ Implementations

Microsoft Language Integrated Query (LINQ) represents an important change in the way developers write code. As mentioned before in this book, if LINQ were only a new version of Embedded SQL for the new millennium, its impact would be limited to a relatively small layer of application architecture. However, the impact of LINQ very likely will become increasingly pervasive in the everyday life of most Microsoft .NET Framework programmers.

This chapter gives you a brief glimpse of other LINQ implementations available on the market. The content is divided into sections that group LINQ implementations by service category and by the type of data each handles. Most of these implementations are community-driven projects, but some are just proof-of-concept exercises. The goal of describing these examples is to give you a broad view of the enormous potential of LINQ.

 Important The LINQ implementations referenced in this chapter were not written or released by Microsoft. At the date of this writing (September 2010), they are publicly available and most are open to contributions from other programmers. The authors do not and cannot guarantee the quality and reliability of the LINQ implementations referenced in this chapter.

Database Access and ORM

As you know, LINQ to SQL supports only Microsoft SQL Server databases (including Microsoft SQL Server Compact 3.5), whereas LINQ to Entities supports all the databases supported by the Microsoft ADO.NET Entity Framework. If you are using a database other than SQL Server, the simplest way to access it through LINQ is by looking for an Entity Framework provider for your database. If you have a provider, you can access your data using LINQ to Entities. However, if for any reason LINQ to Entities is not a good choice for you, an alternative LINQ implementation might offer the support you need. As described in Chapter 15, "Extending LINQ," you sometimes need a custom LINQ provider. The following list describes some of the available LINQ extensions that offer an alternative to LINQ to SQL and LINQ to Entities:

- DataObjects.NET (*http://dataobjects.net/*) includes an Object Relational Mapper (ORM) that is fully compliant with LINQ. It supports SQL Server, Microsoft SQL Azure, Oracle, and PostgreSQL, and has planned features to support an embedded database and MySQL.

- BLToolkit (*http://bltoolkit.net/*) is a free open-source set of components that includes a LINQ provider that supports SQL Server, Microsoft Access, IBM DB2, Informix, Firebird, MySQL, Oracle, PostgreSQL, SQL Server CE, SQLite, and Sybase.

- NHibernate (*http://sourceforge.net/projects/nhibernate/*) has had a built-in LINQ provider since version 3.0. For earlier versions, you can use a separate LINQ to NHibernate provider.

- LinqConnect (*http://www.devart.com/dotconnect/linq.html*) is a lightweight ORM solution that is compatible with LINQ to SQL. It can connect to Oracle, MySQL, PostgreSQL, and SQLite databases.

- LLBLGen Pro runtime (*http://www.llblgen.com*) is an ORM that fully supports LINQ. You can use it as an alternative to other ORM systems, such as LINQ to SQL, the Entity Framework, and NHibernate.

- Telerik OpenAccess (*http://www.telerik.com/products/orm.aspx*) is an ORM that supports SQL Server, Oracle, SQL Azure, Firebird, VistaDB, MySQL, Sybase SQL Anywhere, and Sybase Advantage Database Server.

- SubSonic (*http://blog.wekeroad.com/subsonic/*) is a free open-source light ORM based on a LINQ syntax that supports SQL Server, MySQL, and SQLite.

- Genom-e (*http://www.genom-e.com/*) is an ORM that supports SQL Server, Oracle, DB2, and SQLite.

It is also worth mentioning PLINQO (*http://www.plinqo.com*), which is a set of templates that provide patterns for common tasks and enhancements to the native features of LINQ to SQL. You can read more about PLINQO in Chapter 4, "Choosing Between LINQ to SQL and LINQ to Entities."

Because NHibernate is probably the most famous ORM of those listed, it is interesting to look at a typical query that is written using its LINQ provider. Although the LINQ query itself is identical to one you would write when using another provider, the differences lie mainly in the object being queried. Consider the following sample code:

```
var connection = new SqlConnection( ... ); // Connection to a SQL Server database
var session = GlobalSetup.CreateSession( connection );
var query = from    customer in session.Linq<Customer>()
            orderby c.CompanyName
            select  c.CompanyName;
```

As you can see, the *session* instance is a wrapper to the connection, which can generate typed queryable objects by calling the *Linq* generic method, providing a specific class as a generic parameter that corresponds to the entity type you want to query. Another way to write the same LINQ query is to use a class derived from *NHibernateContext*, which contains typed properties that map to *Linq<T>* method calls with the corresponding type. For example, after creating a *NorthwindContext* class containing as many properties as the types of entities you want to query, you could write the previous example in this way:

```
var connection = new SqlConnection( ... ); // Connection to a SQL Server database
var session = GlobalSetup.CreateSession( connection );
var northwindContext = new NorthwindContext( session );
var query = from    customer in northwindContext.Customers
            orderby c.CompanyName
            select  c.CompanyName;
```

A key feature of LINQ is the improved readability of the code, which is uniform across several providers.

Data Access Without a Database

The title of this section might sound strange. However, it is not that strange if you consider that sometimes you might need to access data without directly accessing a database—even if, in the end, your data is likely to be stored in some relational engine. The first example here deals with this scenario by using Windows Communication Foundation (WCF) Data Services, which uses Uniform Resource Identifier (URIs) as pointers to pieces of data, and simple, well-known formats to represent that data, such as JavaScript Object Notation (JSON) and the Atom Publishing Protocol (ATOM/APP).

Through an Entity Data Model (EDM) that you define in the Entity Framework, you can access WCF Data Services using LINQ to Entities. This way, your program does not have to handle details such as the HTTP verbs (for example, *GET*, *POST*, or *DELETE*) used to interact with the service. These formats have also been used to define the Open Data (OData) Protocol (see more at *http://www.odata.org*). OData is a web protocol used to expose and access information from a variety of sources, including—but not limited to—relational databases, file systems, content management systems, and traditional websites. WCF Data Services supports OData for both producing and consuming OData services. You then expose this data to your code through the EDM.

Other examples of remote data storage are Amazon SimpleDB and Microsoft SQL Server Data Services (SSDS). These services offer a pay-per-use model in which you store data on a remote platform that is completely managed by the hosting provider. Each service has its own application programming interface (API), but their LINQ support makes them easier to use. SSDS natively offers a managed library to support LINQ queries, but there is also a LINQ provider for SimpleDB (*http://linqtosimpledb.codeplex.com*). Considering that each of these services has a proprietary API and does not use standard SQL as the query language, their LINQ compatibility might ease their adoption by reducing the learning curve for developers who opt to use them.

Microsoft Excel is another common source of data. You can find an interesting study about a LINQ provider to access Excel data in this LINQ to Excel provider site at *http://xlslinq.codeplex.com*. The provider is still a simple prototype that does not yet have complete functionality, but it is interesting because it accesses Excel files directly, without using the existing OLE DB provider. This approach makes it possible to define custom LINQ operators and custom entities that are specific to Excel—something that would be difficult to do if you were trying to perform data access through a standard SQL query. This is not to say that using SQL for data access is the wrong approach. However, sometimes you do not have access to all the information available in an Excel document when using the Excel OLE DB provider, which is the standard way to query Excel data using SQL. For example, you cannot use OLE DB to get a list of worksheets in a workbook, but you can obtain such a list easily when using the following *sheets* query in LINQ to Excel:

```
XlsWorkbook book = new XlsWorkbook("sample.xls");
var sheets = from   s in book.Worksheets
             select s;
```

It is worth mentioning that it is also possible to access the Excel object model using LINQ to Objects; however, a custom LINQ provider simplifies that access, because it uses a more straightforward and data-oriented object model.

You can also query Microsoft Word documents saved in the .docx format using LINQ to XML, extracting both text and formatting elements. You can find links to several examples at *http://blogs.msdn.com/b/ericwhite/archive/2007/12/11/using-linq-to-xml-with-open-xml-documents.aspx*.

Microsoft SharePoint Foundation and Microsoft SharePoint deserve a separate mention. You can define queries to SharePoint using the Collaborative Application Markup Language (CAML) language, which is an XML-based language used in SharePoint both to define the fields and views used in sites and lists as well as to write queries over them. Starting with Microsoft SharePoint 2010, the LINQ to SharePoint provider is integrated with the product. You can generate LINQ to SharePoint entities using the command-line tool called SPMetal.exe, provided in the *BIN* folder of each SharePoint 2010 installation.

Using the entities generated by SPMetal.exe, you can not only query SharePoint data using a fully typed approach, but also perform insert, update, and delete operations on SharePoint data. You might think of LINQ to SharePoint as an ORM dedicated specifically to data stored in SharePoint. In fact, LINQ to SharePoint includes concepts such as the *DataContext* object, identity management, object tracking, concurrency conflict handling, and many other features that you are already familiar with from the discussions of LINQ to SQL and LINQ to Entities in this book.

Similar to SharePoint, Microsoft Dynamics CRM is another important repository of data. You can access the data in that repository through FetchXML, which is an XML-based query language used in Microsoft Dynamics CRM. But the Microsoft Dynamics CRM Software

Development Kit (SDK) also provides a LINQ provider as part of the Advanced Developer Extensions for Microsoft Dynamics CRM 4.0, included in the Microsoft Dynamics CRM SDK starting with version 4.0.12. If you have to use an earlier version of the Microsoft Dynamics CRM SDK, you should take a look at the LINQ to CRM project (*http://linqtocrm.codeplex.com*), which implements a LINQ provider that translates queries into FetchXML. Microsoft Dynamics CRM also has third-party LINQ providers such as the AdxStudio xRM SDK (*http://www.adxstudio. com/adxstudio-xrm/xrm-sdk*) and XrmLinq (*http://www.xrmlinq.com*).

Finally, another LINQ to Excel provider, available at *http://solidcoding.blogspot.com/2008/01 /linq-to-excel-provider-25.htm*l, takes a different approach when using Excel as a data source. In this implementation, you can bind a .NET Framework class to data that exists in an Excel workbook, just as you might bind to values in database tables by using LINQ to SQL or LINQ to Entities.

LINQ to SharePoint Examples

As already mentioned, the LINQ to SharePoint provider is integrated into SharePoint 2010. Because SharePoint is more and more a repository of enterprise data, and not necessarily structured in a relational database format, it is useful to have a standard programming interface to access its data without worrying about the underlying physical implementation.

For example, you can query a SharePoint list named Invoices using the following code:

```
using (SampleSiteDataContext spContext = new SampleSiteDataContext(
  "http://sample.sp2010.local/")) {
    var query = from   i in spContext.Invoices
               where  i.DocumentCreatedBy == @"SP2010DEV\PaoloPi"
               select i.Title;

    foreach (var i in query) {
        Console.WriteLine(i);
    }
}
```

The *SampleSiteDataContext* is a class generated by SPMetal that is conceptually similar to a *DataContext* in LINQ to SQL or to an *ObjectContext* in LINQ to Entities. You create the *spContext* instance by providing the URL of the target site. That instance has an *Invoices* property that exposes the content of the Invoices list in SharePoint; you can query it using the LINQ syntax assigned to the *query* variable. Under the covers, the query engine creates a Collaborative Application Markup Language (CAML) query and sends it to the Invoices list by using objects from the SharePoint server object model in a manner similar to the process of generating a SQL query and sending it to a database server by executing LINQ to SQL or LINQ to Entities queries.

When logical relationships exist between entities in SharePoint, you can use LINQ joins to query the different entities in those relationships, as illustrated in the following code:

```
using (SampleSiteDataContext spContext = new SampleSiteDataContext(
  "http://sample.sp2010.local/")) {
    var query = from    c in spContext.DevLeapContacts
                join    i in spContext.Invoices on c.Id equals i.DevLeapContact.Id
                select new { c.ContactID, c.Title, InvoiceTitle = i.Title };
    // Use the query results ...
}
```

However, another approach along the same lines might be to use the equivalent relationships between physical entities contained in *SampleSiteDataContext*. In this case, you also get deferred loading, so related entities are loaded only on demand, when the code accesses their corresponding properties. The following example shows this type of usage by accessing an *InvoicesDocument*, which represents the list of invoices related to a contact:

```
using (SampleSiteDataContext spContext = new SampleSiteDataContext(
  "http://sample.sp2010.local/")) {
    var query = from    c in spContext.DevLeapContacts
                select c;

    foreach (var c in query) {
        Console.WriteLine(c.Title);
        foreach (var i in c.InvoicesDocument) {
            Console.WriteLine(i.Title);
        }
    }
}
```

The previous code executes as many CAML queries as the number of contacts found by the first *query*. This is a default behavior, which you can change by setting the *DeferredLoadingEnabled* property of the *DataContext*-derived class to *false*, as shown in the following example:

```
spContext.DeferredLoadingEnabled = false;
```

If you change the entities read from SharePoint, you can also save those changes by using the *SubmitChanges* method, similar to the way you use the *SubmitChanges* method in LINQ to SQL or the *SaveChanges* method in LINQ to Entities:

```
using (SampleSiteDataContext spContext = new SampleSiteDataContext(
  "http://sample.sp2010.local/")) {
    var contact = (from    c in spContext.DevLeapContacts
                   where   c.ContactID == "PP001"
                   select c).FirstOrDefault();

    // Let's see if we found the target contact
    if (contact != null) {
        contact.Country = Country.USA;
        spContext.SubmitChanges();
    }
}
```

You can also insert new entities by using the *InsertOnSubmit* event, as in the following example:

```
using (SampleSiteDataContext spContext = new SampleSiteDataContext(
  "http://sample.sp2010.local/")) {
    DevLeapCustomer newCustomer = new DevLeapCustomer {
        Title = "Andrea Pialorsi",
        ContactID = "AP001",
        CompanyName = "DevLeap",
        Country = Country.Italy,
        CustomerLevel = CustomerLevel.LevelA,
    };

    spContext.DevLeapContacts.InsertOnSubmit(newCustomer);
    spContext.SubmitChanges();
}
```

Finally, because SharePoint has a Recycle Bin feature, you can choose either to delete an entity permanently, or to move it to the Recycle Bin by calling *DeleteOnSubmit* or *RecycleOnSubmit* respectively, as you can see in the following example:

```
using (SampleSiteDataContext spContext = new SampleSiteDataContext(
  "http://sample.sp2010.local/")) {
    var contact = (from    c in spContext.DevLeapContacts
                   where  c.ContactID == "AP001"
                   select c).FirstOrDefault();

    // Let's see if we found the target contact
    if (contact != null) {
        if (recycle) {
            spContext.DevLeapContacts.RecycleOnSubmit(contact);
        }
        else {
            spContext.DevLeapContacts.DeleteOnSubmit(contact);
        }

        spContext.SubmitChanges();
    }
}
```

LINQ to SharePoint has a concurrency conflict-handling system similar to the conflict-handling system in LINQ to SQL. For example, the *SubmitChanges* method might receive a *ConflictMode* parameter that specifies whether to continue when a conflict occurs:

```
public void SubmitChanges();
public void SubmitChanges(ConflictMode failureMode);
public void SubmitChanges(ConflictMode failureMode, bool systemUpdate);

public enum ConflictMode {
    ContinueOnConflict,
    FailOnFirstConflict
}
```

In case of a conflict, the *SubmitChanges* method raises a *ChangeConflictException* instance, which populates the *ChangeConflicts* property of the *DataContext*-derived class instance with an enumerable collection of objects, each one containing a reference to one conflicting item. You can also inspect the conflicts at the member level by simply enumerating the *Member-Conflicts* property of every *ObjectChangeConflict* instance contained in the *ChangeConflicts* collection.

> **More Info** Although an in-depth explanation of LINQ to SharePoint is outside the scope of this book, you will find a detailed exploration of it in a dedicated chapter of the upcoming book *Microsoft SharePoint 2010 Developer Reference* by Paolo Pialorsi (Microsoft Press, 2011).

LINQ to Services

Chapter 15, "Extending LINQ," showed the implementation of a LINQ provider that simplifies access to a fictitious FlightStatus service. This exercise was useful for providing you with the knowledge to build LINQ wrappers for your favorite services. In the real world, many widely used services already have LINQ implementations. Most of these implementations are community based and are not officially supported by single-service providers.

One of the first LINQ wrappers to an external service was LINQ to Amazon (*http://linqinaction.net /blogs/main/archive/2007/12/12/linq-in-action-samples-source-code.aspx*). Using this service, you can look for books in the Amazon catalog, filtering them by attributes such as publisher, price, title, and so on. Similarly, by using LINQ to Flickr (*http://linqflickr.codeplex.com*), you can search for photos stored in the Flickr photo-sharing service. LINQ to Flickr also offers support for adding or deleting photos, a feature not directly tied to the LINQ query syntax, but which is conceptually similar to the entities you can manage in LINQ to SQL or LINQ to Entities.

Google is another source for accessing data through remote services. The LINQ to Google implementation (*http://glinq.codeplex.com*) actually supports only queries to Google Base, which is a search engine that can index structured entities decorated with customizable attributes. The presence of these attributes makes the use of LINQ meaningful, because you can include them as part of a LINQ query, as shown in the following example:

```
GoogleItems.GoogleContext gc = new GoogleItems.GoogleContext(key);
var r = from   car in gc.products
        where  car.Brand == "Ferrari"
               && car.Price < 200000
        select new { car.Title, car.Price };
```

The Bing search engine offers a LINQ to Bing provider, which is part of the Web Application Toolkit for Bing Search (*http://code.msdn.microsoft.com/webapptoolkitbing*). This provider supports searches on webpages, news, images, and video. Here is an example of a Bing web query:

```
Linq2Bing lb = new Linq2Bing();
var query = from    w in lb.Web
            where   w.Text == "DevLeap"
                    && w.Text == "Conference"
            select w;
```

Yet another LINQ implementation that could be useful for accessing remote services is LINQ to JSON, which is included in Microsoft Silverlight and accessible through the *System.Json* namespace. Another implementation you can use without Silverlight is the Json.NET 3.5 library (*http://json.codeplex.com*). This implementation provides a LINQ-integrated model that simplifies access from a .NET Framework application to data serialized with JSON.

Simplifying access to remote services that provide integration with LINQ queries is an area that will likely see great expansion in the future. The service provider does not need to define its own LINQ wrapper; any service consumer can write a LINQ wrapper for that service. However, the most widely used services will probably be supported either directly by service providers or by projects that are supported by communities.

LINQ for System Engineers

Applications that control an existing infrastructure or that automate administrative tasks might be able to take advantage of LINQ while accessing specific services and APIs useful for their needs.

LINQ to Active Directory (*http://linqtoad.codeplex.com*) is an implementation that simplifies access to Active Directory APIs, such as *System.DirectoryServices* (.NET) and *ActiveDs* (COM). The same author originally wrote (and analytically described) a more general implementation of LINQ to LDAP (*http://www.hookedonlinq.com/LINQ2LDAP.ashx*).

Another interesting LINQ implementation is one that provides access to Windows Management Instrumentation (WMI). You can find an implementation of LINQ to WMI at *http://linq2wmi.codeplex.com*. By using a provider like this, you can query WMI counters in a simple and declarative way.

Dynamic LINQ

The standard result of a LINQ query is considered to be static. It does not change after query execution. However, there are situations in which the definition of a LINQ query should be more dynamic, acting more as a filter in a stream of data or making the query result "live." Chapter 16, "Parallelism and Asynchronous Processing," contains a description of Reactive Extensions for .NET (Rx), which is a prototype available as a Microsoft DevLabs project. However, there are a few other approaches to the same issue.

The LINQ to Streams implementation (*http://slinq.codeplex.com*) focuses on streaming data that changes in real time. Currently, it is a simple prototype, but the approach seems interesting for particular scenarios such as network monitors, financial services, and real-time data acquisition.

Another approach to the same issue is the one used in SyncLINQ. This implementation is focused more on data binding over LINQ queries. To support dynamic updates of the query result, a SyncLINQ query returns collections that implement *INotifyCollectionChanged*, which is the interface provided by the .NET Framework to notify listeners of dynamic changes. The SyncLINQ implementation should establish compatibility with existing user interface components that support *INotifyCollectionChanged*.

These implementations do not provide a solution for every tier of an application's architecture, but they do present an interesting approach to solving some of the issues regarding the use of a common programming pattern (LINQ queries). These implementations attempt to simplify and encapsulate the work necessary to handle dynamic updates to data returned from a query.

Other LINQ Enhancements and Tools

The last section of this chapter is dedicated to other LINQ-related implementations and tools that do not fit into the classifications in the previous sections.

DryadLINQ (*http://research.microsoft.com/projects/DryadLINQ*) is a research project that uses LINQ to access Dryad, a distributed execution engine. DryadLINQ compiles lambda expressions into DLLs and routes the DLLs to remote machines for execution. This is a more complex form of parallelism than the one offered by PLINQ and is an interesting implementation for very CPU-intensive applications.

Indexed LINQ, also known as I4O (*http://i4o.codeplex.com/*), is a class library through which you can create indexes on objects queried using LINQ to Objects. This implementation is particularly interesting for applications that load and maintain a large number of objects in memory. Chapter 15 provided an example of one service that belongs in this category: the FlightStatusService, which monitors all the flights around the world in real time. (There are thousands of flights around the world at any given moment.) Using optimizations like the one provided by I4O, any object graph in memory can seem like an in-memory database, even if LINQ and I40 do not automatically solve the issues of concurrent access in a multithreaded environment.

LINQExtender (*http://linqextender.codeplex.com*) is a tool for building LINQ providers. The LINQ to Flickr provider mentioned earlier was created using this tool. The tool is particularly interesting because it provides an extensible model that supports an object-tracking service similar to the one that exists in LINQ to SQL. Another feature of LINQExtender is that it does not require you to extend a parser for an expression tree. The existing parser converts an expression tree into a simpler object that describes the query itself. This simplification might not be good for every application, but you will probably encounter many cases in which a simple provider cannot support complex queries just because the service that it wraps has very simple and limited query semantics.

MetaLinq, also called LINQ to Expressions (*http://metalinq.codeplex.com*), is a library that allows manipulation of a LINQ query. This library offers an object model through which you can manipulate an expression tree (which could be a query tree) without the limitations imposed by a real expression tree, which is made of immutable objects. The final stage of this manipulation is the creation of an equivalent immutable expression tree that can be used with LINQ.

A useful tool for writing and testing LINQ queries is LINQPad (*http://www.linqpad.net*), which is both an interactive editor and an execution environment for LINQ and SQL queries. It supports queries written using LINQ to SQL, LINQ to Objects, and LINQ to XML.

Another interesting tool is LINQ over C# (*http://linqovercsharp.codeplex.com*), which provides a parser for Microsoft Visual C# that can be used together with LINQ as a solid base for refactoring code and creating software quality assurance (QA) tools.

Finally, LINQ to Geo (*http://linqtogeo.codeplex.com*) is a LINQ implementation for querying geospatial data, and LINQ to Lucene (*http://linqtolucene.codeplex.com*) supports the Lucene Information Retrieval System, which is a free open-source search engine.

Summary

This chapter provided an overview of the rapidly expanding breadth of LINQ implementations, extensions, and tools available at the time of this writing (September 2010). The goal of this chapter was not to explain any of these implementations in depth, but simply to provide you with a brief guide from which to start exploring other LINQ implementations.

You saw that there are alternative LINQ implementations for accessing data in databases as well as data stored in systems other than relational databases. There are LINQ implementations that support ORMs other than the ADO.NET Entity Framework, and wrappers that support LINQ queries over remote services such as Amazon and Flickr, as well as other standard services, such as Active Directory and WMI. Finally, you saw some brief descriptions of other LINQ implementations and tools that can help improve the performance of LINQ providers or simplify the creation of new LINQ providers.

Part V
Applied LINQ

Chapter 18
LINQ in a Multitier Solution

This chapter focuses on using Microsoft Language Integrated Query (LINQ) effectively in common software scenarios. The goal is to learn how and when you can best use LINQ in everyday solutions, and to evaluate the impact of using it in modern software architectures and implementations. You will learn about some architectural patterns and rules, largely concentrating on matters related to the data access layer and the business layer of multitier enterprise-level solutions.

Characteristics of a Multitier Solution

A multitier solution is a software project that usually targets many concurrent users. It is divided into *n* layers—generally at least two or three layers. Applications that use a two-tier scenario are also referred to as *client-server* software. One layer is the back-end server infrastructure, which is generally made up of a database persistence layer. The other layer, the client, includes all the required code to connect to the back-end database and display the user interface. Generally, in two-tier scenarios, the business logic and domain knowledge required for the solution is implemented within the client software. Sometimes such solutions also include database logic, such as intelligent stored procedures, triggers, and so on.

Although client-server architecture is suitable for implementing solutions that will have a relatively small number of users, this book does not cover it in detail because its two-tier architecture has scalability and other limitations compared to other architectural solutions. Software is *scalable* when its performance remains constant and independent regardless of the number of users. Scalable software is not necessarily fast—it simply has a fixed performance score regardless of the number of customers served. The very nature of a client-server solution prevents scalability—specifically, an increase in the number of users can have a huge impact on the back-end database layer.

Partly for scalability reasons, over the past several years, architectures with at least three tiers have become more common. Many modern software solutions are available on a network and the Internet, and serve a large (and unpredictable) number of concurrent users. Three-tier solutions have a data access layer, a business layer, and a presentation layer. The data access layer (DAL) represents the set of code and data structures used to implement information persistence. The business layer (BIZ) defines business logic, business workflows, and rules that drive the behavior of the application. The presentation layer, or user interface (UI) layer, delivers the information to end users. The presentation layer, in particular, has become more complex, because it can (and often must) be implemented in many different ways, one for each kind of consumer (for example the web, Windows, or a smart device). In general, DAL and BIZ are deployed on specific and dedicated application servers, whereas the UI can be deployed on both consumer devices or delivered to browsers from specific publishing application servers (web applications on front-end web servers).

Technologies such as Simple Object Access Protocol (SOAP) services, smart clients, smart phones, or workflow services have influenced many software architects to add other layers. The now-common definition of n-tier solution architecture is one in which *n* designates a value greater than or at least equal to three. In general, as you can see from Figure 18-1, these *n* layers are targeted to meet specific application requirements, such as security, workflow definition, or communication.

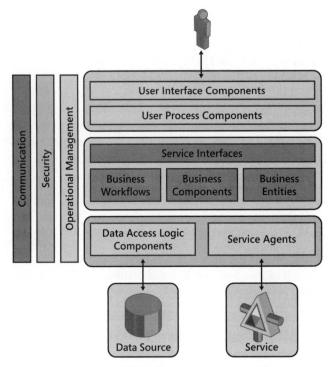

FIGURE 18-1 Schema of an n-tier architecture.

The main reasons for dividing a software solution's architecture into layers are to improve maintainability, availability, security, and deployment.

Maintainability results from the ability to change and maintain small portions (for example, single layers) of an application without needing to touch the other layers. By working this way, you reduce maintenance time and can also more accurately assess the cost of a fix or a feature change, because you can focus your attention only on the layers involved in the change. Client-server software is more costly to maintain because any code modifications must be deployed to each client. Well-defined multitier solutions are also available to users more often because critical or highly stressed layers can be deployed in a redundant infrastructure.

From a security perspective, a layered solution can make use of different security modules, each one tightly aligned with a particular software layer to make the solution stronger. Last but not least, multitier software is usually deployed more easily because each layer can be configured and sized somewhat independently from other layers.

> **Note** This chapter uses the well-known Northwind database as the persistence storage location for a sample multitier solution.

LINQ to SQL in a Two-Tier Solution

From a LINQ perspective, a two-tier architecture solution is an ideal host for a LINQ to SQL implementation. You can use LINQ to SQL entities to model each database table, as well as to query and manage these entities (server tables) from the consumer (client). In a two-tier solution you can also take advantage of the extensibility of the LINQ to SQL *DataContext* object, which is available through partial methods.

For example, consider the Customers and Orders tables of the Northwind database and the corresponding domain model entities (shown in Figure 18-2).

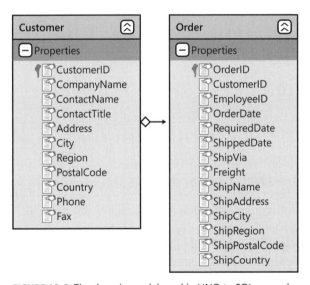

FIGURE 18-2 The domain model used in LINQ to SQL examples.

If you want to save a single *Customer* instance with its related *Order* instances, you can use the approach described in Chapter 6, "LINQ to SQL: Managing Data." The Object Relational Designer (O/R Designer) integrated into Microsoft Visual Studio automatically generates some partial methods that are useful for defining a customized behavior to insert, delete, and update customers and orders. Listing 18-1 shows a code excerpt taken from an autogenerated *DataContext* type.

LISTING 18-1 The partial methods of an autogenerated *DataContext*

```
[System.Data.Linq.Mapping.DatabaseAttribute(Name="Northwind")]
public partial class NorthwindDataContext : System.Data.Linq.DataContext {

private static System.Data.Linq.Mapping.MappingSource mappingSource =
    new AttributeMappingSource();

#region Extensibility Method Definitions
partial void OnCreated();
partial void InsertCustomer(Customer instance);
partial void UpdateCustomer(Customer instance);
partial void DeleteCustomer(Customer instance);
partial void InsertOrder(Order instance);
partial void UpdateOrder(Order instance);
#endregion
// ...
}
```

The autogenerated partial methods *Insert*TYPE, *Delete*TYPE, and *Update*TYPE make it easier for you to customize the behavior of the *DataContext* object during the most common data modification operations.

LINQ in an n-Tier Solution

This section evaluates the role of the various LINQ implementations in an n-tier solution, starting from the data access layer, and then moving to the business layer.

Using LINQ to SQL as a DAL Replacement

The first step in defining any n-tier solution architecture is to identify and describe the domain model, which is the set of entities used by the system. If you want to drive a database design from a domain model, you can create the physical database from the LINQ to SQL entity model by using the *CreateDatabase* method of the *DataContext* object. On the other hand, if your database structure has already been defined, or you prefer to use specific database features in your domain model (such as triggers, functions, views, or stored procedures), you can model LINQ to SQL entities starting from existing tables.

> **More Info** More details about the different ways of working with LINQ to SQL and the tools you can use can be found in Chapter 7, "LINQ to SQL: Modeling Data and Tools."

Regardless of the way in which you define the physical database and the corresponding LINQ to SQL entity model, using LINQ to SQL as your data layer results in LINQ to SQL entities being used by the entire application architecture. This last point means that you can use the types you define for LINQ to SQL, such as the *Customer* and *Order* entities discussed earlier, throughout the application. For example, a presentation layer implemented using Windows Presentation Foundation (WPF) will share these types with LINQ to SQL and can perform data binding against a sequence of type *IEnumerable<Customer>* obtained by executing a LINQ query over an instance of *Table<Customer>* provided by a *DataContext* instance.

This situation has both advantages and disadvantages. The advantages stem from the agility and ease of use that LINQ to SQL offers. By taking a closer look at the code generated and defined by LINQ to SQL tools (such as SQLMetal or the O/R Designer in Visual Studio), you can see that these types implement a set of interfaces targeted to UI data binding: *INotify-PropertyChanging* and *INotifyPropertyChanged*.

On the other hand, the nature of LINQ to SQL means that the data layer will be tightly integrated with the Microsoft SQL Server database. This level of integration might be your goal for a single-database-platform solution, but it can also pose limitations for your architecture.

In general, a data layer is an abstraction of the physical persistence layer, thus allowing changes to the back-end implementation that are transparent to the layers above it. You usually achieve this abstraction by defining a domain model that is independent from the database, communicating between the DAL and BIZ layers by using the entities that belong to the independent domain model. However, when you use LINQ to SQL as a pure data layer replacement, you are limited to SQL Server as a database, and your entities will be widely marked in code with attributes that map to SQL Server-specific information. In addition, you might already have a domain model defined simply because you are extending an existing application, or because you do not want to mark your domain model with data-layer-specific (LINQ to SQL) attributes.

To avoid these issues, you can take a few steps toward true abstraction using one of the techniques illustrated in the next sections.

Abstracting LINQ to SQL with XML External Mapping

To gain abstraction from the database layer, one technique is to define an external XML mapping for your LINQ to SQL entities. You saw an example of this approach in the "Binding Metadata" section in Chapter 6. Using external XML mapping, you can keep your entities free from any LINQ to SQL code attributes, and you can use already-existing entities, mapping them to LINQ to SQL. Listing 18-2 recalls sample excerpts from Chapter 6 for your convenience.

LISTING 18-2 The code to define a *DataContext* based on an external XML mapping file

```
public partial class Northwind : System.Data.Linq.DataContext {

    // Extensibility Method Definitions

    public Northwind(string connection,
        System.Data.Linq.Mapping.MappingSource mappingSource) :
            base(connection, mappingSource) {
        OnCreated();
    }

    public Northwind(System.Data.IDbConnection connection,
        System.Data.Linq.Mapping.MappingSource mappingSource) :
            base(connection, mappingSource) {
        OnCreated();
    }

    public System.Data.Linq.Table<Customer> Customers {
        get {
            return this.GetTable<Customer>();
        }
    }

    public System.Data.Linq.Table<Order> Orders {
        get {
            return this.GetTable<Order>();
        }
    }
}
```

As you can see, the *DataContext* type provides two constructors, both of which require an argument of type *MappingSource*. This argument represents a link to an external XML mapping file such as the one illustrated in Listing 18-3.

LISTING 18-3 The XML mapping file for the Northwind *DataContext*

```
<?xml version="1.0" encoding="utf-8"?>
<Database Name="northwind"
 xmlns="http://schemas.microsoft.com/linqtosql/mapping/2007">
  <Table Name="dbo.Customers" Member="Customers">
    <Type Name="Customer">
      <Column Name="CustomerID" Member="CustomerID" Storage="_CustomerID"
              DbType="NChar(5) NOT NULL" CanBeNull="false"
              IsPrimaryKey="true" />
      <Column Name="CompanyName" Member="CompanyName"
              Storage="_CompanyName" DbType="NVarChar(40) NOT NULL"
              CanBeNull="false" />
      <Column Name="ContactName" Member="ContactName"
              Storage="_ContactName" DbType="NVarChar(30)" />

    ...
```

```
            <Association Name="FK_Orders_Customers" Member="Orders"
                    Storage="_Orders" ThisKey="CustomerID"
                    OtherKey="CustomerID" DeleteRule="NO ACTION" />
      </Type>
    </Table>
    <Table Name="dbo.Orders" Member="Orders">
      <Type Name="Orders">
        <Column Name="OrderID" Member="OrderID" Storage="_OrderID"
                DbType="Int NOT NULL IDENTITY" IsPrimaryKey="true"
                IsDbGenerated="true" AutoSync="OnInsert" />
        <Column Name="CustomerID" Member="CustomerID" Storage="_CustomerID"
                DbType="NChar(5)" />
        <Column Name="OrderDate" Member="OrderDate" Storage="_OrderDate"
                DbType="DateTime" />

        ...

        <Association Name="FK_Orders_Customers" Member="Customers"
                    Storage="_Customers" ThisKey="CustomerID"
                    OtherKey="CustomerID" IsForeignKey="true" />
      </Type>
    </Table>
    ...
  </Database>
```

To load a *DataContext* instance with an external XML mapping file, you can call its constructor and provide an *XmlMappingSource* instance, as shown in Listing 18-4.

LISTING 18-4 The code to load the Northwind *DataContext* with a custom XML mapping file

```
NorthwindDataContext nwind = new NorthwindDataContext(
    ConfigurationManager.ConnectionStrings["Northwind"].ConnectionString,
    XmlMappingSource.FromUrl(
        ConfigurationManager.AppSettings["NorthwindModelUrl"]));
```

The *XmlMappingSource* class is just one of the classes that inherits from the abstract *Mapping-Source* type. The *DataContext* constructor accepts any type derived from *MappingSource*, which means you can define your own mapping using any kind of custom entity schema definition.

Using an external mapping schema might appear to satisfy the needs of abstraction and entity independence, but it is not a real solution. The source code that defines the entities still needs to be specific to LINQ to SQL. For example, consider the relationship between each *Customer* and that customer's *Order* instances. Listing 18-5 shows that the *Customer* type requires a field of type *EntitySet<Order>*. Also, the *Order* type, omitted from the following example, has a field of type *EntityRef<Customer>*. Those types and fields are completely tied to LINQ to SQL.

LISTING 18-5 Code excerpt of the *Customer* type based on external XML mapping

```
public partial class Customer : INotifyPropertyChanging, INotifyPropertyChanged {

    private string _CustomerID;
    private string _CompanyName;

    // ... code omitted ...

    private EntitySet<Order> _Orders;
    // Extensibility Method Definitions
    // ... code omitted ...

    public EntitySet<Order> Orders {
        get {
            return this._Orders;
        }
        set {
            this._Orders.Assign(value);
        }
    }

    // ... code omitted ...
    private void attach_Orders(Order entity) {
        this.SendPropertyChanging();
        entity.Customer = this;
    }

    private void detach_Orders(Order entity)
    {
        this.SendPropertyChanging();
        entity.Customer = null;
    }
}
```

The resulting class is still not truly independent and abstracted from LINQ to SQL. Even so, using an external mapping source is useful for separating entity source code from the mapping information. For example, you might want to translate type names from the database structure to the software architecture, to join a custom mapping source with a LINQ to SQL entity model, or to specify provider-specific attributes that differentiate SQL Server 2000 from SQL Server 2005 databases that use the source code from the same entities.

Using LINQ to SQL Through Real Abstraction

When you need to truly and effectively hide the LINQ to SQL implementation from the upper layers, you should create a real object-oriented abstraction. For example, you can define your domain model to be independent from any particular data layer implementation—including LINQ to SQL or anything else—by defining a dedicated assembly with your own custom entities. This approach implements a concept known as *persistence ignorance*. You can see an example of *Customer* and *Order* types of this kind in Listing 18-6.

LISTING 18-6 The *Customer* and *Order* types defined in an independent domain model

```
namespace DevLeap.Linq.Architecture.NTier.DomainModel {
    public abstract class BaseEntity {
        // Here there could be some common behaviors and properties
    }
    public class Customer : BaseEntity {
        public String CustomerID { get; set; }
        public String CompanyName { get; set; }
        public String ContactName { get; set; }
        public String ContactTitle { get; set; }
        public String Address { get; set; }
        public String City { get; set; }
        public String Region { get; set; }
        public String PostalCode { get; set; }
        public String Country { get; set; }
        public String Phone { get; set; }
        public String Fax { get; set; }
        public ICollection<Order> Orders { get; set; }
    }
    public class Order : BaseEntity {
        public Int32 OrderID { get; set; }
        public String CustomerID { get; set; }

        // ... code omitted ...
    }
}
```

These types are simple and look like data transfer objects (DTO) rather than domain model entities. However, remember that this example is just for the sake of illustration. In a real solution, these entities will probably include some domain model logic such as validation rules or constraints. In Figure 18-3, you can see the class diagram corresponding to the actual domain model.

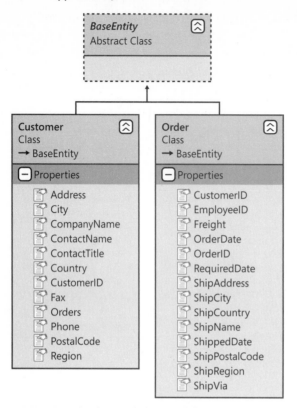

FIGURE 18-3 The abstract domain model.

The sample code in Listing 18-7 works only with *Customer* instances; any *Order* instance will be available solely through its corresponding *Customer* object. To begin, consider the implementation of the data layer as a set of Data Mappers, each one providing a kind of Create, Read, Update, and Delete (CRUD) operation for each domain model entity.

> **Note** A Data Mapper is a software layer that transfers data between the database and in-memory objects. You can find the definition of a Data Mapper at *http://www.martinfowler.com/eaaCatalog /dataMapper.html*.

To keep the business layer independent from the data layer implementation and from the persistence storage, you can define an interface and a *Factory* class or method that creates Data Mapper instances implementing a specific interface. Listing 18-7 shows an example.

LISTING 18-7 An abstract interface for a Data Mapper acting as a CRUD on the *Customer* entity

```
namespace DevLeap.Linq.Architecture.NTier.DataLayer {
    public interface ICustomerDal {
        /// <summary>
        /// Adds a new customer to the persistence storage
        /// </summary>
        /// <param name="item">The customer instance to add</param>
        /// <returns>The customer that has just been added</returns>
        Customer Add(Customer item);

        /// <summary>
        /// Reads a customer instance from the persistence storage
        /// </summary>
        /// <param name="key">The key to extract the customer instance</param>
        /// <returns>The customer instance if it exists</returns>
        Customer Read(String key);

        /// <summary>
        /// Reads all the available customer instances from the
        /// persistence storage
        /// </summary>
        /// <returns>The list of existing customers</returns>
        /// <remarks>In a real scenario, there could be a filtering condition,
        /// eventually expressed using a LINQ query expression</remarks>
        List<Customer> ReadAll();

        /// <summary>
        /// Updates a customer into the persistence storage
        /// </summary>
        /// <param name="item">The customer instance to update</param>
        /// <returns>The customer that has just been updated</returns>
        Customer Update(Customer item);

        /// <summary>
        /// Deletes a customer from the persistence storage
        /// </summary>
        /// <param name="item">The customer to delete</param>
        /// <returns>The result of the deleting operation</returns>
        Boolean Delete(Customer item);
    }
}
```

Listing 18-7 defines a simplified interface dedicated to the *Customer* entity. You could do this for every single entity of the domain model that requires a dedicated Data Mapper. However, starting with Microsoft .NET Framework 2.0, you can use generic types to define a kind of code "prototype." Thus, it is possible to replace the code in Listing 18-7 with a generic interface suitable for many of the entities in the domain model. You can see how to do this in Listing 18-8.

LISTING 18-8 An abstract and generic interface defining a Data Mapper for every entity in the domain model

```
namespace DevLeap.Linq.Architecture.NTier.DataLayer {
    public interface IDal<TEntity, TEntityList, TKey>
        where TEntity : BaseEntity, new()
        where TEntityList : IEnumerable<TEntity> {

        /// <summary>
        /// Adds a new entity to the persistence storage
        /// </summary>
        /// <param name="item">The entity  instance to add</param>
        /// <returns>The entity that has just been added</returns>
        TEntity Add(TEntity item);

        /// <summary>
        /// Reads an entity instance from the persistence storage
        /// </summary>
        /// <param name="key">The key to extract the entity instance</param>
        /// <returns>The entity instance if it exists</returns>
        TEntity Read(TKey key);

        /// <summary>
        /// Reads all the available entity instances from the persistence storage
        /// </summary>
        /// <returns>The list of existing entities</returns>
        /// <remarks>In a real scenario, there could be a filtering condition,
        /// eventually expressed using a LINQ query expression</remarks>
        TEntityList ReadAll();

        /// <summary>
        /// Updates an entity in the persistence storage
        /// </summary>
        /// <param name="item">The entity instance to update</param>
        /// <returns>The entity that has just been updated</returns>
        TEntity Update(TEntity item);

        /// <summary>
        /// Deletes an entity from the persistence storage
        /// </summary>
        /// <param name="item">The entity to delete</param>
        /// <returns>The result of the deleting operation</returns>
        Boolean Delete(TEntity item);
    }
}
```

You can implement this generic interface for each entity to define the entity's generic arguments. The *TEntity* type, should be inherited from *BaseEntity* and requires a default constructor. The *TEntityList* type represents a sequence of entities and should implement *IEnumerable<TEntity>*. The business layer makes queries for this type using LINQ. The *TKey* type is a unique key, which uniquely identifies an entity of type *TEntity*.

From the business layer viewpoint, the data layer is just a set of classes that implement this generic interface. In this way, the BIZ can completely ignore the implementation of the real data layer constructed by the factory.

This book does not cover how to implement the data layer factory, but you can find a fully functional example in the book's sample source code. Of course, the example solution is fictitious; it is intended only to illustrate LINQ concepts. You would need to revise and complete the architecture to use it in a real solution.

To completely abstract the solution from any specific data layer, including a LINQ to SQL implementation, you must define the real data layer implementation in a dedicated assembly that will be loaded through the data layer factory instead of being referenced directly. The code using LINQ to SQL resides inside this referenced assembly. Only domain model entities travel across the boundaries between any DAL implementation and the BIZ layer consumer: not data tables, not LINQ to SQL entities—nothing else.

To meet this last requirement, the LINQ to SQL–based data layer translates its own entities back and forth to the domain model entities. To help organize the code, there is a *BaseDal* abstract and generic class from which every entity-specific data layer type derives. Listing 18-9 shows a possible implementation of the *BaseDal* type.

LISTING 18-9 A hypothetical implementation of the *BaseDal* type

```
using System;
using System.Collections.Generic;
using System.Linq;
using System.Text;
using DomainModel = DevLeap.Linq.Architecture.NTier.DomainModel;

namespace DevLeap.Linq.Architecture.NTier.DataLayer.LinqToSql {
    public class BaseDal<TEntity, TEntityList, TKey>:
        IDal<TEntity, TEntityList, TKey>
        where TEntity : BaseEntity, new()
        where TEntityList : IEnumerable<TEntity> {

        protected NorthwindDataContext Northwind { get; private set; }

        protected BaseDal(){
            this.Northwind = new NorthwindDataContext(nwConnectionString);
        }

        #region IDal<TEntity,TEntityList,TKey> Members
        // ... Code omitted ...
        #endregion
    }
}
```

The definition of the read-only protected property named *Northwind* corresponds to an instance of the LINQ to SQL *DataContext*. Because every LINQ to SQL data layer class needs to access the *DataContext*, and because the *DataContext* should be instantiated and destroyed for each unit of work, this sample uses one *DataContext* instance dedicated to each data layer domain model entity, assuming that you are in a loosely coupled environment because of the n-tier architecture.

Every data layer type inherits the *BaseDal* abstract class, implementing the real behavior related to the entity that it manages. For example, Listing 18-10 contains an excerpt of the *Read* method in the *CustomerDal* type.

LISTING 18-10 The first hypothetical implementation of a part of the *CustomerDal* type

```csharp
using System;
using System.Collections.Generic;
using System.Linq;
using System.Text;
using DomainModel = DevLeap.Linq.Architecture.NTier.DomainModel;
namespace DevLeap.Linq.Architecture.NTier.DataLayer.LinqToSql {
    public class CustomerDal :
        BaseDal<DomainModel.Customer, List< DomainModel.Customer>, String> {

        // ... Code omitted ...

        public override DomainModel.Customer Read(string key) {

            // Get the first LINQ to SQL customer entity
            // instance with the provided key
            var linqCustomer = this.Northwind.Customers
                .First(c => c.CustomerID == key);

            // Convert it into a Domain Model customer
            var result = new DomainModel.Customer {
                    CustomerID = linqCustomer.CustomerID,
                    Address = linqCustomer.Address,
                    City = linqCustomer.City,
                    CompanyName = linqCustomer.CompanyName,
                    ContactName = linqCustomer.ContactName,
                    ContactTitle = linqCustomer.ContactTitle,
                    Country = linqCustomer.Country,
                    Fax = linqCustomer.Fax,
                    Phone = linqCustomer.Phone,
                    PostalCode = linqCustomer.PostalCode,
                    Region = linqCustomer.Region
                };

            result.Orders = new List<DomainModel.Order>();

            // Convert every order obtained from LINQ to SQL
            // into an Order of the Domain Model
```

```
                foreach (var o in linqCustomer.Orders) {
                    result.Orders.Add(new DomainModel.Order {
                        OrderID = o.OrderID,
                        CustomerID = o.CustomerID,
                        EmployeeID = o.EmployeeID,
                        Freight = o.Freight,
                        OrderDate = o.OrderDate,
                        RequiredDate = o.RequiredDate,
                        ShipAddress = o.ShipAddress,
                        ShipCity = o.ShipCity,
                        ShipCountry = o.ShipCountry,
                        ShipName = o.ShipName,
                        ShippedDate = o.ShippedDate,
                        ShipPostalCode = o.ShipPostalCode,
                        ShipRegion = o.ShipRegion,
                        ShipVia = o.ShipVia
                    });
                }
                return (result);
            }

        // ... Code omitted ...


    }
}
```

The code in Listing 18-10 is completely functional and syntactically correct. However, it is a bit verbose and redundant. Never underestimate the power and expressiveness of LINQ syntax! Listing 18-11 shows the same method implemented using a single LINQ query expression.

LISTING 18-11 The final implementation of a part of the *CustomerDal* type

```
using System;
using System.Collections.Generic;
using System.Linq;
using System.Text;
using DomainModel = DevLeap.Linq.Architecture.NTier.DomainModel;

namespace DevLeap.Linq.Architecture.NTier.DataLayer.LinqToSql {
    public class CustomerDal :
        BaseDal<DomainModel.Customer, List< DomainModel.Customer>, String>

        // ... Code omitted ...

        public override DomainModel.Customer Read(string key) {
            // Convert the first LINQ to SQL customer
            // into a Domain Model customer using a
            // LINQ query expression
```

```
        var result =
            (from c in this.Northwind.Customers
            where c.CustomerID == key
            select new DomainModel.Customer {
                CustomerID = c.CustomerID,
                Address = c.Address,
                City = c.City,
                CompanyName = c.CompanyName,
                ContactName = c.ContactName,
                ContactTitle = c.ContactTitle,
                Country = c.Country,
                Fax = c.Fax,
                Phone = c.Phone,
                PostalCode = c.PostalCode,
                Region = c.Region,
                // Converts the list of orders of the
                // LINQ to SQL customer into the list of
                // orders defined in the Domain Model
                // using a LINQ subquery
                Orders = new List<DomainModel.Order>(
                    from o in c.Orders
                    select new DomainModel.Order {
                        OrderID = o.OrderID,
                        CustomerID = o.CustomerID,
                        EmployeeID = o.EmployeeID,
                        Freight = o.Freight,
                        OrderDate = o.OrderDate,
                        RequiredDate = o.RequiredDate,
                        ShipAddress = o.ShipAddress,
                        ShipCity = o.ShipCity,
                        ShipCountry = o.ShipCountry,
                        ShipName = o.ShipName,
                        ShippedDate = o.ShippedDate,
                        ShipPostalCode = o.ShipPostalCode,
                        ShipRegion = o.ShipRegion,
                        ShipVia = o.ShipVia
                    })
            }).First();

        return (result);
    }

    // ... Code omitted ...

    }
}
```

The difference between Listing 18-10 and Listing 18-11 is just syntactic; both method implementations perform the same because they both query SQL Server with the same queries. However, this is only a simple example. There could be more complex situations in which using a single query expression would give you better performance, allowing the LINQ to SQL engine to execute optimized SQL queries. Working with legacy-style procedural code does not allow for any kind of implicit platform optimization.

The key point of this example is that you can replace the LINQ to SQL data layer implementation with any kind of data layer that supports the same contracts (interfaces, base classes, and domain model entities). The technology used within the DAL is completely transparent to the upper layers, so you gain a real abstraction over the DAL and LINQ to SQL without losing the power and simplicity of LINQ to SQL programming. You can find the full implementation of the LINQ to SQL–based data layer in this book's sample code.

Using LINQ to XML as the Data Layer

To demonstrate the real abstraction achieved in the previous section, we built a LINQ to XML–based data layer suitable for a full and transparent substitution of the actual data layer based on LINQ to SQL.

Imagine having an XML file that stores customers and orders (NorthwindCustomersWith-Orders.XML). In Listing 18-12, you can see an excerpt of this file.

LISTING 18-12 An excerpt of the NorthwindCustomersWithOrders.XML persistence file

```xml
<?xml version="1.0" encoding="utf-8"?>
<Northwind>
  <customer>
    <customerID>ALFKI</customerID>
    <address>Obere Str. 57</address>
    <city>Berlin</city>
    <companyName>Alfreds Futterkiste</companyName>
    <contactName>Maria Anders</contactName>
    <contactTitle>Sales Representative</contactTitle>
    <country>Germany</country>
    <fax>030-0076545</fax>
    <phone>030-0074321</phone>
    <postalCode>12209</postalCode>
    <region />
    <orders>
      <order>
        <orderId>10643</orderId>
        <employeeID>6</employeeID>
        <freight>29.4600</freight>
        <orderDate>1997-08-25T00:00:00</orderDate>
        <requiredDate>1997-09-22T00:00:00</requiredDate>
        <shipAddress>Obere Str. 57</shipAddress>
        <shipCity>Berlin</shipCity>
        <shipCountry>Germany</shipCountry>
        <shipName>Alfreds Futterkiste</shipName>
```

```
        <shippedDate>1997-09-02T00:00:00</shippedDate>
        <shipPostalCode>12209</shipPostalCode>
        <shipRegion />
        <shipVia>1</shipVia>
      </order>
      <order>
        <!-- XML code omitted -->
      </order>
    </orders>
  </customer>
  <!-- XML code omitted -->
  <customer>
    <customerID>WOLZA</customerID>
    <address>ul. Filtrowa 68</address>
    <city>Warszawa</city>
    <companyName>Wolski  Zajazd</companyName>
    <contactName>Zbyszek Piestrzeniewicz</contactName>
    <!-- XML code omitted -->
  </customer>
</Northwind>
```

You can build a data layer that works with LINQ to XML and provides data mapping function-alities to the BIZ by abstracting it from the physical persistence storage. In Listing 18-13, you can see a sample implementation of the *CustomerDal* type for the LINQ to XML data layer implementation.

LISTING 18-13 An excerpt of the *Read* method of the *CustomerDal* based on LINQ to XML

```
namespace DevLeap.Linq.Architecture.NTier.DataLayer.LinqToXml {
  public class CustomerDal :
    BaseDal<DomainModel.Customer,
    IEnumerable<DomainModel.Customer>, String> {

    // ... Code omitted ...

    public override DomainModel.Customer Read(string key) {
      var result =
        (from x in this.NorthwindXml.Descendants("customer")
        where x.Element("customerID").Value == key
        select new DomainModel.Customer {
          CustomerID = (String)x.Element("customerID"),
          Address = (String)x.Element("address"),
          City = (String)x.Element("city"),
          CompanyName = (String)x.Element("companyName"),
          ContactName = (String)x.Element("contactName"),
          ContactTitle = (String)x.Element("contactTitle"),
          Country = (String)x.Element("country"),
          Fax = (String)x.Element("fax"),
          Phone = (String)x.Element("phone"),
          PostalCode = (String)x.Element("postalCode"),
          Region = (String)x.Element("region"),
```

```
            // Converts the list of orders of the LINQ to SQL customer
            // into the list of orders defined in the Domain Model
            Orders = new
              List<DevLeap.Linq.Architecture.NTier.DomainModel.Order>(
                from ox in x.Element("orders").Elements("order")
                select new DomainModel.Order {
                  OrderID = (Int32)ox.Element("orderID"),
                  CustomerID = (String)x.Element("customerID"),
                  EmployeeID = (String.IsNullOrEmpty(
                      ox.Element("employeeID").Value) ? null :
                      (Int32?)ox.Element("employeeID")),
                  Freight = (String.IsNullOrEmpty(
                      ox.Element("freight").Value) ? null :
                      (Decimal?)ox.Element("freight")),
                  OrderDate = (String.IsNullOrEmpty(
                      ox.Element("orderDate").Value) ? null :
                      (DateTime?)ox.Element("orderDate")),
                  RequiredDate = (String.IsNullOrEmpty(
                      ox.Element("requiredDate").Value) ? null :
                      (DateTime?)ox.Element("requiredDate")),
                  ShipAddress = (String)ox.Element("shipAddress"),
                  ShipCity = (String)ox.Element("shipCity"),
                  ShipCountry = (String)ox.Element("shipCountry"),
                  ShipName = (String)ox.Element("shipName"),
                  ShippedDate = (String.IsNullOrEmpty(
                      ox.Element("shippedDate").Value) ? null :
                      (DateTime?)ox.Element("shippedDate")),
                  ShipPostalCode = (String)ox.Element("shipPostalCode"),
                  ShipRegion = (String)ox.Element("shipRegion"),
                  ShipVia = (String.IsNullOrEmpty(
                      ox.Element("shipVia").Value) ? null :
                      (Int32?)ox.Element("shipVia")),
                })
            }).First();
          return (result);
        }
        // ... Code omitted ...
    }
}
```

As you can see, the *Read* method implementation works with a LINQ to XML query to extract the required customer element. It converts the customer element into the domain model *Customer* entity using a LINQ query expression. The *CustomerDal* type has a base class that simply implements the light logic to load and save the *XElement* that corresponds to the entire XML storage file. Listing 18-14 shows an implementation.

LISTING 18-14 An excerpt of the *BaseDal* abstract base class for a LINQ to XML–based data layer

```
namespace DevLeap.Linq.Architecture.NTier.DataLayer.LinqToXml {
    public abstract class BaseDal<TEntity, TEntityList, TKey>:
        IDal<TEntity, TEntityList, TKey>
            where TEntity : BaseEntity, new()
            where TEntityList : IEnumerable<TEntity> {

        protected XElement NorthwindXml { get; private set; }

        protected BaseDal() {
            this.NorthwindXml = XElement.Load(XmlDataSourcePath);
        }

        protected void Save() {
            this.NorthwindXml.Save(XmlDataSourcePath);
        }

        #region IDal<TEntity,TEntityList,TKey> Members
        // ... Code omitted ...
        #endregion
    }
}
```

Using LINQ to Entities as the Data Layer

One more option is to use LINQ to Entities and the Microsoft ADO.NET Entity Framework to query and manage data in the persistence storage component, using one of the main features of the Entity Framework: database platform independence. Unlike LINQ to SQL, LINQ to Entities supports many different data providers out of the box, and many third-party software companies also support it.

 More Info   Go to *http://msdn.microsoft.com/en-us/data/dd363565.aspx* for information about ADO.NET third-party providers. For more details on LINQ to Entities and the ADO.NET Entity Framework, see Chapter 8, "LINQ to Entities: Modeling Data with Entity Framework," Chapter 9, "LINQ to Entities: Querying Data," and Chapter 10, "LINQ to Entities: Managing Data."

Because of the native abstraction provided by LINQ to Entities, you might choose to use it whenever you need to abstract from the data layer. On the other hand, you need to think carefully about the overall architecture of your solution, as well as about the persistence model you will use with the Entity Framework. In fact, the standard behavior of the Entity Framework is *not* persistence ignorance. Thus, if you use a standard .edmx model, you would miss out on one of the main requirements for true data layer abstraction: the persistence ignorance of the domain model. On the other hand, if you choose to define persistence-ignorant (that is, POCO) entities, you will gain true abstraction from the persistence layer. You have already seen in Chapter 8 and in Chapter 10 that—with the Entity Framework in

Microsoft .NET Framework 4—you can use your own domain model entities intact, feeding them transparently with the Entity Framework. To achieve that goal, you need to set the "Code Generation Strategy" of the .edmx to *None*, and define a custom class that inherits from *ObjectContext*. Listing 18-15 shows a code excerpt of a sample *ObjectContext* created for this purpose.

LISTING 18-15 Excerpt of a custom *ObjectContext* that uses *DomainModel* entities

```
public class NorthwindEntities: ObjectContext {
    public NorthwindEntities(String connectionString)
        : base(connectionString, "NorthwindEntities") {
        this.Customers = base.CreateObjectSet<DomainModel.Customer>();
        this.Orders = base.CreateObjectSet<DomainModel.Order>();

        this.ContextOptions.LazyLoadingEnabled = true;
    }

    public ObjectSet<DomainModel.Customer> Customers { get; private set; }
    public ObjectSet<DomainModel.Order> Orders { get; private set; }
}
```

If necessary, you can enable lazy loading on your entities by adding the *virtual* keyword to the *Orders* property of the *Customer* type of the Domain Model. However, to make the use of the Entity Framework invisible to the business layer and to the overall software architecture, you still need to define a set of custom data layer components that use the just-defined *Object-Context* implementation internally. In Listing 18-16, you can see an explanatory implementation of the *CustomerDal* class for this situation.

> **More Info** For more information about lazy loading, see the "POCO Support" section in Chapter 8.

LISTING 18-16 The *CustomerDal* implementation using the Entity Framework under the covers

```
public class CustomerDal :
    BaseDal<DomainModel.Customer, List<DomainModel.Customer>, String> {

    public override DomainModel.Customer Read(string key) {
        // Get the first customer using
        // a LINQ to Entities query
        var result = ((ObjectQuery<DomainModel.Customer>)
            (from   c in this.Northwind.Customers
             where  c.CustomerID == key
             select c)).Include("Orders").FirstOrDefault();

        return (result);
    }
}
```

```
    public override List<DomainModel.Customer> ReadAll() {
        // Get the whole list of customers using
        // a LINQ to Entities query
        var result = ((ObjectQuery<DomainModel.Customer>)
            (from   c in this.Northwind.Customers
             select c)).Include("Orders");
        return (result).ToList();
    }

    public override DomainModel.Customer Add(DomainModel.Customer item) {
        // Insert the newly created customer into the ObjectContext
        this.Northwind.Customers.AddObject(item);

        // Save the change
        this.Northwind.SaveChanges();

        // Return the newly created customer
        return (item);
    }

    public override DomainModel.Customer Update(DomainModel.Customer item) {
        // ... Code omitted ...
    }

    public override bool Delete(DomainModel.Customer item) {
        // ... Code omitted ...
    }
}
```

The interesting part of this solution is that, in this case, you do not need to implement a custom mapper from Entity Framework entities to the Domain Model entities, because Entity Framework 4 does the job for you, under the covers. In fact, the CRUD methods accept and output the Domain Model entities directly, as well as the entities used internally by the Entity Framework itself.

As usual, this class inherits from a *BaseDal* type, which centralizes all the tasks and code common to every DAL type. Listing 18-17 shows an excerpt of the code that defines the *BaseDal* type.

LISTING 18-17 The *BaseDal* type implementation based on the Entity Framework

```
public abstract class BaseDal<TEntity, TEntityList, TKey>:
        IDal<TEntity, TEntityList, TKey>
    where TEntity : BaseEntity, new()
    where TEntityList : IEnumerable<TEntity> {

    protected NorthwindEntities Northwind { get; private set; }
```

```
    protected BaseDal() {
        this.Northwind = new NorthwindEntities(
        ConfigurationManager.ConnectionStrings["NorthwindEntities"].ConnectionString);
    }

    #region IDal<TEntity,TEntityList,TKey> Members
    // ... Code omitted ...
    #endregion
}
```

The *BaseDal* constructor creates a protected instance of the *NorthwindEntities* class, which represents the custom *ObjectContext* type, illustrated in Listing 18-15.

Of course, just as in the previous implementations you saw based on LINQ to SQL and LINQ to XML, with LINQ to Entities, you also need to implement a custom factory to provide instances of the LINQ to Entities DAL to the business layer.

LINQ in the Business Layer

Regardless of how you implement your data and persistence layers, modern n-tier solutions have a business layer that provides benefits such as:

- **Security enforcement**   Every activity or operation made by any user should come through the business layer, which should be the central place where you enforce security policies. In this way, regardless of the presentation layer (such as WPF, Microsoft Silverlight, Windows Phone, Windows Forms, and Microsoft ASP.NET) and the communication infrastructure (such as WCF, ASMX, and .NET Remoting) you use, security policies will be checked and enforced in one place. This behavior helps avoid ambiguity and improves maintainability too.

- **Business logic validation and rules enforcement**   In addition to security policies, business logic validation policies and business rules should be enforced in a single place. The business layer is the right place to check these policies and rules. Declarative rules in the domain model, such as attributes, constraints, and referential integrity checks, are only part of the possible logic that a complex application requires. They should be considered complimentary (sometimes redundant) to the rules defined in the business logic layer.

- **Business processes coordination**   Quite often during the last few years, and probably more often in the next few years, business logic consists of complex business processes that coordinate other business components and external services (think about SOA, SaS, and S+S).

- **Transaction coordination**   As we just mentioned, a business process can coordinate many different services and business components and can involve many different data providers. Consequently, the business layer is the only place where a business process can determine the outcome of a transactional activity, regardless of whether it is a local or a distributed transaction.

- **Simplified maintenance**   If all the logic, processes, and rules are defined in a unique place (the business layer), you also gain benefits in maintenance. Any logic or process modification will affect only the business layer, making both testing and deployment of changes faster.

Using LINQ to Objects to Write Better Code

The business layer works with your domain model entities, transferring them back and forth from the data layer and using them in business logic, processes, and rules. On top of the business layer, an application could have a communication layer that separates physical software layers, or it could have a UI. In both cases, you can use LINQ query expressions in the BIZ code to write algorithms and procedures more easily.

For example, imagine having a business process that prints refund forms for all orders shipped later than a *RequiredDate*. The process filters for customers by country. Working with classic procedural code, you would probably retrieve all the customers grouped by country, query all the orders that were delivered late, and then create a refund form, saving the result back to the persistence layer. Because this business process occurs periodically, it is defined as a *Refund* method of the *CustomersBiz* class. Listing 18-18 shows this "legacy style" implementation for such a business method.

LISTING 18-18 A legacy style business method to refund customers for orders delivered late

```
public void RefundLegacy() {
    // Temporary repository for delayed orders, grouped by country
    SortedDictionary<String, List<Order>> ordersToRefundByCountry =
        new SortedDictionary<String, List<Order>>();

    // Get the full list of customers
    // In real life, be careful of these kinds of "full scan" methods!
    var customers = this._dal.ReadAll();
    foreach (var c in customers) {
        foreach (var o in c.Orders) {
            // If the order is late
            if (o.RequiredDate < o.ShippedDate) {
                // Check if the current customer country already exists
                if (!ordersToRefundByCountry.ContainsKey(c.Country)) {
                    // Otherwise create it
                    ordersToRefundByCountry[c.Country] = new List<Order>();
                }
```

```
                // Add the order to the list
                ordersToRefundByCountry[c.Country].Add(o);
            }
        }
    }

    Int32 itemsCount = 0;
    foreach (var itemsGroup in ordersToRefundByCountry) {
        foreach (var item in itemsGroup.Value) {
            // Imagine that here you create and send the refund form
            Console.WriteLine("Country: {0} - CustomerID: {1} - OrderID:
                {2} - DelayedDays: {3}",
                itemsGroup.Key, item.CustomerID, item.OrderID,
                ((TimeSpan)item.ShippedDate.Value.Subtract(item.RequiredDate.Value)).
                    Days);
            itemsCount++;
        }
    }

    Console.WriteLine("Total count of orders to refund: {0}", itemsCount);
}
```

You could rewrite this same business method using LINQ to Objects and LINQ queries as shown in Listing 18-19.

LISTING 18-19 A hypothetical "LINQ style" business method to refund customers for orders delivered late

```
public void Refund() {
    var customersWithOrdersToRefund =
        (from c in this._dal.ReadAll()
        group c by c.Country into customersByCountry
            from    i in customersByCountry
            from    o in i.Orders
            where   o.RequiredDate < o.ShippedDate
            orderby i.Country
                select new {
                    i.Country,
                    i.CustomerID,
                    o.OrderID,
                    DelayedDays = ((TimeSpan)o.ShippedDate.Value.Subtract(
                        o.RequiredDate.Value)).Days }).ToList();

    foreach (var item in customersWithOrdersToRefund) {
        // Imagine that here you create and send the refund form
        Console.WriteLine(item);
    }

    Console.WriteLine("Total count of orders to refund: {0}",
        customersWithOrdersToRefund.Count());
}
```

As you can see, the code is much more readable. It can also be more efficient, even if only under specific circumstances and conditions, as you will see in the next section.

IQueryable<T> vs. *IEnumberable<T>*

Until now, you have worked with LINQ to SQL, LINQ to XML, or LINQ to Entities in the data layer and LINQ to Objects in the business layer. The methods that read the entities from the persistence storage return objects of type *IEnumerable<T>* (or *List<T>*, which internally implements *IEnumerable<T>*) where *T* is the type of the entities to manage. As you know, every *IEnumerable<T>* implementation can take advantage of the benefits of LINQ to Objects. However, the *IQueryable<T>* interface implements *IEnumerable<T>* and can be used to represent LINQ queries as expression trees instead of resolving their definition into LINQ to Objects extension method invocations. Every LINQ query over a LINQ to SQL *DataContext* or a LINQ to Entities *ObjectContext* returns a type that implements *IQueryable<T>*. Thus, you can try to return this type from the data layer types instead of *IEnumerable<T>* or *List<T>*.

> **More Info** *IEnumerable<T>* is described in Chapter 3, "LINQ to Objects." *IQueryable<T>* is covered in detail in Chapter 14, "Inside Expression Trees," and Chapter 15, "Extending LINQ."

Consider Listing 18-20, where you can see an excerpt of a possible implementation of the *ReadAll* method in the *CustomerDal* class. It is based on LINQ to SQL and returns an *IEnumerable<Customer>* to the caller, which should be the BIZ.

LISTING 18-20 The LINQ based implementation of the *ReadAll* method of *CustomerDal*

```
public override IEnumerable<DomainModel.Customer> ReadAll() {
    // Convert the LINQ to SQL customers
    // into Domain Model customers using a
    // LINQ query expression
    var result =
        from   c in this.Northwind.Customers
        select new DomainModel.Customer {
            CustomerID = c.CustomerID,
            Address = c.Address,
            City = c.City,
            CompanyName = c.CompanyName,
            ContactName = c.ContactName,
            ContactTitle = c.ContactTitle,
            Country = c.Country,
            Fax = c.Fax,
            Phone = c.Phone,
            PostalCode = c.PostalCode,
            Region = c.Region,
            // Converts the list of orders of the LINQ to SQL customer
            // into the list of orders defined in the Domain Model
```

```
            Orders = new List<DevLeap.Linq.Architecture.NTier.DomainModel.Order>(
                from   o in c.Orders
                select new DomainModel.Order {
                    OrderID = o.OrderID,
                    CustomerID = o.CustomerID,
                    EmployeeID = o.EmployeeID,
                    Freight = o.Freight,
                    OrderDate = o.OrderDate,
                    RequiredDate = o.RequiredDate,
                    ShipAddress = o.ShipAddress,
                    ShipCity = o.ShipCity,
                    ShipCountry = o.ShipCountry,
                    ShipName = o.ShipName,
                    ShippedDate = o.ShippedDate,
                    ShipPostalCode = o.ShipPostalCode,
                    ShipRegion = o.ShipRegion,
                    ShipVia = o.ShipVia
                })
        };
    return (result);
}
```

If you try to analyze the SQL statements sent to the database when calling this method, you will notice that whenever you enumerate the result of the *ReadAll* method, the code sends a query for the entire set of customers and orders to the database. For example, imagine having a business method called *GetCustomersByCountry* that returns a set of customers filtered by the value of *Country*, as shown in Listing 18-21.

LISTING 18-21 Implementation of the *GetCustomersByCountry* method in the BIZ

```
public IEnumerable<DomainModel.Customer> GetCustomersByCountry(String country) {
    // Check authorization policies

    // Select the data using a LINQ query expression
    var result =
        from   c in this._dal.ReadAll()
        where  c.Country == country
        select c;

    // Eventually check and personalize the entity for the caller

    // Return the resulting customer instance to the caller
    return (result);
}
```

You can use the *GetCustomersByCountry* method to extract some fields (*CustomerID*, *Contact-Name*, *Country*) from the list of Italian customers, as shown in Listing 18-22.

LISTING 18-22 A code excerpt that calls the *GetCustomersByCountry* business method

```
private static void ReadItalianCustomers() {
    CustomersBiz cb = new CustomersBiz();

    // Query the list of customers to extract italian ones
    var query =
        from   c in cb.GetCustomersByCountry("Italy")
        select new { c.CustomerID, c.ContactName, c.Country };
    foreach (var c in query) {
        Console.WriteLine(c);
    }
}
```

The preceding code selects all the customers and their orders from the database persistence layer. The filter by country will be applied to in-memory entities using LINQ to Objects. Here is the SQL query that gets sent to the database:

```
SELECT [t0].[CustomerID], [t0].[CompanyName], [t0].[ContactName],
[t0].[ContactTitle], [t0].[Address], [t0].[City], [t0].[Region], [t0].[PostalCode],
[t0].[Country], [t0].[Phone], [t0].[Fax], [t1].[OrderID],
[t1].[CustomerID] AS [CustomerID2], [t1].[EmployeeID], [t1].[OrderDate],
[t1].[RequiredDate], [t1].[ShippedDate], [t1].[ShipVia], [t1].[Freight],
[t1].[ShipName], [t1].[ShipAddress], [t1].[ShipCity], [t1].[ShipRegion],
[t1].[ShipPostalCode], [t1].[ShipCountry], (
    SELECT COUNT(*)
    FROM [dbo].[Orders] AS [t2]
    WHERE [t2].[CustomerID] = [t0].[CustomerID]
    ) AS [value]
FROM [dbo].[Customers] AS [t0]
LEFT OUTER JOIN [dbo].[Orders] AS [t1] ON [t1].[CustomerID] = [t0].[CustomerID] ORDER BY
[t0].[CustomerID], [t1].[OrderID]
```

If you were using LINQ to Entities rather than LINQ to SQL, it would generate almost the same query. However, it would definitely be better to extract only the Italian customers, and only the fields the consumer truly needs. In fact, in real scenarios, you could extract millions of lines of customers and orders if you were to filter by *Country* only on the BIZ side. One possible solution to this behavior is to move the query to the data layer, defining an ad hoc selection method to extract and project exactly the data you really need. However, this approach moves the filtering logic from the business layer to the data layer, making the BIZ dependent on the DAL. Another possible solution is to return an *IQueryable<T>* from the data layer instead of an *IEnumerable<T>*. The only difference in this approach is the signature of the *ReadAll* method defined in Listing 18-20. The following is the new method signature:

```
public override IQueryable<DomainModel.Customer> ReadAll() {
    // ... exactly the same code as the one in Listing 15-20
}
```

Now, if you execute the code in Listing 18-22 again with the changed signature, the SQL code sent to SQL Server is exactly what you are looking for:

```
SELECT [t0].[CustomerID], [t0].[ContactName], [t0].[Country]
FROM [dbo].[Customers] AS [t0]
WHERE [t0].[Country] = @p0
```

Under the covers, the data layer returns an *IQueryable<T>* that represents an expression tree, not the real set of entities. The *GetCustomersByCountry* method adds a filtering condition to the expression tree, whereas the code in Listing 18-22 adds a custom projection to the same expression tree. Finally, the enumeration (*foreach*) of the query expression determines the conversion of the expression tree into the corresponding ad hoc SQL statement.

This technique is truly powerful, and can dramatically improve an application's performance and scalability. However, as you have already seen in Chapter 14, moving *IQueryable<T>* instances outside the LINQ to relational world can also lead to unpredictable results and issues. For example, the *Refund* method will stop working with LINQ to SQL in the data layer because the filtering condition based on customer orders, which are of type *ICollection<Order>*, cannot be converted into a SQL statement by the LINQ to SQL query provider.

> **Note** The *Orders* property declared in the *Customer* attribute is of type *ICollection<Order>*. The LINQ to SQL entity classes use *EntitySet<T>* to define properties that map a one-to-many relationship. However, *EntitySet<T>* is specific to the LINQ to SQL implementation and cannot be used to define DAL-independent entity classes.

One more thing to consider: if you decide to use *IQueryable<T>* within your data layer interfaces, you should support it from any persistence layer. For example, the DAL based on LINQ to XML presented previously needs to convert its results into something compliant with *IQueryable<T>*. To satisfy this requirement, you can use the *Queryable.AsQueryable* method, which converts any instance of *IEnumerable<T>* into a constant expression queryable via *IQueryable<T>*. However, remember again that not every type can be used within an expression tree and queried by a provider for *IQueryable<T>*. Last but not least, if you use *IQueryable<T>*, you should be very cognizant of the security implications, because someone defining queries from the UI could inject malicious code into the expression tree, making your software unstable or your data insecure.

So although this book recommends that you consider the opportunities offered by using *IQueryable<T>*, be very careful and use the technique only through ad hoc methods and in situations where it is really useful.

Identifying the Right Unit of Work

Another possible consideration that arises from working with LINQ to SQL or LINQ to Entities in an n-tier distributed architecture is to identify the boundaries of a unit of work correctly. A unit of work "keeps track of everything you do during a business transaction that can affect the database" (from "Patterns of Enterprise Application Architecture (P of EAA)," which you can read at *http://www.martinfowler.com/eaaCatalog/unitOfWork.html*). As you learned in the chapters dedicated to LINQ to Relational, the LINQ to SQL *DataContext* and the LINQ to Entities *ObjectContext* both represent a unit of work. Thus, you should create and use them only for single units of work. In general, creating a unique *DataContext* or *ObjectContext* instance and sharing it across multiple user requests is not a good practice.

The examples here created a *DataContext* or *ObjectContext* (termed **Context* to cover both) instance for each Data Mapper instance used by a single business component instance. In this way, different business transactions require different business component instances.

Another option to keep units of work isolated is to apply the *ThreadStatic* attribute to an instance of **Context*, so you can share it across many different domain model entities, identifying the unit of work with the single thread that calls the application server infrastructure. This solution could help in defining services or web applications that map each user request to a specific processing thread. However, caching a **Context* instance for several service requests might require some additional checks when attaching entities.

Whatever technique you define to keep track of the current unit of work, remember that to really abstract and separate the business layer from the data layer, the solution you adopt should be transparent to the BIZ, because the unit of work relates only to the specific DAL implementation.

It is up to you to correctly define the boundaries of your application's units of work and their activation policies, taking your business rules and processes into account. This chapter provides only some hypothetical examples. It is important that you understand that the choice you make could affect the code you have to write—in particular in the data layer. For example, if you keep the **Context* in memory across multiple requests, then when you attach changed entities, you will need to check for their existence in the **Context*.

Handling Transactions

In Chapter 6, you saw how to handle transactions while working with LINQ to SQL, and in Chapter 10, you learned how to manage transactions with LINQ to Entities. Generally, in distributed n-tier architectures, the outcome of transactional activities is determined by the business layer because only the business logic can determine whether a complex business process has been completed correctly or has to be cancelled, rolling back any related data modifications. For the same reasons, you should wrap any activity or operation that involves data modifications through the configured data layer with a *TransactionScope* (*System.Transaction* in .NET Framework 2.0) and you should avoid using explicit transactions in the data layer.

Concurrency and Thread Safety

One last consideration concerns thread safety. Keep in mind that good software solutions work asynchronously on both the application server and on the client side. From a LINQ-based architecture point of view, you need to consider that LINQ to SQL and LINQ to Entities are not thread-safe, so it is up to you to determine a correct threading policy. In general, it is better to avoid sharing instances (such as a *Context* and entities) between different threads, otherwise you will need to use *Lock*, *Mutex*, *ReaderWriteLock* and *ReaderWriteLockSlim*, and so on to synchronize access to resources. This book does not cover how to use these classes, but it is important that you remember this.

 More Info To learn more about threading, synchronization, concurrency, and so on in the .NET Framework, read Jeffrey Richter's book *Applied Microsoft .NET Framework Programming* (Microsoft Press, 2008).

Summary

This chapter provided an overview of the various techniques available for defining two-tier, three-tier, and n-tier architectures using LINQ. You saw how to develop an abstract data layer and how to use custom entities. You also experienced the power of expression trees when defining custom *IQueryable<T>* variables. Finally, you saw a discussion of how to manage a unit of work with LINQ, how to handle transactions, and what you need to do to achieve thread safety.

Chapter 19
LINQ Data Binding

Your code can consume Microsoft Language Integrated Query (LINQ) queries in several ways. When writing the user interface (UI) code layer, you might want to use a LINQ query to bind data to a UI element. This process is called *data binding*. In this chapter, you will see how to use a LINQ query for data binding. One huge advantage of data binding with LINQ is that the queries are independent of which LINQ provider processes them.

The chapter is divided into sections that describe the following UI frameworks:

- Microsoft ASP.NET

- Windows Presentation Foundation (WPF) and Microsoft Silverlight

- Windows Forms

Because most of the sections are independent of each other, you can read just those that apply to you. However, if you are interested in WPF or Silverlight, those sections should be read in sequence.

Using LINQ with ASP.NET

ASP.NET has two controls that implement the *DataSource* control pattern: the *LinqDataSource* and the *EntityDataSource*. Through these controls, you can use a LINQ query to data bind any bindable rendering control using an .aspx declarative approach. For example, you can use a *LinqDataSource* or an *EntityDataSource* control to bind a *DataGrid*, *GridView*, *Repeater*, *DataList*, or *ListView* control.

The *LinqDataSource* control resembles the *SqlDataSource* and *ObjectDataSource* you may have used in previous versions of ASP.NET, but it targets either a LINQ to SQL data model or a custom set of entities using LINQ to Objects. The *EntityDataSource* control targets the Microsoft ADO.NET Entity Framework, and you use it in combination with LINQ to Entities queries, as you will see in the "Using *EntityDataSource*" section later in this chapter.

 Important Be sure to read the "Using *LinqDataSource*" section before the "Using *EntityData-Source*" one. Although they have a similar programming interface, they do have differences, which are highlighted in the "Using *EntityDataSource*" section.

Using *LinqDataSource*

If you have ever used the *SqlDataSource* and *ObjectDataSource* controls, you probably know that you have to define custom queries or methods to support data retrieval, insertion, editing, and deletion features. With the *LinqDataSource* control, you can use the out-of-the-box LINQ environment to get all these capabilities without having to write specific code. Of course, you can always decide to customize the default behavior, but it is important to know that doing so is not mandatory.

For example, imagine the list of customers from the Northwind database. Figure 19-1 shows the complete LINQ to SQL data model schema.

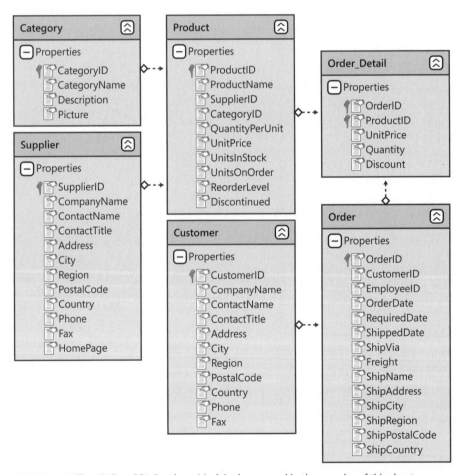

FIGURE 19-1 The LINQ to SQL Database Model schema used in the samples of this chapter.

You can either add the Database Markup Language (DBML) file directly to the *App_Code* folder of your ASP.NET web project, or define it in a separate and dedicated class library project. For a prototype solution or a simple web application, you can declare the data model within the web project itself; however, for an enterprise solution, it is better to divide the layers of your architecture into dedicated projects, thus defining a specific class library for the data model definition.

> **Note** For an enterprise-level solution, read Chapter 18, "LINQ in a Multitier Solution," which discusses how to deal with architectural and design matters related to LINQ adoption.

The .aspx page shown in Listing 19-1 retrieves a list of customers and binds it to a *GridView* control. Note that the *LinqDataSource* control declares a *ContextTypeName* property that maps to the previously defined *NorthwindDataContext* type and a *TableName* property that corresponds to the *Customers* property of the *DataContext* instance. This represents a class of type *Table<Customer>* in LINQ to SQL.

LISTING 19-1 A sample .aspx page that uses a *LinqDataSource* control to render the list of Northwind customers into a *GridView* control

```
<%@ Page Language="C#" AutoEventWireup="true" CodeFile="Listing19-1.aspx.cs"
    Inherits="Listing19_1" %>
<!DOCTYPE html PUBLIC "-//W3C//DTD XHTML 1.0 Transitional//EN"
  "http://www.w3.org/TR/xhtml1/DTD/xhtml1-transitional.dtd">
<html xmlns="http://www.w3.org/1999/xhtml">
<head runat="server">
    <title>Listing 19-1</title>
</head>
<body>
    <form id="form1" runat="server">
    <div>
        <asp:GridView runat="server" DataSourceID="customersDataSource" />
        <asp:LinqDataSource ID="customersDataSource" runat="server"
          ContextTypeName="NorthwindDataContext"
          TableName="Customers" />
    </div>
    </form>
</body>
</html>
```

Using Microsoft Visual Studio, you can define these and many other properties by using the Design view. In Figures 19-2 and 19-3, you can see the steps for graphically configuring a *LinqDataSource* control by using the Configure Data Source wizard. To start the wizard, you simply need to insert a *LinqDataSource* control into an .aspx page, click the control task menu, and choose the Configure Data Source task activity. In the first step, presented on the Choose A Context Object page of the wizard, you can define the main source for the control.

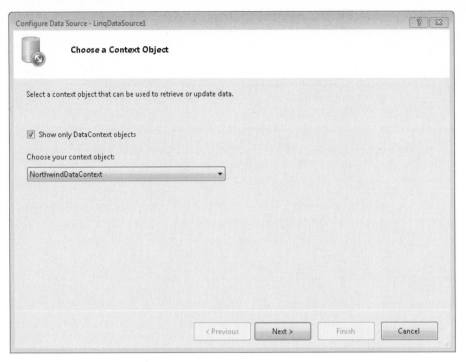

FIGURE 19-2 The Choose A Context Object page of the Configure Data Source wizard.

If you keep the Show Only DataContext Objects check box selected, the drop-down list will show only objects that inherit from the LINQ to SQL *DataContext* type, such as the *NorthwindDataContext* shown in Figure 19-1. If you clear the check box, the wizard shows you any Microsoft .NET Framework type available in the project or in other referenced user-defined projects, including custom entities that you can query using LINQ to Objects, or any instance of *IEnumerable<T>*.

> **Note** When referencing user-defined class libraries, remember that the Configure Data Source wizard for the *LinqDataSource* control works with compiled assemblies. Therefore, you need to compile your solution to access newly created or modified types.

In this last case, the drop-down list will also show all the entity types defined in the LINQ to SQL data model, not only the *DataContext* type. This is useful for querying a property of type *EntitySet<T>* offered by a specific LINQ to SQL entity—for example, the set of orders of a specific customer instance in a master-detail rendering page.

After clicking the Next button in the wizard, the Configure Data Selection configuration panel page appears, as shown in Figure 19-3.

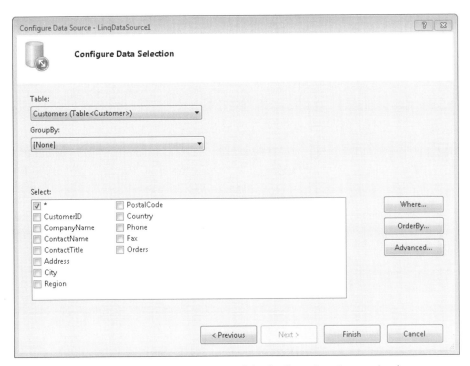

FIGURE 19-3 The Configure Data Selection page of the Configure Data Source wizard.

On this wizard page, you can define the complete set of configuration parameters for the *LinqDataSource* control. For a *DataContext,* you select the *Table<T>* to query using the Table drop-down list; for LINQ to Objects, you select the *IEnumerable* property of a custom type. Use the GroupBy drop-down list to define a grouping rule, eventually with an inner ordering, for each group. In the Select section, choose the fields or properties to select while query-ing the data source. By default, the *LinqDataSource* control projects all the fields (*), but you can define a custom projection predicate. This wizard page also provides a set of buttons so you can define selection rules (the Where button) and ordering conditions (the OrderBy but-ton). Using those buttons, you can define not only static filtering and ordering rules, but also define dynamic parameters, mapping their values to other controls, cookie values, form input elements, ASP.NET *Profile* variables, querystring parameters, or ASP.NET *Session* variables. This behavior is the same as with all the other *DataSource* controls, such as *SqlDataSource* and *ObjectDataSource.*

One last command, named *Advanced*, determines whether you want to allow automatic inserts, deletes, or updates. By default, the *LinqDataSource* control simply selects data in a read-only manner. Allowing automatic data modification can be convenient, but keep in mind that it is allowed only under the following conditions:

- The projection returns all the data source items (*SELECT * FROM...*).

- There are no grouping rules.

- The Context Object is set to a class that inherits from *DataContext,* and consequently the queried collection is of type *Table<T>*.

Unless all these conditions are true, the wizard creates a custom LINQ query, and the projected results will be an *IEnumerable<T>*, where *T* is by design an anonymous read-only type.

> **Note** Think carefully about the previous conditions. Whenever you need to query an updatable set of items using the automatic engine of the *LinqDataSource* control, you need to query its full set of fields/properties (SELECT * FROM ...) even if you need to change only a few of them. This behavior is acceptable in very simple solutions with only one full table mapped directly to the UI, but in more complex and common real-world solutions, it is better to use custom selection and data updating rules.

After configuring the *LinqDataSource* control, you are ready to bind it to any bindable control.

You can define any parameter available through the Configure Data Source wizard by using markup inside the .aspx source code of the page. In fact, the wizard affects the markup of the *LinqDataSource* control instance itself. Listing 19-2 shows an example of a *LinqDataSource* control bound to a list containing the *CompanyName*, *ContactName*, and *Country* fields for Northwind's customers. The list is filtered by *Country*, mapped to a drop-down list with automatic postback enabled, and ordered by *ContactName* value.

LISTING 19-2 Using a *LinqDataSource* control to render a filtered, ordered list of Northwind's customers into a *GridView* control

```
<%@ Page Language="C#" AutoEventWireup="true" CodeFile="Listing19-2.aspx.cs"
    Inherits="Listing19_2" %>
<!DOCTYPE html PUBLIC "-//W3C//DTD XHTML 1.0 Transitional//EN"
  "http://www.w3.org/TR/xhtml1/DTD/xhtml1-transitional.dtd">
<html xmlns="http://www.w3.org/1999/xhtml">
<head runat="server">
    <title>Listing 19-2</title>
</head>
<body>
    <form id="form1" runat="server">
    <div>
```

```
        <br />
        Country: 
        <asp:DropDownList ID="ddlCountries" runat="server"
            AutoPostBack="True" DataSourceID="countriesDataSource"
            DataTextField="Country" DataValueField="Country" />
        <br />
        <asp:GridView ID="customersGrid" runat="server"
            DataSourceID="customersDataSource" AutoGenerateColumns="False">
            <Columns>
                <asp:BoundField DataField="CompanyName"
                    HeaderText="CompanyName" ReadOnly="True"
                    SortExpression="CompanyName" />
                <asp:BoundField DataField="ContactName"
                    HeaderText="ContactName" ReadOnly="True"
                    SortExpression="ContactName" />
                <asp:BoundField DataField="Country"
                    HeaderText="Country" ReadOnly="True"
                    SortExpression="Country" />
            </Columns>
        </asp:GridView>
        <asp:LinqDataSource ID="customersDataSource" runat="server"
            ContextTypeName="NorthwindDataContext"
            Select="new (CompanyName, ContactName, Country)"
            TableName="Customers" Where="Country == @Country">
            <WhereParameters>
                <asp:ControlParameter ControlID="ddlCountries"
                    Name="Country" PropertyName="SelectedValue"
                    Type="String" />
            </WhereParameters>
        </asp:LinqDataSource>
        <br />
        <asp:LinqDataSource ID="countriesDataSource" runat="server"
            ContextTypeName="NorthwindDataContext" GroupBy="Country"
            OrderGroupsBy="key" Select="new (key as Country)"
            TableName="Customers">
        </asp:LinqDataSource>
    </div>
    </form>
</body>
</html>
```

Under the covers, the *LinqDataSource* control converts its configuration to a dynamic query expression and executes it against the source context.

Paging Data with *LinqDataSource* and *DataPager*

If you define a *DataPager* control, apply it to a rendering control such as a *ListView* and map it to a *LinqDataSource* control instance, you can paginate the source data at the level of the LINQ query. In fact, the *LinqDataSource* control will be configured to select a maximum number of records (*MaximumRows*) starting from a designated record index (*StartRowIndex*), depending on the *DataPager* configuration. Internally, the *LinqDataSource* control translates these parameters into a query ending with a *.Skip(StartRowIndex).Take(MaximumRows)* expression.

In Listing 19-3, you can see a sample .aspx page that queries the Northwind's customer list, filters it by country (from a user selection in a drop-down list), and delivers paginated results—five customers per page.

LISTING 19-3 An .aspx page using a *LinqDataSource* control to render Northwind customers in a *ListView* with filtering and paging through a *DataPager* control

```
<%@ Page Language="C#" AutoEventWireup="true" CodeFile="Listing19-3.aspx.cs"
    Inherits="Listing19_3" %>
<!DOCTYPE html PUBLIC "-//W3C//DTD XHTML 1.0 Transitional//EN"
  "http://www.w3.org/TR/xhtml1/DTD/xhtml1-transitional.dtd">
<html xmlns="http://www.w3.org/1999/xhtml">
<head runat="server">
    <title>Listing 19-3</title>
</head>
<body>
    <form id="form1" runat="server">
    <div>
        <br />Country: 
        <asp:DropDownList ID="ddlCountries" runat="server"
            AutoPostBack="True" DataSourceID="countriesDataSource"
            DataTextField="Country" DataValueField="Country" />
        <br />
        <asp:ListView ID="customersList" runat="server"
            DataSourceID="customersDataSource">
            <LayoutTemplate>
                <table cellpadding="5" cellspacing="0" border="1">
                    <tr>
                        <th style="text-align: center">CustomerId</th>
                        <th style="text-align: center">CompanyName</th>
                        <th style="text-align: center">ContactName</th>
                        <th style="text-align: center">Country</th>
                    </tr>
                    <asp:PlaceHolder ID="itemPlaceholder" runat="server" />
                </table>
            </LayoutTemplate>
            <ItemTemplate>
                <tr>
                    <td style="text-align: center">
                        <asp:Label ID="Label1" runat="server"
                            Text='<%# Eval("CustomerId") %>' />
                    </td>
```

```
                            <td style="text-align: center">
                                <asp:Label ID="Label2" runat="server"
                                    Text='<%# Eval("CompanyName") %>' />
                            </td>
                            <td style="text-align: center">
                                <asp:Label ID="Label3" runat="server"
                                    Text='<%# Eval("ContactName") %>' />
                            </td>
                            <td style="text-align: center">
                                <asp:Label ID="Label4" runat="server"
                                    Text='<%# Eval("Country") %>' />
                            </td>
                        </tr>
                    </ItemTemplate>
                </asp:ListView>
                <asp:LinqDataSource ID="customersDataSource" runat="server"
                    ContextTypeName="NorthwindDataContext"
                    Select="new (CustomerID, CompanyName, ContactName, Country)"
                    TableName="Customers" Where="Country == @Country">
                    <WhereParameters>
                        <asp:ControlParameter ControlID="ddlCountries"
                            Name="Country" PropertyName="SelectedValue"
                            Type="String" />
                    </WhereParameters>
                </asp:LinqDataSource>
                <asp:DataPager ID="customersPager" PagedControlID="customersList"
                    runat="server" PageSize="5">
                    <Fields>
                        <asp:NumericPagerField ButtonCount="5" ButtonType="Link" />
                    </Fields>
                </asp:DataPager>
                <br />
                <asp:LinqDataSource ID="countriesDataSource" runat="server"
                    ContextTypeName="NorthwindDataContext" GroupBy="Country"
                    OrderGroupsBy="key" Select="new (key as Country)"
                    TableName="Customers">
                </asp:LinqDataSource>
            </div>
        </form>
    </body>
</html>
```

Figure 19-4 shows the output of the page code in Listing 19-3.

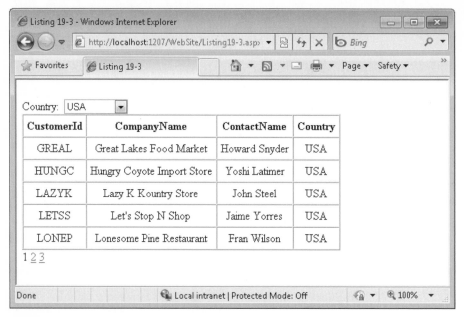

FIGURE 19-4 The HTML output of Listing 19-3.

You can take a closer look at this behavior by subscribing to the *Selecting* event offered by each *LinqDataSource* control instance. With this event, you can inspect the executing query's selecting, filtering, ordering, grouping, and paging parameters. Within the event code, you can also alter the values of these parameters, customizing the query result before its execution. You can see an example of using the *Selecting* event to define a custom filtering parameter in Listing 19-4. The *Arguments* property of the *LinqDataSourceSelectEventArgs* instance received by the event handler describes the paging configuration.

> **Note** Combining a *DataPager* and a *LinqDataSource* for pagination is a good approach from an ASP.NET point of view because it requests only the data displayed in one page from the data source. However, the efficiency diminishes for later pages. For example, when a user selects the last page, running such a query against a large table without filters in a relational database such as Microsoft SQL Server requires a complete table scan. Even if an index exists that corresponds to the desired order, this operation consumes database server resources and requires extra time to complete.
>
> Additionally, if the query is the result of complex filters on a large table, moving from page to page in the *DataPager* control requires this extended execution time, because the query must be executed for each new page. When the table is large and/or the filter operation is complex, you might need to use an architecture that incorporates temporary data caching to reduce the costs of such queries.

LISTING 19-4 An example of using the *Selecting* event of a *LinqDataSource* control

```
public partial class Listing19_4 : System.Web.UI.Page {
    protected void customersDataSource_Selecting(Object sender,
        LinqDataSourceSelectEventArgs e) {
        // Forces sorting by ContactName
        e.Arguments.SortExpression = "ContactName";
    }
}
```

Handling Data Modifications with *LinqDataSource*

Whenever you need to modify data through a *LinqDataSource* instance, you need to configure it with a type inherited from *DataContext* as its *ContextTypeName*, a *TableName* corresponding to the name of a property of type *Table<T>* belonging to the *DataContext* type,
a *NULL* or empty value for the *Select* property, and a *NULL* value for the *GroupBy* property.
You also need to set the *EnableDelete*, *EnableInsert*, or *EnableUpdate* flags to *true* to support
deletion, insertion, or modification of data items, respectively. As you saw earlier in the chapter, you can enable these flags using the Design view or the .aspx markup. Regardless of the
way in which you configure the *LinqDataSource* instance, after enabling data modifications,
you can change the data source by using a data-bound control that supports editing, such
as *GridView*, *ListView*, or *DetailsView*. The .aspx page excerpt in Listing 19-5 uses an editable
GridView to show the Northwind customer list.

LISTING 19-5 A sample .aspx page excerpt using an editable *LinqDataSource* control

```
<form id="form1" runat="server">
    <div>
        <asp:GridView ID="customersGrid" runat="server"
            DataKeyNames="CustomerID" DataSourceID="customersDataSource"
            AutoGenerateEditButton="true" AutoGenerateColumns="true" />

        <asp:LinqDataSource ID="customersDataSource" runat="server"
            ContextTypeName="NorthwindDataContext" TableName="Customers"
            OrderBy="ContactName" EnableUpdate="true" />

    </div>
</form>
```

If you need to modify or examine the values of the fields before effectively executing data
modification tasks, you can subscribe to the *Deleting*, *Inserting*, *Selecting*, and *Updating*
events. When you want to examine field values after data modification, you can handle the
corresponding post-events, such as *Deleted*, *Inserted*, *Selected*, and *Updated*. Keep in mind
that if you want to specify a default value for empty fields, during modification of the data
source, you can add parameters to the control's *InsertParameters*, *UpdateParameters*, and
DeleteParameters properties.

The events that occur before data modification receive event arguments specific to each modification operation. For example, a *Selecting* event handler receives a *LinqDataSource-SelectEventArgs* object, letting you customize the query parameters as well as the result, as you will see in the next section.

A *Deleting* event handler receives an argument of type *LinqDataSourceDeleteEventArgs,* which exposes an *OriginalObject* property containing the data item that will be deleted. It also provides a property named *Exception*, of type *LinqDataSourceValidationException*, which describes any data validation exception that may have occurred within the entity before its deletion. If you want to handle such an exception by yourself and do not want to throw it again, you can set the *ExceptionHandled* Boolean property of the event argument to *true*.

An *Inserting* event handler receives an argument of type *LinqDataSourceInsertEventArgs*. This type provides a *NewObject* property whose value is the data item that is going to be inserted, whereas the *Exception* and *ExceptionHandled* properties work just like those for the *Deleting* event argument, but reference validation exceptions related to data item insertion.

An *Updating* event handler receives an event argument of type *LinqDataSourceUpdateEvent-Args*, describing the original and actual state of the data item through the *OriginalObject* and *NewObject* properties, respectively. Again, you can handle any kind of validation exception using the *Exception* property and *ExceptionHandled* flag.

You might be wondering how the *LinqDataSource* control keeps track of the original values of entities between page postbacks. Under the covers, the *LinqDataSource* control saves each entity field's original value into the page *ViewState*, except for fields marked as *UpdateCheck. Never* in the data model. Using this technique, the *LinqDataSource* control handles data concurrency checks transparently.

> **More Info**   For more details about *UpdateCheck* configuration, refer to Chapter 7, "LINQ to SQL: Modeling Data and Tools."

In Listing 19-6, you can see a code example that validates updated customer information, before the actual data modification occurs.

LISTING 19-6 Code-behind that uses a custom validation rule while updating customer information through an editable *LinqDataSource* control

```
protected void customersDataSource_Updating(
  object sender, LinqDataSourceUpdateEventArgs e) {
    if (((Customer)e.OriginalObject).Country != (((Customer)e.NewObject).Country)) {
          e.Cancel = true;
    }
}
```

The interesting part of this approach is that the *LinqDataSource* control handles all the plumbing transparently. Later in this chapter, you will see how to manually handle data selections based on custom LINQ queries.

Although each pre-event handler receives a specific event argument type instance, all the post-event handlers receive an event argument of type *LinqDataSourceStatusEventArgs*, so you can examine the result of the data modification task. For successful modifications, the event argument's *Result* property provides the modified data item. When data modification fails, the post-event argument's *Result* property is *null* and exposes the exception that occurred in its *Exception* property. As with pre-events, you can set the event argument's *ExceptionHandled* Boolean property to avoid throwing the exception again. Listing 19-7 shows a code excerpt that handles a concurrency exception while updating a data item.

LISTING 19-7 Sample code handling a concurrency exception while editing a data item through a *LinqDataSource* control

```
protected void customersDataSource_Updated(object sender,
    LinqDataSourceStatusEventArgs e) {
    if ((e.Result == null) && (e.Exception != null)) {
        if (e.Exception is ChangeConflictException) {
            // Handle data concurrency issue
            // TBD ...

            // Stop exception bubbling
            e.ExceptionHandled = true;
        }
    }
}
```

Three more useful *LinqDataSource* control events are *ContextCreating*, *ContextCreated*, and *ContextDisposing*.

The first two occur when the *DataContext* is going to be created, or has been created, respectively. When *ContextCreating* occurs, you can specify a custom *DataContext* instance by setting the event argument's *LinqDataSourceContextEventArgs.ObjectInstance* property. If you ignore this event, the *LinqDataSource* control will create a *DataContext* by itself, based on the type name in the *ContextTypeName* property value. You can use this event when you want to customize *DataContext* creation—for example, to provide a custom connection string, a user-defined *SqlConnection* instance, or a custom *MappingSource* definition. The *ContextCreated* event, on the other hand, gives you the ability to customize the just-created *DataContext* instance. Like post-event data modification events, it receives a *LinqDataSourceStatusEventArgs*, but in this case the event argument's *Result* property contains the *DataContext* type instance. If errors occur while creating the *DataContext*, you will find an exception in the event argument's *Exception* property; the *Result* property will be *null*. The example in Listing 19-8 handles the *ContextCreated* event to define a custom data shape for querying data.

LISTING 19-8 Sample code customizing the *DataContext* of a *LinqDataSource* control, just after its creation

```
protected void customersDataSource_ContextCreated(object sender,
    LinqDataSourceStatusEventArgs e) {
    NorthwindDataContext dc = e.Result as NorthwindDataContext;
    if (dc != null) {
        // Instructs the DataContext to load orders of current year with
        // each customer instance
        DataLoadOptions dlo = new DataLoadOptions();
        dlo.AssociateWith<Customer>(c => c.Orders
            .Where(o => o.OrderDate.Value.Year == DateTime.Now.Year));

        dc.LoadOptions = dlo;
    }
}
```

The *ContextDisposing* event is useful for handling custom or manual disposing of the *Data-Context* type instance and receives an event argument of type *LinqDataSourceDisposeEventArgs*. This event occurs during the *Unload* event of the *LinqDataSource* control and provides the *DataContext* that is going to be disposed of in the *ObjectInstance* property of the event argument.

> **Note** Because the *LinqDataSource* control is hosted by an ASP.NET environment, internally the *DataContext* used to query the data source is created and released for each single request with a pattern similar to the one shown later in the "Binding to LINQ Queries" section and in Chapter 18. In the case of an uneditable *LinqDataSource* control, the *ObjectTrackingEnabled* property of the *DataContext* instance is set to *false*; otherwise, it is left to its default value of *true*.

Using Custom Selections with *LinqDataSource*

Sometimes you need to select data by using custom rules or custom user-defined stored procedures. In these situations, you can use a *LinqDataSource* to subscribe to the data source control's *Selecting* event. The *Selecting* event handler receives a *LinqDataSourceSelectEventArgs* instance that you can use to change the selection parameters, as you saw in the previous section. However, it can also return a completely customized selection if you set its *Result* property to a custom value. Listing 19-9 shows how to handle the *Selecting* event to return the result of a custom stored procedure instead of a standard LINQ to SQL query.

LISTING 19-9 Handling a custom selection pattern for a *LinqDataSource* control using a stored procedure

```
protected void customersOrdersDataSource_Selecting(object sender,
    LinqDataSourceSelectEventArgs e) {
    NorthwindDataContext dc = new NorthwindDataContext();
    e.Result = dc.CustOrdersOrders("ALFKI");
}
```

For an editable *LinqDataSource* control, the custom selection code should return a set of items with the same type *T* as the *Table<T>* type of the *TableName* property of the data source control. The code to select the custom result should return a set of items consistent with the configured *TableName*; thus, you can use a stored procedure in addition to customized explicit LINQ to SQL queries. Listing 19-10 shows a *Selecting* event implementation that uses a custom LINQ query to select a customized data source.

LISTING 19-10 A custom selection pattern for a *LinqDataSource* control that uses an explicit LINQ query

```
protected void customersDataSource_Selecting(object sender,
    LinqDataSourceSelectEventArgs e) {
    NorthwindDataContext dc = new NorthwindDataContext();

    e.Result =
        from   c in dc.Customers
        where  c.Country == "USA" && c.Orders.Count > 0
        select c;
}
```

One more thing to notice is that when data paging, the custom result is paged too. The paging occurs because the *Result* property of the *Selecting* event argument is managed by the *LinqDataSource* engine, which applies any paging rule to it. For an *IQueryable<T>* result, as you can see in Listing 19-10, the paging occurs on the LINQ query expression tree, preserving performance and efficiency.

When you programmatically set a custom result during the *Selecting* event, the *LinqData-Source* control does not raise the *ContextCreated* event.

Using *LinqDataSource* with Custom Types

One typical usage of the *LinqDataSource* control is to query data available through LINQ to SQL, but you can also use it to query custom types and entities. If you define a *ContextType-Name* that does not correspond to a type inherited from the LINQ to SQL *DataContext*, the *LinqDataSource* automatically switches from LINQ to SQL to LINQ to Objects queries. Listing 19-11 defines user-defined *Customer* and *Order* types that are not related to a LINQ to SQL data model.

LISTING 19-11 User-defined *Customer* and *Order* entities not related to a LINQ to SQL data model

```
public class Customer {
    public Int32 CustomerID { get; set; }
    public String FullName { get; set; }
    public List<Order> Orders { get; set; }
}

public class Order {
    public Int32 OrderID { get; set; }
    public Int32 CustomerID { get; set; }
    public Decimal EuroAmount { get; set; }
}
```

Now consider a *CustomerManager* class offering a property named *Customers* and of type *List<T>*, where *T* is a *Customer* type, as shown in Listing 19-12.

LISTING 19-12 A *CustomerManager* type providing a property of type *List<Customer>*

```
public class CustomerManager {

    public CustomerManager() {
        this.Customers = new List<Customer> {
            new Customer { CustomerID = 1, FullName = "Paolo Pialorsi",
              Orders = new List<Order> {
                 new Order { OrderID = 1, CustomerID = 1, EuroAmount = 100},
                 new Order { OrderID = 2, CustomerID = 1, EuroAmount = 200}
              }
            },
            new Customer { CustomerID = 2, FullName = "Marco Russo",
              Orders = new List<Order> {
                 new Order { OrderID = 3, CustomerID = 2, EuroAmount = 150},
                 new Order { OrderID = 4, CustomerID = 2, EuroAmount = 250},
                 new Order { OrderID = 5, CustomerID = 2, EuroAmount = 130},
                 new Order { OrderID = 6, CustomerID = 2, EuroAmount = 220}
              }
            },
            new Customer { CustomerID = 3, FullName = "Andrea Pialorsi",
              Orders = new List<Order> {
                 new Order { OrderID = 7, CustomerID = 3, EuroAmount = 900},
                 new Order { OrderID = 8, CustomerID = 3, EuroAmount = 2500}
              }
            }
        };
    }

    public List<Customer> Customers { get; set; }
}
```

You can use the *CustomerManager* type as the value for the *ContextTypeName* of a *Linq-DataSource* control, while the "Customers" string could be the value for the *TableName* property of the *LinqDataSource* control. Internally, the data source control queries the collection of items returned from the *CustomerManager* class, allowing your code to query a custom set of entities instead of a LINQ to SQL data model. Nevertheless, keep in mind that using LINQ to Objects instead of LINQ to SQL requires loading the full set of data into memory—before any filtering, sorting, or paging task takes place. Be careful using this technique because it can be very expensive for your CPU and memory if your code processes a large amount of data or makes many page requests. The code in Listing 19-13 is from an .aspx page that uses this kind of configuration.

LISTING 19-13 Sample .aspx page with a *LinqDataSource* control linked to a set of user-defined entities

```
<%@ Page Language="C#" AutoEventWireup="true" CodeFile="Listing19-13.aspx.cs"
    Inherits="Listing19_13" %>

<!DOCTYPE html PUBLIC "-//W3C//DTD XHTML 1.0 Transitional//EN"
  "http://www.w3.org/TR/xhtml1/DTD/xhtml1-transitional.dtd">

<html xmlns="http://www.w3.org/1999/xhtml">
<head runat="server">
    <title>Listing 19-13</title>
</head>
<body>
    <form id="form1" runat="server">
    <div>

        <asp:GridView ID="customersGrid" runat="server"
            DataSourceID="customersDataSource">
        </asp:GridView>

        <asp:LinqDataSource
            ID="customersDataSource" runat="server"
            ContextTypeName="DevLeap.Linq.Web.DataModel.CustomerManager"
            TableName="Customers" />

    </div>
    </form>
</body>
</html>
```

Using *EntityDataSource*

With the *EntityDataSource* control, you can use an Entity Data Model (EDM) as a *DataSource* for your bindable controls. Setting up the *EntityDataSource* is similar to setting up a *LinqData-Source*. For the following examples, you first define an EDM using the same entities shown in Figure 19-1.

Listing 19-14 shows the code for an .aspx page that uses a *GridView* to display customers. The *EntityDataSource* control requires a *DefaultContainerName* property that maps the EDM used, an *EntitySetName* that defines the entity the *EntityDataSource* will be bound to, and a *ConnectionString* property mapping to the connection that the EDM will use to connect to the external database.

LISTING 19-14 A sample .aspx page using an *EntityDataSource* control to render the list of Northwind customers into a *GridView* control

```
<%@ Page Language="C#" AutoEventWireup="true" CodeBehind="Listing19-71.aspx.cs"
    Inherits="WebSiteEDM.Listing19_71" %>
<!DOCTYPE html PUBLIC "-//W3C//DTD XHTML 1.0 Transitional//EN"
  "http://www.w3.org/TR/xhtml1/DTD/xhtml1-transitional.dtd">
<html xmlns="http://www.w3.org/1999/xhtml">
<head runat="server">
    <title>Listing 19-14</title>
</head>
<body>
    <form id="form1" runat="server">
    <div>
        <asp:GridView ID="customersGrid" runat="server"
            DataSourceID="customersDataSource">
        </asp:GridView>

        <asp:EntityDataSource ID="customersDataSource" runat="server"
            ConnectionString="name=NorthwindEntities"
            DefaultContainerName="NorthwindEntities"
            EntitySetName="Customers" />
    </div>
    </form>
</body>
</html>
```

The Configure Data Source wizard available in Visual Studio for configuring an *EntityData-Source* control has two steps, shown in Figures 19-5 and 19-6. To start the wizard, simply drop an *EntityDataSource* control into an .aspx page, click the control task menu, and choose Configure Data Source. In the first step, presented on the Configure ObjectContext page of the wizard, you define the main source for the control by choosing the connection and the container to use.

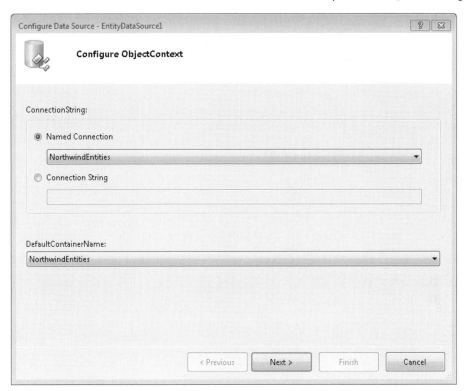

FIGURE 19-5 The Configure ObjectContext page of the Configure Data Source wizard.

After clicking Next, the Configure Data Selection configuration panel page appears, as shown in Figure 19-6.

On this page, you define the configuration parameters for the *EntityDataSource* control. Choose the entity set to query from the EntitySetName drop-down list. You use the Event-TypeFilter drop-down list only to filter entities of a particular type (if you have multiple types in the same entity set), and in the Select section, you choose the entity values you want in the query result. By default, the *EntityDataSource* control projects all the entity values, but you can define a custom projection predicate. The remaining check boxes control whether you want to allow automatic inserts, deletes, or updates. Like the *LinqDataSource*, the *EntityData-Source* allows automatic data modification only when you project all the entity values (when the first check box, Select All (Entity Value) is selected); otherwise the *EntityDataSource* will be read-only.

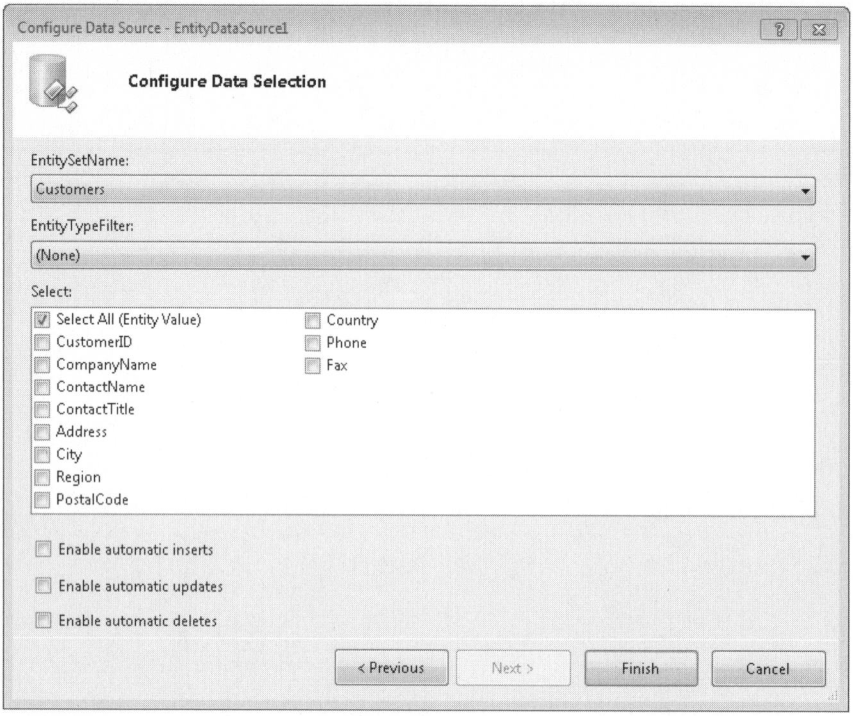

FIGURE 19-6 The Configure Data Selection page of the Configure Data Source wizard.

EntityDataSource and *LinqDataSource* support identical techniques for customizing the user interface; however, because the wizard for *EntityDataSource* does not have a section to define grouping, filters, and ordering condition, you have to modify the corresponding properties available in both the *EntityDataSource* and *LinqDataSource* component manually. The only difference is the syntax, which uses the *it* prefix for an entity value and the @ symbol as a prefix for parameter names.

> **More Info** You can find a complete discussion about data selection by searching for *EntityDataSource* at *http://msdn.microsoft.com/library/cc488529.aspx*.

Listing 19-15 shows an .aspx page that creates the same user interface shown in Listing 19-2, but using an *EntityDataSource* rather than a *LinqDataSource*.

LISTING 19-15 Sample .aspx page with an *EntityDataSource* control that renders Northwind customers into a *GridView* control with filtering and ordering rules

```
<%@ Page Language="C#" AutoEventWireup="true" CodeBehind="Listing19-15.aspx.cs"
    Inherits="WebSiteEDM.Listing19_15" %>
<!DOCTYPE html PUBLIC "-//W3C//DTD XHTML 1.0 Transitional//EN"
  "http://www.w3.org/TR/xhtml1/DTD/xhtml1-transitional.dtd">
```

```
<html xmlns="http://www.w3.org/1999/xhtml">
<head runat="server">
    <title>Listing 19-15</title>
</head>
<body>
    <form id="form1" runat="server">
    <div>
        <br />
        Country: 
        <asp:DropDownList ID="ddlCountries" runat="server"
            AutoPostBack="True" DataSourceID="countriesDataSource"
            DataTextField="Country" DataValueField="Country" />
        <asp:GridView ID="customersGrid" runat="server"
            DataSourceID="customersDataSource" AutoGenerateColumns="False">
            <Columns>
                <asp:BoundField DataField="CustomerID"
                    HeaderText="CustomerID" ReadOnly="True"
                    SortExpression="CustomerID" />
                <asp:BoundField DataField="CompanyName" HeaderText="CompanyName"
                    ReadOnly="True" SortExpression="CompanyName" />
                <asp:BoundField DataField="ContactName" HeaderText="ContactName"
                    ReadOnly="True" SortExpression="ContactName" />
                <asp:BoundField DataField="Country" HeaderText="Country"
                    ReadOnly="True" SortExpression="Country" />
            </Columns>
        </asp:GridView>

        <asp:EntityDataSource ID="customersDataSource" runat="server"
            ConnectionString="name=NorthwindEntities"
            DefaultContainerName="NorthwindEntities"
            EntitySetName="Customers" EnableFlattening="False"
            Select="it.[CustomerID], it.[CompanyName], it.[ContactName], it.[Country]"
            Where="it.[Country] = @Country" >
            <WhereParameters>
                <asp:ControlParameter ControlID="ddlCountries" Name="Country"
                    PropertyName="SelectedValue" Type="String" />
            </WhereParameters>
        </asp:EntityDataSource>

        <asp:EntityDataSource ID="countriesDataSource" runat="server"
            GroupBy="it.[Country]"
            OrderBy="it.[Country]"
            Select="it.[Country]"
            ConnectionString="name=NorthwindEntities"
            DefaultContainerName="NorthwindEntities"
            EntitySetName="Customers" />

    </div>
    </form>
</body>
</html>
```

Paging Data with *EntityDataSource* and *DataPager*

You can use the same data-paging techniques shown in the "Using *LinqDataSource*" section of this chapter to use a *DataPager* with an *EntityDataSource*. Again, the only difference lies in the *EntityDataSource* property syntax, as you can see in Listing 19-16. Refer to the section "Paging Data with *LinqDataSource* and *DataPager*" earlier in this chapter for further details, particularly Figure 19-4, which shows the output generated by the sample code.

> **Note** If you bind an *EntityDataSource* control to a paged control, you must specify its *OrderBy* property; otherwise, you will get a run-time exception. As an alternative, you can use the same technique shown in Listing 19-4, by intercepting the *Selecting* event and providing a valid syntax using the *it* prefix for an entity value.

LISTING 19-16 Using an *EntityDataSource* control to render Northwind customers into a *ListView* control with filtering and paging through a *DataPager* control

```
<%@ Page Language="C#" AutoEventWireup="true" CodeBehind="Listing19-16.aspx.cs"
    Inherits="WebSiteEDM.Listing19_16" %>
<!DOCTYPE html PUBLIC "-//W3C//DTD XHTML 1.0 Transitional//EN"
  "http://www.w3.org/TR/xhtml1/DTD/xhtml1-transitional.dtd">
<html xmlns="http://www.w3.org/1999/xhtml">
<head runat="server">
    <title>Listing 19-16</title>
</head>
<body>
    <form id="form1" runat="server">
    <div>
        <br />
        Country: 
        <asp:DropDownList ID="ddlCountries" runat="server"
            AutoPostBack="True" DataSourceID="countriesDataSource"
            DataTextField="Country" DataValueField="Country" />

        <asp:ListView ID="customersList" runat="server"
            DataSourceID="customersDataSource">
            <LayoutTemplate>
                <table cellpadding="5" cellspacing="0" border="1">
                    <tr>
                        <th style="text-align: center">CustomerId</th>
                        <th style="text-align: center">CompanyName</th>
                        <th style="text-align: center">ContactName</th>
                        <th style="text-align: center">Country</th>
                    </tr>
                    <asp:PlaceHolder ID="itemPlaceholder" runat="server" />
                </table>
            </LayoutTemplate>
            <ItemTemplate>
                <tr>
```

```
                            <td style="text-align: center">
                                <asp:Label ID="Label1" runat="server"
                                    Text='<%# Eval("CustomerId") %>' />
                            </td>
                            <td style="text-align: center">
                                <asp:Label ID="Label2" runat="server"
                                    Text='<%# Eval("CompanyName") %>' />
                            </td>
                            <td style="text-align: center">
                                <asp:Label ID="Label3" runat="server"
                                    Text='<%# Eval("ContactName") %>' />
                            </td>
                            <td style="text-align: center">
                                <asp:Label ID="Label4" runat="server"
                                    Text='<%# Eval("Country") %>' />
                            </td>
                        </tr>
                    </ItemTemplate>
                </asp:ListView>

                <asp:DataPager ID="customersPager" PagedControlID="customersList"
                    runat="server" PageSize="5">
                    <Fields>
                        <asp:NumericPagerField ButtonCount="5" ButtonType="Link" />
                    </Fields>
                </asp:DataPager>
                <br />

                <asp:EntityDataSource ID="customersDataSource" runat="server"
                    ConnectionString="name=NorthwindEntities"
                    DefaultContainerName="NorthwindEntities"
                    EntitySetName="Customers" EnableFlattening="False"
                    Select="it.[CustomerID], it.[CompanyName], it.[ContactName], it.[Country]"
                    Where="it.[Country] = @Country"
                    OrderBy="it.[CustomerID]" >
                    <WhereParameters>
                        <asp:ControlParameter ControlID="ddlCountries" Name="Country"
                            PropertyName="SelectedValue" Type="String" />
                    </WhereParameters>
                </asp:EntityDataSource>

                <asp:EntityDataSource ID="countriesDataSource" runat="server"
                    GroupBy="it.[Country]"
                    OrderBy="it.[Country]"
                    Select="it.[Country]"
                    ConnectionString="name=NorthwindEntities"
                    DefaultContainerName="NorthwindEntities"
                    EntitySetName="Customers" />

            </div>
        </form>
    </body>
</html>
```

Handling Data Modifications with *EntityDataSource*

There are no significant differences between *LinqDataSource* and *EntityDataSource* for data modification operations. Of course, the differences between LINQ to SQL and the Entity Framework apply, but for data binding, which one you use has no impact on syntax and the programming interface. For example, the code excerpt in Listing 19-17 is from an .aspx page that enables updates on a grid bound to an *EntityDataSource* control.

LISTING 19-17 Sample .aspx page excerpt using an editable *EntityDataSource* control

```
<form id="form1" runat="server">
    <div>
        <asp:GridView ID="customersGrid" runat="server"
            DataSourceID="customersDataSource" AutoGenerateColumns="true"
            AutoGenerateEditButton="true" >
        </asp:GridView>

        <asp:EntityDataSource ID="customersDataSource" runat="server"
            ConnectionString="name=NorthwindEntities"
            DefaultContainerName="NorthwindEntities"
            EntitySetName="Customers" EnableUpdate="true" />
    </div>
</form>
```

Using Custom Selections with *EntityDataSource*

As demonstrated in the "Using Custom Selections with *LinqDataSource*" section, you can use the *LinqDataSource.Selecting* event to customize the selection by setting the event argument's *Result* to a custom value. With an *EntityDataSource*, you have to use the *QueryCreated* event instead, because of the underlying Entity Framework architecture. Listing 19-18 shows an *EntityDataSource.QueryCreated* event handler example that is functionally equivalent to using the *LinqDataSource.Selecting* event shown in Listing 19-10.

> **More Info** Go to *http://msdn.microsoft.com/library/ee404748.aspx* for further details about applying LINQ queries to *EntityDataSource*.

LISTING 19-18 Handling a custom selection pattern for an *EntityDataSource* control using an explicit LINQ query

```
protected void customersDataSource_QueryCreated(
    object sender, QueryCreatedEventArgs e) {
    var customers = e.Query.Cast<Customer>();
    e.Query = from   c in customers
              where  c.Country == "USA" && c.Orders.Count > 0
              select c;
}
```

Binding to LINQ Queries

The sections "Using *LinqDataSource*" and "Using *EntityDataSource*" showed LINQ queries that use the *LinqDataSource* and *EntityDataSource* controls. However, in ASP.NET, you can bind a bindable control to any kind of data source that implements the *IEnumerable* interface. Every LINQ query, when it is enumerated, provides a result of type *IEnumerable<T>*, which internally is also an *IEnumerable*. Therefore, you can use *any* LINQ query as an explicit data source. The example in Listing 19-19 uses a LINQ query in its *Page_Load* event to bind a custom list of Northwind products to a *GridView* control.

LISTING 19-19 A sample page code based on a user-explicit LINQ query in the *Page_Load* event

```
public partial class Listing19_19 : System.Web.UI.Page {
    protected void Page_Load(object sender, EventArgs e) {
        NorthwindDataContext dc = new NorthwindDataContext();

        var query =
            from   c in dc.Customers
            where  c.Country == "USA" && c.Orders.Count > 0
            select new {
              c.CustomerID, c.ContactName,
              c.CompanyName, c.Country,
              OrdersCount = c.Orders.Count };

        customersGrid.DataSource = query;
        customersGrid.DataBind();
    }
}
```

This capability means you can use the complete LINQ query syntax—LINQ to SQL, LINQ to Entities, and LINQ to XML—to query custom data shapes and many different content types, and bind the results to an ASP.NET control. For example, Listing 19-20 shows the code for an .aspx page that renders the list of posts from a blog via a LINQ to XML query applied to the blog Really Simple Syndication (RSS) feed.

LISTING 19-20 The code-behind class of a page reading an RSS feed using a LINQ to XML query

```
public partial class Listing19_20 : System.Web.UI.Page {
    protected void Page_Load(object sender, EventArgs e) {
        XElement feed = XElement.Load(
            "http://introducinglinq.com/blogs/MainFeed.aspx");

        var query =
            from   f in feed.Descendants("item")
```

```
        select new {
           Title = f.Element("title").Value,
           PubDate = f.Element("pubDate").Value,
           Description = f.Element("description").Value
        };

    blogPostsGrid.DataSource = query;
    blogPostsGrid.DataBind();
  }
}
```

Querying data sources of any kind and shape using the many different flavors of LINQ is a challenging activity. However, LINQ to SQL is probably the most common use of user-defined explicit LINQ queries. Sooner or later, almost every web application will need to query a set of records from a database. This is far more interesting when you also need to update the data. Using the *LinqDataSource* control, everything is automated; the data source control handles updates, insertions, deletions, and selections by itself, raising a concurrency exception when data concurrency issues occur.

In contrast, when you are querying data manually, you need to take care of those details yourself. First, ASP.NET is an HTTP-based development platform. Therefore, every request you handle can be considered independent from any other—even if it comes from the same user and browser. Thus, you need to keep track of changes applied to your data between multiple subsequent requests, possibly avoiding use of *Session* variables or shared (static) objects, because those reduce the scalability of your solution. On the other hand, you should not keep an in-memory instance of the *DataContext* used to query a LINQ to SQL data model. You should instead create, use, and dispose of the *DataContext* for each request, as the *LinqData-Source* control does. Listing 19-21 shows an example of this technique that explicitly queries the Northwind customer list.

LISTING 19-21 The code-behind class of a page explicitly querying Northwind's customers via LINQ to SQL

```
public partial class Listing19_21 : System.Web.UI.Page {
    protected void Page_Load(object sender, EventArgs e) {
        NorthwindDataContext dc = new NorthwindDataContext();

        var query =
          from  c in dc.Customers
          select new {
            c.CustomerID, c.ContactName, c.Country, c.CompanyName};

        customersGrid.DataSource = query;
        customersGrid.DataBind();
    }
}
```

Listing 19-21 binds the query result to a *GridView* control, configured as editable. Listing 19-22 shows the corresponding .aspx page source code.

LISTING 19-22 The .aspx page code excerpt based on the code-behind class shown in Listing 19-21

```
<body>
    <form id="form1" runat="server">
    <div>

        <asp:GridView ID="customersGrid" runat="server"
            AutoGenerateEditButton="true"
            AutoGenerateColumns="true" />

    </div>
    </form>
</body>
```

Now here is the interesting part. Imagine that your user decides to change some fields for the currently selected customer, using the editable *GridView* produced by running the code from Listings 19-21 and 19-22 (see Figure 19-7).

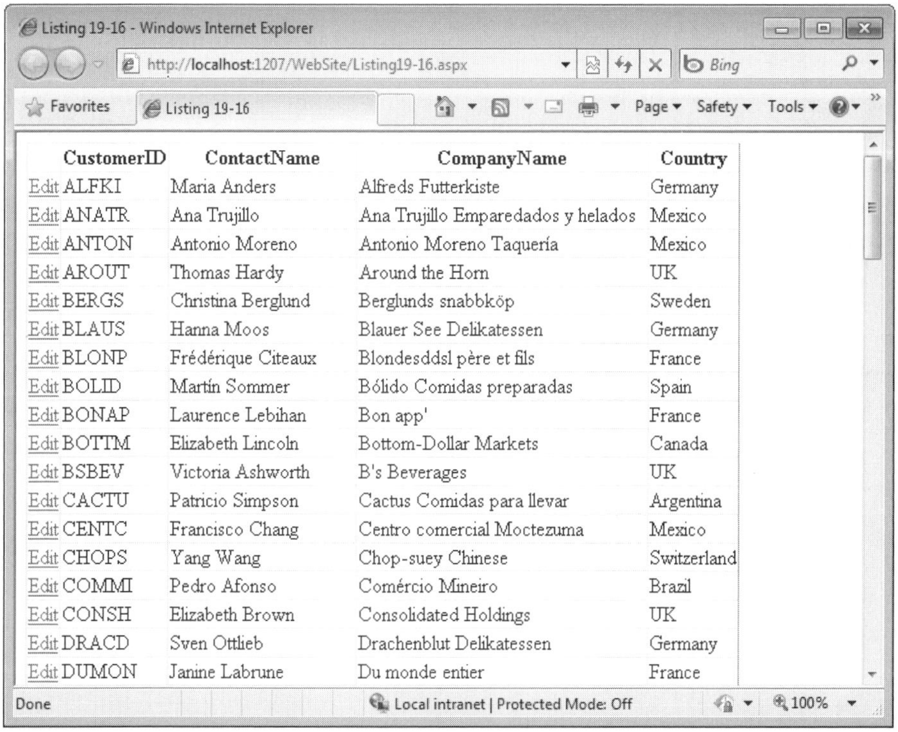

FIGURE 19-7 The HTML output of the page defined by Listings 19-21 and 19-22.

What you get back when the user presses the Update button on the page is the index of the selected/edited item in the *GridView*, as well as the values of the controls rendering the editable row. To update the data source, you need to create a new *DataContext* instance, which will be used during the entire unit of work that handles this single page request, and query the *DataContext* to get the entity corresponding to the data item that is going to be updated.

After you have retrieved the data item entity from the original store, you can explicitly change its properties, handling the user modifications, and then submit the changes to the persistence layer, using the *DataContext.SubmitChanges* method, as shown in Listing 19-23.

LISTING 19-23 Code to explicitly update a Northwind's customer instance with LINQ to SQL

```
protected void UpdateCustomerInstance(String customerID,
        String contactName, String country, String companyName) {
    NorthwindDataContext dc = new NorthwindDataContext();

    Customer c = dc.Customers.First(c => c.CustomerID == customerID);
    if (c != null) {
        c.ContactName = contactName;
        c.Country = country;
        c.CompanyName = companyName;
    }

    dc.SubmitChanges();
}
```

Unfortunately, it is not that simple. The preceding example is missing an important part of the process: the concurrency check. In fact, it simply uses the user input to modify the persistence layer. However, there are no guarantees about the exclusiveness of the operation you are performing. When the user decides to update a data item, you can use a specific *DataContext* method called *Attach*. With this method, you can attach an entity to a *DataContext* instance, which can then provide the entity's original state so you can determine whether any modification occurred, and if so, notify the *DataContext* that the entity has been changed. If the entity type has an *UpdateCheck* policy defined, the *DataContext* will be able to reconcile the entity with the one actually present in the database. Listing 19-24 shows an example of a codebehind class that uses this technique.

More Info For more details about *UpdateCheck* configuration, refer to the "Entity Class" section in Chapter 7.

LISTING 19-24 The code-behind class of a page updating a Northwind customer instance with LINQ to SQL, tracking the original state of the entity

```
protected void AttachAndUpdateCustomerInstance(String customerID,
    String contactName, String country, String companyName) {

    NorthwindDataContext dc = new NorthwindDataContext();

    Customer c = new Customer();
    c.CustomerID = customerID;
    c.ContactName = contactName;
    c.Country = country;
    c.CompanyName = companyName;

    // The Boolean flag indicates that the item has been changed
    dc.Customers.Attach(c, true);
    dc.SubmitChanges();
}
```

Using LINQ with WPF

In this section, you will learn about the support provided by Windows Presentation Foundation (WPF) to LINQ. As you will see, LINQ helps address many situations in which you need to manage data, either as XML or as a collection of entities, to solve data binding needs, rendering needs, or both.

Binding Single Entities and Properties

WPF provides solid and wide support for data binding, allowing user interface designers to bind elements to entities, XML, controls, and so on. In WPF, you can achieve data binding simply by configuring a data source against a target property that supports binding. A property can be bound whenever it is implemented as a *DependencyProperty*. For example, you can bind the *Text* property of a *TextBox*, but you can also bind the *Text* property of a *TextBlock*, or the *Background* property of an *AccessText* element. In Listing 19-25, you can see an example of XAML code that binds the *Text* property of a couple of *TextBox* elements to the properties of a variable of type *Contact*.

LISTING 19-25 A XAML sample window with a simple data-binding definition

```
<Window x:Class="DevLeap.Linq.WPF.SampleBinding"
    xmlns="http://schemas.microsoft.com/winfx/2006/xaml/presentation"
    xmlns:x="http://schemas.microsoft.com/winfx/2006/xaml"
    xmlns:c="clr-namespace:DevLeap.Linq.WPF"
    Title="SampleBinding" Height="146" Width="300">
```

```
    <Window.Resources>
        <c:Contact x:Key="myContact"
            FirstName="Andrea" LastName="Pialorsi" />
    </Window.Resources>

    <Grid Height="106">
        <Canvas Name="canvas1">
            <TextBox Name="firstName"
                Text="{Binding Source={StaticResource myContact}, Path=FirstName}"
                Canvas.Left="10" Canvas.Top="12" Height="29" Width="250" />
            <TextBox Name="lastName"
                Text="{Binding Source={StaticResource myContact}, Path=LastName}"
                Canvas.Left="10" Canvas.Top="61" Height="29" Width="250" />
        </Canvas>
    </Grid>
</Window>
```

Listing 19-26 contains the *Contact* type definition.

LISTING 19-26 The *Contact* type definition

```
public class Contact {
    public String FirstName { get; set; }
    public String LastName { get; set; }
}
```

Figure 19-8 shows the resulting window.

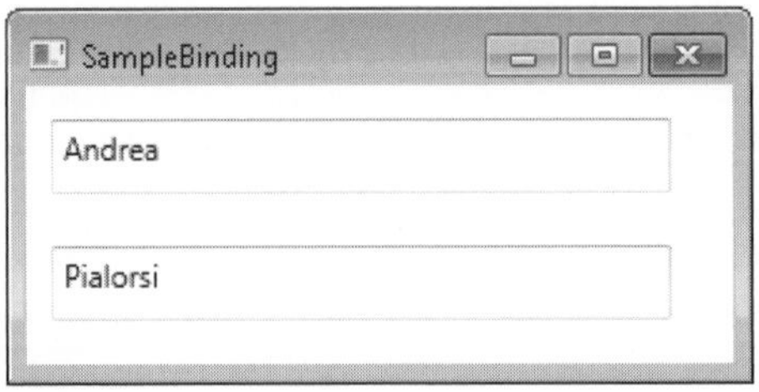

FIGURE 19-8 A XAML window rendered with simple data binding.

Starting from this really simple example, it is interesting to evaluate how WPF binding works when the binding source is a LINQ to SQL or LINQ to Entities entity, rather than a static resource.

Consider the Northwind customer set. Imagine having a XAML window that is bound to a *Customer* instance, as in Listing 19-27.

LISTING 19-27 A XAML window with data binding against a Northwind customer instance

```
<Window x:Class="DevLeap.Linq.WPF.SingleCustomer"
    xmlns="http://schemas.microsoft.com/winfx/2006/xaml/presentation"
    xmlns:x="http://schemas.microsoft.com/winfx/2006/xaml"
    Title="SingleCustomer" Height="222" Width="300" Loaded="Window_Loaded">

    <Grid>
        <Canvas Name="canvas1" Margin="0,0,0,121">
            <TextBlock Height="16" Canvas.Left="10"
                Canvas.Top="14" Width="68.69">Customer ID:</TextBlock>
            <TextBox Name="CustomerID"
                Text="{Binding Path=CustomerID}" Canvas.Left="10"
                Canvas.Top="30" Height="29" Width="250" />
            <TextBlock Height="16" Canvas.Left="10"
                Canvas.Top="64" Width="79">Contact Name:</TextBlock>
            <TextBox Name="ContactName"
                Text="{Binding Path=ContactName}" Canvas.Left="10"
                Canvas.Top="79" Height="29" Width="250" />
            <TextBlock Height="16" Canvas.Left="10"
                Canvas.Top="111" Width="88">Company Name:</TextBlock>
            <TextBox Name="CompanyName"
                Text="{Binding Path=CompanyName}" Canvas.Left="10"
                Canvas.Top="128" Height="29" Width="250" />
        </Canvas>
    </Grid>

</Window>
```

The code in Listing 19-28 binds the first Northwind customer to the window's *DataContext*.

LISTING 19-28 Microsoft Visual C# source for the XAML window in Listing 19-27

```
public partial class SingleCustomer : Window {
    public SingleCustomer() {
        InitializeComponent();
    }

    private void Window_Loaded(object sender, RoutedEventArgs e) {
        NorthwindDataContext dc = new NorthwindDataContext();
        this.DataContext = dc.Customers.First();
    }
}
```

Binding the *Text* properties of the three *TextBox* elements is almost identical to the static binding shown in Listing 19-25, except that Listing 19-28 configures the binding source in code-behind code using the *DataContext* discovering capability, rather than using a *StaticResource* defined in XAML by directly assigning the *Source* property. In WPF, the binding source of a control can be explicitly set against the control itself, or higher in the control hierarchy, because WPF bubbles the *DataContext* lookup across the entire control hierarchy. It is important to emphasize that you can bind a set of XAML elements against a hierarchical data structure, such as a customer that may have a collection of orders, each of which in turn is related to a collection of products, and so on. In fact, a WPF binding path can reference any depth level in an object graph.

For the sake of completeness, Figure 19-9 shows the window resulting from the code samples shown in Listings 19-27 and 19-28.

FIGURE 19-9 A XAML window with simple data binding.

Again, the most interesting part of this discussion emerges when you think about modifying entities bound to a XAML window. Both LINQ to SQL and LINQ to Entities implement a couple of interfaces useful for data-binding purposes: *INotifyPropertyChanging* and *INotifyProperty-Changed*. The first of these interfaces notifies the data-binding environment that a property of a currently bound item is going to be changed, whereas the latter interface notifies the environment about a property change that has already occurred. Listing 19-29 shows the signatures of these interfaces, together with the classes involved in their definitions.

LISTING 19-29 *INotifyPropertyChanging* and *INotifyPropertyChanged* interface signatures and related types

```
public interface INotifyPropertyChanging {
    event PropertyChangingEventHandler PropertyChanging;
}

public delegate void PropertyChangingEventHandler(object sender,
    PropertyChangingEventArgs e);

public class PropertyChangingEventArgs : EventArgs {
    public PropertyChangingEventArgs(string propertyName);
    public virtual string PropertyName { get; }
}
```

```
public interface INotifyPropertyChanged {
    event PropertyChangedEventHandler PropertyChanged;
}

public delegate void PropertyChangedEventHandler(object sender,
    PropertyChangedEventArgs e);

public class PropertyChangedEventArgs : EventArgs {
    public PropertyChangedEventArgs(string propertyName);
    public virtual string PropertyName { get; }
}
```

This behavior, which is available both for LINQ to SQL and LINQ to Entities, implies that the WPF environment is able to intercept and handle any data modification related to data-bound entities. Thus, it can dynamically and automatically refresh portions of the user interface so they are consistent with data changes as soon as those occur.

To test this behavior, add a *Button* to the window created in Listing 19-27, as shown in Listing 19-30.

LISTING 19-30 A XAML excerpt to define a *Button* element

```
<Button Canvas.Left="10" Canvas.Top="171" Height="37"
    Name="changeCurrentCustomer" Width="250"
    Click="changeCurrentCustomer_Click">Change Current Customer</Button>
```

Listing 19-31 shows the *Button.Click* event handler code.

LISTING 19-31 The *Click* event of the *Button* element

```
private void changeCurrentCustomer_Click(object sender, RoutedEventArgs e) {
    ((Customer)this.DataContext).ContactName += " modified!";
}
```

As soon as you press the Change Current Customer button, the *TextBox* displaying the *ContactName* changes, synchronizing its value with the actual *Customer* instance.

In Figure 19-10, you can see the result, just after pressing the button.

FIGURE 19-10 A XAML window showing simple data binding synchronization.

Using this feature, you can define user interfaces that are fully synchronized with their binding sources. Keep in mind that this behavior is automatically available only with autogenerated entities of both LINQ to SQL and LINQ to Entities; if you define your own entities, it is your responsibility to support this useful behavior by implementing the required interfaces.

On the other hand, you need a client-server application architecture to take advantage of this behavior, and in modern applications you will probably have LINQ to SQL or LINQ to Entities on the application server and client-side entities in the consumer environment. For this reason, communication frameworks such as Windows Communication Foundation (WCF), or even ASMX, provide the capability to automatically generate data binding–enabled client-side entities. This capability is provided by implementing *INotify** interfaces on the entities derived from communication contracts, such as those that are part of Web Services Description Languages (WSDLs) and XML Schema Definitions (XSDs).

More Info For further details about distributed architectures, refer to Chapter 18.

Binding Collections of Entities

So far, you have seen how to use single entities as binding sources, but you can also bind a collection of items. From a WPF point of view, you can use any type that implements *IEnumerable* as a binding source. However, only types that implement the *INotifyCollectionChanged* interface can automatically send notifications to the user interface about the insertion and deletion of items. Listing 19-32 shows the signature of this interface, together with its related types.

LISTING 19-32 The *INotifyCollectionChanged* interface signature and its related types

```
public interface INotifyCollectionChanged {
    event NotifyCollectionChangedEventHandler CollectionChanged;
}

public delegate void NotifyCollectionChangedEventHandler(object sender,
    NotifyCollectionChangedEventArgs e);

public class NotifyCollectionChangedEventArgs : EventArgs {
    // Public constructors
    // …

    // Public properties
    public NotifyCollectionChangedAction Action { get; }
    public IList NewItems { get; }
    public int NewStartingIndex { get; }
    public IList OldItems { get; }
    public int OldStartingIndex { get; }
}
```

WPF provides a type named *ObservableCollection<T>* that already implements the *INotify-CollectionChanged* interface, thus offering a set of events useful for monitoring the collection status. In general, you can use this type as the base class for any collection that you want to bind in WPF, supporting the full set of features available.

Unfortunately, the entity collections in both LINQ to SQL and LINQ to Entities do not inherit from *ObservableCollection<T>* or implement the *INotifyCollectionChanged* interface. This implies that you will not be able to automatically handle user-interface updates when the data sources change, which happens whenever you use the *Table<T>* and *DataQuery<T>* classes of LINQ to SQL or the *ObjectQuery<T>* class of LINQ to Entities as sources for binding elements in WPF. This also happens with any LINQ query based on either of these LINQ providers. To visualize this behavior, consider the sample XAML code shown in Listing 19-33.

LISTING 19-33 Sample XAML code for a WPF window with a *ListBox* bound to a LINQ to SQL entity set

```
<Window x:Class="DevLeap.Linq.WPF.ComplexBinding"
  xmlns="http://schemas.microsoft.com/winfx/2006/xaml/presentation"
  xmlns:x="http://schemas.microsoft.com/winfx/2006/xaml"
  Title="WPF LINQ Sample Application" Height="418" Width="616"
  Loaded="Window_Loaded">

  <Window.Resources>
    <DataTemplate x:Key="CustomerTemplate">
```

```xml
      <Grid>
        <Grid.ColumnDefinitions>
          <ColumnDefinition Width="50" />
          <ColumnDefinition Width="200" />
          <ColumnDefinition Width="*"/>
        </Grid.ColumnDefinitions>
        <TextBlock Grid.Column="0" Text="{Binding Path=CustomerID}" />
        <TextBlock Grid.Column="1" Text="{Binding Path=ContactName}" />
        <TextBlock Grid.Column="2" Text="{Binding Path=CompanyName}" />
      </Grid>
    </DataTemplate>
  </Window.Resources>

  <Canvas>
    <TextBlock Canvas.Top="8" Height="18.96"
      Canvas.Left="9.183" Width="113">Customer ID:</TextBlock>
    <TextBox Canvas.Top="5" Name="CustomerID"
      Text="{Binding Path=CustomerID}" Height="21.96"
      Canvas.Left="127" Width="84" />
    <TextBlock Canvas.Top="40" Height="19"
      Canvas.Left="9.183" Width="113">Contact Name:</TextBlock>
    <TextBox Canvas.Top="37" Name="ContactName"
      Text="{Binding Path=ContactName}" Height="22"
      Canvas.Left="127" Width="171" />
    <TextBlock Canvas.Top="72" Height="19"
      Canvas.Left="8" Width="114.183">Company Name:</TextBlock>
    <TextBox Canvas.Top="69" Name="CompanyName"
      Text="{Binding Path=CompanyName}" Height="22"
      Canvas.Left="127" Width="171" />
    <Button Canvas.Left="8" Canvas.Top="105" Height="28"
      Name="reloadCustomersList" Width="151"
      Click="reloadCustomersList_Click">Reload Customers</Button>
    <Button Canvas.Left="176" Canvas.Top="105" Height="28"
      Name="addNewCustomer" Width="151"
      Click="addNewCustomer_Click">Add a new Customer</Button>
    <Button Canvas.Left="344" Canvas.Top="105" Height="28"
      Name="deleteCustomer" Width="151"
      Click="deleteCustomer_Click">Delete selected Customer</Button>
    <StackPanel Margin="8,120,11,10"  Name="panelCustomers"
      Grid.ColumnSpan="2"
      Height="233" Canvas.Left="0" Canvas.Top="27" Width="582">
    <ListBox IsSynchronizedWithCurrentItem="True"
        ItemsSource="{Binding}"
        ItemTemplate="{StaticResource CustomerTemplate}"
        Height="233" Width="582" Name="customerListBox" />
    </StackPanel>
  </Canvas>
</Window>
```

As you can see, this XAML code declares a *DataTemplate* element that defines how to render each Northwind *Customer* instance. Later, the code applies that template to each item of a *ListBox* element. Moreover, the page contains three *TextBox* elements bound to the *Customer* instance currently selected within the *ListBox* element. Finally, there are three buttons that you can use to refresh the list of customers, add a new *Customer* instance, and delete the currently selected *Customer* instance, respectively. Listing 19-34 shows the source code behind the XAML in Listing 19-33.

LISTING 19-34 The code behind the *ComplexBinding* XAML of Listing 19-33

```
public partial class ComplexBinding : Window {
    private NorthwindDataContext dc;

    public ComplexBinding() {
        InitializeComponent();
    }

    private void Window_Loaded(object sender, RoutedEventArgs e) {
        dc = new NorthwindDataContext();
        bindWindow();
    }

    private void reloadCustomersList_Click(object sender,
        RoutedEventArgs e) {
        bindWindow();
    }

    private void bindWindow() {
        this.DataContext =
            from   c in dc.Customers
            select c;
    }

    private void addNewCustomer_Click(object sender, RoutedEventArgs e) {
        Customer c = new Customer {
            CustomerID = "DLEAP",
            ContactName = "Paolo Pialorsi",
            CompanyName = "DevLeap",
            Country = "Italy",
        };

        dc.Customers.InsertOnSubmit(c);
        dc.SubmitChanges();
    }

    private void deleteCustomer_Click(object sender, RoutedEventArgs e) {
        Customer c = customerListBox.SelectedItem as Customer;
        if (c != null) {
            dc.Customers.DeleteOnSubmit(c);
            dc.SubmitChanges();
        }
    }
}
```

Figure 19-11 shows this WPF window in action.

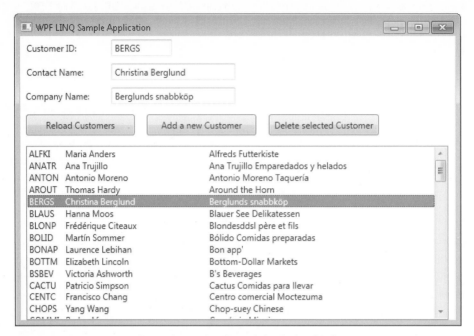

FIGURE 19-11 A XAML window with complex (list and detail) data binding.

Note that whenever you select a *Customer* instance within the *ListBox* element and change its content using one of the three *TextBox* elements, the *ListBox* content gets updated automatically as well. This happens because each entity returned by the query (*DataQuery<T>* in this example) implements both *INotifyPropertyChanging* and *INotifyPropertyChanged* interfaces, which allow it to automatically notify the UI of its changes.

However, if you click the Add A New Customer button, you will see that the newly created *Customer* instance does not appear in the bound list. Because the collection returned by LINQ to SQL does not implement the *INotifyCollectionChanged* interface, it does not notify the user interface of any change. To update the UI, you need to click the Reload Customers button. Similarly, the Delete Selected Customer button requires you to click the Reload Customers button before the deleted customer disappears from the bound list. The same behavior would occur if you were using LINQ to Entities.

Fortunately, this is not really an issue unless you are writing a simple prototype or demo. As stated earlier with regard to single entity binding, modern software architectures should not have client-server scenarios. Still, you will probably have a consumer application that consumes an application server that uses an abstract communication layer. The consumer side will have entities and collections of entities that may differ from the ones on the application server side. The entities on the consumer side should be designed specifically so they can be bound correctly to the UI (for example, Windows Forms, WPF, or ASP.NET).

Using LINQ with Silverlight

Microsoft Silverlight is the cross-browser, cross-platform, and cross-device plug-in promoted as a technology for delivering rich, interactive web solutions. As of this writing, the latest released version is Microsoft Silverlight 4. Silverlight has supported both LINQ to Objects and LINQ to XML since version 2. Silverlight also has ASP.NET AJAX support. By combining these, you can define truly rich Web 2.0 client solutions, using the same syntax and tools available on the server side.

Neither LINQ to SQL nor LINQ to Entities implementations are available in Silverlight, because plug-ins built on top of such a framework must work on the client-side, usually within a browser. For security reasons (browser sandboxing) as well as for location reasons (the database management system is not typically available to a web client), there is no way to connect to a remote database management system from these types of implementations. However, you can use LINQ providers in Silverlight applications that access remote services. (An example of this with the *FlightStatusService* provider was presented in Chapter 15, "Extending LINQ.") You should prefer this method for building scalable web applications, because you have much more direct control over entities transmitted via the wire.

For prototypes or applications that will not have a heavy workload, you might choose to use WCF Data Services to expose data via HTTP web services. Because the EDM is used to represent exposed data as objects, you can use LINQ to Entities on the client side to define queries that are transferred to and executed on the server side, and return only the result of such queries to the client side. However, remember that there is an important difference as compared to using LINQ to Entities in WPF, because every time you execute a query, you are calling a remote service, and Silverlight forces you to make an asynchronous call so that the user interface will not freeze during the service call.

Important The examples shown in this section require you to install Microsoft Silverlight 4 Tools for Visual Studio 2010, available at *http://www.microsoft.com/downloads/en/details. aspx?FamilyID=b3deb194-ca86-4fb6-a716-b67c2604a139*. The following examples use the *DataGrid* control that is included in those tools.

Consider the Silverlight application hosted in the webpage shown in Listing 19-35.

LISTING 19-35 Silverlight application hosted in a webpage

```xml
<UserControl x:Class="DevLeap.Linq.Silverlight.MainPage"
    xmlns="http://schemas.microsoft.com/winfx/2006/xaml/presentation"
    xmlns:x="http://schemas.microsoft.com/winfx/2006/xaml"
    xmlns:d="http://schemas.microsoft.com/expression/blend/2008"
    xmlns:mc="http://schemas.openxmlformats.org/markup-compatibility/2006"
    xmlns:sdk="http://schemas.microsoft.com/winfx/2006/xaml/presentation/sdk"
    mc:Ignorable="d" d:DesignHeight="300" d:DesignWidth="400">

    <Grid Name="orderItemsGrid">
        <TextBlock Height="28" Margin="34,12,0,0"
            Name="orderLabel" VerticalAlignment="Top"
                HorizontalAlignment="Left" Width="65">Country:</TextBlock>

        <ComboBox Height="23" Margin="92,12,198,0" Name="comboBoxCountry"
            VerticalAlignment="Top"
                SelectionChanged="comboBoxCountry_SelectionChanged" />

        <sdk:DataGrid ItemsSource="{Binding}"
                Name="orderItemsDataGrid" Margin="34,46,34,31"
                AutoGenerateColumns="False">
            <sdk:DataGrid.Columns>
                <sdk:DataGridTextColumn  Header="Customer ID" Binding="{
                    Binding CustomerID}"
                     Width="SizeToHeader"/>
                <sdk:DataGridTextColumn  Header="Company" Binding="{
                    Binding CompanyName}" />
                <sdk:DataGridTextColumn  Header="Contact Name"
                    Binding="{Binding ContactName}" />
                <sdk:DataGridTextColumn  Header="Country" Binding="{
                    Binding Country}" />
            </sdk:DataGrid.Columns>
        </sdk:DataGrid>
    </Grid>

</UserControl>
```

The combo box lets users select a particular country. Their choice is then used to filter the data displayed in the *DataGrid*. The columns of the *DataGrid* are configured to display specific values from the customer entities bound to the *DataGrid*. The *ItemSource* property of the *DataGrid* is bound to the *DataContext* that will be set by code when the selection in the combo box changes. You will see how to initialize the list of countries displayed in the combo box later. Figure 19-12 shows this Silverlight application running.

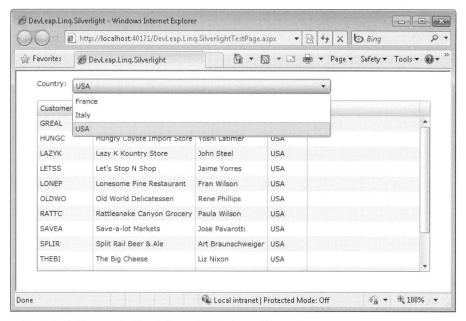

FIGURE 19-12 The sample Silverlight application hosted in a webpage.

When a user selects a value from the combo box, the application runs the code shown in Listing 19-36.

LISTING 19-36 Event handler for selection change in a combo box

```
private void comboBoxCountry_SelectionChanged(
  object sender, SelectionChangedEventArgs e) {
    // Use combo selection to filter customers
    SelectCountry(comboBoxCountry.SelectedValue.ToString());
}
```

The code calls *SelectCountry*, passing the value of the selected item in the combo box, which corresponds to the name of the selected country. Listing 19-37 shows the implementation of the *SelectCountry* method.

LISTING 19-37 Remote execution of a LINQ query with an asynchronous completion event

```
DataServiceCollection<Customer> serviceCustomers;

// Load customers of one country into the grid
void SelectCountry(string selectedCountry) {
    // Load list of Customers
    var context = new NorthwindEntities(new Uri("Northwind.svc", UriKind.Relative));
```

```
      var customersQuery = from   c in context.Customers
                           where  c.Country == selectedCountry
                           select c;
      serviceCustomers = new DataServiceCollection<Customer>();
      orderItemsDataGrid.IsEnabled = false;
      serviceCustomers.LoadCompleted +=
             new EventHandler<LoadCompletedEventArgs>(selectedCustomers_LoadCompleted);

      // Setup the Item Source
      orderItemsDataGrid.ItemsSource = serviceCustomers;
      serviceCustomers.LoadAsync(customersQuery);
}

void selectedCustomers_LoadCompleted(object sender, LoadCompletedEventArgs e) {
    if (e.Error != null) {
        MessageBox.Show(string.Format("An error has occured: {0}", e.Error.Message));
        return;
    }
    else if (serviceCustomers.Continuation != null) {
        serviceCustomers.LoadNextPartialSetAsync();
        return;
    }
    orderItemsDataGrid.IsEnabled = true;
}
```

The *SelectCountry* method initializes a *NorthwindEntities* instance, which handles the communication with the remote Northwind service implemented with WCF Data Services. This service is hosted in the same web application that hosts the Silverlight application. In this way, you do not have to modify the standard security configuration of Silverlight, because the standard configuration allows you to connect to the same web server where the Silverlight application resides.

 Note A description of how to configure the WCF Data Service required for these examples is out of scope for this book. You can find further information about WCF Data Service in Silverlight at *http://msdn.microsoft.com/library/cc838234.aspx*.

Using WCF Data Services in Silverlight might appear similar to using LINQ to Entities in WPF because both use the idea of an entity. However, there are several differences, the most relevant of which is the need to use an asynchronous programming pattern for any remote call in Silverlight. For this reason, the example uses a *DataServiceCollection<T>* instance, which can be assigned to an *ItemSource* of Silverlight-enabled data controls, such as the *DataGrid* in the example. The *DataServiceCollection<T>* class derives from *ObservableCollection<T>* and implements a dynamic entity collection that provides notifications when the collection changes. (However, in this example data is bound in a read-only way.) The *DataServiceCollection* class has a generic parameter that must be the same type returned by the query passed as a parameter to the *LoadAsync* instance method. In fact, the *customersQuery* is defined as an extractor that filters all customers who live in the specified country.

Because the remote query executes asynchronously, you have to specify the code to execute when the remote call returns. The example assigns the *LoadCompleted* event to the *selected-Customers_LoadCompleted* method, which simply enables the *DataGrid* when the remote call completes. To make this check, it checks two conditions. First, if an error occurs, it displays a message box to the user. Second, if the callback has been called with only a portion of the results available, the code simply returns, ignoring the notification. You should note that if you want to load data incrementally, you can use this to display a partial result (the portion of data loaded prior to the notification) so that the user interface does not freeze.

The need to handle asynchronous calls is the more relevant activity for data binding using LINQ and WCF Data Services in Silverlight. The asynchronous calls are important because the time for a remote call depends on several factors and might introduce latency, making the program seem unresponsive to the end user. For this reason, Silverlight supports only asynchronous programming techniques. You can see how to initialize the sample Silverlight application in Listing 19-38.

LISTING 19-38 Remote execution of a LINQ query with an asynchronous completion event

```
readonly string[] Countries = new string[] { "France", "Italy", "USA" };

public MainPage() {
    InitializeComponent();

    // Load list of Countries
    comboBoxCountry.ItemsSource = Countries;

    // Select no country (so that WCF Data Service is bootstrapped in background)
    SelectCountry(String.Empty);
}
```

The *comboBox* is initialized with a fixed array of countries and then the code calls *SelectCountry*, passing an empty string as the argument. Using this logic, the *DataGrid* will be bound to an empty set and will therefore show no data rows. Because *SelectCountry* involves an asynchronous call to complete the operation, these operations do not freeze the UI, but immediately start initializing the connection to the remote service, so that subsequent calls will be more responsive. Avoiding paying the initial startup costs of WCF Data Services is one of the reasons the application initializes the *Countries* string array with a fixed list of country names. The other reason is that there is no *Country* entity in the EDM, so getting the list of distinct countries from the Customers table would require a projection statement and a distinct clause in the LINQ query. Even though Silverlight 4 offers support for projections, the need to use a *DataServiceCollection<T>* instance makes it hard to use such a query to initialize the *Countries* combo box.

Note Another technology available in Silverlight to access data is WCF RIA Services, available as a separate download for Visual Studio 2010 at *http://www.silverlight.net/getstarted/riaservices/*. WCF RIA Services is designed specifically for end-to-end Silverlight and ASP.NET solutions, requiring the client and server to be designed and deployed together. Refer to Chapter 18 for an explanation of the architectural implication of such a choice. It is out of scope for this book to discuss each single technology in detail. The important point for Silverlight is that it imposes the asynchronous programming model for every remote call, including those required by WCF RIA Services—even if that code might be generated automatically by the development environment. You can find more information at *http://msdn.microsoft.com/library/ee707344.aspx*.

Using LINQ with Windows Forms

Windows Forms is the oldest rich client application UI available in the .NET Framework. Although WPF is a more advanced UI framework, Windows Forms is still widely used, and Visual Studio offers very good editors and wizards to support data binding with LINQ queries, particularly for LINQ to SQL and LINQ to Entities.

In Windows Forms, the *BindingSource* component is the main interface between Windows Forms controls and data sources, providing services such as change notification and currency management. This component simplifies working with different LINQ providers, such as LINQ to SQL and LINQ to Entities, because it limits the differences to the *BindingSource* instance assignment code.

Consider the form in the designer shown in Figure 19-13. You will use a form like this to bind data coming from both LINQ to SQL and LINQ to Entities.

The behavior of this form is similar to the ASP.NET and Silverlight applications shown in Figures 19-4 and 19-12. The form loads the combo box with a list of countries, and filters the customers shown in the data grid according to the country selected in that combo box.

The combo box is not connected to any binding source; it is populated by creating an array containing the result of a query that gets a distinct list of countries for the entire set of customers, and then passing that array to the combo box's *Items.AddRange* method, as you can see in Listing 19-39.

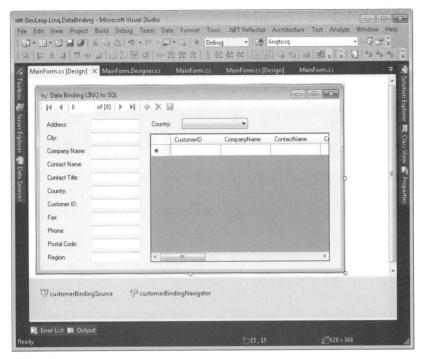

FIGURE 19-13 A form bound to data from LINQ to SQL and LINQ to Entities.

LISTING 19-39 Initialization of controls at a form load event

```csharp
public partial class MainForm : Form {
    public MainForm() {
        InitializeComponent();
    }

    NorthwindDataContext northwind = null;

    private void MainForm_Load(object sender, EventArgs e) {
        northwind = new NorthwindDataContext();

        var queryCountries = (from   c in northwind.Customers
                              select c.Country).Distinct().OrderBy((c) => c);
        var countries = queryCountries.ToArray();
        comboBoxCountries.Items.AddRange(countries);

        this.customerBindingSource.DataSource = northwind.Customers;
    }

    // ...
}
```

Listing 19-39 also shows the initialization for the *DataSource* property of the *customerBinding-Source* instance. It is assigned to the entire *Customers* table of the *northwind* data context, so initially there are no filters on the table. The only code specific to a particular LINQ provider is the declaration and initialization of the *northwind* member instance, which is of type *NorthwindDataContext*, and in this case has been defined in a DBML file in the same Visual Studio solution.

To use LINQ to Entities instead of LINQ to SQL, you just have to replace *NorthwindDataContext* with *NorthwindEntities*, which must be defined by a corresponding EDM in the same solution.

To filter the data grid based on the user's selection in the country combo box, you intercept the combo box's *SelectedIndexChanged* event. In Listing 19-40, you can see that the *Data-Source* property of *customerBindingSource* is assigned to a LINQ to SQL query that applies a filter to the *Country* field based on the selected item in the combo box.

LISTING 19-40 Filtering customers by a country selected in a combo box in LINQ to SQL

```
public partial class MainForm : Form {
    // ...

    private void comboBoxCountries_SelectedIndexChanged(object sender, EventArgs e) {
        var customerByCountry = from   c in northwind.Customers
                                where  c.Country ==
                                       comboBoxCountries.SelectedItem.ToString()
                                select c;
        this.customerBindingSource.DataSource = customerByCountry;
    }
}
```

It is interesting to note that for a LINQ to Entities object context, you have to change the LINQ query slightly because of some differences in the way operator overloading works in the two providers. In LINQ to Entities, the syntax used in Listing 19-40 would raise a *NotSupportedException* at run time because LINQ to Entities does not recognize the *ToString* method properly. To solve the problem, move the assignment out of the LINQ query expression and save the result in a variable, such as the *selectedCountry* string used in Listing 19-41.

LISTING 19-41 Filtering customers by a country selected in a combo box in LINQ to Entities

```
public partial class MainForm : Form {
    // ...

    private void comboBoxCountries_SelectedIndexChanged(object sender, EventArgs e) {
        string selectedCountry = comboBoxCountries.SelectedItem.ToString();
        var customerByCountry = from   c in northwind.Customers
                                where  c.Country == selectedCountry
                                select c;
        this.customerBindingSource.DataSource = customerByCountry;
    }
}
```

Visual Studio offers a useful Data Source Configuration Wizard to generate the required data source elements that you can use to bind controls to data in an abstract way. You can use the wizard to generate data sources for both LINQ to SQL and LINQ to Objects entities, selecting the Object item in both cases from the list shown in Figure 19-14.

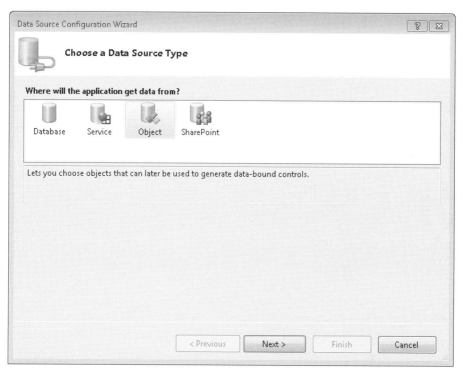

FIGURE 19-14 The Data Source Configuration Wizard generates data sources for both LINQ to SQL and LINQ to Objects.

You do not need the Data Source Configuration Wizard with LINQ to Entities because those entities already show up in the Data Sources pane after you define an EDM.

Summary

This chapter showed you how to use the features and controls available in ASP.NET and Silverlight to develop data-enabled web applications, using LINQ to SQL, LINQ to Entities, and LINQ in general. What you have seen is especially useful for rapidly defining website proto-types and simple web solutions, but keep in mind that for enterprise-level solutions, you will probably need at least one intermediate layer between the ASP.NET or Silverlight presentation layer and the data persistence layer, represented by either LINQ to SQL or LINQ to Entities.

In real enterprise solutions based on ASP.NET, you usually also need a business layer that abstracts all the business logic, security policies, and validation rules from any kind of specific persistence layer. And you will probably have a Model-View-Controller or Model-View-Presenter pattern governing the UI. In this more complex scenario, chances are that the *LinqDataSource* and *EntityDataSource* controls will be tied to entities collections more often than to LINQ to SQL or LINQ to Entities results.

You have also seen that rich client applications should have a multitier architecture in an Enterprise environment. For small applications or those with tiny workloads, a client-server architecture might benefit from the stateful connection provided by LINQ to SQL and the Entity Framework. You get maximum flexibility when data binding under these conditions, but you need to be careful to apply appropriate filters when reading data to avoid loading too many entities in memory.

Index

Symbols

A

B

C

Paolo Pialorsi

Paolo Pialorsi is a consultant, trainer, and author who specializes in developing distributed applications architectures and Microsoft SharePoint enterprise solutions. He is a founder of DevLeap, a company focused on providing content and consulting to professional developers. Paolo wrote *Programming Microsoft LINQ* and *Introducing Microsoft LINQ* both published by Microsoft Press, and is the author of three books in Italian about XML and Web Services. He is also a regular speaker at industry conferences.

Marco Russo

Marco Russo is a founder of DevLeap. He is a regular contributor to developer user communities and is an avid blogger on Microsoft SQL Server Business Intelligence and other Microsoft technologies. Marco provides consulting and training to professional developers on the Microsoft .NET Framework and Microsoft SQL Server. He wrote *Programming Microsoft LINQ* and *Introducing Microsoft LINQ* with Paolo Pialorsi, *Expert Cube Development with Microsoft SQL Server 2008 Analysis Services* with Alberto Ferrari and Chris Webb, and is the author of two books in Italian about C# and the common language runtime.

What do you think of this book?

We want to hear from you!

To participate in a brief online survey, please visit:

microsoft.com/learning/booksurvey

Tell us how well this book meets your needs—what works effectively, and what we can do better. Your feedback will help us continually improve our books and learning resources for you.

Thank you in advance for your input!

Stay in touch!

To subscribe to the *Microsoft Press® Book Connection Newsletter*—for news on upcoming books, events, and special offers—please visit:

microsoft.com/learning/books/newsletter